Praise for *The Sum of It All*

"In *The Sum of it All*, Lewis Lehrman shares with us how he has so effectively directed his commitments to family, country, faith, and conservative beliefs to an extraordinary career in business, politics, and both the writing and promotion of history. His life exemplifies the importance of passion, discipline, vision, and of a knowledge of the past in understanding the present and shaping the future."

—**Daniel Horowitz**, author of *Entertaining Entrepreneurs: Reality TV's* Shark Tank *and the American Dream in Uncertain Times*

"Lewis E. Lehrman has achieved success in so many roles—philanthropist, financier, historian, economist, public servant, businessman, husband, and father—that he calls to mind a statement about Lyndon Johnson, who allegedly had 'extra glands that give him energy that ordinary men simply don't have.' A profound student of Abraham Lincoln, about whom he has written eloquently and extensively, Lehrman followed the Great Emancipator's advice and example, accomplishing much through ambition, determination, industry, generosity, and civic-mindedness. He took inspiration from Lincoln, just as readers of this engrossing autobiography will find inspiration in the story it tells."

—**Michael Burlingame**, author *Lincoln: A Life*

"*The Sum of It All* recounts the fascinating life story of one of the most important businessmen and philanthropists of our time. Readers will discover how Lewis E. Lehrman made Rite Aid a successful national brand, how he influenced American politics and economics, and how he became a leader in history education. In these memoirs, Lehrman also draws from his research on Lincoln, Churchill, and others to offer life lessons that were instrumental to his success. This book is not to be missed."

—**Jonathan W. White**, author of *A House Built by Slaves: African American Visitors to the Lincoln White House*

"I met Lew when he was a young man energetic about his future. Since then he has lived an impressive life full of love and full of knowledge. This book is his account of that life. But it is no mere autobiography. Rather, like Benjamin Franklin, Lew writes it out of gratitude to the country that has given him much. And like Franklin's *Autobiography*, Lew's is meant to help his fellow Americans become 'wise, practical, and good.' All who wish to live a good life should read it."

—**Dr. Larry P. Arnn**, president of Hillsdale College

"Success in life consists in always striving for what is true, good, and beautiful. Lew Lehrman has made it his life's work to do just that. He truly loves his family, his faith, and his country. He has worked tirelessly in the worlds of business and finance, politics, writing, scholarship, and academic enrichment. His gratitude for the blessings God gave him is seen in his generous dedication to the cause of human betterment. This book tells the fascinating story of this inspirational man."

—**Fr. Gerald E. Murray**, pastor at Church of the Holy Family (New York, New York)

"Lewis Lehrman's biography is the riveting story of an American hero who has done 'work worth doing' his entire life and made our world a better place. It is a thoroughly entertaining read."

—**Gay Hart Gaines**, 18th Regent of George Washington's Mount Vernon

"The number of modern figures about whom it may be said with a straight face that he is in the same league with Alexander Hamilton can be numbered on the fingers of one hand. Lew Lehrman is one of those few. His autobiography is instructive not only about the biggest issues facing America but also the character required to still make a meaningful contribution to what Abraham Lincoln called the American 'experiment'."

—**John D. Mueller**, founding director of the Economics and Ethics Program at the Ethics and Public Policy Center

"Personal memoirs are rarely of interest beyond the family and close friends of the memoirist. There are, however, exceptions, and Lewis Lehrman's memoir is one. The reason is that Mr. Lehrman is an exceptional man who has led an exceptional life. The story of his life is, at the same time, the story of what is exceptional about America. The grandson of a Jewish peddler and three other immigrant grandparents rose to prominence in business, politics, philanthropy, and intellectual life. He believed in our nation's principles and promises, and seized the opportunities for success that they made possible. He went to Yale and then to Wall Street. He became a force in civic life and an intellectual whose writings help his fellow Americans to more fully understand, and more deeply appreciate, their principles, their history, and their duties as citizens of the world's most audacious experiment in republican government and morally ordered liberty."

—**Robert P. George**, McCormick Professor of Jurisprudence, Princeton University

THE SUM OF IT ALL

autobiography

LEWIS E. LEHRMAN

LYONS PRESS
ESSEX, CONNECTICUT

LYONS PRESS

An imprint of Globe Pequot, the trade division of
The Rowman & Littlefield Publishing Group, Inc.
4501 Forbes Blvd., Ste. 200
Lanham, MD 20706
www.rowman.com

Distributed by NATIONAL BOOK NETWORK

All photos courtesy of the author unless otherwise indicated

British Library Cataloguing in Publication Information available

Library of Congress Cataloging-in-Publication Data
Names: Lehrman, Lewis E., author.
Title: The sum of it all / Lewis E. Lehrman.
Description: Essex, Connecticut : Lyons Press, [2023] | Includes bibliographical references and index. | Summary: "Filled with interviews, remembrances, quotes, and photographs of the many influential personalities, partners, and associates Lewis E. Lehrman has worked with throughout his life that best testify to his significance. The sometimes unexpected choices Lew has made and delivered on sum up an exemplary life—wide, deep, and well lived"— Provided by publisher.
Identifiers: LCCN 2023016054 (print) | LCCN 2023016055 (ebook) | ISBN 9781493076505 (cloth ; alk. paper) | ISBN 9781493076512 (electronic)
Subjects: LCSH: Lehrman, Lewis E. | Politicians—United States—Biography. | Capitalists and financiers—United States—Biography. | Historians—United States—Biography.
Classification: LCC E748.L566 A3 2023 (print) | LCC E748.L566 (ebook) | DDC 973.9092 [B]—dc23/eng/20230510
LC record available at https://lccn.loc.gov/2023016054
LC ebook record available at https://lccn.loc.gov/2023016055

™ The paper used in this publication meets the minimum requirements of American National Standard for Information Sciences—Permanence of Paper for Printed Library Materials, ANSI/NISO Z39.48-1992.

On the Hunt

"Walking West on East 80th Street"

Dedicated to

Louise Stillman Lehrman, my outstanding wife
Best of friends through thick and thin,
the only love of my life.

With Louise, all things are possible.
Without her, nothing.

CONTENTS

Bronze statue of Abraham Lincoln at the New-York Historical Society by StudioEIS

Father and Son

ACKNOWLEDGMENTS

There are so many people to whom I owe thanks that I could never name each one. If they are missing from these acknowledgments, or the book, it is an inadvertent mistake. I am deeply grateful to all those who gave me their wisdom and shared their memories.

Susan Tang and Deja Hickcox were deeply involved in both the first and the second draft. Deja heroically handled the enormous task of citing all my sources. The final book is a product of myself and my son Leland, with Louise contributing many of the photographs. To Judith Schnell, who published many of my history books and now this one, I owe so many things I cannot even begin to describe them. I could not have paid an outside professional to write this book, so true to my real life it is. Nor could I have undertaken the project by myself, for physical reasons among many others.

Louise was my inspiration, and she generously kept in touch with the book's unfolding. But it was Jim Basker and Richard Gilder who first urged me to write it. In all, it's been a wonderful journey through the past. Since the past is always present, I enjoy it all the more.

Two men from the past, in particular, I would like to acknowledge by name. Abraham Lincoln's defense of freedom—and his advice to "work, work, work"—ennobled the United States and my life.[1] Winston Churchill's advice to study history helped me to understand its supreme importance. For whatever the merits of science and religion—though we justly revere the arts and humanities—*history is the sum of it all.*[2] In order to keep this book mercifully short, I edited several chapters aggressively as the book went to press. I have, however, carefully archived these edits—and a great deal more original source material—all of which can be found at my website: lewiselehrman.com.

One more thing: Each of my children played an indispensable role in bringing the manuscript to fruition, so I would like to honor each of them by name.

R. Leland Lehrman
John Stillman Lehrman
Thomas Dudley Lehrman
Eliza Disosway Lehrman
Peter Rueff Lehrman

Anyone who tries to write an autobiography will face the challenge of rendering their inscrutable life comprehensible. Leland contributed the most to ordering the story, and I thank him for his exceptionally good work. I could not have done it without him. He showed gumption and hard work as I hammered out the final text.

Every man who has children hopes for the best, and I have five children and fifteen grandchildren. All of them have added much to my life, and thus to this story.

Many others to whom I owe thanks will appear in the pages to come.

Rosebud

CHAPTER 1

Walking West on East 80th Street

My mother had a wonderful reputation. To everyone, she was known as "Rose" or "Rosebud." She was friendly with and loved by folks from all walks of life. There was never any distance between Mother and the people she met. She was known as a perfect lady. Mother treated everyone, no matter their work, as princes of their realm. Born to two immigrant parents, she understood what it was to be raised in humble conditions.

Rose Herman Lehrman was the essence of elegance and beauty. She was decorous and dignified. When I was a little boy, we went to the farmers' market on Third Street together. All the farmers in their little stands were delighted to see her. Her humility captivated their hearts. She did not want to attract attention to herself, but she embodied the ethical virtues. In her, I saw the ancient virtue of courtliness: modesty, always standing erect, always speaking fluently with people from all walks of life, and treating everyone with the utmost care—a quality so important in life, but too seldom present.

Even in the most difficult times, Mother was always there for her four children. My twin brother Gilbert remembers her the same way: "Mother came from a very poor family; she never had exposure to what the upper class had. She was a quiet, loving woman who cared deeply about her family, her children, and their education. Everything."[1]

Lois, Gil, Barbara, and I all reciprocated her love and understood her pragmatic approach to problems. "Be that as it may," she would often say in response to an obstacle, "you still have to do your best." And so, we were taught to deal with problems with a generous spirit. "Be that as it may" was her watchword.

For Mother, like my grandfather Louis, reputation was more important than status or wealth. They both took the Ten Commandments seriously. They embodied virtues in ways others recognized. Mother always emphasized these cardinal virtues: honesty and respect for others. She tried to teach us manners for every occasion.

The family is the fountainhead of ordered freedom the world over... Our children, all the children of this land, must be given not only the shelter of a house, but the love of a home.[2]

My father was a hard worker and sometimes a hard man. He emphasized courage as the virtue which secured other virtues, especially in adversity. Benjamin Sachs

Big Ben with Rose

Lehrman was very competitive. He fell in love with Mother the moment he met her. They found each other at a dance on the Pennsylvania State University campus. Mother used to tell me how they would dance the night away to the two-step. Ever beautiful, inside and out, Mother was one of the biggest "catches" in Harrisburg. My older sister Lois remembers that Dad "was quite handsome . . . and people who knew my mother from when she was a girl said she was one of the best-looking girls in Harrisburg."

My friends also fell in love with her. Michael "Biggie" Moore of Denver was one of them. I have a note from him in which he remembers the occasion, saying: "In June of 1957 I visited the Lehrmans as I was riding my Indian motorcycle back to Colorado [from Yale]. I've a picture of Lew's mom riding on the back of my bike. What a fabulous lady!"[3]

Mother was a woman without pretense or pride. At her funeral in 1968, the eulogist delivered a superb remembrance about the grandeur of her character—speaking of the beauty evident both outside and in. He said she was the kind of mother and the kind of grandmother who should be a role model for the entire congregation.

The most important thing my mother influenced was my education. It was she who decided I should leave Riverside Public School after the fourth grade. It was she who decided I should go to the Harrisburg Academy, where I spent grades five through eight. And it was Mother who decided I should go away to The Hill School, in Pottstown, Pennsylvania. When I arrived, the school had a new headmaster, Edward T. Hall, who was very strict, and very knowledgeable about his students. Hill proved to be a turning point for me—socially, athletically, intellectually, and morally.

In my junior year at Hill, I was a hell-raiser and a prankster. Although serious, mine were not expellable offenses. Mother had previously been tolerant of my occasional antics; Father did not hear of them. A strict disciplinarian, he was kept in the dark—even though he had been a prankster himself in high school. Known as "Rip," my father would get on top of the Harrisburg trolley and detach the pole connected to the overhead wires. As a parent, however, he was intolerant of mistakes. Eventually, Mother, Mr. Hall, and I came to an agreement, and so my father never found out about my pranks.

In the decades since, I have often been reminded of the great moral injunctions of my mother and Mr. Hall. When they teamed up again to urge me to apply to Yale, I was enthusiastic. Once upon a time, I had different plans. My fifth-grade teacher, Mrs. Elsie B. Diven, wanted me to go to West Point. She hoped I would become a general. I will forever be grateful to Mrs. Diven for believing in me, but I must thank my mother for her superior insight.

Yale was a life-altering experience for many reasons, yet one in particular stands out above them all. At a fraternity called the Fence Club I met Charles and later, Stanley Stillman. We became good friends, especially Stanley and I, and often stayed

Louise with her mother Frances, and brothers Stanley (left) and Charles

in touch. In the spring of 1964, after active service in the Army, I was in New York staying at the Yale Club. Stanley knew his way around the city, so I gave him a call.

"Come up for breakfast," he suggested.

It was the day that changed my life.

The following morning at 7:30, I hailed a taxi up Madison Avenue to East 80th Street. At breakfast, I had an argument with Stanley's sister Louise about public policy. She thought me too liberal. I disagreed, as diplomatically as I could.

Later that same day, I got a phone call from Howell Scott, who had been one year ahead of me at Yale. Howell said: "We're giving a dinner party. You're invited, but you have to bring a date." I called Stanley back immediately, who said Louise was seeing someone, but that nevertheless I could call her. I did, and she agreed to come to the dinner party the next evening.

The night of the party I headed back to the townhouse on East 80th Street to pick up Louise. After getting out of the taxi, I was so nervous, I walked east intentionally, away from the townhouse. I soon walked back westwards, but instead of knocking at the door, *I turned around and walked east again.* As I walked along, I told myself that if I didn't summon my courage, I might never get another chance to see Louise. I was living in Harrisburg at the time, and my trips to New York were few and far between. Gathering my resolve, I started walking west again, and rang the bell at 15 East 80th Street. A few moments later, I saw Louise coming down the steps. I fell for her immediately. She was so poised, so wholesome, so bright, so sound and full of good cheer. I can still remember the dress she was wearing: a print with flowers, and shoes to match.

Somehow, God blessed me with the insight to see that I had met the girl of my dreams. My life and vocation would have been a mere shadow of themselves had I not come to breakfast on East 80th Street that morning.

Louise was the youngest of three children. Charles Jr. was a year ahead of me at Yale. Stanley, a year behind me, was an intellectual, more interested in politics than I. He went on to become an attorney with Donovan, Leisure, Newton and Irvine, and later a respected journalist.

My father and mother immediately loved Louise. Dad was not easy to impress, but he deferred to Louise, so impressed was he by her character. It was my father who had inspired me with ever higher goals. "Life is worth living if you aspire to great things," was his message. There was no higher goal than my courtship of Louise, which lasted two years. She finally yielded to my blandishments, her all-surpassing common sense notwithstanding.

Louise had grown up in New York City. Her father, Charles Latimer Stillman, had gone to work for Time Incorporated in 1928, six years after its founding. His service as a top executive continued until his retirement in 1971 as chairman of the finance committee, and was interrupted only by work in 1948 on the postwar economic recovery program for China under the Federal Economic Cooperation Administration.

Louise's mother, Frances Disosway Johnson, traced her lineage back to the colonial era. I admired the way she managed her family and her life in addition to pursuing her love of travel by turning it into a profession.

I first proposed to Louise three months after meeting her. To my proposal, Louise responded, "Absolutely not. It's too premature." At one point, we decided to take a holiday from each other. About four months later, I proposed again. We talked about when we should get married in the fall of 1965, and set the date for May 27, of 1966.

I used all my savings to buy a ring.

One of the happiest days of my life was our wedding at the River Club. Years earlier, Louise had come out there, escorted as a debutante by her brother, Stanley. About one hundred members of our family and friends attended the wedding ceremony and reception. We wanted to keep our wedding party small. Gil was my best man and Julie Michel, who had attended The Madeira School with Louise, was the maid of honor. A Civil Court judge officiated.

Louise was a vision of perfection in what the *New York Times* reported was "a gown of white silk organza with appliques of organza flowers. Her veil was of matching organza bordered with the same flowers, and she carried white daisies and ivy."[4] My new wife was a great dancer and she had taught me the two-step, an old-fashioned dance. I liked the pre-1914 quality of it. That night, my friends Yale Kneeland, Bill Beadleston, John Britton, and Johnny Pitts hosted a champagne party for us at the Plaza hotel. Most of the glasses ended up in the fireplace. Louise was not dismayed. She knew that most of my buddies were not conventional.

For our honeymoon, Louise and I went to Mallorca and Madrid. For our first anniversary we went to London and Paris. There, Louise took me to Savile Row to be fitted for a bespoke suit. We also looked at seventeenth- and eighteenth-century American silverware. We saw a pair of Queen Anne candlesticks. They were perfect. I told the shop owner, a man by the name of Mr. Shrubsole, that I would give him $50 as a deposit. I came back the next day, but they were gone. Someone had made a higher bid. I learned a great lesson. When you see something you really want, and can afford, don't hesitate. And when you make a decision, stick to it. Don't hesitate and don't wait.

After we married, Louise and I came back to my home in Harrisburg, Pennsylvania. Mr. and Mrs. George Bailey gave a reception for us. Mr. Bailey was chairman of the Harrisburg National Bank, and the father of my childhood friend, Susie Bailey. Mr. Bailey was also "Mr. Harrisburg," and rightfully shares the name of Jimmy Stewart's timeless character in the classic movie, *It's a Wonderful Life*. He was a friend, and the key banker to our family business. At the party, Louise was naturally the center of attention. Even Mr. Bailey fell in love with Louise. "She is easy to fall in love with,"[5] were Susie's words many years later.

Photo by Yale Kneeland

I rise…

Louise in her wedding dress

When people met Louise, I always went up in their esteem. We made many visits to Paris, starting in 1974, to visit the great French central banker and monetary economist Jacques Rueff. He, too, fell in love with Louise—who spoke much better French than I. During my public career, I was often asked about my marriage. I would usually respond as follows: "I have had only one profound love in my life, and her name is Louise. I married her confident that I had done the right thing. There is not a single detail about my marriage or my immediate family that I would change so perfect a family has Louise given me."[6]

I consider myself a very lucky man—very blessed in all the important things such as my children, my friends, and some of my associates in business. I have avoided insolvency, even in the worst of times, and have been endowed with loyal, devoted, and gifted children. Above all, a perfect wife. As I said on the occasion of our fiftieth wedding anniversary in 2016:

> I have thought about my marriage made in heaven one half-century ago. Walking along, thinking about this, there has been an inescapable reflection. "What would have become of me, were it not for Louise?"
>
> How does one sum up fifty years of marriage? On this, I have reflected, too. I discovered early on, that *with Louise, all things are possible. Without her, nothing.*
>
> Henry Austen confided about his sister, Jane Austen, that "the farthest thing from *her* expectations or wishes was to be exhibited as a public character, under any circumstances."[7] So, too, it can be said of Louise—the farthest thing from *her* expectations or *her* wishes is to be exhibited as a public character, *under any circumstances.*
>
> Still, it can truly be said that my life—so much of what I cherish—is all about Louise. She made my life worth living.[8]

Louis Lehrman, American patriot

CHAPTER 2

The Sum of It All

Like many of you, I was a lucky grandson of four immigrant grandparents—as I was born in America. My immigrant grandfather Louis was a peddler—and a patriot, who believed with the religious founders of our country, that America was the New Jerusalem. At home, I grew up under Grandpa's moral leadership. But, politically speaking, I grew up in the shadow of the legendary "Pop-Pop" Taylor, the Republican boss of Pennsylvania who put Warren Harding over the top in 1920. I can still remember "Pop-Pop" patting me on the head as a boy and giving me some advice: "Lew, never touch cigarettes, whiskey or women—until you reach your twelfth birthday."

Fortunately, my grandpa's moral leadership prevailed, and it was he, my parents, and my teachers who passed on to me the values and standards I learned in my childhood. Like most Americans, I cherish the traditional values I learned growing up in central Pennsylvania. These national standards—family, faith, freedom, and loyalty to the flag for which we stand—these are the things in life worth fighting for. And make no mistake. Today, we are again engaged in a great civil war—an intellectual civil war, testing what kind of nation we shall choose to be in our third century.

The issue is whether or not we shall fulfill the promise, at home, of the Declaration of Independence, and peacefully carry this charter of our liberties to a world longing to be free. This is not the only issue. But it must be the goal of every true American patriot: not only for reasons of self-interest, but more importantly, because America is the preeminent standard-bearer of the sacred code of Judeo-Christian civilization. And no American citizen should doubt that this code of freedom, *by itself*—hammered out in our common law and our Constitution—accounts for the rise of thirteen impoverished colonies by the sea to become the most bountiful nation the Earth has ever known.

Our forefathers believed that all work was sacred, each calling sanctified, every spiritual and economic advance a glory to our Creator. If our earthly end was to increase and multiply, our grandfathers had clear views on the means to this goal. In the realm of commerce, the Founders held—along with our immigrant forebears—that government created the conditions, and some of the incentives, which lead, not to welfare, but to work; not to subsidies, but savings; not to hoarding, but risk taking; not to indulgent consumption, but investment; not to austerity, but growth; not to the dole, but full employment.

Religious and ethical leaders from all walks of life know that "Justice demands the establishment of minimum levels of participation by all persons in the life of the human community."[1] I agree. So do almost all Americans. None of us who have read the Prophets and the Gospels could deny the just claims of the least among us. This doctrine is a goal which we all accept, but the doctrine allows men and women to choose in good conscience the means—the public policy and law—by which to attain this end. And thus many of us ask: Do we give a fish to him who has none, in order to fill him for just one day; or do we make a fisher of this man, and teach him to fish for himself, that he may feed his family all of his days? Do we eliminate poverty by "public service employment and . . . public subsidies," or do we create incentives to bring out the best in free men and women who then create lasting jobs for the least among us in new and growing firms? Which course of action, which means to our goal of full human dignity, is the enduring path of individual progress, the way to self-esteem, and the road to independence for the self-governing family?

Do we really bestow the dignity of economic independence by once again raising the level of welfare payments? During the 1960s and '70s, when I was studying these issues in depth, this scheme gave rise to what has now become trillions of dollars in welfare state spending, with pathetic and ironic results we cannot escape, namely, even more poverty and dependency. For example, the percentage of Americans living below the poverty line rose from 12.6 percent in 1970 to 13 percent in 1980; and teenage unemployment doubled *after* the exponential rise of welfare payments and the minimum wage.

Now, consider the alternative means to our agreed upon goal of full economic participation: We give dignity to life on Earth for all able-bodied men and women who want honest work by creating the conditions for morally guided economic growth, which alone can raise the standard for labor, unskilled and skilled alike.

A low, simple, fair tax rate which rewards hard work, savings, and investment for the making of new jobs; a stable dollar; and a limited government which balances the budget without raising taxes—these are the true incentives for growth. I raise these questions for each of us to examine by the light of conscience and evidence.

For myself, I believe a certain truth; and I also believe this truth can make us free. And it is this: To desire a goal should cause us to desire the most effective means to reach that goal.[2] To do otherwise is to court disaster. I share the goal of a humane American economy with everyone—the faithful and the ethical—and I also believe the means to that goal lie deep in our democratic and republican form of limited government, in the free labor and free enterprise economy, and the 158 million jobs it has created in our country. The evidence is compelling. For example, in the fifteen years between 1970 and 1985, our free economy created twenty-seven million new jobs. In the same time period, the social-democratic welfare state economies of Western Europe lost two million jobs. While America's free farmers still feed the world, government-dominated farm economies in the Sudan, Ethiopia, and throughout Africa often fail to avoid famine, only to be relieved by American alms. Under universal farm socialism in Africa—during those same fifteen years—food production per person fell 20 percent below 1960 levels. And this result, according to scholars, had little to do with the drying up of the water and much to do with the drying up of the incentives to cultivate the land.

Finally, our conscience harkens us again. Faith asks, what of the least among us, those who are literally unable to fish, to farm, or to forge a product on the anvil of the workplace?

Americans have answered this question. They are the most generous givers in history, at home and abroad. I believe our government was created to do those things for our people which they cannot do for themselves. And most Americans agree.

All these American traditions began with the Founders, who guided themselves by a cardinal American economic principle which stemmed from their faith. And the principle was this: In a social order founded on voluntary covenants and consensus, economic justice must mean that before able-bodied citizens make a demand on society, they should first make a supply. To protect this principle the Founders wrote it into the Fifth Amendment of our organic law, stating that private property shall not "be taken for public use, without just compensation." When people and nations act upon this first principle of free enterprise, it completely alters human conduct—to which the history of our nation is a living witness. For some four hundred years in America, we have seen the miraculous fruits of this first moral principle of work. Why should we, or anyone else, be amazed by the American miracle? We know that to supply is, in another form but to give—to offer. And to give is to produce—to make an offering in the market. But to receive is to consume—in another form to take from the market. Thus it is rightly said: Freely do we give. Then we receive.

With this rule of faith and natural law, drawn out and elaborated by great jurists—in Blackstone's Big Book, Chitty's pleadings, Joseph Story's commentaries, and in Chancellor Kent's principles—the Founders and their interpreters had drawn a blueprint, not only for individual and family success; but, in fact, they had passed on to us the revolutionary principles not only for national greatness, but also for global prosperity.[3] Even after nearly 250 years, the American Revolution *alone* still strikes the unmistakable spark of universality in the soul of humanity—bursting brightly upon the face of the Earth, as it did, in the Declaration of Independence—proclaiming that all mankind, not just Americans, but all men and women are endowed by their Creator with unalienable rights.

Despite the truth of this record of American accomplishment, some prominent intellectuals at the most prestigious universities have been teaching that the only truth is that there is no such thing as truth. Such a teaching is both deeply unsatisfying, as well as self-contradictory. Even by its own definition, it cannot be true. So despite the intellectual conceits of modernity, the truth will forever be the perennial human quest, and not just the one truth, but the several truths that make us free Americans.

You see, July 4, in the year of our Lord, 1776 was a world historical event, not because a new nation was founded on the shores of the Atlantic, but because a new nation, the very first of its kind, was founded "under God," begotten, as Thomas Jefferson wrote, according to the "Laws of Nature and of Nature's God." Our nation was dedicated to a religious proposition—a principle of natural theology—and it was this: "We hold these truths to be self-evident: that all men are *created* equal, that they are endowed by their *Creator* with certain unalienable rights, and that among these are life, liberty, and the pursuit of happiness." This proposition, as the Great Emancipator proclaimed, is "the father of all moral principle"[4] among Americans. By reason of this, the Founding Principle to which he held us accountable, Abraham Lincoln anointed his countrymen "the almost chosen people." And it was Thomas Jefferson himself who proposed that the national seal depict Moses leading the chosen people to the promised land. If therefore we elevate the American Revolution above all political revolutions, that is because of this irresistible light of universality with which, in the form of a Declaration to a darkening world, our Revolution burst suddenly upon the face of the Earth—with an elemental spiritual force and a liberating doctrine, the ultimate possibilities of which you and I, even now, can only begin dimly to see. And this is so because *never* before has a Republic of Freedom been conceived and consecrated to a *principle* of natural law, applicable to all people, everywhere, and for all time to come. The American political revolutionaries of 1776, and later the Civil War, did not base their claim to freedom on some ancient title to an ancestral place. They did not assert a parochial claim based on racial or ethnic roots. They did not say—all Americans are equal to all Englishmen, nor that all White men north of the Mason-Dixon Line are equal, nor all White and Black men living in the Western Hemisphere, nor all free men and women living behind the shield of the NATO Alliance. They said *all* people are created by God, *free and equal. This* is what the Founders said and *this* is what they meant. When during our Civil War, the time came for Americans to clarify exactly what this statement really means, we paid dearly to make clear that the human right to freedom is truly universal. And thus we see that the birthright of America is in fact no less than *a title deed to equal rights in every nation and on every continent.*

The link between religion and American politics is thus indissoluble, because the American Revolution itself rests on the natural law written in the hearts of men. And this link Thomas Jefferson himself held to be beyond dispute, writing as he did that the "God who gave us life also gave us liberty. Can the liberties of a nation be secure when we have removed a conviction that these liberties are the gift of God? Indeed I tremble for my country when I reflect that God is just. . . ."[5] The irony would be amusing if it were not a public scandal—but today, critics of American religious tradition argue that our Founding Fathers, in their care to separate an established Church from the State, meant to remove almost every trace of the living God from our public life. This doctrine is not only pernicious; it is false.

In fact, the constitutional debates show that the Founding Fathers sought only to prevent the legal establishment—at the federal level—of a government-owned sectarian church such as the Anglican Church in England. And chief among hundreds of unimpeachable witnesses present at the creation of the Republic, I bring forward President George Washington—"First in war, first in peace, first in the hearts of his

Portrait by Rembrandt Peale. Gilder Lehrman Institute of American History, GLC09119.01

George Washington:
First in the hearts of his countrymen

countrymen"[6]—who declared in his Farewell Address that "of all the dispositions and habits which lead to political prosperity, religion and morality are indispensable supports."[7] It is a fact of early American history that the First Amendment was never a license for government to suppress religious practices in public places; nor was it a pornographic license to destroy the faith, the future, and the mind of a child; neither was it a warrant for the Supreme Court to prohibit prayer in public places. Indeed, the First Amendment, read rightly, according to the common canons of statutory and constitutional construction, means plainly: Congress shall make no law abridging the free exercise of religion. Now more than ever is this true. Moreover, the Supreme Court of the United States cannot maintain much longer the absurd construction of the religion clause itself, wherein it *broadly* construes the free exercise part to include atheism and humanism among protected religions, but *narrowly* construes, on a completely different principle, the establishment clause of the same amendment—with the effect of removing true religion from almost all public life.

Even the Supreme Court, divided against the nation this way, cannot last. Either both parts of the freedom of religion rule shall change and come under one authentic Supreme Court principle, consistent with right reason and the intent of the Founders, or the nation will reform the Court—and vindicate the original principle of free exercise of religion.

If, as a nation under God, our faith has made us mighty and free, so too did we wax prosperous by exalting the family, a way of life grounded in the Bible and in our common law—a common law which stemmed in part from the ecclesiastical courts of Christendom. And if I dwell on these wellsprings of our world greatness—faith, family, and the natural law—it is only because I believe that, cut off from the fountainhead of first principles, the deep river of our national life must eventually run dry—and the hope of the world with it.

Thus, we cannot yield; we shall not yield. We shall never give up. You see, our forefathers were Protestants from England, Germans from the Rhineland, slaves from Africa, later the Irish, Italian, and Jewish immigrants, to mention only a few. And today, from every troubled corner of this Earth they still flee, having no other bond than their common humanity, and the uncommon boldness to break free into our New Jerusalem. There, new immigrants witness, by their work and their way of life, that they know and honor the common watchword of our national faith—the declaration that all people, under God, are created with the unalienable right to life—free and equal.

This declaration alone can be the common bond which joins all Americans together, especially those of us without blood ancestors present at the creation of the Republic. We know, as my grandfather knew, that whatsoever this declaration of rights by the Founders is true—and everlasting—everything I am, everything I could ever be, arises from the fact that I can say: I am an American citizen.

We should have no doubt about the ultimate victory of our faith—and of the American way of life—the faith of our fathers—living still. But if we desire not merely success for ourselves, but triumph, triumph for all Americans who strive for independence, self-respect, and honor—and freedom for all members of the human family on Earth—*we must be bold*; so that for all time to come, this dream of victory, this good news, shall not perish from the Earth.

Let us swear never to be moved from our purpose by fear; by threats; but let us go forward, full in the faith that it is up to us, to you, the standard-bearers of freedom to make this dream come true. And it is time to begin, again.[8]

CHAPTER 3

Getting Started

GROWING UP IN HARRISBURG

My mother's family moved from Boston to Harrisburg in 1927. She was just eighteen. Her father, Lewis Herman, had died at forty of a heart attack, leaving behind a wife, a son, and four daughters. Mother, then still in her teens, went to work at the State Capitol to support the family.

Dad was the "Son" in the family business, Louis Lehrman & Son. He grew up in Harrisburg with two sisters, Martha and Minerva. After meeting each other at the Penn State dance, Mother and Dad married in 1930. Mother gave birth to Lois in 1931 and Barbara in 1937.

On August 15, 1938, my twin brother Gilbert and I were born at the Harrisburg Hospital. The presiding doctor was Alfred Sherman. At that time, my family lived in a "half house" at 2809 North Second Street. Two years later, Dad built a brick house at 2910 Parkside Lane. Overlooking the Italian Lake, our house was just three blocks from the Susquehanna River, and five blocks from the Pennsylvania Railroad tracks going out west. I cherish the memory of my years growing up along the Susquehanna. I pray that I can uphold the authentic American values of central Pennsylvania, the values by which I was educated—faith, family, freedom, and loyalty to the flag of the Republic for which we stand.

Two for the money

There were many people attending our birth. Lois, my sister, was eight years older than I. Barbara was three years older. Lois got a car for her sixteenth birthday, and I remember that because she used to take me and my brother for rides. Otherwise, I remember little of the first years of my life, other than that I always wanted to lead. In July of 1976, my aunt Martha Hurwitz wrote me a memorable

Far, far away lies the Italian Lake

2910 Parkside Lane

c. 1925 Harold M. Brett

The Rockville Bridge over the Susquehanna River

letter, saying that "from the days your mother and I each held a baby and presented the bottle—you yelled the loudest."[1] For the next fourteen years, I shared a bedroom with Gil until, at the end of the eighth grade, Gil went to The Gunnery School, and I went to The Hill School. My brother and I were always a team—especially on the playground. "He and I used to take baths together," Gil would later say. "He was like my father. Taking care of me. Giving me courage to be better than I was. Very grown up. Always supportive of me doing good in football and basketball. Not interested in pushing me in school."[2] Harrisburg, as Lois once said, "was a wonderful place to grow up. It was small-town, and you could get on the bus and go everywhere."[3] Our family was well known in the community. Grandpa had developed a wholesale grocery business from the tiny store he had opened in Steelton, Pennsylvania. Louis Lehrman & Son supplied stores throughout the area from a warehouse under the Mulberry Street Bridge in Harrisburg.

I am named "Lewis" after my maternal grandfather, Lewis Herman. I never met him since he died before I was born. The grandparent I did know well, a real hero in my life, was "Louis" Lehrman. My mother's family came from the Baltic region of what was then Western Russia or Prussia. My father's family emigrated from the same part of Europe, in what is now called Belarus. Grandpa was one of eight brothers who all moved to America.

The family was centered on economic opportunity—the opportunity to build a business. Life at home, as well as at the business, was based upon thanksgiving for the freedom that my grandparents found when they came to America.

Once a week, my grandfather Louis Lehrman came to dinner, usually Tuesday evening. He was a self-educated immigrant who was an unself-conscious apostle of the American Idea. Grandpa was all about America. I was studying at college when I

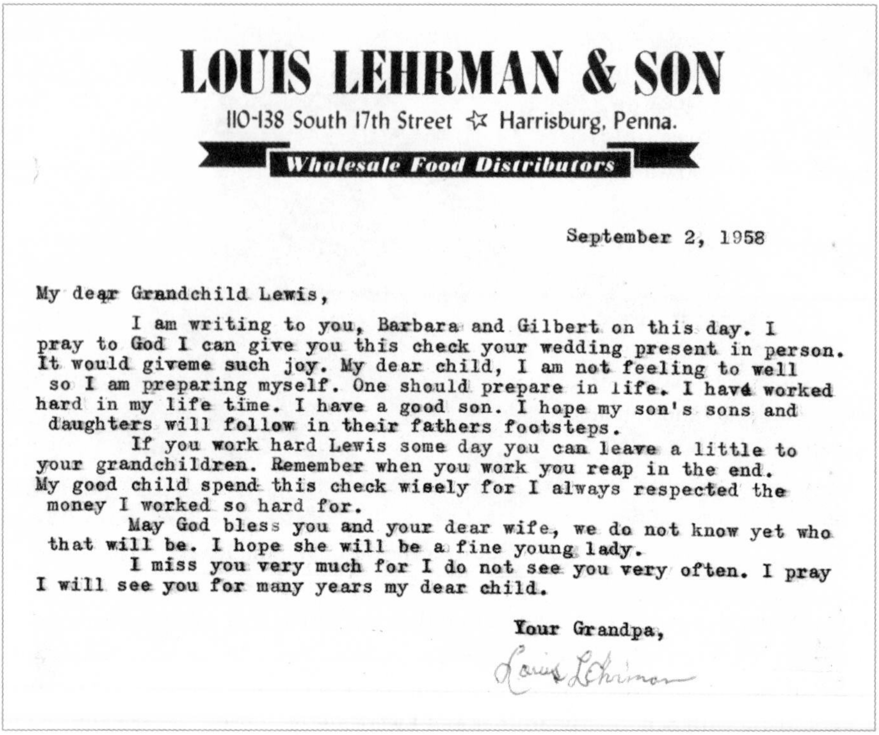

LOUIS LEHRMAN & SON
110-138 South 17th Street ☆ Harrisburg, Penna.
Wholesale Food Distributors

September 2, 1958

My dear Grandchild Lewis,

I am writing to you, Barbara and Gilbert on this day. I pray to God I can give you this check your wedding present in person. It would giveme such joy. My dear child, I am not feeling to well so I am preparing myself. One should prepare in life. I have worked hard in my life time. I have a good son. I hope my son's sons and daughters will follow in their fathers footsteps.

If you work hard Lewis some day you can leave a little to your grandchildren. Remember when you work you reap in the end. My good child spend this check wisely for I always respected the money I worked so hard for.

May God bless you and your dear wife, we do not know yet who that will be. I hope she will be a fine young lady.

I miss you very much for I do not see you very often. I pray I will see you for many years my dear child.

Your Grandpa,

Louis Lehrman

Letter from my grandfather

learned he was near death. At the urging of my father, I visited him in his Harrisburg apartment. In bed, but still alert, he asked me what my plans were. I told him I was studying the culture, the history, and the different nations of Europe, and that I was planning to travel there to learn these subjects firsthand. After all, every sophisticated undergraduate thought Europe was really something special.

My grandfather was scandalized.

He responded indignantly, with words to this effect: "What would you ever want to do that for, going to Europe? Everything is here in America. *This* is the new Jerusalem. America is the place that has everything that you need, everything you want to see, and everything you should aspire to." I tried to persuade Grandpa that there were things he may not have known in Europe that I wanted to see. But he was not to be persuaded. Having left everything there happily behind, he could not understand what I could possibly be looking for in Europe. I never forgot Grandpa's reaction.

As a student of history, I know that there is neither a beginning, nor is there an end to my indebtedness to good teachers. My grandfather and my devoted parents were dedicated teachers and simple patriots. Having raised me in the shadows of the Depression and World War II, in central Pennsylvania, they made me aware of American victories, at home and abroad.

Two decades later, I wrote one of my godsons a bit of advice that reflected how deeply Grandpa's message had been instilled in me: "I want you to know that Paris is a very pretty place," I wrote, "but if you had to live there, you would have to spend all your money to eat three decent meals a day. It is the most expensive place in the whole world. I also want you to know that America is the very best place in which to live; and you will understand this when you get old enough to travel. . . . Sometimes when one is young, these foreign countries and . . . foreigners seem to be impressive and important; but once you get a little older you find out that no country is as good or important as the United States."[4]

Grandpa was a courtly and handsome fellow, well-respected in Harrisburg. Dad was six foot two and 190 pounds. Intolerant of mistakes, he was big and forbidding, and literally all business—arriving at the office before everyone else at 7:00 a.m. I learned from my father the elementary lessons of business—I should not embarrass the family by any major mistake.

Our parents aspired to success for their children. We were driven to excel—morally, spiritually, educationally, financially. Lois excelled at the piano; Barbara as an artist. Gil was an expert at making friends and singing. I was taught as a child that hard work made things easy. I was taught that hard work harnessed to talent makes a difference. Mother was the one who wanted to make sure I got a good education. She was the one who encouraged every student impulse in me. At night, Gil would sit at one end of the kitchen table and I at the other to do our homework.

Gil still has clear memories of those days, saying of me that "[Lew] was always intense. . . . He taught himself to read when we were little, three or four years old. And he'd be concentrating so hard on his comic books, you'd have to call him over and over to come out and play. Then, in school, he was always number one at everything."[5]

Although it is true that I learned to read very early, I did in fact have some help from my mother, Dr. Fred Brown, and Joe Palooka. Although my mother was always quietly there to guide me, serious interest in my intellect also developed in the extended family. My father's sister Minerva had married a psychiatrist named Dr. Fred Brown. A Hungarian immigrant, it was he who called my attention to the *New York Times*, taught me how to read the headlines, and helped me with some words. He wished me well in my studies, and from there, it was Joe Palooka, my comic book hero and a world champion boxer, who helped me finish the job.[6]

Mother wanted me to be a pianist. She sent me to weekly classes with Mrs. Ziegler for instruction in the piano and musical appreciation. I took the bus, but sometimes I was diverted by the opportunity to play football in the field across the street. So I never became an accomplished pianist as Lois did. Both our parents loved musicals, and Mother took me to see some in New York. Her tastes were mostly classical, however—Mozart, Mendelssohn, Beethoven, and Strauss. She would make me stay in some Saturdays to listen to opera, and particularly admired Arturo Toscanini.

Gil and I

Sports were more important to me. One summer when I was about ten, Dad escorted me to camp by train. In New York's Grand Central Station, I saw this man across the terminal who looked very much like my Red Sox idol. My mother had grown up in Boston, so we were both Red Sox fans. "Are you Ted Williams?" I asked the man in Grand Central Station. "You're my hero. I'm a Red Sox fan." Despite the reputation he later gained for being prickly with press and fans, Mr. Williams was very nice to me that day. It was a long time before I washed the hand he shook. I also admired his patriotism as a Marine pilot in World War II, and later in the Korean War. When I was younger, I was also a fan of "Doc" Blanchard and Glenn Davis, the great running backs who were known as the "Touchdown Twins" when they played for West Point in the mid-1940s.

Gil and I went to camp for four weeks in the summer. We played baseball and basketball all day. I avoided swimming because I didn't like being wet. I avoided showers too, except for when the counselor put his foot down.

We started first grade at Riverside neighborhood school, but after fourth grade, Mother decided that Gil and I should go to the Harrisburg Academy. Dad was skeptical, but Mother felt we should get the very best education available, and Mother always prevailed in educational matters.

Dad's advice was consistent as I moved from one stage of my education to another. When I left public school to enter the Harrisburg Academy, my father sat me down and said, "You're now going into the big leagues. We'll see whether you can cut it."

When I left the Harrisburg Academy to go to boarding school in the ninth grade, my father sat me down and said "You're now going into the big leagues. We'll see whether you can cut it."

And when I left boarding school to go to college, my father sat me down and said to me again: "You're now going into the big leagues. We'll see whether you can cut it."

THE HARRISBURG ACADEMY

I arrived at Harrisburg Academy a complete stranger among boys and girls who had been at the school since first grade. They were also much bigger. I was small, and an easy target to pick on. One day I had had enough. I decided to take on the biggest bully. When he continued to pick on me, I found an opportunity to take him down in the schoolyard, right in front of everyone. No one picked on me after that. Like me, Gil was also a feisty kid. Small for our age, we made up for it by being scrappy. It worked. I was elected captain of the football team.[7]

I was equally focused on academic leadership. In 1951, the *Harrisburg Patriot* reported: "Lewis Lehrman, editor of the school paper, has been named president of the 1951-52 Student Council at the Harrisburg Academy. One of the projects now being conducted by the Student Council is the operation of the candy bar which is open every school day."[8]

I learned from some outstanding teachers at the Harrisburg Academy. In fifth and sixth grade, Mrs. Elsie B. Diven was my favorite teacher. She had gone to Columbia, and trained me rigorously, teaching me a disciplined attention to the details of English grammar. An inspired woman, Mrs. Diven inspired me in return. She quickened my interest in the beauty of the English language, and in everything patriotic.

Hers was a strict pedagogy and I minded her. My classmate, Susie Elder Bailey Scott, remembered her commitment to our education with these words: "We both were in Mrs. Diven's class. She was a character out of a Pilgrim storybook—a roly-poly teacher with a will of iron. She would find a way to teach you no matter what."[9]

Mrs. Diven often gave very challenging assignments to her students. I got my earliest training as a teacher helping Mrs. Diven teach my classmates. I loved to help Susie Bailey because she was so cute and cheerful. I will let Susie tell the story: "Lew had an abundant proficiency in math. [Mrs. Diven] would hand out columns and columns of figures [for us] to add them up. Lew could do them in twenty seconds. That infuriated her. She needed to give him something to do, so she set Lew to helping others. He was the big man on campus at the age of 12 at Harrisburg Academy. Extraordinarily nice, kind. Through middle school he held every office there was to hold. In my memory, he never did anything less than A+. Everything he was as a little boy was magnified as he grew up. He had curiosity beyond measure. All the moral characteristics he possessed remain today. . . . It's hard to believe that nearly 40 years and more than four-fifths of our lives have passed since the days of Mrs. Diven's endless columns of addition and the Lehrman twins' merciless mischief and mayhem!"[10]

Elsie B. Diven (left): My Best Teacher

The most important thing that Mrs. Diven taught was her patriotism. She had a special kind of patriotism that came from the heart, less from the intellect. That made it something enduring, which I was lucky enough to learn, boy though I was. I also learned from her to respect ordinary soldiers, for it was they who suffered the sting of battle. There in the fifth grade, after victory in World War II, Mrs. Diven instructed her fledgling students to study Sir Walter Scott's famous poem, *Native Land*. During history class, she would teach us to recite it, insisting that we should memorize these lines:

Breathes there the man, with soul so dead,
Who never to himself hath said,
This is my own, my native land!
Whose heart hath ne'er within him burn'd,
As home his footsteps he hath turned
If such there breathe, go, mark him well;
For him no Minstrel raptures swell,
High though his titles, proud his name,
Boundless his wealth as wish can claim;
Despite those titles, power, and pelf,
The wretch, concentred all in self,
Living, shall forfeit fair renown,
And, doubly dying, shall go down
To the vile dust, from whence he sprung,
Unwept, unhonour'd, and unsung.[11]

Mrs. Diven's claim that our native land is unique still rings true across the decades. Only America, she would declare, can become the homeland for people of every race, creed, and color. Immigrants first become American settlers, but then, they can become Americans in full.

There were other teachers who kept me in line. Mrs. Zack, my teacher in the sixth grade, was a good teacher and a strict disciplinarian. She pulled my curly hair when I tried to dominate classroom discussions. My Latin teacher, Carl Cassara, was also very strict. He had a desk full of erasers, pencils, and pens. His students waged war against him using his own arsenal of writing instruments. Intolerant of bad manners and bad behavior, he slapped me three times. It hurt, but 1949 was a different era with different teacher discipline.

My history teacher was an especially important influence on me at the time. It was he who set my sights on the important turns in history. Duncan Campbell, "a great Scot" and military historian, drove us the forty miles from school to the Gettysburg battlefield. There, he regaled our class with stories of this gravesite of bold warriors, blue and gray, and about the heroic aspects of American wartime statesmanship. For a young man, that kind of exercise can make a big impression. I can still see it all . . . coming down the rocks, at full speed, with Colonel Joshua

Chamberlain, in his great charge defending Little Round Top, on the second day of that pivotal battle.

As an eleven- and twelve-year-old, I got to know Gettysburg at a time when you could still find Algonquin arrowheads and bullets from the battle. If you were lucky, you might find some kind of military tool, such as a bayonet. Then, we were still allowed to search the area for historical artifacts. The day I was there, I found a musket ball. They were all over Devil's Den, where large boulders created a strategic location for Union forces on the second day of the battle.

More importantly, I learned there of slavery and emancipation, of Union and Confederate heroes and heroines. And I learned to revere Mr. Lincoln, who consecrated that battlefield cemetery "to the unfinished work which they who fought here have thus far so nobly advanced."[12]

At that time, President Lincoln's birthday was still a Pennsylvania school holiday. Our family, my teachers, and the families of all my classmates paid much attention to the great moments of American history: the Emancipation Proclamation; the Thirteenth Amendment; the Declaration of Independence; and, of course, General Washington's birthday was a national holiday. My grandfather Louis's daughters, Martha and Minerva, used to dress up in red, white, and blue to celebrate. General Washington was taken seriously as a Father of his Country. There was a natural, unselfconscious and unapologetic patriotism inculcated in young men and women during the early postwar years. It was characteristic, I believe, of the nation as a whole.

We were all planning to do our part, for the country and for the world. My classmate Wheeler "Wheels" Daniels and I had big plans. His father was a lawyer, and sometimes we discussed our ideas with him. "Lew and I go back to Harrisburg Academy days in the '50s," Wheeler said many years later. "We spent a fair amount of time in the woods avoiding our respective social circles, and discussing how to solve the world's problems. We also spent time at each other's homes. Lew would get in heavy discussions with my father."[13]

THE HILL SCHOOL

Lois had been the first in our family to go away to boarding school. After eighth grade, mother sent me to The Hill School in Pottstown, Pennsylvania, and Gil to The Gunnery School in Washington, Connecticut. She believed that in order to be challenged, I had to go away to school. She accepted the proposition that boarding schools had good faculties, *in loco parentis*, that would prepare me to go to a good college.

Hill forever changed my life—instilling the importance of discipline and self-discipline. There were high standards, a strict schedule, and dress code: coat and tie worn every day. I learned how the outer world enters the inner world; how what you wear symbolizes who you are. I learned to challenge teachers. One instructor even remembered me as a "little brash."[14]

In 1952, I was a new boy at a great school. Also new that year was Edward T. "Ned" Hall, who came to Hill as headmaster from Yale. Mr. Hall would play a pivotal role

With Friends at The Hill

in my life, remembering me this way: "Here's a guy that says, 'I'm going to prove that I'm not only as smart, but just as good as everybody else.'"[15]

In the ninth grade, I met Garrett Greene. A very sophisticated history teacher, Mr. Greene thought I would also make a good teacher. He liked to point out bad arguments in my papers by using the Latin phrase defining an informal fallacy—*post hoc ergo propter hoc*—after this, therefore because of this. It wasn't until I got to college that I finally understood his critique of my arguments: just because one event precedes another, doesn't mean that the first one caused the second one.

Peering at me through Edwardian horn-rimmed glasses, Mr. Greene exacted a mighty toll on my memory, always insisting upon mastery of American milestones—dates, names, places, and ideas. Facts and circumstances, I learned from this Hill School master, are the stuff of ideas and decisions. "No big theories, Lehrman," he would thunder. The narrative of past things, he would say, is not only the outcome of impersonal forces, and the history of ideas, but is also the contingent record of individual decisions—of men and women, leaders and partisans, with many motives, caught up in the event. He spoke to us with a conservative outlook and idiom that I have embraced ever since.

At The Hill, Mr. Dawson was a great Latin teacher. I was always seated in the first row. Some phrases stuck with me:

Totum quod splendet ut aurum: All that glitters is not gold.

Gallia est omnis divisa in partes tres: All of Gaul is divided into three parts.

The study of Latin has the virtue of illuminating the English language by shining a light on its roots. I also discovered that quaint things interested people and Latin was surely quaint. Like Mr. Lincoln, I also favored Euclid's sign-off for a proof: *Quod erat demonstrandum*[16] being the Latin translation of the original Greek.

We lived in buildings run by a dorm master. It was a super-masculine environment—all about athletics and academics. It was very 1950s. At the Hill, my teachers remembered me as a "scrapper," a "hustler," and an "intense competitor." My basketball coach, Don Ronnie set the record straight: "He wasn't a very gifted player, but he worked very hard at what he had."[17] I had played varsity sports through junior high school. At Hill, I learned there are a lot of boys more talented in certain things. Most of the guys were bigger than I was. I was 110 pounds when I first went to Hill. I was 140 pounds when I graduated. I went out for the athletic teams and really had to play all out. Sports were serious business. My friends and I kept track of details.

"My best memory," recalled Wheeler Daniels, "was playing JV football where Lew was quarterback and I was an end. Most of his passes went to me. I got moved up to varsity and spent most of my time on the bench wishing I was back playing with Lew on the JVs."[18]

I met my future college roommate on the Hill basketball court in 1954. Marty Gibson eventually became captain of the varsity basketball team. He toured with me, and later remembered that "We had a lot of fun, traveled to different campuses, and played against a couple of college freshmen teams. Afterward, we were off to Yale as freshmen roommates."[19] Marty was a gifted athlete and a superior student who later became an executive with Corning Glass.

I may have been small at Hill, but I was not too small to cause trouble. My most celebrated achievement—even if its authors remained anonymous—was one of the bravest or most reckless things I ever did. One night, Charlie Moore and I lifted a stuffed sixty-pound moose head off the wall of the Pipe Club and took it up to the fifth floor of the Sixth Form dormitory. We clambered out over the roof and tied it by rope

Courtesy The Hill School

Back Row: **Leckonby, Gray, Bryant, Glancy (Mgr.).**
Front Row: **Stark, Lehrman, Gibson, Weiser, Muhlhausen**

Charlie Moore: Moosehead Charlie and best of friends

to the copper tower overlooking the main quadrangle. Charlie was one of my closest friends. Although it has been more than sixty years since our friendship started at Hill, Charlie remembered that night in exactly the same way: "One night, [Lew] and I took the moose head from the Pipe Club and he secured it to the precipice of the roof of the Sixth Form dorm overlooking the quadrangle of the school. So high up, no one dared to remove it!"[20]

After breakfast the next morning, Hill classmates went out on the quadrangle, looked up, and saw the moose, lashed to the ramparts. Both classmates and teachers were astonished. The origin of its elevation was a mystery to all. "Who the hell got it up there?" was the question on everyone's mind. Hill masters were annoyed. I proudly remember that it took eleven men much of the day to get the moose back down. Fifty years later, I got the phone number for my coach and history teacher, Jack Ridell, and apologized for not owning up to my prank. Questioned, I had evaded personal responsibility with the phrase "not on my watch."

Mr. Hall could not prove my involvement, but he did suspect it. Most of the guys at Hill would brag about their exploits. I swore my compatriots to silence, and they never broke confidence. However, there was one classmate who was a great favorite of the headmaster. Mr. Hall was very sophisticated about adolescent behavior, and I believe Mr. Hall ran his suspicions by this student.

The summer between my junior and senior years, Mr. Hall summoned my mother and me to the school for a conference. He respected Mother because she was the perfect lady. He also knew she would be a perfect ally in clamping down on my behavior. Mr. Hall told Mother that I could not ignore the rules of the school. He disclosed in very concrete terms what he knew about my pranks (which did not include the moose incident, about which my mother never learned). Mother in turn warned me of dire consequences if my misbehavior was repeated to my father. That was enough of a warning for me. My senior year I spent setting records in Latin, Math, English, and French.

In future decades, I returned repeatedly to Hill. In 1983, I gave a commencement speech in which I spoke to the students about the responsibilities of being an educated American:

LEWIS E. LEHRMAN
"Lou"
Harrisburg, Pennsylvania

"When I was a child, I spake as a child."
—NEW TESTAMENT

1952-53. Far Fields Football; Junior Basketball; Junior Baseball; Outing Club; Press Club.
1953-54. Far Fields Football; Junior Varsity Basketball; Golf; Outing Club; Press Club; The *News*.
1954-55. Far Fields Football; Varsity Basketball Squad; Varsity Baseball Squad; Fifth Form Committee; Outing Club; Press Club.
1955-56. Far Fields Football; Varsity Basketball; Golf; Outing Club; Press Club; Sixth Form Show; The *News*.

YALE

Courtesy The Hill School

In The Dial, 1956

Your parents could have sent you to a government school. Their property taxes already paid your way there. To have done that, they would have denied you a unique advantage. Here at the Hill you were taught by teachers who love to teach. Here you were taught the values of work, duty, and sacrifice. Here you were taught you must work to learn the skills you need at college and to excel in society. You are very fortunate. While taking advantage of what the Hill and your parents have provided you, you should never lose sight of how lucky you are that you are graduating from one of the foremost schools in America. And above all, that you are an American, destined to give the shining example of faith, freedom, and opportunity to the whole world.[21]

Destined to give the shining example...

There are people in the lives of every individual who have the right chemistry to influence a younger person—just the right sensibility to understand what that individual really needs. In my case, I have experienced a few such mentors—Elsie B. Diven, who really understood me and patriotism; Duncan Campbell, who opened up the wide world of historical studies; and George Bailey—Susie's father—who saw my potential. At the beginning of my time at Hill—guided by the patriotism of Mrs. Diven—I still thought I was headed to West Point. My mother, Mr. Bailey, and Mr. Hall redirected me to Yale.

Neither my mother nor my father had gone to college. George Bailey, our family friend, was a Yale alumnus and recruiter. When I saw him at home during the breaks, he would encourage me to go to Yale. My Hill headmaster had the same idea. He thought I was interested in law and psychology. In my junior year, Mr. Hall asked me: "Have you thought about colleges yet?"

"Frankly, no," I responded.

"I think you should go to Yale. You're a good athlete. You're a good student," he told me. Then he added: "You need an insurance policy, Brown." I had never heard of Brown, but I did as I was told. I applied to Yale and Brown and was accepted at both. But there was never any question in my mind where I was going.

YALE UNIVERSITY

Yale was heaven.

The college captured some of the intimacy and historic social character of boarding school, but on a bigger scale. There were fourteen students from The Hill School in my class at Yale, and then I met all these new guys from Exeter, Andover, and St. Paul's. Mike Moore, Yale Kneeland, Bill Beadleston, Fleming Newbold, Howell Scott, Bart Giamatti, John Pitts, and many others would become lifelong friends.

A great weekend at Fisher's Island

There was another athletic group at Yale that included Eddie Bennett, Matt Freeman, and Rob Hanke. The latter two were from Calhoun College, where I lived. I also met helpful and inspiring upperclassmen, like Anson Beard. Dave Murray was an unforgettable gentleman, whose courtly and inspiring manners would have impressed even my mother.

Howell Scott: "Uncle Howell"

I met John Britton in our freshman year at Yale. He was one of many new friends who had gone to St. Paul's. Our relationship developed slowly; we would run into each other on campus. One day we met at George & Harry's, a classic Yale coffee shop. I had never before drunk coffee. Johnny ordered it for me. I can still see him pouring the milk. After that, I drank one cup of black coffee most every morning.

John Britton: Wise counselor and best of friends

John would provide valuable advice to me for the rest of his life—even when he profoundly disagreed with me on big decisions. In 1981, for example, he wrote a wise and pointed memo about why I should not accept a position on the Presidential Council of Economic Advisors, saying "Your criticisms will irritate and eventually infuriate in proportion to their accuracy; they will yield more enemies than friends (and the enemies will be more powerful)."[22] I valued Johnny's pithy turns of phrase and practical

Office of Public Affairs, Yale University, Photographs of Individuals (RU 686), Manuscripts and Archives, Yale University Library

Bartlett Giamatti: Go Bosox!

insight, and acted on his counsel in this case, even though Alan Greenspan had made the overture. There was simply not enough power in this position to overcome the headwinds I would have faced.

Bartlett Giamatti was a classmate with whom I would develop and nurture a friendship. Bart had gone to Phillips Academy Andover. I met him through our mutual friend, Matt Freeman, a scholar-athlete and a starting end on the football team. Bart and I hit it off right away because he was a total wordsmith. I was, by then, an Anglophile. He was a partisan of the Latinate. Near the school campus was a historic graveyard—the Grove Street Cemetery—where we would go and sit on gravestones talking about philosophy, life, and what we would do with the rest of our lives. He was entirely a man of intellect, a very modern man, but a scholar of the English and Italian Renaissance.

After graduation, Bart would become the secretary of the Class of 1960. I would later become the class treasurer. In the December 1976 issue of *Yale Alumni News*, Giamatti reported on me:

> I thought when Lew Lehrman was made Treasurer of our Class, that would be enough. After all, I was Class Secretary, he would work for me—we could say he would work with me—at his age, that's quite enough. One would have thought. But no, Lew has always kept busy so the *New York Times* did a long story on him this last summer, entitled "From Drugstores to Doctrine." It said his Rite Aid chain was the nation's fourth-largest drug store chain, with 467 stores, six thousand employees, $392 million in sales last year, and that in addition to his company he spent a great deal of time on The Lehrman Institute, of which he is chairman of the board and president. The Institute, in Manhattan, conducts "public policy studies stressing the historical roots and philosophical implications of contemporary economic and foreign policy issues". . . . Nowhere, in the *Times* or anywhere else, does it say he is Treasurer of the Class of 1960 and works for or with me. [All this was said firmly tongue in cheek.] I'm sure Lew told them and I am sure the next time we read about Lew things will be set straight and explained in the proper order.[23]

I wrote Bart back right away:

> As you say, my dear friend, "I am sure Lew told them" of his post as Class Treasurer. You are right. I did. The *Times* chose not to print it.
>
> It seems that the financial section of the *New York Times* does not consider Yale to be quite so fashionable as Main Street and Wall Street. Curious, old boy, but that's the way plain, old, working people see it. Now Bartlett, the truth is, of course, (as you suggest in your opening lines of the Class Notes) that I have always worked for you. At my age, I could never presume to do more. Of that presumption, I am quite sure. (In the new, presidential vernacular, you can count on that).[24]

By the mid-1970s, Giamatti had become a professor of comparative literature, and served as a house master at Yale. When the presidency of the university became vacant in 1977, and Giamatti was rumored to be a potential candidate, he declared: "The only thing I ever wanted to be president of was the American League."[25] In 1986, he would get his wish. Bart and I held our love for the Boston Red Sox in common. I remember the time he called me to ask if I could get him tickets for his family to see a Red Sox game in the World Series. I complied, still amused by his cheeky warnings about my presumption. When I was asked to chair the Yale University Council on the Humanities, Bart arranged my visits, and my engagements with the heads of each department. In 1977, I wrote a letter in support of his candidacy to the Yale committee selecting its next president. Bart replied in August before Yale's decision was announced, saying "The Divine Poet must have been moving your hand when you penned that splendid letter to the Yale Search Committee. Sometime we might chat by phone and I could tell you what the voices whisper here."[26]

When Bart was inaugurated as president that October, I was asked to write a tribute for the *Yale Daily News*. Entitled "Noble and Brown-Bearded Giamatti," the article exhibits a stylistic flourish I used almost exclusively in Bart's company:

> Into the disjoined universe of the present decade the noble Prince alighted. His ascendance to the Presidency of Yale was no accident. It was fortuitous only in the sense that prevision is denied us. But aided by the timid harmonies of reason, all in hindsight is now clear to us.
>
> There is a fitness to it. Angelo Bartlett Giamatti, son of scholars, disciple of the Divine Poet, spiritual heir of the Renaissance, pretender to the throne of baseball commissioners! Who else but he possessed the sense of proportion to transport us from our age of uncertainty into an era at Yale characterized by a feeling for hierarchy and order, traditional Yale virtues of which the inspired Giamatti has written so eloquently in the past.[27]

As you can see, Bart and I were well matched in the cheeky department.

Without the academic model that Bartlett's family provided for him, my own Yale major was less preordained. As a freshman I was pre-med. My grandfather Louis wanted a doctor in the family, and so did Mother. Grandpa had spoken with me directly about his hopes, and I always wanted to please him. Though I did my best, my organic chemistry professor told me the laboratory was not the place for me. I switched to history with relief and enthusiasm. I had developed a natural interest in the subject which would stay with me my whole life. I had excelled in the history classroom at the Harrisburg Academy, and at The Hill School. The decision proved to be a wise one. At Yale, history and English were, I believe, the dominant departments. A. Whitney Griswold, then president of Yale, had emerged from Yale's history faculty. At the time, history was perhaps the largest and most important major in the University.

I thrived in those history classrooms. In the fall of 1957, Anson Beard and I took our inaugural American History class. This is how Anson remembered it years later:

> You were a sophomore, I was a senior, majoring in American studies for which this course was a pre-requisite. With great pride in recollection, despite my 10% seniority in age, I spotted you as "the smartest guy in the room." Those days began a six-decade friendship, which I still cherish to this day.[28]

Another Yale classmate, Daniel Horowitz, was a keen observer of the social and academic scene on campus. He noted that:

> Scorning or avoiding competition in the classroom, many of those who graduated from prep schools were more likely than others to cut academic corners—cheating on assignments, paying someone to write their papers, and cramming at the last minute. Even if they obeyed the rules, as many of them did, they had learned skills before coming to Yale that they might share with others.[29]

Always interested in teaching, I managed to earn a mention for it in Daniel's book, *On the Cusp:* "I remember walking to an exam with Lew Lehrman, a classmate who had gone to the Hill School. I listened intently while he told me that the way to handle an exam question was to focus an answer on the premise underlying the topic the professor asked us to explore."[30]

One of my Yale professors was William H. Goetzmann, who taught a survey of American history and a graduate seminar. With his encouragement I chose to look more into the Civil War and Abraham Lincoln, not least because I was born and raised near Gettysburg. Around this time, I first began to read Roy P. Basler's *Collected Works of Abraham Lincoln*, noticing especially the importance of Lincoln's October 1854 antislavery speech at Peoria, the defining moment in his political career that set the tone for the rest of his life and work.

Another influential professor was Bardwell Smith, who taught "Religion and Literature." He had been a student of Richard Niebuhr, a theologian's theologian.

Bardwell taught me that things, *invisible* but true, are just as important as things *visible* and true.

As a freshman and sophomore, I concentrated on how to stay on the honor roll. In my junior year, I developed a real passion for scholarship. At Yale, the "summa" of learning was the comprehensive exam at the end of the senior year. I ended up with the highest grade for history, a 94.

After a meeting with Professor George Wilson Pierson, chairman of the History Department, my goal was to be a full professor on the Yale history faculty. My father did not think it was a good idea. He wanted me to be a lawyer or a doctor.

Mother always encouraged me, however. She believed in my star. Even though both she and my grandfather also wanted me to be a doctor, Mother supported my choice to major in history.

SCRAPPING, COMPETING, AND RIDING MOTORCYCLES

I was always very competitive. My friends said I was scrappy. When the choice was to fight or flee, I always fought. In elementary school, I fought on the playground every recess with one boy. At Harrisburg Academy, I was challenged by a couple of boys who were bigger than I was.

In 1982, I admitted to a reporter that I was combative and competitive as a kid. "I say that life is a struggle because, among other things, it's a struggle to impose self-discipline upon oneself," I went on. "And you learn to discipline your passion and your temper, or you can't win."[31]

"My earliest contacts with Lew were glancing blows," recalled my friend John MacMurray.

> There were no spectators to speak of at the early 1950s contest on the Camp Hill gridiron.
>
> This one-off encounter, played on the big boys' field, pitted the visiting squad of the Harrisburg Academy (and its outsized game face) against us, everyman adversaries of the "West Shore"—the left bank of the Susquehanna River. It had the look of a Norman Rockwell sandlot scrimmage—mostly boney knees, elbows, and leather helmets.[32]

Matt Freeman also emphasized our football connection noting that "Lew played, as he loves to say, some real high school football in Eastern Pennsylvania. I was elected captain of the Yale freshman football team, and I think that's how our bond started."[33]

At Yale, we exercised in the basement of Calhoun College. My strongest friend was John Pitts, the toughest guy, pound-for-pound, I ever knew. He and I would go to Yale-Princeton games and stay at John's Rumson home. We went prepared to "defend Yale's honor," which meant that at the end of the game we were bound to get into a fight at the goalpost.

John Pitts: Pound for pound the toughest guy I ever met

Mike Moore: "Uncle Biggie," yodeler genius and best of friends

I was still a prankster, even at Yale. Matt Freeman remembered details even I have tried to forget, describing "late nights on Chapel Street when Lew would throw a forearm shiver into parking meters with devastating effect."[34] Matt had a few other humorous remarks to make about our life together: "In our junior year I became Vice President of the Delta Kappa Epsilon fraternity, the big jock house on campus, full of football, hockey players, and swimmers. I remember Lew's hilarious descriptions of brothers having to turn sideways between massive shoulders to get a seat at the bar."[35] And Matt wasn't just an athlete, he was a dazzling student, remembering that "During our shared Calhoun College experience, I think Lew became enthralled when I would morph from stereotypical jock mode into a would-be Shakespearean scholar, and quote whole stanzas from the Bard's classics. We used to have contests about the meanings of the Bard's emanations."[36]

There was also a Yale motorcycle group that included John Pitts, Mike "Biggie" Moore, Rob Hanke, Franklin Roosevelt IV, and me. One evening, a few of us decided to go to New York City on our bikes. Some of us did not have windshields or crash bars. We were traveling at tremendous speed when I hit a bee and a bump in the road at the same time. I was knocked off balance—my legs flew up straight behind me—but I never let go of the handlebars. It was a miracle I didn't kill myself.

We arrived in New York City but needed gas to return to New Haven. None of us had any money. We met a guy at a gas station who lent us $20 and gave us his card. Several months later, I was in New York, and paid him back.

Rob Hanke: "The Protector"

I still had my motorcycles in the early years after university—a Triumph T120 and a BSA. I bought them used and very cheap. Louise used to ride on the back when we went to dinner. I used to scout for store locations on them, as Louis Lehrman & Son branched out into discount drugstores. They are easy to park in a hurry.

TEACHING AT YALE

Professor Charles Garside, my European History teacher, nominated me to be a Carnegie Teaching Fellow in History. But it was Professor George Wilson Pierson, chairman of the History Department, who made it happen. Professor Pierson was a formidable mentor, and a de Tocqueville scholar. When he heard that my father was opposed to the nomination, he called him directly. I don't know what he said, but somehow he persuaded my practical and business-minded father that I should accept the Carnegie Teaching Fellow appointment, even though the pay would be low. Professor Pierson, a harsh-looking fellow who was nonetheless deep and personable, thought I would make an excellent teacher, and he was prepared to see it through.

As an assistant instructor of history on the Yale faculty, I was paid $3,500 for the year. Although it's true it was a modest stipend, it was certainly adequate for a bachelor. And I was never more at home. Professors Howard Lamar, Charles Garside, Ralph Turner, William H. Goetzmann, and Robin Winks, among many others, pressed me deeper into the field. My teaching experience at Yale had an impact on my intellectual development which I can trace to this very day.

The Carnegie Fellowship allowed me to spend part of my time on graduate studies, while spending two-thirds of my time teaching. I told the story of that year for an article in the *Yale Alumni Magazine* in May of 1961, just as I was concluding the Carnegie Fellowship:

> As an undergraduate I was quite certain that I would go to law school, and all during my graduation year I debated with friends the relative merits of this law school and that. To tell the truth, I had no desperate desire to become an attorney. Rather, law seemed an appropriate profession for a liberal arts graduate who was unsure of what he really wanted to do.

It was in December of my senior year that I was approached by a member of the faculty, Charles Garside, director of undergraduate studies in history, and told that I had been nominated for a Carnegie Teaching Fellowship and that if I were interested I would be interviewed by the committee in charge of the program within a few weeks. Not yet having made any definite commitment to law school, I was more than willing to listen to other suggestions. Fortunately, I had known two of the 1959-1960 Carnegie Teaching Fellows, and I was familiar, through them, with the general purpose and nature of the program. After further conversation I became genuinely excited about my prospects for an appointment.

Strangely enough, this concern suddenly died out and I "definitely definitely" made up my mind that I would go to Harvard Law School and stop vacillating between the various professions. I was eventually interviewed by the Carnegie committee, at which time I said that if offered a Teaching Fellowship I would probably not take it since I was planning to go to law school. A week later, the appointment was offered—and to my surprise, I promptly accepted.

After assuring my family that I was determined to enter law school, I now had to inform them I had changed my mind again and that I was remaining at Yale as a Carnegie Teaching Fellow in history. Although they were obviously disturbed at still another change of mind, they acquiesced in my decision, probably because they felt that at least I made up my mind about something—for a year at least.

As far as the Carnegie program was concerned, the rest of my senior year was devoted to finding out what I was to teach, how, and to whom. Particularly helpful in this regard was a dinner meeting with the outgoing Fellows, at which

Yale Alumni Magazine, May 1961

The budding teacher

certain common problems were raised and freely discussed. Fortunately, I was to teach History 10, a survey course in European history which I had taken as a sophomore. . . .

As June drew near I was anticipating my teaching experience with a new feeling of commitment and a genuine attitude of excitement. To strengthen this commitment, I took off for Cambridge, Massachusetts, and Harvard Summer School, where I was determined to learn enough German to really help me in my graduate course in history. During the course of the summer I somehow managed to involve myself in the Massachusetts gubernatorial campaign, but when I returned to New Haven I had learned some German and a great deal about Massachusetts politics.

Life in New Haven, I soon found out, was going to be somewhat different from that which I had experienced as an undergraduate. As part of the Carnegie program, Fellows are required to live off campus so that they will have a taste of some of the domestic problems that face the young instructor, and I, in conjunction with a friend, had leased a small beach cabin near Milford, just twenty-five minutes from the university. Here I laughed into my first cook-it-yourself attempts—with a minimum of success and a maximum of distress. I can say, however, that endurance pays off, and now in April I seldom experience the kitchen paralysis that was my permanent condition in early September.

Around the middle of the month I went to my first History 10 faculty meeting where the instructors are briefed on the material they will teach in the following week's classes. Here Peter Garlock and I, the two Carnegie Fellows in history, got our first chance to see from the inside the way in which courses are formally organized. Here, too, we almost immediately found ourselves placed on a first-name basis with the one-time Brahmins of the faculty, and we soon found ourselves discussing various problems in European history on equal terms with men who only a short while ago had been our mentors. It was all very new and exciting, and I loved it.

The first day of classes quickly rolled around. Armed with a new briefcase filled with books and suggestions, I marched into my first class at ten o'clock of a Thursday morning to face a group of extremely composed sophomores and juniors. No doubt some of them at first thought I was one of the class, but since no one else was talking, they quickly concluded that I was their somewhat underaged instructor. Class began with my fumbling search for a piece of chalk, the misspelling of my own name on the blackboard, and a few nervous laughs. Then everything settled down, and the serious business of learning and teaching began.

The laughs are no longer nervous, but the business, for the most part, remains serious. From feudalism to German unification, from the philosophy of history to the John Birch Society, the class never seems to run out of ideas. Teaching, awesome at the beginning, is now a part of my life, taken in a still somewhat hesitant stride, but with a new sense of confidence born out of that most traumatic of experiences—holding a class together.

Yet teaching itself is not the all-in-all of the Carnegie program. Equally demanding has been the graduate seminar in American history in which I was enrolled and which has introduced me to the real and confusing complexities of the field in which I will probably teach. This graduate seminar has accomplished precisely what the Carnegie program intends: an introduction to graduate study, an association with graduate students, and an initiation into the demanding world of scholarship.

A short year has drawn to a close, and one now asks whether the Carnegie program has accomplished its purpose. In my case, the answer is a resounding "yes." A year ago, you will remember, I was "set" on law school, so set that I accepted a Carnegie Teaching Fellowship. Next year I am off to Harvard on a Woodrow Wilson Fellowship to do graduate work in history. . . .[37]

My seminar students also encouraged me to pursue a career in teaching. In evaluations submitted to the faculty they wrote:

- "Mr. Lehrman is probably the best teacher I've ever had. He has a real interest, not only in the course itself, but in each individual student. He set forth the course in a logical, systematic fashion and I can honestly say I never lost attention and enthusiasm in the course for one minute. I think he is an excellent teacher and would be a great credit to Yale University."
- "Mr. Lehrman was definitely one of the finest teachers I've had—I only wish I could have taken more advantage of his abilities."
- "Mr. Lehrman, through 1) his enthusiasm, 2) his knowledge of the subject, and 3) his ability to communicate ideas effectively, has captured my attention all year. In fact, this semester the only class I looked forward to attending was history discussion."
- "I regarded my discussions in History 10 as unquestionably the best of any offered by any of the courses I took this year. I cut them less than any of my other lectures or discussions and quite frankly found them consistently interesting."
- "Give the guy a professorship—he's pretty hot as a teacher."

To all those who have ever encouraged me I wish to again offer thanks. I truly hope my life and work has honored your faith in me.

CHALLENGING MALCOLM X

I have a coherent political philosophy which I deploy in moments of intellectual combat. Because I was competitive, I enjoyed intellectual combat—sometimes a bit too much as a student. As an adult I did not always prevail, but I have been privileged to enter the arena with worthy opponents, one of whom was Malcolm X.

In October of 1960, as I began my Carnegie Teaching Fellowship, Malcolm debated the NAACP's national youth secretary in the Yale Law School auditorium. Malcolm was extremely bright, articulate, and impassioned. I had read some of his writings and was interested in his work. He did not disappoint me. At the outset of his talk, he said:

Malcolm X: I respected him

Library of Congress, Prints & Photographs Division. New York World-Telegram & Sun Collection

> In this crucial hour in which we live today, it is essential that our minds constantly be kept open to reality. We have both races here in this Yale Law School Auditorium tonight. Let us not be emotional. Let us be governed and guided only by facts. . . .
>
> My friends, surely you will agree that no other people in history, biblical or otherwise, have been so completely stripped and robbed by their slave master of all knowledge concerning their own kind, and because of this, no other people in history, biblical or otherwise, have ever presented such a problem to their former slave masters or to the world . . . as the problem created by the presence of the twenty million so-called Negroes here in America today. . . .
>
> We have accepted your invitation to come here to Yale University Law School this evening to let you know firsthand why twenty million so-called Negroes cannot integrate with White America, why White America, after one hundred years of religious hypocrisy and political trickery will never accept us as first-class citizens here . . . and why we must therefore seek some separate territory of our own.[38]

After his brilliant, impassioned lecture, Malcolm remained at the platform to answer individual questions. I went down front to speak with him. We immediately got into a debate about the right way to interpret and implement the Declaration of Independence. "Emancipation is the great story of Black people in America, not slavery," I said. "The implication that violence will be needed to advance the rights of Black Americans detracts from your argument." A crowd of people gathered around, but Malcolm turned to respond to a question from someone else. I reached out to grab his arm to get his attention back, but one of his bodyguards knocked my wrist hard, and so, I regret, the debate had to end there.

In his book, *Class Divide: Yale '64 and the Conflicted Legacy of the Sixties*, Howard Gillette, Jr. covers my involvement in the event:

> Paired in debate with the NAACP's national youth secretary, Herbert Wright, Malcolm rejected the central premises of integrationist civil rights activism he had embraced only months earlier, calling instead for the complete separation of the races. Among those he made an indelible impression on was Lewis Lehrman, 1960, who as a Carnegie teaching fellow on the Yale faculty instructing a freshman history class recorded Malcolm's chilling effect and warned his students of Malcolm's potential influence.[39]

Concerned though I was about Malcolm's ideas and tactics, still, when he was assassinated in February of 1965, I mourned his death. He was a charming man and I respected him very much. Three decades later, I shared my impressions with one of my sons, who had written a paper about Malcom X. "I know well the impact Malcom X had upon you. I felt the same tingling sensation in 1960 when I met him at Yale. More important than any 'tingling sensation' however, is the judgment, indeed, the wisdom to know the correct lesson of his life."[40] No matter how much you are rejected, hard work and organization will overcome it.

In 2002, at a reception following a New-York Historical Society presentation by Harvard professor Henry Louis "Skip" Gates, I got a chance to make a prediction. My friend and colleague Daniel Jordan was able to record the scene: "I was standing by Lew. We could hear these two African-American businessmen discussing the negative portrayal of African-Americans in American history. Lew interrupted them, 'You are winning. It's just the sixth inning. But by the ninth you will have won.' He was very civil, but very emphatic. He made the case."[41]

Today, I can be certain I was right. In fact, my work at the Gilder Lehrman Institute of American History has been part of the movement that made it so.

A EUROPEAN EDUCATION

If you wanted to be a historian, it was thought best to learn German—because the PhD was first awarded in Germany in the seventeenth century. Leopold von Ranke, a papal historian, had developed primary-source-based history in the nineteenth century and set the standard for the research and writing of modern history. Although I never quite mastered the German language, I was certainly wise enough to embrace the importance of primary-source-based-history. I have been devoted to its principles—and grateful for its wisdom—ever since.

After all, who can be trusted with the interpretation of history? When it comes to matters of such importance, the original artifacts must be consulted again and again, by each succeeding generation, so as to mine and apply their wisdom freely in every unfolding circumstance.

My first trip to Europe was in the summer of 1961 after completing the Carnegie Teaching Fellowship year at Yale. I flew first to visit Italy. I then flew from Rome to Berlin, where I was to arrange lodging for myself and my good friend John Britton. John had been in my Yale class initially, but had taken a year off. He would go on to earn a PhD in the History of Science and Medicine for his study of ancient mathematics and Babylonian astronomy.[42]

When I landed at Flughafen Templehof, I needed to find a room where Johnny and I could stay. Coming out of the terminal, I saw a big heavyset German in a 1949 Cadillac, easily recognizable by its trademark fins. Though I did not speak German and the driver did not speak English, I approached him and tried to convey to him that I was looking to rent a room.

The driver took me to two or three places that were not suitable, before taking me to the Kaiserdamm 100 near the lake called the Lietzensee.

We climbed three flights of stairs to reach the Westfall household. When two beautiful young women answered the door, I thought my guide had misunderstood my intent and taken me to see some prostitutes. After I protested "No, no," he calmed me down. A bedroom and small sitting room awaited. With the help of their son, Hans Volker, who spoke some schoolboy English, we arranged the rent.

The household consisted of Herr Wernhoff, his wife whom I called "Müti," Ilsegunda, Gabriela, and Hans. Müti had lost her first husband, Herr Westfall, during the Second World War, and the family had kept his name.

In preparation for future studies in Western Europe, John and I had signed up to study German at the Goethe Institute. Most days we attended our lessons, and a friend of the Westfalls, Herr W. P. von Lietzner, worked hard to help us take advantage of the opportunity. Nevertheless, Johnny and I found the classroom less instructive than our conversations with the Westfall family, where Herr Wernhoff knew enough English to be helpful. Furthermore, Johnny and I just couldn't help but spend some days poking around Berlin in summertime, chasing after Gabriela, and sometimes touring with von Lietzner. One day Johnny and I went to see the old Olympic Stadium. Site of the historic 1936 Olympics, it was one of the monumental holdovers that had escaped destruction during Hitler's rule. I can still remember gazing upon that massive stadium, dreaming about the triumph of Jesse Owens—and the humbling of Hitler's racist

In Germany for a summer with W. P. von Lietzner

philosophy represented by the four gold medals Jesse won there—for freedom, for equality, and for America.

At the time, the Berlin Airlift was still on the front pages, but the crisis seemed less real in Berlin than it did when reading about it in the American papers. It occurred to me in that moment that he who is on the spot of contest may know more about events than can be found in the newspaper coverage.

My hosts were old enough to have been through World War II. Frau Westfall asked me where my family came from. I said my grandfather came from West Russia. It was a difficult question to answer at the time, no matter what kind of Russian origin you had. Frau Westfall often complained about the Soviet Russian treatment of civilians during the final invasion and occupation of Germany.

The Westfall family had a close relationship with Dr. Helmuth Roos, chief of surgery at East Berlin's largest municipal hospital, and a member of the East German communist elite. He was contemplating defecting to the West, and needed to act quickly before the Berlin Wall, then under construction, was completed. Through the Westfall's eldest daughter, Ilsegunda, we got tickets for a performance of the opera in East Berlin. Ilsegunda in turn had gotten the tickets through Dr. Roos.

The morning of the performance, however, it was announced that the East Germans had closed the border. Ilsegunda was very concerned for Dr. Roos. Almost immediately, she, John, and I drove from the American zone to his apartment in East Berlin. According to the postwar agreement, Americans had free access to all of Berlin. Dr. Roos's wife and children were on vacation in West Germany. Their family lived in a luxury of material convenience that few East Germans under communism could dream of.

For two hours we looked on, bewildered, as Ilsegunda and Dr. Roos argued about whether he should immediately flee to the West. At that time, Dr. Roos decided to stay, but as a precaution, he asked the three of us to take his medical files across the border in our rented Volkswagen—which we did.

Early that afternoon, however, we got a call that Dr. Roos had actually decided to escape by visiting a patient on one of the border roads called the Berneuer Strasse, a checkpoint in the middle of the chaos not yet sealed by the East German police. He asked, however, that John and I pick up some baggage that he had not been able to bring with him. Boldly, we drove back across the city in our VW Beetle, following instructions to the Roos apartment.

In East Berlin, we stopped at a traffic light where a nineteen-year-old kid jumped into the car. We followed his instructions and rendezvoused with a second car carrying part of the Roos luggage. Unfortunately, so had half a dozen East German policemen. Luckily for us, the *Volkspolizei* thought the other car had broken down. After they departed, we accomplished the second rendezvous. There we picked up the rest of Dr. Roos's baggage, after which our East German accomplices quickly disappeared.

By the time we got back to the border checkpoint, a series of barriers had been erected, and a long line of cars was trying to make the crossing. As we and our contraband moved toward the head of the line, John and I had second thoughts about the wisdom of our actions. Suddenly, we realized that we could end up prisoners in an East German communist jail.

Just then, a white Porsche came careening through the border barricades at about 60 miles per hour, heading directly toward the car at the front of the line. The guard on the front car's right made a graceful leap over its hood to avoid imminent extinction. He survived, but the Porsche escaped, flying past the line of cars and through the barricades at breakneck speed.

The East Germans—perfect bureaucrats all—headed straight for the telephones, presumably to report the incident and deny responsibility. Seldom have I ever been so grateful for bureaucracy. When the processing began again, the guards merely looked at our passports—and not at the suitcases full of silverware, and Mrs. Roos's fur coats.

John and I were lucky. Dr. Roos got his silverware, and we got back to the American zone in West Berlin. We later learned that nearly everyone connected with the escape had been arrested. The police were even said to have pictures of two foolish young Americans. In our zeal to rescue a fur coat for Dr. Roos, we had risked spending ten to twenty years in an East German jail.

The incident taught me a new respect for freedom, stainless-steel forks, and wool outer garments. It also taught me how easily and quickly the freedom we cherish can be lost. The distinction between Yale and jail was a narrow one, and one which I deeply appreciate. We can never take freedom for granted. Vigilance—and Providence—will always be required to maintain it.

In the summer of 1962, I went back to Germany to study again at the Goethe Institute. Herr Wernhoff and the Westfalls had relocated near Marburg, a university town where Herr Wernhoff worked for a chemical company. I wanted to meet the great historian Ludwig Dehio at the University of Marburg, but he was away. At Harvard, I had read Dehio's classic text on the European State system, *The Precarious Balance: The Politics of Power in Europe, 1494–1945*. It was the one of the key sources for what would become my master's thesis.

Frau Westfall had a friend who worked as a lumberjack. I got a job working for 25 cents an hour with a crew of four. A lumberjack would fell the trees, and we would lift the logs onto a truck. It was all muscle work, no brains involved. My fellow lumberjacks, strong as oxen, treated me like someone off the streets. They could lift a hundred pounds more than I could. The first day, I was so sore from lifting that I took my first bath since I was five years old.

I may have exercised my body more than my mind that summer.

A MASTER'S DEGREE AT HARVARD

"I was very serious about school and teaching," I would tell a journalist in 1979. "But during that year of teaching, I came to be skeptical of the extent to which the university prepared men for the world. I began to believe that academics and students had to know in a firsthand way what people in factories and businesses were thinking."[43] My experience in business further convinced me of this truth.

Nevertheless, after I finished my Carnegie Teaching Fellowship, I competed for and won a Woodrow Wilson Fellowship at Harvard. Professor Howard Lamar had encouraged me to apply for the Harvard fellowship, where I would be subsidized with the princely sum of $2,500 for the year. Even though it was a further pay cut, at that time I was still convinced I wanted to study some more, even teach some more.

My undergraduate studies had focused more on Europe than America. My Carnegie fellowship was for the *study* of American history, but the *teaching* of European history, where I helped certain professors prepare their classes. At Harvard, the international politics and diplomacy among Germany, France, England, and the Austro-Hungarian Empire's major countries would be my focus.

I needed to pursue a doctorate if I expected to teach at an elite college. At Harvard, Professor Ernest May was a complete master of late nineteenth and early twentieth century diplomatic history. Professor Merle Fainsod was master of Soviet history. I studied their courses with zeal. Fainsod believed the Soviet form of government was very fragile. His personal view was that slavery has existed in many different forms over the centuries—from slavery proper to serfdom, and from colonialism to communism. For me, the inescapable conclusion is that fighting for freedom may therefore be both a universal and eternal preoccupation.

I was fascinated by World War I and the Versailles Peace Conference which followed. I read *The Economic Consequences of the Peace* by John Maynard Keynes, which was one of the most significant commentaries on the event. He was a beautiful writer and an excellent mathematician, but argumentative and self-righteous. One of his most important and widely believed theses, that inflation was necessary to prevent dictatorship, was later refuted by the great French philosopher Jacques Rueff. In later chapters, we shall explore the ongoing significance of the famous debates in Switzerland between these two intellectual giants, and we will see that Rueff had the better argument.

There were no heroic figures who prevailed at Versailles, but I did study the example of Vance C. McCormick. Another Harrisburg native, McCormick provided an inspiring model for me. Commissioner McCormick was a Yale All-American football player from central Pennsylvania who served as chairman of the American Commission to Negotiate Peace at the Paris Peace Conference of 1920. He was also a graduate of the Harrisburg Academy who later became the school's board chair. He was well born, well connected, well educated, socially prominent, and blessed with boundless energy.

A Harrisburg businessman, McCormick became the head of the Harrisburg morning newspaper, the *Patriot*, and later the mayor. He had a tremendous influence on local and state politics and served as chairman of the Democratic National Committee.

As chair of the DNC, McCormick was instrumental in the nomination of Woodrow Wilson for president, and as early as 1914 became an advisor to Wilson himself. He also became a good friend of financier Bernard Baruch, who was an economic advisor to

Wilson at Versailles. Although no longer famous, McCormick had a significant influence on public policy, and on me.

I also came to admire General John "Blackjack" Pershing and George Marshall—an aide to Pershing—for their roles in World War I. The French leader at Versailles, Georges Clemenceau, was a hero to Winston Churchill, who thought him the greatest Frenchman since Napoleon. I was also struck by the boldness of the young Churchill, and his plans for the Gallipoli Campaign in 1915. It was an attempt to end the mass slaughter on the western front by taking Turkey out of the war. His brilliant strategic effort was, however, poorly executed. The naval breakthrough failed. It was supposed to be coordinated, but Lord Kitchener's troops landed too late. Though the man in charge gets the credit for victory, he also gets the blame for failure. In this case, Churchill's effort at Gallipoli is known as a failure. Eventually I would write the book *Churchill, Roosevelt & Company: Studies in Character and Statecraft*, published in 2017. There, Churchill, in all his glory, is among the primary subjects.

Library of Congress, Prints & Photographs Division, photograph by Harris & Ewing (LC-DIG-hec-08002)

Vance McCormick: Harrisburg's big shot

My master's thesis at Harvard took a different tack on Anglo-French history and the European State system. Inspired by Ludwig Dehio's work, it focused on the British purchase of the Suez Canal in 1875 with the help of a loan from Baron Lionel Rothschild.[44] The Suez Canal was the key to the Mediterranean, which then became a British lake. Ownership of the Suez Canal was also important in that it solidified British dominance of the trade routes to the East. France and Turkey had been the only significant competitors for the canal. The British victory in the bidding war solidified its position as a global empire until the end of World War II. My thesis was ultimately destroyed in the Pennsylvania flood of 1972, and unfortunately, no copy of it remains. The reason I chose the subject was for its ability to illuminate the balance of power in the European State system, a well-documented historical period that provides a wealth of material with which to understand the nature of power in commercial civilizations.

With commerce comes power. When Great Britain won the battle with Napoleon for dominance of the world trading system, the British pound replaced the French franc as the key reserve currency, a position which was firmly solidified by the British acquisition of the Suez Canal, and the resulting control of world trade.[45]

QUESTIONING ACADEMICS, HEADING HOME

I had reunited with my former Yale classmate, Dan Horowitz at Harvard Graduate School. Dan wrote of my departure from Harvard in his book *On the Cusp*, saying:

> He and I shared an apartment with two other history graduate students. I remember him with considerable admiration . . . , but also as a compelling person who possessed a fierce and brilliant intelligence. . . . When he left Harvard in the spring of 1963, Lehrman told me he planned to make enough money so he could devote himself to history and public affairs. Lots of people have such dreams, but few fulfill them so abundantly.[46]

I left Harvard at my mother's request. She wanted me to come home to deal with some problems in the family business. I had also begun to doubt that scholarship was what I wanted to pursue. I was more than half a commercial man. My father, dealing with these family and business problems, also wanted me close by. Gil had trouble with our father, Lois had chosen her own direction, and Barbara was trying to find her way. My parents had faith in me. Mother's primary objective was stabilizing family relationships. She also believed I was made for both business and scholarship. She sensed, and encouraged my move toward business, and was happy because it would also improve the family dynamics.

Still, I was torn, because at the same time, I was recruited by several Princeton faculty members. They convinced me to come to Princeton to complete my PhD under the auspices of Arno Mayer. It was an easy commute from Princeton back home, approximately two hours by car, and so I hoped it would be a workable compromise. At Princeton, I studied American History under Professors Cyril Black and Eric Goldman. And it was then that the example of Lincoln drew me away from Europe, and back to American history.

But the issues in the family business wouldn't go away. Leaving Princeton after one semester, I temporarily closed the door on my academic career.

IN THE US ARMY

"I loved boot camp."[47]

That summer, in 1963, I worked for Louis Lehrman & Son, opening our sixth discount drugstore in Binghamton, New York. However, my parents knew I wanted to serve in the military to fulfill my duty to my country. Indeed, I had always wondered how I would fare in battle. There was never any question in my mind about military service. I was determined to serve, even if I was not required to. In 1945, Victory in Japan Day had arrived on my seventh birthday. While in school, I made it my business to learn about the great World War II battles in the Pacific such as Iwo Jima,

Midway, and Guadalcanal. Mrs. Diven thought I should be a general, a graduate of West Point, and I minded her.

That August, I first went to the local Marine recruiter. He wanted me to sign up for Officer Candidate School. The Marines guaranteed I would emerge a second lieutenant, and that I would advance very rapidly. I was attracted by the Marines' *esprit de corps*, their team approach. "You're going to be an outstanding officer," I was told. The problem was that it required a five-year, full-time commitment—away from our family and its company.

In uniform, US Army

Next, I went to an Army recruiter in Harrisburg, who said "We have a perfect arrangement for you—six months active and six years in the active reserves." They had a long waiting list, but I explained my family situation and was called up in September of 1963.

I had received $3,500 to teach at Yale. In my second year as graduate student at Harvard, they gave me a $2,500 scholarship. With a 30 percent pay cut every year, it was clear that I needed a new vocation. The Army only promised to pay me seventy bucks a month, but there were three meals a day . . . and service to my country.

I enlisted in the US Army on September 3, 1963, and was ordered to active duty on October 25. I flew to Kentucky and reported for basic training at Fort Knox. I loved it. I liked the people. I liked the challenge.

I never rose above the rank of platoon guide, but I loved the Army life of an enlisted man. Sergeant Hall, my platoon sergeant, was fond of drink. In the mornings, he often slept in. He appointed me platoon guide, which meant I took charge at meals and marches. I loved command and still do, to this very day. The boot camp experience was very important to me.

The "Field First" was Sergeant Baggat. One day, while organizing the company, he called out: "LAR-MAN! LAR-MAN, I want you to come out here and show everyone you need a HAR-cut just like everyone else does." He had read my 201 File and knew that I went to Yale and Harvard. From then on Baggat made fun of my education at every opportunity.

People from all walks of life were there at boot camp. The competition was fierce. We boxed every Sunday in a space roped off between the barracks and played pickup football on weekends. Bill Hutchinson was my best friend in basic training. He was a Kentucky boy, born in Jefferson County. Bill and I were among the better athletes of our platoon. There was a chin bar at the entrance to the mess hall, where you had to do ten chin-ups to get a meal. Bill and I would challenge each other to see how many chin-ups we could do. I managed to beat Bill regularly, but it was our intellectual relationship that really mattered to Bill. Bill was humble, not very learned. He had not gone to high school. When we were exercising or playing sports, we talked, and our conversations had a profound effect on him into the future. Later on, Bill described our days together in basic training:

> In our first meeting, Lew was talking with several squad leaders around him. I was so impressed with his ability to communicate with them. I wondered: "What in the world is he doing here?" So I asked him: "What are you doing here? You are officer candidate material. You have leadership written all over you." He said: "I am interested in entering politics later. I want to understand how the blue-collar workers think." That started me to thinking, that's exactly what we need in the political arena.
>
> Those who seek to understand how the people can be helped. I listened to him. He had a lot of common sense. Obviously, he had not been among blue collar workers very much [there Bill was wrong], but he had the ability to make people like me understand. He made everybody understand. Everyone respected him after the second week there and looked up to him. He had the leadership capacity about him. There was never talking down to anyone. Lew said, "Money is a tool. It does not define me, or people like me. It is a tool." That got me to thinking, we, as blue-collar, must try and provide as many tools as we can for our kids.
>
> Lew was the platoon guide, acting NCO. Often that goes to people's heads. Lew helped a lot of folks. We were together when John Kennedy got killed. We were on the firing range when we were told he was assassinated. Lew said "one man doesn't run this country." There were a number of things that he quietly pointed out about Kennedy. He had a way of telling you things you didn't want to hear.
>
> I began to realize he was multinational—he understood more about the world than I did. There were no blanks where he was concerned. He was concerned with everything. He knew what he was talking about.
>
> We had a guy in the platoon who couldn't fire his rifle to pass a proficiency test . . . who was going to be a missile expert. Lew made me do the firing so this guy could pass the test. That basically may have influenced other people's thinking about him. The Executive Officer knew. He came up and said, "Good job." We got our missile expert qualified.[48]

Decades later, after Bill had undergone surgery, his son called me saying "Dad has been talking about you ever since he met you." Then he handed Bill the phone, who spoke from his hospital bed as we reminisced.

"I talked to my children about you," he said. "I learned from you a completely different world. My sons know people like that are out there. I was able to do what I wanted to do. The blue-collar guys want to do the best they can for their families."[49] Bill sent all his kids to high school and college so they could have better lives.

In January 1964, I received a letter from Captain Heyward W. Riley, commanding officer.

> I have had occasion to observe your conduct, which is further substantiated by your company commander, that your performance as a Sergeant, Platoon Guide, during basic combat training with this battalion has been outstanding. . . ."
>
> To hold such a position you have demonstrated your ability to be the kind of leader the Army needs. . . . Many times in the absence of your Platoon Sergeant you have taken charge and ably fulfilled the obligations of a man who would normally be far outside the realm of your experience. . . . I'm certain that you will find that the experience you have had as a "Leader" will be of value to you in your future assignments.[50]

I was grateful for the friendship, the recognition and the opportunity, but I was ready to get back to business. I left boot camp in March of 1964. For five-and-a-half years thereafter, I went almost every month to a weekend of ready reserve duty, and did two weeks at Army camp during the summer.

In 1965, I almost got called up. President Lyndon Johnson announced in July that forty-four combat battalions would be sent to Vietnam to help General William Westmoreland launch an offensive. I was on the list to go, but President Johnson and General Westmoreland called off the attack.

In May 1967, I was transferred to 2153 Corps Augmentation Unit at Indiantown Gap Military Reservation. The following year, Major H. W. Gleason wrote to Pvt E2 Lewis E. Lehrman:

> You are commended for your outstanding instruction during the two-week course in administrative procedures conducted by this unit during ACDUTRA 1968.
>
> The quality of your preparation and presentation distinguished you as first among all the instructors and brought favorable comments from both our evaluators and your students. Your contribution to the success of our training missions reflects credit upon yourself and your unit.[51]

In 1969, I was winding down my monthly reserve commitment, and had just taken Rite Aid public. I was assigned to complete a history of our unit and the training we had completed the previous summer at Fort Devens, Massachusetts. It began:

Jonathan Bush: "All hell broke loose!"

Six a.m., Saturday, July 13th, the 441st Personnel Service Company departed Harrisburg by bus for Fort Devens, four days after the advance party, led by Major Gleason and Warrant Officer Sabol, had arrived at camp to clear the way.

Fort Devens is a very hot Army camp. Most evenings find the mosquitos in bed with the soldiers, and as a result, a 441st instructor might arise in the morning not as well-rested as he should be. A bit uncomfortably the first night passed; and Sunday followed uneventfully, as briefing sessions in preparations for the morrow's first classes occupied the day.[52]

That same summer, in August of 1969, my very witty Yale buddy Jonathan Bush wrote me tongue-in-cheek during the last two weeks of my service: "At last, after fifty weeks of worry and tossing at night, I can once again sleep peacefully knowing that you are defending Jody, myself, and John, Jr. Is there any way that you can be persuaded to serve for more than two weeks a year since the remaining fifty weeks we feel vulnerable?"[53]

CHAPTER 4

Down to Business

LOUIS LEHRMAN & SON

Louis Lehrman & Son was founded by my grandfather. He started out as a peddler in Indiana after emigrating from Russia in 1896 at the age of fifteen. His mother had urged him to leave. The story he told to relatives was that she gave him several packs of cigarettes to bribe his way to Hamburg, where he boarded a ship to New York. Louis Lehrman arrived at Ellis Island in New York without a penny to his name. When he came down the gangplank, a man presumably from an immigrant aid group gave him $10, more money than he had ever seen in his life. He worked odd jobs and sewed buttons on shirts in New York City before he moved on to the US Steel town of Gary, Indiana. There he worked among the steelworkers as a peddler, selling sugar and shoelaces on foot, saving money to open his own store.

In his early twenties, Louis moved back east to Steelton, Pennsylvania. Two of his brothers had already located there in that booming industrial center, home to one of the larger Bethlehem Steel plants. There he was finally able to open his own grocery store at Second and Chestnut Streets, around the corner from the steel plant. From house to house and on to restaurants, he made deliveries by horse and carriage, the side of which was specially painted in bold lettering: "Louis Lehrman, Groceries and Notions, 2nd and Chestnut Sts." In 1906 he married Sarah Sachs, who had lived in Baltimore. The Sachs family had been in America for a number of years.

One family member recalled that "Uncle Louie had his grocery store at Second and Chestnut Streets, and had living quarters behind and over the store. The store was clean and well-stocked. He catered to the better trade in Steelton. My father would tell us with awe that Uncle Louie was worth $20,000, and had built this up in approximately six years."[1]

In 1917, Grandpa Louis moved to the bigger market town of Harrisburg. There, building on his experience in Steelton, he started a wholesale grocery business in the industrial area near the train lines and the Susquehanna River. In 1927, my father Benjamin became a partner in the business, which then became Louis Lehrman & Son. Together, with the help of Charlie Graf of Central Trust, they weathered the Flood of 1936, and kept on growing.

Because my family was a commercial family, I grew up with and respected commercial values: hard work, thrift, competition, and success. My historical

Things change

imagination caused me to identify with the tradition of Lincoln, civil liberties, and equal opportunity.

Work was something I was taught to respect, and I did. Beginning at age twelve, I worked holidays for my Dad and Grandpa in the family business. I started out working Christmas vacations and summers—even through my college years.

In 1955, when I was seventeen, I worked as a substitute salesman. My father told me he would rent me a car if I worked for the summer. It was a two-tone Chevy—white and red. I had previously ridden with all six salesmen on their rounds, so I knew the drill. The routes were generally defined geographically and were about thirty square miles each. In order to figure out where I was going, I had to take copious notes on the details of Pennsylvania's back roads while traveling with the salesmen.

Every week, Dad put some specials on items for which he had obtained a concession from the manufacturer. He paid salesmen a bonus for meeting a quota on these items. The proprietors of the stores I visited were the owners of their castles. Without exception they were friendly, even avuncular, when I would walk in saying "I'm Lew Lehrman. I'm taking the place of your salesman, who is on holiday. I've got something special to sell you." There was a bonus on stationery and envelopes that summer. I got a bonus of 50 cents on each case of stationery and envelopes I sold.

It was a wonderful experience dealing with people. I learned how to ingratiate myself to the owners. I learned how to present something in a positive manner. I learned how to navigate in strange territories. I learned how to take advantage of opportunities in the here and now, and I learned how to operate in unfamiliar environments with older, independent men.

The Flood of 1936

When the regular salesmen returned from vacation, they complained that the stores were overstocked. I made $2,000 that summer. Dad said to his friends: "We had to hire the cheapest salesman we could get. My son works only on a bonus." Dad was proud, but standoffish. It was his way of being a coach.

In the late 1950s, Alex Grass married my oldest sister Lois Lehrman and took a job in the tax department at the State Capitol. It didn't work out, so my father invited him to join the business.

To their credit, my father and Alex decided to expand the business and move into new markets. At that point we took on some non-food lines like health and beauty aids. Diversification had already begun before I joined the company full-time. In 1958 the company started Rack Rite Distributors to sell health and beauty products in retail outlets and drugstores.

In 1959 while I was still at Yale, Dave Sommer joined the family business. Dave had experience purchasing health and beauty products. He was only sixteen years old when his father had died, so from an early age he had learned to keep his family's grocery store alive.

RITE AID

In 1960 and 1961, several small companies, White Cross and Revco among them, began opening discount health and beauty stores in Pennsylvania. We also noticed independent drugstores opening up on Main Streets, and we studied them.

White Cross, a subsidiary of A. Robinson & Company out of Pittsburgh, had opened a store in Harrisburg. I stood by the cash register to check out their operations. The average purchase was $2.50. That was big money back then. I counted the number of people who came in during the noon lunch hour. White Cross would merge with Revco in 1972. The owner of White Cross, Donald Robinson, was known in the trade for having said that "competition was one thing, but the competitive Lehrman was another."

The first investment in the company's expansion came from my father, who lent Rack Rite the money to open some new stores. Dad kept earnings in the company as a general practice. It is easier to finance a business this way. Dad was completely indispensable, and he was especially confident when I came into the business. He risked his own capital behind our efforts. Without him, it would have been a different story.

In the late 1950s, Dad, Alex, Dave Sommer, and I began to talk about opening a discount drugstore. I had been closely involved since around 1956. My father had chosen me to represent the Lehrman family because there were adversarial interests at work. There were often secret meetings with the company's lawyer, Franklin Brown, which Alex did not attend. Franklin had gone to work for the firm founded by Solomon Hurwitz, who had married my dad's sister, Martha. It took us until the fall of 1962 to resolve all the factors needed to work out the supply chain and the company structure. Dave became the chief buyer. Alex was in charge of the warehouse. I was the outside man finding locations and opening stores. It became a great team effort.

In a March 1981 article in the *Harrisburg Evening News* Paul B. Beers wrote:

> Back on September 20, 1962, the Lehrmans, Alex Grass, Dave Sommer and friends drove to Scranton to see the first store open at Washington and Lackawanna Streets. 'They didn't even go by airplane or any of that fancy stuff, but they were as excited as kids," recalled an old-time employee. . . .
>
> Grass, like Dave Sommer, was born in Scranton but was raised in Florida, where he graduated from the University of Florida Law School. He came to Harrisburg in 1951 and worked for two years in the Bureau of Corporation Taxes. When he was thwarted in his efforts to join the IRS, he signed on with the Lehrmans in the wholesale food business.
>
> It was Grass, now 53, and Lew Lehrman, 42, who masterminded Rite Aid.[2]

We didn't invent the discount health and beauty business, but we took an idea, and with more determination, energy, and system made it into a very large enterprise. We engineered the most efficient store. The innovations we made were put together in a way that gave us the capacity to sell cheaply at retail. We were determined to be the lowest cost, lower price retailer of medicines and beauty aids. We succeeded because our cost structure was also the lowest.

We understood that the American system of business was changing. The interstate highways made delivery accessible over long distances. I appeared at a New York Society of Security Analysts conference and spoke on the revolution in marketing over long distances. We could open stores far away and deliver to them cheaply. Our efficiency meant we needed less capital to open stores, which, in some cases, were profitable by the sixth or seventh week. Our credit was satisfactory for downtown stores which were threatened by shopping centers. Shopping centers did not want

The Lehrmans on the Rite Aid Board

us because we did not have the required balance sheet. That's why you can still see Rite Aid stores on Main Street all over northeastern America.

Strategy counts, but sometimes it is not the origination of the idea itself, nor is it any complicated and systematic planning which gives rise to the success of an enterprise. Just as often, it is the relentless will to organize things more efficiently, to apply oneself with a certain discipline and commitment to one's goals. We had those virtues.

In the spring of 1964, I came back to Harrisburg from boot camp. We opened a store each month that year. By the end of 1964, we had opened about twelve Rite Aid stores, and the discount drugstore business was as big as the wholesale grocery business. As a result, we decided to go all out.

After I came into the business, I identified the locations and signed the leases for most of our new stores. It was impractical to set up new stores during weekday business hours, so on weekends we would get moving using employees from neighboring stores. By Monday morning, we were ready to do business. It was a seven-day workweek. We would also place a full-page advertisement in the local newspaper and follow up with more advertising. We had a substantial impact on the merchants of health and beauty aids.

Dave Sommer and I set up every single store until we went public. Dave, Alex, and I established a good working relationship. The work that we did together provided the model for expansion. At that time, Benjamin Lehrman was the chairman and head of the family business, Louis Lehrman & Son. In turn, Louis Lehrman & Son was the sole owner of Rack Rite Distributors, Rite Aid, and all their subsidiaries. To avoid exorbitant estate taxes, Louis gave Benjamin all the remaining shares of the parent company prior to his death in 1959. From then on, Benjamin was the sole owner of the company's stock until just before we went public.

Our lawyer, Franklin Brown, told the story of those years for an April 1982 *New York* magazine article:

> During those very early years, when only a few stores were opened up, Lew would come home from college and participate in all the planning decisions. He was 18 and I was 28 then, but it was clear to anyone that this was a dynamic and brilliant man. His reasoning was scary. He challenged my legal opinions, and he was often right—and he was still just a boy.
>
> Lew pushed to expand the business rapidly. Everything was go, go, go.

> And, suddenly, stores began to open all over the place. Lew put together a cadre of people to do the work, while Alex was the desk executive. Lew would go out on his motorcycle and scout locations for Rite Aid stores, but he wasn't just some gifted real-estate guy. He was a genius, and I don't know what the verb for "charisma" is, but he just charismated people. He got landlords to believe in us, to let us sign leases on credit when we were so small that we weren't entitled to credit. And he'd get us into the best locations when other, established drugstore chains wanted the same space. He caused the stores to open, and that was the key thing because, after all, this is a storekeeping business.[3]

We did not want, however, to threaten the company's grocery business in central Pennsylvania. Our own grocery stores also sold toothpaste and sundry drugs. For that reason, we opened our first store in New York State during the summer of 1963 and focused on New York from then on.

One day I went up to Binghamton, New York, near our first store in Scranton. There I found a real estate man by the name of George Ealy. We walked around the streets, and he showed me a storefront at 37 Court Street, the old United Shirt Shop. I thought it was a good location, and we leased it. It became our sixth store. At that time, New York was the biggest and richest state. Even then, I could tell that if we were really going to build a big business, we had to concentrate on New York State.

I also decided that the business could grow much faster than it was growing. When one is from rural Pennsylvania, one can see the opportunity of expanding in New York. There were almost seventeen million people in the state. It was an economy as big as the entire nation of Canada.

We hit an obstacle in 1965 when we attempted to launch a store in New Rochelle, New York. We were opening our twenty-second store at 544 Main Street, next to what was then a branch of Bloomingdale's. It was to be Rite Aid's first store with a pharmacy. Up until that time, our stores were strictly health and beauty aid outlets.

None of the principals in the corporation were pharmacists, but to open a pharmacy we had to get a license to operate from the New York State Pharmacy Board. The Pharmacy Board felt that the name we had used on our first twenty-one stores—"Thrif-D"—was unprofessional.

That precipitated a crisis. I had already hired Fred Shenker as the chain's first pharmacist. We were committed to paying his salary whether or not he was dispensing prescriptions. But the notion of paying someone to do nothing was completely foreign to a struggling young company like Rite Aid. Indeed, the whole notion of opening a pharmacy made me so uncertain that I had brought Louise—then my fiancée—to New Rochelle to provide reassurance in case I fell flat on my face.

We simply could not afford to carry a non-working pharmacist. Every penny counted, especially when you came from the grocery field where a penny's profit on a dollar's sale was considered a success. As my grandfather Louis used to say, "All the money is made between the cracks in the floor."

We were already selling rubbing alcohol and aspirin under a private label called "Rite Aid." We had come up with the name several years earlier when we started the private label business, so we agreed to use the name Rite Aid for the store. The Pharmacy Board was also agreeable, so I called the sign maker back. It was a rush job, but the next morning—only one day late—the first "Rite Aid" store opened. By 1967, we had introduced more than seventy Rite Aid private-label products and many more Rite Aid pharmacies.

GOING PUBLIC AND EXPANSION

We were expanding Rite Aid very rapidly and needed more capital. At that time, we were borrowing from the Harrisburg National Bank, where the avuncular Mr. George Bailey was still chairman, and a mentor to me. But bank loans were not going to be enough.

In 1967, I discussed with my father the idea that it was time to go public. Then, I talked to Alex. At the time, all the stock was owned by my father. He was preparing to share it among the family—on the merits. Dad was a very powerful man. He wanted to protect his children. I spent a lot of time with my parents and lawyers trying to figure out how to insulate my sister Barbara and my brother Gil in the distribution of stock before we went public.

The splits within the family had continued. Lois and Alex treated me with great respect, but Mother was angry about their treatment of Dad. The problem was that Alex wanted to split the company with me 50-50, and freeze out everyone else. At one confidential meeting, Mother said "Ben, you've got to do something here." Dad saw that the business was expanding, and he didn't want to mess things up by starting a fight within the family. I was very diplomatic. My mother was my model—"never say an evil word about anybody, be cheerful and friendly."

George Bailey: Mr. Harrisburg

Necessity is very compelling. You don't pick a fight with a family member when there is an alternative. Alex was a good executive, but his proposal was not going to work for the family. On the other hand, I still wanted to protect my sister Lois, Alex's wife.

In the deal Dad and I finally worked out, I received about 32 percent. Alex got 16 percent, and Lois got 16 percent. As I remember it, Gil got 16.9 percent. Barbara also got a fair share which has helped to finance her family to this very day. I saw to it that Dave Sommer and his wife also received their share, and that Aunt Martha and Aunt Minerva—Dad's sisters—got theirs. Dad had wanted to keep a bigger share of the company himself, but I convinced him not to because federal estate tax laws were, and still are, confiscatory.

Langdon and Lyn Cook: "The other L&L"

Desmond and Muffie FitzGerald

Splitting the company's equity was one problem. Selling it to the public was another. But I had allies on Wall Street, formed in friendships at The Hill School and Yale.

At JPMorgan I met and became friends with Langdon Cook and Desmond FitzGerald. Desmond remembered my presentation well, saying, "I first met Lew about 50 years ago, when he was running Rite Aid and I was in the investment department at the Morgan bank. Lew stood out as so much younger, smarter, more energetic, and more effective than just about all the other CEOs who came to woo the bank."[4]

Mingling with friends while working the Wall Street beat, I had cultivated a relationship with investment banker Gus Levy, chairman and CEO of Goldman Sachs. Gus had introduced me to the philanthropic community of New York City. At one event, I met Max Rabb during the campaign for Catholic schools organized by Cardinal Cooke, who had brought in Gus Levy. Gus thought it was important—and he was hard to refuse. I got involved because I thought it was a good cause. Max Rabb was a senior partner at the law firm of Stroock, Stroock and Lavan, and a former

Cabinet secretary in the Eisenhower Administration. It was he who introduced me to a legal expert by the name of Erwin Milliment. I developed a close relationship with both Max and Erwin. I was at every meeting. Together we worked on the IPO prospectus, and Max joined the Rite Aid board.

Max Rabb

Don Miller: There from the beginning

At White Weld, I met with Paul Hallingby, a partner of George Montgomery who was several years ahead of me at Yale. Paul said he would set the price at $16 per share. Several other investment bankers bid on the IPO, which was ultimately handled by two companies, G. H. Walker & Company and Merrill Lynch.

Jonathan Bush—the brother of my Yale classmate William H. T. "Bucky" Bush—handled our account at G. H. Walker & Company.

Merrill McGowan was my contact at Merrill Lynch. He was also a Yale classmate, and the grandson of Charles Merrill, cofounder of the famous brokerage firm. Don Regan, then CEO of Merrill Lynch, managed our account for the company. I would encounter him in the future on a political matter which no one, including me, could have foreseen.

At a lunch Regan hosted for me, I made the case that Rite Aid would be a leading company. Merrill Lynch offered to set the price at $25 per share, which was considerably higher than any other offer. At G. H. Walker & Co., I met with Don Miller and Bill Mayo-Smith in addition to Jonathan Bush. They agreed to co-manage the public offering with Merrill Lynch at $25 per share. At that price, Rite Aid was valued at $25 million, which was enough to finance the company's expansion for several years.

The April 26, 1968 prospectus for the initial public offering included the company history, reading as follows:

> The Company was founded in 1927 by members of the Lehrman family, who operated a wholesale grocery business under the name Louis Lehrman & Son. In 1958, its operations were expanded into rack service merchandising under the name Rack Rite Distributors. In September 1962, the Company opened its first retail store and in the following five years an additional 47 stores were added, including 12 stores in 1967. In February 1968, the Company acquired the 10 store Martin's chain of retail health and beauty stores in the Philadelphia area.[5]

By the time of the stock offering, the company operated sixty stores. Most were in Pennsylvania and New York, with twenty-one and twenty stores respectively.

The prospectus noted that Rite Aid retail store sales had grown from $1.4 million in Fiscal 1964 to $17.3 million in Fiscal 1968. Moreover, those stores accounted for about "75% of the consolidated net income of the Company." The sales of Louis Lehrman & Son, which supplied about 370 restaurants, cafeterias, and other grocery stores had also grown, but slower, from $9.8 million in 1964 to $13.2 million in 1968. The sales of Rack Rite Distributors had grown from $3.4 million in 1964 to $4.6 million in fiscal year 1968.

At the time of the offering, Benjamin Lehrman was chairman of the board. The eight-member board included Alex Grass, president; myself as executive vice president and treasurer; D. Gilbert Lehrman, vice president; David Sommer, vice president; Franklin C. Brown, secretary; Fred M. Alger and Maxwell M. Rabb, directors.

Fortunately, it was a bull market on Wall Street in 1968. The firm made its first public offering of stock at $25 per share in June 1968 and changed its name to Rite Aid Corporation. Shortly thereafter, the board of directors elected me president.

Leslie Wayne later chronicled the success of the IPO in an October 1982 *New York Times* piece:

> As a young businessman, Mr. Lehrman dazzled Wall Street with his ability to sell investors on the Rite Aid Corporation, the discount drug chain founded by his family. "He was like a Pied Piper," recalled Bruce Greer, a financial analyst with Drexel Burnham Lambert. Taken by his promotional abilities, investors eagerly put their money into Rite Aid, causing its stock to soar.[6]

Business was booming, but it was a tough time for the family. Mother was diagnosed with cancer in the spring of 1968. She had known about the symptoms but did not go to a doctor until it was too late. When she underwent surgery, the doctors removed half of her stomach. She died six months later on November 13, 1968. It was a devastating loss for myself and the entire family. Rose Lehrman was known and beloved by all of Harrisburg, and we let ourselves be depressed. It was the first, but not the only setback. We could not be joyous about the public offering, but eventually we managed to get back to work.

In 1969, the firm's first major acquisition was the forty-seven-store Daw Drug Co. of Rochester, New York. Philip Neivert from Daw joined Rite Aid as a vice president and director. Other additions included Martin's (1968), Save Right (1970), Fountain (sixteen stores in 1970), Cohen Drug (forty stores in 1971), Keystone (fifty-two stores in 1976), and Reads (1977).

Alex had apparently harbored doubts about the company's future. "I didn't think this business would be anywhere near this successful," he explained to the Harrisburg *Patriot-News* in 1995. "But apparently our method of operation was superior to a lot of the other competition."[7]

My friend, the investor and philanthropist Richard Gilder, and I first met in those days. He described our first encounter and earliest collaboration for C-SPAN's Brian Lamb in a 2005 interview:

> We hiked down there, and Lew and his brother-in-law are running this company. And Lew was all business. I mean, this was a great stock, and I was doing very badly in the market then. It must have been '69 or '70. I was just having a dreadful year. I'd started the firm a year earlier. We're down 80 percent. And so I only held Rite Aid—it was one of the few stocks I bought that went up that year. And I just was so excited I sold it.
>
> But Lew was—I mean, he was right on the ball, smart as hell. He didn't smile. I don't think his lips [moved]—you know, we got about an inch and a half, that was the most.
>
> He was the outside man, making acquisitions, but had the strategy. His brother-in-law was the inside guy, dealing with the unions and the internal controls and the merchandise. So, they were a terrific team.
>
> But I never forgot that . . . a) because it was one of the few stocks that went up that year for me, and b) you don't meet a guy like Lew that often. And so, I had this riveting impression of him.[8]

In 1971, I decided to investigate the British drugstore market. That year, Rite Aid acquired a 49 percent share of Superdrug, a British firm that had started building a health and beauty aid chain in 1966. My Yale classmate Billy Beadleston had introduced me to the British investment banker Nicholas Baring of Baring Brothers. I investigated the firm walking around the high streets of England after receiving a wire from Nicholas urging me to come and see the stores. They were so much like ours. That led to a series of negotiations, culminating in a transaction that gave us co-control of the company. In 1987, Rite Aid would sell its shares of Superdrug for much more than we paid.

BUILDING THE TEAM

As I told the *Discount Merchandiser* in 1971, the company's organization consisted of "three senior operating officers: Alex Grass, chairman of the board, myself as president, and David Sommer, senior vice president."[9]

"One of the unique advantages our management team had was simply that we were not hung up on any of the prejudices that handicapped all the old-line retail drug chains," I said. "We didn't know whether a pharmacist was necessary to a store or not. We opened the discount health-and-beauty aid stores along the lines of what we knew from our own rack jobber operations. If we had decided to incorporate pharmacies at the beginning, we would never have been able to open so many units. What we [did was] to go back and review specific locations and install prescription departments in many of our older successful stores."[10]

I matured very quickly between the ages of twenty-two and thirty, developing the kind of responsibility necessary to manage a public company during those years. At Rite Aid, I had to manage people who were much older than I. I had to develop a relationship of equality and respect. I was very pleased with the relationships and the standards I set. I wrote all of the operating manuals for Rite Aid.

I looked for and brought onboard other talented, ambitious managers. We actively looked for talent, recognizing and advancing those who showed it. Among the best I recruited was Tim Noonan, who had this to say about the experience:

> In 1969, Rite Aid acquired Daw Drug, where I had just started working fresh out of Pharmacy School. Lew held a meeting in Upstate New York to talk about this acquisition. I was very impressed with him as I had never met a person who was so charismatic and very intelligent.
>
> A short time later, as I was being promoted to a pharmacy supervisor, I met Lew in his office. Lew had a way about him that made you feel good about yourself and the company. Yet, you knew he was interviewing you for the job—which I got.
>
> The '70s were a very active and busy time at Rite Aid—opening stores, acquiring stores, adding pharmacies to stores, and opening warehouses. Rite Aid was also expanding store size and buying and expanding product mix. It was very busy, but Lew was always involved and wanted to know what was going on. He wanted to meet store and field people and to hold meetings to inspire them to help the company grow. The opportunity

Tim Noonan: "Aye aye Captain!"

Duane Ruble, center: "Aye aye Lieutenant!"

> was there for you to get ahead in the company and he was willing to share it. We were opening or acquiring a store a day. Lew was always on the go—to meet people in the stores. He was the visible person of Rite Aid. Everyone knew Lew and he passed this priority on to me.[11]

I moved Tim out of his store, and put him in the senior executive position responsible for the success of the pharmacies. He was a deep, thoughtful, and honest man. We were both football players. I remember discussing with him that there was something in business of the competitive nature of football. He was a top-quality executive. Tim eventually rose from pharmacist to president and chief operating officer of the company.

In management, presence is vital. I looked out for everybody. If they could see that your interest in them was sincere, they would be very loyal to the company. It wasn't just a company. It was a team. Alex didn't share that approach to leadership. Nevertheless, we worked well together. I even taught Alex's sons to play football.

As in all the professional relationships I pursued, I sought an alignment of interests with partners. I looked carefully at what was important to that partner. Alignment of interest is necessary. I learned the virtue of true sincerity and humility.

John Szelest remembered our first meeting at the grand opening of the Niagara Falls store, saying that "the highlight was meeting the real boss, Lewis E. Lehrman. When introduced I called him Mr. Lehrman. I was immediately corrected as he said, 'Mr. Lehrman was my grandfather, my name is Lew!' This was a man of the people."[12]

I met Duane Ruble while serving in the Army Reserves. He had worked with Sears Roebuck before joining Rite Aid in 1968. I recruited him straight out of the barracks. I put him through a special course of training and helped him buy his new home.

I sent him to the toughest store in Buffalo. He rose quickly. I trained him the way I trained Tim, and he eventually became vice president of operations.

At Rite Aid, we worked all the time, but I communicated a sense of fairness to each employee . . . and a sense of interest in each employee and his family. I felt it my responsibility to inspire these guys, given how hard we were working. On Saturday, the regular leadership came to Harrisburg to plot strategy. Tim Noonan still remembers those weekends too, saying that "At Rite Aid we worked 6 to 7 days a week. Quite often on Sunday morning I would bring my five children into work with me. Lew would always spend time talking with them. You knew he cared about your family—to him, family was first."[13]

There was a gentleman I hired in Newark, New Jersey. I noticed he never smiled. That led to a series of questions and it turned out he had decayed front teeth. He said he didn't have the money to fix them; I told him to get his teeth fixed and I paid for them out of my own pocket. We communicated a sense of caring for employees and their problems. We promoted quickly, according to merit. The officers came from the ranks of regional managers and supervisors. They rose rapidly.

The real estate team was the center of growth. We always had twenty-five to fifty leases ready to be used to continue expansion. I spent weeks on the road. I knew all the managers. I paid very careful attention to their honesty, their character, and their candor. John Szelest was able to accelerate his young career by capitalizing on his hard work. He was also Hollywood handsome. This is his story:

> In 1969, I made the move from my first job (Kentucky Fried Chicken) to a clerk's position at the local Leader Drug Store in Tonawanda, New York. The store was owned by the pharmacist James Goldstein. At the same time, Rite Aid was expanding its retail presence in Western New York. Acquisition of the Leader stores did not take place without resistance from older, established store personnel. The Rite Aid "model" separated the pharmacy activities from the retail "front end" . . . . As a teenager I saw this as an opportunity. I became acquainted with the Rite Aid area supervisor Jim Spyvak and was given more responsibility. I was a freshman at Niagara University and was able to arrange my classes to work as Assistant Manager at store #776 my entire undergraduate career.[14]

CHALLENGING DICK CHENEY AND DONALD RUMSFELD

In 1971 my business interests began to collide with the government. Though Richard Nixon was socially conservative, he was a radical in his economic policy, even suborning the chairman of the Fed to his electoral objectives. On August 15, 1971, Nixon imposed the first peacetime wage and price controls in American history. I was running a business where ten thousand products from major manufacturers were involved. The wage and price controls made it impossible to run a business intelligently, not just for Rite Aid, but for every small and medium-sized business in America. Major corporations got all kinds of exemptions. The Economic Stabilization Act of 1970 had authorized the president to stabilize prices. On the same day that he defaulted at the gold window, Nixon proclaimed "a freeze on all prices and wages throughout the United States,"[15] to last ninety days. Because of the simultaneous nature of his actions, it is likely that the Nixon Administration was fully aware of the inflationary effect of suspending the gold standard. It is likely they wanted to be able to control prices in order to avoid the economic and political repercussions of increased inflation. Ironically, just two months earlier at the end of June, the president had proclaimed his opposition to such controls, which had not been imposed in the United States since World War II. "We will not have a wage-price board, we will have jawboning."[16] Dick Cheney was then the top aide to Donald Rumsfeld during Rumsfeld's time as the head of Nixon's Cost of Living Council. Cheney recalled the crisis in his memoirs:

> The two entities that were supposed to write the regulations, the Pay Board and the Price Commission, wrangled and dithered. When it looked as though they were going to miss a crucial deadline for getting regulations published in the Federal Register, Rumsfeld decided to take things in hand. He assembled Jack Grayson, the chairman of the Price Commission, and about a dozen of our CLC [Cost of Living Council] staff and said that we wouldn't be leaving until we had the regulations ready for the printer. We set up in Rumsfeld's outer office, and as others paced and dictated, I sat at one of the secretary's desks and typed everything on an IBM Selectric typewriter.[17]

Donald Rumsfeld never wanted to emphasize that he and Cheney were the architects of the wage and price controls. It was clear to everyone that such controls would lead to the end of free markets. George Shultz, who became secretary of the treasury in 1972, once told me with a certain amount of amusement how he had once told Rumsfeld and Cheney "I don't see on your resume that you ran the wage and price controls." Those two may have been concealing their roles because they usually voiced support for free markets. Milton Friedman had predicted the wage and price controls would end "in utter failure," and he was right. Nevertheless, the administration set up a huge bureaucracy to enforce their mandate. They were rigorous in their application, and it affected Rite Aid stores. When we received their orders regulating prices, we saw that it would have a serious adverse impact on the company. That was when I went to Washington.

I knew both Rumsfeld and Cheney from past connections, though I did not endorse their political plans. They had approached me during the Nixon campaign and one of their colleagues had maintained the relationship with me.

In Washington, I met with Rumsfeld and Cheney at the White House. I told them we had absolutely no alternative but to bring an action in federal court for relief. They were very gracious, and yet they were unable to do anything, so I filed a complaint in the Federal District Court of Scranton, Pennsylvania. When Rumsfeld, Cheney, and the administration refused to budge, Rite Aid proceeded with the lawsuit and was given injunctive relief by the Court. Shortly thereafter, Nixon dropped the whole idea of wage and price controls. Perhaps he was influenced by the outcome of our case.

OVERCOMING FLOOD AND RECESSION

Tropical Storm Agnes hit central Pennsylvania in 1972—including Harrisburg. According to the *Evening News*, on June 24, the Susquehanna River crested 32.57 feet—fifteen feet above flood stage.[18] I lost all of my papers in the flood—my papers from my early years, my school years, and all of my correspondence. We had to work quickly to make repairs to the company's headquarters and affected stores. After the flood, I began to keep a personal archive in a climate-controlled environment. The loss of those papers has made it harder to document the parts of this autobiography before the flood's destruction. The archive I created made the rest of this autobiography much easier because there is so much material to work from. Keeping the archive has confirmed the value of documentary history, and the respect I developed for it at Yale.

In 1972, Alex Grass and Lois Lehrman divorced, but it had little effect on the company. Rite Aid had more serious problems with the recession of 1973. The years 1973 and 1974 were difficult years. A recession was accompanied by high debt from a high expansion rate. We had borrowed a lot of money. The problems deepened in 1974 when the price of oil went up ten times. Most prices went up at supermarkets and drugstores. The oil price was carried on the swift tide of inflation resulting from the US default at the gold window and other inflationary policies including direct purchases of government bonds by the Federal Reserve. Rite Aid was over-leveraged. There were six quarters of flat or declining earnings after twelve straight years of growth. The stock dropped substantially. The share price went from $55 in 1972 to $2 and a fraction in 1974. Short-sellers made a lot of money. There were rumors about the insolvency of the company. We cut back on expansion—completely halting new store openings—gradually righted the ship, and then proceeded with expansion again. By 1974, earnings had turned around.

As Rite Aid expanded, the company's financial needs also expanded. We had graduated from Central Trust in Harrisburg to First National Bank of Harrisburg. By 1977, we were in good shape. Friends at JPMorgan such as George Rowe took over our banking relationships.

CHAPTER 5

The Farm and the Family

BUILDING THE FARM

We are a farming family. After our marriage in 1966, Louise and I rented a small ranch house for $200 a month. A year later, Louise found a farm in Monroe Township, a farming community half an hour from Harrisburg. We started with forty-five acres, ten arable, and an old farmhouse that we bought for $55,000 on a twenty-year mortgage. Both Louise and I love country music—especially Willie Nelson and Waylon Jennings.

Ours was a deliberate decision to keep our roots deep in the soil of Pennsylvania.[1] For half a century, we have worked to turn the "Home Farm" into a heavenly property by combining about fifteen separate-but-large farms. When our neighbors wanted to retire, they would come to me. I would buy their farms on purchase money mortgages, generally twenty years in length. They would get the equivalent of a pension, because I had the cash or credit to purchase their farms. We would get the benefit of economies of scale.

The first farm Louise and I purchased this way was the Sollenberger farm across the road. His property was contiguous to the "Home Farm." Mr. Sollenberger didn't have a pension, because his was a family farm. The purchase money provided for his retirement. That form of purchase benefitted both parties, a good example I followed often when building the farm up to sixteen hundred acres. I also bought the Simmons farm from a neighbor and friend I had known for many years. That added two hundred acres to our farm, and it was the means of sustenance which allowed Mr. Simmons to retire at a young age.

Our children all learned farming, and how to drive tractors, haybalers, and combine harvesters. It was a project that Louise and I shared throughout our marriage—creation and cultivation. Louise has created gardens throughout the property that extend to fifty acres and planted two thousand trees throughout the fields. She may not know how to run the tractors, but she surely knows how to create gardens out of nothing. We were planning for the future, and the trees now provide shade throughout the farm for walking, running, and horseback riding. We have also now created a family cemetery where all the family can choose to be buried under mammoth oaks, if they so wish.

Before we arrived

The Home Farm today

By the 1970s, the farm had expanded to 150 acres. By 1982, it totaled 400 acres, and it now occupies 1,600 acres in the township. With Sheldon Brymesser and Daryl Alger we farm all arable land in wheat, corn, soybeans, and hay. Daryl and Sheldon are truly the best farmers in the county, and I remain involved in every decision.

Louise and I learned the farming business from scratch. Louise became an accomplished photographer as well, taking photographs of the farm and family through its whole history. I learned the seed machinery businesses. The number of dairy farms in the township dropped from sixty in 1967, to five or six in five decades. Farming is very hard. Developing a profitable farm is harder, you have to reach a certain scale. Fewer and fewer people want to work on a farm.

Nevertheless, a farm is a wonderful place to welcome friends and their families. As John Britton wrote:

> The farm always seems a place of tranquility, refreshment, and renewal, and this trip was no exception. It's such a wonderful combination of physical beauty, closeness to nature and growing things. . . . Suffice to say that being there with you is a very special treat for all of us, and one which we are grateful to be able to enjoy.[2]

We tried the sheep business and raised Black Angus cattle. I learned that if you don't know what you're doing, don't farm livestock. The only thing that was profitable for us was raising corn, soybeans, and wheat in rotation. In order to make money, we needed scale. One combine can cost as much as $500,000. A planter can cost $300,000. At sixteen hundred acres, we have finally achieved our goal—profitability due to economies of scale. Many of our employees on the farm stayed with us from the beginning, and that has made it easier to train them. We learned early on that farmers can be inspired to do good work that they never did on their own farms. The farm managers are Sue and Tom Zerbe, who have been with us for over twenty years. I find that treating employees with adult judgment produces an employee who tends to have good judgment as well. I also found that employees that have a natural inclination to do good work set the example for new folks on the farm.

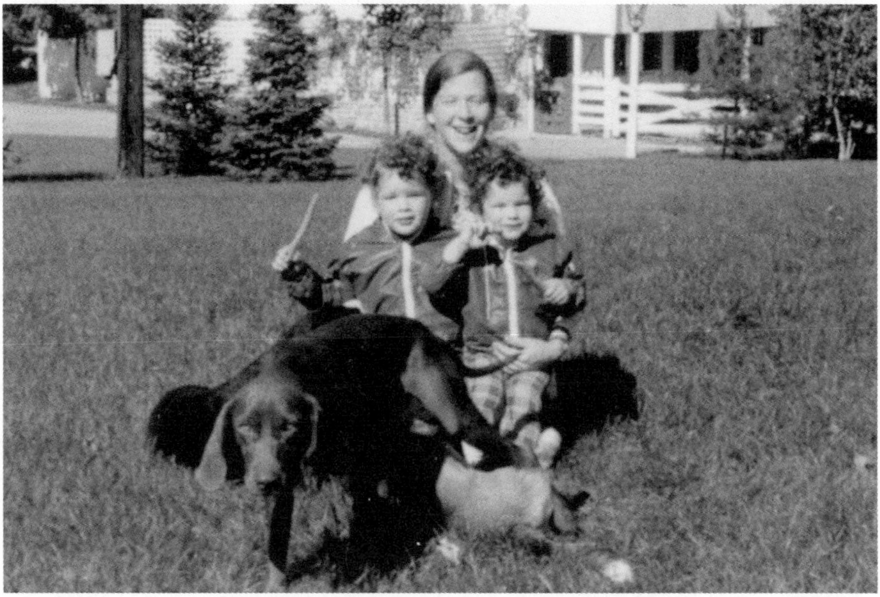

Louise with Leland and John: Good old days

You have to be in farming for the long haul. City folks do not know the effort that is required, the issues that must be addressed—the nature of the soil, planting at the right time, spraying for weeds at the right time, harvesting at the right time. Farming is a time-oriented business subject to the elements and a host of factors over which you have little control.

For the children, the farm was a learning experience in many, sometimes unexpected ways. Our sheer persistence was one lesson. For all five of our children, another lesson was watching us piece the farm together bit-by-bit over more than fifty years. The children all brought their friends to the farm, as did my friends. Johnny Britton brought his sons, John and Sam, and they always had a good time. They would beg their parents to come to the farm all year long, until the summer allowed them time to come. Sammy MacFarlane—the grandson of my dear friend Sam Reeves—felt the same way.

In 2019 I asked my children to send me a few words about the farm and how they remember it. Thomas said:

> Mom and Dad got us to appreciate the value and dignity of an honest day's work. I picked and carted apples for a penny an apple until my hourly wage surprised my parents and required a downward adjustment. We built forts in the hay mows and listened to farmer Jerry tell us about his childhood days jumping from 25-foot rafters to land on the hard wood floors. There probably is a grain of truth to that story. We cleared woods on the Farm and watched carpenter Buddy flip the Bobcat while operating on an incline behind the garden. Dad would take me down to the Monroe Township baseball field in 90-plus degree heat, and he'd pitch me baseballs until I tired out, then he would run and fetch them from the outfield.[3]

It was not all work. The farm was the family playground. Eliza often rode horses with Louise and me on the bridle trails. This is how she remembers those days: "We used to float down the Yellow Breeches in tractor tire tubes. We would play every imaginable game you could create while floating along a creek bed."[4]

Peter made an amusing confession:

> I was a pretty curious and mischievous kid and one day at age six decided to climb into the tractor mower parked outside the front door and turn the key. I turned it on, popped the clutch, and all of a sudden, the tractor took off. I was so terrified of what I had done that I ran off the tractor while it was moving. It slowly turned left, drove right into the garage, smashed right into the wall and destroyed the sink and everything else. I ran upstairs and hid under my bed. I was scared and ashamed and knew I'd made a big mistake.[5]

Neither Louise nor I punished him. We took the position that all children make mistakes.

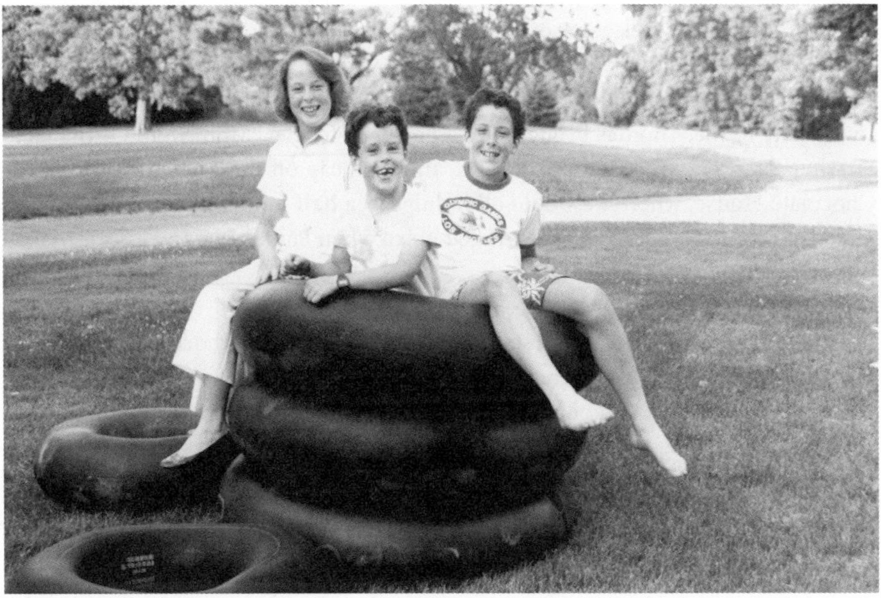

Eliza, Peter, and Thomas: Inner tubes for floating down the Yellow Breeches creek

Above all, the farm was a gathering place for the family. Eliza remembers how

> we used to sit in the small library at the Home Farm [with its huge cooking fireplace], listening to Cat Stevens on the record player.
>
> Dad would be in the rocking chair, giving us airplane rides on his extended leg. We would all sit around on the floor and sing along. I remember those evenings, being all together for hours in that room, feeling the love and beauty of our family home.[6]

Lee sent me a nostalgic note saying "I remember holding Dad's hand and walking down the old farm road. And I remember him reminding me of when I was holding his hand, walking down the old farm road."[7] Peter enjoyed "building huge forts with the wood shavings in the barn." He also remembered "practicing my racing starts on the straightaway between the fields and the pond with my motocross racing gate. Mom would drop the gate when Dad dropped his hand. I practiced and practiced this and it made me a really good starter on the track."[8] The farm was a place where family memories were made.

John listed some more of them: "Running to Allenberry, ice cream at Matteson's, dinner at Rillo's when I was young, Dad and Uncle Charlie grilling ribs and playing kick the can."[9] Thomas added a few more: "Mom and Dad would take us to Rillo's and Dad would let us drive on his lap and we would close up the evening with ice cream at Matteson's, while at least one of us would drop a scoop onto the parking lot."[10] Peter also remembered "kick the can after dinner. I loved this so, so much and always was begging my siblings to play."[11] Eliza described the game well, saying this "nighttime hide and seek game of tag went on for hours into the beautiful firefly-filled nights of Central Pennsylvania."[12] The children also loved the world-famous Hershey Park, home of the famous candy company. It was only half an hour from our farm. In his note to me, Thomas brought the scene back to life: "Mom would bring us to Hershey Park, endure six hours of rides, and then cap off the day with a trip to the Chocolate House, where we would all indulge in a half pound chocolate bar which took us a month to eat."[13] Eliza reminded me of when Paul Fabra and his son visited us during the family's famous

> summer outing, packed in the station wagon, to the famous chocolate town and home of the "Comet," the greatest roller coaster on the East Coast.
>
> We flew around that park with our parents, ride after ride, culminating in each of us getting to pick out a one-pound Hershey chocolate bar that had to last us the remainder of the summer. Dad would always get a Hershey's Golden Almond Bar (with gold wrapping) for his birthday in August, and we would all vie for a chance to sit in his lap and be the one to help count how many almonds were in the chocolate bar.[14]

Even when it was just a weekend, time at the farm was always special.

Peter was there sometimes when I flew in on a helicopter from work. We would land right at the front door. He remembered those weekends much the same way I do:

> I always remember looking forward to when Dad arrived and for some reason there was one week when he came to the Farm on a Wednesday instead of on Friday. It was late afternoon, the sun was shining, and I saw him walking across the lawn in front of the old kitchen, still in his suit. He was wearing a white shirt, which he rarely wore, and I remember being so happy to see him, knowing that he was going to be there for five days versus the more usual 2.5 days.[15]

In 2001, Tom and Sue Zerbe replaced Patrick and Veronika Kelley as the onsite managers. About the same time, we recruited Daryl Alger and Sheldon Brymesser to oversee the farm's operations. Daryl farms most of the land, namely fifteen hundred acres, and Sheldon farms the rest. Daryl Alger proved to us in virtue he is the best farmer east of the Mississippi. He is the master of efficiency, innovation, and productivity.

RIDING TO THE HOUNDS

From the earliest days, when we were just beginning as stewards of the farm, horses have been present. Horses played a major role in our family. Louise was an accomplished horsewoman when I met her. Previously, I had ridden just a little at summer camp.

One of the first things we did after we bought the farm was to buy two horses. We used to ride all over Monroe Township, from field to field, after the harvest was in.

Louise the accomplished horsewoman

On Gallatin: To horse!

Later we bought three Connemara ponies in Ireland and transported them to the farm by boat. We loved Ireland and returned several times. We bought nine horses for $15,000, three brood mares in foal, each with a foal by their side. Louise cared for them, bred them, and showed them in Harrisburg at the Farm Show building. Louise and I taught all the kids to ride and gave one of the ponies to Eliza. It was a beautiful life, but not a good business. Generally speaking, the cost of maintaining a horse is both more than you pay for it, and more than you can sell it for.

Louise wanted me to go fox hunting with her. I was in the hunt field almost immediately after we settled in Pennsylvania. Later, we joined the Golden's Bridge Hounds in northern Westchester County, New York. We were also members of the Beaufort Hunt in central Pennsylvania.

While Louise was an accomplished horsewoman, I was a survival horseman. I had to become a fast learner to preserve myself. You learn quickly that if you're not a disciplined horseman, you are taking your life in your hands. Guiding a horse teaches respect for the will of another. I had some magnificent falls—going over fences too fast. I knew how to tumble from my athletic background, so I survived. Falling off over fences in the field, I had several life-threateningly close calls. Re-mounting in the field is not easy. We hunted on weekends until 1982, when my public life interrupted our normal schedule.

Over the years, we have owned about twenty-five horses, whom Louise managed. My favorite horse was named Gallatin. He could jump anything on the field. The horses were sometimes sold at auction at Keeneland. Our best transaction was selling a horse for $29,000.

Eliza eventually became a professional equestrian. She is a Grand Prix rider and trainer, married a Belgian-born horseman, Filip de Wandel, and built a stable while restoring one of the historic farmhouses on the property. It was once just a shell of a building, but is now a magnificent equestrian center, with beautiful, yet down-to-earth architecture, fitting to the area.

At the outset of our life on the farm, Louise and I also bred the rough and tumble sheep dogs, Cardigan Welsh corgis. My favorite one I named Lloyd George. It was not a good business, so we instead settled for companionship. My favorite dog overall was a wide-ranging German short-haired pointer. I named him Bismarck after the famous German chancellor who consolidated the German principalities and was one of the most famous statesmen in the second half of the nineteenth century. One day I heard a pounding on the door. When I answered, I saw a big man filling the doorway who said, "Is this your dog? He ate my dog's lunch, so keep him to yourself." At the time, Bismarck didn't have quite enough room to roam, as the farm was only 160 acres.

SETTLING IN NEW YORK

In 1969, after Lee was born, we decided we wanted to raise our family in New York. Louise wanted the children to grow up in a bigger pond where they would have more competition for attention. In New York, "everyone" was more successful than

Emilie Betz: "Mimi"

I was, and Louise did not want the children to be spoiled. In addition, she was familiar with its educational opportunities from her own experience, as her family had deep roots in the city, fifth generation at some New York schools.

I still had responsibilities in Pennsylvania where I would continue as president of Rite Aid until 1977. I would spend the week in the field, hiring managers and supervising them, opening new stores and locations, and negotiating leases. I was at company headquarters on Saturdays and often Sundays, meeting with other executives of the company. I would visit New York during the week when I was nearby. As president, I handled all the field operations for the company. We had an office in New York at 425 Park Avenue, which made home visits convenient. New York was the center of the Northeastern Region where the company had switched its focus.

In early 1969, a twelve-room apartment became available on Fifth Avenue. We bought it at auction. The Fifth Avenue apartment had only four bedrooms however, and as the family grew, we needed more room. In 1978 we moved to 778 Park Avenue where my friend Bill Buckley lived on the ground floor.

After Leland was born, we hired a German nurse by the name of Emilie "Mimi" Betz. Mimi and I would speak German while she helped Louise with the babies. After our first three children were born, the elderly Mimi realized she needed to retire, but we still needed someone to help full-time. Louise took charge and, through Mimi and other mutual friends, we eventually met Genevieve Lengard, a very bright, very capable, tough-minded French native who tolerated no nonsense from the children. She had very strong, traditional values. Genevieve remained with us for fifteen years. She formed a very strong relationship with all the children, especially Eliza and Peter. When she retired, Genevieve settled back in her native France. Eliza eventually handled the complicated questions regarding her finances because Genevieve trusted her with all of her affairs.

We also had household help including our beloved cook from Jamaica, Ivy Baldwin. Ivy was always laughing and answered "yes" to every question. The lilt of her voice and the taste of her brownies, oatmeal raisin, and chocolate chip cookies still linger with the family. She was a deeply faithful and educated woman, and after she retired to Florida, she used to write lovely letters to our family bestowing "God's

Genevieve Lengard: "Bonjour!"

Ivy Baldwin: "Cookie Master"

richest blessings," just as she had once nourished us so well at the table. I bought her a house when she retired. She was eternally grateful, and I never thought twice about my decision.

AT HOME IN GREENWICH

In 1972, we bought 444 Round Hill Road in Greenwich as a weekend retreat, but Louise never liked it. She wanted a farmhouse, so we sold the property in 1975. That sale financed the purchase in 1976 of Cherry Valley Farm, where there were twelve acres on which to build stables, room for the horses to roam, and flower beds where Louise could work her horticultural magic. In 1987, we were also able to buy the property next door.

Greenwich was a place for our kids to enjoy sports. The boys, Eliza, and I would play football, hockey, and baseball every weekend. I was always game. Leland remembered me on the field. "The way he would throw the ball, the enthusiasm of his own play, his earnest effort in all things comes out beautifully in sports."[16] We sometimes played with the family of Sam Sammis, himself a great athlete. Peter remembers running football patterns with Thomas and me, and that "My dad also taught me step by step how to play basketball. He and I really dug in on this one and he taught me a lot of the fundamentals of the game."[17] Eliza has always been an athlete. "I loved playing football with Dad and my brothers," she remembered. "Dad always made it feel like you were really playing with a purpose and not just in a backyard. It was important to try as hard as you could, all the time, in every arena. He really made it fun to try to bring your 'A-game' every time. It was always about achieving excellence. I remember actually catching a long throw from Dad, scoring a touchdown,

In the country (Greenwich)

and Dad being incredibly proud of me. Since I was the only girl, it meant a lot that it was just as important to him that I was playing good football."[18]

There were accidents. Thomas remembered that "Among the most memorable was our touch football game in the yard, where I ran into a tall, fat pine tree trying to chase down a long Hail Mary pass from my Dad. It was among the hardest tackles I ever faced in my football career from grade school to high school."[19] John still remembers skating on the frozen Mianus River with friends, and biking down Cherry Valley hill. Years later, he recalled my advice "to give up the running shoes for the bicycle,"[20] not least because I eventually had two hip replacements. That said, I loved running. With hindsight I might have done things differently, choosing lower impact aerobics, but regular exercise improved my life in many ways. I ran when on the road for business, at home in Central Park, and on high school tracks during my public

Thomas (at left) and Leland in the autumn leaves

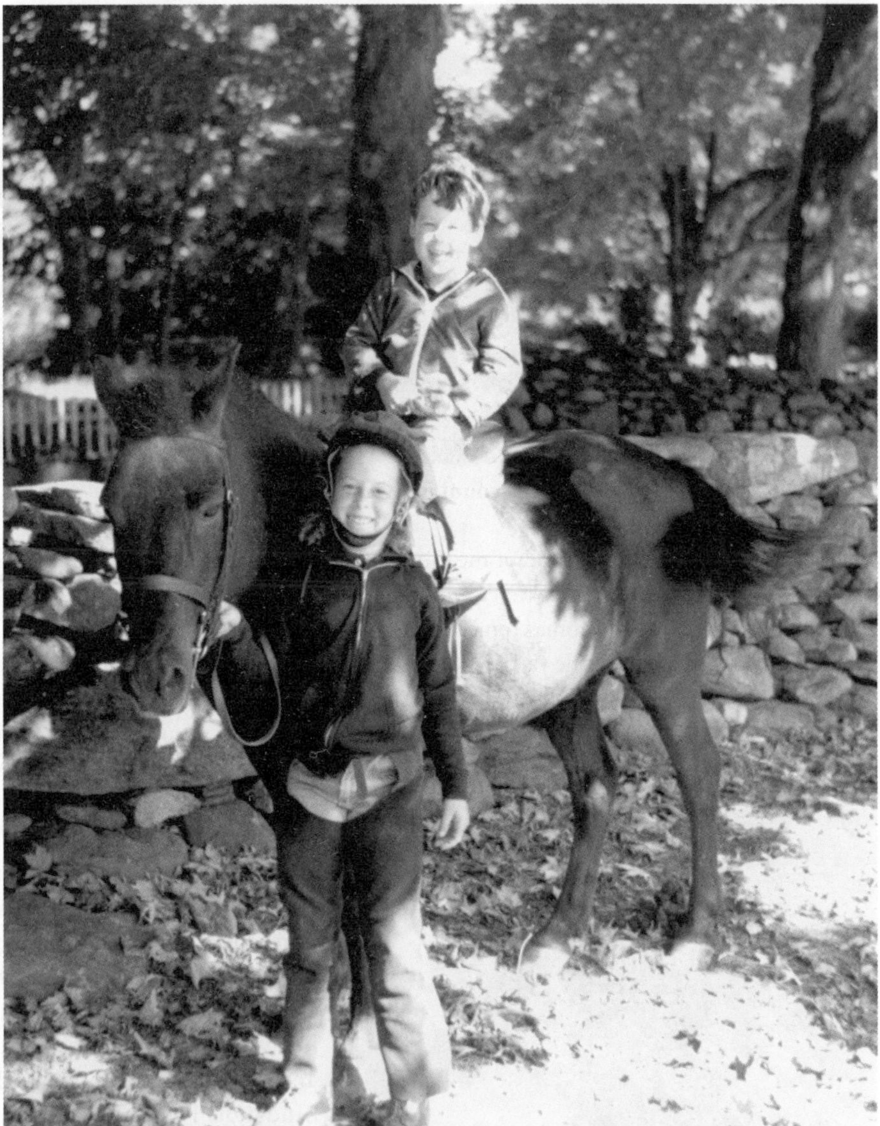

Mighty Mouse and his riders, Eliza and Peter

campaigns. The high point of my running career was finishing the 1978 New York Marathon with a time of three hours and twenty-seven minutes, almost exactly eight minutes a mile.[21]

I loved running because all you need is a pair of shorts and sneakers. My love of running was as legendary as it was religious. My godson John D. Britton never forgot it, saying "For all of Lew's evident intellectual and business achievements, I remember as a boy that Lew made a huge impression as a rugged and tough athlete."[22] He can still remember me

> training to run the New York Marathon and going on long runs, [for] a few of which my dad accompanied him on a bike. I recall visiting the Lehrmans in Nantucket and Lew getting out of the car a seemingly impossible distance from the house so he could run home. I remember having contests in our Vermont house with wall sits and simulated downhill tuck positions to see how strong the competitor's legs were. I recall Lew winning.[23]

As an adult, I joined the Over-40 Group of Businessmen-Athletes in Greenwich. This was a wonderful group of men who played football in the fall, basketball in the winter, and soccer in the spring. It brought joy to my heart, and I always had my children by my side. We showed up around ten o'clock on Sunday mornings at the Greenwich Country Day School sports field, and away we went. After playing with the kids at home in the mornings, I would often relent when they begged to come and see the big boys play. There, at the sports field, the "munchkins" would play their own games with a football on the sidelines, and there were no happier children than they.

Record time

I called Barton Biggs of Morgan Stanley "the Commissioner." There were about a dozen members—eight regulars. We played without substitutes for two hours straight. The group consisted of several Morgan Stanley executives in addition to Barton and me, including Jonathan Clark, John Hill Wilson, Robin Prince, and Jim Gantsoudes. Other good friends like Fergus Reid, Gerry

Once a football player, always a football player

Jones, Billy Morton, Rick Salomon, Jim Donley, Fred Filoon, Bill Finn, Bob Campbell, Irv Hanson, and Sam Sammis rounded out the company. As I recall, Barton and Jonathan Clark would pick teams at the beginning of each session, carefully choosing members to balance the ever-changing sides. Visits to the Greenwich Hospital emergency ward during or following a game were a fairly regular occurrence, but the good fun, exercise, and camaraderie made it all worthwhile. Starting in 1980, I missed the Over-40 football games—including the group photograph day—because of my commitment to public life. Thankfully, my friend Jonathan Clark was there when I wasn't. He helped me to accurately reconstruct this story, and sent me photographs of our teams.

The family often bicycled together. Physical exercise was an article of faith in the family before its benefits became widely accepted. "The only thing I would urge you to do—one hour of running, biking, swimming or gym work at least 5 out of 7 days,"[24] I wrote one of my sons—a sentiment I frequently repeated in correspondence. "Sustained athletic exercise will enable you to concentrate on your demanding reading more easily. It will give you great stamina in the evening; I know from experience. You will sleep better, you will eat better and if I do say so myself, it will increase your general self-confidence."[25]

CHAPTER 6

The Lehrman Institute and Monetary Policy

At Lehrman people tend to ask unvarnished questions that go to the core of the thing.
—Professor Robert Heilbroner, The New School for Social Research[1]

Although I left the academy in 1963, I did not abandon my interest in history, diplomacy, and public affairs. I continued to read intensively over the next decades. I began to study the great economists, and to contemplate how a rejuvenated university like Yale might be reconstituted. I put my ideas into practice at The Lehrman Institute.

FOUNDING THE LEHRMAN INSTITUTE

I started thinking about the Institute even before I left graduate school. I had decided the universities were not good places to do policy studies, or historically oriented policy analysis. Faculties were very partisan, and esoteric. They could neither hear, nor articulate, the authentic voices of public opinion.

In 1961, when I was still a Carnegie Teaching Fellow, I attended a Yale seminar on the Paris Peace Conference of 1919 with Nicholas Rizopoulos. Two years ahead of me as an undergraduate, Nick was by then working on his PhD in history. The discussion at the seminar that day was uninspiring. Afterwards, at a New Haven diner, Nick and I talked about starting a small institute dedicated to the study of economics and foreign policy. "Nick, if I ever become rich, one thing I would love to do is to set up a small, independent think tank," I told him.

By 1972, I had made some money as a result of Rite Aid's growth and was ready to put $3 million worth of seed money into the Institute. I called Nick, then an assistant professor of diplomatic history at Yale. As Nick recalled the conversation, "Lew asked me if I was willing to drop everything I was doing and help organize, then direct, the institute of the sort he had talked about."[2]

Nick later told Karen Heller of the *Rochester Democrat and Chronicle* about my passionate enthusiasm for policy studies. She called her article "A Hurricane Named Lew," and wrote that "Rizopoulos says that evenings with him at The Lehrman Institute in New York City, discussing foreign and economic policy are far from peaceful. 'Never, never,' Rizopoulos says, chuckling into the phone. 'With Lew there's always an argument, always fighting, screaming, and a lot of laughter.'"[3]

THE LEHRMAN INSTITUTE

The Lehrman Institute: intellectual debate headquarters

I had come to the conclusion that universities were no longer midwives of American progress. The better American colleges had been established to train people for the workplace, for business, and for the professions. But it was clear to me that over time, the elite universities and divinity schools had become separate from the workaday world. I thought America needed fresh approaches. I would take the same position in 1976 when I served as chairman of the Yale University Council on the Humanities and reviewed the humanities curriculum for undergraduates. Eighteen departments constituted the humanities section of Yale. It was a vast undertaking.

At The Lehrman Institute, I turned my academic dreams into reality. My concern was that the universities did not draw *working* men and women into them. They were apart and separated. At the time, I felt the "ivory tower" metaphor was in fact correct. I wanted the United States to have a public policy institution that was firmly planted in the commercial world—where lawyers, doctors, journalists, and businessmen could continue to study and have a real impact.

We made a special application to the New York State Department of Education for a charitable exemption. I visited the liberal Brookings Institution and the conservative American Enterprise Institute in order to understand their positions. I knew people I wanted to recruit to the enterprise. David Calleo was two years ahead of me at Yale. He was concerned with the same things I was, namely nineteenth-century Europe and the European State system, foundation stones of the current international world order. David had joined the faculty of the Johns Hopkins School of Advanced International Studies (SAIS). He would become one of The Lehrman Institute's trustees. In December 1972, we held an organizational meeting.

About that time, I purchased a townhouse on the Upper East Side of New York City to be the center for Lehrman Institute activities. Its layout helped to frame our work. A typical Institute event would involve sitting around a third-floor roundtable discussing the opinions of authors, adjourning to the drawing room on the second floor for continued conversation, and finally enjoying dinner on the first floor. Behind its green front door, the Institute was the perfect place to discuss the fields of economics, history, foreign policy, and urban policy.

Some of the articles written about the Institute are illustrative.

"Lehrman had planned the think tank as a 'small, elegant research institution,'" wrote Laurie Bennett in an interview with Rizopoulos.

> The 62-year-old townhouse on Manhattan's upper east side is just that. Scholars and politicians meet and debate in rooms decorated with parquet flooring, marble fireplaces and terraces adorned with begonias and roses [to which Louise gave her nimble touch]. Yet although Lehrman has a Bachelor's degree from Yale, studied at Princeton, and received a Masters degree from Harvard, he was never meant to be an academic, Rizopoulos says. "He is the kind of person who has to do something, rather than sitting back and taking the long view at what was happening in 14th Century Venice."[4]

Lise Bang-Jensen also esteemed the quality of the varied participants at Institute functions, writing:

> The two men [Nicholas and I] began inviting provocative thinkers to seminars, "roundtables", and dinner parties. . . . Participants are as diverse as the topics. Conservative economist George Gilder, author of *Wealth and Poverty*, the handbook of supply-side economics, has had to fend off intellectual attacks from avowed Marxists. Robert L. Heilbroner and Irving Kristol, economists with conflicting ideologies, appear frequently at Institute events, while the Dalai Lama and ex–CIA chief William Colby have spoken at the Institute's "occasional meetings."[5]

Edmund Newton of the *Soho News* appears to have enjoyed the interior of the Institute, writing that:

> Up on East 71st Street is a handsome, five-story brick front townhouse—once the home of Alan Jay Lerner, who presumably was responsible for the interior of the tiny elevator being painted like a view from the gondola of a hot-air balloon.
>
> This is The Lehrman Institute, which . . . Lehrman founded ten years ago [1972] to serve as a center for policy studies. Here, among tasteful modern art, plushly upholstered furniture, sitting rooms and meeting rooms, an elegant garden, and bathrooms with toilets that flush soundlessly, is where Lehrman lets his intellectual hair down according to friends.
>
> The idea was one that came to Lehrman as a graduate student at Yale, says institute Director Nicholas Rizopoulos. "He had this idea in his head that when he grew up, he was going to start this scholarly, but not academic, institute for policy studies," says Rizopoulos, Lehrman's fellow student and fraternity brother at Yale.[6]

We were soon fortunate enough to bring Professor Robert Tucker onboard. Like Calleo, he, too, had taught at the School of Advanced International Studies at Johns Hopkins University. Tucker would later serve as president of the Institute from 1982 to 1987. Bob was one of the best-known international relations professors of his time. Among many other ideas, he had formulated the argument that the United States should end the OPEC cartel by military force.

Each year, the Institute chose fellows to conduct research and present material from the books on which they were working. One of the earliest fellows was Doris Kearns Goodwin, who worked on a biography, *Lyndon Johnson and the American Dream*, shortly after Johnson's death in 1973. Historian Ronald Steel worked on *Walter Lippmann and the American Century* at the Institute.

In a piece on the Cold War for the *Washington Post*, Sidney Blumenthal remarked on the connection between our fellowship program and contemporary policy-making:

> It was unsurprising that two books warning of America's inability to maintain its economic ballast while financing the Cold War were published virtually simultaneously; for [Institute authors David] Calleo and [James] Chace were both on the committee to develop programs for a small think tank in Manhattan, the Lehrman Institute. On the surface, the Lehrman Institute might appear an ironic setting for the rethinking of the Cold War. Its founder and funder, Lewis Lehrman, the drugstore mogul, was an ardent conservative—one of the first disciples of supply-side economics. . . . But the institute that bore his name was a place of genuine and independent scholarship. . . .[7]

British economic historian Robert Skidelsky presented early work on his multivolume biography of John Maynard Keynes. Skidelsky became one of the century's greatest biographers and was eventually knighted for his work. He and I subsequently continued our correspondence. A sensible liberal, he was well acquainted with the debates between Jacques Rueff and John Maynard Keynes, especially their public debates in Switzerland. In my opinion, Rueff won all those debates. Despite Skidelsky's dissenting view, I was very impressed with his work, and decided to use it as an example of excellence. In March 1975, I wrote to David Calleo, saying:

> I suggest we should take Skidelsky's four essays and seminars as a standard by which we should measure all future Research Fellowships.
>
> Truly, he achieved distinction in all those facets which characterize the type of fellowship we have been trying to develop. His four papers, although they were related to his research on the Keynes book, were not merely "chapters." They were papers written exclusively to achieve the purposes intended by the seminar, namely, to help the Research Fellow understand better the issues with respect to his main line of inquiry, in this case, the critical issues surrounding the life of Lord Keynes. They were distinguished essays.
>
> Surely, the seminars were an equal success. [Skidelsky] was articulate, well-prepared and, more importantly, modest and receptive when confronted by a hostile point of view, not the least of which was mine. I was particularly impressed that his strong views were put forward with a forbearance that was not always reciprocated by some. He was unruffled.[8]

In a piece for *Change* magazine, Stan Luxenberg emphasized our collegial environment, and the confidentiality that made full expression possible. All discussions were off the record. "Though it is small," he began, "operating on an annual budget of about $275,000, the foundation has managed to attract a growing core of dedicated supporters, including some of the country's best-known scholars. What draws people to its seminars and research projects is the fact that Lehrman has created a neutral forum where sharp thinkers can meet to swap ideas."[9]

Stan's article went on to point out some of the unique attributes of the Institute. "Participants feel free to speak their minds," he continued. "'The seminars are possibly the best I've ever attended,' says Robert L. Heilbroner, Norman Thomas Professor of Economics at the New School for Social Research. 'Very often when you go to a seminar everybody is wary and you don't want to make a fool of yourself. At Lehrman people tend to ask unvarnished questions that go to the core of the thing.'"[10]

In 1979, the same year in which the *Change* article was published, the Institute sponsored about seventy-five seminars and supported three research fellows then writing books. "The Lehrman staff expends considerable time and money to insure that projects are worthwhile," Luxenberg added. "Seminar topics are carefully checked and participants are selected to provide a stimulating mix of views. Grant recipients are chosen for the quality and timeliness of their work by a five-person committee whose composition reflects the foundation's nonpartisan emphasis."[11]

While it was important to me that the Institute engage with experts from all political circles, I was also committed to representing the best of the historical tradition and defending it from what I regarded as merely fashionable or convenient. In that commitment I was forever joined to my mentor, Jacques Rueff.

MEETING JACQUES RUEFF

One of the Institute's initiatives in which I took the most pride, and on which I expended the most effort, was the publication of the five-volume *Complete Works of Jacques Rueff (Oeuvres Complètes de Jacques Rueff)* by Plon, the publisher which had also been entrusted with the memoirs of Charles de Gaulle. In 1979, the trustees of The Lehrman Institute and the Association Jacques Rueff also jointly established a Jacques Rueff Memorial Prize in honor of one of France's greatest economists and statesmen.

Rueff was a younger contemporary, friend, and peer of the English economist John Maynard Keynes, with whom Rueff often debated. After Keynes died in 1946, Jacques Rueff never again had a peer throughout the second half of the twentieth century, excepting perhaps Robert Triffin, the Belgian-American economist, who held many of the same views. Rueff did become friends with Milton Friedman, but Rueff was older, and more than Friedman's peer. At the epicenter in France of monetary theory and diplomacy throughout World War I and World War II, Rueff remained at the vital center of intellectual, economic, and monetary debates in the postwar Bretton Woods era until his death in 1978. He was the most profound economist of the twentieth century.

At Yale and Harvard, I saw the success of Rueff's financial reform plans for France fully embraced by General Charles de Gaulle, president of the Fifth Republic. During the 1960s, I admired Professor Rueff from afar by reading newspapers and economics journals. His work regularly appeared in *Le Monde*, and sometimes in the *Wall Street Journal* and *Fortune*.

In 1958, France was collapsing under the pressure of inflation and the Algerian war. When De Gaulle was called to power on an emergency basis by the National Assembly, he promptly appointed Rueff to reform the French economy. Rueff was the master of theory, policy, and administration at the French Central Bank and

Jacques Rueff: The outstanding French philosopher

Treasury. He was called "Cassandra," because he forecast disaster both in the 1930s and the 1940s, but he was right. Despite his critics he was the most powerful person at the French Treasury in the 1920s, and forty years later he became responsible for the successful economic plan of the Fifth Republic.

In 1963, I was staying at the Yale Club while on business in New York City. I was going through back issues of *Fortune* magazine when I came across Rueff's article in the July 1961 edition. That article, "The West Is Risking a Credit Collapse," focused on the problems created by the Bretton Woods agreement of 1945. It begins with this admonition:

> A grave peril hangs over the economy of the West. Every day its situation more and more resembles the one that turned the 1929 recession into the great depression. The instability in our monetary system is such that a minor international incident or a small economic or financial disturbance could set off worldwide disaster. There is a great deal of concern about this instability, though rarely expressed in terms as stark as I have used, and a number of measures have been suggested for dealing with it. But instead of going to the roots of what is wrong, these would rather prolong for several months or years the erring ways that are responsible for the danger.
>
> The West has no task more urgent than to recognize the disease that infects it, and by curing it, to re-establish in the free world a monetary system that generates lasting stability.[12]

Rueff had been the youngest secretary of the treasury in French history. He became deputy governor of the Bank of France in 1939, serving until 1941. Jewish by birth, Rueff was pressured by the Vichy regime to resign after the French surrender to Germany, even though he had converted to Catholicism at the age of twenty-four. Off duty, he wasted no time. During World War II, he wrote one of his most influential works, *L'Ordre Social*, a monumental tome of social and economic theory. But it was what he accomplished in his later years that had caught my attention. In May of 1981, I went over the history in an interview for *Human Events* magazine:

> Twice in his lifetime, Jacques Rueff saved the French currency.
>
> Once during the 1920s—between 1926 and 1928—after the catastrophe of World War I. The second time, in the midst of the collapse of the Fourth Republic, President de Gaulle called Rueff to power to end inflation, reform the French currency, balance the budget, and renovate French economic institutions. Both times he was successful. *The key element of both French financial reforms was the restoration of convertibility of French currency into gold and the establishment of budgetary equilibrium.*
>
> The economic consequences of Jacques Rueff in 1959 were very simple and very dramatic. They are part of living memory. The Fourth Republic was collapsing; the economy of France was uncertain; inflation raged; French foreign

De Gaulle and Rueff: Heroes of the Fifth Republic

exchange reserves equaled about 45 days of foreign payments. The currency was declining. The government was virtually bankrupt and immobilized. De Gaulle had been called to power from his home in Colombey-les-deux-Eglises. Rueff was summoned by him to restore financial order.

De Gaulle created the Fifth Republic, the constitution and the presidential system that went along with it, a fact which was not unrelated to his admiration for the American Republic. But it was Jacques Rueff who created the financial conditions which led to the restoration of the French economy.[13]

Rueff's ideas were the same in 1918 and 1958. Thus, they were out of fashion. It was assumed by jealous academics that he could not be right twice. That point of view overlooks the fact that some principles are eternal. His article in *Fortune* and the success of his policies encouraged me to read his economic writings. Following Rueff's reforms, there was a boom throughout the 1970s in France. I sought out and read his books and articles, including the untranslated ones. My French improved enormously as I waded through all six of his collected works in the original. Rueff's ideas—included in books such as *The Age of Inflation*, *Balance of Payments*, *The Monetary Sin of the West*, and *L'Ordre Social* struck me with the same force as Mr. Lincoln's 1854 speech at Peoria.

Jacques Rueff became my most influential teacher and colleague. Inspired by his voluminous writings and studious example, I read the best of the free-market economists, and the best of the socialists. Very quickly, I identified the leading scholars from the past and the present. Indeed, I met some at The Lehrman Institute. I read William Stanley Jevons, one of the key economists in the United Kingdom. I studied Rueff's conservative intellectual opponents and his historical influences, focusing on Germany's Ludwig Erhard, France's Jean-Baptiste Say, Austria's Ludwig von Mises and Friedrich von Hayek, and America's Milton Friedman. While there were differences among them, they respected each other as conservatives, and their differences of opinion were minor, except to them.

I have always made a distinction between reading and studying. I didn't just read John Maynard Keynes. I *studied* him. Study was necessary to understand the essential differences between Keynes and Rueff, differences which could tip the scales between war and peace, depression and prosperity. I often wrote about these differences for the *Wall Street Journal* and other outlets. My first Lehrman Institute book, *Money and the Coming World Order*, also compared the teachings of Keynes and Rueff.[14] But in 2010, Christopher S. Chivvis did such a good job summarizing the significance of their debate that I choose to cite him here. In his book *The Monetary Conservative: Jacques Rueff and Twentieth Century Free-Market Thought*, Chivvis wrote:

> Rueff and Keynes met in the 1920s, when Keynes was rising to stardom and Rueff was just beginning his career. To Keynes, Rueff was a leading French proponent of the "Treasury view" Keynes thought so recondite. To Rueff, Keynesianism was a disease, a drug politicians used to placate the masses. Keynes saw activist fiscal and monetary policy as a means of salvaging liberal democracy from the threat posed by the unemployed masses—otherwise tempted by fascism. By contrast, Rueff thought Keynesianism inevitably created inflation and that, in the democratic context, this would have precisely the opposite effect—inflation would make the masses more susceptible to the allure of tyrants masquerading as conservatives and promising to restore order.[15]

Studying Rueff's successful modern implementation of a gold standard in France led me to study the history of the gold standard. The gold standard is perhaps the most important aspect of the economic history of the United States from 1776 until 1971. The monetary and currency issue has been among our nation's most continuous political and financial preoccupations. Beginning with the collapse of the Continental currency during the Articles of Confederation, the issue remained at the forefront until the coinage powers were established by the US Constitution. Then, from the Bank of the United States controversies through the restoration of the gold standard in 1879 after the Civil War, it never left the public mind. It dominated discussion from the free silver question to the definitive Gold Standard Act of 1900, and erupted anew with the still controversial Federal Reserve Act of 1913. The monetary issue remained paramount through the currency wars between 1914 and 1944, during the Great Depression when FDR took the United States off the gold standard, under the Bretton Woods regime, and since its collapse in 1971. There is nothing unique about my historical focus—namely, the saliency of the currency question throughout American history.

This currency question is not just a domestic issue. It has universal importance. I described the historic impact of monetary policy for the *Cato Journal* in 2014, saying:

> No one knew better than Jacques Rueff, a soldier of France and a famous central banker, that World War I had brought to an end the preeminence of the classical European states system and its monetary regime—the classical gold standard. World War I had decimated the flower of European youth; it had destroyed

> the European continent's industrial primacy. No less ominously, the historic monetary standard of commercial civilization had collapsed into the ruins occasioned by the Great War. The international gold standard—the gyroscope of the Industrial Revolution, the common currency of the world trading system, the guarantor of more than 100 years of a stable monetary system, the balance wheel of unprecedented economic growth—was brushed aside by the belligerents. Into the breach marched unrestrained central bank credit expansion, the express government purpose of which was to finance the colossal budget deficits occasioned by war and its aftermath.[16]

With respect to Rueff and France, my study focused on newspaper reporting about the affairs of Europe in the late 1950s and early '60s. When the National Assembly called De Gaulle to the rescue in 1958, they authorized him to rule by decree for six months. De Gaulle then called up Rueff, and together as a team they wrote one of the most important chapters of twentieth-century French economic history. In fact, it is one of the most important chapters in the history of France, and had a major effect on all her trading partners. Professor Rueff's plan for the restoration of the French economy was grounded in the restoration of the convertibility of the franc to gold and to the dollar at a level *which ensured that nominal French wage rates would not fall.* Rueff chose this level consciously and deliberately to avoid the mistake made when Winston Churchill, as chancellor of the British Exchequer, had overvalued the pound sterling against gold in 1925. This mistake had led to widespread unemployment, and downward pressure on British wages.[17]

In a word, the Rueff plan worked. Rueff was a genius, more than a peer of Keynes. De Gaulle decreed Rueff's franc restoration plan *in toto.* The subsequent decade was one of the best in French history. Economic growth in France was the most rapid among the developed countries. Rueff's plan worked, but it would have been better had the United States cooperated, for it then would have stabilized the global financial system. This entire period from 1958 onward inspired my careful reading of the American and the available European press on the subject of the French economy.

I am a small-c conservative, not in the English or Burkean tradition, but in the classical liberal tradition of Cobden, Bright, Acton, Hamilton, and Lincoln. I favor a strong but limited constitutional government which acknowledges the constitutional monetary standard, namely gold and silver. I insist upon this point not merely because of Article I, Sections 8 and 10 of the US Constitution, but because the institutions of trust, integrity, and respect for the wages and savings of the least powerful and pensioners depends on the stability and long-term purchasing power of the monetary standard. All other economic issues may be important, but in the absence of long-term stability for the purchasing power of the monetary standard, only insiders, the rich, those well-endowed by the wealth of forebears, and the financial-banking speculative class, can deal effectively with inflation, not least because of their privileged access to cheap or free money from the US Federal Reserve and its member banks.

In August 1971, when President Richard Nixon "closed the gold window," he ended the last American link between the dollar and gold. *I have come to believe that the overturning of the gold standard was not just an economic issue, but can be seen as a metaphor for the collapse of all objective cultural and moral standards during the past century in the so-called advanced, developed countries.*

A decade later, President Nixon reached out to me. He invited me to come see him. He was interested in the fact that I had become a prominent conservative Republican in Nelson Rockefeller's liberal state. When we met, I told him he had made a serious mistake in removing that last link to the gold standard. He asked me what I would have done in his position. I told him that he made it inevitable that America's economic situation would get worse. He could have reformed the international monetary system. The obvious alternative was to raise the price of gold and redeem the debts owed by the United States to all free world countries with dollars. At that time, the United States was protecting the free world for free, and had the moral and political power to secure a gold price adjustment such that nominal wages and industrial competitiveness *would not decline in the United States.* It would have required a substantial increase in the dollar price of gold, but it would have worked just as the Rueff plan had worked for France. Rueff had faced a similar situation. He had to think carefully about the reintroduction of the gold standard in France. When he did, he made sure to set the gold price in francs high enough so that French citizens and industries would be left in a competitive position. Nixon could have done the exact same thing for the United States. Readers interested in the method for accomplishing this goal in the United States can consult my book *The True Gold Standard, a Monetary Reform Plan without Official Reserve Currencies* (2011, revised and enlarged second edition in 2012).

It was in the early 1970s that I began to correspond directly with Jacques Rueff. I wrote to him at first to sympathize with his work on the "twin evils of reserve currency and budget deficits." When he wrote back to invite me to meet with him in Paris, I was elated. In 1972 I finally met my economic mentor when Rueff testified before the Joint Economic Committee of Congress.

Stanley Stillman: Louise's brother "Steamboat"

My brother-in-law, Stanley Stillman, had interviewed him for *Time* magazine. Rueff argued before the congressional committee that the United States had tried for more than a decade unsuccessfully "to balance external payments by administrative manipulations."[18] Stanley wrote penetratingly on the subject, saying:

> Despite his views on gold, Jacques Rueff still commands the attention of those in America familiar with the international monetary situation. Last fall, he was called to testify before one of the groups most skeptical of his views, the Joint Economic Committee of Congress and its subcommittee on international monetary affairs.
>
> Only a deep residual respect for the man's integrity and idealism can explain why those whose anti-gold [views] are among the most vehement and publicly held in the world would consult him. How carefully they listened to him remains to be seen; but superficially at any rate they paid tribute to his position. This week, he traveled again to the United States to participate in a conference on the monetary situation sponsored by Columbia University.[19]

When I met him in Paris, Rueff told me that he had checked on my background, and that it caused him to take me seriously. He recognized that I really understood his theory, and we immediately began to compare notes. We both felt an urgent concern that the so-called experts had learned nothing from the inter-war economic experience, which had demonstrated so clearly the links between inflation, dictatorship, and war. In 1974, after continued correspondence, I followed up on his invitation to visit with him again in France.

When we got to Paris, Rueff wanted me to meet the chief economic editor of *Le Monde*, Paul Fabra, a master of the history of economic thought. We went out to the famous restaurant, Brasserie Lipp, where Rueff had his own table. Fabra was an economist, who was also the financial editor of *Le Monde* during the De Gaulle–Rueff restoration of the French franc. He was well respected by the entire De Gaulle government, including Jacques Rueff. Fabra's coverage of De Gaulle's great speech of 1965 on the gold standard had been reported worldwide. Paul was a very modest man with a wonderful temperament. He had a powerful ego that never showed. We became fast friends. Back at the Institute, I hired a gifted editor and researcher, May Wu, fluent in French, to work on the Rueff manuscripts we would publish as part of a transatlantic partnership with the Rueff family. She also translated the speech I gave to the inaugural Rueff Prize Dinner.

In presenting the first Rueff Prize to Paul Fabra in November 1979, I observed:

> Our era—preeminently an age of inflation—has . . . become an age of unparalleled disorder. For Jacques Rueff, . . . the goal of statecraft, the mission of every *Inspecteur des Finances*, in our times, must be "*Le Combat Pour l'Ordre Financier*," the struggle to restore financial order. Jacques Rueff's mission as a scholar and a statesman was to demonstrate the ineluctable connection between

Paul Fabra: Le Fils Spirituel de Jacques Rueff

> the idea of order and the idea of freedom. His life was, above all, a struggle to achieve his goal of a free and ordered world.[20]

It appears to be a riddle, that you cannot have freedom without order. But by considering the risk to freedom under anarchy, the riddle may be solved. If we do not achieve the goal of a free and ordered world, anarchy will be the outcome, making way for tyrants and false prophets to seize control of the state.[21]

I made several visits to Paris. Rueff and Fabra both fell in love with my wife, Louise, who spoke much better French than I. My pursuit of Rueff's thoughts and economic model would lead to the appellation "spiritual son of Jacques Rueff,"[22] as one French magazine would describe me. I treasure the award.

Professor Rueff died in April 1978. I did not go to the funeral because I was on the road with the New York Republican Platform Committee. I had become friends with Rueff's daughter Passerose, and his son-in-law, Henri Pigeat, during my visits to France, and through publishing Rueff's collected works. Like Fabra, Henri was a gifted journalist who rose to become head of Agence France-Presse (AFP).

In 1996, I returned to Paris to give a speech at the French Assemblé Nationale. In my remarks entitled "Jacques Rueff, the Age of Inflation, and the True Gold Standard," I began:

> The ideas I set before you originate in the proven genius of an extraordinary teacher, a selfless servant of the French people, and a peerless citizen of the world—in the words of General de Gaulle—"un poète de finance."[23]

I tried to put Rueff's pathbreaking work in the context of his life, saying "This is the reform plan set out for us by Jacques Rueff two generations ago . . . Indeed, domestic and international monetary reform, i.e., the gold standard—a common, neutral, non-national currency, is the only true and lasting road to full employment."[24]

With Professor Rueff as a mentor, my studies at The Lehrman Institute were similar to a post–doctoral degree in global economic and monetary policy. I spent a lot of time working on the "Rueff Plan" and considering its application to the United States. I met a lot of opposition. Michael Barone, however, called the views I developed original. He wrote a fair-minded and vivid article that focused on my relationship with Jacques Rueff, and our commitment to ordered freedom. Quoting me, Barone included the following distillation of our point of view:

> "A free people will tolerate financial disorder for only about 15 or 20 years," [Lehrman] says, with a steeliness that echoes off the panels of the Citicorp Center. He is speaking of the American economy after the 1971 decision to let the dollar float free; one hero is Jacques Rueff, de Gaulle's economist, whose hard-money currency reform led to the vast prosperity of Fifth Republic France. Lehrman believes something analogous will happen here within the next 10 years; and if it does, he will have something to do with it. "Simple ideas," he says, speaking of Rite-Aid and of politics as well, "are the ones that have worked. It takes a very firm hand to direct it, and a clear vision."[25]

MONETARY REFORM

Monetary and economic policy seminars at the Institute attracted particularly strong panels of economic thinkers and active businesspeople. Some of them I met for the first time at the Institute, including for example, Malcolm S. Forbes, Jr., editor-in chief of *Forbes* magazine.

Another was Columbia professor Robert Mundell. Bob won the second Jacques Rueff Prize at the Palais de Luxembourg in October 1983. Nineteen years later he would be awarded the Nobel Prize. In presenting the Rueff Prize to Mundell, I noted: "He has called for a restoration of the gold standard in order to save the Western world from the twin catastrophes of deflation and inflation."[26]

My work on the gold standard led me to contribute to what became known as supply-side economics. The Lehrman Institute was a place where Friedmanites met the emerging supply-siders like Arthur Laffer, Jude Wanniski, and Robert Mundell. I differed with some of the latter in my belief in the importance of monetary stability and balancing the budget as opposed to simply cutting taxes. Cutting taxes alone can lead to inflation if the Federal Reserve just turns around and monetizes the deficit.

Edmund Newton did a good job clarifying the different positions, writing the following for the *Soho News*:

> Lehrman quietly denies that he is a supply-sider, one of those who shaped the Reagan approach to tax reform . . . "I've always been much interested in a balanced budget . . . and the composition of public spending," [Lehrman] says. "I was always interested in whether or not social programs actually do work. Supply-siders are primarily interested in marginal tax reform."[27]

Supply-side economics was part of an economic and policy framework that had The Lehrman Institute as one of its headquarters. According to the *Washington Post*'s Glenn Frankel:

> The supply-side gospel was hammered out in the mid-1970s by Laffer, economist Robert Mundell of Columbia University, Wanniski, Kemp and others in endless seminars at the Michael restaurant on Trinity Place in lower Manhattan, at business tycoon Lewis Lehrman's New York think tank, and in Kemp's congressional office. It holds that broad tax cuts combined with a stable currency can unleash entrepreneurs and investors and trigger a wave of growth and prosperity. One of its fundamental features is the curve that Laffer first drew on a napkin at Michael purporting to show how cuts in marginal tax rates can lead to a burst in economic growth large enough to make up the lost taxes from the initial cuts.[28]

Among those who attended The Lehrman Institute sessions was Robert Bartley, editor of the *Wall Street Journal* editorial page. I wrote to him in October 1974, saying "I noticed that you were able to attend the Tucker session at the Institute last week. I am also an admiring follower of your editorial page. My brother-in-law, Stanley Stillman, has suggested that the three of us get together for lunch or dinner, and I would like to know if you might have an opening on your calendar in the near future."[29]

Some of New York's top bankers attended Lehrman Institute seminars. Among those who participated was Harold Van B. Cleveland, chief economist for Citibank who had helped set up the Marshall Plan early in his career. Mr. Cleveland served on The Lehrman Institute's Board of Trustees and co-wrote an Institute book with me, *Money and the Coming World Order* (1976). A third coauthor of the book was economic historian Charles P. Kindleberger, who had also worked on the Marshall Plan before becoming a professor of international economics at the Massachusetts Institute of Technology. In our book, I wrote:

> On a larger scale, the interdependent world economic system grows steadily more precarious. The disorders of the global economy, and in particular the disequilibrium of its monetary system, are inextricably tied up with this problem of inflation. Internationally as well as nationally, power replaces the market. The unrestrained use of political power, in pursuit of particular national economic interests, exemplifies an increasing tendency to both circumvent market disciplines and to brush aside temporarily inconvenient systems of

> international rules. Nowhere, of course, has this tendency toward accentuated nationalism been more obvious than in the growing disorder of the international monetary system.
>
> I believe that the problems of world monetary disorder, endemic inflation, cartelization of raw materials, and unemployment are, in fact, closely linked. They originate in the excessive fiscal and monetary policies of the nation-states which compose the postwar international economic system. These harmful national policies derive their support not only from partisan groups and individuals, whose political influence displaces true national interest with narrow sectarian goals, but also from a widespread intellectual misunderstanding of the nature of the international economic system. Popular economic doctrines have exacerbated rather than checked the spread of inflation. This potent combination of greed and fallacy has made it increasingly difficult for the world economic system to achieve stability.[30]

I also got to know Mr. Cleveland's boss Walter Wriston, the president of Citibank. He was infamous for insisting that all sovereign government securities were safe and profitable instruments, a statement disproven almost immediately after he said it. Wriston, a devoted admirer of Milton Friedman, insisted that Citibank had a foolproof system of lending. In 1973 and '74, however, sovereign governments would default around the world. Citibank almost went broke, and Wriston's foolproof system of lending had to get bailed out by the Federal Reserve.

David Rockefeller, CEO of Chase Manhattan Bank, was caught in the same financial crisis as Citibank's Walt Wriston, but he was much more reserved in his prescriptions than Wriston. I met David through Rick Salomon, a friend with whom I played touch football in Greenwich. Rockefeller was a very disciplined man. Very modest, he was a practical banker. He listened. He was not doctrinaire.

On November 15, 1978, I chaired a roundtable at the Institute in which Robert Bartley presented a paper on "The Fate of the Dollar." I wrote Bartley the next day, saying:

> I think your "critics," both academic and business, could have been better informed and more inspiring. I'm not sure they ever really challenged your view, in a rigorous or compelling way. I do hope you found it all worthwhile.
>
> May I just add my own words of encouragement to you, though I know you need none. You are teaching a whole new generation of businessmen, bankers, lawyers and journalists to understand the economic world from neither a Keynesian nor a monetarist point of view. Rather you are teaching them about the world of a real economy and a real financial economy, composed of real business institutions and real factors of production, and of the organic relations among them. . . .
>
> I pray that "Bartley's essays" have the same success in our time as [Walter] Bagehot's[31] did in his.[32]

In a 2011 interview with Morton Kondracke, I observed that to describe those early meetings at Michael's and the Institute

> as a movement, then, is too large an idea. It was just generally a small group of people, a meeting at The Lehrman Institute, and then some of them going off to [write articles for the business press, or to] drink and eat at Michael's Restaurant. But the sort of serious sessions where there was no food and no drink were the seminars at The Lehrman Institute on economics, and the participants are well known . . . Jack [Kemp] in the area of monetary policy, was much influenced by Bob Mundell, who was at Columbia at the time—and, of course, Bob came to The Lehrman Institute seminars. . . ."[33]

During the mid-1970s, I began submitting articles to the *Wall Street Journal* editorial page at the invitation of Bob Bartley, who had assumed editorship of the page in 1972. The *Wall Street Journal*'s op-ed page published my shorter pieces, while Barton Biggs of Morgan Stanley published the more thorough research as white papers.

In an article for the *Washington Post* about the impact of Bartley's editorial page, Dan Morgan wrote:

> In addition to his own writings and those of Wanniski, Bartley also began to open the page to outside contributors with unorthodox economic views. These included Laffer himself, whose early articles argued that currency devaluations did not help countries' trade balances; Norman Ture, a supply-sider recently named assistant secretary of the treasury for tax policy; and businessman Lewis Lehrman, a leading gold standard advocate."[34]

My effort to bring together decision-makers for a serious policy discussion was rewarded when in December 1979, I chaired a roundtable at the Institute on "The Goals and Conduct of Monetary Policy." The speaker was Paul A. Volcker, chairman of the Federal Reserve Board of Governors. He had been appointed by President Jimmy Carter in 1979. A couple years earlier, I had met Volcker with Jerry Milbank, then chairman of the Republican National Finance Committee. Volcker was a trustee of the Milbank Foundation, a position in which I later served. I had lunch with Milbank and Volcker, who was astounded by my order—just a plate of lettuce. At the time, I was running regularly after lunch, and so ate lightly at the midday meal. I knew that Volcker had played a key role in 1971, when the Nixon Administration ended the function of gold in international finance. At that lunch, I directly criticized him for it. Volcker's alternate policy: high interest rates and an overvalued dollar led to the de-industrialization of America. Volcker's defense at lunch amounted to little more than financial gossip by way of passing the buck.

I hoped that the roundtable at The Lehrman Institute would lead to a more thorough discussion, and made sure that the audience for Volcker's talk was significant, and included journalists. Even though the discussions were off the record, the presence of journalists played an important role in holding Volcker accountable.

The distinguished guest list for the Volcker dinner included:

- Robert Baldwin, President, Morgan Stanley and Company, Inc.
- Jeffrey Bell, President, International Center for Economic Policy Studies.
- Barton Biggs, Director of Research, Morgan Stanley and Company, Inc.
- David Calleo, Professor of European Studies, The Johns Hopkins S.A.I.S.
- Jerry Corrigan, Vice President, Federal Reserve Bank of New York
- Richard Debs, President, Morgan Stanley International
- George Goodman, Executive Editor, *Esquire*
- Lawrence Kudlow, Chief Economist, Bear Stearns
- George Melloan, Deputy Editor of the Editorial Page, *Wall Street Journal*
- Zygmunt Zagorski, Vice President, The Lehrman Institute
- Perry Neff, Executive Vice President, Chemical Bank
- Nicholas X. Rizopoulos, Executive Director, The Lehrman Institute
- David Rockefeller, Chairman of the Board, Chase Manhattan Bank
- Jude Wanniski, President, Polyconomics
- Albert Wojnilower, Managing Director, First Boston Corporation

I was generally satisfied with the outcome of the roundtable, and grateful for the opportunity to get to know the participants more intimately. Several months later, I wrote Max Rabb:

> Take a look at these two descriptions of the Volcker dinner at the Institute during the third week of December. One is written by Barton Biggs, managing partner in charge of research at Morgan Stanley, the other by Jude Wanniski. Also enclosed is the list of attendees. You will observe that my entire Volcker relationship has much to do with this meeting and with the subsequent paper I wrote [later published in *Harper's*], in which you may observe that I divulged no part of the Institute discussion.
>
> Barton M. Biggs, Dinner with Volcker. Last week I went to small dinner meeting with Paul Volcker hosted by Lew Lehrman in his exquisite Georgian town house on Seventy-First Street. I liked and was impressed by Volcker . . . Volcker repeated over and over again that he was going to "to stick with it [namely, his austerity policy]." He went on to say that the problem is that everyone has a different view of what "it" should be, but as he described his definition, the impression was clear that "it" was a policy of gradual, persistent monetary restraint. Of course, this kind of talk comes easily over 10-year-old red wine served in cut glass decanters and drunk in a high-ceilinged dining room with tall French windows.
>
> Jude Wanniski, Polyconomics, FYI: Volcker Dinner, December 27, 1979. I spent several hours last night with Federal Reserve Chairman Paul Volcker, from 5:15 pm to 8 p.m. in a round table discussion with 15 or so high-powered financial types at The Lehrman Institute in NYC . . . . Overall impression:

> Discouraging. Volcker needs plenty of help, and I don't mean in terms of learning the supply-side model. He seemed unsure of what his role is as the nation's central banker.[35]

Barton Biggs: The Commissioner

I had similar concerns, and the several crises of the following years only confirmed my doubts about the stability of the nation's economy, and the capacities of the policymakers overseeing it. For example, in 1979, the Hunt Brothers (Nelson, Bunker, and Herbert) tried to corner the silver market. They bought silver on margin, driving up the price of silver to record heights, before it collapsed in January of 1980. The silver crisis was threatening the broader markets because it increased inflation expectations. Gold and commodities speculation had been rampant since the default at the gold window in 1971. Investment in the productive economy and government bonds had collapsed in the same time period, because inflation was eroding returns on savings and investment, and destroying the incentive to work. Insiders like Volcker were especially concerned because the Morgan Bank was directly exposed to the Hunt Brothers collapse, having provided them with leverage. A collapse of the Morgan Bank could have caused a depression. The markets and the nation were in real crisis when Volcker invited me to Washington. He had read my Morgan Stanley paper "Monetary Policy, the Federal Reserve System and Gold," which came out that same January. I had sent it to him with a personal note. Alan Greenspan also remarked on it at the time, saying that "Your paper is raining all over Washington."[36]

Despite our differences, Volcker respected me. He knew I understood the relationships between gold, silver, commodities, inflation, and the broader economy. We talked about the problem and the crisis; he asked my advice. I advised him to provide the Hunts with unlimited credit to meet their loan obligations to Bache, Halsey, Stuart, and Shields, but to take Hunt Brothers' assets as collateral. Instead, Volcker simply refused to provide the Hunt Brothers with credit. A substantial portion of Bunker Hunt's fortune was liquidated. Volcker and the government were eventually able to stabilize the crisis, but their ongoing policy prescription—high interest rates and an overvalued dollar—eventually led, along with other causes, to the de-industrialization of America.

As I wrote long essays for Morgan Stanley, I would continue to try to influence Volcker about the deficiencies of the monetary system. I wrote to him after a dinner in April 1980, saying "I enjoyed dinner. I appreciate how busy your schedule is.

Therefore, I was genuinely grateful for the chance to have several hours to talk monetary policy and central banking with you." I was intent on making the following additional points in my letter:

> First, your remarkable openness and willingness to review different points of view is quite striking for those in power in Washington. Second, though my critique of 1977-1979 Fed policy was severe in the Morgan Stanley manuscript, it is clear to me that you understand that I do have the same goals in mind as you: namely, reasonable price stability, a sound currency, and a stable monetary and economic policy framework in which businessmen and consumers can plan sensibly for the future.
>
> I am aware that some of my views—with respect to the discount rate and open market operations, not to mention the "price rule" I propose in the gold standard over against the "quantity" rule of the monetarists—are at the moment unorthodox. It is for that reason, moreover, that I appreciate your willingness even to discuss it.
>
> I do hope you will consider yourself welcome at the Institute whenever you are in New York. I know you have all the equipment you need to do the job you want to do, but if the privacy of the Institute can ever be of service to you, please don't hesitate to call on us.[37]

By the mid-1970s, I had also begun making other friends in Washington. Greenwich resident Langdon Cook introduced me to William Simon when he was treasury secretary under President Ford. Lang thought I should join Simon at the Treasury. Instead, I began a long and cherished friendship with both men.

I began to make friendships in Congress as well. In March of 1976, I wrote to Representative Jack Kemp:

> For some time now I have been aware of your efforts to advocate effective but unfashionable policies to solve the economic problems of our times. I should like to offer my assistance and would look forward to discussing these issues with you in New York or Washington. Perhaps you will have a few moments on your next visit to New York City; or on my next visit to Washington, I could stop by to see you.[38]

After several missed opportunities, we met. Jack had a very winning personality and a team-building style developed playing football for the Buffalo Bills. I would occasionally visit Jack's office and home to discuss economics. There, I met one of his key advisers, John Mueller. John later wrote about that 1979 meeting:

> We met in Jack Kemp's congressional office in the Rayburn House Office Building, where Lew was conferring with Kemp. I don't recall the exact occasion for the meeting, but as I was Kemp's recently hired speechwriter and soon also

staff economist, it would have been natural for us to have met. We immediately found in one another a kindred spirit, despite our difference in age (I am 15 years younger) and experience. . . . In that first meeting, Lew outlined with some rigor the ideas of the French economist Jacques Rueff. After familiarizing myself with Rueff (which, before long, led me to study French to read him in the original) and thinking through the issues, I soon became an advocate of Lew's "Rueffian" version of economics—an approach that is at once comprehensive, systematic and rooted in the realities of human nature, as reflected in history, particularly American history. In particular, the Rueffian approach explains how to restore financial order by restoring monetary order with a metallic currency [gold or silver] and long-term balance to the federal budget and international balance of payments.[39]

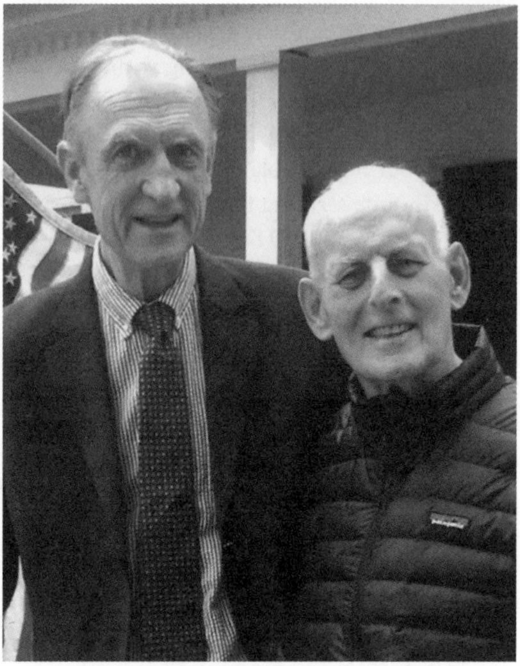

John Mueller: Profound intellectual

In October of 1981, Jack would invite me to address members of the House Republican Conference on monetary policy. Although this committee proved unable to understand or act on my ideas, the ongoing relationship with Mueller was productive. As I told Mort Kondracke in 2011:

> I was able to conduct my campaign for the convertibility of the dollar and [fixing the] weaknesses of Bretton Woods through John Mueller. John and I became close. John read the original works [of Rueff]. He had mastered the subject, and, as a result, I was always confident, after John went to work for Jack, that on a day-to-day basis Kemp would be hearing the case for the historic American monetary standard [—namely gold]. . . . John is, himself, a remarkable man. He's the rare bird who is very, very learned and very, very modest, and he's a master of economic policy, but of so much more in addition to that. . . .[40]

At The Lehrman Institute I was also an occasional seminar leader. I was able to resume my own writing and research which I had put aside in 1962. I got fulfillment from writing, especially about political philosophy and economic policy. I was much less of a rover than some of the people with whom I was aligned. They lived in Washington. I was in New York. I was in business. They were full-time at intellectual campaigning, not just political campaigning.

While I was advocating classical economics on the national stage, I was also familiarizing myself with New York's regional issues. One series of Institute seminars concentrated on municipal problems. Both Mayor Edward Koch and Lieutenant Governor Mario Cuomo participated. On January 25, 1979, I presented a paper entitled "The Decline and Fall of the Public Interest in New York" to the Institute's Seminar on Local Government. I began:

> The decline and fall of The City of New York occurs simultaneously with one of Manhattan's greatest commercial booms. Parts of the boroughs rot. Other parts flourish. Private well-being accompanies public bankruptcy.
>
> Virtually all analysts agree that this crisis is largely a fiscal crisis in public finance. Some contend that it is merely a question of municipal access to the credit markets. Others emphasize civil service problems, union problems, or government management problems. I believe public bankruptcy can be nothing else but a leadership problem. The City Fathers, private and public, appointed and elected, have failed.[41]

My work on this subject would soon lead to direct involvement.

INFLUENCING THE REAGAN ADMINISTRATION

My writing on monetary policy expanded in 1980 as inflation heated up and the presidential campaign accelerated. Increasingly, my writing was geared toward influencing an expected Republican administration in Washington. Because of my friendship with the Bush family, I began the presidential contest as a supporter of George H. W. Bush. But when Reagan won the primary, I spoke in support of the Republican nominee.

Ronald Reagan "has always been the candidate of the small-business man," I told the *New York Times* in an interview at the July 1980 Republican National Convention in Detroit. "The crucial difference between the admirers and critics of Governor Reagan in the business community is that his admirers have studied his record on tax, monetary and regulatory policy and on reducing the size of the government. In general, his critics have not made the effort to study his record [instead concentrating on his career as an actor]."[42]

In August the *Syracuse Post-Standard* quoted me, "the New Yorkers who will benefit most from Governor Reagan's election are the middle-income New Yorkers struggling to find a way to send their teenage children to college, the struggling young couples who figure and refigure their finances to determine how they can afford their first home, and the inner-city youths whose futures have been short-changed from real jobs and meaningful economic advancement."[43] In September, I wrote in the New York *Daily News* that Reagan "is not promising to give *more* to New

York—but to take *less* of what we earn. He believes that New Yorkers, not Washington politicians and bureaucrats, should control their own paychecks."[44]

When "Monetary Policy, the Federal Reserve System and Gold" was published by Morgan Stanley in January of 1980, its publication kicked off a year in which potential restoration of the gold standard attracted widespread attention. *Barron's* journalist Jim Grant would later point out that "In an introductory note, Barton M. Biggs, the head of investment research at Morgan Stanley, speculated that Lehrman had hit on 'what could be the economic and political issue of the 1980s—why the world must return to the discipline of the gold standard.'"[45] Articles in the *Wall Street Journal* led to other writing opportunities—such as an essay for *Harper's* magazine in the summer of 1980. The intervention of Congress gave my views more attention in political circles when that fall, Congress passed legislation requiring the designation of a presidential commission to evaluate a return to the gold standard.

My ideas were not always popular—particularly with the conventional economists who populated the Nixon and Ford Administrations and dominated the academic world. But my supporters became leaders in the field. Jim Grant became the most influential journalist-economist in the Anglophone world. John Mueller became one of the most powerful voices for economic sanity in Congress through his advice and influence on Jack Kemp.

After Ronald Reagan triumphed over Jimmy Carter in November of 1980, I analyzed what his victory meant in the context of recent American history. There was a resurgence of the conservative party in America, which I repeated over and over again in the newspapers, and in this article for *Harper's* magazine:

> The Reagan victory was no surprise to some thoughtful analysts of the trend of public policy in America. The old public philosophy, born during the 1930's, had begun to tire during the 1960's—neo-Keynesianism was exhausted in the late 1970's. For two generations, our nation had been governed by a world view and public institutions which originated during the worst period in our nation's economic history, the Great Depression. I think it is fair to say that Franklin D. Roosevelt's New Deal was a profound [but in some ways errant] American social and legislative response to the catastrophe of unemployment and deflation. Out of the suffering of the 1930's came the Roosevelt coalition which gave us a set of liberal, big government, social-democratic values which have endured to this very day.
>
> For 30 years, fundamental questions about the New Deal consensus haunted the Republican Party. After 1940, the Republican Party had followed in the wake of the successful Democratic Party. It, too, had become a New Deal Party. As a result of this fundamental shift in the 1950s and 1960s, the Republican Party became a battleground between those who wanted to [reverse] the New Deal [and those] who wanted to manage the welfare state [namely, the liberal, Northeastern Republicans]. In 1964, the first presidential candidate of the

conservative reformers was Barry Goldwater. As we know, Lyndon B. Johnson campaigned against Barry Goldwater by branding him a warmonger and a reactionary—and defeated him. I was told in 1964 that, if I voted for Barry Goldwater, there would be inflation and a major American war in Asia. I [voted for Goldwater], but the war and inflation came under Johnson and the [victorious] Democrats! The irony of the next four years, as Johnson escalated the war and ignited the price level, was [ignored by virtually all] Democrats.

Then came the Nixon years. A Republican-Democratic coalition of moderate and neo-conservative public philosophies and legislators came together during this period to reorganize and manage more efficiently the New Deal heritage—but not to reform or repeal it. Pat Moynihan of Harvard called this experiment Tory Democracy.[46] Evoking Prime Minister Disraeli of Britain and his clever words, Moynihan called upon the Republicans (the "Tories") to "dish" the Democrats, (the "Whigs"), by co-opting the welfare state of the liberals. The experiment failed. The catastrophe of peacetime price and wage controls, inflation, and Watergate engulfed the Nixon Administration before it was able to fulfill any of its [announced] electoral mandates.

In spite of the astonishing [majority of Nixon's win] in 1972, there were some who would argue that President Nixon was neither temperamentally nor philosophically convinced that New Deal economic and social institutions, the status quo, needed to be reformed. It was Nixon, we should remember, who said that, "We are all Keynesians now." John Maynard Keynes, a social democrat, was one of the chief inspirations of the economic policies prevailing in America during the era of Democratic Party hegemony.

Jimmy Carter's election in 1976 suggested that the liberal Democratic New Deal Coalition was intact, that its public philosophy still prevailed, and that little fear of reform from the right was justified or likely. Many insouciant liberals did not perceive the gradual change in American attitudes toward the welfare state, huge and growing government spending, the depreciation of the dollar, and the assault on many of our social institutions such as family, faith, and work. Those liberals were setting themselves up for a great political shock—what will be recorded by historians as one of the great tremors of American political history.

That tremor is the Reagan victory. Confounding the early conventional wisdom that he was too conservative to win, Reagan swept the field in the primaries, just as, in spite of the early skepticism of the self-appointed experts about his competence and intelligence, he decisively swept all before him in the general election. What does it all mean? The election results mean that we are about to witness a conservative experiment which holds great promise and much risk for Americans from every walk of life. If it succeeds, then we could very easily look back on this period as the forging of a new and productive coalition in American politics—to replace permanently the Roosevelt coalition put together over 40 years ago. As depression was the forging block of the

> Roosevelt coalition, inflation has tempered the steel of the new coalition. The Reagan coalition is essentially a middle-class coalition of working people. These Americans now believe in less government intervention and spending, fewer government subsidies and programs, [and] diminished government regulation of the private and public lives of every aspect of human affairs.[47]

Those in power took note of my thesis. As the election approached, E. Pendleton James, personnel chief of the Reagan transition, sent me a formal letter. He asked me to provide policy ideas for what was expected to be a new administration. Brian Domitrovic wrote about our encounter in his book *Econoclasts: The Rebels Who Sparked the Supply-Side Revolution and Restored American Prosperity*:

> Reagan put Los Angeles headhunter E. Pendleton James in charge of recruitment. "Pen" James sent out scores of elegantly appointed letters to candidates for cabinet and other executive posts. The letters often asked for a precis of policy views. The response of Lehrman, the supply-siders' darling and a candidate for a Treasury post, was that the stock, bond, and loan markets were in a state of imminent collapse. The new president had to do all that he could, as soon as possible, if a national financial calamity were to be avoided."[48]

It was fourteen pages long, that urgent and highly charged memo I wrote for Mr. James. I called it "The Struggle for Financial Order at the Onset of the Reagan Presidency," and sent it off to James two days after the election. Rowland Evans and Robert Novak would later write in *The Reagan Revolution* that the memo's title "was deceptive because nothing written by Lehrman's lucid economic pen was dry and because its impact was anything but academic."[49]

I also sent confidential copies of the memo to Congressmen Jack Kemp and David Stockman among others. I wrote a "memo to file" on December 15, saying "As it turned out, they not only did not keep it confidential but they took the memo, elaborated on it, and sent it to all members of the press thereby exposing the analysis and the plan to excessive publicity. [They] thereby rendered the plan less effective than it might have been."[50] Jonathan Bush, my close friend and political advisor, wrote me to say that the memo was overexposed. Kemp and Stockman also claimed that the memo had started with them, but then, the press pounced.

Author Michael Kramer noticed that I was getting traction in Washington, and that others were trying to ride on my coattails. His article "When Lewis Lehrman Talks, Ronald Reagan Listens" was published in *New York* magazine, on February 9, 1981, and focused on the difficulty my colleagues and I were having getting the Reagan Administration to do more than just listen. "Having won the initial skirmishes," the article began, "the supply-siders should be happy.

> They aren't. Now they are worried about gradualism (or, as it has come to be known, Thatcherism)—the slow and unrelated implementation of their policies.

> They fear that their program will be dissipated because the president will fail to see that the entire program must be undertaken as a whole if it is to succeed.
>
> Among those worrying most about this possibility is Lewis Lehrman, a 42-year-old New Yorker who is one of the supply-side school's most brilliant and articulate advocates. You may not have heard of Lehrman, but you may well be familiar with his work. Remember that famous "Dunkirk" memorandum sent to the president-elect from Dave Stockman and Representative Jack Kemp? Well, a first-grader could determine that the "Dunkirk" paper was inspired by an earlier memo written by Lew Lehrman.[51]

Dunkirk was a good description for the paper I had written, because having seen the carnage of the 1970s at close hand, and having studied the history of financial collapse, I was aware that in an inflationary environment, disaster lurks around any corner. The original November 6th memorandum for Pen James began:

> Inflation is the transcendent issue of our times. Inflation is to our generation what depression was to our parents and grandparents. Inflation, if unstopped, will revolutionize our nation and its social institutions. . . .
>
> The previous administration sowed chaos, and, I regret to say, President-elect Reagan may very well reap the whirlwind. If he is not ready, if he does not understand what is happening, he could easily be swept away by its hurricane velocity. The extraordinary coincidence is that these were very much the same conditions which greeted Margaret Thatcher when she inherited the whirlwind from her predecessors—the big spending socialists. I might add that these were the very same conditions that caused the collapse of the Fourth Republic in France in 1958. Except that President de Gaulle understood the causes of collapse. The Fifth Republic, his creation, was born amidst his program for currency stability, budgetary equilibrium, and economic renewal and growth. . . .
>
> The following policies must be presented to the President-elect. Only he should reject them, for only he, in the end, must bear the consequences or the fulfillment of failure and success.
>
> 1. His administration must move much more rapidly than originally planned to establish budgetary equilibrium in the federal government.
> 2. The budgetary policy must be coordinated with Federal Reserve monetary policy in a planned and coherent way. This coherence has been lacking in every economic and monetary program with the goal of stabilization in the past 20 years. Such a program in no way would compromise the independence of the Federal Reserve System. On the contrary, new procedures of monetary control, combined with budgetary equilibrium, could lead to the rehabilitation of the Federal Reserve System now, fairly or unfairly, discredited in the marketplace.
> 3. Simultaneously we must move on a tax reform bill—to be introduced not in November, but after the inauguration. The bill will implement marginal tax

rate reduction and further reduction in capital gains taxes, while abolishing the inane distinction between taxes on income from savings and taxes on income from wages and salaries.

4. There are six months in which to decide and to act. . . . We are now in the midst of an ongoing financial crisis which has characterized the Carter Administration and the markets since the November 1, 1978 foreign-exchange panic which occasioned the first unsuccessful Fed-Treasury financial plan. . . . President-elect Reagan's transition has now been overtaken by a financial market crisis and economic events which are moving rapidly beyond control. This financial tidal wave has been coming in for years. It is now upon us.
5. It is now necessary for the President-elect to act discreetly but immediately. As he waits upon January 20, he must become prepared to undertake an emergency plan for economic stabilization and renewal at the onset of his Presidency. At this very moment he should organize a task force with the specific purpose of designing a program for economic stabilization and economic recovery—the plan to be completed by Inauguration Day.[52]

While sharing my ideas on the importance of urgent action, Kemp and Stockman were maneuvering themselves into position in preparation for a November 16 policy meeting in California. Economic historian Brian Domitrovic also covers this meeting in his book:

> Because Kemp was the one passing out the paper, the battle for Reagan's soul seemed to have resolved itself. Here was the author of Kemp-Roth becoming a hawk on spending and regulation. Lehrman might have been on to something when he had said that the new administration must do it *all* [a comprehensive, coordinated policy . . .]. Reagan offered Stockman the job on Thanksgiving, eleven days after the Los Angeles meeting at which his paper had made the rounds.[53]

Stockman admitted his reliance on my work to Mort Kondracke in a 2011 interview. He went on to say:

> You probably are aware of one of the things I wrote at the time, which sort of kicked this thing all off, was in December [*sic*] 1980, after Reagan was elected, "The Danger of a Dunkirk." I got a lot of that rhetoric from Lew Lehrman. So he was very influential in those days of transition. In fact, he was in the lineup to be Secretary of the Treasury, a great tragedy that he was not chosen, because he knew what the whole doctrine was about both on the monetary side as well as on the fiscal policy side. Don Regan didn't have a clue. He was a stock trader.[54]

Sidney Blumenthal went even further and deeper, writing:

> After the election the President-elect summoned his issue task forces to his Pacific Palisades home to outline an agenda for the first 100 days of his Administration. An internal memo was drawn up by George Shultz and unanimously agreed to by Reagan and the participants in the economic task force, including Kemp, the only supply-sider on the team. But then Stockman, together with Kemp and Lewis E. Lehrman, owner of the Rite Aid drugstore chain and a leading supply-sider, wrote a 23-page statement, "Avoiding a G.O.P. Economic Dunkirk." It was not inconsistent with the Shultz memo, but it was far more dramatically written, giving the issues a heightened sense of urgency within the ranks, and it placed greater emphasis on the supply-side aspects of the program. . . . Reagan essentially accepted this analysis. In December, when Wanniski, without consulting anyone, leaked the "Dunkirk" analysis to Leonard Silk, economics columnist for the *New York Times*, the public for the first time became aware of the new influence wielded by supply-side theorists in the Reagan camp. They also became aware of David Stockman. Says Wanniski: "It elevated Stockman into a pivotal force."[55]

My warnings were having an impact, but not all of my policy prescriptions—lower taxes, less regulation, a balanced budget and sound money—were given the same attention. Conventional politicians and economists thought my views were out of the mainstream. I thought they were wrong because my views were grounded in my understanding of American history and economics.

My writings would continue to generate publicity . . . and controversy . . . for the next few years. James Glassman's article in the February 1981 issue of the *Atlantic Monthly* portrayed me in a serious mood:

> I tracked down Lewis Lehrman in his office on the twenty-fifth floor of a building at Lexington Avenue and 54th Street. At the time, Lehrman was considered a candidate for high office in the Reagan administration, perhaps even secretary of the treasury. But Lehrman himself had his doubts: "The problem with me is that I'll actually do all the things that Reagan talked about during the campaign."[56]

Politics would triumph over policy, as Stockman himself admitted in his book, *The Triumph of Politics*. The economic plan that the Reagan Administration pursued was incomplete, and in Stockman's words "flawed." It thus fell far short of that which was needed.

On December 18, Kemp brought Stockman to New York in an attempt to detoxify him in the eyes of Wall Street. Stockman was so ambitious that Wall Street was frightened he would cause chaos in the markets with well-intended but insufficient policy prescriptions that would fail. After meetings downtown, there was a dinner at the Century Association which I hosted. As Bob Novak reported a few days later, "Stockman ran into static when he and Kemp dined in New York that night with some leading exponents of supply side (pro-tax cut) economics. Among those present were businessman Lewis Lehrman, politician Jeff Bell, scholar Irving Kristol, journalist Robert Bartley and business consultants Jude Wanniski and Richard Whalen. Even economist Alan Greenspan, no supply-sider but an ardent free-enterpriser, dropped by."[57]

Although Greenspan was a friend of mine, he was conventional by any stretch of the imagination. In love with the Fed, he was of no use in the effort to bring sound monetary policy to Washington.

In his memoir, Stockman complained: "No sooner had dinner begun than Wanniski turned from digging into his food to digging into me."[58] Wanniski wanted the emphasis on tax cuts, not spending cuts. Stockman would recall: "Together, Jude Wanniski and Lew Lehrman were the Odd Couple of supply side. Wanniski was very easygoing and a bit unkempt. Lehrman was very formal, rigid, austere. He wore suspenders and never had a hair out of place. What they had in common was their revolutionary temperament."[59]

We may have had some things in common, but Wanniski was intellectually careless, with disastrous results for the United States. As I recalled in a 2011 interview:

> Jude in his own way read me out of the supply-side movement because I insisted that you could not have sound economic policy without the aim being a balanced budget. Jude taught a whole generation of people [including Rumsfeld and Cheney] that deficits don't matter, and he had certain political reasons for doing that. [Namely, Wanniski wanted to use deficit-spending as a method of reducing taxes without having to reduce spending.] He believed that you had to get away from "root-canal economics," as he called them, and for him, a balanced budget was root-canal economics. For me, a balanced budget was not root-canal economics; it was the only sound way to run a national government."[60]

Wanniski's theory turned out to be a disaster. Deficits don't matter? What drivel.

At the end of December, the *New York Times*' influential columnist Leonard Silk summarized our efforts, writing:

> In the shorter of these two memorandums, Mr. Lehrman urged that the new Republican administration avoid repeating the "tragedy" Britain had suffered as a result of the monetarist policies of Prime Minister Margaret Thatcher. Unemployment and inflation had been worsened, he said, because the Conservatives had failed to understand the relations among budget deficits, central bank monetary policy and high marginal tax rates on "working people's inflation-boosted incomes."
>
> Mr. Reagan could avoid the Thatcher trap, said Mr. Lehrman, if he moved with speed and conviction to attain these three objectives:
>
> - Achieve a balanced budget much sooner than originally planned (in the 1983 fiscal year according to the Sept. 9 Reagan budget projections).

- Harmonize the new budgetary policy with Federal Reserve monetary policy in a planned and coherent way—but without compromising the independence of the Fed.
- Move immediately after the inauguration on a tax reform bill that would cut marginal tax rates and capital gains taxes, while abolishing the distinction between taxes on income from savings and from wages and salaries.

> Such is the doctrine championed by Mr. Lehrman and Mr. Reagan's other radically conservative supply-siders.[61]

Although the importance of the gold standard was not often covered by the mainstream press, Tom Redburn of the *Los Angeles Times* focused on it. In fact, his article recapitulated the central justification for the use of a gold standard very well, stating:

> Gold, according to Lehrman, is the perfect tool to control money growth because, unlike the current system of paper money, it is difficult to expand the gold supply. . . . Over time, gold advocates maintain, production of gold has increased at a rate of about 2% a year, almost the same as the growth in real economic output. The gold standard, by providing an explicit "error signal" to the Fed that it is creating money too fast or too slow, would put severe limits on the power of the central bank. According to Lehrman . . . this would provide "virtually a constitutional guarantee of the purchasing power of money and therefore of the future value of savings."[62]

As Pen James and the rest of the Reagan transition team mulled over my urgent and historically informed economic policy prescriptions, the financial establishment at the Federal Reserve and Treasury started to panic. They feared they might lose the monetary policy discretion to which they had become accustomed, and in which I saw the root causes of inflation.

Over at the *Times*, Leonard Silk warned that if I was appointed to a Reagan Administration post, "this will point the direction in which the Reagan administration economic policy is moving. But it is not yet there and there is strong opposition among more traditional conservatives."[63] I am not quite sure what Silk was trying to say. He must have been referring to academic conservatives or centrists, because my policies were right in line with traditional conservative economics as practiced by Alexander Hamilton. He, in turn, had inherited the time-tested principles of stability and prosperity from the English and European traditions, which are based ultimately upon the work of Aristotle and Augustine as combined by Thomas Aquinas.[64]

Traditional or not, the fact is, I had been asked to write the memorandum because the Reagan Administration was considering me for secretary of the treasury. Pen James had been explicit about their interest. Reagan's chief of staff Edwin Meese came to see me at the American Enterprise Institute to discuss how I would handle the job.

Jude Wanniski and Bob Novak were perhaps the most public proponents of my candidacy. According to John Berry:

> Columnists Rowland Evans and Robert Novak... rarely miss an opportunity to tout the pure supply-side approach to tax policy. With almost the same breath, however, they have pushed hard recently to have New York businessman Lewis Lehrman named to an administration post, beginning with Treasury secretary.
>
> Each time they have urged Reagan to hire Lehrman, the columnists have described him as a supply-sider. In fact, he is not, Lehrman says the two most important economic policy moves the administration should make are to balance the budget and to get the value of the dollar to a gold standard. Cuts in marginal income tax rates take a back seat with him, and that, by definition makes him no supply-sider at all.[65]

To be thoroughly clear, it is also necessary to make the dollar convertible to gold at a price which takes account of inflation in order to protect wage earners and pensioners. The key is to make sure the relative prices of goods and gold are in equilibrium. In 1980, we had to consider the forty-odd-years of inflation since Bretton Woods when proposing the equitable dollar price for an ounce of gold. Now, that price would have to take into account the equally vast inflation that has occurred since Reagan's presidency.

Former secretary of the treasury William Simon was the early favorite to return to that post, but his demands proved prohibitive. Citibank CEO Walter Wriston was also considered, but he had too many financial conflicts, and the sovereign defaults had discredited his ideas on banking and economics. The choice came down to two men: Merrill Lynch CEO Don Regan and myself. We were both interviewed by Ed Meese and Pen James in the cafeteria of the American Enterprise Institute—which attracted the Republican establishment types with government experience.

Two decades later, Wanniski wrote: "When Ronald Reagan won the presidency in 1980, we were sure we could get Lew a high post at Treasury, but Milton Friedman and his monetarist allies used their clout with Reagan aide Ed Meese to block any appointment."[66] Regan was a banker, who was already head of Merrill Lynch when I took Rite Aid public with his firm in 1968. Merrill Lynch was one of the bulge bracket underwriters of the Rite Aid shares for the initial public offering. Don was a good Marine and a disciplined executive. But he was never interested in public policy. Nevertheless, the Marine got the job. His appointment was announced on December 11, 1980. Years later, Pen James moved to Greenwich. Every time he would see me, he would call me "Mr. Secretary." One day at the Round Hill Club, he confessed that not pushing me for treasury secretary was the worst mistake he made during the Reagan transition.

In his memoir, *For the Record: From Wall Street to Washington*, Don Regan would write that he was urged to "placate my critics by appointing Lewis Lehrman, a prominent New York conservative, as Deputy Secretary of the Treasury."[67] Regan did not want to do so however, writing: "Although Lehrman was a capable, even a brilliant, man, I declined. I knew that he and I would clash because he would not be content to take a backseat. I wanted an administrator, not a person with policy objectives of his own."[68] Regan also refused to appoint me for the position of undersecretary for monetary affairs. For each of the important Treasury jobs, I was rejected. Milton Friedman appeared to have veto power over anything that had to do with monetary or exchange rate policy. His monetarists filled all the posts to which I had aspired.

Finally, two jobs were found for which it was thought I would be sufficiently removed from any real power—ambassador to France and ambassador to Portugal. I rejected both posts. The press caught wind of events, and Steven R. Weisman of the *New York Times* spelled it out, writing "In 1981 Mr. Lehrman was blocked from a job in the Administration by someone who worried that he was overly zealous in his views."[69] Although I am not exactly sure who that someone was—it could have been Milton Friedman—I ultimately came to believe that I had been blocked by James Baker and George H. W. Bush. Although George's brothers, Jonathan and Bucky Bush, were lifelong friends of mine, George might have been worried about me as a likely challenger to his political future. Although James Baker had a positive attitude toward me, and he reportedly said I was the "brightest guy he had ever met," Jim, like Regan, didn't want anybody who would contest the Administration's policy. Although I did not get an appointment, neither did I abandon my economic and constitutional beliefs in search of a job. Indeed, my beliefs undoubtedly cost me the appointment. That was fine with me, because I had come to the conclusion that I wanted to get hired by the people . . . directly.

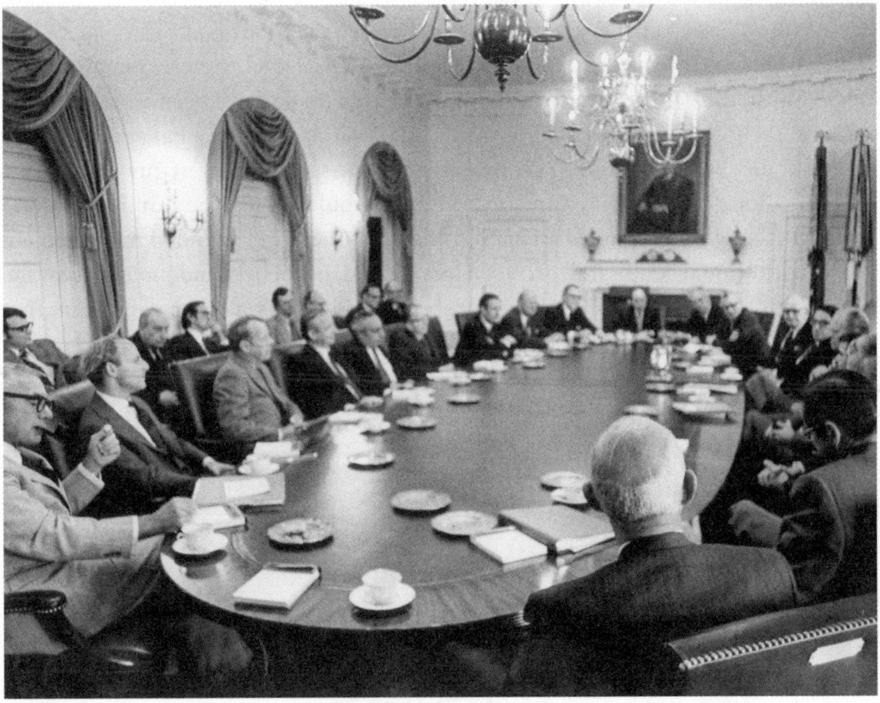

Gerald R. Ford Presidential Library

At the White House:
Policy roundtable with President Ford, May 7, 1975
I am seated second from left

CHAPTER 7

Into Politics

There are lots of reasons to go into politics. If you believe a certain set of standards should prevail, and that ideas have consequences, you concentrate on public policy.[1] In the mid-1960s, I went to Washington and made financial contributions to a few congressmen. I was not pleasantly surprised at the quality of representatives and governors I met. I resolved to get more involved in politics as a result. My experience with wage and price controls taught me that direct action produced results. In 1976, I began to get serious.

JOINING THE BUCKLEY CAMPAIGN

My first major political project in New York was Senator James Buckley's 1976 re-election campaign. I knew and liked Senator Buckley and was happy to raise money for him. He was a man of character. He was very sophisticated, and he knew what he was doing. He was a purist intellectual without being self-righteous. Jim had won the election in 1970 running as a Conservative in a three-way race—winning with just 39 percent of the vote—to 37 percent for the Democrat, and 24 percent for the Republican.

In 1976 Buckley had both the Republican and Conservative lines, but his chances for victory evaporated when, in the five-way Democratic primary, former UN ambassador Daniel Patrick Moynihan narrowly edged out the more radical Congresswoman Bella Abzug. Moynihan went on to win the general election 54 to 45 percent. Buckley went on to serve as a distinguished justice on the US Court of Appeals in the District of Columbia.

The Buckley-Moynihan campaign gave me a chance to get to know some of the major Republican contributors in New York. I also learned from that race the truth of Jesse Unruh's comment: "Campaigns don't run on enthusiasm alone. Money is the mother's milk of politics."[2] It started me to thinking about running for office, and whether I could afford it. I took a very careful look at how much it would cost being a complete unknown in the world of politics. Just as important, I got to know the leaders of the New York State Conservative Party—Daniel J. Mahoney, Mike Long, and Serf Maltese.

In 1976, I was still president of Rite Aid, and spending considerable time in Pennsylvania, where Congressman John Heinz, a fellow member of the Yale class of 1960, was running for US Senate. I was drafted to help with a fundraiser for Heinz by John

Tuten, head of National Central Bank of Pennsylvania. I had met Tuten through my father. National Central Bank had been the financial backer for Louis Lehrman & Son for many years. The day of the event, Heinz did not show up, and I was called on to speak. I must have done well because Tuten asked me if I would run for governor of Pennsylvania. He was very influential in Republican politics statewide. I apologized, saying, "I would like to help you, but I've decided to move to New York." Still, John Tuten was very encouraging.

Former treasury secretary John B. Connally of Texas also came to see me in 1976. He asked me to host a fundraiser for President Ford at our New York apartment. At the event, my young son Thomas went up to the former Texas governor, asking him who he was and what he was doing. Thomas captivated Connally, who picked him up and put him on his lap.

Five years later, as I was contemplating a run for governor of New York, Connally wrote to me on his own initiative, saying, "I don't know enough about New York politics to advise you one way or the other, but I think you have got the bug and whether it's the governor's race or some other one, I don't think you will ever be happy until you get it out of your system—win, lose, or draw."[3] Connally remembered the cocktail party at our house, and developed an avuncular attitude toward me. Lots of people felt that way about me. I think it was because of my readiness to engage with serious people, and to include them on my own initiative.

ORGANIZING THE PLATFORM COMMITTEE

After the 1976 presidential election, New York Republican politics entered a new era. Governor Malcolm Wilson, who had served as lieutenant governor under Nelson Rockefeller, had been defeated in 1974. Although he had been appointed vice president under Gerald Ford, "Rocky" was now out of New York politics. His political lieutenant, Richard Rosenbaum, stepped down as Republican state chairman after the defeat of the Ford-Dole ticket.

Max Rabb had introduced me to Rosenbaum, who in turn introduced me to Dr. Bernard Kilbourn, who was elected Republican state chairman in 1977. Bernie, a dentist from upstate Oneida County, was anxious to get to know New York City Republicans who could help get the party out of debt.

Bernie asked to meet with me. He came to the city to inquire if I would be interested in becoming chairman of the 1978 Republican Platform Committee. I saw an opportunity, and I took it.

Bernie would remain a very strong and loyal supporter. He resisted the criticism of those who thought I was an outsider from Pennsylvania. I had, after all, only become a New York State resident in 1977—when I resigned as the full-time president of Rite Aid.

I saw the Republican State Platform Committee as an opportunity to master New York policy and politics. I also saw it as an opportunity to establish my reputation as a doer. I did not want public office except as an example of what could be done by changing policy in New York. Former *New York Times* reporter Samuel Freedman wrote about my plans for his book *The Inheritance*:

> [Lehrman's] goals for the party went far beyond solvency or an orderly transfer of power. What was needed was a populist uprising with a manifesto to match. Lehrman planned to create both the same way he had created the Rite-Aid network, by driving to cities and towns and paying attention to Main Street. As a retailer, he had never rented a storefront until he stood outside it at noon, three, and five, counting foot traffic with a hand-held clicker. As a politician, he intended to listen to those walkers talk. If his intuition was right, they wanted lower taxes, less government, and a crackdown on crime. And in a party rebuilt from below and realigned to the right, Lewis Lehrman himself might well figure as a candidate for governor four years hence.[4]

In January 1978, I put together a small staff for the platform committee including Richard Behn. I had met Dick in January 1977 when he interviewed me for an issue of the *Empire State Report* about the post-Rockefeller Republican party. Dick had written that I was a potential Republican candidate for governor.

Tim Carey, who had broad experience in Republican campaigns at the local and state level in New York, also came in for an interview that ended up lasting five hours. Freedman captured the importance of this meeting, noting that it eradicated any preconceptions Tim might have had about me.

> What [Tim] noticed about Lehrman was not aristocracy, but its absence, the difference between a man born into money and a man who earned it. This multimillionaire executive used a stark dining-room table for a desk. The leather on his briefcase was cracking with age. His fedora had a hole in the brim. When Lehrman spoke of hailing from the [modest background] of Harrisburg, Pennsylvania, he meant it as a compliment to a place he associated with the values of thrift, discipline, and hard work.[5]

Tim remembers that same meeting this way, writing:

> Lew was looking to hire a field operative to work with Dick on developing a plan for the 1978 Platform Committee. Lew was very intense in asking questions about my education, family, military background and political involvement. I remember that he was somewhat surprised that I had done some research on his background and asked him questions of his knowledge of New York State and its politics. He hired me. [6]

Four years later, Tim would tell a reporter, "I knew the first time I met him back then that there was a man who was destined to play a significant role in government."[7]

Freedman really understood what I believed in and was trying to do. The story he discerned in the way I built a team for the new Republican Party was right on target. He emphasized the importance I assigned to the working class and its values, as shown in these two excerpts from his book:

> Cerebrally, Lehrman had convinced himself long ago that the working and middle classes should abandon their sentimental attachment to the party of Franklin Roosevelt and the New Deal. But thinking was so different from seeing the evidence in the person of Tim Carey of Crotonville. Behind Tim, Lehrman imagined every manager he had ever hired for a Rite Aid store, multiplied by the millions into an army of revolution.[8]
>
> In Tim, meanwhile, Lehrman found someone ineffably familiar. There was a kind of guy Lehrman had often hired to run a Rite Aid store—usually Irish or Polish or Hungarian, a decent athlete with a sense of humor and a big family, ambitious enough to aspire to management, unaffected enough to unload a delivery truck. Tim exuded those qualities, plus some college polish and political savvy.[9]

With Tim doing advance, we prepared to take an unorthodox approach to the platform operation—holding hearings all around the state and meeting political, civic, and business leaders. Tim described our working model this way: "Two to three days on the road working with local Republican Committee representatives to set up next week's hearings, Lew arrives (flies or driven in) for two days for hearings, and then it starts all over again."[10]

Dick "Rosey" Rosenbaum would later acknowledge that the job was tailor-made for someone with my instincts and ambition. "It gave him an opportunity to be exposed in the party, get around the state, get to know some of the hierarchy in the party."[11]

"I worked with all 62 county chairmen and I got to know the state committee," I explained four years later. "I campaigned for the Republican candidates in 40 counties for a full day and in as many as 50 counties for a short period. I gave of myself in 1978 in a way which caused the Republican Party all over the state to remember the work I did."[12]

The work of the platform committee made a small splash in the greater scheme of New York State politics in 1978, but it allowed me to make a big splash in some small counties where I would meet people like Esther Twentyman in Cortland County and Bill Winans in Madison County. Also helping the committee were people like Frank Trotta and John Szelest, who would be central to my 1982 campaign team.

Some of the county representatives I met would become my earliest and most enthusiastic supporters in the 1982 gubernatorial campaign. Unlike the New York business executives who dabbled with the idea of running for governor, I became a known quantity around New York. I wasn't just a name. I was a face with whom they had shared breakfast or lunch. I listened to their frustrations with state mandates and regulations, their anger about unresponsive politicians. In politics, like business, people need to think you care before they care what you think.

While meeting county chairs, local officials, and newspaper editors, I was still able to criticize the existing political establishment—and denounce state legislators and politicians "who say one thing to get elected but then don't follow up on those promises."[13]

John and Susie Szelest: Hollywood Handsome

Under the banner "The Republican Party Listens," we got to hear voter frustrations in more than sixty meetings. "What we have heard over and over is that people are tired of all the mandates from Albany and Washington," I told one Albany reporter. "There's no question that they want a redress of the balance of power back to the local level."[14]

I told a Binghamton journalist that "whether they are Democrats or Republicans, liberals or conservatives, the public is distinguishing between talkers and doers."[15] In Utica, I said, "Rarely have parties paid attention to smaller, rural, less populated counties, but it's not going to be true anymore."[16]

Gus Bliven, veteran political editor for the *Syracuse Post Standard*, sized up my work and decided that "Lehrman happens to be one of those strange people who has the old-fashioned idea that the country and state were good to him and he owes something in return and he is prepared to pay the debt."[17]

I got to present the platform to the Republican State Convention at the Americana Hotel on June 13, 1978. The real news was the nomination of Assembly Speaker Perry Duryea as the Republican candidate to contest the re-election of Governor Hugh Carey. "Our economic crisis has become a moral crisis," I told the delegates. In the platform's introduction, we stressed opportunity:

> Republicans believe in opportunity.
>
> They believe in opportunity for men and women of all ages to find employment for their skills.

> They believe in opportunity for all New Yorkers to develop those skills to the limit of their capacities.
>
> They believe in opportunity for all children to become fully literate members of society with adequate education to assure their access to tomorrow's job market.
>
> They believe in the opportunity for citizens to see their tax dollars spent in a frugal, efficient manner.
>
> They believe in the opportunity for young families to buy and furnish a home in a neighborhood of their own choosing.
>
> They believe in the opportunity for older New Yorkers to live their lives in their own homes, free from the twin assaults of tax collectors and thieves.
>
> They believe in the opportunity for citizens, regardless of residence to work, to shop, to relax, and to sleep free from the constant threat of violence.
>
> They believe in the opportunity for local government officials to pursue the legitimate interests of their constituents without the shackles of state fiscal mandates.
>
> And Republicans believe in the opportunity for all New Yorkers to express their views to elected officials—and to receive a receptive audience for those views.
>
> Opportunity is the key to New York State's future. But opportunity for New Yorkers requires the leadership and commitment of New York's elected officials, particularly its governor. Only with leadership can laudable goals be turned into tangible progress. Only with leadership can these goals withstand the onslaught of conflicting pressures. Only with leadership and integrity in Albany can the future of all New York State be assured.
>
> The Republican Party pledges itself to the creation of conditions in which all New Yorkers will once again feel a larger measure of control of their destiny.[18]

"I believed that ideas would rule,"[19] I told the *New York Times* in 1982. There were a lot of similarities to my business experience, I explained. "Look, I know New York cold from opening Rite Aid stores. I know labor halls. I know Rotary Clubs. I just know."[20] Mickey Carroll of the *New York Times* captured my enthusiasm, style, and disappointment:

> He made friends with a lot of people, listened to local leaders, bought them breakfast, made a mailing list, promised to keep in touch. "And we completed the platform," Mr. Lehrman says, "and then"—he makes the motions of typing and binding and tidying a report—"we presented it." He laughs. Politely, party leaders accepted the platform and, just as politely, they ignored it, as they usually do. "I discovered then," says Mr. Lehrman, "that ideas don't always rule."[21]

TACKLING ISSUES WITH THE ECONOMIC ADVISORY COMMITTEE

Hampered by an eighty-eight-day newspaper strike in New York City, the Duryea-Caputo ticket was unable to oust Governor Carey, who prevailed by a 51 to 45 percent margin. Carey had replaced Lieutenant Governor Mary Ann Krupsak—who had challenged him for renomination by the Democratic Party—with Secretary of State Mario Cuomo.

Both Bernie Kilbourn and I wanted to continue the work of the Platform Committee—and maintain the grassroots work it had started. Bernie also needed help with the debts that the Republican Party had incurred in the mistaken belief that Carey could be defeated. I had my own reasons to stay involved. I was ambitious for true change.

In order to keep the issues and my participation active, Bernie and I launched an Economic Advisory Council (EAC) within the New York Republican Party. The EAC attempted to publicize some of the important work done by Republican state senators and assemblymen, and to adopt their initiatives for Republican Party use. The staff of the Republican State Senate majority and Assembly minority were helpful in sharing their data.

But the EAC also attempted to explore other areas in which the Republican Party could make a unique contribution to public policy. Ultimately, I knew the EAC and the Republican State Committee would be judged not by their words, but by their ability to affect public policy and to make New York State a better place for working people to live and to raise their children. During 1979, I held meetings and forums for the EAC throughout New York State and helped to produce a series of newsletters on topics like small business, government waste, energy, local government mandates, transportation, tax cuts, gambling and the black-market economy.

In March, I told Republicans that "these times are no less catastrophic than the days of Lincoln." I called inflation "the acid that is dissolving the bonds of our society."[22] In Elmira that April, I said New Yorkers were the "most overspent, overtaxed and overregulated people in America."[23]

My criticism of New York politicians ranged from the implicit to the explicit. In April I said that "I see no alternative but to eliminate people who say one thing to get elected but then don't follow up on those promises."[24] The *Corning Leader* wrote that "the three major problems [Lehrman's] council has identified are inflation, the level of government spending, and the level of taxation. No candidate who 'hitches his wagon to any of those three stars' stands a chance in New York State today, he believes."[25]

When asked if I planned a run for political office in the wake of reports that I was "being eyed for a future run for governor or senator," I responded with a grin:

> Right now, the only thing I'm running for is reelection to the board of the Rite Aid Co. But I wouldn't rule it out. I want to see the present political situation altered and I'm prepared to work to that end. . . . You have to get out of the office and find out what the people really need. That's the way you build drug stores and that's the way you win elections.[26]

In June I told the truth about my efforts, and it was not hard to understand where they might be leading: "We gotta find folks who can win. A winner is someone who can understand where the working people stand."[27]

On October 15, we held a Republican Issues Conference in Albany—bringing together 150 Republicans involved in liaison committees working on agriculture, education, criminal justice, health, labor, local government, mental health, small business, and the death penalty.

This was a period in which the national economy was being devastated by inflation, and crime was out of control everywhere, especially in New York City. I also used my appearances around New York State to criticize the Carter Administration: "It is our government which we must control. The government printing press is fueling inflation, and the legislation generated in Washington and Albany is hindering business,"[28] I told the Albany County Republican dinner in February. "Just as the Jeffersonian Democrats took over from the Federalists and ruled for two generations, the Republicans of Lincoln's day also ruled for two generations, about 60 years. After two generations, the Democrats again took over the government."[29] I was well aware of Mr. Lincoln's travels around Illinois in support of the fight to limit the spread of slavery. His exertions did not immediately lead to public office, but they did ultimately lead to the presidency. "The goal," of this exercise wrote Jim O'Hara of the *Elmira Sunday Telegram*:

> is to recommend policies for Republican officeholders and the state committee on taxation and economic growth. It means that Lehrman is once again on the circuit. In two days he hit Watkins Glen, Corning, Elmira and Ithaca. He met with politicians and newspaper editors. Later it was four more communities. And on and on through the year. That's what they mean by exposure. It's the kind that will catapult Lehrman into competition with Rep. Jack Kemp and State Comptroller Ned Regan, who've been put on the pedestal by a lot of Republicans. . . . Lehrman has the unique opportunity of calling himself an upstater and a downstater all at the same time. He lives in Manhattan but claims he's spent a lot of his adult life in the rest of the state.[30]

Speaking in the Buffalo area in August, I made reference to my business experience: "As a merchant, whose sixth store opened in Binghamton 15 years ago, I saw New York State go from being the preeminent state economically to being one of the least prosperous in the United States. I have reflected on this fact and I now ask, Why?"[31]

In February 1980, I told Oswego County Republicans: "Inflation is like a tumor and must be cut immediately. If we let it continue, even at a reduced rate, over a period of years, we would still suffer from it."[32] I also attacked New York State's tax rates.

> It is not the Sunbelt or Texas or California which are the main competitors to New York, it is the adjacent states. . . . While local and state and federal taxes take over $1,300 per capita in New York, the amount is only $990 in New Jersey, $900 in Pennsylvania, $660 in New Hampshire, and only $1,110 in Massachusetts. The average for the entire nation is only $800.[33]

Talking to Binghamton journalists in February 1980, I said: "I want to learn from you what you think the economic issues are in our state. Where do you feel our state is economically, and what do you think of the economic policy coming from Albany."[34]

I was finally ready to publicly admit my aspirations:

> There are times I get so mad, yes, I think of getting into politics . . . getting directly involved. . . . New Yorkers are worried how they will meet this winter's exorbitant fuel bills and they have little confidence in either the government of the state or the nation to reverse the decline in their purchasing power. . . . Americans are Americans wherever you go. They want economic opportunity for themselves, their children, and their children's children.[35]

Over a two-year period, the Economic Advisory Council issued papers on property reassessment, the shadow economy, indexing taxes to inflation, and meeting New York's energy and transportation needs. Dick Behn and I wrote the papers; I made the final edits. At the press conferences where we made them public, I would speak to the media and answer questions.

During the Republican presidential primaries in early 1980, I avoided direct involvement to remain friendly with all the candidates, but was very clear about my beliefs, saying that "The candidate who can identify the causes of inflation in a compelling and understandable way that will appeal to a broad range of voters, and then come up with a workable remedy, is the one who is going to win."[36]

The *Binghamton Press and Sun-Bulletin*'s Clark Walter wrote that I:

> levied the blame for current economic problems facing the state on government and taxes. "Going around New York in the '60s and '70s I concluded that small businesses were successful only in spite of government policy." . . . Lehrman said the average of $1,300 a year in local and state taxes New Yorkers pay is more than 50 percent greater than the national average. He said Connecticut and New Hampshire citizens pay $900 and $600 respectively . . . Lehrman cited higher personal, corporate, and sales taxes as the main reason business is leaving the state. He said the state loses millions each year when residents shop and do business in contiguous states with lower taxes.[37]

In March 1980, we held an "Agenda for the Eighties" forum with Republican county executives in Syracuse. Our work drew a less than enthusiastic response from some Republican legislators in Albany because lower taxes meant less revenue for government projects, including their own.

However, we had an influential fan to whom I had sent our position papers. *National Review* editor William F. Buckley Jr. admired the work of the Economic Advisory Council. He wrote to me saying "I must congratulate you on those brilliant papers. They are lucid, to the point, and helpful. I'll write a lug in the next day or two."[38] Buckley was the most influential Republican journalist of his time. In addition, he had always maintained the conservative position. It would not be the last boost Bill provided for my political ambitions. His support was continuous throughout my political career.

When the "lug" finally came out, I was delighted. With his signature literary flair and ironic disposition, Buckley introduced me to the political world, saying:

> There is in New York City an institution called Lewis E. Lehrman, a relatively young man of substantial means who runs an industrious think-tank which is receptive to differing opinions. But in private life he is an active partisan of the private sector and serves as chairman of the Economic Advisory Council for the New York Republican State Committee. His reports are miracles of economy and lucidity, and his November issue is devoted to the subject of "Cutting Government Waste." Brace yourself.[39]

I had a good working relationship with the Republican state chairman, Bernard Kilbourn, but in the spring of 1981, Kilbourn resigned and was replaced by the Brooklyn GOP chairman, George Clark, who had been an early Reagan supporter. Bernie himself took a job with the incoming Reagan Administration.

I had not been so lucky. I felt like Congressman Lincoln in 1849. After working hard to elect President Zachary Taylor, the only official positions Lincoln was offered were ones he did not want.[40] I recognized that if there was going to be the kind of political change I favored, I could not wait for someone else to appoint me. In September 1982 I told the *Rochester Democrat and Chronicle*'s Karen Heller:

> I realized if you had very strong feelings of your own, if you have your own world view, if some of your ideas are unorthodox, if you go about things in not the established or conventional way, then probably the very best thing is to run for public office so that people say, "Yes we want you to do it the way you say you are going to do it."[41]

LEAVING THE COMPETITION BEHIND

By the summer of 1981, there was a shifting cast of characters for the Republican gubernatorial nomination. State Senator John Marchi, who had defeated John Lindsay for the 1969 Republican mayoral nomination, was a favorite. So were Suffolk County Executive Peter Cohalan and Nassau County state senator Ralph Marino.

Three prominent New York City businessmen considered and then backed away from a candidacy—John P. Holmes, Estée Lauder heir Ronald Lauder, and erstwhile Wall Street veteran William Donaldson, who had served as dean of the Yale School of Management.

Bill Donaldson came to see me. He pulled out and lit one of his big cigars. "There's only room for one of us," he announced.

"I agree," I replied. "You're not going to be the one." In April, Donaldson dropped out.

I had an advantage over Donaldson and most other potential Republican candidates. While others had been flying over the state at thirty thousand feet, I had been on the ground talking to Republican leaders. I wasn't a household name, but I didn't need to introduce myself. I had done that already. And unlike Donaldson, I liked being among the people.

I made the decision to run in June. The key thing was Louise. With Louise, all things were possible. She told me: "If that's in your plan of life, if that's your destiny, that's your destiny." It was a continuing conversation. We had five kids, and the campaign would cast a big shadow over them. We knew there would be a lot of distractions. I gave some serious thought to the impact of politics on our children.

I had abandoned hopes that the Reagan Administration would find a suitable post for me where I might make an impact on economic policy. The press noticed the change in my course and an article by Evans and Novak announced it:

> Millionaire New York City businessman Lewis Lehrman, a leading supply-side economic theoretician, turned down separate offers to become ambassador to France and Portugal in order to launch a long-shot bid to be elected governor of New York. After Lehrman had been passed over early this year for any economic policymaking post in the Reagan administration, he was suddenly offered the coveted Paris embassy last month. When he said no, he was offered the Lisbon post to finish Portuguese base negotiations. His reason for turning down diplomatic service: At age 43, he feels his role is to stay home and fight to bring Reaganism to Albany. Some friends of Lehrman were deeply suspicious that the sudden White House interest in him coincided with the beginning of deliberations of the U.S. Gold Commission, where Lehrman is advocating a gold standard in opposition to top Reagan policymakers.[42]

While it is true I was deeply involved with the Gold Commission, my priority had shifted to the campaign for governor.

I began putting together a campaign staff. First, I hired Karl Ottosen, who had been the campaign manager for Senator Al D'Amato's insurgent but successful campaign in 1981. I added John Steele, a direct mail and polling wiz, who had been the driving force behind Bill Donaldson's trial run. With Karl, John, and Tim Carey, the campaign had instant organizational credibility among Republicans who stayed up on New York politics.

We began rolling out the campaign in stages—starting in August 1981 when we filed the campaign committee. On August 25, a letter went out from Cortland County Republican chairman Bill Winans. He was a true loyalist on my side from the center of upstate New York. I had met him in 1978 during the Platform Committee hearings. Bill would become my central New York coordinator and deliver a vital block of votes at the Republican State Convention. He joked with me about his involvement, saying "My business was lousy along with the rest of the economy, so it gave me something to do."[43] In his letter to New York Republican Party members, Winans wrote:

> The "New Yorkers for Lew Lehrman" Committee has been filed with the State Board of Elections in Albany.
>
> Lew Lehrman needs, and deserves, your support as our Party's candidate in the crucial 1982 gubernatorial election. I have known Lew for years and have seen him develop from a successful businessman to a national leader on key issues, particularly the vital economic ones. Along with members of his family, Lew helped take the family's local grocery business, redirected it into the discount drug trade, and made Rite Aid a billion-dollar-a-year business and a household name.
>
> In 1978, Lew came to Madison County as chairman of the New York Republican Platform Committee. He visited 42 counties that year and has been doing spade work for the Party as the chairman of the State Republican Economic Advisory Council since then. Lew has also been carrying the banner of our State Party high on the national front: As a member of the RNC's Advisory Council on Economic Affairs, as New York Chairman of Business for Reagan-Bush, as the writer of a paper on our country's economic problems which became the basis of the "Economic Dunkirk" Memorandum, and now as an advisor to the administration and member of the President's Gold Commission.
>
> Lew has the assets that our candidate for Governor will need to win. He has earned both the personal resources and community respect that will enable him to raise the money necessary to finance a campaign against Democratic guru David Garth. He has an in-depth knowledge of the issues. He has the physical stamina to go the distance. And he has a strong background in management. Equally important, he has no ties to past mistakes in Albany.
>
> Lew is the candidate who best understands that effective government is based on responsible politics. Too often, candidates think the Party is only a vehicle to win office. Lew understands that the Party can make government more effective and that it has the potential not only to elect the Governor but to lead the state. Just as Lew listened to the Party in 1978 when he chaired the Platform Committee, he will listen to the Party's leaders as Governor.
>
> Lew is a dramatic contrast to the man who liberal columnist Jimmy Breslin calls "Society Carey." Unlike the latter, he has first-hand knowledge of what it's like to run a farm, a small business, and a large corporation. He has had to meet payrolls and the taxman.[44]

That summer, the core campaign staff met at The Century Association in Manhattan to go through our plan. Halfway through the meeting, I suggested we take a break. When I went out into the corridor, I was surprised to run into US senator Daniel P. Moynihan. I invited the senator into the room and introduced him to my "friends." But Moynihan was no fool. Surveying the room, he noticed the planning notebooks laid out on the table. "Is this the plan?" he demanded as he picked up one of the super-confidential notebooks. We were all frozen in place since no preparations had been made for a Democratic invasion of our discussion.

Genially, Moynihan put down the notebook and went back to his own senatorial campaign planning in the room next door. At the end of the night, Karl Ottosen and Dick Behn carefully picked up all the planning materials when they left the meeting room. With several notebooks under their arms, they walked out of the club and into the night, there to be confronted again by a somewhat inebriated Senator Moynihan who demanded: "Where's the plan? I must have the plan!"

I'm afraid the senator was disappointed when it was not forthcoming, but I had often tried to help Senator Moynihan deliver results for the people of New York State. Since Moynihan had done nothing constructive in response, I was not about to share "the plan."

While my campaign was starting, others were stopping. Judge Sol Wachtler of the State Court of Appeals—a favorite of the Nassau County machine—unexpectedly took himself out of contention in September. "I was ready to run for governor and even told [Chief Judge] Larry Cooke that I was going to run," Wachtler recalled.

That was on a Friday. On a Sunday, I went to the Forest Hills tennis matches and Donald Trump was there. Donald Trump was just emerging; no one had ever heard of him. He came over to me, pointed his finger in my face and said, "People say you're running for governor. We're going to talk." I went home to Joan and I said, "I just can't do this. I can't go around raising funds and having people like him point their finger at me."[45]

Wachtler was widely described as a "formidable" candidate against Carey. So was Congressman Jack Kemp. Publisher Rupert Murdoch personally and persistently pushed Kemp to run. But years later, Kemp aide David Smick told Murdoch: "I could tell [Kemp] was just diddling you. He had no interest in that. He didn't want to run the state of New York. He didn't want to be a manager. . . . That was not his thing."[46] Jack, with whom I had long worked on economic questions, made no move to announce his decision. William Buckley pressed Kemp to make a decision in early October. Bob Novak covered the question of Kemp's candidacy, but also introduced me favorably writing:

> Republican county chairmen who have been kept on hold by Kemp for months are about to get some very unpleasant news. They consider Kemp the best chance to elect a Republican governor of New York for the first time since 1970, with the rest of the GOP field consisting of dubious prospects. Former state Republican chairman Richard Rosenbaum is probably the frontrunner, but Lehrman has been picking up support in conservative quarters.[47]

Newsday's Dick Zander wrote, "A number of prominent Republicans say Lehrman's friendly relationship with top Conservatives, plus his personal wealth, make him an especially palatable potential candidate. These Republicans do not believe a

GOP candidate can win a statewide race without a cross-endorsement by Conservatives. That's what makes him worth keeping an eye on."[48]

Buckley then wrote the newspaper column that changed the course of my political life. On October 20, he abruptly closed the door on Kemp, and opened a window on me, writing:

> Such is his essential modesty and anxiety to please that [Kemp] has never said, in as many words, "No I wouldn't." But a week or so ago he ran past a deadline which he himself accepted as reasonable. Accordingly, those who believe that he had, in virtue of seniority and service performed, primary right to the designation, have—in many cases— decided whom, in the absence of Kemp, they want.
>
> His name is Lewis Lehrman.
>
> I must not give the impression that Lehrman is less than an enthusiastic choice of those who know him and his potential for public service. . . .
>
> Lewis Lehrman, at age 43, has conquered the economic world and the world of higher thought. There is no academic company whose conversations would leave him embarrassed or silent. His fierce concern for his country, for his wife and children, has brought him to incline to run for public office, and it is the objective of his admirers to persuade him to do so.
>
> . . . as governor of New York he would not, obviously, be situated to bring us to gold convertibility. But he would be situated to elaborate, from his high public position, on the theme that inflation is the most pressing of our domestic dangers. You hear this, mind you, not from a yahoo who makes Archie Bunker-type emunctory noises every time Edith complains of the high price of tomatoes.
>
> Lehrman understands that the disease of inflation can affect the soul strings of a society. He opened up an essay in *The Washington Post* last winter by quoting Cicero, "The budget should be balanced, the Treasury should be refilled, public debt should be reduced, the arrogance of officialdom should be tempered and controlled."[49]

Wikimedia Commons

William F. Buckley Jr.: "Saint Bill"

I wrote in grateful response to Buckley, "Your essay inaugurated my campaign. I pray

I prove worthy of your faith. I shall never forget your interest, nor shall I forget the inspiration which you have given me and the whole movement."[50] Buckley's column provided the conservative stamp of approval that my new campaign desperately needed.

BUILDING AN ORGANIZATION

While other candidates were deciding whether or not to run, or deciding whom to hire for their campaign and how to pay for them, I put together a complete campaign organization, opened a campaign office, traveled to campaign stops around the state, and made it clear that I was in the race until the election and victory. My determination was intended both to reassure supporters and to scare opponents.

My plans to announce on January 11, 1982, put pressure on the Republican state chairman George Clark, who in turn put pressure on the new establishment favorite, Comptroller Edward Regan, to announce his candidacy. By December, at least four serious candidates—William Donaldson, Sol Wachtler, Jack Kemp, and Warren Anderson—had all backed away from the race.

My campaign mobilized to fill the power vacuum. Jonathan Bush, younger brother of then vice president George H. W. Bush, signed on as my campaign chairman. He was one of my most treasured friends and contributors. Ever genial and perceptive, Jon was very loyal and very, very influential. He made an eight-minute video for potential contributors.

From the start, we planned for a statewide Republican primary. My campaign manager Karl Ottosen wrote a confidential memorandum to Jon Bush on November 4, 1981:

> Our first objective is to get on the Republican primary ballot. There are two ways to do this. We can either get 25% of the Republican State Committee to vote for Lew; or we can get 20,000 signatures from enrolled Republicans. . . . When people get to know Lew, they are always impressed with him. Therefore, I cannot conceive of us having any difficulty getting 25% of the weighted votes of the Committee's 402 members, nor 20,000 signatures.[51]

On November 7, 1981, Congressman Kemp publicly took his name out of contention for governor and Comptroller Regan put his name into contention for the Republican nomination. On November 9, the State Assembly minority leader James Emery and former state Republican chairman Richard M. "Rosey" Rosenbaum suggested they, too, would run for the Republican nomination. Rosey had the advantage of the connections he had built up running the GOP for Nelson Rockefeller. Emery had the advantage of the State Assembly payroll on which many county chairmen had jobs.

Regan had indicated his interest in running but temporized about his commitment. His failure to commit provided an important opportunity for me. Still, I was running at the back of the pack. In December, the Regan campaign released a poll by Market Opinion Research showing that he would beat Governor Carey, 56 to 32 percent. The poll also showed Regan leading the Republican pack: Regan, 54 percent;

Warren Anderson, 18 percent; Richard Rosenbaum, 8 percent; Lehrman 3 percent. My response to this poll was to call myself "Lew, Who?" But it was a nickname that would not last long.

On December 3, when State Senate majority leader Warren Anderson announced that he would not run for governor, I was fortuitously in the Albany area meeting with newspaper editors. "Oh, my golly!" I said, then rather optimistically added: "I hope I can get his support." I told the press that "there is a season for every man . . . and it's my season. New York needs a businessman or woman" as governor. I told a reporter that voters were "looking for a fresh face—a chance to start over."[52]

Republican leaders, led by George Clark, wanted a tried and tested face. They were determined to maintain control of the nomination and prevent the Conservative Party from directing the nomination process. Clark pushed Ned Regan to declare his candidacy so he could be endorsed by the Republican State Committee before the Conservative Party acted. Somewhat comically in retrospect, Republican and Conservative leaders raced to see who could anoint their choice first. Fortunately for me, the Conservatives won.

I began my gubernatorial campaign as a self-acknowledged underdog. An outsider, I would be opposed by my own Manhattan Republican organization. A committed conservative, I was distrusted by the stalwart liberal Republicans of the legislature and the many Republican county chairs on legislative payrolls. I would be viewed with suspicion even by ideological allies like Jack Kemp. My supporters, however— such as assemblyman Bobby D'Andrea—were few but vocal. And some of these supporters—notably those at the top of the New York State Conservative Party—were powerful.

The keys to my campaign were will, organization, money, and friends. I never expected to be "anointed" as the Republican Party candidate. I expected to fight for it and knew I would need an organization to do that—a bottom-up organization, not a top-down one. In a May 1982 memo to campaign manager Karl Ottosen, organizational expert John Steele would lay out how the many slots were to be filled in each county organization structure: county coordinator, volunteer coordinator, finance chair, headquarters director, legal coordinator, materials coordinator, press coordinator, recruitment coordinator, special committees coordinator. . . . We had a role for any man or woman willing to work to win.

Enthusiastic county coordinators like Schenectady's Margaret "Mugsie" Buhrmaster put together comprehensive organizational structures early in the campaign—even though her Republican county leader was supporting another candidate or uncommitted.

The key to the effectiveness of our county organizations was their strong relationship to our field organization around the state. Suffolk County coordinator Gustie Schneider wrote me after the election:

> I would be remiss if I didn't take one last opportunity to comment on a few people I worked with on your behalf. John Steele, whose guidance, inspiration, ceaseless energies and nagging helped Mary MacLachlan and me to achieve

> some impossible tasks. John is such a pro and I hold him in the highest regard. Carmine [Guadagnino] was invaluable, not only in carrying out his own jobs, but was always very supportive and considerate of others. Andy Cowin, a great back-up man, really saw to it that all the loose ends got tied.[53]

My campaign staff was a diverse group. Some had already been working with me for several years, like Bob Palombo, Tim Carey, and Carla Saunders. Others, like Karl Ottosen, John Steele, and Mary Mower Mitchell were experienced campaign professionals. Many supporters had worked on the fringes of Republican and Conservative politics. Some, like Jim Miller and Adam Walinsky, were veterans of Democratic campaigns. My nephew Louis Lehrman sometimes did extra duty as a surrogate for the candidate.

For Susan (Yu) Tang and Lilly Eng, the campaign was one of their very first jobs as they entered college. "Lilly and I started on February 29, 1980," remembers Susie.

> We were at 641 [Lexington Ave.] and Lew, wearing his suspenders came down the hall to say hello and introduce himself. I said, "Hello, Mr. Lehrman."
>
> "Nope, that was my grandfather." He had an aura about him—very confident, very forceful. I had no idea who he was or why we were doing what we were doing—copying names from *Who's Who in Finance*. Next thing, Tim Carey sits us down and tells us that Lew is going to run for governor. Our response was "no way." I was totally clueless about politics.[54]

Carla Saunders: Devoted secretary

For Susie,
who knows more about the gold standard
than the Wall St. Journal - with deepest gratitude, Lew

Susan Tang: All around loyalty, with me for forty-three years

Some of the finance working group like Diana Colgate and Leslie Horn had experience working on George Bush's presidential efforts in 1980. Others in the finance group like Jim Killough, Andy Baxter, and Price Paschall brought finance experience.

Several of the campaign staffers—Tim Carey, Leslie Maeby, Karl Ottosen, and Frank Trotta—had known each other for years having worked together on young Republican politics in Albany. Tim, Leslie, and Frank were later featured in Samuel G. Freedman's *The Inheritance* about conservative Republicans who grew up in Democratic households. The full title of the book well expresses one of my own political theses: *The Inheritance: How Three Families and America Moved from Roosevelt to Reagan and Beyond.*

In the book, Frank told Freedman why he joined my campaign: "When I was deciding whether to leave Weil, Gotshal & Manges to join Lew's campaign for what was to be a one-year assignment, one of the most compelling reasons to leave the safety of a Wall Street law firm was Lew's intellect and gravitas. Lew spoke eloquently to me and other young conservatives of the 1980s."[55] Freedman decided that "There was no small measure of the Old Testament prophet in Lehrman, a mixture of personal magnetism and ideological purity."[56] Friends and family members of these staffers were also important. For a commercial about New York State's economy Frank recruited an unemployed cousin to stand outside a closed factory talking to me. He also recruited a fellow lawyer to be part of a commercial filmed in Tim Carey's living room early in the campaign. Tim's wife was recruited to be part of a commercial filmed at the Rite Aid store in New Rochelle.

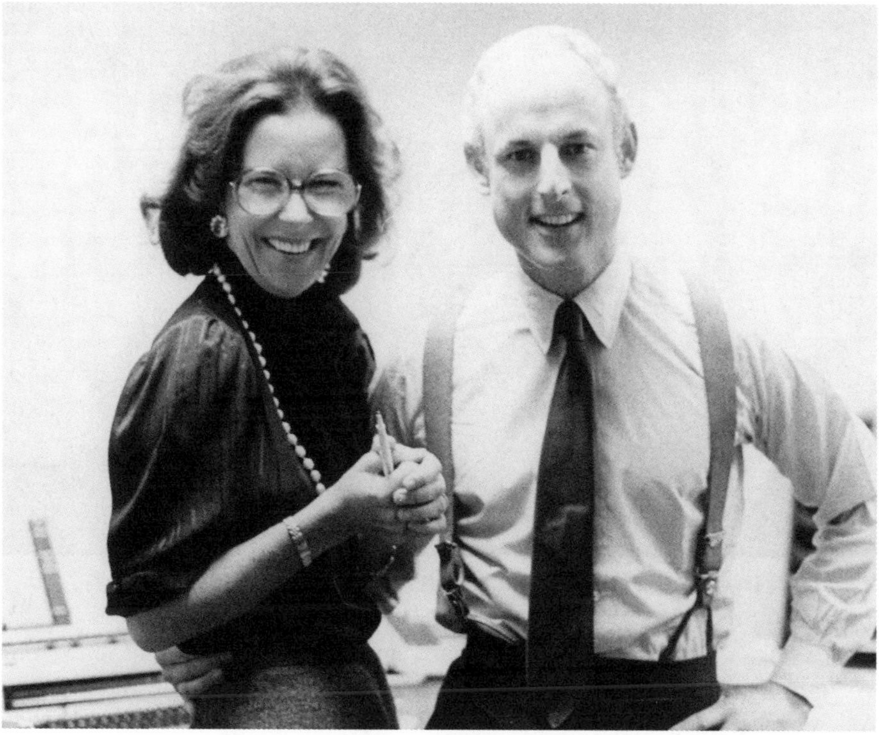

Diana Colgate . . .

Others, like press secretary John Buckley, nephew of William F. Buckley Jr., and James Buckley came from a long Conservative Republican heritage. Staffers Jerry Weil and Arnie Moskowitz were veterans of Jim Buckley's Senate campaign. Others came directly out of the Conservative Party like Carmine Guadagnino, Rob Ryan, and Allen Roth. And some like Joe Rogers (Harvard) and Kevin Rooney (Columbia) came directly out of the Ivy League.

. . . and Leslie Horn
The Long Island Girls

Ours was an assault team—ready to take on the establishment without alienating it completely. We were a real threat to the party's status quo in Albany.

It takes a team: Diana Colgate, Karl Ottosen, Carla Saunders, Lewis Lehrman, Leslie Horn, Andy Baxter

We took organization—and organizational techniques—very seriously. As at Rite Aid, we even had operating manuals, all of which I again wrote myself. I set the tone and agenda with top campaign officials in mid-March of 1982, writing:

> We must develop now a technique for recruiting systematically into our volunteer organizations . . . our county volunteer group should welcome people outside the organization. We should welcome Democrats, liberals, conservatives, anybody who wishes to work in our volunteer operation.[57]

We knew that no one was going to "give" me the GOP nomination. Knowing the opposition of the Republican establishment, the key to the early work by our volunteers was the compilation of a prime voters list: potential voters in the Republican primary that we expected to get from the beginning. We expected and planned for a primary—and we put our volunteers to work on the mammoth challenge of preparing for the first-ever Republican gubernatorial primary in New York State history. It is a little-known fact that prior to the 1982 primary, *all Republican nominations for Governor had been uncontested.*

The campaign manual for our prime voters initiative began:

> The project you are about to work on is of the utmost importance to the Lehrman for Governor Campaign. You will be identifying those Republican voters in your County that have a history of voting in Primary elections. This project is based on the concept that people who have voted in past Primaries will tend to vote in future Primaries. . . . Once these Republican Primary voters have been identified,

> the Lehrman Campaign will be able to efficiently target its voter contact effort. We estimate that there are about 650,000 Republicans in New York State that can be identified as Primary voters. The Lehrman Campaign's ability to identify those voters in your County rests upon you.[58]

We took nothing for granted. We brought on two campaign advisors with national reputations who brought us the instant credibility we needed and the expertise we required. First, we hired Richard Wirthlin, owner of Decision Making Information, the polling firm used by Ronald Reagan. Dick was "originally hired to give an unknown candidate the gravitas that was needed early on,"[59] recalled Karl Ottosen. Wirthlin's familiarity with the New York electorate, however, was something less than ideal, as was his work ethic. Tim Carey recalled that "Doctor Dick asked us what we wanted the polls' outcomes to say . . . [That] shocked me at the time, as we were looking for the truth."[60] We paid less and less attention to Wirthlin as the facts revealed themselves.

On the other hand, advertising wiz and Fox News founder Roger Ailes worked by the book. Although I was later disappointed by news of his bad conduct, at that time, he was tough-minded, talented, and great fun. Years later, Roger wrote of me that:

> Never did I meet a person running for office who was more passionate about his ideas than Lew Lehrman. Sometimes he believed that pure passion could overcome political opposition. Many times it worked, sometimes it didn't. Also, I never saw a man grow as much as Lew throughout his campaign. He became more tuned to people, more adept at handling any situation, and more aware of others' concerns. I don't think there is a man who understands principle, integrity, and values more than Lew.
>
> At the same time, he could wear anyone's rear end completely out arguing a point because he was always certain, but not always right. After a time, however, he came to develop a sense of humor about this, which is the real sign of growth. . . . No one is more committed to God, country, and family than Lew. If all of our leaders had Lew's intellect, drive, and courage this would be a better America.

My opponents' campaigns had their own formidable consultants—John Deardourff, Bob Teeter, and Roger Stone for Ned Regan, Arthur Finkelstein for Paul Curran, George Humphreys and Judith Press-Brenner for Jim Emery, and John Sears for Richard Rosenbaum—but my "well-oiled machine" drew more attention, respect and, ultimately, votes.

We kept two would-be advisors, Roger Stone and Arthur Finkelstein, out of the campaign. Stone started with Kemp. Finkelstein would orchestrate Paul Curran's attacks on me. No less than Richard Nixon urged me to push aside my young campaign staff in the summer of 1982—and bring Stone and company on board. Stone, who had planned on helping Kemp, was also promoted by New Jersey Senate candidate Jeff Bell. I refused.

On the suggestion of refreshing my campaign staff, my liberal friend Adam Walinsky, a former Robert Kennedy aide, might have agreed with Nixon and argued in favor of hiring cynical, "centrist" professionals. But the people I hired—such as campaign counsel Frank Trotta, scheduler Leslie Maeby, and press secretary John Buckley—were young, hungry, loyal, and dedicated conservatives. I had no doubts about their ability or any alternative agendas. I stuck with my team, and they stuck with me. After the Republican state convention in June, the *Daily News*' Beth Fallon recited their qualities: "Based on their performance at the three-day state committee meeting that ended yesterday, the Lehrman forces are smart, meticulously well organized, computerized, opportunistic and fielding an aggressive, telegenic candidate with a genius for publicity."[61]

Finances would be critical to success. Although I expected to contribute a large portion of the campaign budget, it was essential to develop a fundraising operation that could both galvanize the base *and* secure the loyalty of big givers who might otherwise be tempted to support more established candidates. Investment expert Fred Alger, who had been one of the original Rite Aid board members, became finance chairman. He was assisted by Dick Gilder, Jonathan Bush, Andy Baxter, Price Paschall, and Mary Mower. There was also a group of talented, dedicated, and incredible women—mostly from Locust Valley, Long Island—who were family friends, and friends of friends. They were essential to the campaign, loyal and hard-working. Their dedication and energy was behind all of our successful fundraising.

FLASHBACK: CHALLENGING JACOB JAVITS, SOLIDIFYING CONSERVATIVE PARTY SUPPORT

In 1976, there was a meeting of about three hundred supporters of Senator Jacob Javits at a New York Hotel. Javits was a liberal Republican who had repeatedly run with both the Republican and the Liberal Party lines ever since his election two decades earlier.

I was already known to Javits through my philanthropic activities. At the event, I objected to the way that Senator Javits referred to the Conservative Party so negatively—as if we didn't have a right to exist. I stood up and challenged him, very politely and very respectfully, regarding his disparaging attitude.

I got pushback from some liberal Republicans such as Arch Gillies, but more importantly, the news of my challenge got back to Conservative Party leaders. Dan Mahoney, Mike Long, and Serf Maltese invited me to dinner at their favorite New York steakhouse. They asked me if I had considered running for office. They expected I would want to run for the US Senate. I told them: "I've been an executive all my life. I would want to be an executive —not a legislator beating my gums. I want to make New York #1 again."

They asked me when I expected to run. I said: "In five years, in 1982." They were shocked, and responded: "Are you really going to run for governor in 1982?" I said: "I'm going to do it. You can count on it." They couldn't believe that I could commit to a date so far in the future. Mike Long would later say, "I was confrontational

Daniel Mahoney: Founder of the New York Conservative Party

with him . . . I looked at him and said, 'You mean you're telling us exactly what you are going to do five years from now.' And Lew replied, 'That's exactly what I'm doing.'"[62] Although there was a lot of bobbing and weaving over the following five years, my decision remained firm.

In this case, a challenge to leadership led to an opportunity to engage other leaders. I saw an opportunity to get Conservative Party support, and I seized it. My candidacy was thus only contingent on my willpower, my bank account, and my ability to get on the Republican primary ballot. Having committed my will and finances to the campaign, I had an advantage over Ned Regan—whose candidacy was hampered by indecisiveness and worries about fundraising.

We prepared our alliance carefully. In September 1981, Karl Ottosen and I had dinner with several of the top metropolitan leaders of the Conservative Party—Howard Lim, Michael Long, Serphin Maltese, George F. McGuinness, James P. Molinaro, and Wilson Price. Karl remembers that at the outset, "Lew was 'Lew who' to everyone in New York politics except for Mike Long and the Conservative party."[63] Of Mike Long's support he then said:

> Mike was an early and true believer. Mike would call every day all day, to see what he could do, what we were doing, what we should be doing, what he was hearing and what were we hearing. I don't want to make it sound as if Mike was a pain, just the opposite, he was extremely knowledgeable and helpful, just intense.[64]

In November I attended a Conservative Party panel discussion with Senator D'Amato and Congressman Kemp. Conservative Party support had been critical to D'Amato's upset victory over Senator Jacob Javits in 1980. History might repeat in 1982.

Ned Regan understood that he needed the Conservative Party line to be elected governor. He did not want to announce his candidacy unless he was assured of the Conservative line. "Conservative Party support is also critical," Regan told reporters. "It would therefore be premature for me to accelerate my decision until after I have met with state and county Conservative Party leaders."[65]

If we could take away that opportunity from Regan, we could effectively block his candidacy. So, as a critical meeting of Conservative Party leaders on December 12 approached, my campaign worked to box him out. Not everyone in the Conservative Party was happy with our efforts. Some had their own favorites like Regan or Rosenbaum. Others wanted to maintain Conservative flexibility. Still others resented giving Dan, Serf, and Mike the power to determine the party's nomination.

Mike Long: The family man of the Conservative Party

We left little to chance as we prepared for the meeting at which party members interviewed prospective candidates for the nomination: Regan, Marino, Emery, Rosenbaum, Marchi, myself, and Democrat John S. Dyson. The expectation was that the Conservative Party would announce their party's preference by early January—thus exasperating GOP chairman George Clark who did not want the Conservative tail to be wagging the Republican dog.

Ray Herman of the *Buffalo Courier-Express* took a close look at the proceedings:

> Perhaps seeking a psychological edge, Lehrman . . . phoned Maltese. Would it be all right if he showed some hospitality to the Conservative leaders who were to come in from across the state—breakfast at Lehrman's campaign headquarters on Lexington Avenue and East 54th Street, a Lehrman-financed lunch down the hall from the conference room at the Halloran, and post-audition drinks back at Lehrman's headquarters. If Maltese had any reservations about the high-octane Lehrman, they were removed a week before the Halloran House soiree. Lehrman invited Maltese to a 7 a.m. breakfast a block away from the Lehrman campaign headquarters. They finished at 8:15, walked a block down Lexington to 54th, took an elevator to the 25th floor of an office building. The Lehrman headquarters take up the entire floor and staff was at work. Surveying the hustle and bustle at a time when most strap-hangers are en route to work, Maltese thought: "There are certain advantages to running a hard-headed businessman for governor."[66]

At that same December meeting at the Halloran House, Regan's uncertainty was evident. "Nothing is resolved yet," he said of his candidacy. "There must be some coalescing of opinion and some real sign of support for me in the Republican Party and soon. If it doesn't develop fast, I don't know. . . . The situation is fluid."[67] While other candidates were testing the waters, I was ready to take the plunge.

Ray Herman, who continued to chronicle the gubernatorial campaign for the *Buffalo Courier-Express*, wrote that our "press kit, in short, smacks of a self-assured conservatism and an impending campaign which will not lack for money."[68] Presciently, Herman wrote, "Most qualified observers feel that it may take up to $15 million to be competitive for governor in 1982."[69]

George Borrelli, Herman's veteran counterpart at the *Buffalo News*, filled in some gaps in the story:

> Lehrman . . . rolled out the red carpet for Conservative leaders from around the state eight days ago when they met in New York City to interview candidates for governor. He hosted a breakfast for the leaders at his campaign headquarters in the Bowery Bank Building on Lexington Avenue. While the Conservatives were munching on Danish pastry and drinking coffee and orange juice, they were shown a video presentation by Jonathan Bush highlighting Lehrman's credentials to be governor. . . . Conservative leaders were given a tour of the Lehrman headquarters, which are equipped with computers, telecopiers and communications equipment . . . Lehrman, who also hosted a luncheon and post-meeting cocktail party for the Conservatives, was attempting to impress the minor party officials that he is fully committed to a gubernatorial campaign and that he has the best and most efficient organization assembled.[70]

Serphin Maltese: "Kingpin of the Right"

Our work paid off. By the end of December, the Conservatives announced they would quietly back my candidacy. In not backing Regan, the Conservatives had a convenient excuse— their worry that only Regan could retain the comptroller's office. Maltese told

Regan that "we didn't want to turn that over to a Democrat of Carol Bellamy's ilk."[71] Conservatives wanted my assurance that I would not leave them in the lurch by taking a job in the Reagan Administration. That, I gave.

The *New York Times*' Maurice Carroll broke the news the following day writing that I had "been promised the Conservative Party nomination for Governor of New York . . . even if it would mean splitting the right-of-center opposition against the Democrats." Carroll continued, quoting me, "'Conservative leaders have told me you need both lines to get elected, and I agree with them.'"[72] The rest of the article focused on the thoughts of Conservative Party leaders, and their power within the organization:

> "A majority of our leaders favor Lew Lehrman," said Serphin R. Maltese the Conservatives' executive director. "Right now the party is leaning to Lew," said J. Daniel Mahoney, the state chairman. Over breakfast in a Manhattan restaurant the two had unsuccessfully urged Mr. Regan to run instead for re-election as Comptroller. . . . Mr. Lehrman has been close to the Conservative leaders. The party is pretty much controlled from the top; what Mr. Mahoney and Mr. Maltese want, they customarily get, and they are said to want Mr. Lehrman.[73]

In some quarters, the Lehrman-Regan battle was viewed as a surrogate for a future Bush-Kemp battle for the presidency. That added a layer of complexity to what was already an unusual situation for Republicans—a multi-candidate race for the GOP nomination. While others believed that their past experience and record should have given them preference for the nomination, I relied on strategic preparation. Ironically, it was the obscure and complex Wilson-Pakula Act of 1947 that gave me a key strategic advantage.

The irony was that Malcolm Wilson—for whom the Wilson-Pakula Act is named—would become my most prominent antagonist in the Republican primary. I had gone to meet with him before I announced my candidacy for governor. Wilson suggested I should run for the State Assembly and reconsider the governorship in a decade or two. Needless to say, I ignored him.

Years earlier in 1947, then Assemblyman Wilson had sponsored a state law that required a candidate *to get permission to run in a party primary if he was not a member of that party.* The law was designed to limit the influence of the American Labor Party in New York City politics.

Without a Wilson-Pakula pass, one would have to circulate petitions to get on the ballot of any party to which the candidate did not belong—a tedious and costly process. I paid special attention to the Conservative Party's New York City leaders, who assured me that I would not have any problem with the Conservative Party designation. They also implied that a Wilson-Pakula pass would be denied to my opponents—thus making it very difficult for anyone else to combine both the Republican and Conservative lines. Some Conservative leaders such as Nassau County's John J.

O'Leary—who was allied with Nassau GOP chairman Joe Margiotta —were aware of the risk to their own candidates. They were intent on breaking the Wilson-Pakula lock in favor of their candidate, the former US attorney, Paul Curran.

In his autobiography, O'Leary recounted this moment:

> The State Executive Committee met in New York City on March 25th. . . . At this meeting I offered a proposal for the Executive Committee to go on record to give a Wilson-Pakula authorization to any candidate from another party who receives the necessary 25 percent of the vote at the State Committee meeting for any statewide office to show that the Conservative Party has an open leadership. Leo Kesselring and several of the other dissidents presently supported me in this effort but Serf Maltese who was presiding at the meeting ruled the motion out of order for not having proper notification. Gauged by the sentiments expressed by the members present in the room, this motion would have passed, opening the door for a primary contest between Lehrman and Curran; unless Maltese made the unprecedented move of voting the proxies which I was certain always gave Mahoney or Maltese a majority vote.[74]

As he noted, O'Leary was not alone. Dissidents like O'Leary, Monroe's Leo Kesselring, and Erie's George Vossler, had interviewed other candidates at the Conservative Party Political Action Conference in Albany in early February. In March, Paul Adams and Kieran O'Doherty, who had been the Conservative Party's first gubernatorial ticket in 1962, wrote to state committee members saying, "The spirit and essence of a true Conservative-Republican partnership means that the cross-endorsement process has to allow for a two-way, not just a one-way street."[75]

The Conservative Party leadership, however, stuck with me. They were placing a big bet on me, and given my lack of name recognition, it was a very big bet. Frank Lynn of the *New York Times* did a thorough analysis of the implications of the situation on January 26, 1982:

> If the Conservative Party and its candidate, Lewis E. Lehrman, a Republican, are successful all the way to November, the Conservatives would be a major influence in a Lehrman administration—very likely more so than any other third party in the state's history. The Conservative Party would also have demonstrated its political muscle for future dealings with the Republican Party. On the debit side, if the Conservatives nominate Mr. Lehrman and then he fails to win the Republican nomination, they could split the Republican-Conservative vote in the general election and help elect a Democrat.[76]

The Mahoney-Maltese-Long team remained stalwart. Lynn cited the simple reason why I was the Conservatives' preferred candidate: "'Regan was invited to Kings County over the years,' said Mike Long, 'but he never had the time to be there.'"[77]

As Conservative Party support solidified behind me, the angst among some Republican leaders was reflected in a March column by *Newsday*'s Dick Zander:

> The Conservative leadership seems to be trying to dictate the selection of the GOP candidate just as they did successfully in 1980. In that race, the Conservatives picked Republican Alfonse D'Amato for the Senate long before the Republicans met to make a choice. . . . To a degree the Conservatives have already tested success with Lehrman. They are as responsible as Mayor Edward Koch for convincing the front-runner for the GOP gubernatorial nomination, State Comptroller Edward V. Regan, to drop out of that race and seek re-election.[78]

After a key meeting of Republican county chairmen in January, state chairman George Clark said: "There was a strong feeling that nobody wants the Conservatives telling us who our Republican candidate should be."[79] I didn't have time to get involved with the inter-party bickering. I just kept right on challenging the establishment, one step at a time.

George Marlin, in his history of the New York Conservative Party wrote:

> Lew Lehrman was what Republican insiders pejoratively labeled "a true believer." The old-line establishment opposed him because he was devoted to the fundamental principles of conservatism. Sure, his optimistic vision was in tune with Ronald Reagan's—lower taxes and supply-side growth—but New York's Republican hacks saw Lehrman as an outsider, and feared most of all that they would be left out in the cold if he were elected.[80]

They were right.

Sewing up the Conservative Party nomination was in fact critical to the campaign strategy to win the Republican nomination.

In the *Rochester Democrat and Chronicle*, I was quoted:

> "[T]he Republican county chairmen, indeed George Clark, the state chairman, have encouraged all of us to get the Conservative line as well, even though it is a different party. That's because the Democrats have about a million registration advantage over Republicans in the state. In 1978, Ned Regan won the comptrollership; the margin of victory was provided by the Conservative Party. Ronald Reagan won in New York state in 1980, and the margin of victory was provided by the Conservative Party. Al D'Amato won in New York State, and the margin of victory was provided by the Conservative Party. . . . I cannot influence the Conservative Party. I can present my point of view and my qualifications. They will choose me if they think I can win the general election. They will not if they don't."[81]

My alliance with Conservative leaders Mahoney, Maltese, and Long was not based on self-interest alone. It was an alliance based on a similar vision of American history. These men felt I had the guts to overturn the liberal order. I liked Daniel Mahoney. He said they weren't used to candidates in the Republican Party being policy-oriented or students of politics. Dan was historically-oriented. They were all well-tutored.

I respected Serf Maltese, whose wife Constance was a gifted artist. Serf and I fell in as partners almost immediately.

And I loved Mike Long. The Longs had nine children. Louise and I respected them as parents. They were a family dedicated to public service. Mike was a civic leader in his Brooklyn neighborhood who later became a city councilman. He became statewide head of Conservatives for Lehrman. As Mike recalled: "Lew realized that to have real leverage with Republicans, he had to secure Row C. He also wanted to head off a Ned Regan candidacy. We assumed correctly that Regan wanted to be crowned."[82]

But this is the United States, and that doesn't happen here.

THE COMPETITION

On December 30, 1981, Comptroller Regan announced his candidacy for governor of New York—while on a ski vacation in Vermont—through a statement issued by the press secretary of his state comptroller's office back in Albany. His remarks to the press were also indecisive. "I am a committed candidate for governor of the State of New York,"[83] he said unconvincingly, "because I have been assured by state Republican Chairman George Clark that I have a significant majority of the votes needed for governor at next year's Republican convention."[84] Apparently, his own convictions and principles were not much involved. I was not impressed, and not concerned.

Clark gamely pretended surprise: "That is one of the exciting things about Ned. He is a kind of spontaneous person. I'm rather delighted. I support him. He will be the Republican choice."[85] The *New York Times*' Maurice Carroll reported on Regan's announcement:

> In his statement issued in Albany, Mr. Regan said he looked forward to a "demonstration" of party support at a meeting of county leaders next Wednesday in Albany. Friends said he had been promised the backing of at least three leading Republicans—Representative Jack Kemp, his Buffalo neighbor; Senator Alfonse M. D'Amato of the Town of Hempstead, L.I., and the State Senate majority leader, Warren M. Anderson of Binghamton. After Republican support "coalesces" around his candidacy, Mr. Regan said, he will "contact the leaders of the state's Conservative Party to seek their support as well."[86]

We sailed right through. To reinforce the determination and seriousness of our campaign, we announced a $600,000 radio advertising buy starting right away to show that Lew Lehrman was the guy to beat. The campaign wanted radio commercials to influence and impress county leaders traveling to Albany by car for that meeting of the county chairs Regan had announced. Frank Trotta introduced Karl Ottosen to Jack Cookfair, who produced radio ads which flooded the New York State Thruway. The commercials began on January 4th, saying "If you think Hugh Carey is doing a good job as governor, you must not live in New York,"[87] and concluded with the tag line: "Lew Lehrman, a leader to make New York work again."[88] The campaign stayed on the air virtually continuously through Election Day on November 2.

Having pushed Ned Regan into the gubernatorial race, Clark sought to push Republican county chairmen to back Regan's candidacy at their meeting in Albany. The meeting seemed timed to deflate the impact of the announcement of my own candidacy scheduled for January 11. On January 5, the day of the meeting, Clark's attempts to crown Regan failed when Republican county chairmen balked, and refused to fall into line behind the comptroller. I had little support in that group, but Emery and Dick Rosenbaum had sufficient backing to help block Regan . . . and provide an opening for me. The GOP chairmen did not want to back a loser, and they didn't want to back a candidate who might not go the distance. Frank Lynn of the *New York Times* keenly observed the dissension within the Republican leadership:

> The Republican State Chairman, George L. Clark Jr., and his choice for Governor, State Comptroller Edward V. Regan, had hoped to paint a rainbow of unity behind Mr. Regan's candidacy at a meeting of the state's 62 Republican county chairmen last week in Albany. Instead, they evidently encountered something more nearly approaching what State Senator Roy M. Goodman called "an explosion in a paint factory." The G.O.P. leaders, many of whom resented that Mr. Regan ignored them, their chicken dinners and their patronage requests until he decided he needed their support, refused to endorse him —at least for now. Clearly, Mr. Regan has fences to mend.[89]

The next day, I met with supportive Republican county chairmen for breakfast at the Fort Orange Club in Albany telling them, "If you are looking for a man with a business track record who can raise money from every nook and cranny, you got it right here."[90] Nevertheless, I faced tough questions about my relationship to Conservative Party leaders and whether they would "control" me.

Part of my work during January and February involved putting out fires. The first, at the Republican state chairmen's meeting, did not take much effort. In truth, Regan put out his own fire. His sense of pompous entitlement—by nature of both his personality and his statewide office—undermined his candidacy. Michael Kramer got it right when he wrote:

> Problem is, Regan thinks he should be the only contender—and his arrogance just might do him in. Regan resents the entry of "outsiders" into the race. "I've worked hard for sixteen years," he says. "I started by helping people get stop signs, and now I keep the books. I deserve the nomination, and, yes, I do find it hard to accept that there are others challenging me."[91]

But challenge is how the political—and commercial—systems are supposed to work in America. Only free competition with a focus on merit—under the Constitution—can even theoretically lead to just *and* popular government.

Meanwhile, national political issues were moving under the surface, and I found myself having to block Ned's attempts to suggest that President Reagan was backing Clark's maneuvers. There were rumors, and some journalists were intent on reporting them. Ray Herman credited my efforts in the *Buffalo Courier Express*:

> The Lehrman clout in Reagan's Washington soon became apparent. During a Washington visit Lehrman, who had served as chairman of a business committee in New York for Reagan and George Bush during the 1980 campaign, sought out White House chief of staff James Baker, seeking "clarification" of the Reagan-Regan press speculation. It was blunting the Lehrman drive. Baker advised Lehrman that the president would be neutral in any New York struggle for the nomination for governor. Lehrman advised Baker of the press reports. "Show me the stories," Baker replied. The next day, Lehrman dispatched the clips to the White House. And in early January, Reagan, through his chief political operative, Lyn Nofziger, proclaimed his neutrality in New York, a development which helped sidetrack a Regan drive to sew up the party endorsement early.[92]

The statement by Nofziger was telegraphed to Clark on January 6. It read "There have been some false rumors and inaccurate media reports that the President has endorsed or will endorse one of the primary candidates. President Reagan, in keeping with his long-time and often-stated policy, is and will remain neutral in all primary races involving nonincumbents, including those races in New York State."[93]

Ned Regan had a natural base of support among New York bankers interested in his financial sway. Once again, I was engaged in a game of chicken. I spoke to one of his supporters in the banking community in a very direct way.

I also spoke very directly to Congressman Kemp, when my friend Jack curried favor with the Erie County base he shared with Regan, and with the legislative Republicans who controlled the shape of his congressional district.

Regan seemed to be feeling the pressure. Michael Kramer described his efforts to get serious:

> Regan has hired some high-priced talent—campaign consultants Roger Stone and John Deardourff. He is on his way toward raising $10 million through a finance committee that includes William Spencer, the president of Citibank. And there is little doubt that Regan is prepared to wage whatever kind of campaign is necessary—in both the primary and general elections. "I didn't enjoy beating up on Jay Goldin every day," recalls Regan of his [1978] race for state comptroller. "but I know how to, if I have to do it to get elected, I will."[94]

I was unperturbed.

"Today, I announce my candidacy for Governor of the State of New York"

CHAPTER 8

Through the Primary

ANNOUNCING MY CANDIDACY

On January 11, 1982, I began my gubernatorial announcement tour around the state—in unexpectedly frigid, single-digit weather downstate, and a blizzard upstate. The first stop in the early morning was the upper mezzanine of Grand Central Station in Manhattan—a location that some thought "unorthodox."[1] The text of my announcement began:

> Today, I announce my candidacy for Governor of the State of New York. I have never been a politician. I have never before run for political office. Therefore, an introduction may be helpful. I am the grandson of immigrants. Louis Lehrman, my paternal grandfather, came to Ellis Island in 1896. My first job after college was as a college teacher, working on a fellowship. I left the university, went to boot camp at Fort Knox, and then returned to my family's grocery business. We built the Rite Aid corporation from a local business into one of New York's fastest growing enterprises. Today Rite Aid is an international company.
>
> Rite Aid brought me to Binghamton, New York in the summer of 1963. Six years later, my wife Louise and I took our apartment in New York City and decided to raise our family here. In 1977, I gave up the presidency of Rite Aid and returned to the public concerns I left behind as a scholar. Five years earlier, I had established The Lehrman Institute, where we do research on economic and foreign policy issues—as well as on state and local government.
>
> But this day, above all, I am primarily a citizen of New York—the husband of Louise Lehrman, and the father of five children. Today, I feel and say, as all parents do, that these children are our hope and our future. I believe that if my immigrant grandfather's dreams are to live, they must live also for millions of others less fortunate. All New Yorkers must be entitled to a full opportunity to share the blessings of this land and the fruits of our labors.[2]

Beth Fallon called the announcement "a thoroughly professional affair, orchestrated by top Republican campaign managers, pollsters, and media specialists he has hired." She then faithfully reported highlights of the speech, saying:

> Slight, intense, dramatic, the candidate came over rather well in person, delivering a scathing attack on the policies and personal qualities of Hugh L. Carey, "In the fable, the ant worked and ate; the grasshopper played and starved. Our problem is that the people work, and the governor plays," Lehrman snapped scornfully. "Yet somehow he eats, and it is we the people who suffer. . . ." "Unacceptable" that in 1981 more New Yorkers died by violence than did victims of strife in Lebanon and Northern Ireland . . . "unacceptable" that the State Court of Appeals ranks the rights of pornographers above those of the wounded children they exploit . . . "unacceptable,'" Lehrman said leaning over his three-ring blue notebook, that after billions are spent, hundreds of thousands "languish on welfare without the hope of honest work" while nearly 800,000 New Yorkers "were driven out of this state" from 1975 to 1980 [by uncompetitive tax and economic policy].[3]

After the announcement in Grand Central Station, I rode by train to White Plains with Frank Trotta and Gannett Westchester's Milt Hoffman. I then flew to Albany for the next stage of my announcement. The plan had been to move on to Buffalo for a third announcement. Instead, we were grounded by two feet of snow at our destination. The next morning when our plane arrived in Buffalo, John Szelest and Tim Carey had to help shovel the way to our press conference.

We moved on to Rochester and Syracuse to announce again. A few days later, we made a second "announcement" tour of smaller upstate cities. Our campaign took the attitude that anything truly worth doing was therefore worth doing multiple times to reach multiple audiences. I found that approach to be effective in business as well as in politics. It was a relatively unconventional approach at that time, when an announcement was thought to be a one- or perhaps two-time event. We wanted to reach each of the many small upstate media markets with newspapers, radio, and TV. These were cities where simply showing up made news. Richard Meislin noticed my outreach to the smaller political districts:

> Whether he can win the support of the average voter in, say, Oneonta, as he has with those in the upper echelons of public policy remains to be seen, but Mr. Lehrman is confident. "They'll remember that I was the guy who came to Oneonta and opened up the Rite Aid pharmacy," he said.[4]

During this time, we launched the rest of the advertising campaign we had announced earlier in January. Meislin explained our strategy:

> The candidate has begun a $600,000 schedule of radio and television advertisements. They are intended largely to increase public awareness of his name and, to a lesser extent, to explain his views. The commercials stress the two issues Mr. Lehrman plans to make the keystone of his campaign—job development (he favors restructuring state taxes to encourage small businesses to invest in

New York) and crime control (he supports the reinstitution of the death penalty and putting criminals "away for a long time, because that's what people want").[5]

As we were gearing up, others were wearing down. Two-term governor Hugh Carey bowed out of the race on January 15. He had apparently tired of the relentless press assault. There had been "an incessant string of stories critical of his use of state planes and cars, his attempt to seize a dentists' property next to his family home on Shelter Island, his promise to swallow a glass of PCBs in Binghamton,"[6] and on his lifestyle. Our campaign no longer had Hugh Carey to challenge for re-election, but we would continue to question the impact of his policies.

MOVING OUT FRONT

Buttressed by the certainty of the Conservative Party nomination, my own willpower and resources were still essential to eventual success. It was evident that I would be on the Republican primary ballot—by designation or with enough signatures. It was certain that I would be on the general election ballot—on the Conservatives' Row C. My opponents were, however, hobbled by uncertainty. Their campaigns were based on "if." Mine was based on "will."

At best, Ned Regan's campaign was a half-hearted effort. It got off to a weak start when he announced while on vacation in Vermont and the press hardly noticed. Shortly afterwards, he failed to win endorsement from a majority of Republican county chairmen, and then was rebuffed by leaders of the Conservative Party. He seldom displayed real enthusiasm for the fight to win the nomination of his party. He limited his public appearances to carefully chosen Republican gatherings and avoided taking shots at his opponents. He never seemed to be sure whether he wanted to be comptroller or governor. Many observers predicted he would quit as soon as the going got tough, despite his statement in late January that he was "irrevocably" in the race.

There were other candidates to contend with, however. On February 2, Richard Rosenbaum announced his candidacy for governor. Unfortunately for Rosey, his announcement took place in a major snowstorm that paralyzed Rochester and made it impossible for him to duplicate what we had done in January.

In addition to his weather problems, Rosenbaum's message didn't fit the moment. "Even though politics is a dirty word to some people, I'm proud of my political background, proud to say I am a politician,"[7] declared the former Republican state chairman.

The electorate was not so sure.

Regan was still looking for money and was still unconvincing. "I have been assured that there is $5 million out there," Regan told a reporter. "I know what it is to campaign without money. I wouldn't even consider taking myself this far if I didn't think we could raise the money."[8]

My announcement was accompanied by a heavy television wave of "biographical" TV ads featuring my work at Rite Aid. Less than a month later, a poll by Decision Making Information (DMI) showed me leading my Republican opponents. We had instructed DMI's Dick Wirthlin to conduct this poll by the book, so we were truly pleased by the results. Wirthlin focused on gauging voter awareness, saying "We knew we had low name ID. 'Lew Who?' was clearly our major political problem. His success in getting identification is far beyond our expectations."[9] On February 6, we released the poll results. They showed me leading Regan by 26 to 22 percent with Rosenbaum at 6 percent and Emery at 4 percent.[10]

Regan scoffed at the poll when opening his Buffalo headquarters on February 8. "Look at it, if being governor was as easy as getting yourself on TV in drug stores in two weeks, why hasn't it been done before? If it was that easy you don't need my 16 years [of experience in government]. You don't need it. Come on, it is just so inconceivable."[11] Ned's problem was that bureaucratic political experience cannot be relied upon to win a contested primary during a national economic and ideological crisis.

On February 11, Congressman Kemp endorsed Regan, calling the comptroller a "capable leader and fiscal expert."[12] Rowland Evans and Robert Novak, always keen to report any disagreement between Kemp and myself, wrote that Kemp's announcement had provoked "long-simmering animosity."[13] I might have had a few choice words with Kemp when I called him. Kemp's announcement was meant to stall my campaign and create momentum for Regan. But it did not.

On February 22, New York City mayor Ed Koch jumped into the Democratic party fray. At the same time, Regan again announced, "I'm in the race to stay."[14] This time, however, he had an escape route: "We've got to be sure we can raise the kind of money needed to beat Ed Koch."[15] If he decided the money wasn't there, he could just jump through the hatch.

Regan's top political supporter, GOP chairman George Clark, complained bitterly that Koch had reneged on a pledge he made twice not to run for governor. Koch's own political aide, John LoCicero, confirmed that Koch had indeed made the promise, but Regan had bigger problems than Koch. George Borrelli listed them in detail:

> State Comptroller Edward V. Regan of Buffalo is leading in most polls measuring the contest of the GOP nomination for governor, but his campaign organization is a model of inefficiency, a number of Republicans agreed today. . . . One common complaint from politicians, campaign workers, and the media is that Mr. Regan is either inaccessible or extremely difficult to contact.[16]

On March 9, Assembly Minority Leader James Emery announced his gubernatorial candidacy. Jim had already served in the State Assembly for eighteen years with over three years as minority leader. He had also served as a colonel in the Air Force Reserve and on active duty during the Korean War. His campaign was premised on the support of Republican county chairmen, twenty-two of whom were on his Assembly payroll.

Emery's announcement seemed to put Regan over the edge. On March 12, Regan dropped out of the gubernatorial race and announced his campaign for re-election as state comptroller. It was no surprise. Richard Benedetto sketched out the response to Regan's announcement saying that "State Comptroller Edward V. Regan's decision to abandon his Republican race for governor [came] as little surprise to many political insiders who said from the start that he didn't have the guts for a tough fight."[17]

Koch himself sympathized with Regan, saying: "It's regrettable that Regan is done in by Lehrman's money."[18] In truth, Ned had taken Republican officials for granted, and they declined to come to his aid when he beckoned. As Regan himself admitted: "I don't want to take a major chance (now) of terminating a public career. I really like this job [as state comptroller]."[19]

George Clark had finally come to realize that Regan's "heart was never really in it,"[20] observing: "It was a question of whether the Conservatives or Ned's people would blink first, and Ned blinked."[21] Dick Zander agreed, writing that:

> A prominent Long Island Republican said: "Lehrman's big trump card from the beginning was the Conservative Party and now it becomes a tremendous trump card." Serphin Maltese, executive director of the party, informed of Regan's intentions, said: "it was the statesmanlike thing to do." Regan aides had approached Conservative leaders to make certain nothing stood in the way of Conservative endorsement to a second 4-year term as comptroller. Nothing did, Maltese said.[22]

JOCKEYING FOR POSITION

A few days before Regan's announcement, former congressman Bruce Caputo took himself out of the US senatorial race against Moynihan. I made it clear I was not interested in shifting my goal, telling a reporter:

> I made an irrevocable decision and I am in the governor's race to stay until victory. Under no circumstances would I run for the Senate. I am not running for an office simply because it is vacant, but I am running for governor because that way I can most directly affect the lives of the people of New York.[23]

With Regan out of the race, the pressure from onetime Regan supporters on former US attorney Paul Curran to announce grew. I had few concerns about Curran as a candidate, but there were other, more serious problems. President Reagan visited New York in late March and undermined all the Republican candidates when he praised Koch. Evans and Novak reported that Reagan had not read the memo prepared for his trip:

> The new memo was put in the President's briefing book for his visit to New York City. It detailed the state's political situation, making clear that a heated race for governor was shaping up in the fall with Democrat Koch and Republican Lewis Lehrman leading for the major party nominations. "I'll bet the president never got around to reading that," one aide confided. There was no oral briefing of Reagan describing how Koch's praise of him had more recently

> turned to criticism. So, when asked at a *New York Post* interview whether Koch would make a good governor, Reagan replied in words reminiscent of an out-of-date memo written for the White House last fall. That memo, prepared by Republican political consultant Roger Stone, justified Koch's nomination by Republicans as well as Democrats for 1981 re-election as mayor.[24]

Reagan's slip may not have been entirely his fault, but it was emblematic of other problems in New York's Republican Party. Frank Lynn revealed our struggle for the *Times*:

> With election campaigns for Governor and Senator already under way, the New York State Republican Party is in such disarray that Republican leaders say privately that the party's chances of victory in November are in jeopardy. They concede that the party is at its weakest point since the heyday of Nelson A. Rockefeller. Even President Reagan acknowledged in his visit Tuesday to New York City that "you don't like to see that happen in a party." New York Republicans confess privately that they are not optimistic about the chances of recapturing the Executive Mansion in Albany, the most important office for building up a party through patronage and contributions.[25]

While others in the party wrung their hands, my campaign staff put theirs to work. Party officials had looked for a "savior" to lead the party's ticket—Wachtler, Kemp, Anderson, Regan. The ambition of those men was strong, but their willpower was insufficient. Because I had never run for public office, some Republican leaders thought me unprepared. But politics is about contrast. My determination contrasted with the lassitude of those who dropped away.

Journalists saw the contrast between my determined quest for the governorship and the tentative approach taken by Curran, who finally announced his candidacy in mid-May. Curran had filed preliminary papers of candidacy with the State Elections Committee in January, but he had been reluctant to give up his law practice to campaign full-time. There was a clear contrast between my four years of traveling throughout New York State and Curran's daily commute between his Westchester home and his Manhattan law office.

Curran had been talking about running but delaying the announcement. "I don't want to announce now and be a part-time candidate," said Curran in January. "When I announce, I want to devote full time to my candidacy."[26] While Emery sought to control the retail vote supply chain through small county chairmen, Curran wanted to replace Regan as the candidate of the big box bankers—county chairmen with major blocks of votes.

I intended to compete everywhere.

When Curran entered the race on May 18, he had little to offer in terms of message, organization, or personality. As Sam Roberts would write in the *Daily News*, "There's nothing flashy about Curran, from his Brooks Brothers and Burton Clothing

Ltd. pinstripes to the white handkerchief protruding from his pocket. No suspenders—red or otherwise. He does wear garters to keep his socks up."[27]

Despite Curran's praise of former governor Nelson Rockefeller, some of Rockefeller's inner circle went with Rosenbaum, and others with Emery. Despite Curran's assertion that money would not be a problem for his campaign, money would remain a problem. Furthermore, although Curran had substantial support from the New York, Nassau, and Erie County GOP organizations, his state-wide organization continued to struggle.

Former governor Malcolm Wilson appeared to be the driving force behind the Curran candidacy. Like Wilson, Curran had also once served in the State Assembly. Senate Majority Leader Warren Anderson, who would nominate Curran at the Republican State Convention, backed him a few days later in May. The establishment was joining ranks against me, even if they were divided.

I was ready for them. I was an outsider, an independent businessman. I wanted to change things. Both Rosenbaum and Emery were well liked among Republican Party leaders across the state, but there were lingering doubts about whether they had the resources to win, even among their loyal supporters. With Curran in the race, he, Rosey, and Jim split the old Rockefeller establishment wing three ways.

All four of the Republican candidates had the potential to get close to the magic 25 percent we would need at the Republican State Convention to avoid having to circulate petitions to get on a primary ballot. Until the convention, doubt would remain as to which candidate, including me, could reach that threshold.

UPSETTING THE CONVENTION

My goal was to win the 25 percent of the weighted votes of 402 delegates necessary to get into the Republican primary without the necessity to petition our way onto the ballot. We secured petitions anyway, to stir things up and get ourselves better known. The convention promised to be an unscripted event—and therefore very much out of character for the Republican Party in New York since Nelson Rockefeller's days.

Concerned that I might doom Republican chances by remaining on the ballot as a Conservative, some Republican county chairmen sought to impose a loyalty oath in early June. I responded: "I intend to support the winner of the Republican primary for governor. I fully expect to be that candidate."[28]

Emery and Rosenbaum's campaigns were based on their extensive contacts with Republican county leaders built up over the past decade—leaders who could deliver their delegations. Curran's campaign was built on trying to organize an influential set of Republican officials to deliver the nomination wholesale on the grounds that he represented the moderate middle of the electorate.

In contrast to these wholesale efforts, I had built a retail operation—much as I did with Rite Aid—patiently and repeatedly visiting upstate counties over a four-year period. I visited not only politicians and business leaders, but journalists and editorial boards. I was not a household name when the campaign began, but I was known by those who might eventually give me their support. And in many cases where I was not their first choice, I was their second. That turned out to be really important.

In early June Michael Kramer wrote that the Republican bosses "have declared Lehrman *persona non grata*. They don't control him, so they don't want him. Their candidate is Paul Curran, a colorless former U.S. attorney and longtime party stalwart whose main qualification for the job seems to be that he isn't Lehrman."[29] The major threat to my victory was a potential coalition of the Curran and Emery forces. To counteract the attempt to block me, my campaign released a list of thirteen Republican county chairs who had endorsed me—most from relatively rural counties upstate. That's when the farming came in handy. I had been in Syracuse for the State Fair, and I was the only one who could milk a cow. Here are the county chairs who endorsed me, to whom I am forever grateful:

Gerard Fitzpatrick, Cattaraugus County
Jane Westervelt, Columbia County
William Ames, Cortland County
Ethel Block, Dutchess County
James Traub, Madison County
Anthony Shaheen, Oneida County
Norman Rothschild, Onondaga County
William Sinnott, Rensselaer County
George Hart, Richmond County
James Foley, Saratoga County
Hyman Klionsky, Seneca County
Anthony Prudenti, Suffolk County
Rose Marie Gregory, Washington County

"All I wanted was the chance to compete in a Republican primary," I told the *Binghamton Evening Press*'s Steve Geimann. "I wanted the opportunity to show the Republican leaders, the Republican Party as a whole, that I could win a primary election."[30] Then on June 14—a day before the convention opened—a crucial piece of my convention math fell into place. Kings County Republicans led by Chairman Fred Panteleone endorsed me. Behind the scenes, my friends in the Conservative Party had been making phone calls to their Republican counterparts. Some of them knew and respected one another. With Brooklyn's support, I seemed assured of the 25 percent of the convention vote. I was still an outsider, but now one with an inside track to the nomination. I also continued to earn respect from the press. "Only rarely does a man of dignity step out from normal society with solid achievements behind him and speak with freshness and sagacity," wrote R. Emmett Tyrrell in the *Finger Lakes Times*:

> Such a candidate is right now campaigning for New York's gubernatorial nomination. Because of his singularity and because he is campaigning in one of the nation's showcase states—the state that has brought us such epoch makers as Roosevelt I and Roosevelt II—his campaign has national significance. He is Lewis Lehrman. . . .

> Balmy liberalism has quite obviously lost touch with ordinary Americans' yearnings for security from crime, inflation, and higher taxes. Lehrman is one of the few candidates who understands this, and he is among an even smaller minority of candidates who have something thoughtful to prescribe.[31]

That year, the convention was held at the Sheraton Hotel in New York City. When we arrived, my team was ready for action. A fundraising dance at the Roseland Ballroom was orchestrated by Diana Colgate, Leslie Horn, and Carla Saunders. We had the cast and the props—a red pickup to contrast my upstate support with Mayor Koch. Patsy Matzye and Marnie Pillsbury organized a rally that included an appearance by Uncle Sam. Our five children were media stars. With Louise, they were still my most important priorities.

Tim Carey and the Staten Island Republican chair George Hart helped direct our floor demonstration—which miraculously produced more tickets for supporters than had been authorized. Frank Trotta had cut the authorized ribbons in half. It was truly a team effort—one recognized by delegates and journalists alike. John Britton Sr. had used Lotus 123 to develop a program that allowed the campaign to track the voting. The program used both its own projections, and the actual voting, to project a final result—a technological "advance" that we made sure the press reported.

Andy Logan was covering the convention for the *New Yorker*:

> The song that Lehrman chose for his supporters to march to at the Sheraton Centre was the one from "Applause" that urges all hands to step to the rear and let a winner lead the way—a reminder that the Republicans lost the last two gubernatorial races to Hugh Carey. Lehrman not only chose this message for his supporters to march to but, coatless and wearing bright-red suspenders, which he had flaunted as a kind of trademark throughout the convention, broke with precedent by joining the parade that celebrated his superior qualifications for the nomination.[32]

My only dispute with Andy's report is that I did not *flaunt* my suspenders, having worn them at home and at work for years. Louise used to buy them for me at L.L. Bean.

Convention drama ensued. Emery was plagued by rumors he fueled that he would drop out of gubernatorial contention to run for Senate or other office. The *Times* wrote "the rumors of possible rearrangements were a sign of how things had changed. Until four years ago, Republicans played follow-the-leader [namely Rockefeller] when they picked their state ticket. But leaders will not be in control of this meeting."[33]

George Clark tried to reduce the number of gubernatorial candidates in order to allow for a more clear-cut decision by the convention. On the first ballot, I led with 26 percent of the delegates—but Emery and Curran also qualified with the necessary 25 percent to get on a primary ballot without needing to circulate a petition for signatures. Rosenbaum fell about five points short of that goal. No candidate was close to the 50 percent needed for an endorsement. The following hours were a complex round of strategizing, negotiations, threats, and rumors. Key meetings took place in crowded hotel room bathrooms. Some of my supporters shifted to Rosenbaum on a second ballot to help him qualify, but the second ballot showed little change in the candidates, and Rosenbaum soon dropped out of the race.

Curran had meanwhile endorsed cosmetics heir Ronald Lauder for lieutenant governor. I called Lauder and asked to visit him. I took a taxi to his apartment that very day to explain why he did not want to get involved. I wanted him to feel uncomfortable. Lauder's money might have helped make Curran a more credible candidate—even though candidates for governor and lieutenant governor run separately in a primary. The two run as a ticket only in the general election. Lauder never officially entered the race.

A negotiation conducted in a hotel kitchen storeroom proved to be the turning point. As Tim Carey recalled: "Frank Trotta set up a meeting with Westchester County Republican Party Chairman Tony Colavita in an empty kitchen off the convention floor. Westchester County Republican Vice Chairwoman Margaret Soter told Tony she didn't care what he threatened her with, 'She was voting for Lew' and she did."[34] The entire delegation of Westchester County—where both Curran and former governor Malcolm Wilson lived—switched behind me.

Curran supporters made a key tactical error that would doom his candidacy. After trying to add Lauder to their ticket for lieutenant governor, they tried to block Emery from getting that post. The order of nominations then changed. Many Republicans had been suggested as possible candidates for lieutenant governor—including Suffolk

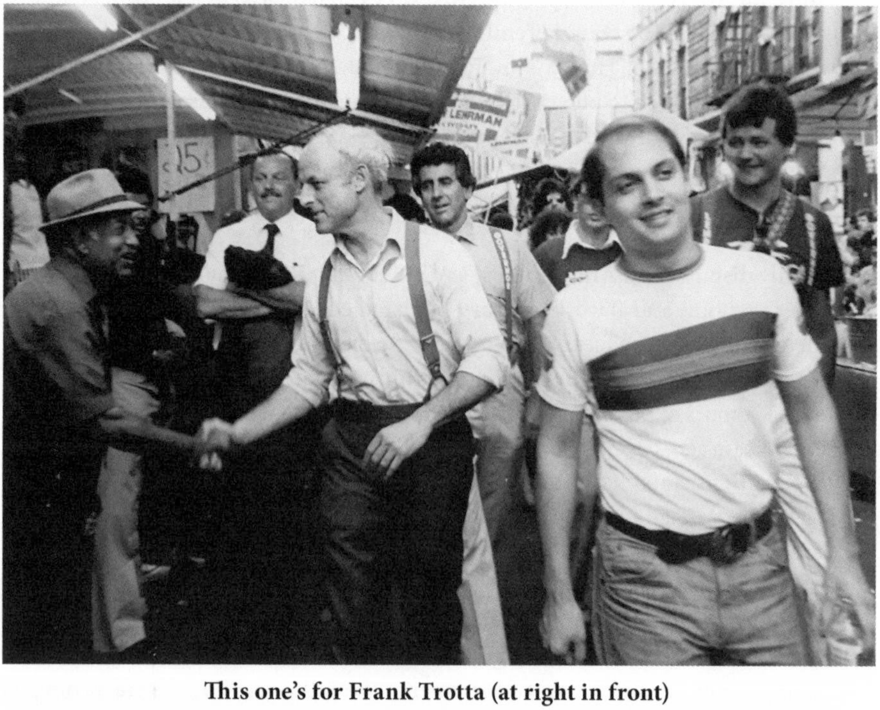

This one's for Frank Trotta (at right in front)

County Executive Peter Cohalan and Erie County Comptroller Alfreda Slominski, but most had attracted only local support.

Jim Emery, on the other hand, had a network of support throughout New York. His candidacy was important for me. He had tied up a key block of Republican delegates who might otherwise have moved to Curran or Rosenbaum. Just then, the convention vote for governor was interrupted by a motion calling on Emery to accept the Republican nomination for lieutenant governor. "We want Jim, we want Jim," chanted delegates. I announced I would "be proud to campaign"[35] with Emery. Convention delegates steamrolled the Curran forces, and Emery was *nominated by acclamation in the middle of the gubernatorial balloting.* With Emery and Rosenbaum having gracefully bowed out, the stage was set for a shocking turn of political events. We had planned for many eventualities—except for overwhelming victory.

CONSOLIDATING THE REPUBLICAN PARTY

The day after the convention, I sat next to President Reagan at a fundraising event in Manhattan. The *New York Post* featured a front-page photo of us convulsed in laughter with the headline, "That's a good one, Lew!" Not bad for a candidate about whom a prominent Republican consultant had said in February: "He is the fourth-place candidate, and I don't see how he gets much farther than that between now and June."

At the Conservative Party Convention in Colonie on June 19, Louise and our children made another star appearance. Curran was not even nominated—because he did not have the 25 percent support necessary to get on the primary ballot, much less the votes of the executive committee whose permission was also needed to run in a primary.

My previous opponents progressively fell into line behind my candidacy in early July. Albany County GOP leader George Scaringe and Ulster County leader Peter Savago quit the Curran campaign to support me.

In Buffalo, I was endorsed by Congressman Kemp, County Executive Ed Rutkowski, and Erie County Chairman Victor N. Farley. "I never believed Christmas would come before July 4, but it happened today in Buffalo," I declared. "Today we stand together. Our goal is victory in November."[36]

Asked about his switch, Farley "cited St. Paul. When he was on horseback, lightning struck him, and he had a change of view."[37] Curran's stumbling campaign and lack of finances helped generate this kind of lightning. On July 23, George Clark abandoned his neutrality and endorsed my candidacy.

On July 8, Jim Emery endorsed me at a press conference at the Roosevelt Hotel. Jim declared: "Lew and I share a vision of a strong New York; with an economic system based on the tenets of free enterprise, a penal system based on the swift but fair administration of justice, and a tax and spending policy that is conservative, yet compassionate."[38] Afterwards, the "unified Republican ticket" embarked together on a tour of upstate New York. Treating my pre-convention opponents with respect had paid off. The *Rochester Democrat and Chronicle*'s Michael Clements would point out, "indeed, an alliance forged between Emery and Lehrman during the convention

The *New York Post* ran a similar photograph of President Reagan and me on June 18, 1982, with the headline "That's a good one, Lew."

seems to be working well. While Lehrman has handled the major cities like New York, Buffalo and Albany, Emery has covered the less-populous, 'B-circuit' places like Lockport and Rome."[39]

"I've always held to the desire to have a primary," I told reporters at an Albany press conference on July 9. "A primary is one of the best ways to energize a party. The Democrats have proven that to be the case."[40] In Marc Humbert's account of events he quoted me, "'I welcome a primary,' said the former president of the Rite Aid drugstore empire. 'That kind of competition produces really strong athletic teams and produces strong business enterprises. And I believe it will produce a stronger Republican party'. . . . In fact, Lehrman seemed to be doing his best Friday not to criticize Curran too much. Asked about some of Curran's attacks on his background and lack of political experience, Lehrman soft-pedaled his way by the question. 'In politics one is free to do as one pleases and each person will be responsible for his own conduct,' [Lehrman] said."[41] I was in the middle of the primary I had already expected—but I was also trying to unify the party sooner than expected. "Granddaddy always said don't knock the competition,"[42] I told a reporter.

Curran was very lawyerly. He was stuck on the idea that he had experience as a US attorney. That was not a compelling credential on its own. His underfunded and undermanned campaign never established a rationale for his candidacy. Instead, Curran carped relentlessly about my "credibility." His issues had little traction, and so did Curran's campaign.

At the *New York Post* debate on August 3, I moved from defense to offense. Ray Herman noted the change in his articles for the *Buffalo Courier Express*:

> The morning of the debate, Lehrman arrived early. After three days of prepping with his staff, the candidate appeared serenely confident as he table-hopped during the breakfast hosted by the *Post*, greeting friends and foes alike with a luminous affability. True to his game plan, Lehrman, employing the somber tone of an Old Testament prophet, ticked off a cavalcade of murder, rape and robbery statistics for New York as he called on the courts to come down hard on violent criminals instead of continually "questioning the testimony of police officers."[43]

At a debate on August 20 sponsored by the *Buffalo Evening News*, I took off the gloves. "Paul Curran traded his own U.S. Attorney's legacy for the support of Joe Margiotta by writing a letter to try and influence the judge,"[44] I declared, hitting him in the soft spot of his alliance with the convicted Nassau leader. Ray Herman reported: "Lehrman and Curran really don't like one another, a point which was underscored in the debate. In the two or three minutes prior to airtime, the debaters and panelists were asked to remain seated. Lehrman and Curran exchanged no banter. There was palpable tension."[45]

The real focus of the campaign was defining my candidacy in opposition to business as usual in Albany. I opposed unneeded public works projects and overstaffing at state facilities. I said of Koch and Cuomo: "It is the difference between Tweedle-dee and Tweedle-dum. It's the difference between two big city Democrats who favor tax, tax, tax, and spend, spend, spend. I'll be happy to compete with either or both of them."[46]

Curran's campaign was running out of ideas and running out of money. I had plenty of both—along with plenty of energy and growing recognition. Our campaign commercials continued to have an impact—driving up my name recognition in all sections of the state and among all ages of New Yorkers. The most talked-about commercial—called "Outtakes"—would not air until October. I was sitting on a stool, jacket off, explaining my tax reform proposal. I flubbed the script, but the camera kept rolling as I laughed: "That one blew me right off the chair. Holy mackerel! Too much energy."[47] Then the camera pulled back to reveal that the segment was on a TV monitor. I spoke to the camera with the monitor in the background: "Hey, I make some mistakes, even taping my commercials. I'll make some mistakes as governor. . . ."[48]

The commercials seemed to be making the impact we had hoped for. "It's no longer Lew who? Now the voters recognize Lewis E. Lehrman as a candidate for governor,"[49] noted George Borrelli:

> Mr. Lehrman, a multimillionaire who has the endorsement of the Republican and Conservative parties, is stopped on the sidewalks, in restaurants and even on the highways by well-wishers and voters who are attracted to his candidacy.

> He was carrying his suit jacket and wearing a blue shirt and conservative tie, along with his trademark, red suspenders, when he left his Park Avenue apartment early Thursday for another full day of campaigning.
>
> A middle-aged woman stopped him to wish him luck as he entered a car that would take him to Westchester County for a series of quick-paced interviews and speaking engagements.
>
> After a radio interview, the car carrying Mr. Lehrman and his party was stopped at a State Police checkpoint just outside Peekskill.
>
> "Pull over," a trooper ordered Mr. Lehrman's driver after noticing the car's registration sticker had expired.
>
> Mr. Lehrman bounded out of the car, trotted over to the cadre of troopers manning the checkpoint, introduced himself and was back in the auto within a matter of seconds, cleared to continue his trip.[50]

That encounter, as captured in Borrelli's article, was one of the high points in my campaign. In truth, I had lots of experience with troopers from a life on the road.

SEALING THE DEAL

With polls predicting an overwhelming victory over Curran in the Republican primary, I tried to shift my focus to Ed Koch, the expected winner of the Democratic primary. Just two days before the election, I admitted: "Make no mistake—we're running against Koch right now."[51]

On September 23, both parties held gubernatorial primaries. As expected, I defeated Paul Curran by a 4–1 margin. *New York Times* reporter Maurice Carroll highlighted the significance of the event for Republicans. "That Mr. Lehrman, a newcomer with more foes than friends among the party's leaders, has won the Republican nomination on the strength of a television blitz aimed right at the voters calls into question the effectiveness and very meaning of the party organization."[52] Kevin McCoy did a great job capturing the flair of our victory celebration in a piece for the *Journal News*:

> Tim Carey impatiently barked out a command telling the band in Lewis E. Lehrman's Sheraton Hotel headquarters to resume playing. Carey . . . then turned his attention to campaign security personnel, organizing them in a double line flanking an aisle leading from a corner doorway to the balloon adorned podium. A moment later, holding his hands aloft, alternately as clenched fists or in victory signs—Lehrman, now the Republican gubernatorial candidate, strode proudly down the aisle, hitting his pre-arranged entrance time on the mark.[53]

I was proud of our team and our "military-like efficiency and precision," which McCoy declared was "a key to Lehrman's role in helping build a small family business into the sprawling Rite Aid Corp. pharmaceutical empire. [It] was symbolic of the millionaire businessman's campaign and his plans for the state government."[54] But

I knew we needed to stay humble in the face of the two million Democratic voter registrations. The day after the September 23 primary, former state attorney general Louis J. Lefkowitz, who had backed Curran, campaigned with me at a Manhattan subway stop. The general election campaign was underway.

Unexpectedly, Mario Cuomo had defeated Ed Koch, 52 to 48 percent, for the Democratic nomination. Cuomo's victory shocked New York. Koch had advantages in name recognition and fundraising (more than twice that of Cuomo), but even in his very own New York City he only received four thousand more votes than his opponent. Cuomo's running mate was fellow Italian-American Alfred DelBello. They were not the best of friends, but they brought the Liberal and the Democratic Party together. Governor Carey, who had backed Koch over his own lieutenant governor in the primary, finally gave Cuomo his support.

The New York Times Magazine
OCTOBER 31, 1982/SECTION 6
A NATIONAL TEST IN NEW YORK
The New Right
vs.
The Old Liberalism
Republican gubernatorial candidate Lewis Lehrman, left, and his Democratic opponent, Mario Cuomo.

Mario and I

CHAPTER 9

Running the Race

The general election campaign was extraordinarily short—just forty-four days—after the long and brutal primary. Our campaign contrasted the abstract goals of politics-as-usual with a serious champion of political reform. The world took note. As the *Economist* of Great Britain reported in July 1982, "Lehrman has run a clever campaign so far, making the most of his experience as a corporate executive who will bring efficiency into government, and displaying contempt for professional politicians whom he blames for New York's economic difficulties."[1]

DEBATING MARIO

Mario complained in his book *Diaries of Mario M. Cuomo* that the Lehrman campaign avoided debates, whereas it was just the opposite. The first proposed debate—on *This Week with David Brinkley*—was turned down by Cuomo's campaign and accepted by the Lehrman campaign. Although Mario was an excellent debater, I was often able to knock him off balance. In the *Daily News* debate, I took aim at Mario's tendency to avoid specifics, saying "My opponent has a very point-blank approach to the issues. Every time you point to the issues, his mind goes blank."[2] Although Mario had good reason to worry about my rhetorical skills, reporters often enjoyed them. Richard Wolf reported one of my quips for Westchester County's *Journal News:* "Confronted in Syracuse Tuesday with the heretical question, 'Would you fly on a plane where the pilot has no experience?' Lehrman shot back, 'Would you fly on an airplane where the pilot has crashed?' The remark brought the partisan house down."[3] Cuomo's designated debate negotiator was his son, Andrew Cuomo, who bickered at length with my debate advisor, John Buckley about debate formats. He even threatened that Mario would not show up for the *New York Post* debate if there were prepared opening and closing statements.

John recalled that "the night before the breakfast debate, Roger Wood of the *Post* had Andrew and me do a walk-through of the debate logistics and staging at the Sheraton. And the whole time we were there, Andrew—complaining about how the *Post* was in the bag for Lehrman—insisted he didn't know if Mario would be well enough to show the next day. He claimed he'd been felled by the flu, and maybe, possibly, he could pull himself off his death bed, but we shouldn't count on it. It was all BS—he just wanted to get us off-balance wondering if the debate would proceed. It didn't work. But it was a remarkable bit of political theater by a future Governor."[4]

At the *New York Post* debate

When the *New York Post* debate began on October 8 at the Sheraton Centre, the moderators soon abandoned their roles controlling the debate. Mario Cuomo took full advantage of the situation. He was determined to get in his talking points—the rules of the debate be damned. It was, all acknowledged, a lively affair from the very start, when the predetermined length of two-minute opening statements was ignored by Cuomo. I like to know the rules and follow them. Mario knew the rules but was intent on breaking them to talk as long as he desired. He confessed as much in his diaries, writing "I am going to make the most of this. I can't match him in 30-second commercials. This is my shot today."[5]

Reaganomics and wealth were Cuomo's target. Tiring of his filibustering, I looked at my watch. Cuomo thought he saw an opening: "That's a very expensive watch, Lew."[6] Of all Mario's comments that morning, that was perhaps the one best remembered—but even journalists thought it was a soundbite too far. I got in my shots. "It won't take me the ten minutes it takes my opponent for each of his answers,"[7] I said after one of Mario's monologues.

Mario also acknowledged in his diary that his approach that day was too harsh and too hot—a judgment confirmed by many analysts. Veteran liberal columnist Murray Kempton wrote "The high scorn that Cuomo brought to his treatment of Lehrman yesterday suggested that he may be at peril of traveling the same route [as Mayor Ed Koch, and becoming a bully]." Kempton went on to say "It is just possible that, during the next 25 days, by mere stubbornness, Lehrman may come to seem to us the idealistic, beleaguered amateur bullied by the professional."[8]

AT THE FINISH LINE

On the final weekend of the campaign, I crisscrossed the state in an energetic appeal for the votes we needed to win. Our campaign chartered a fifty-seat turbo-jet to carry the members of the Republican ticket and our families around New York.

"Unlike most campaigns, which wind down the weekend before the election," wrote George Borrelli, "Lehrman's rolled on relentlessly, even as voters went to the polls. His TV and radio commercials saturated the airwaves on Sunday and Monday before the election and on Election Day. In addition, millions of pieces of literature from the Lehrman campaign, some of them second and third mailings, arrived at the homes of voters just before the election. It was the most massive use of the electronic media and the mail by a candidate in the history of New York State politics."[9]

In those final days before the election, as I flew throughout the state rallying voters, Andy Logan reported on my strategy. Two years prior, the United States hockey team had come from behind to beat the heavily favored Soviet Union in what has come to be known the "Miracle on Ice." Remembering the classic confrontation, I "urged the crowds at each stop to remember the words of Herb Brooks, the legendary coach of the 1980 American Olympic championship hockey team: 'This is your moment. You were born to play this game. Victory will be yours.'"[10]

John Buckley, who had faithfully accompanied me on airplanes around New York State for ten months, and jogged with me around high school tracks when time allowed, recalled: "I remember driving into the city with you and Louise, on the final car ride home from Teterboro. The two of you were like young lovebirds, so happy the campaign was over, knowing you had done your best. Manhattan sparkled with light and the evening was crisp. There was an air of finality to the slog and joy of the campaign, and we were on the cusp of something . . . new and exciting."[11]

COUNTING THE VOTES

The weather was gorgeous and turnout was heavy on Election Day. In Queens, Mario Cuomo was getting very nervous, according to *Daily News* columnist Jimmy Breslin, who spent the day with him. Cuomo had discussed the consequences of a possible defeat, even with his wife.

But the news I was receiving election night was not good. Mario was going to win even though the early returns from upstate New York put me on top. Nevertheless, it seemed foolish to concede while the posted totals showed me ahead. We had compiled signatures for a third ballot position —the Statewide Independent Party—and we were uncertain as to whether these third-party votes had been counted in the totals reported. The author of the strategy, Adam Walinsky, had apparently engaged in some freelancing on election night—without any authorization—that effectively delayed my decision to concede, and had repercussions in the press and party. "For agonizing hours," John Omicinski wrote, "it seemed that Lehrman could pull off one of the biggest shockers in New York political annals. But his long run, which started way back in January, fell inches short at the wire. Over the weekend Lehrman stumped the state insisting it was a 'neck-and-neck' race, and he proved it wasn't campaign talk. In the space of less than a week, he turned around a lead of 10 points or more which pollsters gave to Cuomo."[12] Because of the late hour, I sent my supporters home and prepared to concede the following day when it would be clear that although I had won fifty-five of the sixty-two counties in New York, Cuomo's margin in New York City had brought him victory. The final vote tally as recorded by history was Cuomo, 2,675,213 to Lehrman, 2,494,827, or 50.9 to 47.5 percent.

The next morning, I called Mario to congratulate him and then prepared for an early afternoon press conference at the New York Sheraton. Accompanied by Louise, State Republican Chairman George Clark, State Conservative Chairman Dan Mahoney, and running mate Jim Emery, I announced: "Congratulations to Mario Cuomo. He ran an outstanding race. We were beaten not for the lack of trying but because we met a worthy opponent."[13]

Mario "won a marvelous victory in the primary and earned his victory in the general election. . . . I've always believed that in a contest of any sort, the competition always determines the quality of the game. Mario was a worthy opponent, a strong opponent, a man of ideas. As I began this campaign as a campaign of ideas, so we were able to finish it as a campaign of ideas. We played as close to errorless ball as we could. We hit singles and doubles, but my opponent hit a home run. . . . As Louise said to me, we didn't lose. We came in second."[14]

John Omicinski was kind to call my concession "composed and gracious." He went on to observe that:

> After expending a king's ransom and a great deal of energy, he took the first major loss of his 44-year-life with aplomb and class. After months of appearing stiff and reserved, he also demonstrated that he has a funny bone. He revealed that he had a "secret plan" for winning the election. He was going to go on radio and television, he said, on Election Day and tell New Yorkers that if they didn't vote for him, he'd continue to run his television commercials for three more years.

Beth Fallon was also touched, and mused that:

> It's not often that a loser is as cheery as Lehrman, for as a wise old pol once told me, "In a car crash or an election, an inch is a good as a mile. Either you hit the thing or you don't." Nonetheless, Lehrman has plenty to be cheery about. He came within 165,000 votes of the governor's mansion, out of more than 5 million cast, on his very first try for public office. He is only 44 years old. He reinforced the Conservative Party's dominant role recently in choosing Republican candidates [and he] established a highly efficient organization, which will remain in place. . . .
>
> It is rare that the loser of an election remains as interesting, or almost so, as the winner. But so it was and is for Lewis Lehrman this week, and in the weeks to come. While the old, moderate-to-liberal Republican state leadership profoundly wishes that Lehrman would disappear, it was clear at his concession press conference on Wednesday that he has no intention of doing so. For a loser, Lehrman was positively buoyant. At times, I thought I must have wandered into the wrong press conference.[15]

From the point of view of the future, I had re-established the Republican Party on a conservative basis, something which was widely recognized by the 1990s. In fact, I established this trend throughout the Northeast. I even won a few votes in Canada and Quebec, just like Rockefeller.[16]

The closeness of the election was disappointing. "If we had another two or three days, I think we would have taken it," Conservative leader Serf Maltese told *Newsday*'s Dick Zander. Referring to the unseasonably warm and sunny election day, Serf said: "We could have used rain in the city, maybe a little hurricane or two."[17] The Cuomo majority was eventually tallied at 180,386 votes. There was a 1.2 million voter Democratic registration advantage. It was just too large a gap to overcome.

I may have conceded, but as the *New York Times* noted at the end of my concession speech: "he planned to keep some of his campaign staff together as a 'loyal opposition' that would continue to expound his views, particularly on the need for sharp tax cuts to generate jobs. 'We shall be observing,' he said. 'We shall be commenting on the conduct of the administration.' Mr. Lehrman said he 'positively' planned to run again for office, but he said he did not know now what office he would seek."[18]

FOLLOWING UP ON THE RESULTS

There was recognition that *had I won*, New York State politics would have been transformed. Maurice Carroll had penned a *New York Times* profile at the end of October, writing "A Lehrman victory would, in fact, turn politics and government in New York State upside down. A Lehrman win on Tuesday would change dramatically the character of New York State Republicanism. Following the election of conservative Senator Alphonse M. D'Amato in 1980, it would represent the final demise of the liberal Republicanism that has lingered on after the death of Nelson A. Rockefeller in 1979. It would also confirm a major role for the Conservative Party, whose programs and objectives would have to be incorporated into the Republican legislative agenda."[19]

The *Washingtonian* magazine concluded that I was the "biggest winner who lost," saying that "Lew Lehrman of New York gave Governor-elect Mario Cuomo a real scare and in the process became a force in the Republican party."[20] Even for conservatives, my narrow loss seemed to carry instructive lessons. The noted *Washington Post* author, Bob Novak, defied conventional opinion by praising the losing gubernatorial campaigns that I and Richard Headlee of Michigan had waged. "While the President was urging Americans to stay the course," Novak wrote, "Lehrman and Headlee took a hard right-populist turn: cut taxes to induce prosperity."[21]

New York Republican leaders like George Clark were less kind than the journalists. Two years after my loss, he argued that I lost because I had not catered to Warren Anderson, John Marchi, and Ned Regan. "He was too intent on being his own person," Clark opined, "removed from government and politics. He was the outsider running against the establishment, even though it was a Republican establishment: That turned a lot of [Republican officials] off."

Clark did, however, have the gumption to add: "He feels that nobody can do it better—and he may be right."[22]

I had lost but was not forgotten. A decade later, Richard Vigilante wrote in *Newsday*: "Lew Lehrman, who 10 years ago came within a whisker of saving us from 12 years of Mario Cuomo, gave a speech a few days ago that reminded me what a big mistake we made. Lehrman is the class act of the New York Republican party: as articulate as Cuomo, more intellectually honest, with a clear vision of what's wrong with government here and why." Vigilante argued that I was right that New York had "too little politics. Albany is occupied not by Democrats or Republicans but by cozy incumbacrats, who defer to the same interest groups and value reelection above all. Voters cannot make choices because they are not offered any."[23]

FIGURING OUT THE FUTURE

At the time, I had not lost my taste for politics. In the aftermath of the election, I kept my core team together to assess what I should do next. There were those like Richard Viguerie who were disappointed in Reagan's first year and wanted me to consider a presidential race. Seeing what I had accomplished in New York and fearing what I might accomplish in a national campaign, the Reagan White House sought ways to keep me occupied.

Many people saw a future for me. What that future was remained unclear. The assumption, however, was that whatever I started, I would finish. The conventional wisdom was that I was mobilizing for a return match with Governor Cuomo. I formed two political action committees—The Committee to Make New York #1 and the Fund to Keep America #1—but they had no staff and only limited funds to distribute to campaigns.

Eventually I resolved never to run for governor again because of the shadow it might cast over the future of my children. I no longer kept the personal interactions with the grassroots that fuel a genuine candidacy. Although I ruled out another race for statewide office, I did roil the political waters on occasion.

My name was mentioned for a rematch with Cuomo in 1986 until I took myself out of contention in November 1985. By then I had taken a job with Morgan Stanley. In 1988 I was considered a possible opponent to Senator Moynihan, but by then I was a managing director with partnership status at the firm. I knew Pat on a first name basis and thought him a bit of a bully and a comedian. I let the rumors fly because I wanted to scare him a little, and shake up his reputation as a consensus player. He had suggested that he could, like Benjamin Disraeli, "dish the Whigs," by which he meant that he would use liberal positions on social policies to offset conservative economics as a way to win elections. I knew him pretty well, had tried to advise him without success, and from my point of view, Moynihan was a phony and a prestige monger. I had no interest in making things easy for him.

Still, after the 1982 election, I slowly began turning my back on elective politics and devoted myself to family, business, and writing. If I had learned nothing else from the gubernatorial race, one thing was absolutely clear: Such a campaign cannot be waged without total commitment.

I wanted to play football with my family and friends.

I think all the kids learned by the example I set—even while watching their father campaign and lose. Specifically, they learned a lesson in manners from what newspaper writers called my gracious speech in defeat.

"Dad's race for the governorship of New York in 1982 had the greatest impact on me," recalled Eliza.

> He ran for an office that he knew would be a very tough win, but he believed so deeply in what he knew to be the right next choices for New York. So, he grabbed his bayonet and charged the front line. He made a tremendous effort, took a big risk and with no reservation, committed to his passionate drive. He stayed committed to the drive because he was committed to bringing the best ideas and changes to a people and a state he had grown to love. The accomplishment was the commitment to doing good things and helping to change lives for the better. I learned that you may not accomplish your original goal, so the actual accomplishment becomes the kind of effort made and the honor behind the drive itself. I believe his tenacity and commitment to helping the people of NY was the accomplishment; and while I was only 8 years old, from that point on, I knew my father was a great and honorable man. [24]

REFLECTIONS ON CHALLENGING MARIO CUOMO

For six intense weeks in 1982, Mario Cuomo and I had contested the leadership of New York. Mario and I were a study in contrasts—which made us good copy for journalists. The *New York Times* had begun its endorsement of Cuomo:

> Lewis Lehrman, the Republican from nowhere, draws inspiration from a French economist. Mario Cuomo, the Democratic Lieutenant Governor, explicates medieval philosophers. In a political world often marked by botched sentences, both speak in complete paragraphs. They may be the best-read gubernatorial candidates ever.
>
> But that's where the similarity ends. Mr. Lehrman has a vision. Take the handcuffs off the police—and also off business, he says, with a cold light in his eye. He offers no assurance that he knows how to get from here to there.
>
> Mr. Cuomo, who does know how to turn goals into action in Albany, offers little in the way of goals. But his view of the duty of government—to help those who need it most—is warmer. We share that view, and urge his election.[25]

When I saw Governor-Elect Cuomo at the restaurant in Manhattan called 21, a couple of his companions acknowledged how terrified they had been that I would surpass Mario. Confirming these remarks, Cuomo told me that he really did think he would lose in those last days of the campaign, so fast were we taking the lead. He congratulated me on a "supersonic campaign." One of his aides even said that with two more days, Mario would have lost.

For some reporters, even those not inclined to support my ideas, the campaign provided a model for the spirited intellectual contest of ideas. In May 2000, liberal *Washington Post* columnist E. J. Dionne, who had covered the 1982 campaign for the *New York Times*, wrote:

> The best election campaign in New York's recent history was about issues, not outsized personalities. It cast an unabashed supply-side conservative against a liberal who called himself a "progressive pragmatist."
>
> The conservative Republican said he would cut spending and be tough on crime—thus establishing "a limited government state that is strong enough to protect 'free people.'" The liberal Democrat defended the "charitable" state. "The purpose of government," he said, "is to make love real in a sinful world." Voters appreciated the clarity of the choice, and gave both candidates exceptionally high approval ratings. There are worse things for politicians to do than argue about issues. The election was the 1982 contest for governor between Republican Lew Lehrman and Democrat Mario Cuomo, who won narrowly.[26]

A few days before the election, I told a reporter that "No one promised me success. It's been prayers and hard work from the beginning. I feel we've done the very best we can, and that we're going to win."[27] Ultimately, I failed in my race with Mario. I may not have been ready for the challenge—despite how close to victory I came. I would expound on the differences at the heart of the campaign in a 1985 interview:

> I think the campaign of 1982 was much less a campaign of personalities than it was a struggle between two points of view. Mario is probably the best exponent of the old Liberalism—of a militant secular liberalism. He makes that school of thought as interesting as it can be. My campaign was for a restoration and a reformation of the social and economic institutions of New York and, by the logic of public policy, also for our country. I campaigned on the application of the objective moral code to crime and punishment.[28]

My campaign had been a high-risk effort. We went all out but fell short of the goal. In retrospect, I was perhaps too young. I might have been better off to have achieved all my other objectives before entering politics. Nevertheless, one final story from long after the campaign illustrates a most important principle that we were able to uphold.

My friend the historian Harold Holzer sent me this tale. He had spent many years working for Governor Cuomo, and so was the only person in a position to orchestrate this event. Harold described the situation as:

> an interesting "reunion" I helped arrange in the late 1990s. The New-York Historical Society, with Lew's support, was to exhibit an early printed copy of Abraham Lincoln's immortal Second Inaugural Address. Organizers asked

me to write the gallery notes, and wondered if I could get my onetime boss and longtime friend, former Governor Mario Cuomo, to collaborate. (We [he and Mario] had co-edited the 1994 book, *Lincoln on Democracy.*) Of course, Mario had run against Lew for Governor back in 1982, a close, tough race remembered for one of Cuomo's rare slip-ups in debate: watching Lew gesture during one response, Cuomo glanced at his opponent's timepiece and cracked: "Nice watch, Lew!" It was an attempt to mark Lew as an opulently rich man, but it backfired; Cuomo endured so much flak for being too glib and too personal.

So years later, here we are at the opening event at New-York Historical. Mario and Lew both attend. I decide it's on me to bring both of them together at least for a conciliatory handshake, for they have not spoken since the 1982 campaign. I ask Lew if I can bring him over to greet the former Governor. Ever-obliging, he agrees. "Governor," I say, "look who's here to say hello." Cuomo glances up, aware that Lew has helped fund this project, and the two men shake hands. Lew says, "Good to see you, Governor."

"Happy to see you, Lew" comes the reply. Here is a classic moment of bipartisan coalescence around Lincoln, made possible by a man who is very decidedly *not* a sore loser. But dear Mario cannot help himself when it comes to the last word. As Lew extends his arm for the handshake, revealing his wrist as his shirt cuffs recede, Cuomo smiles: "It's still a nice watch, Lew." And the two dissolve in laughter next to a vitrine holding the "malice toward none" words of Lincoln.[29]

WEARING SUSPENDERS

All through the campaign, I literally ran hard—often in running shorts and a T-shirt, and sometimes without a shirt in the summer heat. Those jogging pictures were a staple of press coverage—and contrasted nicely with my more formal attire—suspenders. The suspenders, however, were what I was wearing when my family toured the State Fair in Syracuse in late August—when I was photographed milking a cow.

The day before, I had spent the night at the farm of Esther and Gerald Twentyman in Homer. The *Cortland Standard*'s Mark James reported: "It was just another quiet evening around the dinner table in the classic old farmhouse off Route 11—almost. A guest in red suspenders is settling down from a long trip, sitting quietly after dessert, while the children run in and out."

"I wear them to keep my pants up," I repeatedly explained to whomever asked. Democrats and reporters might ignore me. But no one could ignore my red suspenders. Some thought them a gimmick. Some thought them outlandish. But they quickly became part of my political brand. I had first started wearing suspenders when my weight fluctuated during the mid-1960s. Louise presented me with a pair in 1965—the year before we married. I grew accustomed to wearing them. I also needed them when training for the marathon, when my weight again plunged.

Noted conservative journalist and friend R. Emmett Tyrrell offered advice in the early days leading up to the campaign, "I remember one time having Lew to breakfast at the New York Athletic Club and doing a critique of his approaching race for the governorship. I remember telling him that the power of the press in politics is overwhelming. I pointed to his trademark red suspenders and told him no matter how clever the trademark was it was the press that would decide if they were chic, clever, or they stood for anything of substance. It turned out the press did not think them in bad taste as I recall. Red suspenders in his race stood for something that mattered," Tyrrell said. "Even the media agreed."

Journalists looking for "color" when writing campaign profiles found the suspenders a useful foil and focus. "I'm a jogger, so I lose weight when I run, usually in the summer. This way I don't have to keep paying to have my pants taken in," I explained to the Associated Press in January 1982.[30] Hardly a profile would be written for the rest of the campaign without mention of my suspenders, which came inadvertently to represent my disdain for politics as usual. One of those profiles made the connection explicit, writing "As for those red suspenders, his friends and handlers insisted that he stash them for the duration of the campaign and find a more conventional replacement, such as a belt. He resisted. He is, in short, independent."[31]

As long as others were going to weave a narrative around my clothes, I made an occasional attempt to weave my own. Delivering the commencement address at Eisenhower College in 1982, I warned: "You have to watch how you dress, too. It's hard to believe, but there are people in this world who don't like red suspenders."[32]

The suspenders became a campaign symbol. Lew '82 suspenders replaced hats and T-shirts as my customary attire. The suspenders—and reporters' questions about them—became a staple of the campaign. They became part of the language of Lew '82.

I was not an experienced politician, but I *did* know how to expose my political assets. In the middle of my speech on primary night in September 1982, I took off my jacket. As Lisa McCormack wrote, at the sight of my suspenders, "The large crowd went wild and began chanting, 'We want Lew.' Flamboyance, energy and polish are communicated in the 10 seconds it takes him to shed the jacket of a perfectly tailored black pinstriped suit, revealing bright red L.L. Bean suspenders, roll up his shirt sleeves and announce that he just came back from his daily six-mile run."[33]

After the campaign, the *Buffalo Evening News* arts critic, Jeff Simon, wrote favorably about the "incredibly savvy TV image of Lehrman in his commercials—a youngish, vigorous guy who was always photographed without a jacket and wearing red suspenders. It was the red suspenders that did it. So help me, they probably added a half a million to his vote total."[34]

Inadvertently, I believe I contributed to a sartorial trend—perhaps the only one in which I have ever participated. Paul Winston of Winston Tailors argued in June 2016 that "In 1982 Lewis Lehrman ran for governor of NY. He was pictured in all his campaign ads wearing red suspenders and no jacket. It became the rage in NYC—many young attorneys and bankers began wearing suspenders with jackets off in the office."[35]

Can you believe it?

CHAPTER 10

Citizens for America

THE LONG JOURNEY TO CONSERVATISM

Even though he died when I was seven, Franklin D. Roosevelt had a strong influence on me. My social attitudes were influenced by the effect Roosevelt had upon my family. We were Republicans, but we were much impressed by him as a leader. Nevertheless, as I matured, I realized that his political solutions were tailored to a particular stage of the economic cycle, and were counterproductive—and could be dangerous to freedom—except during deep depressions.

In September 1981, I wrote an op-ed for *USA Today*, writing that "The old public philosophy, born during the 1930s, had begun to tire during the 1960s and was exhausted in the late 1970s. For two generations, our nation had been governed by a world view and public institutions which originated during the worst period in our nation's economic history, the Great Depression. I think it is fair to say that Franklin D. Roosevelt's New Deal was a profound American social and legislative response to the catastrophe of unemployment and deflation. Out of the suffering of the 1930s came the Roosevelt coalition which gave us a set of liberal, big government, social-democratic values which have endured almost to this very day."[1]

As a student at Yale, I would meet FDR's widow. I was doing a paper on World War II and wanted to interview Mrs. Roosevelt about her ideas. She had her own constituency, separate from her husband's. Smarter than her husband, and a more astute liberal, Eleanor Roosevelt was a person of great learning and great passion for the underdog. I wanted to know how she wielded her influence.

When we met, Mrs. Roosevelt was very generous with me; she never made me feel she was watching the clock. She taught me to think about the humanity of the politicians, not just their ideologies. She was a good influence on me. She had something to do with my passion for ideas and politics. She had this unique voice which I remember from the radio. Every time she wanted to criticize her husband—on for example women's issues or the color gap—she would raise her voice. Her voice would rise and fall with her passion.

Although the Roosevelts were an enduring presence, the most striking president for my generation was Jack Kennedy. You had to be twenty-one years old, as I was, to know the effect JFK had on the whole country in 1960, especially on the younger people. Jack Kennedy gave us a sense of excellence and honor about public service,

Ronald Reagan Presidential Library & Museum

President Ronald Reagan: The Gipper

despite what has been said and written since then. Though I did not agree with some of his views—and I was later disappointed to learn about some of the troubling facts of his life and career—he inspired us. I was not then as partisan as I am now. In fact, I campaigned for the Democrat Endicott Peabody in his race for governor of Massachusetts when I was at Harvard for summer school. Being close to the political action was the key thing for me. My attitude toward politics was much determined by my study of history. I preferred men and women who intended to do great things, regardless of their ideology. As an example from British history, both Benjamin Disraeli and William Gladstone fascinated me. Although I ultimately came to see only Gladstone as motivated by first principles, I was equally interested in Disraeli because of his towering ambition. I was not as certain about ideas then as I was of the character of the statesmen who interested me.

With time, my political beliefs grounded themselves to the American Founding in the Declaration of Independence and Constitution, and to the Refounding by Abraham Lincoln in the constitutional amendments he inspired, namely the Thirteenth, Fourteenth, and Fifteenth Amendments. I believe the governing American philosophy held by the vast majority of Americans will still be the same when you are holding your grandchild on your knee, and it will still be the Declaration of Independence and the American Constitution.

New York Conservative Party leaders Daniel Mahoney, Mike Long, and Serf Maltese had seen that I shared their conservative, constitutional values—as a matter of principle rather than convenience. They had adopted me as their candidate for governor in 1982 over several other candidates who had more conventional qualifications. Ours was not an alliance based on self-interest alone. It was an alliance based on a similar vision of American history.

Over the next several years, I continued to attend Conservative Party meetings across New York State. I got to know the party's leadership at the county level. I established a relationship of mutual trust and shared vision that had made me their preferred candidate for governor in 1982. Conservatives responded to my presence as well as my principles. My work, my writing, my friendships were all of a piece in support of my vision of American ideals.

The *American Spectator*'s Bob Tyrrell remembered those early days of the Conservative Renaissance for his magazine:

> [I]t seems that [Lew] was at about every important meeting of conservatives in the early 1980s. One meeting was at a breakfast I think he held at the Carlyle. . . .He footed the bill for *The American Spectator* to hold its 15th anniversary at the Lehrman Institute, which was just the right touch. We were considered by the limousine Liberals to be hicks from Indiana. You could not call us hicks at the Lehrman Institute. In the first 25 years of *The American Spectator*, Lew and I met regularly and he was always eager to help. He was the man who introduced me to Teddy Forstmann, soon to be a close friend

and Board Member. . . . In recent years, of course, he wrote extensively for the magazine. Every time he did we all learned something from Lew even as we were learning from his books.[2]

Alan Eyesen accurately described the relations between my values, my prospects, and the political situation at the time, writing:

Personal ambitions aside, Lehrman believes that a struggle for the soul of the Republican Party began in 1976, with Reagan's unsuccessful bid to seize the GOP presidential nomination from Gerald Ford. The conservatives succeeded in 1980. "And that's an ongoing struggle which will continue," he said. Lehrman believes that because a second-term Reagan presidency would be a lame duck presidency, moderates will mount a vigorous challenge to the dominant conservative element that now controls the party. "That will be decided in '88," he said, as may Lehrman's role in public life. . . . As Lehrman put it, "The issue simply is for what the national Republican Party stands."[3]

NAVIGATING CONSERVATIVE STREAMS

The Conservative movement had many strands. I was called a paleoconservative—a conservative on every front. Daniel Patrick Moynihan was a neo-conservative, as were Irving Kristol, Norman Podhoretz, Jeane Kirkpatrick, and a host of others. Mike Long was a dyed in the wool conservative who saw neo-conservatives as a boarding party trying to take over the conservative movement. A lot of neo-conservatives found their way into the Reagan Administration. There was envy and jealousy. I was aligned with the conservatives in the Heritage Foundation—Ed Feulner, Joe Coors, Bill Middendorf, and Robert Krieble. In fact Middendorf, former secretary of the navy, was explicit in his desire that I take the mantle from Reagan. In the following series of quoted speeches and articles, I present the core of my conservative values as I articulated them at the time. I still stand for them all, to this very day.

Speaking to the Conservative Political Action Conference in February 1983, I presented my vision for an active conservatism, saying:

There are at least two schools of conservatism. One believes stability and predictability are the highest political values. It is incrementalist as it strives honestly and painstakingly to grapple with the nation's deep problems. The other school acknowledges the need for stable institutions. But its members argue that, on occasion the times demand activist solutions, a fundamental reformation, in order to make conservative principles work in the world . . .

Historians speak of the American Revolution as a conservative revolution. And I agree. But the American Revolution was an actively dynamic reconstruction of an entire social order, conservative as it was. It was an ambitious era of

> fundamental reform, but it was also, indisputably, a popular revolution. . . . In Second Kings, it is told how Israel fell upon evil times and descended [into] Assyrian bondage. But in Judea, two conservatives, King Hezekiah and his son Josiah resisted the evil practices and institutions they saw around them. . . .
>
> Ours is a similar predicament today. As conservatives, we know our nation has fallen on hard times. The times call for a reconstruction of the Federal government which many desire, but as many will think difficult. In Lincoln's words "As the problems are new, so must we think anew." It is time to stop trying to accommodate ourselves to the failures of the past. We must move out, completely beyond the discredited liberal policies which have undermined our national security, our prosperity and our values.
>
> We do not have to settle for the mess which we find in Washington. We can go forward with traditional American goals and policies which made this country great—policies of financial order and a sense of our manifest national destiny and prudent belief in the democratic example we can set for the world, a belief in low taxes, economic growth, and a respect for individual liberties in a strong, but limited government. . . .
>
> Throughout our history, Americans have marched to a different drummer. Conservatives hear more clearly today the beat of the drum. They respond to its rhythm. Once again, I too can hear the drumbeat of American conservatives calling our country to restore the basic principles on which it was founded—evoking the principles by which we can grow and prosper in our third century—the true American century.[4]

My activist approach and philosophy were both based on traditional American values which I made every effort to define.

In 1980, I was inducted into the Babson Institute Academy of Distinguished Entrepreneurs. As I told the Babson College Commencement in May 1981:

> We live in an age preoccupied with value. There are many different standards of value. Most of us have learned never to take value for granted—no matter what level we are accustomed to, we want to get something out of life and we want to get something out of what we put into life. We want value and values. We want to get our money's worth and our soul's worth. Education seeks to do both—to advance our minds and our morals—and to advance our financial success. Education teaches us to value ideals, to value truth, to value progress and success. All who look around today must question both the value and the values in our society.[5]

Years later I wrote down the core of my own theory of value for *Crisis* magazine. I titled it, "Capitalism, Only One Cheer," which gives you an idea of what I think capitalism itself is worth. The one cheer is for its effective role in wealth production, where everyone is responsible for producing the wealth by having jobs or otherwise serving. But there are other, more important issues, which I articulated for that article in this way:

> A free society is, in fact, not free. That is, a free society does not come free. More intellect, more effort, more decentralized power is required in the aggregate to sustain a free society than to uphold an authoritarian society. In a free social order, every man and woman must work each day to think and to do right. But in a despotism, the rulers must. In a constitutional republic, one that respects the laws of persons and property, it is the duty of each citizen freely to choose to do the lawful thing—not the unlawful thing potentially licensed by his autonomy in a free society. In particular, for a just market order to flourish, each person—despite the human passions of avarice, ambition, and lust—must summon the will every day freely to respect the human and property rights of his neighbor. That is to say, each citizen in a free society must properly govern himself such that a limited self-government of the whole might lightly regulate the general welfare of all.
>
> But we learn from history, reason, and experience that men can be moved to do the lawful thing primarily by two social mechanisms: a morally grounded conscience or the external threat of civil and criminal penalties—monetary damages, prison, and the loss of freedom. If a majority is moved to do the lawful thing by coercion, penalties, and jail, who would deny that a free society must necessarily become, in time, an armed camp of police, prosecutors, and prisons? This outcome does not even consider the economic costs of a regime wherein a majority is moved to right-minded action primarily by force and fear. The cynical admonition "Follow your inclinations with due regard to the policeman around the corner" is no practical rule for a lasting social order. For when moral anarchy prevails, there can never be enough policemen! Thus, a free society can remain free; the creative mind of man can achieve its loftiest aims; and capitalism can be sustained in the long run, only if the vast majority is moved by the inner dictates of a well-formed conscience. Such a conscience, by itself, enables every person in the community to transact his business without fear of unaccountable theft and bodily harm. The well-formed conscience is also the simplest, least expensive, and most efficient regulator of a free social order.[6]

When I announced my candidacy for governor, I had explained to everyone that my philosophy dated back to America's Founders, saying:

> You see, the idea of a democracy like our own, certainly the idea of Washington, Jefferson, and Madison, was that everybody would do public service—blacksmiths, merchants, grocers, doctors. . . . And the idea was that in the United States, men and women from all walks of life would do public service, run for offices in the state or federal legislatures, and then go back to work so they could

see how the world worked and what it was really like in the neighborhoods and communities for which they were legislating and making the rules.[7]

Although they were clearly traditional, my values and ideas were sometimes unfashionable, especially because I held them to be objective and actionable. Dismayed by the state of academic discourse and its effect on politics, I criticized it passionately at the Philadelphia Society in April, 1983, saying:

> Today, we live in a society dominated by intellectual elites for whom relativism replaces religion, and perverse "situation ethics" displaces the Judeo-Christian moral code. Within the liberal academic and media elites, a faithless and melancholy social determinism has taken deep root. The hopeless mess of the welfare state competes for primacy with the *true* birthright of free people in America—individual responsibility, and optimism about the special destiny of our country.
>
> Some fashionable left-wing academics in our elite universities publicly scorn the historic American values of patriotism, right conduct, and self-reliance. This alienated intellectual "new class" teaches our children that traditional family values are not only irrelevant, but false.
>
> In fact, our historic American values are not only still relevant for the life of a great nation, but, more than ever, necessary for a world desperately in need of confident and hopeful American leadership.[8]

I was fully transparent about the revolutionary nature of my efforts, telling Ronald Brownstein:

> I wake up thinking about the conservative revolution and how we can move it giant steps forward every day. I go to bed thinking about how we can make America the model for the entire world. How can we peacefully move the failed Soviet and Swedish and Social Democratic experiments into the ash heap of history where they belong and substitute our own as the model for what was supposed to have been a world revolution anyway, the revolution of the founders?"[9]

When Sidney Blumenthal and I spoke at length regarding my campaign and the conservative shift America was making, I even mapped out for him the stages of the conservative revolution. After we spoke, he quoted me extensively for his article:

> Lehrman views Reagan's presence in the Oval Office as just the beginning of the conservative movement, not as its culmination. "The big issue," [Lehrman] told me recently, "is whether we're at the Menshevik or the Bolshevik phase, whether it's 1905 or 1917. Maybe I should talk about this in terms of the American Revolution. I think we're all at the Committee of Correspondence stage of the Revolution, the early stage. Reagan has made all of this possible through his charm and his vision. But it's incomplete. The triumph is partial

until dominant institutions of the 'liberal establishment' are vanquished. The conservative movement is less strong than the liberal establishment," Lehrman says. "We don't control the high places—the great foundations, the organs of communication, the elite universities, the cosmopolitan newspapers. It made the challenge all the more desirable and the taste of victory all the more exciting. The taste is in my mouth a little bit."[10]

SUPPORTING THE HERITAGE FOUNDATION

I met Ed Feulner shortly after he founded the Heritage Foundation with the help of Paul Weyrich and Joseph Coors in 1973. In addition to free market economics, Heritage advocated a strong peace-through-strength foreign policy.

Paul was the first president. In 1977, Ed left Capitol Hill where he was executive director of the Republican Study Committee, to become president of Heritage. I hit it off with Ed, who would earn a PhD from the University of Edinburgh in 1981. Right around that time, Ed called me, and said I should be with them rather than with the American Enterprise Institute (AEI), whose board I had joined in 1979. At the time, AEI was primarily a board of corporate executives. Indeed, I felt much more comfortable at the Heritage Foundation because they were entrepreneurial, and the board was entrepreneurial. In addition, they were more conservative than AEI. Heritage became a driving force in the conservative movement and the Republican Party over the next four decades.

Compared to AEI and Brookings, however, Heritage was an upstart. When I joined in 1979 at age forty-one, compared to other Heritage trustees I was the young buck on the board. When Heritage was celebrating its tenth anniversary in 1983, Feulner chose me as the first chairman of its capital funds drive, "Heritage 10—Funding the Conservative Decade." He also asked if he could put my family name on the Louis Lehrman Auditorium, now a chief meeting place for Heritage events on the first floor of its new Massachusetts Avenue headquarters on Capitol Hill. I had already invested a substantial amount of money in Heritage, and at the same time I honored my grandpa by using his spelling, instead of my own. "'But he ain't just a pol for hire,' Mr. Feulner insisted. 'Lehrman is not in this for Lew Lehrman, he's in it for principles. He's a genuinely feeling, caring person. That's something we don't always see with conservatives in this town. That's pretty rare.'"[11]

I would continue to serve on Heritage's board for nearly two decades. I resigned at the beginning of my run for governor in 1982 and was renamed to the board in 1984. I retired again in the late 1990s, by which time they had become so dominant that they did not need my help anymore. My involvement with Heritage briefly became an issue in the 1982 campaign. Marc Humbert wrote it up, saying "When Lewis Lehrman announced he was running for governor of New York state earlier this year, one of the many positions he resigned was a seat on the board of trustees of the Heritage Foundation. For most New Yorkers, the Heritage Foundation probably sounds like something which publishes a glossy magazine about old houses and history. The sort of things filled with advertisements for polished brass eagles and other bits of Americana. . . . For New Yorkers who view Lehrman simply as a multi-millionaire businessman who wants to cut taxes, the foundation connection again points up that Lehrman has some strong ties to the most conservative forces in the Republican Party."[12] At least Humbert got that right.

FOUNDING THE MANHATTAN INSTITUTE

In 1978, Bill Casey, Bill Simon, Antony Fisher, and I started what became the Manhattan Institute. It was first called the International Center for Economic Policy Studies (ICEPS), and it was founded to study and promote free market approaches to problems. Simon had been treasury secretary under President Ford. Casey would be CIA director under President Reagan. British businessman Antony Fisher would go on to found many libertarian think tanks.

In 1981, there was a discussion about changing the name to something more memorable. Conservative Washington insider Bill Hammett, our first full-time director, had suggested the "New York Institute." We had lunch at the Racquet Club, where in a bout of intellectual jiu-jitsu, I convinced him to call it "The Manhattan Institute."

Jeff Bell was the first president of ICEPS. He had just lost a Senate race in New Jersey to Bill Bradley. Journalists Irving Kristol and Leslie Lenkowsky helped arrange Jeff's appointment. Bill Hammett succeeded Jeff in 1980 when Jeff's political activities on behalf of Ronald Reagan became problematic for a nonprofit. "I'd become president of what became the Manhattan Institute," Jeff said, "and Bill Casey was the chairman of the Manhattan Institute at the same time. We both resigned at the same time. Casey became the Reagan campaign manager, but I had to leave because my name had appeared in the 'Periscope' section of *Newsweek* as putting together the television commercials for Reagan's primaries, and the people on the board of what became the Manhattan Institute . . . said 'You're getting too political.'"[13]

Under Larry Mone, who was president of the Manhattan Institute for nearly a quarter-century beginning in 1995, the Institute became the prime conservative think tank in New York City. Occasionally, they would call on me to address one of their events on either economics or history.

CHALLENGING RONALD REAGAN

In the 1982 gubernatorial campaign, I had always qualified my support for the Reagan Administration. I had to walk a tightrope between a president I supported and a number of his policies with which I disagreed.

I had advocated a coordinated, four-pronged attack on the nation's economic difficulties. The policies that I presented were different from the ones the White House wanted to follow. In October of 1982, I told the Associated Press's Marc Humbert that "unlike many of the candidates for appointment as cabinet secretaries, I had laid out my policies [in magazine and newspaper articles] and so it was very clear where I stood." The Reagan Administration preference was for someone who would adjust their opinions to fit the priorities of the White House. The rest of Humbert's article, "Lehrman: Budget Stand Cost Him Federal Post," explained the nuances of the situation well.

> Republican gubernatorial candidate Lewis Lehrman says his "insistence on balancing the [federal] budget" even at the expense of no increased defense spending probably cost him a top-level job in the Reagan administration.
>
> The millionaire businessman said late last week during a campaign swing across upstate New York that he was interviewed several times by top-level aides to then President-elect Reagan in the fall of 1980 concerning the U.S. Secretary of the Treasury job . . .
>
> The explanation of his differences with Reagan's top aides [whom] he would not publicly identify might appear politically self-serving for Lehrman as his Democratic opponent, Lt. Gov. Mario Cuomo, has attempted to link Lehrman repeatedly with Reaganomics.
>
> But during the in-flight interview Friday, Lehrman appeared hesitant to talk about his differences with Reagan aides and did so only under repeated prodding by several reporters.
>
> "I don't think anybody gets elected governor attacking the president of the United States or riding his coattails," he had said earlier in the day.
>
> So what was it the president elect's men didn't like?
>
> "My insistence on balancing the budget at the same time as you reduce taxes. Whatever the tax rate reduction, it had to be accompanied by a drive to bring the balanced budget," said Lehrman. "We had to balance the budget more rapidly."
>
> Lehrman said he told Reagan aides that the administration had to eliminate enormous wasteful political boondoggles such as the B-1 bomber which has since been continued by the Reagan administration.
>
> "I said we cannot increase Pentagon spending until we rebuild the economy," said Lehrman, "a coherent economic policy to work had to be linked to a foreign policy that we could afford . . . and I believed we could not afford a very rapid increase in Pentagon spending."
>
> "I laid out my views in unmistakably clear terms," said Lehrman. "Indeed, the memos I submitted were dropped like snowflakes all over Washington by Dave Stockman (Reagan's director of the Office of Management and Budget) himself."[14]

Michael Kramer saw the bigger picture of what I was proposing, writing:

> Whether he makes it to the inner councils or not (and Reagan is missing a bet if he doesn't take him on), Lehrman is sure to continue as one of the administration's leading economic gurus. Here's how Lehrman sees the economics we thought we were getting when we elected Ronald Reagan:

"To begin with," argues Lehrman, "it is impossible to overemphasize that everything must be done together. Everything is interrelated. A failure to understand that is what has doomed [the policies of] Margaret Thatcher in England. That failure need not be repeated here. Theirs was a failure of will, and a failure to comprehend the relations among budget deficits, central-bank monetary policy, and the high marginal tax rates that hit everyone.

"Unless President Reagan moves simultaneously in all three areas—monetary reform, budget restraint, and a substantial reduction in the marginal tax rates—he cannot succeed in his war against inflation. Absence of any one of these elements could well doom the other two. Simply holding the line on taxes and spending while permitting the Federal Reserve to manipulate the money supply without working in conjunction with the administration's program is almost certain to yield continued stagflation and economic instability, which in turn would lead to further breakdowns in the economy."[15]

In a January 1982 letter, I appealed directly to the President, saying:

I pray you will reconsider the decision to raise taxes on working people. Higher gasoline taxes will penalize all Americans who drive to work and to school. Higher taxes on beer and cigarettes reduce the wages of those working Americans who elected you as President.

In a recession Americans have few enough small pleasures. It is unfair to tax them.

Corporations may be able to shift their investment tax credits to lower their tax burdens. But for working Americans, the alternatives to a gallon of gas, a pack of cigarettes, and a glass of beer are few.

Americans want your economic program to work. They believe in it and in your leadership. But they do not believe that the budget deficit should be reduced by taxing working people more. Simple fairness demands that these proposed new taxes be rejected. I hope you will reject the insensitive advice of some members of your Administration who think otherwise.[16]

President Reagan responded positively to this letter on February 22, writing:

Dear Lew,

I know by now you're aware that I have decided against those who suggested higher taxes as a part of our program. But, I wanted you to know how very much I appreciated your letter of January 23rd. It made me more confident of my decision and more comfortable. You were kind to write as you did, and I do appreciate it.

I have confidence in our program, and I wish I could convince people they should just have a little more patience. I'm getting tired of hearing that the program is a failure when the first and smallest phase of it only began on

October 1st. I worry, at times, that the constant drum beat by the press might begin to affect people, and create a fear that I believe would be harmful to what we're trying to do.

Again, thanks and best regards.

Sincerely,

Ron [17]

This letter again confirmed my sense that his instincts were good, and that he legitimately needed help from active citizens. Although he did not always act on his words in the most thorough way, I was grateful for his efforts, aware the challenges were real, and certain of his good faith.

Periodically during the campaign for governor, I would make clear my differences with the Reagan Administration. In covering my campaign announcement, Dick Zander noted that "Questioned about welfare funding, Lehrman, a staunch supporter of President Reagan, said he disagreed somewhat with Reagan in proposed federal cutbacks. 'I'd never cut public programs during a time of recession. The time to cut is in a period of expansion,' Lehrman said." [18]

It was easier for Democrats and some reporters to downplay my opposition to these Reagan Administration economic policies. In the general election campaign, as unemployment hit 10 percent, Cuomo's strategy was to tie Reaganomics around my neck. A forty-four-day campaign is a short time to explain the nuances of my complaints with the administration. Sometimes, I was misrepresented by journalists, too. My idea that "government's main purpose is to ensure public safety," and should otherwise "pretty much . . . get out of the way of free markets and free people,"[19] was paraphrased by E. J. Dionne to paint me as more of a supply-sider than the president himself. "With these views, and a program for a 40 percent tax cut that resonates with the President's supply-side economics, Mr. Lehrman is widely regarded as a Reagan lookalike. In fact, Mr. Lehrman is a truer believer in small government than Ronald Reagan himself—to the point of wanting to cut the national defense budget. 'Work, save, invest' are Lew Lehrman's words, the words of a man who prides himself on having grown up, as he puts it, 'in the land of Babbitt'" [a phrase I borrowed from Sinclair Lewis].[20]

Sometimes the press even decided that my ideas were unpalatable to Republicans. I went back and forth on these issues with Alan Emory of the *Watertown Daily Times*, who wrote that:

If reporters ever get Lewis Lehrman talking about national economic issues this year, some Republicans are going to shudder.

Talk to the unemployed, the GOP gubernatorial hopeful says, and you will find out "we are already in a depression. The tragedy," he adds, is that "both Republicans and Democrats are willing to live with high unemployment rates." Not just Democrats, mind you. And there is more. He finds the "small business community is being disassembled before your eyes" due to high state taxes and the exodus to neighboring states.[21]

Since the Reagan White House had decided that President Reagan would not come to New York to campaign for me, I carried the label of an advocate of "Reaganomics" without the overt support of the president. On September 28, White House Chief of Staff James Baker had come to New York City to support my campaign. But it was Baker who had decided that *President Reagan* was not going to come. The Chief of Staff saw me as an obstacle to the prospects of George H. W. Bush, his preferred future candidate. Baker was well known as one of the smartest political operatives in presidential politics. "We happen to be of the view that Lew is going to win the governorship without the president coming in here,"[22] he had declared during a press conference in Manhattan. Perhaps they did believe that, but my campaign would have preferred the President come. John Buckley told the larger story in a statement for Jane Perlez:

> The decision not to send Mr. Reagan to New York was made despite a request by the campaign 'a long time ago' for his presence.[. . .] [Lehrman's] press aide said today that Lehrman campaign staff members would talk to Mr. Baker about a visit by the President. The apparent reluctance by the White House to schedule a campaign swing for Mr. Reagan on Mr. Lehrman's behalf may be based only in part on the priority of assisting Republican Congressional candidates elsewhere.[23]

The excuse was that Reagan was too busy campaigning for congressional races to come to New York. The absence of the President even became an issue raised by Cuomo in the *New York Post* debate: "President Reagan said he would come here and campaign for you, but he hasn't been asked. I ask him. Come campaign,"[24] said Mario. When I was asked a few weeks later by Sam Roberts if I really wanted Reagan to campaign in New York, I was ambivalent but diplomatic: "I think that it would be of no consequence either way. I don't believe in the coattail theory of politics."[25]

When asked about rising unemployment and the policies of the Reagan Administration, I tried to shift the blame. "It's up to us to take the positive approach and develop a program for renewal in New York and quit blaming all of our problems on people far away,"[26] I said in early October. "It was Jimmy Carter who gave us 21 percent interest rates, and two recessions in a single term."[27]

I told journalist Michael Clements that I thought the Reagan program would succeed in the long term—perhaps ten years—because

> in the long term, we will reform the Federal Reserve System so that we get a sound dollar. . . . And over the long term I believe that the American people will insist on a balanced budget, and over the long run I believe we will match our existing domestic economic resources to the scale of our foreign policy. . . . [but the programs won't] be as successful as we want them to be until he adopts the full economic reform program . . . including some fundamental reforms in monetary policy, Pentagon policy and the big pork barrels to bring the budget under control.[28]

I told the same story to ABC's *This Week with David Brinkley* on October 24:

President Reagan's economic plan has not been as successful as it could be because they, in fact, have only done one part of the program which many of us recommended in November of 1980. First, we do not yet have sound money. We do not have an honest dollar. The dollar in Washington is kicked around like a political football, and it's been depreciated into a small fraction of what it was worth, even since the presidency of Jack Kennedy, who himself called for a sound and honest dollar.[29]

In the final debate in October, I tried to give the Reagan Administration the benefit of the doubt: "The jury is not in yet . . . I think that it might very well be that the president will alter his policies. He may very well see that we're giving too much money to the Pentagon. He may see that we don't need to build the B-1 bomber."[30]

As the campaign reached its conclusion and unemployment remained high, I expressed my frustration to reporters aboard my campaign plane:

"I believe the Reagan administration should be making a major effort to show clearly how we are going to rebuild the economy and create 20 million jobs in the next 10 years. . . . A slogan like 'stay the course' is inadequate to the point of folly." [The press went with it, writing] "Republican gubernatorial candidate Lew Lehrman, in an unexpected move, yesterday criticized President Reagan for not clearly explaining how he planned to rebuild the economy. Lehrman also for the first time admitted that the 10.1 per cent national unemployment rate was hurting his campaign."[31]

I was just as specific with Sam Roberts of the *Daily News*, whom I told:

I had recommended a comprehensive economic program. No changes have been made in monetary policy, the dollar is still a political football, deregulation has been very modest, the balanced budget is even further off in the distance and the tax rate reduction policy was reduced. If the comprehensive economic program had been implemented, we'd be in the midst of the biggest economic boom in American history.[32]

In an end-of-the campaign profile for the *New York Times*, Mickey Carroll wrote:

The outcome of this gubernatorial race will have significance for President Reagan's future as well. While Mr. Lehrman has sought to demonstrate that his economic ideas differ from the President's, he has been bombarded by Mr. Cuomo's assertion that the New York election represents a "referendum on Reaganomics," and doubtless that is how the outcome will be viewed.[33]

The cagey way that the Reagan White House dealt with me—even before his inauguration—continued. I was respected, but not fully trusted, because I did not endorse all of Reagan's policies. Periodically during the campaign, I had to intervene to make sure that the White House was not meddling in New York politics in a way that might undermine my candidacy.

After the election, I was somewhat more pointed about my differences with the Reagan Administration in interviews with New York and Washington reporters. In a joint piece for the *Daily News,* Marcia Kramer and Sam Roberts would write:

> Defeated Republican gubernatorial candidate Lew Lehrman has said that his party's plans to salvage the national economy are "utterly inadequate" and that White House policies concerning future economic growth are "outrageous and unacceptable" and "must be repudiated."
>
> In a candid, sharply worded interview with the *Daily News*, Lehrman warned that "no President will survive without adopting a program for full employment and a 4% interest rate."
>
> And he placed part of the blame for his gubernatorial defeat on President Reagan's performance and the "deep effect" national policy had on New York politics.
>
> Lehrman said flatly that if the White House had taken his advice two years ago, he would have beaten Democrat Mario Cuomo earlier this month. . . .
>
> While he agreed that it "may have been helpful politically" to have drawn a distinction earlier in the campaign between what the President was doing and what Lehrman believed ought to be done, Lehrman recalled that, "I thought loyalty was more important than public criticism."
>
> Lehrman said, however, that while he had thought Reagan should be given the time to pursue his program, "I think he has now had enough time.'[34]

In an article for *Human Events* called "Lehrman Ready to Catch the Flag," John Lofton presented a lively and nuanced picture of my challenge to the President:

> In his superb address here before the Conservative Political Action Conference (CPAC), Lew Lehrman did not openly challenge President Reagan by throwing down any gauntlet. Instead, being the first-class guy he is, Lehrman firmly but gently laid the gauntlet on the table. And his message was crystal clear: For conservatives, now is the time to act against and move beyond—not seek a compromise with—the discredited policies of liberalism which have undermined our national security, our prosperity and our values.
>
> Correctly praising Ronald Reagan for setting forth conservative beliefs and dreams in a way no one else has, Lehrman called the President a "prophet" who "caught the falling flag and, in November 1980, hoisted it high."
>
> But in a series of cleverly phrased rhetorical questions, Lehrman revealed just exactly where he parts company with the President.

Quoting scripture, the New York Republican asked his fellow conservatives: If our trumpet gives an uncertain call, who will prepare themselves for battle?

Referring to the situation conservatives face today, Lehrman asked: "Do we need gradualism to restore the liberties and values that liberalism has systematically undermined for a generation? Or do we need activism, comprehensive reform and social reconstruction to set right the corrosive upheaval of yesteryear?"

Insisting that conservatives must adopt an activist strategy, Lehrman, by implication, criticized the President for supporting tax increases to reduce the deficit—tax increases on gasoline, the self-employed, Social Security benefits, petroleum production and contingency taxes on personal and corporate income.

Lehrman asked his conservative audience: "Do you really believe that at the end of this road to higher taxes, upon which we have already embarked, we will be closer to President Reagan's original goal of a more limited federal government—or will we be further away?

"Do you believe that the Congress will actually use these new federal taxes, proposed by President Reagan, to bring our budget in balance, as he hopes; or will Congress use this money to increase federal spending as a share of the nation's income and still allow the deficit to grow?"

In another obvious allusion to the President, Lehrman observed: "Though we must respect the sincerity and dedication of those conservatives who feel that new federal taxes are the only way to bring our budget into balance, we must also ask ourselves whether there's a better path, one that is truer to our conservative values."

Indeed, Lehrman believes there is a better path. Specifically, he favors a "fair and flat-rate tax system for America." To those hand-wringers who fear that such an imaginative substantial reform could never be achieved, he argues persuasively, "If the American people were not ready to consider major change, they never would have elected Ronald Reagan in the first place."[35]

DEVELOPING CLOSER RELATIONS WITH THE REAGAN ADMINISTRATION

Although President Reagan did not campaign for me directly when I ran for governor, he had appeared with me at a dinner in June, at the end of the Republican State Convention. The classic photo of us laughing together had appeared in the *New York Post.*

There was friendship, but also a competition, which can be summarized like this: During the campaign, I had been critical of some aspects of the Reagan program. The narrowness of my defeat gave hope to some conservatives that I could be a more authentic advocate for conservative policies than the President. The 1982 race had also demonstrated that I had the will, the message, and the resources to wage an effective campaign. My success and independence were both duly noted. The mandarins of the White House did not want me *inside* the tent, but neither did they want me *outside* the tent pursuing my own agenda.

Bill Peterson described the tense situation for the *Washington Post*:

> A small group of conservatives, disturbed by what they consider a leftward drift in the Reagan administration, has begun shopping for a "fresh new face" to run for the Republican presidential nomination.
>
> The group, led by New Right fund-raiser Richard A. Viguerie, thinks Ronald Reagan probably will not run for reelection, but it may try to field a candidate against him even if he does. . . . Another person mentioned is Lewis Lehrman, who ran a surprisingly strong race as the GOP gubernatorial nominee in New York last fall. He met with Viguerie recently but said in a subsequent interview that he and Viguerie did not discuss running for president.
>
> Lehrman clearly intends to keep his political prospects alive, however. He has arranged to speak before several national conservative groups, scheduled a trip to meet with world leaders, kept much of his campaign staff intact and formed an organization called the "Committee to Make New York Number One Again" to provide help to conservatives running for state and local offices.[36]

Although I was seriously considering the conservative interest in my candidacy, I remained friendly with the administration. In early 1983, I went abroad on behalf of the US State Department. Diplomatic arrangements were handled by Charles Z. Wick, who had been appointed by President Reagan to head the US Information Agency. For nearly fifty years, the USIA was responsible for American public diplomacy, until it was folded into the State Department in 1999. The motto of the USIA was "Telling America's Story to the World," and Wick liked to say he wanted the job more than any other Cabinet position because telling America's story to the world was the most important job in government.[37] Wick had been a close personal friend of the president going all the way back to the 1950s in California. A musician, movie producer, and successful businessman, Wick was an early and senior member of Reagan's so-called Kitchen Cabinet, the name given by the press to the influential businessmen who had supported Reagan's election. I already knew Wick because he had previously been involved in the discussions with the president about appointing me ambassador to France or Portugal. It was Wick who told me that President Reagan had specifically requested my assistance on behalf of America's foreign policy. He also agreed to my request that Louise come with me, since she loves to travel. The opportunity to meet world leaders on behalf of the State Department—particularly in a limited engagement that preserved my options—was appealing and I took it.

Traveling throughout Europe and Asia, Louise and I met with top political and economic leaders. There I lectured to audiences on the history and promise of America. I explained the origin of our country and the challenges we met successfully. Invariably, I would meet with the head of the Central Bank in each country. To my dismay, none of them knew enough about central banking to be effective in their positions. In particular, the head of the Italian Central Bank was remarkably uninformed. On my return, Wick invited me to speak to employees of his agency. Charles was impressed. He was also friends with the influential California businessman Jaquelin "Jack" H. Hume, another member of Reagan's Kitchen Cabinet.

A few weeks later, Hume came to see me. I think he was the first major Northern Californian to get behind the candidacy of a private citizen running for governor in 1965 by the name of Ronald Reagan. Jack wanted to form a civic organization to support the agenda of President Reagan. He already had support from some fellow members of the Reagan Kitchen Cabinet such as auto dealer Holmes Tuttle and steel magnate Earle Jorgensen. "For Hume, Lehrman was perfect: a driven man who was also a builder," wrote Ronald Brownstein. "For several years, Hume had harbored the dream of linking conservatives across the country; after the reversals in the 1982 elections, he went to see Reagan and Reagan said go ahead."[38]

Hume had been pushing the idea for a year, but the 1982 elections—in which Republicans were roundly defeated in Congress—had given his project new impetus. Saul Friedman sketched out the timeline:

> Hume proposed the grass-roots organization in a letter to Reagan, who approved and suggested formation of a committee. He assigned presidential counselor Edwin Meese to work with the panel. Longtime Reagan sponsors joined up: Earle Jorgensen, a steel distributor, Justin Dart, whose Dart Industries owns drug stores, bookstores and auto-parts stores; Fred Hartley of Union Oil and Joseph Coors whose beer wealth has financed many conservative causes. Hume went after Lehrman for chairman in April and found him reluctant, but the president intervened.[39]

I guess I met the requirements for what Hume wanted in a leader of the new organization, which we eventually called Citizens for America. Sidney Blumenthal described Hume's aspirations for the *New Republic* in December of 1983:

> Hume had no desire to lead the group himself. He wanted someone younger to assume responsibility. Choosing the chairman of C.F.A. was a way of advancing onto the national stage another potentially "very effective individual." Hume knew what the resume of his ideal chairman should include. "I wanted to get a successful businessman;" he says, "who was reasonably young, retired from active business, a conservative with proven executive ability." In discussions among other conservative leaders he consulted, one name kept surfacing: Lewis E. Lehrman. "I'd never met him before," says Hume. Lehrman, 45 years old, neatly fit Hume's bill of particulars. . . .
>
> Entrepreneur, intellectual, citizen-politician—Lehrman is the kind of son a Kitchen Cabinet member might like to have: just like the old man, only better. Hume decided Lehrman was the man for the movement. Once again, the Kitchen Cabinet anointed a promising leader of the future, who, like Reagan in 1964, had never held public office.[40]

ENTERTAINING PRESIDENTIAL AMBITIONS

With Heritage Foundation president Paul Weyrich pushing me as a conservative alternative to Reagan, I considered my options about how to express my differences. In 1982, James Perry wrote an article for the *Wall Street Journal* about whether Ronald Reagan would seek re-election. Perry cited disappointment among some conservatives such as Richard Viguerie about Reagan's performance in office. He also quoted Lyn Nofziger, Reagan's political guru: "Mr. Nofziger is even more adventurous. 'What,' he asks, 'would happen if Lew Lehrman was elected governor of New York?'"[41]

Speculation about Reagan's succession was stimulated somewhat by the launch of Citizens for America (CFA) in the summer of 1983. Columnists Evans and Novak were often good to promote either collaboration or competition between Jack Kemp and myself—competition being good for newspaper sales. Kemp was also considered a prominent conservative successor to Reagan. In the event, Robert Novak promoted me. He wanted to be the first person invited to the White House if I was elected president.

Apparently presidential aspirations were widely presumed, although they were not true except in an abstract way. In November 1983, the *Arizona Republic* editorialized: "Lehrman makes no secret of his ambition to someday become president, and CFA could well serve as a steppingstone."[42] Talk was also fueled by *New York Times* columnist Russell Baker, once called "The Great Mentioner."

In August 1983, columnist Jeffrey Hart wrote:

> Normally we expect our presidential candidates to have held lesser office before trying for the top, but Lewis Lehrman of New York appears to be testing that political assumption. . . . Lehrman is considered to be a conservative, which is true, but it might be more accurate to call him a reformer. He is a descendant, in a different time and in different circumstances, of another New York reformer—Theodore Roosevelt. Lehrman wants to cut taxes steeply, break the stranglehold of government bureaucracy, and stimulate the private sector by bringing businesses back to New York. He would apply the same philosophy nationally . . . Lewis Lehrman's projected presidential candidacy has a special quality. It is not based upon experience in previous political office, but upon the validity of his ideas.[43]

Sidney Blumenthal followed Evans and Novak when writing about the contest between Kemp and me, saying that "The high priests of conservatism view this contest with bemused and critical detachment. 'May the best man win,' says Irving Kristol, the neoconservative who is Kemp's intellectual mentor and serves as a trustee of the Lehrman Institute. 'The last time I was at Jack's, about two months ago, Lew was there. It's like watching the Jets and the Giants playing in the Super Bowl. I'm for both.'"[44]

Blumenthal fueled the speculation with a December 1983 cover story for the *New Republic* called "Let Lehrman Be Reagan." In the article, he helped me sketch out my vision for the conservative future, writing:

> Lehrman is enormously confident about the future. To him, Reagan's Presidency is only the glimmering of what will follow. The movement will inexorably gather strength. "If that past is prologue, some great crisis, some great event, will make the conservative idea a reality," he says. "The Depression was the event that created the coalition in which the social democratic idea in America triumphed. It's hard to predict what the event will be. But I have little doubt that there will be *the* event. I am struck by the Lincoln experience. He was unusual for an ideologue in that he was a good inside politician. And he was relentless. He made unavoidable the irrepressible conflict. Lincoln didn't know the context in which it would occur, the timing of the event, but he knew it would happen. We change the climate of opinion and we await the event and then we win. Total victory."[45]

Still, a presidential campaign was a large leap for a man without prior elected or appointed office. Much as I believed in the gold standard, I was well aware of how few voters shared my conviction—and of how many members of the chattering classes opposed it. It's true I was interested in ideas—but my ideas were not always popular. Ronald Brownstein described some of my challenges in a perceptive 1984 profile for the *National Journal*:

> It is, by any conventional measure, absurd to talk about Lehrman for President. He has never won elective office. Conservative leaders love him and think he would be a great President, but they loved Philip M. Crane and John B. Connally—two early candidates for the 1980 GOP presidential nomination—and it didn't get them very far that year. Lehrman would have some support from the CFA cadres he has recruited, but by no means is everybody signing up with the group a Lehrman partisan.[46]

I may have had the bug, but I did not have the bucks or the political bureaucracy that a presidential campaign would have required.

FORMING CITIZENS FOR AMERICA

When we met in April 1983, Jack Hume described his organizational vision for what he had been calling "The Council for Reagan's Ideas." The new group would be composed of committees of community leaders organized in all 435 congressional districts. These opinion leaders would be joined together by a single thread, mainly their commitment to the success of President Reagan's conservative programs. I came up with a name, "Citizens for America," and we adopted it for what we described as a "national civic league."

Sidney Blumenthal quoted Jack when writing about the formation of CFA:

> "I've felt for a long time," [Hume] says, "that a large number of conservatives who are opinion leaders in each Congressional district would like to function as a group." He broached the idea to his close friends. Holmes Tuttle and Earle

> Jorgensen gave generously. So did others who were approached: including Fred Hartley, the chairman of Union Oil, and Robert Anderson, chairman of Atlantic Richfield. "Naturally," says Hume, "you turn to the people you know." In March [1983] he traveled to Washington to meet with some old friends from California to see if they would lend their moral support. Ronald Reagan and Edwin Meese were both enthusiastic and urged him to continue his efforts.[47]

Jack proved an expert wielder of political power. Hume told me that the president was considering me for a Cabinet appointment. He was very expansive, saying "You would make a great secretary of the treasury. President Reagan knows that, and he is considering you for that position." Hume's vague promises and controlling personality were effective, and they distracted me from other options I might have exercised.

The morning following my meeting with Hume, one of the secretaries in my office, Carla Saunders, came running down the hall saying "Lew, the President is on the phone!"

"The president of what?" I asked.

"It's the President of the United States!"

I waited a moment for the White House operator to click me on, and when I heard the president say, "Lew?" I said, "Yes, sir."

The president continued saying, "Congratulations, Lew. Jack Hume and I are really thrilled that you have decided to become chairman of our new enterprise. I'd like you to come down to talk about it."

I was delighted to hear from the president, but surprised to hear that I had already accepted the position. I had done no such thing, but it was an embarrassing situation. Although I had actually put Jack off when we met, I told the president I would take on the project. I told him that I would do the job for three years. At the end of three years, I would quit.

Behind the scenes, other factors were at work. Those in the White House who had kept me out of government—and would continue to do so—did not want to keep me out of the Reagan orbit. Fred Barnes broke the story in the *Baltimore Sun* on June 18. "Because he was approached by some conservatives eager to field a challenger to Mr. Reagan for the 1984 GOP presidential nomination, Mr. Lehrman has been viewed warily by Reagan political strategists. He rejected the idea that he run against Mr. Reagan, and his selection to head Citizens for America ties him firmly to the president."[48]

An August article in the *Baltimore Sun* accurately described the events on my calendar at the time:

> Several months ago Senator Paul Laxalt (R., Nev.), general chairman of the Republican party, telephoned Paul Weyrich, New Right leader. Was Mr. Weyrich trying to get Lewis Lehrman the Republican from New York, to challenge Mr. Reagan in the primaries next year? Yes, Mr. Weyrich said.

> Suddenly Mr. Lehrman found himself inundated with phone calls from Mr. Laxalt, White House aides, and members of Mr. Reagan's "kitchen cabinet." Not long after, Mr. Lehrman was ushered into the White House for a lengthy conference with Mr. Reagan, then was named to head Citizens for America.
>
> And, you guessed it, he's not running against the President in the primaries.[49]

I confess that I never stopped thinking about becoming treasury secretary until Reagan left office. I had this vain expectation that circumstances would require my engagement. Hume knew I was a candidate for treasury secretary and kept that carrot in front of me. As Louise said, "Jack out-traded you." I would be passed over by the Washington establishment, *and* I would be kept from criticizing any Reagan Administration policies. In truth, I got boxed in. Political operatives around President Reagan knew that Richard Viguerie and company were searching for a candidate to contest him in 1984. A political journalist had seen Viguerie and me walking down the street, and that gave rise to rumors. Reagan's friends found a way to keep me in line.

I wasn't the only one who could see what was happening. As John McLaughlin wrote:

> A few weeks ago there was such strong speculation in Washington that Mr. Lehrman was envisioning a presidential bid for himself that Paul Laxalt, the President's '84 campaign manager, put a call through to an establishment New Righter seeking verification. Laxalt was told that a number of conservatives were encouraging Lehrman to declare his candidacy because, even though he has not held any public office, with the right kind of campaign he could stake a claim on the conservative future. For many years conservatives rallied around Goldwater, and then, for a while, Agnew. Then came Reagan. Now a lot of people are big on Jack Kemp, who has massive national conservative appeal. But a lot of conservatives also think that Kemp, like a splendidly groomed racehorse at the gate, may refuse to run, so Lehrman was being encouraged to stay down the track. But he said no.[50]

Despite my ambivalence, I remained enthusiastic about supporting President Reagan and most of his policies. It was time to get to work. Within the White House, it was decided that I would coordinate with Ed Meese and the White House Office of Policy Development. Once there was agreement in principle, we went to work on the legal framework for the organization.

On May 19, 1984, I headed over to the White House where the president laid out the basic idea for CFA and its purposes. He gave me the encouragement and support I needed. McLaughlin went into the details, writing that CFA was an organization

> whose purpose would be to set up a grass-roots cluster of businessmen [or conservative political activists] in each congressional district to lobby for the Reagan agenda. Lehrman was then whisked into the Oval Office where President

> Reagan explained for twenty-odd minutes why the new organization was so important. With Lehrman as a partner in the strategy for '84, the Gipper had very nearly pulled the plug on the New Right.[51]

That night Reagan wrote in his diary: "Lew Lehrman and Jack Hume came by. They have a great plan for getting our supporters organized at the Cong. District level."[52]

"The President and I had a long talk," I would later explain to a journalist. "The conclusions of our discussion were very simple.

> We agreed we needed a national civil league, an activist enterprise, people who agreed on first principles, that would focus on economic and national security policies. Our first purpose is to induce a mutation in the climate of opinion in America among opinion leaders. We would join the intellectual debate in every town, village, and city through our Congressional district committees. We would also lobby Congress. Finally, we concluded that this would be the work of a lifetime. Just as the social democratic ideas took two generations to complete, so our work requires the remainder of the working lifetimes of the people involved.[53]

But I only committed to the chairmanship for three years, which meant I would be free of responsibilities to CFA in October of 1987.

Hume was careful both to encourage my ambition for a prominent Cabinet post and simultaneously to limit my powers of independent action. Hume insisted on Wendy Borcherdt, a longtime Reagan and Hume loyalist, as vice chair. Borcherdt had been special assistant to President Reagan for Public Liaison until she clashed with Elizabeth Dole (then director of that office) and was moved out of the White House in mid-1982. She had been nominated to be deputy undersecretary for education, but was never confirmed. Wendy was loyal to Hume and the Kitchen Cabinet. She and Jack opposed some of my initiatives—and wasted opportunities to advance President Reagan's agenda. Not everyone in the president's orbit was happy. It was Hume who told me that because CFA was a nonprofit, nonpolitical enterprise, some members of the Republican National Committee saw it as a competitor for donor dollars. So did the Heritage Foundation, of which I was a board member.

Nevertheless, Citizens for America attracted a wide array of talent during the 1980s. Among the executive directors were Marc Holtzman, Jack Stevens, Jack Abramoff (eventually fired for cause), Frank Trotta, and Bill Wilson. Andrei Bogolubov, who eventually became chief communications officer for AOL-Europe and is now CEO of Hook Life, served as executive assistant to the chairman. Phil Hamilton, also an executive assistant, went on to become a distinguished history professor. Trish Blake worked with me for more than a decade before moving to Colorado to work for the American Heart Association among other nonprofits. David Carmen, who went on to found The Carmen Group, was an early director of policy and communications. He was extremely well informed and very effective at public relations.

One of his first coups was a cover story on me by Sidney Blumenthal that appeared in the December 1983 issue of the *New Republic*. In a Capitol Hill bookstore, the article would leave a lasting impression on Andrei Bogolubov:

> There, on a sunny Saturday, while perusing magazines, I was suddenly confronted by a caricature of Lew on a cover under the headline "Reagan's Heir?" I read the article twice, transfixed by Lew's unapologetically optimistic articulation of a modern American conservatism grounded in first principles—the founding, free markets, sound money, and a strong defense. Lew's vision was as striking as it was inspirational. People didn't talk of such things and in such a manner, certainly not in Washington. America under President Reagan was just beginning to emerge from a liberal ascendancy that began in the 1930s. Washington was still dominated by a liberal, Club of Rome worldview uninformed by, or openly hostile to, the American tradition . . . Lew answered the President's call to lead the insurgency and organized Citizens for America as the Reagan Revolution's Committees of Correspondence. Like their colonial antecedents, Citizens for America committees in every congressional district across the country kept the growing conservative movement informed and in touch.[54]

Given Andrei's enthusiasm and rhetorical skill, it will be no surprise to learn that he would soon come to work for me as CFA's press secretary. The president was also continuously supportive of our efforts, writing in his diary: "Went over to the Exec. Bldg. where [Lew] Lehrman & Jack Hume had about 150 or 200 people gathered who

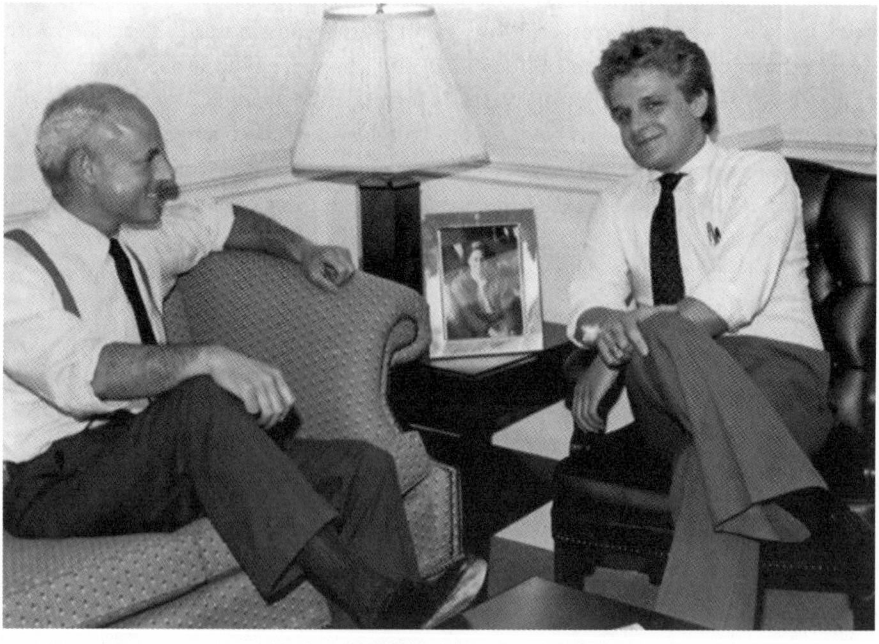

Andrei Bogolubov: Fisher of men

are volunteers in Citizens for Am. They will be regional directors. It was a morale boost to meet them. I did Q&A & then took a photo with each."[55]

CFA established an office in space sublet from the Heritage Foundation on Massachusetts Avenue near the Capitol. I also sublet space for my business there. The group organized rapidly and moved into the arena in the second half of 1983. As I told the *New York Times:* "[T]o be successful, you don't sit in an office, you don't build a business in an office, and you don't build a grass-roots citizens lobby campaigning for the President's programs and a peaceful conservative revolution in an office."[56] I explained the structure and function of CFA in an interview with *Human Events:*

> We will have a headquarters office on the third floor of the Heritage building on Capitol Hill. There we have a small research staff headed by David Carmen, who is in charge of our Policy and Communications Group. We gather the best evidence and data we can from the research of the Heritage Foundation and the American Enterprise Institute and the Hoover Institution, among others, as well as from the White House, the Treasury, National Security Advisor's office, the Secretary of Defense, and the CIA headed by Bill Casey, among others, and we reproduce it in a usable form for our volunteer leaders of Citizens for America in every congressional district—three-by-five cards to set out the basic questions on a particular issue. In addition to that, there is a three-page memorandum which lays out the issue facts, the policy alternatives before Congress, the President's choice, and why. And then there's often a 10 to 20-page memorandum which sets the issue in its historical context. Any one of our members briefing themselves on this material will probably be better informed than his liberal counterpart, when debating him or her on the radio or TV station, and almost invariably, better informed than the interviewers who cross-examine them on radio and television shows.[57]

Bob Tyrrell would invoke Paul Revere as he documented CFA's growth:

> Reaganite principles for spending and taxing, defense and revived federalism are widely held. It is just that the story is being ignored by our political and media elites. Lehrman believes they must be bypassed if the conservative revival is to continue. [CFA organizers] are trying to bring in citizens who never before have been in politics, and they believe that these organizations will bring Ronald Reagan's message to the locals and reverberate that message back to Washington. "Conservatism in America has reached a critical mass, but needs an instrument to galvanize its various parts," Lehrman has said. He believes there are social conservatives, religious conservatives, economic conservatives all "waiting to be brought together." With Ronald Reagan's blessing he is now attempting to do just that.[58]

I approached my job with missionary zeal, as I told an Easton, Pennsylvania journalist in October of 1983:

> This is the fourth peaceful American revolution, just like the Roosevelt revolution of the '30s; it is designed to bring America out of the terrible decade of the 1970s, which has caused us to become poorer instead of richer, caused our opportunities to shrink instead of expand. We have been recruiting without any concern for party. The single thread which binds all of the district chairmen is a view about what our country should be. That view is very simple. We believe in rapid economic growth, full employment, low long-term interest rates, the historic American dream, and we believe President Reagan is the man who can bring it about, provided that Americans from all walks of life get behind him.[59]

A few days later, I told a reporter in Manchester, New Hampshire: "We want to decentralize the communication of ideas we believe are held by most Americans . . . Second, we will take the ideas of conservative reform and lobby that in each congressional district. It's not unlike the Committees of Correspondence of 1776."[60]

In 1984, we worked hard to establish CFA in congressional districts across the country. The bulk of this work fell to district directors like John Szelest. John had been with me at Rite Aid, and now took charge of the Northeast. President Reagan would continue to boost morale, noting another visit in his diary: "Went over to the E.O.B. & met with Lew Lehrman & Jack Hume's Citizens for Am. Shook hands & was photographed with each of the 240 there."[61] Louise sat next to President Reagan during lunch and they hit it off very well indeed.

In Washington, the staff put together communication packages in support of the Grenada Rescue Operation, Enterprise Zones, the "Central American Democracy, Peace and Development Initiative Act," and the MX missile program. In December 1984, I explained the CFA program to *Human Events*:

> We tend to do about one issue a month. We have made the case nationally for the President's strategic defense program, the only promise of an end to the military strategy of Mutually Assured Destruction. We made that campaign in the midst of the national press relations developed about the ABC movie, *The Day After*.
>
> We had done several programs on our central American policy—our El Salvador and Nicaragua policies, in particular. We did a major campaign for the line item veto, enterprise zones, and the Balanced Budget Amendment. . . .
>
> My goal is to serve our President. Our goal at CFA is total victory for all Americans by means of the peaceful conservative revolution which President Reagan inaugurated in 1980.[62]

We established a presence at the 1984 Republican National Convention in Dallas. Sometimes members of the press thought our activities were in competition with Jack Kemp's presidential ambitions. Sometimes, we were portrayed as his supporters.

Both points of view were correct. We were concerned that Kemp might refuse to run as the conservative alternative in 1988, and wanted to make sure everyone knew we were ready to field a candidate. CFA had become a visible force in Washington politics. In January of 1985, Lisa McCormack wrote about our pre-inaugural activities for the *Washington Times*:

> Rushes replaced gushes at Lewis Lehrman's party . . . that afternoon. The president of Ronald Reagan's grass-roots lobbying group, Citizens for America, had sent out 1,700 invitations, expecting only a fraction of those invited to actually show up. Instead, over 1,000 enthusiastic conservatives . . . streamed up three flights of stairs to listen to short speeches by presidential counselor Ed Meese, Defense Secretary Caspar Weinberger and United Nations Ambassador Jeanne Kirkpatrick.[63]

In early 1985, CFA concentrated on tax reform. As I told the *Washington Times*, "Tax reform is on the front burner. Whether or not the particular reform that I would recommend is on the front burner, I don't know. I would say this is about the president: I've never heard him in private or in semi-private circumstances where his instinct . . . was not right on the money. I have absolutely no doubt he recognizes, in the privacy of his own considerations, that a 25 percent marginal tax rate is the right rate."[64]

In June 1985, I traveled to Jamba, Angola to meet with anti-communist resistance leaders from Angola, Laos, and Nicaragua. I brought with me a letter from President Reagan which stated: "Around the world we see people joining together . . . to free their nations from outside domination and an alien ideology. It is a global trend, and one of the most hopeful of our times. Those of us lucky enough to live in democratic lands have been moved by the example of men and women who struggle every day, at great personal risk, for rights that we have enjoyed from birth. Their goals are our goals."[65]

In a joint statement, the resistance leaders agreed, saying "Colonialism denies the right of free people to legitimate self-determination.

> The old colonialism of the eighteenth and early nineteenth centuries has passed into oblivion with the success of the Independence Movements of the 1950s and 1960s. Today, there is only one colonial power in the world—the Soviet Empire. An empire more vicious and oppressive than all others that passed before. Soviet Imperialism is the common enemy of mankind. Today, the Tide of History has turned against Soviet Colonialism. The Soviet Empire is fated to fall—just as all previous empires have collapsed, because Soviet Imperialism violates the true nature of man.[66]

I continued to write for the newspapers but was now focused broadly on political subjects. I was an outspoken proponent of the Strategic Defense Initiative, and described its promise for the *New York Times* in February of 1985, saying "President Reagan's proposed strategic defense, known popularly as 'Star Wars,' promises to bring about a revolution in our national security policy in the next generation. Most significantly—and quite unlike the nuclear doctrines that we currently rely upon to keep the peace—a strategic defense would be a win consistent with the ethical principles that matter to Americans."[67] In January 1986, my colleague Gregory Fossedal and I wrote a *National Review* article which expanded on the strategic defense theme:

> As long as the Soviets have an undemocratic government that threatens peace abroad and suppresses its own people at home, we must be prepared to defend ourselves. Such relatively peaceful levers on Soviet behavior as the Voice of America, economic pressure, and aid to freedom movements around the globe will all be more effective as we inch away from the strategy of mutual assured destruction. A space shield, in this sense, is far more than just a particular piece of hardware or a set of satellites. It is a fundamental change of foreign policy and military strategy, part of a peaceful forward strategy that seeks to dismantle Communism, and to extend freedom and constitutional democracy to all nations.[68]

After Holtzman left to plot a 1986 run for Congress in Pennsylvania, I was urged by Jeff Bell to hire Jack Abramoff as his successor. It was one of Jeff's few bad ideas. Abramoff, who had already burned his bridges at the Republican National Committee when he chaired the College Republicans, did not understand limits or budgets. Abramoff also had conflicts with some of the CFA staff who had survived previous turnovers. He effectively forced out David Carmen and brought in Grover Norquist as his deputy. Together, they put on big, splashy, attention-getting events—similar to those they had initiated at the College Republicans—regardless of whether they fit with CFA's core mission. As Jeff Bell eventually told the *Weekly Standard*: "He and Grover were just wild men."[69]

On July 27, 1985, Sidney Blumenthal accurately described my response to Abramoff's mismanagement for the *Washington Post*:

> Last week seven members of the CFA national staff were fired or quit. Apparently, Lehrman concluded that the organization's $3 million budget was being mishandled, although he declined to comment on the reasons for the shakeup. (In the previous six months, more than half the staff of 40 had left the organization, CFA sources said.)
>
> Lehrman has not been closely involved in the group's day-to-day activities. Instead, he has raised money and traveled.[70]

Andrei Bogolubov helped me get the truth out about the transition at CFA. "When Lew had enough," he remembered, "a group of us met after work at Terry Henry's house to prepare a transition plan.

> We worked most of the night and arrived at CFA early the next morning. Lew came in from the airport and went to the conference room. Once he was settled, I went to get Jack. In this way, Lew fired Jack Abramoff, Grover Norquist, and the rest of his College Republican contingent one-by-one.
>
> At the time I was serving as the press secretary for Citizens for America and received a call about the firings from Sidney Blumenthal of the *Washington Post*. My alarm bells went off. . . .
>
> Over several days, I worked with Sid on the phone to get the facts on the record and keep him from using Jack's firing to cast Lew or Citizens for America in a bad light. For the next four nights, at 11:00 pm, I parked my car outside the printing plant in northern Virginia to wait for the next day's *Washington Post* to roll off the presses. I ended my first three vigils shuffling through the still-moist paper only to find no story. Finally, on the fourth night, it was there and was about the best we could expect given the source. Years later the story turned up as a minor footnote to the Abramoff lobbying scandal, an example of Jack's early transgressions. Lew turned out to be prescient in firing Mr. Abramoff.[71]

After I fired Abramoff and his friends in July 1985, Frank Trotta took over as interim executive director. Frank restructured the organization and reduced its footprint at the Heritage Foundation.

Frank was succeeded by Bill Wilson, who had worked for the National Right to Work Committee for a decade. Bill, who was very much a movement conservative, went on to become an advisor to US Term Limits, founded by Howard Rich, and president of Americans for Limited Government. Bill stayed only a year.

Jack Stevens served as CFA's western regional director from 1983 to 1986 before his appointment as executive director in 1986. Jack was a good man. He was the one who really did the work after we fired Abramoff. Nothing was too much for him to take under his wing.

CFA's talent extended to its board, which would include Hume, Joseph Coors, Holly Coors, Richard M. DeVos, Edwin J. Feulner, Theodore J. Forstmann, Richard Gilder, Fred Jones Hall, Richard Headlee, Robert H. Krieble, Frank L. McNamara, Holmes P. Tuttle, and myself.

Late in 1986, I turned over the reins of CFA to Ambassador Gerald Carmen, David Carmen's father. When I resigned, Jack Hume was very upset. He objected to my departure. "We need you," he said. "You're indispensable." I replied: "My loyalty is to President Reagan's policies, but I have a family in New York." I had originally told Jack that I would see my way to doing it for three years. I quit on the very day my three years were up.

I had finally woken up from the dream of being Reagan's secretary of the treasury.

At the White House, the President told a changing-of-the-guard ceremony that:

> Lew Lehrman has stepped down as national chairman. Lew is not only an outstanding leader. He's one of America's most thoughtful voices. His writings on monetary reform, on anti-communist freedom fighters, and on many other issues have been among the most important in our time. And let me tell you, it's like advice from a certain broker—when Lew Lehrman talks, I listen.
>
> So, Lew, though you're stepping down, I have a feeling it's just to get ready to step up to an even greater future and that, when it comes to Lew Lehrman, we ain't heard nothing yet.
>
> I can't think of any better choice for replacing Lew than the one you've made—Ambassador Gerald Carmen.[72]

I continued to support President Reagan in op-eds even after I resigned from CFA. In January 1987, the *New York Times* published an essay in which I argued:

> American foreign policy has always been mindful of a special national purpose—that all mankind should be free—while nevertheless adapting to the circumstances and possibilities of American power at each stage of our history. In this, the Reagan Doctrine of support for anti-Communist insurgents in Nicaragua, Angola, Afghanistan and elsewhere is a modest natural development of historic American foreign policy—a discreet combination of principle and interest.[73]

Throughout my life I have always been available to make the case for freedom. On behalf of American ideals, I have traveled all over this country and large parts of the world. Usually, I was on a mission, but sometimes I took a break for lunch.

THREE SQUARES ON THE ROAD

Much of my life was spent on the road. My workload was heavy, and my travel budget was sometimes limited. If there was a little yellow splash on the Rand-McNally map, there was usually a McDonald's and a potential Rite Aid store. I wanted a steady, consistent meal.

After I had been to about ten to fifteen restaurants, I decided to have a rating system, rating each McDonalds from one to five. The decisive criteria were the warmth of the french fries, the right cooking time on those fries—how crispy they were—the correct amount of salt, and how fast the food was delivered. The Elmira and Jamestown, New York, McDonald's were superb. They were the first franchises of the owner in that location. Years later in Ames, Iowa, we were wowed. The french fries were so good I didn't eat my hamburger.

John Buckley, my press secretary, recalled some of the finer points of the rating methodology:

> Every McDonald's we went to—including memorably one in the Bronx whose arches you could see from the Triboro [Bridge]—were subject to a grade. Lew,

> whoever was driving, and whoever was with him besides me, would then rate the McDonald's when we finished eating, typically in the car. The principal categories that made up the grade were the burger and fries, but there were points awarded or deducted for cleanliness, friendliness, etc.[74]

With a complete grasp of my system, you could go anywhere in the United States and be well fed. John also remembered that "A typical McDonald's would be graded a B. But a McDonald's with freshly made fries, a Goldilocks level of salt, and a Big Mac that was hot and not oversaturated with special sauce might get an A-. And if it did, we'd remember, and would try to make sure we got back there if possible."[75] John remembers only one A given, and it was in Ithaca. "We ate there before Lew and I went running with the cross-country coach of a local high school who was his supporter. I regretted running so quickly after lunch, but it was an A-grade McDonalds. It was worth it."[76]

During my 1982 gubernatorial campaign, reporters dutifully followed the high-toned positions and the low-toned debates. They also covered such important questions as "What is your favorite hard drink?" My answer: "beer." I responded similarly to a question about my favorite food: "McDonald's hamburgers, beer, and french fried potatoes."[77]

The *Washington Post*'s Martin Schram wrote: Lehrman "attacked his lunch of two McDonald's french fry bags with both fists, as he attacks in the same style a man who is not yet his opponent."[78] (Martin was probably referring to Ed Koch.)

The *Buffalo Evening News* documented one of our meal breaks on the campaign trail. "He stopped at a McDonald's restaurant a few miles away and stood in line to order a hamburger, small bag of french fries and a soft drink. A half-dozen patrons recognized him, pumped his hand and wished him luck. One man sought his opinion on nuclear power plants—Mr. Lehrman is against the construction of new nuclear power plants until safety problems are resolved. 'What do you think?' Mr. Lehrman asked a young lady ahead of him on the line. 'I'm against them,' she replied." [79]

"Lew's favorite place to eat on the road was McDonald's," noted Andrei Bogolubov of our time together at CFA. "We visited McDonald's restaurants in many states, and we took these visits seriously. At that time, Lew was the only person I had ever witnessed returning insufficiently warm fries at a McDonalds." Accordingly, we kept a list that rated the McDonald's we visited to our exacting standards. For the record, America's top-rated McDonald's under the Lew Lehrman Golden Arches Standard was the one in Ames, Iowa."[80]

Campaign reporters sometimes commented on my intense metabolism. Paul J. Browne of the *Watertown Daily Times* was one of them, writing that "before he officially announced his campaign for governor, Lewis Lehrman agreed to do an informal interview over dinner.[. . .] You could imagine Mr. Lehrman consuming plates and plates of pasta, ferret-like, never gaining an ounce. He is trim at 43 and attributes this condition to running. You could also imagine, however, that Mr. Lehrman is capable of burning pounds away while standing in place."[81]

Around the family campfire

CHAPTER 11

Spreading Wings

HOME AWAY FROM HOME

Louise expanded my world in so many ways. She taught me to ski, backpack, canoe, and ride horseback. I taught her about business.

Louise taught me to ski when I was about thirty. I had only skied once before, had an accident, and was on crutches for weeks. In the second year of our marriage, we went to Zermatt. My instructor took us high up on the glacier. Embarrassed by my awkwardness, I ended up losing control, and had to fall down in order to avoid sliding all the way into Italy and France. Over time, I got somewhat better, until I could even handle the intermediate slopes. But there are some things that if you don't master when you're young, you never get good at it.

In 1992, we bought a house in Woody Creek, Colorado, not far from Aspen. We took the kids there on holidays. Thomas started by skiing between my legs and

Skiing with Uncle Biggie (in front with headband) and family

blaming me for every fall he took. He and Peter went on to become accomplished skiers; however, John took the sport to the limit, going on to master the art of back-country skiing, becoming a professional ski guide at his own lodge. All the children surpassed me after three years of skiing.

Louise's grandmother had a house on Nantucket where our family once spent part of the summer. The kids loved the old-time seafaring feel of the place, biking through the streets and going to the movies. We owned property there, but in 1985 and 1994, Louise sold part of it, and donated the rest to the Nantucket Conservation Fund.

LIFE'S GREATEST JOYS

I think of myself primarily as a father and husband, with the great satisfaction that comes along with that. I consider fatherhood a fundamental part of authentic patriotism, and especially American patriotism. Becoming a father reminds me of one of Samuel Johnson's quotes. Permit me to interpolate: "There is nothing like having children to concentrate the mind."[1] Raising children is the most gratifying thing a human being can do, but you have to be all in.

The loss of the governorship had benefits. Many good things occurred because of that loss in 1982. One of the most fulfilling parts of my life was the time I got to spend with Louise and the kids. I had time to teach my children—in both academics and athletics.

My mother had been such a strong influence on us growing up that I immediately delegated the leadership of the child rearing to Louise—so sturdy were her values and her example. I felt my job was to set the example, she was the line executive. I was staff to her and played a supporting role. "All real teaching is by example, and my father knows it," recalled Lee. "He always practices what he preaches, whether in writing, religion or business."[2]

We understood our importance as role models for the five kids. They saw Louise and me working day and night, for example, building the farm in Pennsylvania. Louise and I saw what the farm could be. It took us our entire marriage to achieve it, but we persisted. I would tell Rick Johns of the *American Economic Council*:

> My hopes for the future grow out of my own personal life.
>
> Above all, I care about my family. I have five small children and my wife and most of our hopes for the future are based upon a commitment to a way of life that gives our children an even better chance than I had. I think every parent feels that way. I want my children to grow up in a world where they say, "You know, the 'old man' really worked hard so that America could be the kind of country in which we would want to raise kids." Now, in concrete terms, that means a world where the least advantaged have an opportunity to go to the very top of an economic ladder.[3]

Make that every ladder.

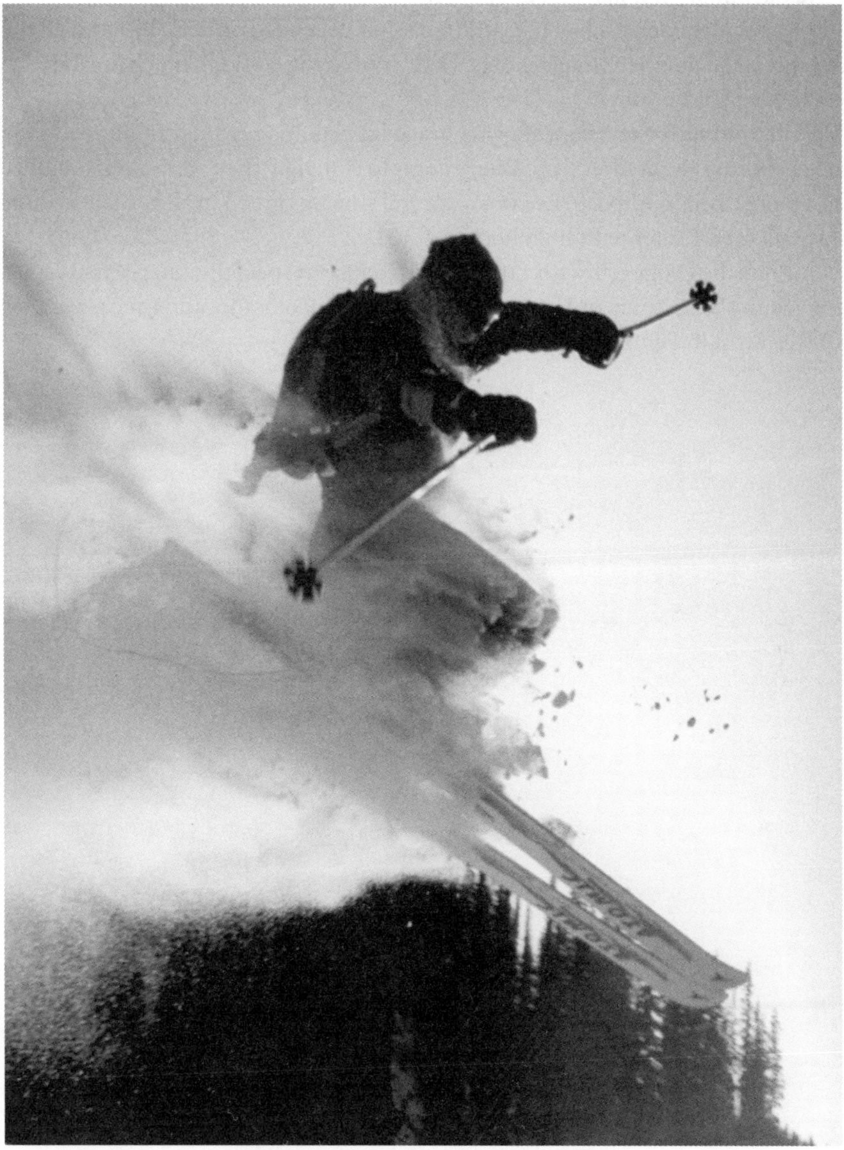

Thomas Lehrman: Powder jumper

Together, Louise and I established values for the children: "Don't brag . . . be modest . . . don't talk about yourself all the time . . . always show respect for your elders and friends by asking about their lives." We understood, however, that we had to live our values, not just talk about them.

Louise understood each of her children. They depended on her. She handled their education. She got them into schools. I taught content. I told them "I am staff. I am here to help your mother."

We discouraged television. We encouraged sports and reading. Thomas and Eliza came home and went directly to their rooms to complete their work. John and Peter had a more casual approach. Lee was a natural—he was gifted in all academic studies and graduated Exeter with high honors.

Our families engaged with families of friends—especially in sports. We went skiing with the Brittons in Vermont, the Moores in Colorado, and they played with us at the farm in Pennsylvania.

CHAPTER 12

Faith in Action

I have long recognized the importance of the Judeo-Christian religion in economic and political life. I explored these connections in the same *Crisis* magazine article wherein I had formulated my theory of value: "Capitalism: Only One Cheer." No matter how good an idea is—whether capitalism, the gold standard, or democracy—in the end, a system, like any tool, can only be as good as the people who use it. For the April 2000 issue of *Crisis*, I wrote:

> Properly conceived, capitalism is primarily an economic mechanism that, given a certain social and political order, may produce remarkable wealth. While it is from the sweat of his brow that man must toil for his bread, no economic principle is, by itself, sufficient to guide his social order. Indeed, no economic institutions, even the efficacious mechanism of capitalism, are sufficient to maintain the free markets themselves.... In the end a lasting free market order depends on the formation of right conduct deep in the character of each citizen. But what forms the well-formed conscience, this indispensable gyroscope of a free society? This is the supervening question of social policy. . . . The text of *Rerum Novarum*—a [papal] encyclical as magnificent in English as it is in the original Latin—unselfconsciously gives us the answer: "Christian morality when adequately practiced leads of itself to temporal prosperity; for it merits the blessing of God . . . who is the source of all blessing; [Christian morality] powerfully restrains the greed of possession and the thirst for pleasure, twin plagues, which too often make a man who is void of self-restraint . . . miserable in the midst of abundance.... No success would exceed that of Christian love."[1]

The attentive reader will please allow me to repeat an important section of that article in which I continued:

> A free society can remain free; the creative mind of man can achieve its loftiest aims; and capitalism can be sustained in the long run, only if the vast majority is moved by the inner dictates of a well-formed conscience. Such a conscience, by itself, enables every person in the community to transact his business without fear of unaccountable theft and bodily harm. The well-formed conscience is also the simplest, least expensive, and most efficient regulator of a free social order.[2]

Pope John Paul II: The Saint for all Seasons
John Buckley and I at the Vatican

Regarding the formation of that conscience, I note the injunctions given by President George Washington in his Farewell Address: "Of all the dispositions and habits which lead to political prosperity, Religion and morality are indispensable supports. In vain would that man claim the tribute of Patriotism, who should labour to subvert these great Pillars of human happiness, these firmest props of the duties of Men and citizens."[3]

EARLY DAYS

My interest in religion was formed in childhood. Grandfather Louis Lehrman was a pillar of the Jewish community. A Reformed Jew, he was an assimilationist and a leader in the Reform community. He was so honorable and gracious, he was wooed by every single Jewish woman in Harrisburg and Florida after his wife died. Faith was still the keystone in the foundation of American values when I grew up by the Italian Lake.

In Harrisburg there were distinct Jewish and Christian communities, as Susie Bailey Scott reminded me recently. She went on to observe that "My father and Lew's father did a lot to bridge the gap. Lew learned a lot from his father."[4]

Rabbi Bookstaber at Ohev Sholom Temple influenced me spiritually. The preparation for my bar mitzvah on October 26, 1951, was demanding, but memorizing Hebrew was easy for me. The milestone made the *Harrisburg Patriot*, "As part of the regular Friday night services of Reform Temple Ohev Sholom, being held during temple construction at the Jewish Community Center, an unusual religious ceremony will take place tonight. The twin sons of Mr. and Mrs. Ben Lehrman, Lewis and Gilbert, will go through the Bar Mitzvah consecration in accordance with a traditional ceremony.[...] A reception in honor of the two sons will be held in the auxiliary auditorium after services."[5]

For all that, Anna "Nana" Simmons, a Presbyterian, had a more profound influence on me than my parents regarding religious questions. She was the babysitter for our family and helped my mother through thick and thin. It was she who taught me the "Lord's Prayer" and "Jesus Loves Me, This I Know, For the Bible, Tells Me So." We recited the Lord's Prayer before we went to bed. Her faith intersected with my soul's sensibility and stimulated an early interest in Christianity.

At The Hill School, I was required to join the other students at chapel every evening and twice on Sunday, even though I was Jewish. And it was a good thing. I profited in the same way that Saul did, on the road to becoming St. Paul. There were only about three Jewish students in the entire school. The faculty were religious Christians. My history teacher Garrett Greene had a very positive attitude toward the Christian faith. He took neither American history nor faith for granted. The traditional way of life at The Hill School was *de rigueur.*

At Yale, I took several religion courses—Early Christian Doctrines and also Religion 24B, Religion in Literature. The latter was taught by Reverend Bardwell Smith of the Merrill Lynch Pierce Fenner & Smith family. When I was an undergraduate, Bardwell was an Episcopal priest and an assistant chaplain under William Sloane

Coffin Jr. Bardwell's mother Gertrude Behanna had been a missionary and wrote a book about her experience, which Louise later read and recommended to me. I got to know both Bard and his mother Behanna very well. I was sufficiently close to them to call her "Reverend Behanna." The key insight I learned from Bardwell was that things *invisible* and true are just as important as things *visible* and true.

I continued to be interested in deepening my faith after I got out of Yale. I knew religion was *historically* important. I just did not know how important it was to me, personally. Over the years, I had often asked myself these two questions:

1. Was Jesus Christ the Son of God?
2. If so, did He found a church?

Those two questions preoccupied me from my days at Yale. I asked myself those two questions over and over again. I was tempted by my friend Nelson Thayer at Yale to come into the church, but did not take the step. Meeting Louise was a big step forward. Louise was a practicing Christian. Anything she took seriously, I took seriously. Because she was Episcopalian and I Jewish, our wedding had been a civil ceremony. Our children occasionally attended religious services of both faiths, especially at Christmas and Easter.

FAITH IN THE CAMPAIGN

During the campaign, it was journalists who raised the issue of my religion—and that of Louise. When at the time of my announcement it was suggested that I might have difficulty winning a Republican primary, I responded: "When a person goes into a drugstore to buy something, they don't ask the religion of the cashier, or the salesman, or the owner."[6] I didn't intend to minimize the importance of religion by the use of that metaphor, but I knew that well-intentioned people of all faiths in America would be able to understand my point. That said, I did not use the metaphor again. It was too easily misunderstood.

The campaign understood that a large proportion of Jewish voters in New York City would vote Democratic, but we appealed to them anyway. We aggressively pursued Catholic voters of Italian and Irish descent because they were more likely to vote conservative. My standing with the hierarchy of the Archdiocese was obvious at the Al Smith Dinner held late in the campaign. "They had Lehrman and Bush lined up with the Cardinal, and they had me with the waiters,"[7] Mario Cuomo would complain. Nevertheless, I did better on the West Side than any previous Republican candidate.

When Louise was interviewed by the *New York Times* in October 1982, she observed: "It's difficult for people to understand. When you don't go to church every Sunday or to the synagogue every week and your children don't go to Sunday School, it's hard to say that you're religious people. But, in fact, we both have a strong sense of values and a lot of that comes from our religious heritage."[8]

Reporters wanted to make religion into a political issue, and I wanted to keep my religious life personal.

STEPS TO CONVERSION

After settling in New York, I had gotten to know some of the hierarchy of the Archdiocese, including Cardinals Terence Cooke and John O'Connor. I was introduced to Cardinal Cooke by Gus Levy, the head of Goldman Sachs, who had taken an avuncular attitude toward me. One day, I got a call from Levy to come to a meeting with Cardinal Cooke, who was a sweet, gentle, orthodox Catholic, always finding the golden mean. Levy had been asked by Cardinal Cooke to form the Inner-City Scholarship Fund (ICSF). When Gus asked me to join the board, I was honored. Max Rabb, a former secretary to the Eisenhower Cabinet and ambassador to Italy, asked me as well. The opportunity to help children from the slums and first-generation immigrants really appealed to my teaching and equal opportunity instincts. When I taught at Cardinal Hayes High School, I found Monsignor Thomas McCormack to be an old-fashioned headmaster. I found there the traditional beliefs with which I sympathized upheld in the classroom, on the basketball court, and in daily mass.

When I chaired the Fund Dinner in 1979, I became well-acquainted with the ICSF leadership—including Sister Eymard Gallagher and Father Robert J. Robbins. Sister Eymard was director of the Inner-City Scholarship Development Fund and a born executive. She was constantly raising funds to support the education of New York children at Archdiocese schools—regardless of their chosen faith.

Cardinal Cooke: "Saint Terrence"

Sister Eymard Gallagher: Ready for the drill

Sister Eymard later became president of Marymount College in Virginia. I supported her every effort. She was an amazingly disciplined woman, enormously capable. It was she who built Marymount into a great college.

Father Robbins served as director of the archdiocesan Community Outreach Office and the Interfaith and Ecumenical Commission before becoming pastor of Holy Family Church near the United Nations for two decades. In 2013, he became pastor of the Church of Our Savior as well as Our Lady of the Scapular and St. Stephen's. These parishes are now under the supervision of Father Gerald Murray, a very good friend of our family.

A soft-spoken, angelic man, Cardinal Cooke died in October 1983 after battling leukemia for years. That December I was honored at the ICSF Dinner at the Waldorf Astoria hotel. There I was given the Cardinal Cooke Award. *Catholic New York* covered the event, and included some of my remarks at dinner:

> "Cardinal Cooke grasped the centrality of value-centered education in a democracy," added Lew Lehrman, recipient of this year's Inner-City Scholarship Fund Award. The Cardinal's commission on the archdiocesan school system "established the financial basis which kept open our schools in hard economic times," said Lehrman, the Republican candidate for governor last year. It was a tribute to Cardinal Cooke's "sharp eye for the bottom line" and his love for children, Lehrman added. "Foremost came the children, and then the means to pay for their education." A member of the Fund's board for the past 10 years, Lehrman has given scholarships to many young people, personally charting their academic progress and helping some get jobs.[9]

It was my way of honoring the Cardinal's legacy.

Earlier that year, I had met Pope John Paul II in Rome during a European trip for Ronald Reagan. John Buckley was with me in the third row at the Vatican. The Pope, who clearly had been briefed said: "Vhere are you from? Are you American? Vhy are you in Rome? I have been told that you represent Ronald Reagan." I was moved by his humble character and plain talk, and told him I was a conservative from New York.

I got such a good feeling from my work with the Catholic Church that I started quietly contemplating conversion as early as the late 1970s. After the campaign for governor, I began to think seriously about it, and spent some time with a priest I will call Father John. He was a good man and a good priest. He told me that every man has to choose for himself, and I chose the Catholic Church.

Looking back, I can now see that I had been prepared for this choice at Yale, by the Religion and Literature course of Reverend Bardwell Smith, and by the personal example of his mother, Reverend Gertrude Behanna.

In 1983, Louise and I discussed my conversion. She thought I should be baptized at St. Thomas More Church on the Upper East Side, and that I should do it regardless of my boyhood religion. I took the three eldest boys for a walk along Highland Farm Road near our Greenwich home. I explained what I was about to do and asked if they wanted to attend. Thomas was the most enthusiastic, but everyone agreed to be there.

With the encouragement of Louise, I made plans. Father Gerald Murray, a young priest who was ordained in 1984, concelebrated my conversion on Sunday afternoon April 13, 1985, at the beautiful St. Thomas More Church in New York. Father Murray and I had been introduced by Bill Buckley, with whom I had consulted about the wisdom of converting. Buckley had said "go for it" and when he wrote a piece in the *Daily News* about the conversion, he cited for support the ancient conversion of Saul becoming Paul.

Father Murray would later become pastor of St. Vincent De Paul Church and Holy Family Church and is a respected multilingual theologian and canon lawyer. We are still friends to this day, and he comes for dinner or lunch regularly.

The conversion and associated sacraments took place with only a few friends and family members in attendance. I called a number of them just days beforehand. St. Thomas More is a beautiful church. Louise and I admired its similarity to country Gothic Anglican churches in England. Four of the seven sacraments were part of the service: baptism, communion, confirmation, and the blessing of marriage. Afterwards, there was a small reception at our apartment. I did not think my conversion was "news," but I was surprised.

The *New York Post* printed a front-page picture of me, and story to boot. Three days later, an article about my conversion appeared in the *New York Times*. Subsequent news articles included a variety of misinformation and inaccurate analysis. As unfortunate as that was, I was hesitant to make corrections or discuss the matter publicly at all. "I can appreciate why you would want to know all about it," I told the *Times*, "but it's just my feeling that one's faith is really a private matter and has not been customarily part of public discussion, so I'd rather not talk about it."[10]

I was surprised at the reaction to my conversion. It apparently affronted some who thought religion was a matter of birth, rather than conviction. "I didn't expect there to be newspaper stories," I told the *Daily News*. "I read some of the stories with the understanding that people have strong feelings on this kind of subject . . . I have

Father Gerald Murray: My canon lawyer

always recognized that every American is entitled to an opinion about what I do. That particular decision remains private."[11]

And that was that. I do remember calling *New York Post* editor Roger Wood and saying "Don't your reporters have something better to do than follow me around from church to church?" Wood called off the paper's coverage.

Some of the news stories were contradictory—suggesting that conversion was political suicide on the one hand, and political expediency on the other. The Republican establishment was beside itself. "I must have gotten 8,000 telephone calls the next day," claimed state GOP chairman George Clark. "People would call and say, 'The guy's nuts. That's the end of his career. What's he trying to do?'"[12] I was indifferent to the political consequences of my actions. Faith is faith.

Even my journalist friends Rowland Evans and Robert Novak, criticized me: "Lewis Lehrman . . . did nothing to prepare either party leaders or his political lieutenants for his surprise conversion from Judaism to Catholicism," they wrote. "Republican politicians felt Lehrman erred in not informing New York State GOP Chairman George Clark in advance."[13]

What was a matter of personal faith was somehow seized upon as a matter of political apostasy. As was often the case, my friend Bill Buckley came to my defense in a late April column, complaining that "What saddens is the callousness of secular commentary, which supposes that any decision, if reached by a man of public affairs, is dictated by political considerations."[14]

My conversion had an impact on associates and family members. Many years later, two of my sons would comment on it directly. Thomas was inspired by my "conversion to Christianity and showing by example what it means to be a good father and husband and the joys that come with that vocation." Leland observed that "changes of that nature take more spiritual courage than anything else, and it is that kind of courage we need in the world today."

My colleagues offered these reflections:

- John Mueller: Though a cradle Catholic, I had become an atheist by the time I got out of college. By the time Lew ran for governor, my wife and I had become Methodists. But a question from Lew helped clarify my choice: "If you are going to be a Christian, why not the real thing?" I said to myself, "So this is what the Catholic Church looks like from the outside."[15] (John is now a confirmed Catholic.)
- Trish Blake: When I worked in Washington, DC I had the opportunity to see Mother Teresa. She was speaking at an event at the Hilton Hotel just down the street from Citizens For America. Security back then was lax as it was prior to 9/11 and I was able to walk in and stand and listen in the back of the meeting room. She spoke about the importance of and the dignity of all life. Several years later, Pope John Paul II said Mass in Central Park. Because of his work with the Archdiocese of New York, Lew secured a ticket to the event and he gave it to me. I sat next to John Murnane and his young daughter Jessica. All these years later, Mother Teresa and John Paul II have been canonized. My work with Lew provided me with an opportunity to personally witness two Saints. I will always appreciate and never forget this.[16]
- Chris Potter: Early during my time (working with Lew), after a broker inappropriately asked me to reveal the nature of a short position we had, Lew told me to be "wise as [a] serpent, and harmless as [a] dove" quoting Jesus (from Matthew 10:16). When a great teacher quotes the *greatest* teacher, it is impactful. In 2000, when I had a crisis of faith, Lew pointed me to *The Confessions of Saint Augustine*.[17]
- Andrei Bogolubov: One day Lew called me into his office in New York City, sat me down and told me he had converted to Catholicism. It caught me by complete surprise and I confessed I didn't know what to say. "Say congratulations!" he said. We embraced and I congratulated him.

  Before this announcement, Lew had met regularly with a young priest who left a budding career on Wall Street to serve God. But Lew's interests, friendships, and correspondents were so diverse and eclectic that I never gave any thought to why Lew was meeting with a Catholic priest. Even when he told me that there are two questions for anyone serious about their faith—was Jesus Christ the Son of God, and if so, what church did He found?—I still didn't put two and two together.

  The phones blew up when the news came out. I must have taken 150 calls from the media. Everyone from the *New York Post* to the *Jerusalem Post*. Lew

> and I agreed to put out a simple statement—this is a matter of faith and we have no further comment. Hearing this, virtually every reporter asked if this was a political move. No, I would repeat, it's a matter of faith. And invariably they followed up by asking if his conversion hurts Lew politically. I would gently note the contradiction and even the most hard-bitten journalists had to chuckle and concede the point.
>
> Soon after, Lew and I dropped into St. Patrick's Cathedral. The great cathedral was nearly empty. We separated and found places in pews. My prayers said, I looked up and saw Lew kneeling alone in a pew before the altar, his head bowed. And I said to nobody in particular, "it's a matter of faith."[18]

I viewed faith as a piece with the rest of life—not separate from it. In a 1993 *Wall Street Journal* review of Michael Novak's *The Catholic Ethic and Spirit of Capitalism*, I wrote:

> The conventional wisdom of our age decrees economics and religion mutually exclusive; commerce and faith the works of separate and sometimes hostile authors. Those enemies of democratic capitalism—mostly socialist academics—like to paint religion as "the opiate of the masses" and a tool of oppression. Even some capitalists lean to reductivism, seeing the economics as only dealing with the bottom line or other inhuman calculuses.

Cardinal O'Connor: "Saint John"

> And so, we are led to ask, where does one discover the inner sovereign by which one freely does right rather than wrong, such that rights of a person might be respected—without threat of "dungeons to ourselves?"[19,20]

Many of my relations with senior members of the Church stemmed from my writings on the right to life. I got to know a lot of the cardinals, especially the conservative ones. In January 1986, I became a Knight of Malta under J. Peter Grace's initiative. I resisted, thinking I was not worthy, but Grace sent my papers to the papacy.

I met future cardinal Edward Egan when he was chancellor of education for the Archdiocese and later bishop of Bridgeport. I met future Hartford archbishop Henry J. Mansell as he rose in the hierarchy of the Archdiocese of New York. I also got to know Cardinal Edwin Frederick O'Brien, coadjutor archbishop for the military services and later archbishop of Baltimore, when he served under Cardinal Cooke.

But it was Cardinal John O'Connor, a former bishop of Scranton, Pennsylvania, who was smitten by my forward stance on abortion and cover stories for *National Review*. Knowing of my relationship with Cardinal Cooke, he had sought me out.

COMMITTING TO THE RIGHT TO LIFE

In the 1982 gubernatorial campaign, I had declared my opposition to abortion, saying "I do not believe taxpayers should be forced to subsidize unrestricted abortion on demand."[21] I had not, however, made the right to life a central part of my campaign, or my political philosophy.

Over the next three years, I began to think about and study the issue from a historical point of view. I connected the work of the Founding Fathers to their religious convictions, and gave speeches all over the country, simultaneously writing articles on the issue for many different newspapers and journals. In a speech at Pepperdine University in November of 1984, I said that "the Founders of our country believed every American a principal player in the drama of salvation of an Almighty God. They held also that America had a providential destiny in that plan."[22] Increasingly, I also connected Abraham Lincoln's fight against slavery with the assertion regarding the right to life in the Declaration of Independence. When I finally put pen to paper, I was thorough.

For the Shippensburg, Pennsylvania *News-Chronicle* I wrote:

> Thirteen years ago, in *Roe v. Wade*, the Supreme Court overthrew the common law of centuries and the statute law of 50 states, and authorized abortion on demand. It severed the child-about-to-be-born from the Declaration of Independence, in which the Founding Fathers proclaimed the self-evident truths of our fundamental law; that all men are created equal, [and] that they are created by God with the unalienable right to life . . . to liberty, and to the pursuit of happiness.
>
> But the Declaration of Independence does not give perfect guidance to the resolution of everyday political disputes, even though it best expresses our ultimate reason for national being. When our positive law, the Constitution, fails

> in some critical way to uphold the first principles of our national founding, it becomes necessary for Americans—who seem now, as they seemed in 1853, too concerned with progress and payrolls—to reconsider the organic law written in their hearts.[23]

In my 1986 commencement speech to Thomas Aquinas College, I got serious, and spelled out what that might mean, saying:

> We are taught to see clearly that today in *Roe vs. Wade* we Americans face for the second time in our history, as first we did in the *Dred Scott* Supreme Court Decision of 1857, the legalization of a crime against the ultimate law of God and moreover, the Supreme Law of the Land. It is no use, in extenuation, to invoke the pluralism of opinions or, falsely, the absence of consensus as if, in the struggle over *Roe vs. Wade*, all were merely a friendly historical debate; that, indeed, there were no lives at stake, no ultimate judge to whom we make an appeal—neither to the binding rule of the Declaration of Independence, nor to the eternal law of the Decalogue. It is this binding appeal to the higher American tribunal we must understand, that is, to the natural law of life enshrined in the Declaration of Independence. But there is also the Pontifical teaching that "The life of a child prevails over all opinions." Both the organic law of the American nation, and the divine law prevail over all positive law, and, *a fortiori*, over all the litigious subtleties and the cunning dissimulations of politicians and judges.[24]

There are times in history when moral issues displace all other political and economic considerations, even in the public consciousness. At the time I wrote these articles, I believed America was facing just such a moral crisis, and compared the sea change in our national politics with events that had occurred in the previous century. In August 1986, *National Review* published a cover story by me entitled "The Right to Life and the Restoration of the American Republic," which was then reprinted in *Crisis* magazine in November. I carefully sketched out the historical parallels between slavery and the right to life, saying:

> The Declaration of Independence and the Constitution of the United States inaugurated not only the American experiment, but also one of the greatest economic booms in history. Americans moved West and South, labored North and East to till the soil, build roads, finance banks, invest in new technologies, discover new methods of farming, mining, and manufacture. "We made the experiment," Lincoln wrote during the prosperity of 1854. In America "we proposed to give all a chance." Now "the fruit is before us. Look at it—think of it. Look at it in its aggregate grandeur, of extent of country and numbers of population—of ship and steamboat and rail."
>
> In 1854, almost fourscore years had gone by since the Founding, and nearly as many years divided the abject poverty of Thomas Lincoln from the prosperity

of his son Abraham, the "lone Whig star" of Illinois. In twenty years of hard work before 1854, Lincoln had been preoccupied with personal advance in law and politics, during which time he focused on the great issues of economic nationalism: the tariff, the National Bank, and internal improvements. It is true that he was only one among thousands of apostles of national development and economic growth; but he was utterly devoted to their cause.

In 1853, all America basked in the glow of a prosperity Americans took as their just desserts. The period stretching from the inauguration of James Monroe in 1817 through the early 1850s has gone down in American history as the Era of Good Feeling and of Manifest Destiny—an era during which, despite the great perils faced by the infant nation at the turn of the century, America had conquered a continent and established her independence of Europe. The new nation had finally settled down.

Then, out of the Great Plains, the Kansas-Nebraska Act of 1854 blew in upon American politics with the force of a tornado, sweeping aside the economic issues paramount in the immediate past. The old Whig Party disintegrated under the pressure of the new politics, and so in all but name did the Old Democracy, the party of Jefferson and Jackson—both parties swept aside by the gale force of a single moral issue, or what our pundits today would call a social issue. That issue, the extension of slavery to the territories, led ineluctably to the great national debate over the "unalienable right to liberty" of the black slave. It was neither the first nor the last, but it was, up to that time, the greatest debate over the first principles of the American Republic.

At first, Americans—Democrats and Whigs alike—refused to believe that the work and wealth of recent decades, not to mention the pocketbook politics of the era, would be swallowed up in a moral struggle over a single issue. But, in opening all the Western lands to slaveholding, Kansas-Nebraska shattered the spirit of the Missouri Compromise of 1820, which had limited slavery to states south of 36°30'. If it were true, as Lincoln would later say, that eventually the nation must be all slave or all free, there could be little doubt in which direction the new act was taking us.

In the words of one distinguished historian of the period, Professor Gabor Borritt of Gettysburg College, Kansas-Nebraska shook national politics like Jefferson's "firebell in the night." So abrupt was the transition from preoccupation with economics and national security ("Manifest Destiny" and "Western Lands") that Abraham Lincoln, himself one of the most knowledgeable of Whig leaders on tax, tariff, and banking issues, abandoned further discussion of them. After 1854, he became almost mute on economic issues, claiming in the year he stood for President that "just now [tax, tariff, and financial affairs] cannot even obtain a hearing . . . for, whether we will or not, the question of slavery is the question, the all-absorbing topic of the day."

Today, six years after President Reagan's first victory, we are far along with economic expansion and just as far along with rebuilding our national defense.

> Financial markets have risen to new highs. Employment levels and new business formations have reached new peaks. . . . Politicians of both parties will speak as if they expect Americans, riding the wave of new prosperity at home and restored prestige abroad, to continue to focus on economic and defense issues as they have for a generation. As Vice President Bush declared in an interview in June, "Today, people vote their pocketbooks." We shall see.
>
> For I believe that today the American people are prepared to put their pocketbooks back into their pockets. I believe that Americans once again are preparing to ask fundamental questions, about life and death, about our special purpose as a nation, and about the first principles and fundamental law by which, as a nation under God, we have dedicated ourselves to live. I believe that national politics during the late 1980s and the 1990s will be dominated by the great constitutional, moral, and social issues of our time.[25]

Questions of life and liberty involve not just the Constitution but the Declaration of Independence in particular. In a 1987 article for the *American Spectator*, I wrote:

> Today in the great debate over the authentic Constitution, inaugurated by Attorney General Ed Meese, conservatives are faced with several unresolved but fundamental issues: Are the legal positivists and legal realists, heirs of Justice Oliver Wendell Holmes and Justice Charles Evans Hughes, right when they declare the American Constitution to be essentially what Supreme Court Justices or elected legislators say it to be—their rulings and statutes thus unappealable—even if such "law" plainly violates not only the organic law of the nation but also the law written in our hearts?[26]

In a piece for the *Human Life Review* I asked Americans some very hard questions:

> Are we finally to suppose that the right to life of the child-about-to-be-born—an unalienable right, the first in the sequence of God-given rights warranted in the Declaration of Independence and also enumerated first among the basic positive rights to life, liberty, and property stipulated in the Fifth and Fourteenth Amendments of the Constitution—are we, against all reason and American history, to suppose that the right to life as set forth in the American Constitution may be lawfully eviscerated and amended by the Supreme Court of the United States with neither warrant nor amendment directly or indirectly from the American people whatsoever? Is it not a biological necessity, if it were not manifestly plain from the sequence of the actual words in the Declaration and in the constitutional amendments themselves, that liberty is made for life, not life for liberty? Is it to be reasonably supposed that the right to liberty is safe if the right to life is not first secured; and, further, is it to be maintained that human life "endowed by the Creator" commences in the second or third trimester and not at the very beginning of the child-in-the-womb?[27]

I often made the comparison with slavery explicit:

> The leadership of Abraham Lincoln in the struggle to abolish slavery and to establish the unalienable human rights of black men and women, serves as an inspiration to those who today seek to overturn *Roe v. Wade* and establish the unalienable human rights of the child-about-to-be-born. And it is fitting to recall that Lincoln was by nature as much politician as prophet—he was not inclined to fanaticism. But when the crucial issue was joined, Lincoln exposed the counsels of timidity for the sophistries they were. Thus, with Lincoln, it is the Declaration's principles we must follow unapologetically and uphold the right to life of the unborn child.

I based my approach to constitutional questions regarding the right to life on the Declaration of Independence, and in particular, on its primary position in American law.

In the June 1989 issue of *Crisis* magazine, I described the difficulty lawyers and judges have when trying to minimize the Declaration's significance in court:

> Based as it is on self-evident principles of natural justice, and given its preeminence in American organic law, the Declaration [of Independence] suggests rules of constitutional interpretation which are too often ignored by contemporary constitutional scholars, who focus narrowly and exclusively on the positive law of the [Constitution] elaborated in 1787. But legal . . . positivists have one hard historical nut to crack: the Declaration was, and is, placed first in the *United States Code of Laws*—even ahead of the Constitution.[28]

"Moreover," I'd ask readers of the *American Spectator*, "is it true, as historicists, relativists, and nihilists argue, that original intent—the actual meaning of the framers—is undiscoverable in the history of the Constitution, or even by a deep reading of the document itself?

> And, further, are strict text-based considerations now irrelevant as "non-interpretivists" imply, when finding and applying the fundamental law of the land. . . . Or, on the other hand, are Jefferson, Madison, Washington, Adams, and Lincoln right when, affirming the Declaration and "the laws of nature and of nature's God," they "hold these truths to be self-evident, that all men are created equal"; and further that all men "are endowed by their Creator" with the unalienable right to life, and to liberty? And did the founders imply correctly that any law or judicial ruling which violates these *unalienable human rights* is, by nature unenforceable, indeed unconstitutional since, according to the Declaration of Independence—the congressional act which united the Colonies and legitimated independence—it is primarily "to secure these [unalienable human] rights" that "governments are instituted among men"; further, that

> governments hold only "just powers derived from the consent of the governed"; and finally "that whenever any form of government becomes destructive of these ends [namely, the unalienable right to life and liberty] it is the right of the people to alter or abolish it, and to institute new government". . . ? Indeed, even the people are here constrained in the Declaration of 1776 to consent only to a government of just powers and law. In their absence, the people—dedicated to the proposition that all men are created equal and endowed by their Creator with unalienable rights—should institute new government.[29]

My thesis attracted the attention of both advocates and opponents of the right to life. My articles became the center of a controversy when Clarence Thomas was nominated for the US Supreme Court in 1991. Opponents of his confirmation cited Justice Thomas's earlier praise for my article's support of natural law and my opinion on abortion. In a 1987 speech to The Heritage Foundation, Justice Thomas had said:

> The need to reexamine the natural law is as current as last month's issue of *Time* on ethics. Yet it is more venerable than St. Thomas Aquinas. It both transcends and underlies time and place, race and custom. And, until recently, it has been an integral part of the American political tradition. Martin Luther King was the last prominent American political figure to appeal to it. But Heritage Foundation Trustee Lewis Lehrman's recent essay in *The American Spectator* on the Declaration of Independence and the meaning of the right to life is a splendid example of applying natural law. Briefly put, the thesis of natural law is that human nature provides the key to how men ought to live their lives. As John Quincy Adams put it: Our political way of life is by the laws of nature, of nature's God, and of course presupposes the existence of God, the moral rule of the universe and a rule of right and wrong, of just and unjust, binding upon man, preceding all institutions of human society and government.[30]

I continued to write and speak on the issue for more than a decade—stressing that a careful reading of American history and jurisprudence reveals that Americans still hold many false beliefs. In a speech before the Catholic Campaign for America on September 21, 1996, I emphasized the dangerous presence of falsehoods, even in the opinions rendered by the 1857 Supreme Court:

> That both Chief Justice Taney and Justice Blackmun, in rendering their opinions, relied not only on false biological theories, but also on false American history, should *never* be forgotten. Contrary to Taney's recitation of American history, blacks *were* truly citizens at birth of the Constitution in 1789, voting in at least five states, including the slave-state of North Carolina, for and against ratification of the Constitution. And in 1857, [Black men] were still recognized as lawful citizens in several states, despite Taney's ruling in *Dred Scott* that [they] were not, and could not be, American citizens. Similarly, the

child-in-the-womb was also treated as a person in state law and in federal law at the very moment of the ratification of the Fourteenth Amendment in 1868, the constitutional amendment which secured legal personhood for [Black people].[31]

For *Crisis*, I finished the thought:

> Thus, by their actions, and, I believe, by their intent, the congressional lawmakers who framed the Fourteenth Amendment implicitly included the unborn child in the due process and equal protection clauses of the Fourteenth Amendment. Indeed, before *Roe v. Wade* (and since), the unborn child was and is treated in certain tort and negligence law explicitly as a person—all this, under the same Constitution which Justice [Harry] Blackmun announced in 1973 did not recognize the personhood of an unborn child.[32]

In an interview with Bill Slocum for the *Greenwich News* I again pointed to President Lincoln's example. "'When Abraham Lincoln wrote the Gettysburg Address in 1863, he said the country was founded "four score and seven years ago." Now four score and seven years ago minus 1863 is not 1789, it is 1776. He was speaking not of the Constitution, but of the Declaration of Independence. I rest my case with Mr. Lincoln.'"[33] Slocum noted the passion in my position, writing that "Mr. Lehrman's eyes blazed again as he made his point. It is, he explained, why he distances himself from other anti-abortionists who argue that the Supreme Court's sole job is to interpret the Constitution as a legal document, and joins with those judicial activists, left and right, who say the court must reach beyond a single document in answering fundamental social questions."[34]

"The present slaughter of the innocents," I declared, "is an ultimate, extraordinary, and unprecedented threat of destruction to innocent human life in America, and thus to the foundation of the Constitution itself."[35] I then asked what I consider to be the most important and difficult question facing Americans grappling with the issue, namely "Should all the fundamental laws but one be executed, even though that one, the unalienable right to life, be the basis of all the others?"[36]

Unlike many conservatives, I was unfazed by the seeming impossibility of overturning *Roe v. Wade*. The analogy to slavery was useful once again. It took a long time, and a difficult struggle to obtain emancipation for Black people. In a speech to the Connecticut Catholic Forum in April 1991, I noted:

> In the 1850s the anti-slavery movement was perplexed that slavery . . . advanced with . . . inexorable drive toward universal acceptability. That slavery had gone with the [corrupted] doctrine of Manifest Destiny and the cotton gin throughout the South and West before the Civil War is an indisputable fact of antebellum history. Historical research on the economics of slavery has confirmed Mr. Lincoln's view in 1858 that slavery was not a dying institution. Moreover, while the Constitution had expressly conferred upon Congress the power in

> Article IV, Section 3 to make all the territories free, [Chief Justice Roger B.] Taney's *Dred Scott* opinion set this power aside in an extra-constitutional ruling. Indeed, he nullified it [the Constitution that is], making the spread of slavery potentially universal throughout the vast open territory of the United States. On all fronts slavery spread across the nation, stronger in 1858 than in 1807, the year before the African slave trade was abolished. Can there be any more obvious analogy with the spread of abortion across the face of our nation after [the *Roe v. Wade* decision of] 1973?
>
> But in 1860 the American people elected a new President at the head of a new party. How then did Mr. Lincoln contend with Supreme Court sponsorship of the advance of slavery in the free territories? Invoking the precedents of Jefferson and Jackson, President Lincoln argued in his inaugural speech of 1861, "if the policy of the [national] government . . . is to be irrevocably fixed by decisions of the Supreme Court—the people will have ceased to be their own rulers." Only a year later came the congressional statute of 1862, which effectively reversed part of the *Dred Scott* decision and prohibited the extension of slavery to all American territories. Then in 1863 came the Emancipation Proclamation which overthrew slavery and the *Dred Scott* Supreme Court permanently.[37]

Speaking to Legatus in 1992, I said,

> In Article III, Section 2, Congress is given explicit constitutional power to remove Supreme Court jurisdiction of all abortion questions. But nowhere in the four corners of the Constitution can anyone discover an explicit power of judicial review, now exercised by the courts over Congress. Thus, those who, [invoking judicial review], argue against Congress' power to make exceptions to the Court's appellate jurisdiction find themselves . . . in an uncomfortable bind. They are forced to deny an explicit power of Congress, granted by express words in the Constitution—in order to protect the Court's implicit power of judicial review, nowhere even hinted at in the document.[38]

In 1996, I proposed a solution to the Catholic Campaign for America. "Given no other means of redress, under present circumstances, there is left to us but one response to the Supreme Court's sponsorship of the unrestrained abortion power.

> We, the people of the United States, must ourselves reverse the Court [if need be through Presidential action in the absence of greater legal power]. *This is urgent and necessary, I say, because the Supreme Court has, through its abortion opinions, overturned the essential principle of the American Republic.* But how may Americans reverse the Court and restrict abortion, even without a constitutional amendment? Liberals argue, since the *Casey* decision, that the Supreme Court has finally settled the matter—with few restraints —in favor of abortion on demand. Liberal elites and some Supreme Court justices, echoing the 1857

Justice Samuel Alito: The majority opinion

> *Dred Scott* opinion, even argue that two decades of pro-abortion Supreme Court rulings are themselves the supreme laws of the land. Americans have generally responded with respect for Supreme Court holdings in particular cases. But, to ask the American people, the sovereign national authority, to be quiet about first principles of the Constitution, no, never. And furthermore, one may reasonably deny that the Supreme Court can, by itself, permanently decide the supreme law of the land, in matters of fundamental constitutional principle. And, as authority for this opinion, one relies, among others, upon President Thomas Jefferson and President Andrew Jackson—the founders of the Democratic Party. It was Jefferson who wrote, "to consider [Supreme Court] Justices as the ultimate arbiters of all constitutional questions [is] a very dangerous doctrine indeed, and one which would place us all under the despotism of an oligarchy." Moreover, he emphasized, "the Constitution has erected no such single tribunal." A generation later, President Jackson, in a dispute with the Supreme Court, declared, "the opinion of judges has no more authority over Congress than the opinion of Congress over the judges."[39]

In closing this section, I would like to say that I rejoice in the recent overturning of *Roe v. Wade*. Finally, in the majority opinion of Samuel Alito, justice was done by the highest court in the United States of America. No matter how one feels about the subject, the Alito opinion is an authoritative guide to the history of the issue, the science, and the controversy. I recommend it to the attention of all Americans, and to all people of good will.

PHILANTHROPY IN THE NATIONAL INTEREST

I took an active interest in many organizations focused on public policy and history. I served as a trustee of the American Enterprise Institute (AEI), the Eisenhower World Affairs Institute, the International Center for Economic Policy Studies (Manhattan Institute), the Pierpont Morgan Library, and the Heritage Foundation among other nonprofit institutions. Other philanthropic boards on which I have served include the Capitol Foundation, the American Civil War Museum, the Boys' Club of New York, the International Center for the Disabled Rehabilitation and Research Center, Harrisburg Hospital, Lenox Hill Hospital (Manhattan), and the US Committee on Refugees.

For more than two decades, the Lehrman Institute concentrated on charitable gifts as well as research. Educational recipients of major Lehrman gifts include, among others, Brunswick School, Buckley School, Cardinal Hayes High School, Claremont Institute, Collegiate School, Duke University, the Garrison Forest School for Girls, Groton School, Harrisburg Academy, Hill School, Madeira School, Princeton University's James Madison Program, the University of Virginia's Jefferson Scholars, and Yale University.

My devotion to the study and teaching of religion, philosophy, economics, science, and history has been reflected not only in my writings, but in Lehrman Institute grants. Among the institutions which have received major research grants are the American Enterprise Institute, the Cold Spring Harbor Laboratory, the Federalist

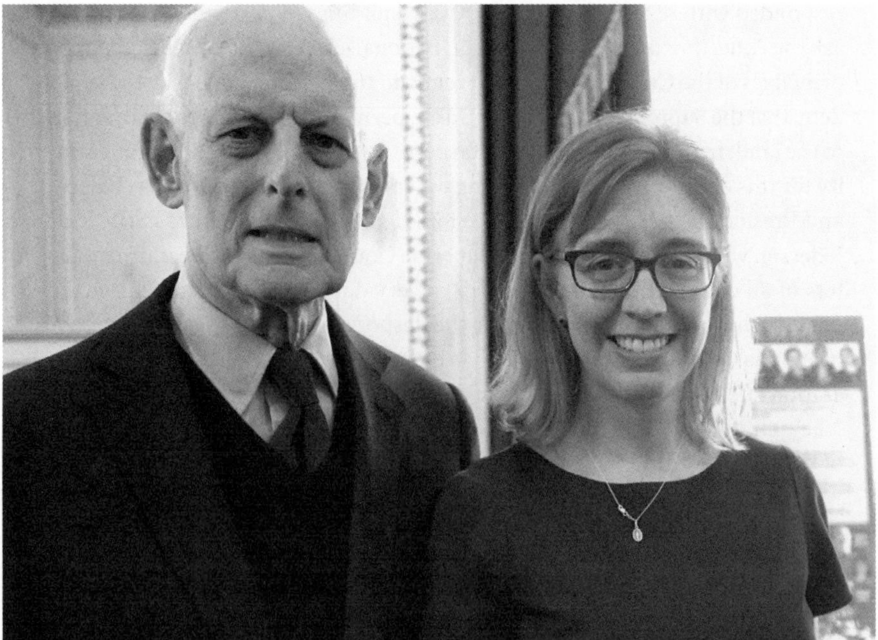

Anna Halpine: A sister for all seasons

Society, the Heritage Foundation, the Empire Foundation, the Ethics and Public Policy Center, the Foundation for Teaching Economics, and the Morgan Library. My philanthropy has also actively aided organizations concerned with the environment and wilderness education such as the Keewaydin Foundation, the Audubon, and various nature conservancies. A few of the major religious organizations which have received grants include the Archdiocese of New York, Kolbe House, Life Athletes, UJA of New York, the Woodlawn Foundation, the Witherspoon Institute, the Diocese of Bridgeport, the St. Thomas More Center and Chapel at Yale, and the World Youth Alliance.

I met Anna Halpine in her early twenties when she was working to establish the World Youth Alliance and to assure its funding. Anna remembered that I helped them early and often, writing that I provided "critical and substantial startup funding," and that "Later on, Lew became a critical funder as we started the development of our school's curriculum. And then, when we hit our hardest times, Lew was there for me. While others expressed their doubt and held off to watch and see, Lew encouraged, insisted on my capacities, and took the time to meet and support me when I needed it most. Month after month he walked with me, handing me this most precious gift of his deep and trusted friendship. When I was plunged into darkness and doubt, he relentlessly maintained his confidence. He gave it back to me, month by month."[40]

I also quietly aided other authors in the publication of their books through research grants provided by the Lehrman Institute. Such books include the University of Illinois–Springfield professor of history Michael Burlingame's magisterial, two-volume biography *Abraham Lincoln: A Life*, *The Street Stops Here* by Patrick Jameson McCloskey, about one year in an inner-city Catholic school, and *Redeeming Economics* by John D. Mueller, director, Economics and Ethics Program of the Ethics and Public Policy Center and The Lehrman Institute Distinguished Fellow in Economics.

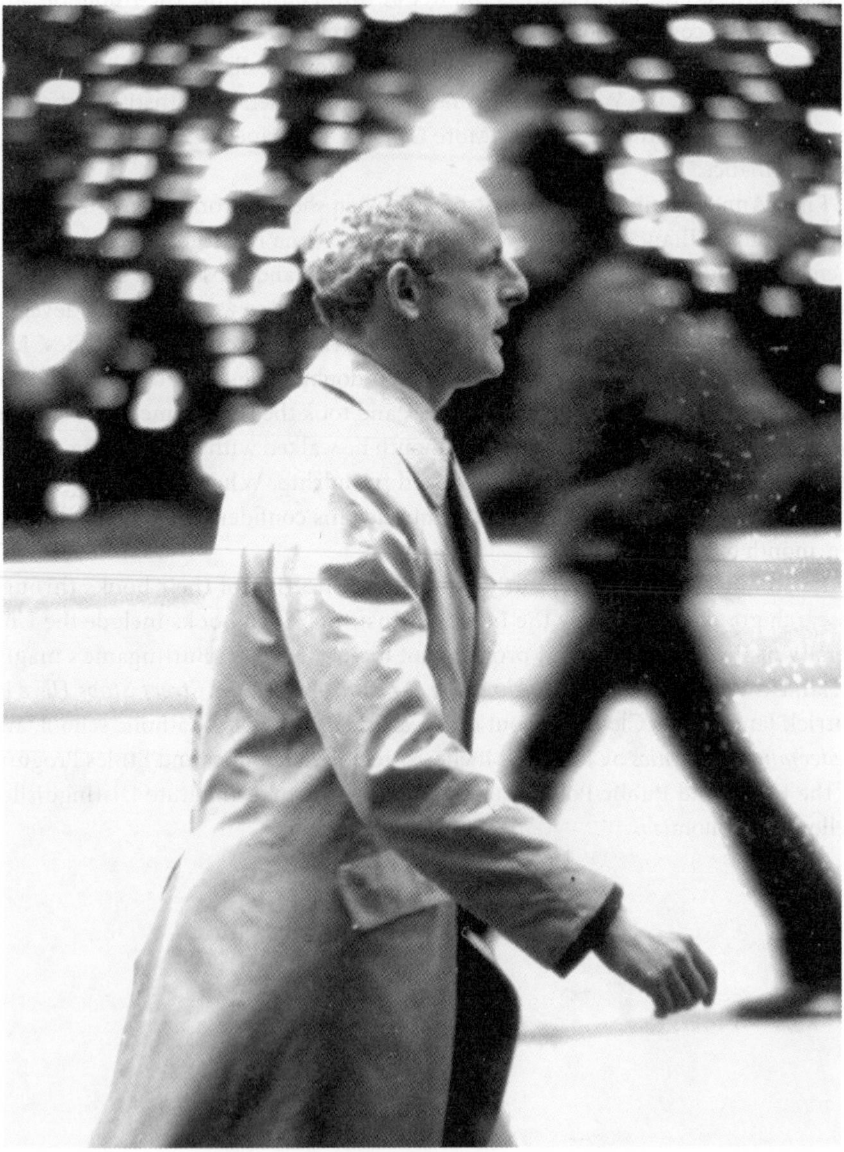

On the double

CHAPTER 13

Business and I

Pigs get slaughtered.
—Steve Szymanski

BUILDING AN INVESTMENT BUSINESS

The First Principles of Investing:

1. Don't run with the crowd.
2. Do your homework.
3. Meet the managers.
4. Understand the world.
5. Maintain constant vigilance.

I learned about the commercial world from my father and grandfather. Even my interest in the stock market came from Dad, who read *Business Week*, *Fortune*, and all the commercial magazines.

As my first stock pick, I chose Jaeger Machine—which I bought with savings when I was about twelve. I lost money on that original investment, and soon learned to do my research about companies. I was always interested in the details and applied that principle to my public life as well.

As I was preparing to leave the presidency of Rite Aid, I set up an investment office in New York with Louise's brother Charles Stillman Jr. Our first office was at 425 Park Avenue. We then moved to 641 Lexington Avenue—taking all of the twenty-fifth floor.

One investment I made would later get considerable publicity. Arbusto Energy, sometimes referred to as Arbusto Oil, was a petroleum and energy company formed in Midland, Texas, in 1979, by future president George W. Bush. It was funded by a group of investors which included his grandmother Dorothy Bush, Celanese CEO John D. Macomber, Prudential-Bache Securities CEO George L. Ball, venture capitalist William Henry Draper, and George's uncle, my friend Jonathan Bush. Recruited by Jonathan, I was also one of the early investors. After meeting George in March 1979, I wrote to Jonathan, saying:

> Just met George. I knew I shouldn't let him through the door. I told him I was overextended. Like his Uncle John and his daddy, he just went on talking

and by the time he was finished, I was completely charmed.

He is smart, educated, has great presence, and is an impressive man.[1]

Charles Stillman Jr.: Louise's brother Uncle Charlie

George himself wrote to me in August 1979: "I have your investment in the Arbusto '79 Ltd. Fund. . . . A few investors have not yet sent in the forms, and one large investor decided not to invest on July 30. Hence, I will raise more money during the next three weeks and close the fund toward the latter part of August. Our first well will start in the first week of September."[2] Arbusto had attracted a wide array of top-notch investors. Unfortunately, though it was a top-notch company, it drilled a number of dry wells.

After the gubernatorial campaign in 1982, we wound down the New York business office. Charlie moved to Texas with his family, but continued to handle some of the family investments. I was increasingly focused on Washington, DC. During the mid-1980s, my business office was located in Washington on the second floor of the Heritage Foundation building. Carla Saunders, Lilly Eng, and Susan (Yu) Tang moved to Washington with me. Larry Henry acted as my business manager, while Frank Trotta was legal counsel to the enterprise.

JOINING MORGAN STANLEY

In March 1987, I joined Morgan Stanley as a director of Morgan Stanley Asset Management, to concentrate on the growth and development of the business in the United States, Europe, and Asia. Our unit managed portfolios for institutions, international organizations, and individuals.

When the *New York Times* asked about my new career choice, I said, "They asked me, and I suppose it's the New York Giants of investment banking. They made me an offer I couldn't refuse . . . I gave them a [three-year] commitment to help them build a world-scale investment management company."[3]

I had known Barton Biggs, the famous Morgan Stanley investment commentator, as an intellectual colleague, friend, and commissioner of the "Over-40 Football League" in Greenwich. Barton had published four of my detailed analyses of the international monetary system. He was one of my closest friends. "Barton's values were inner-directed, born of an era gone by," I would later remark at his memorial service. "Surely there was poetry in his soul. But his character was one hard nut to crack. Grit, determination, and unstinting hard work pervaded his every calling and commitment—to his family, to Morgan Stanley, to mastery of the English language, to emerging markets, to exercise, to tennis."[4]

I also knew Morgan's president Dick Fisher, and CEO Parker Gilbert, both of whom had presided over the dramatic growth of the firm. Parker was one of the most subtle CEOs I ever met. He ruled by character.

Bob Niehaus and I met at Morgan Stanley in the '80s. We both liked to work out at lunchtime in the Morgan Stanley gym. More recently, Bob shared his recollections with me:

> Lew and I would run on treadmills that were next to each other. Being the social creatures that each of us are, we introduced ourselves, discovered that we had some similar interests, and began to have a quick lunch together after our workouts in the Morgan Stanley cafeteria. Both of us had played high school football in eastern Pennsylvania (which we viewed as "real" football), and believed that our football experience had taught us some great life lessons about hard work, teamwork and perseverance. [Bob was the superior football player, and he had proven it at Princeton.] Both of us were also devout Catholics and devoted family men, and tried hard to live and do business by a strong moral code in the rough and tumble world of Wall Street. We both had a tremendous passion for history, and a strong belief in the founding principles of the United States.[5]

Bob and I remain active together to this day, as Bob is now a director of the Gilder Lehrman Institute of American History.

Bob Niehaus: Princeton football player par excellence

At Morgan Stanley, I relearned that it's crucial to set the example—to be the first one in the office, and the last one to leave. There were only a hundred partners then. Susan Tang came with me from the campaign, to CFA, to Morgan Stanley. My political career had an impact on my approachability. According to Susie, "Everybody was leery and afraid to talk to us. They were nice, but questioned why Lew was there. I thought it was funny. Some employees would attempt to brownnose us."[6] But I made other impressions as well.

Trish Blake, who came to Morgan Stanley from CFA, later said that

> It was interesting sitting right outside of Lew's office . . . he had an uplifting, powerful, motivating effect on

**Trish Blake:
Loyal and steadfast
through thick and thin**

**Anson Beard:
"The Duke of Equities"**

> everyone who walked by, especially some of the younger employees . . . they would pick their heads up, put their shoulders back, quicken their step, look a little sharper . . . excited for the chance to run a thought by or interact with Lew, who was always interested to hear what they had to say. Susan and I used to call the set of doors adjacent to and leading into the hallway outside of Lew's office "the magic doors" because of the transformation that took place when people walked through them in anticipation and hope of seeing Lew.[7]

I also learned what I didn't know about the investment business. Morgan Stanley was highly educational. I got valuable investment experience there while learning how to run the firm's equities division. I also deepened many friendships, and occasionally had a good laugh. My Yale friend, Morgan Stanley senior partner Anson Beard, appreciated my observations on company politics, saying "I will never forget your astute analysis regarding Morgan Stanley's governance: 'it is a collection of fiefdoms, and you anointed me as the 'Duke of Equities!'"[8]

There was one serious crisis. During the crash of 1987, Susie remembers "sitting there, Ted Forstmann calling, and the tape was running two hours late. I did not know what to say to people."[9] Ted was one of my largest clients. I told Susie to tell him we've got it in hand; we are not overextended. And it was true. We bounced back almost immediately and then went on to further highs in Ted's portfolio.

By 1990, I felt I had completed my tasks at Morgan Stanley. What I learned at Morgan Stanley helped me to set up my own hedge fund. I resigned in May.

FOUNDING A HEDGE FUND

In 1987, I moved my personal business back from Washington, and opened the office next door to my home on Cherry Valley Road in Greenwich, Connecticut. When I left Morgan Stanley behind, I left a great place full of great people and great friends. But I had decided I wanted to establish my own business. My ever-present friend and advisor John Britton thought I would do much better on my own. In order to keep the farm, which was very capital intensive, I needed to make money. I also had five kids in private school.

So I set up an investment management company in 1991, calling it Ten Squared. The partnership office was on Fawcett Place in downtown Greenwich. At Ten Squared we concentrated on investment themes like early entry into wireless email, and on markets like South Korea, Russia, Canadian technology, mining, oil service, oil drilling, fertilizer production, and agricultural technology.

"Ten Squared" was a very ambitious idea—ten times your money in ten years. People like Dick Gilder, Bob Wilson, and Clark Winston were already accomplished hedge fund operators. I had no reputation.

The biggest difficulty was rounding up money to invest. Sam Reeves was one of the most successful men in the California cotton industry. He had found me when I was at Morgan Stanley, where he attended one of my speeches, and sought me out based on an appreciation for my ideas, my patriotism, and my character. Barton Biggs made the formal introduction.

Sam Reeves: Friend in the faith and superb businessman

I formed a fast friendship with Sam and one of his daughters, Annesley, who married David MacFarlane. Sam eventually moved east with some of his children. I wrote a letter of recommendation for each of his grandsons. It was part of my philosophy to help friends, and Sam was certainly a friend. He proved it.

When I went to him to set up the investment fund, he said yes promptly. I shall ever be grateful to him for entrusting me with money to invest even though I was a rookie. Sam was a superior investor, and he told me the one thing I never expected: that among all the hedge funds he had enlisted in his interest, I had the best long-term performance. There is nothing better than to satisfy a client, and nothing worse than losing money for one. I needed people who were prepared to risk investing with a rookie. Every person was a different struggle.

Samuel, William, James, Annesley Reeves, and David MacFarlane: First, last, and always

Raising money was hard, but it was made much easier by the work of my team. Frank Trotta had been with me since the gubernatorial campaign. So had Susan Tang. Susie had an upbeat personality from the very beginning. She worked for the office while in college, following me from New York to Washington and then back to New York. She eventually replaced Trish Blake as my assistant, when Trish and her husband decided to move to Denver. Susie did a brilliant job, handling a wide variety of complex tasks. She is always willing to do what has to be done, and accomplishes the almost impossible. In the period of my deteriorating health, she has been irreplaceable, and brilliant.

Trish followed me from CFA in Washington, to Morgan Stanley in New York, and finally to my investment operations in Greenwich. In 2019 she wrote a summary of our activities that give a sense of what we did together:

> Working at CFA and at Morgan Stanley were two of the most exciting chapters of my life. Even so, I think the time that I spent at Ten Squared and establishing the office in Greenwich was the most rewarding. It was thrilling to work side by side with Lew and Frank in the successful establishment of this new business. Lew was thoroughly intellectually engaged in this enterprise, yet still had the flexibility and the time to pursue his other passions . . . research, writing, American History, economics, Presidential leadership, the gold standard, political commentary, Catholic philanthropy, family activities and so many other undertakings. I loved supporting every aspect of the work: administrative, organizational, logistical, client service, marketing, moral support. No two days were alike, and the diversity and fast pace were inspiring and exhilarating.

The greater the logistical or operational challenge, the more fulfilling it was to help find a solution or bring about a good outcome. I once arranged to have a horse Federal Expressed from Ireland back to the United States. I retrieved a briefcase that had been left on a train from New York City to Greenwich, a needle in a haystack. I loved organizing Lew's Lincoln Day Card mailing. I was thrilled to help orchestrate the client outing to Gettysburg and the stay at Lew's farm in Mechanicsburg for the MacFarlanes, the Reeves, and some of Lew's other best clients and good friends. Working for the Lehrmans became more than a job to me, more than a career . . . it felt vocational. I always tried to conduct myself with energy, enthusiasm, generosity and joy—exactly as I had witnessed Lew reach out to others for so many years. In every interaction, I hoped to reflect as positively as I could on the Lehrman family.[10]

When Deja Hickcox first came to work with me, a quarter-century after Susie, she took on the administrative work. Thinking back to her interview, Deja remembers:

[I was] sitting in the conference room at Fawcett Place and he came in. I was very nervous to meet with him because of how much procedure and formality there had been for all of the interview process. We talked about my resume. At the time I was 24, had not yet finished college, but was attending a local community college studying business management. He asked about my course load and I mentioned that I was taking accounting. Lew started asking me, with a very stern look on his face, very intently about my familiarity with double-ledger

Barbara Feeney, Deja Hickcox, and Mary MacKenzie: The team

accounting methods and I remember being scared to death. I was taking accounting, but it was an entry-level course, and here he was asking me CPA-style questions . . . I remember being very nervous to work with him after that, and soon learned that he was always that intense, but that it wasn't a bad thing, it was just his energy.[11]

Chris Potter: My partner, my friend

We got Deja involved in producing *Lincoln at Peoria*, and all of my other books, and her attention to detail was extraordinary. She had an offer from another firm and left, but later let it be known she wanted to come back. When she returned, she became involved in every part of the business. After Frank retired as chief operating officer, Deja became chief administrative officer. She was totally attentive to all dates and assignments. She is rigorous and determined, and she has natural administrative leadership and skill which she has perfected through practice.

I had known Chris Potter from his childhood. He had just graduated from Columbia Business School. I knew his parents very well. His father Nicholas was a year behind me at Yale. Nick was a very hard-working guy, inspired to do well, and a loyal friend. Chris recalled his first day of work for me:

He gave me homework on day one—read the 3 classic works of Phil Fisher (*Common Stocks and Uncommon Profits*, *Conservative Investors Sleep Well* and *Developing an Investment Philosophy*) and then write book reports on them. From the start, I remember being immersed in company research, building huge Excel models, visits to Houston, Singapore (at the end of the Asian financial crisis) and many other places with Lew and Ben Atkinson to meet with company executives, and long conversations with Lew as he patiently explained his investment methodology. He even took the time to show me how he read *Barron's* and which sections he focused on. It was a fast-paced, intense and always exciting time. Lew had assembled a great team . . . Susie, Trish, Frank, Ben, Steve, Denise, Jennifer, and others. I remember it being so much fun and rewarding to be part of this group.[12]

Chris's sister Jennifer also came to work for me. Hired as an assistant to Chris, she did a great job. Both have said that they learned—in our office—everything they needed to go out on their own.

We didn't run with the crowd. We looked for special companies doing something remarkable. We spent a lot of time researching Canadian equities. Chris followed a talented bunch of entrepreneurs in technology and mining that were largely ignored by Wall Street. He eventually came up with a company called Research in Motion. We got to know their co-CEOs. We did our homework and met the managers. Chris went the extra mile. In order to explain the virtues of the Blackberry, he had management bring me one of the first red Blackberrys. I'll let him tell the rest of the story: "I met with Research in Motion (RIM) in New York City, and the CFO showed me how their two-way pager could send email wirelessly. It was like a light bulb went off and all that preparation from Lew allowed me to see the opportunity. I wrote Lew a one-page memo on November 5, 1998, outlining the investment merits of RIM. Lew then came into my office, asked for the annual report, sat down, read through it quickly and thoroughly (as Lew can do). Without much further discussion, he said 'let's do it.' The rest was history."[13]

Investing in Canadian stocks was very difficult, but Chris was not intimidated by even the biggest challenges, including the dramatic case of Slater Steel. "During the six years we worked together at Ten Squared, Slater Steel was not our biggest winner," Chris recalls, "but I think it was our most elegant investment.

> We accumulated 19% of the outstanding shares [which was 20% of the Ten Squared portfolio at the time] around $11/share and sold at close to $20/share, near the all-time high. We made a huge bet at a low price and managed to sell near the top. It was a tough battle, with a pivotal meeting that Lew organized at Tiger Management's offices in June of 1999. Frank, Lew, and I faced off against Slater's management and the Co-Steel bankers with Lew's friend Julian and his team visible to all the participants of the meeting through the conference room glass walls. It was great theater.[14]

"I think Lew threw a lot at me during that initial period," Chris remembered, "so that when the moment was right, whenever that might be, I'd have a fighting chance when it came to deciding between good and bad investments. I feel like I was slow to get comfortable investing though. At one point, Lew and Ben even gave me a very small part of Ten Squared's capital to invest, but I was too unsure or nervous to make a bet."[15]

Steve Szymanski came to work with me as CPA and chief financial officer. He did a great job. He was a very learned securities CPA. He agreed with our "honor strategy," saying that:

> The tech bubble years were heady years.
>
> While everyone was piling in, Lew was skimming off the top, keeping the amount invested in highflyers at a certain level. At the time, I did not understand why he was pulling so much money and not letting it ride. In retrospect, valuations for many of these companies were abnormally high. Nonetheless,

> most everyone I knew was thinking "this time it's different." In the end, many people got hurt when everything went bust. For [Ten Squared], the damage was contained and the profits considerable. Lesson learned . . . Pigs get slaughtered.[16]

Steve Szymanski: "Pigs get slaughtered"

Running a hedge fund is a character test and a skill test. One has to understand that you can't always make profitable decisions. There's a lot of intuition as well as analysis. One has to be flexible, make mistakes, and move on. There's no room for pride.

I remember Charlie Allen telling me that you only have time to gather 20 percent of the information on any investment. He was one of the most successful investors of my generation, and I was grateful for the several opportunities we had to speak. He made a big impression on me and some of his recommendations form the core of my investment philosophy.

I relearned the same lessons again and again: Research, research, research.

My investment strategy was simple:

- Don't run with the crowd.
- The crowd will amplify the risk of loss.
- Look for the specialized company doing something remarkable.
- Do your homework as best you can.
- Meet the managers. In Russia, it was hard. The oil industry was easier.

The investment business requires you to understand the world around you. You have to maintain constant vigilance. It engaged my full attention.

By 2002, I was back on my feet financially again. I decided to give back the money to investors and close Ten Squared—while continuing to invest on behalf of my family. As my partner Frank Trotta, summed it up: "Lew grew tired of worrying about other people's money."[17]

THE GERSON LEHRMAN GROUP

The Gerson Lehrman Group (GLG) was founded in 1998 by Mark Gerson and my son Thomas. Mark was a Yale Law School graduate and author. Thomas had just finished working as an investment analyst at Tiger Management for two years. Steve Bodow offered a perspective on the early days of the business for the *New York Times,* writing that:

They commissioned industry guidebooks for institutional investors but sold none. Fund managers were interested in talking with the authors, explaining that many of their best insights came through casual conversations, not from formal reports. "We thought it was kind of ridiculous that the hedge fund business got so much information by asking for favors—'Could I please have 15 minutes of your time?'—when they would certainly pay for that information," said Mr. Gerson, 29. "And the people who have it would love to talk. We just thought there should be a way to get the two connected." In early 1999, Gerson began offering subscriptions to its network of consultants. By June of that year, the company had abandoned the publishing business. For now, Gerson makes its money mainly by charging a fee for unlimited access to its advisers: doctors, engineers, sales agents, academics, software consultants. The initial rate is $48,000 for six months for each industry, and renewal rates are based on use. Clients, on average, spend about $70,000 for each industry every six months, Mr. Gerson said. Renewals are running at more than 85 percent, the firm said. "If our $300 million fund is up 10 percent and we can attribute a good percentage of that to Gerson, it easily pays for itself," said [David] Beard [a hedge fund manager]."[18]

Mark Gerson: Loyal partner to Thomas at The Gerson Lehrman Group

GLG would go on to bill itself as "the world's largest membership network for one-on-one professional learning."

My time with the company provided me an opportunity to mentor not only Mark and Thomas—who served as co-CEOs of the company—but also my son Peter, who joined the company in 2001 after his graduation from the University of Virginia.

Although Thomas left GLG's management in 2001 to attend Yale Law School and serve in the US State Department, I was active on the board of directors until 2011. The entire top management of GLG has changed since then, but Thomas and Mark still serve on the board and play important roles in guiding and advising the company and its team of over twenty-five hundred employees.

Jacques Rueff: Le Poète de Finance

CHAPTER 14

Forward to Gold

A disordered currency is one of the greatest political evils.[1]
—Senator Daniel Webster

I began to write about economics in the mid-1970s. Privately, I wrote long essays, namely "Reflections on the Monetary History of the West," "Inflation and Civilization: Man's Fate and His Money," and "The Origins of Money—4000 B.C.–1700 A.D." Those essays presented my studies on the history of money over five millennia. My work included original research that both uncovered and articulated the ancient foundations of what had eventually become the international gold standard. Many of these essays are now contained in my book *Money, Gold and History*.[2]

Through The Lehrman Institute, I also contributed a chapter to *Money and the Coming World Order* (1976).

The rest of my efforts focused on newspaper and magazine articles.

I was prolific.

For the *Washington Post*, in July 1981, I briefly outlined the American experience with the gold standard:

> For most of our life as a nation, we had stable prices and low interest rates under the gold standard. After mercantilist trade wars had wrecked the world economy and the international monetary system, President [Franklin] Roosevelt abandoned the gold standard domestically in 1934. President Johnson abandoned international convertibility in 1968 [substituting IMF SDRs and a two-tier system: one for speculators and one for governments], and President Nixon officially ended [the gold convertibility portion of the Bretton Woods system on] August 15, 1971.[3]
>
> The economic situation we have faced since 1971 is not unique. It is all too similar to the inflations of the Revolutionary and Civil wars. During the Revolution, the Continental Congress reduced the value of its currency to a pittance. But in 1792, after the inauguration of President Washington, Congress established the [specifics of the] gold and silver standard. During the Civil War, the U.S. government issued Greenbacks that were not convertible into gold, and the price level doubled.

> Inflation was [again] a problem until Congress began the transition to a gold standard in 1875, completing it in 1879. For more than a generation, the price level was stable, because the dollar was as good as gold.[4]

For the *Wall Street Journal,* I characterized the historic impact of abandoning the gold standard, saying "Irredeemable paper money has almost always been accompanied by unbalanced budgets, high inflation and high interest rates. But the true gold standard has been associated with balanced budgets, reasonable price stability and low interest rates. Paper money has been the handmaiden of war, protectionism and big government. But the gold standard was the symbol of peace, free trade and limited government."[5]

The problem seemed obvious to me. The solution seemed equally obvious. We need to return to the true gold standard. Thus, I eventually wrote a book on how to do it in the contemporary American context. It's called *The True Gold Standard, a Monetary Reform Plan without Official Reserve Currencies.* It went through two editions. The last one is a finished product.

On a more personal level, I tried to educate lawmakers about our national dilemma. After dinner with Senator Daniel Patrick Moynihan, I wrote him a long letter in May of 1977 wherein I avoided the arcane terms of economists. Instead, I broke down complex issues into a series of linked, simple arguments that are still relevant to voters and policy makers today. I wanted to demonstrate that there are simple cause and effect relationships in economics that have moral consequences. Because this is true, policymakers need to be confident of their understandings when they act. To this end, I wrote the following:

> To create conditions which enhance the prospects for savings means to enhance the incentive to save. To save means to defer present consumption in order to ensure future security and future consumption. In order for a laborer to choose not to consume today, he must have confidence that the wages he saves will preserve their purchasing power in the future, when he chooses *then* to expend them. Money wages must preserve their purchasing power over time, or saving becomes a meaningless act of foolishness. If the value of saved money wages is dissipated in the future by a sustained rise in the general price level (i.e., inflation), no working man should be fraudulently encouraged to save against his better instincts. To create sufficient conditions in order to encourage saving means simply to end inflation. To end inflation means to create a stable money. To create stable money means to establish budgetary equilibrium in the *National* income accounts while, at the same time, establishing balance in the monetary policy of the Federal Reserve System (through the Gold Standard). If inflation is conquered, saving will ineluctably triumph. Establish a stable money and free working people will save those resources necessary to finance new capital formation.

But an end to inflation is a necessary, but not a sufficient condition for the purposes of enhancing capital formation. *Investment returns* (to the laborers and working people who save and thereby create capital) must rise. Moreover, the level of uncertainty among working people, entrepreneurs and business managers must fall. Whenever the level of uncertainty rises in any economic system, the level of investment falls, as the predictable future returns to saving and investment will be less quantifiable. How does one establish *freedom of person* as an important objective of a stable and productive economy? By that I mean, simply, an end to violent crime against working people and businessmen in their homes, on the streets, in the factories and on their playgrounds. Extinguish the more obvious forms of criminal violence and you will at once lower the level of uncertainty. When freedom of person is secure, all the conditions of an exchange economy are enhanced. And the stable expectations necessary for investment will give rise inexorably to the business confidence which only an ordered society experiences.

We must also end *economic violence.* By economic violence I mean confiscatory levels of taxation resulting from an ever more progressive tax structure, which takes more and more of the income from the rising (nominal) money wages of the lower and middle class. Because of our progressive income tax structure and because of the secular rise in the price level, more and more people are transported into higher and higher rates on the scale of a progressive tax structure. [In other words, every pay raise is consumed by higher taxes.] Plain people cease to realize an economic value commensurate with the extra effort typical of the most productive working people.

. . . You see, Pat, it is very much like the many things you have said in other places. It is all of a piece. One cannot legislate and make policy successful for one segment of the economic system without taking into account other segments, not to mention the planetary system as a whole.

It is for these reasons that I believe you are on the right track with your emphasis on the impact of imports on American jobs. It is for the above reasons that I believe you are on the right track with your concentration on the connected problems of unemployment, welfare and work. It is for the above reasons that I believe you must also bring to bear your intellect upon the problem of the international monetary system. And if you do, you will come to understand these problems better than anyone in the United States Senate. And for all Americans, that will be a good thing.[6]

CHALLENGING MILTON FRIEDMAN

Beginning in 1976, I engaged in a lengthy correspondence with Professor Milton Friedman in which we debated our disagreements over fixed and floating exchange rates, as well as the benefits of a renewed gold standard. I tried to persuade Friedman that fixed exchange rates and a gold standard were morally and practically superior to monetarism, where the central bank tries to directly manage currency and interest rates in an international system based on fiat currency and floating exchange rates.

At the time, Friedman was still convinced that monetarism would work. Although his arguments were well informed, he waved away historic evidence, and stated that "we have no alternative" to the floating system. He described classical economic solutions that had worked as recently as 1959 in France as "hypothetical," and eventually stopped responding to me after he received the Nobel Prize in Economics. Although he continued to promote targeting the "domestic money supply" for a long time, he did finally have the intellectual honesty to admit that it was not good monetary policy. In a remarkable June 7, 2003, interview with the *Financial Times*, he concluded that "the use of quantity of money as a target has not been a success. I'm not sure that I would as of today push it as hard as I once did."[7]

THE ONGOING CAMPAIGN FOR GOLD

Although at the time, I could not move Friedman, my friendships with Robert Bartley and Barton Biggs were more valuable associations in the effort to promote sound money. I wrote numerous editorials about the gold standard for Bartley's editorial page at the *Wall Street Journal*, and detailed policy papers on the same subject for Biggs at Morgan Stanley. My studies of economic history formed the basis of a forty-four-page paper for Morgan Stanley Investment Research in January of 1980. This essay, "Monetary Policy, The Federal Reserve System and Gold," was disseminated all over Wall Street. It also landed on desks at the Federal Reserve in Washington, DC. In it I criticized the confusion of economic intellectuals, comparing their fashionable theories with easily observed hard facts:

> Gold and silver were "outdated," declared the "experts." Professional economists—Keynesians and Monetarists alike—proclaimed the coming of a new era of central bank "managed money." Monetarists promoted a steady growth in the money supply, a fixed "quantity rule"—*to be achieved* through open market operations by the Fed in the buying and selling of U.S. government securities for the portfolio of the central bank. Keynesians offered "countercyclical monetary management," a *variable* quantity rule, largely to accommodate their hyperactive fiscal policies.
>
> Within these same schools of thought, the Bretton Woods fixed exchange rate regime was also found wanting. But what both Monetarists and neo-Keynesians sought was not the reform of Bretton Woods, but rather, its demolition. They advocated managed currency, floating exchange rates and the demonetization of gold—in a word, an end to fixed-exchange-rate regimes. These monetary doctrines soon became the fashionable credos propagated by academic economists and policy makers. Henry Reuss, Chairman of the House Banking and Currency Committee, went so far as to predict that when gold was demonetized,

it would fall to $6 per ounce. (As of April 2023, gold is worth more than $2,000 per ounce. So much for the experts.)

Nixon followed Johnson and gradually went through his own conversion to Keynesian economics, announcing, "We are all Keynesians now." But he also absorbed some of the teachings of the Monetarist School—floating exchange rates in place of the Bretton Woods fixed rate system. On August 15, 1971, Nixon defaulted at the gold window: he refused to redeem excess dollars for gold as the British government had demanded a few days earlier. Thus Nixon globalized in 1971 the demonetization of gold, begun—on the domestic front—by FDR in 1934. The last vestiges of an official domestic and international gold standard had been abrogated by the undisputed leader of the free world.

Most of the conventional economic forecasts of the day predicted a secular fall in the gold price. Lenin had once observed that gold should henceforth adorn the floors of latrines. Since, according to the experts, gold was no more than a "barbarous relic," its value must decline. The price of gold remained below $40 until 1972. [But] it rose to $200 in 1974 as Watergate, inflation and war upended the Nixon administration. . . .[8]

Once again, most of the "experts" were wrong.

I often develop my ideas through intellectual partnerships—such as those with John Mueller, who was working in Congressman Jack Kemp's office when we first met. In a 2011 interview, Mueller summarized our work and its implications for Mort Kondracke:

> [Lew] had known Jacques Rueff, the French economist, who understood the peculiarities of having one nation's currency—it's now the dollar—but when Rueff started it was the pound sterling and the dollar, as international money. Lew . . . published the complete works of Rueff through the Lehrman Institute, in French unfortunately. I learned French in order to read [Rueff] well enough to understand him. So I was introduced to these ideas and understood there was a flaw in the Bretton Woods system, the same flaw that led to the breakdown in the 1920s and early thirties caused by the massive expansions and contractions that are possible under such a system and they're still at the center of what's been going on in the world economy lately. So being exposed to the Rueffian theory through Lehrman, I became convinced that Lehrman was correct, Rueff was correct, and that Bretton Woods was not a viable solution. It had broken down the first time, and it would break down again.[9]

For the interested reader, translations of Rueff's key works in English are available, and can be found in the bibliography. In addition, there is now underway a project to translate the entire *Collected Works of Jacques Rueff* into English.

James Grant: Kingpin of the financial journalists

James Grant was another intellectual ally who would become a friend. Jim was writing for the weekly business newspaper *Barron's* when he first profiled me in 1980. He went on to become the most famous journalist-economist in the Anglophone world. In *Money of the Mind* Grant later wrote:

> Lehrman was a student of central banking, and an apostle of Jacques Rueff. He was impartially hostile to the opposite wings of conventional economic thought—Keynesian and monetarist—and single-mindedly devoted to the idea of the classical gold standard, which, in its very obsolescence, had acquired an *avant-garde* capacity to shock. Morgan Stanley & Co., a top-tier investment bank that was not usually moved to champion long-shot causes, agreed to publish the Lehrman essay, all forty-four pages of it, "*Monetary Policy, the Federal Reserve System, and Gold.*" (In an introductory note, Barton M. Biggs, the head of investment research at Morgan Stanley, speculated that Lehrman had hit on "what could be the economic and political issue of the 1980s—why the world must return to the discipline of the gold standard.")
>
> Lehrman's diagnosis was elegantly simple and persuasive. He observed that the world's monetary system had been going downhill ever since 1914[10], retrogressing from the international gold standard as the gold-bullion standard to the gold-exchange standard and finally to the full-paper standard of 1971, each new regime less rigorous and more inflation-prone than the one preceding it. His prescription was equally simple but, again, in its very orthodoxy, discordant to many Morgan Stanley clients, for whom monetary heresy had long since become gospel. It was drawn in part from Rueff and in part from the nineteenth century British thinker Walter Bagehot.[11] The world must return to gold, Lehrman insisted, and the Federal Reserve must stop its frenetic buying and selling of government securities. It must throw in the towel on trying to control the nation's money supply, which it could not even count.[12]

I have ever been grateful for the support of Jim Grant, who became a dear friend.

As President Reagan's administration began in early 1981, it became increasingly obvious that I was not going to be a part of it. Nevertheless, I was determined to be a part of the discussion about its policies. I regularly wrote or contributed to articles about how to handle budgetary, inflation, and trade issues. Brian Domitrovic later wrote about these efforts, stating that "Since the Dunkirk memo, Lehrman had been devoting his energies to the cause of gold. When the Reagan administration assumed power, he was confident that it would succeed in cutting taxes and regulation, even if it was not as successful in slashing spending. But he worried that the monetary component of doing it 'all' was in jeopardy. Even though the administration had called for slow and stable money growth, the responsibility for achieving this lay outside the administration, with the Federal Reserve, and Lehrman had no confidence in the Fed. After all, in early 1981 the Fed, purportedly governed by strict quantity targets, was pumping up the money stock by 10 percent, many times in excess of the rate of economic growth."[13] Not only was this an inflationary policy, but the growth in the money stock caused undesirable volatility in the currency exchanges, which made the fair conduct of the international system more difficult.

In a long article in the *Washington Post* two days before Reagan's inauguration, I refuted the absurd notion that "excess demand" by ordinary Americans created inflation. I called it "How to End Inflation," and wrote that "a true understanding of inflation begins with a second and entirely different view of its causes and origins. In this view, the correct one, the government causes inflation. Not the oil sheiks, not the oil companies, not greedy labor or avaricious big business. Inflation is a monetary and a financial disorder, engendered by the federal government. This interpretation explains why working people voted on November 4, 1980, to reduce the size of government, not to restrict further the world of work and enterprise."[14]

About two weeks later, Senate Majority Leader Howard Baker placed my article in the *Congressional Record.* I was grateful for Senator Baker's vote of confidence, but although he was a fair-minded expert, he tended to confuse policy with politics. As a result, he was not a particularly effective ally in Congress.

In an interview for a February article in *The Atlantic*, I emphasized that the gold standard was not really a political issue, but that it was really all about stability. I told economic journalist James K. Glassman that the "gold standard has little to do with gold as a commodity. The gold standard is a political and social institution. It's a special means to achieve a particular end: a reasonably stable price level. We have this same goal—price stability. The argument is no longer over the goal but over the means."[15]

Later in February, I wrote "The Means to Establishing Financial Order" for the *Wall Street Journal.* In that article I once again laid out a commonsense prescription for stable money in a stable society, saying "To establish financial order, a sound Fed credit policy is a necessary condition; but it is not sufficient. History and classical economic analysis [namely pre-Keynesian economics] show that the policy best-suited to ensure stable money over the long run is to define the dollar as a weight [unit] of gold. But a domestic standard is not enough, because our national economy is fully integrated with the free world economy. It follows that only a world monetary system can provide an impartial common currency, not subject to sovereign political manipulation. Such a world monetary system is the international gold standard. This is the classical monetary policy."[16]

In May of 1981, I deepened the analysis. In basic terms that anyone can understand, I explained exactly what is at stake in this argument over how to configure economic systems and establish stable money. For the magazine *Human Events* I wrote:

> In recent years we have not had stable money. But we did have it throughout American history when we had a monetary standard—the gold standard. You can have a nominal money, a paper dollar; or you can have a real dollar, defined by its gold weight. Let us resume the historic American monetary standard, a

gold dollar, in order to end inflation. . . . If we truly desire to restore the future of America *by reviving the will to save and invest*, and if we genuinely desire to renew the spirit of capitalism around the world, then we shall have to give the world a real money, a true and reliable measuring rod of economic value, the gold standard. That's why I believe no economic program in this country will ever yield the American Renaissance we hope for unless we restore the international gold standard. It is the unique monetary institution and sovereign symbol of a peaceful, open and growing world market order. Only the United States, as the leader of the West, has the power to establish and maintain a capitalist world market order. Let us get on with our destiny.[17]

One of the ideas in the *Human Events* article is particularly important, namely the importance of reviving the will to save and invest. Although it is second nature to those of us Americans who grew up in the postwar, patriotic, and commercial culture, I would also like to make its value clear to those for whom the will to save and invest is less well understood. Often overlooked by modern intellectuals and journalists, the will to save and invest is a social phenomenon which forms the bedrock of both cultural and economic activity. It is also connected to the passion for family, community, and national development.

Without the will to save and invest, you don't have a country. Instead, you consume your own seed corn, and have none for next year's crop. Individuals hope—and vote accordingly—that their own aspirations will be mirrored in their nation's policies. The American version of this phenomenon was known as "the right to rise" in the days of Hamilton and Lincoln. It is one of the fundamental positive characteristics of the capitalism of the United States of America.

But the right to rise cannot thrive in an economy where inflation keeps undermining prosperity. Where inflation settles in, the will to save and invest withers, along with long-term planning, quality of life, and the public interest. Main Street gives in to an understandable, but frenetic effort to stay ahead of price increases, and Wall Street retreats to stable, but not necessarily productive assets. The lack of stable money acts throughout the economy to impact the character of the nation and its people. Indeed, it can poison the deepest wellsprings of human creativity, and set the stage for war.

In July of 1981 I spoke urgently about these fundamental values with the American Economic Council: "Probably the most important reason why the gold standard upholds peace is that government cannot resort to printing money in order to finance a war. It's much easier for a government to go to war if it knows that it can issue paper money. Another important reason is that a true gold standard is an international standard. When the people of civilized nations can count on the future purchasing power of a common money, they cooperate in production throughout the world. Now, a gold standard in the United States alone, is not sufficient to insure a prosperous and dynamic world economy. And only a dynamic world economy can insure the growth and prosperity of our own country. That's the reason why I believe that national monetary reform is no more important than international monetary reform."[18]

I further argued that "to uphold the gold standard as a Frenchman, an Englishman or an American, is to seek to rule out trade warfare and military warfare in the interest of a free and open world economy. But to abolish the gold standard is to free national governments from restraint and discipline and allow them sufficient autonomy and license to manipulate their currencies, manipulate the exchange rate in the interest of their export industries, and impose tariffs and quotas."[19]

Licentious and disordered policies such as these are the historic precedents for war, even if national governments have no such intent when implementing them. Such a policy framework constitutes a degenerate form of capitalism called mercantilism, and it has been the scourge of the world since the lead-up to World War I, when restricting free and fair access to markets became a major driver of competitive national economic and foreign policies. And before they were called mercantilism, these policies—in their more obvious forms—constituted the method of colonialism, with all of its attendant injustice.

Milton Friedman said that "in the end," the gold standard would not be sufficient to prevent war and economic crisis. We agree on that point. In fact, however, Friedman's floating exchange rates are much worse, exacerbating the international economic tensions known as "currency wars." Despite the dominant role of morality in international affairs, the technique of the gold standard does provide a serious check on unprincipled and expensive military policy. As long as one wants to maintain peace, a gold standard may be part of the answer. As an example, the Nazis were well known for wanting to manipulate or get rid of the gold standard. In the end, they succeeded, and flooded the market with Deutsche Marks. In their desire to restore hegemony in Europe, they devalued the Mark to a fare-the-well.

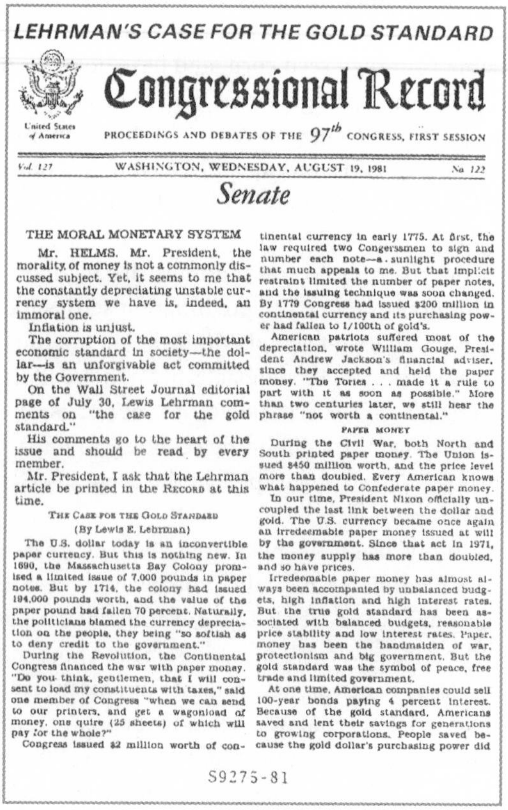

LEHRMAN'S CASE FOR THE GOLD STANDARD

Congressional Record

United States of America

PROCEEDINGS AND DEBATES OF THE 97th CONGRESS, FIRST SESSION

Vol. 127 WASHINGTON, WEDNESDAY, AUGUST 19, 1981 No. 122

Senate

THE MORAL MONETARY SYSTEM

Mr. HELMS. Mr. President, the morality of money is not a commonly discussed subject. Yet, it seems to me that the constantly depreciating unstable currency system we have is, indeed, an immoral one.

Inflation is unjust.

The corruption of the most important economic standard in society—the dollar—is an unforgivable act committed by the Government.

On the Wall Street Journal editorial page of July 30, Lewis Lehrman comments on "the case for the gold standard."

His comments go to the heart of the issue and should be read by every member.

Mr. President, I ask that the Lehrman article be printed in the RECORD at this time.

THE CASE FOR THE GOLD STANDARD

(By Lewis E. Lehrman)

The U.S. dollar today is an inconvertible paper currency. But this is nothing new. In 1690, the Massachusetts Bay Colony promised a limited issue of 7,000 pounds in paper notes. But by 1714, the colony had issued 194,000 pounds worth, and the value of the paper pound had fallen 70 percent. Naturally, the politicians blamed the currency depreciation on the people, they being "so softish as to deny credit to the government."

During the Revolution, the Continental Congress financed the war with paper money. "Do you think, gentlemen, that I will consent to load my constituents with taxes," said one member of Congress "when we can send to our printers, and get a wagonload of money, one quire (25 sheets) of which will pay for the whole?"

Congress issued $2 million worth of continental currency in early 1775. At first, the law required two Congerssmen to sign and number each note—a sunlight procedure that much appeals to me. But that implicit restraint limited the number of paper notes, and the issuing technique was soon changed. By 1779 Congress had issued $200 million in continental currency and its purchasing power had fallen to 1/100th of gold's.

American patriots suffered most of the depreciation, wrote William Gouge, President Andrew Jackson's financial adviser, since they accepted and held the paper money. "The Tories . . . made it a rule to part with it as soon as possible." More than two centuries later, we still hear the phrase "not worth a continental."

PAPER MONEY

During the Civil War, both North and South printed paper money. The Union issued $450 million worth, and the price level more than doubled. Every American knows what happened to Confederate paper money.

In our time, President Nixon officially uncoupled the last link between the dollar and gold. The U.S. currency became once again an irredeemable paper money issued at will by the government. Since that act in 1971, the money supply has more than doubled, and so have prices.

Irredeemable paper money has almost always been accompanied by unbalanced budgets, high inflation and high interest rates. But the true gold standard has been associated with balanced budgets, reasonable price stability and low interest rates. Paper money has been the handmaiden of war, protectionism and big government. But the gold standard was the symbol of peace, free trade and limited government.

At one time, American companies could sell 100-year bonds paying 4 percent interest. Because of the gold standard, Americans saved and lent their savings for generations to growing corporations. People saved because the gold dollar's purchasing power did

S9275-81

The moral monetary system

Throughout the summer of 1981, I continued to write about the gold standard with articles entitled, "A Glittering Economy," in the *Washington Post*, "Should We (and Could We) Return to the Gold Standard?" in the *New York Times*, "The Road to a Balanced Budget Is Paved with a Return to a Gold-Based Currency," in *Conservative Digest*, and "The Case for the Gold Standard," in the *Wall Street Journal*.

This last article was placed in the *Congressional Record* on August 19, 1981, this time by Senator Jesse Helms of North Carolina. I disagreed with Senator Helms on many things, but he was dead on with respect to monetary policy. Senator Helms introduced the printed article with a flourish, calling it: "THE MORAL MONETARY SYSTEM." Rising to speak to the Senate he said:

> Mr. President, the morality of money is not a commonly discussed subject. Yet, it seems to me that the constantly depreciating unstable currency system we have is, indeed, an immoral one.
>
> Inflation is unjust.
>
> The corruption of the most important economic standard in society—the dollar—is an unforgivable act committed by the Government.
>
> On the Wall Street Journal editorial page of July 30, Lewis Lehrman comments on "The Case for the Gold Standard."
>
> His comments go to the heart of the issue and should be read by every member.
>
> Mr. President, I ask that the Lehrman article be printed in the RECORD at this time.[20]

In the *Christian Science Monitor* that September, I explicitly tackled the direct relationship between economics and ethics, writing that "inflation is a moral problem as well as an economic one. Government contractors, large debtors (such as the government itself), spendthrifts, and speculators all benefit from inflation in the short run. Workers, savers, pensioners, and the poor are robbed just as surely as if they had been mugged. This immoral transfer of wealth, which totals hundreds of billions of dollars each year, violates our religious heritage, makes a mockery of honest work, and erodes our faith in constitutional government."[21]

For *U.S. News & World Report* that month, I described exactly what the effect of stable money is on working people and the business community: "What the gold standard does is give working people confidence in the future purchasing power of their saved wages. I would predict that true savings committed to productive investments would double within one year after the establishment of a gold standard. Therefore, businesses would have an enormous pool of savings from which to draw the capital to invest in new plants and new equipment. This investment [which is typically twice the rate of savings] would create a huge demand for labor, end unemployment and lead to the creation of new wealth and economic opportunity for the poor."[22]

In my private thoughts, I call this the heavenly process, which constrains war in the sense that popular discontent is low, leading to support for the prohibition of war at the nation-state level. When the major countries keep the peace, the result is an example of prosperity and benevolence.

In an article for *Leaders* magazine that autumn, I emphasized that gold is "the Ursache," as they say in German . . . *the fundamental cause or source* of the world economy's stability. Continuing to speak to the fundamentals of the gold standard and its rationale, I wrote that "It is an indispensable and vital *standard*, a measuring rod, of economic value. [It] takes a relatively constant rate of application of capital and human labor to produce a constant quantity of gold. *Like the yardstick for length, gold is a metering device which gauges the relative productivity, over time, of capital and labor. For this reason, gold money is the best economic measuring rod of the value of other products desired in the market, all of which require capital and labor to be produced.* Over the long run [measured in centuries], the value [or purchasing power] of gold is more constant than that of any single commodity, product or standard assortment of goods which could be used as a monetary standard. Stable gold money encourages people to save. The security and plenitude of savings enhances the ability of industry to plan long-term growth."[23]

In subsequent decades, even as America's trade deficits worsened, the pernicious role of the dollar as the world's reserve currency decimated America's manufacturing base. This process occurred because the need to hold dollars and US Treasuries as reserves created an excess demand for dollar reserves worldwide. The resulting overvalued dollar made the prices of American-made goods and services uncompetitive on the world market.

APPEALING TO THE PRESIDENT

When I was repeatedly bypassed for an appointment to the Reagan Administration, I recognized that any opportunity to make an official impact on monetary policy had been lost. Nevertheless, I continued to exert an educational impact. My writings on the gold standard had provided one vehicle. My personal interactions with President Reagan in the upcoming years would provide another. But the most immediate vehicle for my work on the gold standard would be the creation of a federal "Gold Commission" to investigate the issue at the outset of the Reagan Administration.

Ronald Reagan had told me directly that he felt favorably toward the gold standard. He thought that reform would require full cooperation from other big countries. The gold standard, however, was unfashionable among Reagan's more "politically correct" backers. At one point in Governor Reagan's 1980 campaign, he was even persuaded to film a TV commercial backing the gold standard. Someone must have intervened at that point, however, because he quickly backed away in a phone call to Jeff Bell. Reagan "didn't mention anyone by name," recalled Jeff, "but I think he was talking about Milton Friedman, who was at the Hoover Institution at Stanford at that time. Friedman was the founder of monetarism who had won the Nobel Prize in economics. He was a Reagan supporter, but he'd argued that the gold standard was at least partly responsible for the Great Depression. So Friedman would not be in favor of returning to any kind of gold standard. And I don't think Reagan wanted to rock the boat at that time. So he asked me to hold off on it."[24] However, Reagan did instruct Bell not to erase the tape, which confirmed that Reagan's understanding was similar to mine.

Bell went on to state that:

> What [Reagan] said in the ad, which is something I think he always believed, was that we'll never have stable prices until we get back to some form of gold backing for the dollar. He didn't blame labor for inflation. He blamed the government.
>
> He didn't say that it was only inflation that was a problem. He said, in effect, that the uncertainty of paper money is a problem in itself, even at times when the dollar is strong. It winds up disrupting the world economy, disrupting the terms of trade. Reagan's message holds up very well to this day.[25]

Friedman's argument that the gold standard was responsible for the Great Depression is false. Nevertheless, it is the one most often cited in objection to the gold standard. The pain of the Depression was such that to be accused of making the same mistake causes most people to buckle under the moral pressure of such responsibility. But the argument is wrong.

The historic reason the argument is false is that the gold standard was not considered responsible for any of the previous financial crises, and during its preeminence, the world witnessed unprecedented prosperity and peace. In addition, the Great Depression was caused largely by human moral failures at the Federal Reserve and in the banking industry, as well as trade wars. All of these moral failures were due more to territorial political ambition than concern for the public welfare. The gold standard, like gold itself, has unfortunately seemed mute, unable to defend itself from unprincipled men willing to make it the scapegoat. Giving gold and the gold standard a voice has been one of my life's true callings.

Leonard Silk described the president's interest in the gold standard for the *New York Times*: "In seeking to reconcile the main ideas of his two principal groups of economic supporters, the supply-siders and the monetarists, President Reagan set aside one of his own economic beliefs: that the country should go back to the gold standard to end inflation.... The contemporary advocates of gold maintain that the perpetual inflation under the dollar standard and floating rates is ... dangerous for economic and political stability.... Mr. Reagan's supply-siders are now urging him to appoint a [gold] commission [to include] some sympathetic friends of gold like Lewis Lehrman...."[26]

The 1980 Republican National Platform, to which Jeff Bell, John Mueller, and I had contributed, suggested that a shift in monetary policy was under consideration. The relevant portion states: "Ultimately, inflation is a decline in the value of the dollar, the monetary standard, in terms of the goods it can buy on the world market. Until the decade of the 1970s, monetary policy was automatically linked to the overriding objective of maintaining a stable dollar value. The severing of the dollar's link with real commodities [like gold and silver] in the 1960s and 1970s, in order to pursue economic goals other than dollar stability, has unleashed hyper-inflationary forces at home and monetary disorder abroad, without bringing any of the desired economic benefits. One of the most urgent tasks in the period ahead will be the restoration of a dependable monetary standard—that is, an end to inflation."[27]

My argument has always been that economic goals other than dollar stability are inherently questionable. As a merchant and businessman, I was intimately familiar with the damage that currency or any other type of financial instability could do to business confidence. In particular, when Nixon ended the gold standard in 1971, the resulting crisis of 1973 severely damaged my company's operations in a way that was impossible to forget. Therefore, the advantages of dollar stability were as plain as day to me, and no amount of academic or political posturing could move me from my position. As long as it is not vitiated, a policy of monetary stability and full employment is sufficient, even ideal, in the effort to induce prosperity in a healthy, productive, and ethical economy. Rather than trying to destabilize the monetary standard in pursuit of supposed social goals, better to focus on low taxes, a high savings rate, and fair-minded regulation that does not unnecessarily burden productive enterprise. Most social goals will be better served by such a policy than direct aid, although of course government can play a role in helping those unable to care for themselves.

Tom Redburn of the *Los Angeles Times* called those of us advocating for a gold-backed currency "a mixed lot." But he went on to clearly articulate many of the essential benefits of the gold standard. "At a recent conference sponsored by the National Committee for Monetary Reform . . ." Redburn continued "they ranged from currency trader Nicholas Deak to gold bug James Dines to the conservative scholar and businessman Lewis Lehrman. . . . They all agree on one point—without a restoration of gold as the backing for its currency, the United States will never get inflation under control. . . . 'Gold,' according to Lehrman, 'is the perfect tool to control money growth because, unlike the current system of paper money, it is difficult to expand the gold supply [in most cases] . . . The gold standard, by providing an explicit 'error signal' to the Fed that it is creating money too fast or too slow, would put severe limits on the power of the central bank [and the federal government's borrowing power.] According to Lehrman . . . this would provide 'virtually a constitutional guarantee of the purchasing power of money and therefore of the future value of savings.'"[28]

The term *monetary standard* was a euphemism used by those who fear the potentially controversial words "gold standard." In the '70s I allowed Jude Wanniski and Bob Mundell to convince me we have to use euphemisms like "monetary reform" or "a dollar as good as gold" or any of the other euphemisms invented to placate the self-appointed cognoscenti. But the euphemisms did not work, for they are empty of meaning, while the term *gold standard* has five thousand years of definition, and two thousand years of history. Indeed, there is no substitute for the gold standard, and no substitute for the term *gold standard*. I have since resolved not to use any euphemisms to hide the true sentiment behind my philosophy on gold.

In a December 2011 interview with Morton Kondracke, I told a story about President Reagan's interest in the gold standard that few people remember and even fewer will understand. Nevertheless, it is a crucial piece of history that made its way into the mind of a young man who would one day become president.

"Reagan was old enough," I began "to have remembered the early debates in the forties and the fifties about the consequences of Roosevelt's actions in appropriating privately-owned gold in 1934 and the executive orders that he used to terminate the gold standard, and then, of course, the great gold-clause litigation at the Supreme Court in 1936, so that when he came along . . . as a Democrat in the forties, he remembered those debates and he knew that the dollar had lost 50 percent of its purchasing power from the time that he'd gone to work. . . . So . . . he was receptive to the idea."[29]

Asked why President Reagan never moved to enact a new gold standard, I said: "My explanation has always been that he had only so much that he was physically capable of doing. I mean, he was a man well over seventy as he got into the best years of the presidency."[30] No matter who is in the White House, it will require a firm hand at the presidency to reform the monetary system.

In his book, *The Prince of Darkness: 50 Years Reporting in Washington*, Robert Novak suggested that President Reagan was boxed in by advisors:

> In one other peculiar exchange during the lunch, I asked Reagan: "What ever happened to the gold standard? I thought you supported it."
>
> "Well," the president began and then paused (a ploy he frequently used to collect his thoughts), "I still do support the gold standard, but"—At that point, Reagan was interrupted by his chief of staff, Don Regan. "Now, Mr. President," said Regan, "we don't want to get bogged down talking about the gold standard."
>
> "You see?" Reagan said to me, his palms uplifted in mock futility, "They just won't let me have my way."[31]

I had my own, more productive conversation with President Reagan at a fundraising dinner. I sat next to him for two hours, during which he articulated his working knowledge of the history of the gold standard and its abrogation by Roosevelt and the Supreme Court in the 1930s. At the president's request, I then told him how I would reestablish the gold standard. He asked several very good questions. I had considered every political problem, but the president said: "That sounds very thorough, but it seems to me that it is a little harder to do than to say." I cited the Rueff-de Gaulle example and said its success in America depended on political will and leadership, as well as a sound theoretical foundation. His response was memorable, and was consistent with my position, namely that gold is the ideal standard for trade among the biggest countries as long as they do not cheat in a mercantilist fashion. Although I am sure he was telling the truth, we did not get much farther than these remarks in our conversation, nor in his administration.

But we did not quit.

WORKING IN THE MINORITY AND THE GOLD COMMISSION

By the autumn of 1980, Senator Helms was making news by blocking legislation to fund the International Monetary Fund. In order to release the bill, Helms's aide, Howard Segermark, maneuvered to get congressional approval for a "Gold Commission." Helms and Congressman Ron Paul of Texas had sponsored a bill to "conduct a study to assess and make recommendations with regard to the policy of the U.S. Government concerning the role of gold in domestic and international monetary systems." In the heat of the presidential campaign and the continuing hostage crisis in Iran, the Carter Administration had made no move to implement the legislation. It remained for the Reagan Administration to follow up, and it took five months to announce the appointments to the seventeen-man panel.

In early June of 1981, Thomas O'Donnell of *Forbes* wrote that "At the moment, the key battle is being waged around the staffing of the gold commission. That's the body set up by an amendment that Helms and Paul tacked on to a law, last fall. It will probably have 17 members and is scheduled to complete a report by October. If the 'right' individuals are chosen and a favorable report results, the gold standard would then take a giant step forward, say the hard money optimists."[32]

On June 22, appointments to the US Gold Commission were announced. I was named one of four "distinguished citizens" whom Reagan appointed. However, Congressman Paul and I were the only two strong backers of a gold standard on the entire commission. Other members included three senators—Democrats Christopher J. Dodd and Harrison H. Schmitt, and Republican Roger W. Jepsen. The other members from the House were Democrats Henry S. Reuss and Stephen L. Neal, and Republican Chalmers P. Wylie. The Council of Economic Advisors was represented by Chairman Henry C. Wallich and Jerry L. Jordan. The Federal Reserve was represented by J. Charles Partee, Wallich, and Paul C. McCracken. These appointees were not merely agnostic when it came to the gold standard. They were confirmed antagonists.

With my appointment to the Gold Commission, I thought I finally would have a vehicle for making the case for monetary reform. The vehicle that had been constructed, however, was designed to stop, not promote forward movement to the gold standard. A week before the commission, I wrote a memo to Ed Meese that built on my earlier policy piece now remembered as the Dunkirk memorandum. This time I called it "The Return of Gold":

> President Reagan was elected to end inflation and restore the economy. His administration moves in that direction: slowing the growth of the money supply and Federal spending, cutting taxes, and eliminating costly government regulations. Some of its advocates call such a program "monetarism." But the President's program is missing the crucial element—a prompt implementation of a balanced budget and a gold backed currency. Without such a policy, interest rates will come down slowly from 20%. Demoralized financial markets will yield little relief.

Some Reagan advisers and the Federal Reserve may, however, force a recession and unemployment in order to bring down interest rates more quickly. But no sound and compassionate person can really desire to cure inflation and high interest rates with worklessness. That is why a policy other than austerity and monetarism must be considered. Budgetary equilibrium and a gold standard policy will reduce interest rates by finally stabilizing the currency and the market for government securities. Such a policy is the clear implication of the 1980 Republican National Platform which stated: "Ultimately, inflation is a decline in the value of the dollar, the monetary standard, in terms of the goods it can buy. One of the most urgent tasks in the period ahead will be the restoration of a dependable monetary standard—that is, an end to inflation. . . .

An effective program for enduring financial order must include the gold standard and a balanced budget. Together they establish a stable legal framework, a monetary constitution, within which the central bankers and the prime ministers and presidents must work. Under such a program, deficits cannot be financed by printing currency, or by forcing false new credit at the banks and the Fed because free Americans would otherwise exchange undesired excess paper or credit money for gold. Under a gold standard, authorities must maintain the convertibility of the currency to which they are pledged by law or the constitution. Hence a balanced budget and equilibrium in the balance of payments follow from the decision to adopt the gold standard. Moreover, stable money, like a gold currency, encourages people to save again. The security and plentitude of savings enhances the ability of American industry to plan long-range growth and full employment. As a result of the mutation in the savings rate under the gold standard, we could also count on permanent, low, long-term interest rates."[33]

Such was the basic state of affairs that characterized the American price level from the adoption of the American Constitution until the Civil War.

The first private meeting of Reagan's Gold Commission was held on July 16, 1981. The members of the commission were heavily stacked against the gold standard. In addition, Treasury Secretary Don Regan knew next to nothing about the gold standard or economic policy in general. Both the Friedmanite monetarists and Congressman Henry Reuss's Keynesians opposed the gold standard. Regan chaired the commission, and he was no more inclined to consider the gold standard than he had been to consider my appointment to the Reagan Administration. Beryl Sprinkel, the monetarist, whom Regan had appointed as undersecretary for monetary affairs in my stead, was designated to sit in for Regan as the commission's de facto chair.

The executive director, Dr. Anna Schwartz, was a first-class Friedmanite. Professor Friedman, with whom I had corresponded extensively, was opposed to the gold standard. Schwartz was very capable, very smart, and a good scholar, but she was

Milton Friedman's intellectual partner. Still, it must be said of Dr. Schwartz that she was not as hostile to the gold standard as Friedman was. She wanted both sides to have their say.

Not everyone in the media understood the seriousness of our situation, nor recognized the risks we faced due to currency debasement. With shallow cynicism, William Safire made light of my push for integrity and gold. In his article for the *Chicago Tribune*, he wrote:

> [...] Lewis Lehrman, a New York businessman, has been peppering the papers with literate projections of a glittering economy. With Rep. Kemp staying in Washington, he will run for New York governor waving the standard, to which the wise and honest can repair.
>
> Will their brilliant E.P.M.P. [Eco-Political Media Process] campaign succeed? The odds are 16 to 1 in favor—their triumph will be limited, but significant. Evidence comes from an authentic White House insider, who says "'Ronald Reagan wears one of those watches with the face made of a $20 gold piece. Every time the President checks to see what time it is—maybe 30, 40 times a day—he gets reminded to do something about the Gold Standard."[34]

Safire may have been dismissive, but there was a big hullaballoo in Washington the day of the first public meeting of the Gold Commission. Robert Hershey wrote it up for the *New York Times*, saying "Whether the gold enthusiasts will eventually prevail depends largely on the President himself. Mr. Reagan has indicated he would wait for the commission's findings before taking any action. But his basic sympathy toward gold, though rarely expressed since last fall's election campaign, is well documented." Reagan's statement did not give me confidence, but I stayed optimistic for the record anyway, telling Hershey that "We've moved light-years just in the last six months."[35]

But we still had light years to go.

Most of the initial hearing was devoted to a detailed presentation of the history of the gold standard in the United States by Dr. Schwartz. In response, Federal Reserve Governor Emmett J. Rice declared: "The weight of the evidence suggests none of the automatic systems, the rigid systems (such as a direct gold standard) has performed satisfactorily."

I replied: "I must deny the assertion of Governor Rice," and explained that even the data presented by Dr. Schwartz showed that under gold, "the monetary standard was stable and the price level was stable also."[36]

The next day, Caroline Atkinson reported out a bland but revealing story to the *Washington Post*:

> The administration will not make up its mind on a possible return to the gold standard until well into next year, despite recent calls by some supply-side Reagan supporters for an immediate move towards gold as the only way to bring down interest rates, Treasury secretary Donald Regan said yesterday.
>
> After the first public meeting of the U.S. Gold Commission yesterday, Regan said the issue is very complex and there is no chance of coming up with a "fast or simple" answer. He added that it will be at least six or nine months before the commission, which he heads, can complete its report, and that the administration will not take a position until some time after that. . . .
>
> Although gold adherents appear to be in a minority on the commission, almost all the members were careful yesterday to appear open-minded about the issue. But it was immediately clear that there is little chance of a unanimous report emerging from the commission's deliberations.[37]

One problem was that Don Regan had not studied the relevant issues carefully. He had learned to be a skilled manager of America's leading stockbroker—but the currency issue requires a deeper understanding of monetary policy. Under the Fifth Republic, Jacques Rueff had been able to implement a convertible currency in less time than Regan wanted to take talking about it. The real issue was lack of resolve, not lack of understanding.

The hearings of the Gold Commission did little or nothing to change the views of the commission members. Even Dr. Schwartz doubted that the commission was a "serious attempt to study what a gold standard could contribute to the public welfare."[38]

In general, she was right.

Because the jury was rigged, I had to make my case in the court of public opinion—sometimes wholesale, in articles and interviews, and sometimes retail, as in conversations with Seth Lipsky, then working for the *Wall Street Journal*. Recently Seth wrote to me about those heady and dramatic days, saying "I will never forget your wonderfully patient, erudite, and logical explanations—delivered between sessions of the United States Gold Commission—of the centrality of gold to a moral and just political economy. I learned more in those taxicab rides back to National Airport than I did in any course at college (not that they were lacking). Everyone I know who is invested in this great cause looks to your leadership. Jacques Rueff would say the same thing, I'll warrant."[39]

About five years after the Commission presented its 226-page report, Schwartz wrote an article entitled "Money in Historical Perspective," saying "The creation of the Gold Commission served one paramount objective of its sponsors. It promoted discussion of gold in the media, on television, and among a lay public committed to the view expressed in the minority report that only gold is 'honest' money. The minority report itself is a rallying call for the faithful. Both Helms and Paul were committed to the immediate objective of the minting of gold bullion coins by the Treasury. As the minority report noted: 'We are extremely pleased that the Gold

Commission has recommended to the Congress a new gold coinage. It has been almost fifty years since the last United States gold coins were struck [as legal tender] and renewing this Constitutional function would indeed be a cause for celebration and jubilee.' Short of the appointment of a Commission committed to restoring the gold standard, the sponsors probably view the limited results attained as a gain in achieving their ultimate objectives."[40]

Although I had far more expansive plans, I too was pleased that the United States had begun to mint gold coins. In 1981, the one-ounce gold coins called double eagles were issued to banks with a $50 face value. Since that time, they have appreciated to over $2,000, and now constitute a substantial portion of America's gold reserves. Much of it is held in private hands or abroad.

Although the Gold Commission was clearly not going to be receptive to my ideas, the publicity of the event did create speaking and writing opportunities. With only two gold standard advocates on the Commission, there were not many prominent alternative advocates for the media to approach. I had an open field—for both my own writing, and for inclusion in newspaper and magazine articles. I took advantage of the media's demand to make an intellectual supply.

If I could not play an *executive* role in the implementation of a gold standard, I could still proselytize, and play a *pedagogical* role explaining the deficiencies of the current monetary dysfunction. I wanted to present the options for the restoration of a monetary order that would also restore monetary sanity . . . *and* America's manufacturing base. Although I was isolated, I optimistically told *Business Week* that August: "The Administration's views on gold are agnostic but not hostile."[41] This I knew for a fact, having spoken with the president himself.

In a September *New York Times* op-ed I again wrote on behalf of the working people of America, speaking in simple terms about the way in which a gold standard could again protect them and the value of their work:

> The gold standard gives people today confidence in the future purchasing power of the dollar. As a result, working men and women, believing in an honest dollar begin to ask for reasonable wage increases, proportional, that is, to the gain in the productivity of their own labor.
>
> It's almost as if the gold standard were an insurance policy, an actuarial reminder to all who participate in the market that the dollar in 10 years instead of being 50 percent of what it is worth today would be approximately equal in purchasing power as it is today. . . .
>
> I'm a businessman and I'm very concerned about the just character of our monetary standard. Under the gold standard, the paper dollar is a promissory note. It is a claim to a real article of wealth defined by law as the [monetary] standard. . . .

> In the abstract, especially in the classrooms of Yale where I went to school, it was always easy for professors to draw on a blackboard equations which showed why bank reserves could be provided rationally to the market. As a businessman I have learned that under the gold standard, these reserves were provided much more rationally by virtue of the operations of markets.[42]

In the fall of 1981, I was simultaneously preparing for an intensive political campaign for governor of New York State and running an educational outreach campaign for the gold standard. In a November interview published in *Fortune* magazine I wrote about the value of the gold standard for the business audience:

> A true gold standard simply causes nations to settle promptly the deficits they accrue as they go along. You don't have to export gold. You could simply export more textiles, or more steel, or more automobiles. You could export, in the case of the U.S., more high technology, more plants and equipment, more wheat, more services.
>
> A deficit can be settled by shipping out a real good like gold, but it can also be settled by shipping out a real good like wheat. . . .
>
> What we need is a true gold standard, similar to the one we had until 1933. That would be a modernized gold standard where the value of the currency was defined by law as a weight unit of gold. [The gold standard we had until 1914 was better still.] There would be minting of gold dollars for anyone who wished to bring his bullion to the mint for free coinage, and all paper currency and bank deposits would be a claim on the monetary standard. Convertibility [into gold] would be universal and unrestricted.[43]

THE CONNECTION BETWEEN THE GOLD STANDARD AND MINING

In an interview with *Newsday*, I again laid out the significance of the more important events in the nation's monetary history, especially in light of the inflation then ravaging the country:

> Since 1971, when President Nixon ended the last vestiges of the U.S. dollar's convertibility into gold, consumer prices have risen 137 per cent, the money supply has grown 186 per cent and real wages [inflation adjusted wages that is] have fallen 14 per cent. Ending the link to gold led to 'the worst inflation in U.S. history' and extremely volatile foreign exchange rates. . . .
>
> There are 2.6 billion ounces of gold in the world. The Soviet Union each year produces one-third of 1 per cent of that total, and South Africa produces less than that. . . .
>
> The worst inflation for any one year when the U.S. was on the gold standard was 4 per cent [and that was when they discovered gold in California]. And

> during the worst period, from 1896 to 1912, the average rate of inflation annually was 2 per cent.[44]

That 2 percent inflation rate is a key number, about equal to the long-term average increase of the gold supply to the market from mining. That is part of the secret to the gold standard's success. The annual increase in gold supply from mining is roughly equal to the annual increase in global economic activity, at around 2 percent. *Thus, the gold standard remains stable over long periods of time.* Even if we increase the money supply to add sufficient currency to enable increasing economic activity in a growing population, if the amount of gold in circulation also increases by the same amount, the price level will not rise. In general, population increases and gold output tend to change slowly over time, keeping population and natural resources in a carefully considered relationship.[45]

In another interview, this time with Jim Cook of *IRI Insights*, I highlighted what the short-term and long-term benefits to the American people would be from the gold standard. Confident of both the evidence of history and its theoretical foundations, I flatly predicted:

> Within a year of its establishment, the gold standard would stabilize the value of money, end inflation, and tell all working Americans that the price level and the value of the dollar would be stable in the future.
>
> Therefore, all working Americans would save much more. And what they saved would not be invested in antiques, second homes, stamps, raw land, and every other inflation hedge. . . . They would invest their savings in stocks and bonds and other forms of real wealth and real production. People would put their savings into financial assets, stocks, and bonds, because their future purchasing power would be assured. . . .
>
> The demand for labor and capital equipment [would also increase] as new bonds and new shares brought new capital to enterprise. . . . When the demand for stocks and bonds rises, the rate of interest falls . . . the monetary policy of the gold standard is expansionist. But it is a *true* economic expansion, based on the production of real wealth [not an inflation boom]. The gold standard provides all the money that people want to hold and use. Working people can make all the profitable investments they decide to make by borrowing . . . and [they can] invest knowing their money's future value will not be destroyed by inflation.[46]

THE REPORT OF THE GOLD COMMISSION

The report of the Gold Commission was finally issued in March of 1982, although under the original legislation it was due in October of 1981.[47] A footnote in the main report did in fact accurately portray both my position and my policy prescription in the most succinct possible way. The note read: "Mr. Lewis E. Lehrman—I favor the restoration of a gold standard with a fixed price of gold. It is the means to achieve discipline in the U.S. monetary base which will then increase or decrease with gold purchases and sales by the monetary authorities."[48] In a cover letter, Secretary Regan wrote: "In forwarding this report, we acknowledge the wide public interest in the issues examined by the Commission and are grateful for the cooperation the Commission received from many individuals in testifying before us and submitting written statements of view."[49]

At the time of the report's release, I was preoccupied with the intense battle for the Republican nomination for governor.

I faced a dilemma.

I had no time to prepare my own minority report. I also had difficulty with Congressman Ron Paul's text, which appeared overly simplistic, and insufficiently anchored in history. It was authored primarily by the libertarian economist Murray Rothbard. Ron appealed to me as a friend to sign on however, and he deserved to be honored for his leadership. As Anna Schwartz wrote, "[Lehrman] did not want to distance himself from Paul and therefore endorsed the minority report."[50] In 1987, she added some more details, writing "Volume 2 of the Report is described as 'annexes.' The bulk of the volume is occupied by a minority report. The existence of a minority report was not revealed to the Gold Commission until a few days before the final revision of the Report that was intended to represent all views. The minority report was prepared under the direction of Congressman Paul and mirrors his views rather than those of Lewis Lehrman who endorsed it."[51]

At the time I consented—to some lasting regret—on a policy formulation with which I had disagreements. I did not leave the field, but it would be thirty years before I could finish the job.

We were not able to directly implement a gold standard through the Gold Commission, but we made the case for it so public that the monetary authorities were constantly under the microscope during the economic turbulence of the 1980s. It may even be the case that one result of our work was that the Federal Reserve and Treasury Department decided to use gold standard theory to stabilize the economy without directly implementing a gold standard. Instead, they appear to have pegged the value of the dollar to the gold price, if only for a brief time.

Economic historian Brian Domitrovic is convinced that the Federal Reserve's Open Market Committee realized they needed to align their monetary policy with the gold price in order to control inflation. In his book, *Econoclasts*, Domitrovic explains how they did it. Making a persuasive case in support of our efforts, he was direct and forceful. "The Fed was scared it might be put out of business by the Gold Commission," he began.

> Over Paul Volcker's first two and two-thirds years as Fed chairman, from the summer of 1979 through the spring of 1982, the progress he made on coordinating monetary policy with real economic growth was zero.

> But after the spring of 1982 [when the Gold Commission released its report], there all of a sudden arose a close sequential relationship between a declining price of gold and Fed easing, and a rising price of gold and Fed tightening. It's probably the single greatest secret in the history of modern monetary policy. After mid-1982, it looks like the Fed followed a gold price rule for quite a while. This, of all things, is where we got both the defeat of the horrible stagflation of the previous dozen years and the mega-boom of the 1980s and 1990s.
>
> The secret wasn't Volcker or monetarism or anything like that. It was adherence to the market price of gold. One piece of evidence we can all look up: As the Gold Commission was gathered and convened, the price of gold tumbled from the 1980 peak north of $800 and in 1982 began to hover around a $350 price, give or take a few gyrations, totally mild by today's or the 1970s standards, for the next two decades of boom-time economic growth.
>
> I'm ready to say that the Gold Commission of 1982 is by rights one of the unsung heroes at the origins of the Great Moderation. Ultimately the recommendation was the wrong one, but what with Paul, Lehrman and the scold Schwartz on it, the commission put a good fright into the Fed. The fear was that a substantial part of its "beloved discretion" might be removed from it. Therefore, the Fed's top men set to watching the price of gold like a hawk for two decades. In the meantime, unheard-of prosperity deadened everyone's senses to the fact that there was ever a problem with the Fed to begin with.[52]

And that is precisely the reason why a gold standard must remain at the foundation of economic policy. With each passing year, the institutional memory of its use and management grows dimmer. Without the gold standard, and an institutional respect for its efficacy, there is nothing to put the brakes on the Federal Reserve and the federal government when they lose sight of fundamentals. Unbalanced sectarian policy interests, war, and financial crises may enable policymakers to tempt fate. This is not a theoretical problem. Even as I write this, in October of 2022, policymakers have once again implemented inflationary measures in the face of financial crisis and war. As we know, these measures disrupt business confidence. And once more they rob the working people and the vulnerable of the purchasing power of their wages and savings.

Unhappy with the minority report of the Gold Commission, I started to work on my own version of a plan to re-implement the gold standard in America. In April of 1983, I told *Barron's* that "I began working on my book within a week of the campaign's end. Worked hard right through Christmas. It's done in manuscript form, although it needs a lot of editing. And I'm adding a few chapters . . . I put the book aside when I decided that I had to learn a little bit more about what's going on with our allies and maybe a little less about the main streets of New York. So I went off on a State-Department-sponsored trip to London, Paris, Frankfurt, Bonn, Berlin and Rome. I visited the defense ministries, the foreign ministries, the central banks to get caught up with what had gone on in Europe over the last 18 months."[53]

I worked on the book through the whole trip. At the time it was called *The Nature of the Gold Standard*, but it was eventually published as *The True Gold Standard: A Monetary Reform Plan without Official Reserve Currencies*. In that *Barron's* interview, I continued my criticism of the Federal Reserve:

> One of the great flaws of monetarism is that it looks only at the supply side, if you will, of the market for credit. If the supply of credit is equal to the level of credit actually desired for the purpose of production in the market, then the rate of interest will tend to be stable and so will the price level. It is only when the supply of credit being issued by the central bank exceeds the demand for credit by profitable producers in the market, that the price level will tend to rise and the value of money decline.
>
> *The relative desirability of a gold standard should be determined by its stability.* . . . The most efficient gold standard is one in which the currency of each country is convertible into gold. Such a system is generally known as multilateral convertibility of individual national currencies, each into a fixed weight of gold. That is a fixed exchange rate regime because all of the currencies have a proportionality, one to the other, based upon the gold weights of the currency. Then fixed exchange rates, you see, are not a discretionary matter for central bankers to decide, but the incidental by-products of the ratios of the gold values of the individual currencies.
>
> And [the silver and gold standard is] what characterized the whole period of America's rise from 13 impoverished colonies by the sea to the greatest world power. . . .
>
> A convertible currency is the only proven way, theoretically and historically, to bring about low long-term interest rates. It is the only way to bring about conditions of rapid expansion. It is the only way to restore the long-term bond markets so that we can create conditions where capital will be invested for long periods in new industries and new technologies. It is, in fact, the only way to create boom conditions which will once more restore full employment, without money and credit inflation.[54]

A year later, I dug into the details for another *Wall Street Journal* op-ed about the problems of Fed discretion. I again highlighted the way in which a stable monetary standard encourages sufficient savings to unleash productive investment. I also explained how the nation's early history had resulted in the formal creation of the gold standard, writing:

> By means of open-market operations, the Fed creates and destroys bank money [and credit] without creating or removing new goods and services during the same market period. Thus, on the one hand, too expansive open-market purchases of government securities by the Fed cause demand to exceed supply at

> prevailing prices and inflation gets under way, as happened between 1977 and 1980 [among other periods]. . . .
>
> Only a fixed monetary standard [namely gold and silver] can abolish this risk premium in long-term interest rates and renew faith in the fixed value of all future money payments on borrowings (bonds, mortgages, stocks and other long-term financial contracts). Confidence in the stable future purchasing power of a convertible dollar into gold leads directly to a boom in the supply of savings offered for long periods at fixed, low rates.
>
> This new supply of savings will tend to lower the price of credit, i.e., interest rates. Only a real currency, legally convertible to gold at a fixed rate, can bring about these effects in the capital markets. That is why the Constitution of our country— Sections I and VIII—originating as it did in 1789 after a catastrophic inflation of the previous currency of the Continental Congress—upholds a gold or silver-backed currency.

This history explains how the expression "not worth a Continental" entered the American lexicon. In addition, our nation's history also records the fact that at the height of the gold standard, in 1900, one-hundred-year fixed rate bonds were purchased in large numbers, so confident were Americans in the long-term purchasing power of the dollar, and the future of their country.

With enough study and information, the savings boom that results when Americans have faith in the stable future purchasing power of the dollar can be observed on the balance sheet of the Federal Reserve. You start with the total bank credit number and remove all the other credit line items until you have isolated total savings. This data and methodology was the one I used in my Morgan Stanley analyses of the Federal Reserve. As far as I know, I invented the analysis of the Federal Reserve balance sheet for investment and certain economic policy purposes. The most important of these analyses was the Morgan Stanley paper called "Monetary Policy, the Federal Reserve System and Gold."

ON THE BURDEN OF TAXES IN TIME OF INFLATION

One of the problems that emerges in an inflationary economy without a sound money is that people begin to resent paying their taxes, because inflation is already a hidden tax. For this reason, I often wrote in favor of simplifying the tax code to make it fairer, such that citizens would not feel overly burdened by both inflation and high taxes. In a February 1985 op-ed for the *New York Times*, I took on the issue of taxes in the context of the general prosperity, writing:

> Our present high marginal tax rates destroy incentives for job growth. Before the 1981 tax reductions, the top personal income tax rate was five times as high as the lowest bracket. The disparity has been reduced, but existing rates remain counterproductive. High marginal tax rates actually reduce net tax revenues at certain levels, thus deepening government deficits at any given level of Federal spending.

> High marginal tax rates also foster unproductive tax schemes. As a result, we have a scandalous situation in which some wealthy individuals and certain corporate taxpayers are able to escape their fair share of the tax burden. The diversion of scarce capital into tax gimmicks holds back new business development, and keeps joblessness high—while it increases the amount that the government must pay out in unemployment compensation and welfare payments. If we establish low, fair tax rates, we can enlarge the tax base, spreading the burden more equitably. Most important, we can create jobs for all Americans who want to work.[55]

In August of 1985, I again wrote about taxes, this time for the *Wall Street Journal*, saying "Ronald Reagan has handed New York state an opportunity. His tax reform program, by ending the deductibility of state and local taxes, throws a spotlight on the flaws of the state's own tax system—which like the federal code, is loaded down with numerous special-interest loopholes and burdened with tax rates that are too high. State leaders could have seized this opportunity for creative leadership by enacting a significant reform of the New York tax system, badly needed whether or not, as now seems possible, Mr. Reagan's own tax reform passes."[56]

In response to this sentiment, Secretary of State George Schultz wrote to me: "I just read your article in today's *Wall Street Journal* and I want to say to you what an important article I think it is. You hit the nail right on the head in both the rightness and quality of your argument. You expressed your thoughts so clearly that I can't help but feel the article will have a major impact."[57]

THE HIDDEN PROBLEM OF THE RESERVE CURRENCY

In November of 1985 I wrote my third Morgan Stanley paper, "Protectionism, Inflation, or Monetary Reform: The Case for Fixed Exchange Rates and a Modernized Gold Standard." One problem with recent gold and gold exchange standards, such as Bretton Woods, is that they have been implemented within a reserve currency system. In the Morgan Stanley paper, I trace the history of a reserve currency's problematic impacts on trade:

> The reserve-currency system was first devised in 1898 as an imperial expedient in colonial India and subsequently was copied in other colonial possessions, like the American Philippines. But general use of a national currency as an official reserve currency came into vogue among industrial countries after the First World War when at the conference in Genoa in 1922 they agreed on the practice as a temporary method of dealing with the so-called gold shortage. The "shortage" was caused by the fact that credit-inflated prices were 50% higher than before World War I, while the convertibility price of gold in the two major currencies—the pound sterling and the dollar—had been reinstated at prewar parity, *without a rise in the value of monetary gold to its prewar parity.* Without a rise in the value of monetary gold to its proportional place

> in the hierarchy of prices (a step that was urged at the time by the economist Charles Rist[58] and others), the inevitable result would be an overvalued dollar and pound, and deflation of wages and prices to prewar levels, something one could expect during the first major financial crisis. And, indeed, this occurred in the United States between 1929 and 1934. The gold-exchange standard was liquidated, first by world deflation, then by Great Britain's default and devaluation of sterling in 1931, as well as by the rising economic nationalism of the thirties, which effectively closed financial [and some export] markets. Meanwhile, the world economy literally disintegrated in a free-for-all of beggar-thy-neighbor policies of managed floating-exchange rates, combined with all forms of capital controls and protectionism. Such systematic and global protectionism almost always leads to a depression. Finally, in a desperate but deliberate move, President Roosevelt devalued the dollar in 1933-1934 ("raised the price of gold"), which, together with the previous deflation, reliquefied the financial system, brought down interest rates, stimulated gold production and investment, discouraged hoarding, and led to a gradual upward drift in prices, profit margins, and output.[59]

Furthermore, a worldwide stock market boom was the result, although it was somewhat influenced by the prospect of another war.

In early 1986, I again sketched out the domestic and trade problems associated with the dollar's role as the international reserve currency—a problem that could also be solved by an international gold standard. In an article for *Challenge* magazine, I wrote:

> The trade deficit is closely associated with the unprecedented rise of the dollar that began in 1980. That is a monetary and financial problem [due to the buying up of dollars by foreign central banks for reserve currency purposes]. The trade-weighted dollar in February of 1985 was almost double its 1980 low. Experts estimate that the dollar has risen by 30 percent to 50 percent above the value of its true purchasing-power parity against key currencies. So it can hardly be surprising that the protectionist bomb has exploded in Congress. The protectionist impulse has become a fulcrum giving rise to a serious and healthy debate over what represents the best solution to the trade problem—protectionism or monetary reform. Few of our national leaders seem to realize that, despite our professed policy of free trade, nearly 30 percent of the market for manufactured goods in America is already covered by various quantitative restraints. That is particularly dangerous since quotas effectively eliminate further trade, while tariffs and taxes on imports merely raise their prices. We have learned over many decades of experience that defenders of free trade have to demand an essential precondition: fixed exchange rates based on a fair and stable value of the dollar. Free trade without stable exchange rates is a fantasy.

> The administration has proposed no coherent, comprehensive financial reform to remove permanently the true monetary cause of protectionism in the form of ever-worsening exchange-rate disorders.[60]

In February I pointedly hit the same theme for the *New York Times*: "The damage inflicted on our workers and industries by the overvalued dollar has demonstrated that free trade without stable exchange rates is a fantasy. [In addition, the government and banks add insult to injury by failing to use our additional reserves to finance American industry.] The argument for gold as a stable currency has rarely been stronger than it is today."[61]

MODERN MERCANTILISM

I continued to diagnose the same problem, and government authorities continued to ignore the necessary prescription.

For the *National Review* in November 1986, I wrote: "Modern mercantilism—generally ignored by economists and politicians alike during the past 15 years—has been practiced circuitously through the smokescreen of unrestrained monetary policies. This ruthless monetary struggle takes the form of a competitive depreciation of currency values similar to that which led us from the Depression of the 1930s into the nightmare of World War II. Managed floating exchange rates have become the hidden proxies for explicit tariffs, quotas and export subsidies—and, ironically, the new exchange-rate wars provoke protectionist trade retaliation in response, dangerously retarding world economic growth."[62]

That December, I told the Congressional Summit on Debt and Trade that the details matter: "Budgets will never be balanced before there is effective monetary reform," I said. "Moreover, until the budget is brought near balance, the secular [or long-term] trade deficit will continue—not least because sufficient U.S. produced domestic goods, now absorbed by [or purchased with] the budget deficit and financed by the reserve currency system, cannot be released for export abroad in order substantially to reduce the trade deficit—without a [domestic] recession."[63]

In January 1987, I returned to the op-ed page of the *Wall Street Journal* to further explain the budget and trade deficits, writing that "The 'twin deficits' and the protectionist effects of floating exchange rates are now out of the financial section and onto the front pages of the national print media. The present budget and trade crises cannot be exaggerated, even if their elusive monetary causes may now lead to mistaken tariff and quota policies. Indeed, after 25 years of fruitless debate over international monetary reform, recent signs of a steep inflation in the value of financial assets suggest the world may be in for yet another round of shocks, even while the conventional price indexes appear stable."[64]

BATTLING WITH BLACK MONDAY AND ITS AFTERMATH

For the next several years, while I concentrated on the creation of real wealth at Morgan Stanley Asset Management, I continued to write on the subject of sound monetary policy. Sometimes, my words had a special audience, even if that audience had not previously paid attention to my policy recommendations.

When the Black Monday crash of 1987 overwhelmed central banks on both sides of the Atlantic Ocean, the Bank of England came calling. Gordon Richardson was then the head of the Bank of England. The day after the crash, I received a note from the executive suite at Morgan Stanley—where Dick Fisher and Parker Gilbert had their offices—stating that Richardson wanted to see me. He had come to the United States to meet with Fed Chair Alan Greenspan, but he also came to see me in person at Morgan Stanley. Neither Richardson nor Greenspan appeared to know what to do.

I had called Greenspan the day of the crash. At the time, I told him to lend to the banking system without limit. Speed was everything. I told him to act fast, and to act generously. I remember telling him to put out a wire the following morning at eight o'clock saying that no bank will fail. When Richardson came to see me, I told him to lend the financial system the necessary credit to prevent it from collapsing, or the Bank of England would get blamed for letting the crisis get out of hand.

We did not have much of a choice.

I told Richardson and Greenspan to lend to any failing bank on equity capital, allowing the banks to use their equity holdings as reserves. I also suggested that they allow the banks to mark their equity holdings at pre-crash parity. I acknowledged the difficulty of their position and gave them a way out, but I also told Richardson and Greenspan that bank lending to the investment houses had gotten way out of hand. Nevertheless, I told them to wake up in the morning and put the word out that central banks were prepared to lend at whatever rate was necessary, asking for repayment with penalties only after the crisis was past. Both Greenspan and Richardson were historians. They both knew that the Bank of England had solved previous financial crises in much the same way.[65]

By 1988, things had settled down in the markets. When I wrote "Gold in a Global Multi-Asset Portfolio"—the fourth in my series of essays on gold—I looked at the use of gold as an investment. In this paper I focused on the fact that "since gold is uncorrelated, rather than negatively correlated, with financial assets, it is not surprising that the addition of gold to a financial portfolio can have very different effects."[66] My paper went on to discuss these effects in detail.

THE SPIRITUAL SONS OF JACQUES RUEFF—REINTRODUCING RUEFF

In contrast to the still-growing number of Americans interested in the work of Jacques Rueff, my efforts to reintroduce Rueff's ideas to his native France were ultimately disappointing. I had become acquainted with a rising generation of French economic thinkers and politicians in the 1970s and 1980s, and in March 1993, traveled to Paris with John Mueller, at the request of Jacques Raiman, the founder of the French software company G.S.I. We were there to meet with Edouard Balladur, who had just been appointed prime minister of France under Socialist Francois Mitterand in a "cohabitation government." We presented our comprehensive analysis of the

French economic and political situation and recommended "A 'Rueffian' Economic Plan for France."

We began by warning against a complacent "incremental" plan, pointing to Bill Clinton's defeat of George H. W. Bush in the November 1992 election as a cautionary example. We identified the main cause of France's high and rising unemployment rate as the relative disadvantage for French industry due to the rising cost of social benefits, which also necessitated rising payroll taxes. We traced the chronic weakness of the French franc to the French monetary authorities' continual purchases of French Treasury debt, and high French interest rates to a premium for expected future devaluation.

In opposition to the incremental approach, we proposed an integrated plan to Balladur with the following key components:

a) Refix the Franc/Deutschmark parity higher by about 9 percent. This proposal devalued the French currency to make the French economy more competitive. At the time, Germany was in a powerful boom, and was able to afford the increased competition from France;

b) Prohibit the Bank of France by law from purchasing any French public debt;

c) Undertake a fiscal reform designed to increase incentives for hiring and working. The reform would also increase funds for private investment by balancing the French budget and reducing French government spending from about 50 percent to 45 percent of GDP. This we accomplished by adjusting the tax code for inflation, but not the spending programs;

d) Pursue a bold program of privatization by ending wage and price controls, and allowing private enterprise to operate in sectors of the economy normally reserved to the government, and

e) Remove regulatory and administrative obstacles to economic efficiency.

Although he listened politely, Balladur took only very limited action. He did pursue privatization, but his tax reform was limited to abolishing the wealth tax, without cutting income or payroll tax rates. We found this rather strange for a supposedly socialist government. In addition, he failed to implement the social security reforms we had proposed. We felt the elderly would benefit more from a healthy French economy than from having their already limited pensions eroded by an inflationary currency. Rather than refixing the French franc to permit lower interest rates, French interest rates were raised on the theory that only a "*franc fort*," or strong franc, would permit an eventual easing of interest rates. In the event, the French unemployment rate was higher when Balladur left office in 1995 than when he took office in 1993. Balladur unsuccessfully ran for re-election in 1995, coming in third. Jacques Chirac, with whom Balladur had needlessly quarreled, then became the prime minister.

I should add that in addition to the special contribution of John Mueller, many other extraordinarily talented individuals have been involved over the years in the effort to popularize the sound economic principles of Jacques Rueff. All number among those whom Paul Fabra fittingly called "*Les fils spirituels Americains de Jacques Rueff*"[67]—the American spiritual sons of Jacques Rueff.

THE RESERVE CURRENCY CURSE

Even though the markets had settled down after the 1987 crash, the American economy was still struggling, and inflation remained a problem on Main Street. In ongoing essays for the *Wall Street Journal*, I would continue to emphasize the "curse" that making the dollar the world's reserve currency had placed on the American economy. In a 1993 op-ed, I wrote:

> Just as with the dollar shortage of the 1950s, the apparent dearth of [German] marks is partly a plethora of pounds (and lira and francs). The balance sheets of Europe's central banks reveal that the weakest currencies are almost invariably those whose central banks "monetize"—that is purchase—government debt on a large scale: the lira, the pound, the peseta and even, lately, the French franc. By contrast, the mark and those currencies that have had no problem remaining tied to the mark—for example, the Belgian franc and the Dutch guilder—have central banks that don't monetize government debt in significant amounts.
>
> Yet, also like the U.S. under Bretton Woods, Germany is still suffering from inflation caused by the rapid recent expansion of its reserve currency role. [U.S. inflation has been much higher since the end of dollar-gold convertibility, but U.S. consumer and producer prices also doubled even under the gold exchange standard of Bretton Woods.]
>
> To describe the problem simply: For other countries to increase their foreign exchange reserves, the reserve currency country must purchase more wealth abroad than it sells—i.e., run a balance of payments deficit. This demand for wealth without a matching supply causes inflation of either goods or securities prices [in the reserve currency nation]—usually both, in succession.[68]

In November 2014, John Mueller and I described for the *Wall Street Journal* how our concerns about the reserve currency curse had been borne out by events. "For more than three decades," the article began, "we have called attention on this page to what we called the 'reserve-currency curse.' Since some politicians and economists have recently insisted that the dollar's official role as the world's reserve currency is instead a great blessing, it is time to revisit the issue."[69]

This time we went into the history, hoping policymakers would understand that they had alternatives to their failed policies. We again demonstrated the way in which Milton Friedman was wrong when he claimed that the gold standard was the cause of the Depression. In fact, it was quite the opposite. The end of the true gold standard, and its replacement by a debased "gold-exchange" standard institutionalized the inflationary "reserve currency system," and thus produced the inflation-fueled speculation of the 1920s. Our *Journal* article summarized the history:

> The 1922 Genoa conference, which was intended to supervise Europe's post-World War I financial reconstruction, recommended "some means of economizing the use of gold by maintaining reserves in the form of foreign

balances"—initially pound-sterling and dollar IOUs. This established the interwar "gold exchange standard."

A decade later, Jacques Rueff explained the result of this profound change from the classical gold standard. When a foreign monetary authority accepts claims denominated in dollars to settle its balance-of-payments deficits instead of gold, purchasing power "has simply been duplicated." If the Banque de France counts among its reserves, dollar claims (and not just gold and French francs)—for example a Banque de France deposit in a New York bank—this increases the money supply in France but without reducing the money supply of the U.S. So both countries can use these dollar assets to grant credit. "As a result," Rueff said, "the gold-exchange standard was one of the major causes of the wave of speculation that culminated in the September 1929 crisis." A vast expansion of dollar reserves had inflated the prices of stocks and commodities; their contraction deflated both.

The gold-exchange standard's demand-duplicating feature, based on the dollar's reserve-currency role, was again enshrined in the 1944 Bretton Woods agreement. What ensued was an unprecedented expansion of official dollar reserves, and the consumer price level in the U.S. and elsewhere roughly doubled. Foreign governments holding dollars had increasingly demanded gold before the U.S. finally suspended gold payments in 1971.

The economic crisis of 2008-09 was similar to the crisis that triggered the Great Depression. This time, foreign monetary authorities had purchased trillions of dollars in U.S. public debt, including nearly $1 trillion in mortgage-backed securities issued by two government-sponsored enterprises, Fannie Mae and Freddie Mac. The foreign holdings of dollars were promptly returned to the dollar market, an example of demand duplication. This helped fuel a boom-and-bust in foreign markets and U.S. housing prices. The global excess credit creation also spilled over to commodity markets, in particular causing the world price of crude oil (which is denominated in dollars) to spike to $150 a barrel.[70]

I worked everywhere to expose the weaknesses and defects in the Keynesian and monetarist theories. Speaking to Grant's Spring Credit Conference in May of 1991, I said:

> It seems difficult to believe today, but floating exchange rates were actively desired by a majority of a whole generation of economists and investment experts, both monetarist and Keynesian. In the late 1960s, both schools believed that stable exchange rates stood in the way of their economic policy objectives: Full employment via budget deficits and [central bank expansionism] for the neo-Keynesians; price stability through control of the domestic money supply for the monetarists.
>
> The Keynesians complained that the Bretton Woods system of fixed exchange rates that prevailed until 1971 overvalued the dollar. They argued that devaluation of the exchange rate, by reducing the real value of U.S. wages, could

> stimulate exports and thus employment. And they insisted that "fine-tuning" of fiscal and Federal Reserve policy could control whatever inflation resulted from devaluation. History proved them wrong. (The 1970s featured the most dangerous inflation since the 1920s.)
>
> The monetarists pointed out the inflationary bias in Keynesian domestic economic policy. But, curiously enough, they were, for reasons of their own, prepared to accept floating rates. Fixed exchange rates stood in the way of the monetarist prescription for stable prices—that is central bank control of the domestic money supply. But it is impossible to target both the price of a currency (the exchange rate) and its quantity (the money supply) at the same time. If the exchange rate is fixed, then manipulation of the money supply must be constrained. Thus, monetarists wanted to float the exchange rate in order to manipulate the quantity of money in circulation.
>
> But in freeing exchange rates, the monetarists unhinged their own theory. This is because monetarist central banking strategies depend on the assumption that the demand for cash balances is more or less stable. If the demand for cash becomes unstable, the monetarists, like Archimedes, are left trying to move the earth without a place to stand. Thus, it becomes impossible for the Federal Reserve Board to predict what effect open market operations will have on the supply of money and the price level.[71]

This fact is probably what forced Milton Friedman to finally admit that his monetarist policy ideas had not worked and could not work.

Mueller and I consistently explained that one bad system—Bretton Woods—had been replaced by another bad system, namely floating exchange rates and a reserve currency fiat standard. In July 1994 we wrote an op-ed for the *Wall Street Journal*, arguing that "The Bretton Woods system contained the seeds of its own destruction. Like the interwar gold-exchange standard, Bretton Woods differed from the gold standard in one essential respect: the use of foreign exchange along with gold as international reserves. And this turned out to be its fatal flaw. Steady expansion of dollar reserves contributed to rising prices [in dollars], and rising prices steadily diminished the supply of new gold. [This was true because the price of gold was fixed. Gold miners' costs increased, but not the price they could get for their gold. Under a true gold standard, although the price of gold does not increase, neither does the price of anything else.] In 1960, Jacques Rueff and Robert Triffin, economic-statesmen, predicted the eventual run on the dollar. This would lead to either deflation or suspension of gold payments and continued inflation."[72]

Their prediction came true when the British demanded gold for dollars in 1971. Rather than redeem British dollar reserves for US gold, President Nixon defaulted at the gold window and suspended the Bretton Woods system. This one single act was a primary cause of the most inflationary and unstable period in recent American history.

Alas, Rueff and Triffin were ignored—as was I. But I was committed on the merits, and I knew that history would have the last word. That September, I told the Empower America Conference that "Historians will record that President Clinton's economic policy was as much a hostage to a flawed monetary system as that of his predecessor. But I also believe that, in a democracy, voters will eventually require politicians to change. One day politicians will come to understand the wrong choices of the 1930's and the 1970's, and, among them, a far-seeing statesman will emerge to reject our 'cross of paper' and lead us forward—to restore the least imperfect monetary standard that has worked for civilized man: the gold standard."[73]

I had hoped to be that statesman—and still I pray—that these words, these ideas, this history will be helpful to you, the wise and earnest Americans of tomorrow.

I will never stop speaking out, even though the issue is no longer as well understood by the nation or its politicians as it was in the 1980s. Despite the best efforts of Jim Grant, John Mueller, and myself, the nation's political and economic elite just could not understand—or continued to ignore—the value of our historical and theoretical evidence, even when the inevitable crises continued to hit with increasing severity.

Mueller and I were not surprised when the Crash of 2008 hit and caused the Great Recession of those years. By December we had diagnosed the situation in its proper context for the *National Review*:

> "The most disturbing aspect of the current financial crisis is that no U.S. official has correctly identified its primary cause. Experts variously attribute the economic reverses to subprime lending, derivative trading, excessive leverage, and regulation that was either too lax or too strict (take your pick), but these are symptoms rather than causes. Ignored is the main culprit: the dollar's role as the world's main official reserve currency. Though he almost certainly doesn't realize it yet, President-elect Barack Obama will either set the dollar's reserve-currency status on the path to extinction or risk becoming the next victim of what we call 'the reserve-currency curse.'"[74]

Monetary policy blindness and ignorance has left our nation in the dark. The Great Recession and other financial crises are easier to understand if you study the history of monetary policy. Decades of easy money had increased the money supply without a corresponding demand for currency from productive enterprise and a growing population. This led to inflation, destroying Main Street's purchasing power while pumping up asset prices. But asset prices fall when investors realize that productivity increases have not kept pace with investor expectations. The dollar's strength and high dollar asset prices were artificially induced by the artificial demand for dollars as reserve currency. The collateral damage was that American companies and their dollar-denominated exports were priced out of the market. American industry continued to struggle and go overseas. Wages could not keep pace because American industries could not compete. Struggling Americans turned to flipping houses, lured by an unscrupulous mortgage-backed securities market. Finally, when this lack of productivity became visible in the poor performance of American assets from housing to equities, prices tumbled across all asset classes.

REVIVING INTEREST IN THE GOLD STANDARD—AGAIN

Public attention to the gold standard revived yet again in 2011 when Republicans took control of the House of Representatives. It was the sixty-seventh anniversary of the Bretton Woods Agreement, and those who understood the significance of its collapse in 1971—and its relevance to the Great Recession—again began to call for the gold standard to be the keystone of responsible monetary reform.

That year, Congressman Ron Paul became chairman of the House subcommittee on domestic monetary policy. He invited James Grant, Professor James Salerno, and myself to testify before the committee on March 17. Prior to that hearing, John Mueller and I laid the groundwork with articles about the various economic problems that had their roots in the absence of sound monetary policy.

Writing for the *Washington Examiner*, we argued:

> Under President Reagan, Congress reformed the income tax code and balanced pay-as-you-go Social Security despite deep partisan divisions. Yet by Reagan's self-assessment, the Reagan Revolution was incomplete when he left office. We believe the monetary and budget reforms left unfinished in the 1980s now seem finally doable.
>
> "When a conservative says it is bad for the government to spend more than it takes in, he is simply showing the same common sense that tells him to come in out of the rain," Reagan had remarked in a February 1977 address outlining his presidential strategy.
>
> He was restating in common language the first principle of successful economic policy that went back to George Washington and Alexander Hamilton: don't give the central bank credit to finance the deficit.[75]

Those years also saw suffering and unrest develop around the world due in part to bad American monetary policy. In the *Weekly Standard*, I described the creeping but serious danger of dollar inflation overseas. When inflation hits in the reserve currency, dollar prices also rise overseas. But dollar inflation can hit developing markets even more brutally than at home, especially in nations that depend on dollar-denominated food and energy sources. "Since the beginning of 2009," I wrote, "oil prices have almost tripled, gasoline prices are up about 50 percent, and basic food prices, such as corn, soybeans, and wheat, have almost doubled around the world. Cotton and copper prices have reached all-time highs; major rises in sugar, spice, and wheat prices have been creating food riots in poor countries, where basic goods inflation is rampant. That inflation is in part financed by the flood abroad of excess dollars created over the last couple of years by the Federal Reserve."[76]

Later in March, Jim Grant again invited me to speak at his firm's semi-annual conference. There, I again pointed out the relationship between monetary policy and the export markets:

> Between 2009 and 2010 we have experienced a major, emerging market equity and economic boom—but at the very same time, sluggish growth in the United States. Foreign authorities are now reacting to inflation, raising interest rates, just as relative growth shifts to the U.S.[77]

The problem for America was this: the nature of the financial markets is such that emerging markets with high growth opportunities often receive the first wave of dollar investment from an inflation-fueled boom. But by the time those countries are ready to make purchases of US goods and services, they often adjust their financial policies for their own benefit, raising interest rates so that their people and businesses have less capacity to invest in US products and services. The result is that dollar purchases become more expensive, American exports have insufficient markets, and American earnings and wages suffer.

In April 2011, I wrote what was effectively an open letter to Congressman Paul Ryan for the *Wall Street Journal.* In it I implored him to include monetary reform in what was otherwise an impressive effort to fix problems exposed by the Crash of 2008 and the Great Recession:

> No man in America is a match for House Budget Committee Chairman Paul Ryan on the federal budget. No congressman in my lifetime has been more determined to cut government spending. No one is better informed for the task he has set himself. Nor has anyone developed a more comprehensive plan to reduce, and ultimately eliminate, the federal budget deficit than the House Budget Resolution submitted by Mr. Ryan on April 5.
>
> But experience and the operations of the Federal Reserve system compel me to predict that Mr. Ryan's heroic efforts to balance the budget by 2015 without raising taxes will not end in success—even with a Republican majority in both Houses and a Republican president in 2012. . . .
>
> The problem is simple. Because of the official reserve currency status of the dollar, combined with discretionary new Federal Reserve and foreign central bank credit, the federal government is always able to finance the Treasury deficit, even though net national savings are insufficient for the purpose.
>
> Paul Ryan's plan won't succeed without legislation to prevent the Federal Reserve from monetizing the national debt.[78]

The reason for my concern was that only by an Act of Congress could the government finally be *compelled* to balance the budget. Although the Federal Reserve Act of 1913 explicitly forbids the monetization of the national debt, both the Fed and Congress still violate the act with impunity. The violations began almost immediately after passage of the act, and continue to this very day. Incredible as it may seem, the sections of the Federal Reserve Act forbidding the monetization of the national debt have, in fact, *never been repealed*.[79]

In 2011, I also used the fortieth anniversary of the August 1971 default at the gold window to retrace the folly of that action. This time I described some of the details of the presidential meetings leading up to the disaster. In some cases, I had learned about the events from personal conversation with the participants. In an op-ed for the *Wall Street Journal*, I wrote:

> On the afternoon of Friday, Aug. 13, 1971, high-ranking White House and Treasury Department officials gathered secretly in President Richard Nixon's lodge at Camp David. Treasury Secretary John Connally, on the job for just seven months, was seated to Nixon's right. During that momentous afternoon, however, newcomer Connally was front and center, put there by a solicitous president. Nixon, said by his staff, was smitten by the big, self-confident Texan whom the president had charged with bringing order into his administration's bumbling economic policies.
>
> In the past, Nixon had expressed economic views that tended toward "conservative" platitudes about free enterprise and free markets. But the president loved histrionic gestures that grabbed the public's attention. He and Connally were determined to present a comprehensive package of dramatic measures to deal with the nation's huge balance of payments deficits, its anemic economic growth, and inflation.
>
> Dramatic indeed: They decided to break up the postwar Bretton Woods monetary system, to devalue the dollar, to raise tariffs, and to impose the first peacetime wage and price controls in American history. And they were going to do it on the weekend—heralding this astonishing news with a Nixon speech before the markets opened on Monday.
>
> The cast of characters gathered at Camp David was impressive. It included future Treasury Secretary George Shultz—then director of the Office of Management and Budget—and future Federal Reserve Chairman Paul Volcker, then undersecretary for monetary affairs at Treasury. At the meeting that afternoon Nixon reminded everyone of the importance of secrecy. They were forbidden even to tell their wives where they were. Then Nixon let Connally take over the meeting... First July 1944, and then August 1971: the dog days of summer have been momentous for the American dollar. It was 67 years ago that 44 nations from around the world gathered at Bretton Woods, New Hampshire, to plan the postwar framework for international money and trade.[80]

There, an ailing John Maynard Keynes and Harry Dexter White prevailed in their basic plan for a revived financial system. The Bretton Woods location had been chosen by White, who was the chief international economist at the Treasury Department, and the chief American negotiator at Bretton Woods. White had been influenced in his choice of location by Keynes, who strongly objected to the torture of hot, humid Washington. More importantly White was also a Soviet Communist spy, making the subject of Bretton Woods—and its highly problematic policies—even more worthy of scrutiny.

White's communist affiliations were significant, and he was by no means the only example of the systemic infiltration of American political institutions by global communism. Communism's stated aims are one thing, but in effect it typically empowers the state at the expense of the citizen. The facts of the White case are well known and well documented in scholarly articles and book length treatments. Readers interested in my own history of the events can consult the closing chapters of my book *Churchill, Roosevelt and Company.*[81]

To my consternation, no one in the decades since Bretton Woods has attempted to reconfigure what was always a patchwork and deficient system. Instead, the nations of the world stumble along from crisis to crisis. As I had written in June of that year, "The economic crisis we endure today is only the latest chapter in the century-long struggle to restore financial order in world markets—a struggle whose outcome is inextricably bound up with U.S. prosperity and the promise of the American way of life."

In September 2012, Representative Paul invited me to appear again before the House Subcommittee on Domestic Monetary Policy & Technology. These were among my remarks:

> The Federal Reserve System has in fact manipulated interest rates since the first year of Federal Reserve operations in 1914. Professor Allan Meltzer's magisterial, two-volume history of the Fed is the definitive witness to unrestrained Federal Reserve credit operations and their consequences. The problems created by Fed interest rate manipulation are very similar to the problems of government wage and price controls. [In addition, all are features of communist or authoritarian regimes.] . . .
>
> The extravagant and unprecedented Fed credit policy of Quantitative Easing, now intensified by QEIII announced Thursday, September 13, 2012 is one more extraordinary experiment in central bank interest rate and credit manipulation [also known as money printing]. These episodes of interest rate suppression and excessive Fed credit expansion—with effects similar to wage and price controls—have well-studied precedents in earlier economic and financial history. For example, the effects of the President Nixon-Arthur Burns (chairman of the Fed) credit expansion (1970–1973); and their wage and price controls of 1972 led to the collapse of financial markets in 1973 and 1974, and the worst economic decade in American history since the Great Depression. Indeed, during the late 1970s, the highest interest rates and inflation in American history were the ultimate result of previous Federal Reserve credit expansion, and government wage and price controls. The effects of substantial Fed interest rate suppression and credit expansion have, in the end, led to inflation of food prices—or oil,

> or natural resources, or real estate, or equities; or in the 1970s consumer price inflation—followed by a fall.
>
> The most important economic and monetary issue before the Congress is how, through institutional reform of the Fed and the monetary system, to solve this Fed-created monetary problem of cyclical booms and busts—largely the results of unrestrained Fed interest rate manipulation and quantitative easing . . . [quantitative easing being another euphemism for money printing].[82]

Although cyclical booms and busts *are* present in gold-standard private economies, they are much diminished in severity. The mistakes of ordinary people tend to be less severe than those of politicians and so-called experts.

In an article for the *American Spectator* the same month, I summarized the case for a modernized gold standard. The article starts with the basics: "Gold, a fundamental, metallic element of the earth's constitution, exhibits unique properties that enabled it, during two millennia of market testing, to emerge as a universally accepted store of value and medium of exchange, not least because it could sustain purchasing power over the long run against a standard assortment of goods and services. Rarely considered in monetary debates, these natural properties of gold caused it to prevail as a stable monetary standard, the most marketable means by which trading peoples worldwide could make trustworthy direct and indirect exchanges for all other articles of wealth. The preference of tribal cultures, as well as ancient and modern civilizations, to use gold as money was no mere accident of history. Nor has this natural, historical, and global preference for gold as a store of value and standard of measure been easily purged by academic theory and government fiat. Gold, by its intrinsic nature, is durable, homogeneous, fungible, imperishable, indestructible, and malleable."[83]

Just as I had done three decades earlier, I stormed the intellectual, political, and media establishment with articles, speeches, and testimony. Again, I fell short of the goal. Knowing that a full policy paper was necessary given the increasing ignorance of the historical issues, I resumed work on my book about the gold standard. I had started it back in 1981 with a $4,000 advance from Jason Epstein at Random House for *The Nature of the Gold Standard*. I had returned the advance long before, but many of the theoretical arguments—and the evidence to prove them—are published in my books, *Money, Gold and History* and especially in *The True Gold Standard, a Monetary Reform Plan without Official Reserve Currencies*.

Thirty years later, I was better prepared to make the case for the gold standard, and to explain how to get there. I wrote the original manuscript for *The True Gold Standard* in a Paris hotel room one afternoon and evening during the spring of 2010. I strained my back because I refused to get up until I finished it. I started at 11:00 a.m. and finished at midnight. Louise was with me at the time and saw how important it was to me, noticing that I even went without a shower. I worked hard to make it comprehensive. I worked totally from memory. I didn't have one book with me.

"America and the world need monetary reform," I wrote in the introduction.

> Indeed, they need a twenty-first century, international gold standard. The gold standard— i.e., national currency convertibility to gold—is the simple, proven, global monetary standard by which to transmit reliable price information worldwide. Unlike manipulated, floating, paper currencies, the true gold standard—a dollar defined in law as a specific weight of gold—exhibits the optimum, impartial, networking effects characteristic of the electronic age of reasonably transparent, global standards.
>
> America should lead in the age of monetary reform by unilateral resumption of its historical constitutional monetary standard—namely, the gold dollar. (America should also work hard to persuade its major trading partners to do the same.) Unilateral resumption of the gold standard means that the United States dollar will be defined by Congress in federal statute as a certain weight unit of gold—as the dollar was so defined from 1792–1971. The Treasury, the Federal Reserve, and the banking system will be responsible for maintaining the statutory gold value of the United States dollar.[84]

With the cooperation of allies like Ralph Benko, The Lehrman Institute worked to educate the American public about the gold standard through a website. We also engaged the field of presidential candidates in 2012. In one of the Republican presidential debates, former House Speaker Newt Gingrich proposed a new gold commission, to be chaired by Jim Grant and myself. Earlier, Congressman Paul had pledged to appoint Mr. Grant as chairman of the Federal Reserve Board. When he learned of Paul's proposal, Jim ratcheted up his trademark irony, saying it was "the very best way to get a federal office: you just wake up and are coronated."[85] On the need for the commission Gingrich said, "Hard money is a discipline. . . . It is very important for us to understand in finance that the entire contraption that has been built up over the last thirty or forty years has so much paper in it, so much debt, so much leverage, that we probably have a fifteen- or twenty-year period of working our way out of it. And yet, the alternative is to get sicker and sicker and sicker."[86]

For the *New York Sun* I wrote on the prospects for such a commission, saying:

> The next gold commission . . . must be different from the Reagan Gold Commission, the majority of which endorsed the managed paper dollar and floating exchange rates. As the two dissenting minority members of the 1981 commission, Ron Paul and I filed a minority report. We called for the restoration of the gold standard—that is, a stable dollar defined by law as a certain weight of gold. The minority report, entitled "The Case for Gold," was later republished in book form.
>
> My views on monetary reform have not changed, except that my sense of urgency is even greater. The Constitution in Article I, Sections 8 and 10, makes clear that Congress has the full and unique authority "to coin money" from gold [and silver] to be the monetary standard of the United States. Since 1792,

> Congress by statute established a stable dollar, defined in law as a specific weight unit of gold, but a 1971 executive order effectively changed that. . . .
>
> It is clear that a Gold Commission II must not be an academic exercise, nor the means by which a paper money majority is enabled to "deep-six" serious consideration of the means by which to reestablish a stable dollar convertible to gold. The purpose of Gold Commission II should be to spell out a plan whereby Congress and the President are enabled, effectively and successfully, to restore the gold-backed dollar. (My thoughts regarding this plan went into the text of *The True Gold Standard*.)
>
> All relevant evidence and points of view must be considered, but the fundamental purpose of the Gold Commission II should be to render judgment on the era of the declining paper dollar—its consequences, and above all, the remedies for inflation.
>
> Jim Grant and I have recommended that Gold Commission II should focus on the following agenda in order to show how a stable dollar engenders economic growth and tends toward full employment. The purpose of the agenda should be to demonstrate that a dollar convertible to gold is the missing link in presidential growth plans limited to deregulation, tax reform, and balanced budgets.[87]

In the wake of the Great Recession, central banks propped up both tottering economies and tottering privileged businesses. I criticized these bailouts in the *American Spectator* edition of June 3, 2013:

> Central banks worldwide, led by the U.S. Federal Reserve, mint new money ceaselessly to bail out insolvent governments, insolvent banks, and insolvent but politically powerful corporations and labor unions. This new money goes first to insiders in the financial sector, who exchange the cheap credit for commodities, stocks, and real estate at ever-rising prices. This is the so-called carry-trade, monopolized by a financial class that uses free money from the Fed to front-run the authorities for "insider" profits.[88]

The Great Recession was so severe that there really was an opportunity in its aftermath to implement the gold standard. But the political headwinds remained steady. In the *Weekly Standard* for February 2013, I wrote that "A winning agenda for a political party must simultaneously satisfy the requirements of economic effectiveness and political success. Ronald Reagan had such an agenda in the 1980s. Subsequent Republican presidential candidates have not."[89]

The idea of a second Gold Commission died with Newt Gingrich's candidacy. The opportunity for transformative change remained unmet, for there was no other presidential candidate prepared to take up the challenge.

Over the course of my life, my writing and speaking about gold had given my advocacy weight. When reviewing the second edition of *The True Gold Standard*,

Paul Brodsky acknowledged the cogency of my arguments and the lifetime of study supporting them:

> Lewis Lehrman is one of a very small group of contemporary gold advocates able to successfully bridge the gap separating practical conservative intellectualism from fleeting, half-baked idealism. . . . Lehrman frames well the intractable issues associated with baseless fiat currencies, a toxic global brew that can lead to only one thing in liberal democracies: ongoing inflation ending in gross economic imbalances. . . . Such a nightmarish scenario was not the premonition of a bitter command-economy fortune-teller in a frigid Soviet state building 30 years ago. It describes precisely the chain of events occurring today across most of the largest advanced global economies, including the United States. . . . Only someone erudite and elegant in demeanor could hope to pull it off. . . . Lehrman's views are considered, and his convictions carry weight. He brings gravitas to his cause, and he does so from within as a member of the club.[90]

"In an imperfect world, peopled by imperfect human beings, there can be no perfect monetary system," I wrote in *The True Gold Standard*. "Nor is the case for gold the case for investment in gold. Based on a prudent consideration of monetary history, it is an argument from principle by which to establish the optimum monetary standard for a stable, growing economic and social order."[91]

The remarks in this chapter are *positive* proof of the superiority of the gold standard. For refutations of all the chief objections, please consult the many books on the subject, including the two I wrote.

Imperfect though we all are, by the test of centuries, the true gold standard without official reserve currencies, is the least imperfect monetary system of history.

IN CONGRESS, JULY 4, 1776.

The unanimous Declaration of the thirteen united States of America,

When in the Course of human events, it becomes necessary for one people to dissolve the political bands which have connected them with another, and to assume among the powers of the earth, the separate and equal station to which the Laws of Nature and of Nature's God entitle them, a decent respect to the opinions of mankind requires that they should declare the causes which impel them to the separation. — We hold these truths to be self-evident, that all men are created equal, that they are endowed by their Creator with certain unalienable Rights, that among these are Life, Liberty and the pursuit of Happiness. — That to secure these rights, Governments are instituted among Men, deriving their just powers from the consent of the governed, — That whenever any Form of Government becomes destructive of these ends, it is the Right of the People to alter or to abolish it, and to institute new Government, laying its foundation on such principles and organizing its powers in such form, as to them shall seem most likely to effect their Safety and Happiness. Prudence, indeed, will dictate that Governments long established should not be changed for light and transient causes; and accordingly all experience hath shewn, that mankind are more disposed to suffer, while evils are sufferable, than to right themselves by abolishing the forms to which they are accustomed. But when a long train of abuses and usurpations, pursuing invariably the same Object evinces a design to reduce them under absolute Despotism, it is their right, it is their duty, to throw off such Government, and to provide new Guards for their future security. — Such has been the patient sufferance of these Colonies; and such is now the necessity which constrains them to alter their former Systems of Government. The history of the present King of Great Britain is a history of repeated injuries and usurpations, all having in direct object the establishment of an absolute Tyranny over these States. To prove this, let Facts be submitted to a candid world. — He has refused his Assent to Laws, the most wholesome and necessary for the public good. — He has forbidden his Governors to pass Laws of immediate and pressing importance, unless suspended in their operation till his Assent should be obtained; and when so suspended, he has utterly neglected to attend to them. — He has refused to pass other Laws for the accommodation of large districts of people, unless those people would relinquish the right of Representation in the Legislature, a right inestimable to them and formidable to tyrants only. — He has called together legislative bodies at places unusual, uncomfortable, and distant from the depository of their public Records, for the sole purpose of fatiguing them into compliance with his measures. — He has dissolved Representative Houses repeatedly, for opposing with manly firmness his invasions on the rights of the people. — He has refused for a long time, after such dissolutions, to cause others to be elected; whereby the Legislative powers, incapable of Annihilation, have returned to the People at large for their exercise; the State remaining in the mean time exposed to all the dangers of invasion from without, and convulsions within. — He has endeavoured to prevent the population of these States; for that purpose obstructing the Laws for Naturalization of Foreigners; refusing to pass others to encourage their migrations hither, and raising the conditions of new Appropriations of Lands. — He has obstructed the Administration of Justice, by refusing his Assent to Laws for establishing Judiciary powers. — He has made Judges dependent on his Will alone, for the tenure of their offices, and the amount and payment of their salaries. — He has erected a multitude of New Offices, and sent hither swarms of Officers to harrass our people, and eat out their substance. — He has kept among us, in times of peace, Standing Armies without the Consent of our legislatures. — He has affected to render the Military independent of and superior to the Civil power. — He has combined with others to subject us to a jurisdiction foreign to our constitution, and unacknowledged by our laws; giving his Assent to their Acts of pretended Legislation: — For Quartering large bodies of armed troops among us: — For protecting them, by a mock Trial, from punishment for any Murders which they should commit on the Inhabitants of these States: — For cutting off our Trade with all parts of the world: — For imposing Taxes on us without our Consent: — For depriving us in many cases, of the benefits of Trial by Jury: — For transporting us beyond Seas to be tried for pretended offences — For abolishing the free System of English Laws in a neighbouring Province, establishing therein an Arbitrary government, and enlarging its Boundaries so as to render it at once an example and fit instrument for introducing the same absolute rule into these Colonies: — For taking away our Charters, abolishing our most valuable Laws, and altering fundamentally the Forms of our Governments: — For suspending our own Legislatures, and declaring themselves invested with power to legislate for us in all cases whatsoever. — He has abdicated Government here, by declaring us out of his Protection and waging War against us. — He has plundered our seas, ravaged our Coasts, burnt our towns, and destroyed the lives of our people. — He is at this time transporting large Armies of foreign Mercenaries to compleat the works of death, desolation and tyranny, already begun with circumstances of Cruelty & perfidy scarcely paralleled in the most barbarous ages, and totally unworthy the Head of a civilized nation. — He has constrained our fellow Citizens taken Captive on the high Seas to bear Arms against their Country, to become the executioners of their friends and Brethren, or to fall themselves by their Hands. — He has excited domestic insurrections amongst us, and has endeavoured to bring on the inhabitants of our frontiers, the merciless Indian Savages, whose known rule of warfare, is an undistinguished destruction of all ages, sexes and conditions. In every stage of these Oppressions We have Petitioned for Redress in the most humble terms: Our repeated Petitions have been answered only by repeated injury. A Prince, whose character is thus marked by every act which may define a Tyrant, is unfit to be the ruler of a free people. Nor have We been wanting in attentions to our British brethren. We have warned them from time to time of attempts by their legislature to extend an unwarrantable jurisdiction over us. We have reminded them of the circumstances of our emigration and settlement here. We have appealed to their native justice and magnanimity, and we have conjured them by the ties of our common kindred to disavow these usurpations, which, would inevitably interrupt our connections and correspondence. They too have been deaf to the voice of justice and of consanguinity. We must, therefore, acquiesce in the necessity, which denounces our Separation, and hold them, as we hold the rest of mankind, Enemies in War, in Peace Friends. —

We, therefore, the Representatives of the united States of America, in General Congress, Assembled, appealing to the Supreme Judge of the world for the rectitude of our intentions, do, in the Name, and by Authority of the good People of these Colonies, solemnly publish and declare, That these United Colonies are, and of Right ought to be Free and Independent States; that they are Absolved from all Allegiance to the British Crown, and that all political connection between them and the State of Great Britain, is and ought to be totally dissolved; and that as Free and Independent States, they have full Power to levy War, conclude Peace, contract Alliances, establish Commerce, and to do all other Acts and Things which Independent States may of right do. — And for the support of this Declaration, with a firm reliance on the protection of divine Providence, we mutually pledge to each other our Lives, our Fortunes and our sacred Honor.

John Hancock

Button Gwinnett
Lyman Hall
Geo Walton

Wm Hooper
Joseph Hewes
John Penn

Edward Rutledge
Thos Heyward Junr.
Thomas Lynch Junr.
Arthur Middleton

Samuel Chase
Wm. Paca
Thos. Stone
Charles Carroll of Carrollton

George Wythe
Richard Henry Lee
Th Jefferson
Benja. Harrison
Thos. Nelson jr.
Francis Lightfoot Lee
Carter Braxton

Robt Morris
Benjamin Rush
Benja. Franklin
John Morton
Geo Clymer
Jas. Smith
Geo. Taylor
James Wilson
Geo. Ross
Caesar Rodney
Geo Read
Tho M:Kean

Wm. Floyd
Phil. Livingston
Frans. Lewis
Lewis Morris

Richd. Stockton
Jno Witherspoon
Fras. Hopkinson
John Hart
Abra Clark

Josiah Bartlett
Wm. Whipple
Saml Adams
John Adams
Robt Treat Paine
Elbridge Gerry
Step. Hopkins
William Ellery
Roger Sherman
Sam.el Huntington
Wm. Williams
Oliver Wolcott
Matthew Thornton

The Stone Declaration of Independence commissioned by John Quincy Adams

CHAPTER 15

Getting Right with the Founders

AN AMERICAN IN FULL

"Boy though I was among the academic skeptics in New Haven, and at Cambridge—I was still, as a graduate student, dare I say, man enough to embrace, unselfconsciously, the greatness of American history." So I told an event of the Gilder Lehrman Institute of American History in 1995. "Americans were unlike citizens of all other nations," I continued. "They were not united by race, neither were they anchored by ancestral territory, nor joined by common genealogies. Immigrants all, Americans were set apart—because they were bound together by a less obvious, but much more profound link with their past. That link was a principle that all men are created equal, enshrined forever in the Declaration of Independence and President Abraham Lincoln's Gettysburg Address."[1]

America can become the native land for peoples of every race, creed, and color. Only in America, among all the countries of the world, and of history, can such a primordial transformation take place. If I emigrate to Germany, am I a German? If to India, am I an Indian? If to Japan, am I Japanese? If to China, am I Chinese? But if I come to America, from any and every foreign land, I can become an American-in-full.

After leaving Harvard, I had kept up with the scholarship in American history. The example set by my teachers in middle and secondary school stayed with me. At The Lehrman Institute, I shared discussions with some of my generation's great emerging historians.

My single-minded focus on American history began at Harvard. JFK caused everyone to be interested in American politics. I started to read Roy Basler the way I had read Jacques Rueff. I read his *Abraham Lincoln's Collected Works* straight through in the 1970s without interruption, and then again in 1982. I studied Lincoln's words. I wanted to be able to quote him. I instinctively knew that Lincoln was the man who opened doors. He was *the* American.

In a campaign profile, Michael Barone had written that my "interest in ideas was always there. After college he studied history in graduate school. On the road . . . for Rite-Aid locations in the mill towns and small cities of upstate New York and central Pennsylvania, he would eat dinner at McDonald's and retire to a Holiday Inn to read history. The crinkled book jackets in the bookcase behind him are testimony

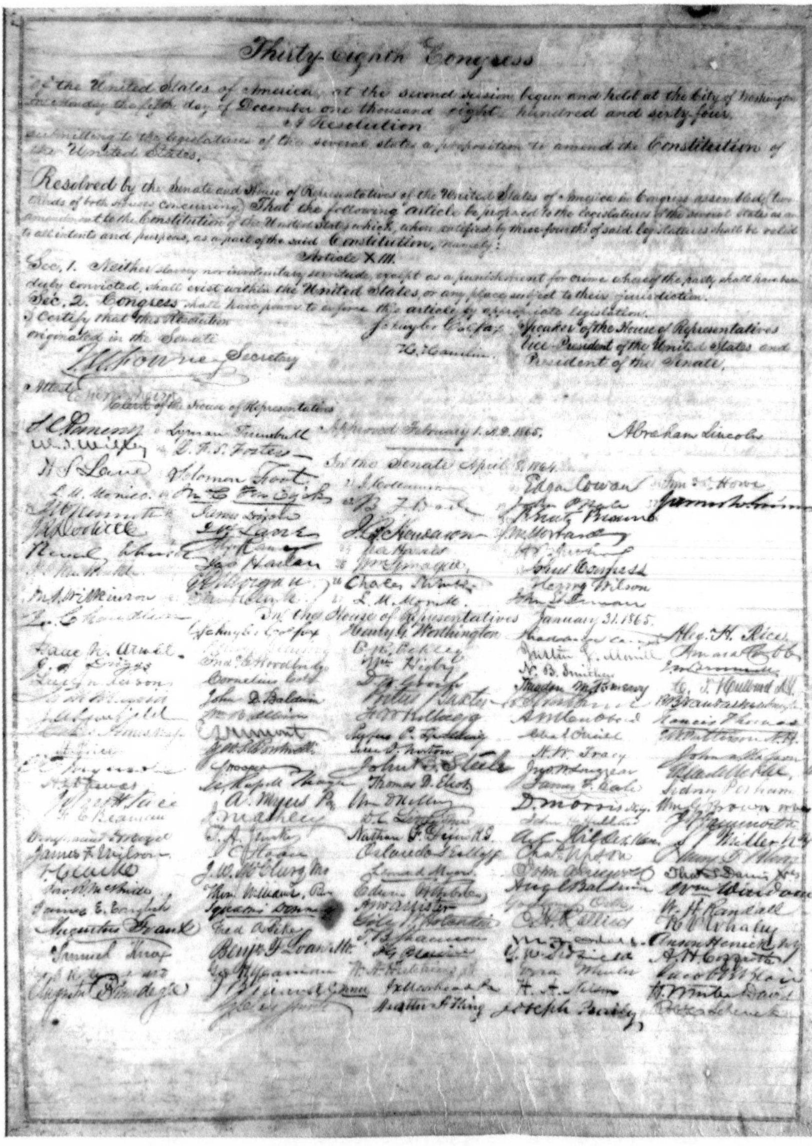

Thirty-Eighth Congress of the United States of America; at the second session, begun and held at the City of Washington, on Monday, the fifth day of December, one thousand eight hundred and sixty-four.

A Resolution

Submitting to the legislatures of the several States a proposition to amend the Constitution of the United States.

Resolved by the Senate and House of Representatives of the United States of America in Congress assembled, (two-thirds of both houses concurring,) That the following article be proposed to the legislatures of the several States as an amendment to the Constitution of the United States, which, when ratified by three-fourths of said legislatures, shall be valid to all intents and purposes, as a part of the said Constitution, namely:

Article XIII.

Sec. 1. Neither slavery nor involuntary servitude, except as a punishment for crime whereof the party shall have been duly convicted, shall exist within the United States, or any place subject to their jurisdiction.

Sec. 2. Congress shall have power to enforce this article by appropriate legislation.

I certify that this Resolution originated in the Senate.

J. W. Forney Secretary

Schuyler Colfax Speaker of the House of Representatives

H. Hamlin Vice President of the United States and President of the Senate.

Attest Edw. McPherson Clerk of the House of Representatives

Approved February 1. A.D. 1865. Abraham Lincoln

In the Senate April 8. 1864.

In the House of Representatives January 31. 1865.

The Thirteenth Amendment: Second Revolution

to his continuing interest in history, economics and politics and the breadth of his knowledge."[2]

Reverence for our American heritage was part of the parenting Louise and I provided our children. When our five children were young, on the Fourth of July, Louise and I would emphasize the great paragraph from the Declaration of Independence: "We hold these truths to be self-evident that all men are created equal. . . ." We talked about the Declaration of Independence as the founding document of our country. We emphasized that the remarkable liberty we enjoy as citizens of America entails duties as well as rights. Indeed, for every right, there is a corresponding duty. After years of repetition, I believe every one of our five children has absorbed this truth. Now our children can communicate it to our grandchildren.

The Founders of America, led by General Washington, made the United States of America a true union. However, in order to establish that union, they had to accept slavery in the states where it existed. Abraham Lincoln recognized that accepting slavery was incompatible with the premises of America's founding document. Thus, beginning in the 1850s, Mr. Lincoln campaigned relentlessly to put slavery "in the course of ultimate extinction."

After his re-election in November 1864, he pushed equally relentlessly for passage of the Thirteenth Amendment, abolishing slavery. This he called a "King's cure." We esteem President Lincoln because he created a country where all men and women can be free.

I met Professor Harry Jaffa after I read his book, *Crisis of the House Divided*, about the Lincoln-Douglas debates. Dr. Jaffa was an incomparable political philosopher, who saw in Lincoln the same greatness that I did. As I said at the time, "in Jaffa's evangelization of Lincoln, one discovers not the temperament of a lawyer but of a lawgiver, not the profession of a judge, but a prophet of first principles of jurisprudence."[3]

I met Professor Gabor Boritt after reading *Lincoln and the Economics of the American Dream.* As I studied, I began to appreciate the connection between Mr. Lincoln's early focus on economic growth and freedom, and his later preoccupation with extending freedom to those who were victims of slavery. Although most of my writing in the

Wikimedia Commons

Harry Jaffa: Lincoln's philosopher

1970s and 1980s focused on economics, I was deepening my own understanding of the linkage between the Founding in the eighteenth century and America's Refounding under Lincoln in the mid-nineteenth century, with the Thirteenth, Fourteenth, and Fifteenth Amendments to the Constitution.

Some of the first fruits of my study can be found in my writing and speeches connecting Lincoln's antislavery crusade to the movement to preserve the right to life during the late 1980s and early 1990s.[4]

In the mid-1990s, I began writing short essays on President Lincoln that were published in the *Wall Street Journal*, the *Greenwich Time*, and newspapers across the country (collected and published in 2013 as *Lincoln by "Littles"*). In so doing, I began to turn my attention back to the academic study and teaching of American history I had left behind at Harvard. My study was informed by the work Dick Gilder and I had begun for the Gilder Lehrman Institute of American History.

Scholars and professional historians responded favorably to my writings, and would be generous enough to recognize my efforts. "Lew's early scholarship were compilations of essays," said the former President of Monticello, Daniel P. Jordan. "With *Lincoln at Peoria*, he progressed to a monograph. His recent books on World War II show remarkable research and fresh thinking . . . People can look at Lew and see a guy who is a real scholar. This is not an academic historian. He's a businessman, and a champion of history."[5]

REVERING THE DECLARATION

Increasingly, I wrote and spoke about two periods of American history: the Founding, and the life of Abraham Lincoln. In a 1991 address to The Hill School, I began: "July 4, 1776 was a unique event in the history of the world, not because our forefathers declared themselves for a new nation, but instead, for a nation founded on new principles. We must remind ourselves . . . that we were not in 1776, as we are not now, bound together by the ties of a common religion, nor joined by common race, nor even by ancestral territory. Rather, in both independence and war we have been bound together as we are today, by dedication to a common proposition, the American proposition—that all men are created equal."[6]

In one op-ed, I focused on the signing of the Declaration, and in particular, Lincoln's reverence for it. "The debate, which John Adams derided as an 'an idle Mispence of Time,' came to an end on a hot, humid July 4. To alleviate the oppressive heat that day, windows of the State House were opened. The final vote was hastened by an invasion of horseflies from a nearby stable. Their aggressive behavior caused the delegates to vote, adjourn, and quickly retreat from Independence Hall. As Abraham Lincoln would later say of this event: 'Four score and seven years ago our forefathers brought forth on this continent, a new nation, conceived in Liberty, and dedicated to the proposition that all men are created equal.' That is [doing the math], the United States of America was inaugurated by the Declaration of Independence in 1776 [and not the ratification of the Constitution]."[7]

The dream of the Founders was firmly grounded in the promise of opportunity and freedom in the Declaration. Not only Thomas Jefferson, but also James Madison, Father of the Constitution, held the Declaration of Independence to be in the latter's words "the fundamental act of union"—the organic law in virtue of which the union of the colonies was consummated and the American nation inaugurated. In a 1983 speech, I noted: "The everlasting principles of our forefathers—free men, free markets and equal opportunity—the fundamental covenants by which the Founders gave birth to a new nation, are 'the sacred truths' which Thomas Jefferson, in that room on 6th and Chestnut in Philadelphia, set forth in the Declaration of Independence."[8]

The promise of the Declaration continues to shine like a beacon through American history. In a 1996 speech to Thomas Aquinas College, I described its progress: "Our ancestors were Protestants from England, Catholics from the Continent, black slaves from Africa, later the Irish, Italian and Jewish immigrants, to mention only a few—and today, from every forsaken corner of the earth they flee, having no other bond than their common humanity, and the uncommon boldness to break free into our New Jerusalem. These new immigrants witness, by their work and their way of life, that they know and honor the first watchword of our national faith—the Declaration of Independence. Thus now do we see why the founding American proposition, all men are created equal, must also be the first proposition of a future America; for this proposition is the only common bond which can join all Americans together, especially those of us without blood ancestors present at the creation of the Republic. We know, as my grandfather knew, that whatsoever the faith of the founders is true—and everlasting—just so you know, and I know, that everything I am, everything you could ever be, arises from the fact that we can say—our lives, our liberty are gifts of God, not of the government."[9]

The promise of the Declaration further extends to the whole world. In 1985 I met in Angola with resistance leaders fighting communism in four countries on three continents. I could think of no more fitting gift than framed copies of the Declaration of Independence. As I said in one 1985 interview: "The Declaration of Independence is a universal document."[10]

Upon the Declaration, my view of American history is founded. As Winston Churchill said at Fulton, Missouri, in March of 1946. "We must never cease to proclaim in fearless tones the great principles of freedom and the rights of man which are the joint inheritance of the English-speaking world and which through Magna Carta, the Bill of Rights, the Habeas Corpus, trial by jury, and the English common law find their most famous expression in the American Declaration of Independence."[11]

CELEBRATING THE FOUNDERS

Benjamin Franklin—The Nation's First Entrepreneur

I came to appreciate the interrelationship between the Founders' pursuit of economic success and political freedom, easily demonstrated by the life of Benjamin Franklin.

"Benjamin Franklin was a typesetter who became America's greatest printer," I would tell an audience in December 1983. "He was a writer who became early America's greatest publisher. He was a property owner who organized America's first insurance company to protect it. As a book collector, his small investment brought forth the first library. As a student of medicine, his enterprise led to the first hospital."[12]

As I told the Pennsylvania Society: "To Franklin, the greatest of Pennsylvanians, freedom meant the right to follow your own star in peace without regard to education, income or background. [Franklin was] America's foremost self-made man. His life's work—no matter Franklin's few years of formal learning—symbolize the astonishing creativity of free enterprise. He is, in fact, America's most famous entrepreneur. He was the eighteenth century's most celebrated small businessman. He was our first venture capitalist."[13]

In a 1984 speech at Pepperdine University, I said "Benjamin Franklin had a coherent economic philosophy and he expressed it through the sayings of Poor Richard. To Franklin, government played a part, but only a strictly limited part, in a free and ordered society. Government assured stable money, frugal spending practices, low taxes, and public safety. Government created the conditions, and some of the incentives, which lead to hard work, not welfare; savings, not subsidies; risk-taking, not reclusive hoarding; investment not indulgent consumption; growth not austerity. These were the cardinal principles of Poor Richard, all of which give rise to economic opportunity, new enterprise, new jobs, and full employment. These virtues—and their just desserts—made up, not only the commercial code of Franklin, but they were the hope of the new nation."[14]

Alexander Hamilton—America's First Nation Builder

Like Franklin, Alexander Hamilton symbolized the classic American rags-to-riches success story. Hamilton was Washington's second-in-command, wrote most of the Federalist Papers and founded the American financial system. An immigrant from the Caribbean, this penniless fifteen-year-old boy came to America and created a truly extraordinary American legacy.

In a speech at Princeton University in June of 2007 I would say:

> Alexander Hamilton was, in a word, a prodigy. He was America's first Secretary of the Treasury at age 34, indeed by all accounts, the first minister of the cabinet assembled under President Washington. At 21 he had been an early leader of the revolutionary party in New York. At 24 he was de facto Chief-of-Staff to General Washington. . . . And the origins of this aspiring statesman were no less implausible than his rapid ascent.
>
> Hamilton's birth was advertised in an infamous description by President John Adams, whose self-importance was again on display, when Adams referred to Hamilton as "the bastard brat of a Scotch Pedlar." Alexander Hamilton had been born out-of-wedlock into the slave and sugar culture of the Caribbean—abandoned by his father, put to work penniless at 11, then left alone at 13 by the

Gilder Lehrman Institute of American History GLC08343_0

Alexander Hamilton: "We are all Hamiltonians now."

death of his mother. Four years later, sponsored by a Caribbean merchant, he arrived in America. Only seventeen years thereafter, he was Secretary of the Treasury in President Washington's first administration.

The exertions and achievements of Hamilton's founding statecraft were a match for his ambitions. . . . The Hamiltonian economic revival of the 1790s vindicated the new constitution of 1789. In the first National Bank of the United States, in the design of the U.S. monetary standard [on the basis of gold and silver], the refinancing of federal and state debt, and in his report on manufactures, to mention only a few Hamiltonian initiatives, he . . . elaborated a pathbreaking economic vision. . . . And, in the building of our government institutions, he displayed a practical wisdom, *rare* among intellectuals. In sum, he was a lawgiver, a teacher, and a nation-builder."[15]

Hamilton shaped both ratification of the Constitution and the early American economy. My view of Hamilton was confirmed in biographies of the first treasury secretary by Rick Brookhiser and Ron Chernow. In a review of Brookhiser's book I wrote: "Hamilton most assuredly had his flaws, and, like his talents, they were outsized. But still, if Brookhiser is right in describing him as a great man, why have historians concentrated on his errors and flaws rather than his remarkable achievements? In fact, Brookhiser's account of Hamilton's legacy is nothing less than the authentication of a great deed of statecraft—of nation-building. Moreover, no reasonable scholar can dispute the fact that most of Hamilton's plan as Secretary of the Treasury had been well-crafted. Paradoxically, while he rebuilt the wellsprings of the wealth of his adopted nation, he manifestly cared nothing for riches himself. Born poor, he died poor. His ambitions were for fame, sought in the leadership of his country, designed in policies aimed at creating a unified nation—rich, powerful, well-respected."[16]

James Wilson—The Lawyer's Lawyer

The Founders studied political philosophy and applied its lessons to the American experiment. Like his contemporary Hamilton, Supreme Court justice James Wilson was a "study in ironies." So I wrote for the Cumberland County Historical Society in 1994, continuing: "Born poor, become rich, James Wilson died poor, but he spent much of his life pursuing wealth and status. He was a successful Carlisle attorney for a rural community who became a cosmopolitan advocate for the Philadelphia elite. He was a university failure, turned constitutional architect, who had the self-confidence to call his handiwork at the Constitutional Convention 'the best form of government which has ever been offered to the world.'"[17] Like Hamilton, Wilson's public life was marred by scandal but also marked by dedication to conservative economic principles. Wilson's work helped finance the American Revolution. His thinking helped formulate the Constitution. "One sees in James Wilson, writ larger than life, the conflicts which inflamed the revolutionary generation. For example, Wilson moved to Carlisle because he saw in the frontier an opportunity to advance his legal career. Then he moved from Carlisle to Philadelphia to enlarge the stage of his ambition. There he was comfortable, it seems as a proud signer of the Declaration of Independence while, at the same time, he was a prominent attorney for Philadelphia Tories accused of high treason [prior to and during the Revolutionary War]."[18]

Gilder Lehrman Institute of American History GLC04842.40_2

Justice James Wilson:
Enigmatic Founder from Pennsylvania

Wilson was as imaginative as he was brave, and took part in the last battle of the Revolution at Yorktown. A Washington circular had called him into battle, where he succeeded mightily, according to contemporary accounts.

The Ambitions of the Founders

The Founders were admittedly ambitious men—ambitious for themselves and ambitious for their country. We in the United States of America are the beneficiaries of their ambition. Sometimes their ambitions were in conflict. In 2013, I published a book of my essays called *The American Founders*. As I wrote in the introduction to one of those essays, "The Founders were keenly aware that those who wrote history, influenced how history was interpreted. John Adams, a bit jealous, but still able to preserve his sense of humor, declared: 'The history of our Revolution will be one continued lie from one end to the other. The essence of the whole will be that Dr. Franklin's electrical rod smote the earth and out sprang General Washington. That Franklin electrified him with his rod—and thenceforward these two conducted all the policies, negotiations, legislatures, and war.'"[19] John Adams tended to complain—in conversation and in writing—which may explain why history has not always been kind to him. He worried deeply about his reputation. Most of the Founders thought virtue part of their legacy. This we know because they were writers who left an impressive record of their thoughts. Historian Gordon S. Wood wrote: "No doubt writing was important to the Founders. Indeed, it was often through their writing that they first gained a reputation."[20] And they understood that it was through writing—their own and the writing of others about them—that their reputations would be sustained.

Winston Churchill summed up this tendency by suggesting that history would be kind to him, for he intended to write it.

ABRAHAM LINCOLN—FOUNDER

I was born and raised just under forty miles north of America's greatest battlefield. There my sixth-grade teacher, Duncan Campbell, maintained the tradition of annual student treks over the field to awaken in us the "mystic chords of memory"[21] linking young Americans to the gravestones of the men who had given their lives that a great nation might live. There, with my classmates, I recited the peerless funeral oration delivered by the greatest American who ever lived. There, inspired by his example, I realized that only in America could anyone go to that house at 1600 Pennsylvania Avenue. There I learned that the untutored chief magistrate of a great nation, Lincoln, could be the unsurpassed master of his enemies, above all, the master of himself.

There for the first time I sensed the meaning of true American statesmanship. I became fascinated by this man who was, I think, a unique literary genius, as well as a unique statesman. Here is a man who had fewer than twelve months of formal education. He was born absolutely dirt poor and grew up literally on the edge of the frontier with bears and panthers in the deep woods of Spencer County, Indiana. Out

On the Lincoln Trail in Kentucky

Gilder Lehrman Institute of American History GLC04200_0

Abraham Lincoln: Our best president

of nothing in terms of inheritance and education, he taught himself to be a surveyor, and he taught himself to be a lawyer. He didn't go to law school, but studied the law books on his own. After taking the test directly before the Supreme Court of Illinois, he became one of the most successful appellate lawyers in the state by both reputation and achievement.

Abraham Lincoln was not an important topic in any of my Yale undergraduate courses, except by my own choice, with Professor Goetzmann. I regret I never took a course with David Potter at Yale, for Professor Potter was teaching Lincoln. With Dr. Robin Winks for one year when I was a Carnegie Teaching Fellow, we studied Carl Degler's historiographical monograph *Out of Our Past: The Forces That Shaped Modern America*. That monograph focused on the way American history was written. At Harvard, I focused on diplomatic history. But I never forgot Mr. Lincoln.

Roy P. Basler's *Collected Works of Abraham Lincoln* became available in the 1950s. I read these volumes word for word in my twenties, which is, I think, the best way to read and retain what is effectively—in his own hand—the autobiography of Mr. Lincoln. A complete rookie, I stumbled through the volumes, inspired, reading some letters and speeches more carefully than others.

There was, in Volume II of Basler, a speech that Lincoln gave at Peoria. The Peoria speech struck me then as the greatest speech I had read to that point in my life. I could actually hear it in my mind's ear. The speech entirely suffused my consciousness, and preoccupied me for days. It was a brilliant *tour de force*. It would take another four decades, during which I continued to study Mr. Lincoln's life and works, before I could complete *Lincoln at Peoria: The Turning Point* (2008).

Unlike his debate opponent Illinois senator Stephen A. Douglas, Mr. Lincoln insisted that the equality principle applied to Blacks as well as Whites. At Peoria and thereafter, Lincoln made the case against slavery's expansion, and for its ultimate extinction. The moral and political principles Lincoln defined at Peoria formed the basis of his thinking and actions until his death in 1865. Getting right with the Declaration of Independence was a driving passion of Mr. Lincoln as he fought his way back into state and national politics in 1854. Armed with

Wikimedia Commons

Roy P. Basler: Lincoln's autobiographer

the "sheet anchor" of American republicanism, as Lincoln called the Declaration, he was determined to set right the historical record, and redefine America's future by stopping the spread of slavery.

Prior to the passage of the Kansas-Nebraska Act, Mr. Lincoln had been largely retired from politics after a single term in Congress. Writing a sketch of his life in 1859, Mr. Lincoln observed: "From 1849 to 1854, both inclusive, [I] practiced law more assiduously than ever before. Always a whig in politics, and generally on the whig electoral tickets, making active canvasses, I was losing interest in politics when the repeal of the Missouri Compromise aroused me again. What I have done since then is pretty well known."[22] Mr. Lincoln was a life-long Whig, but politics was breaking down over slavery extension. Old political divisions were no longer effective. It was a new coalition which would elect him president.

On October 16, 1854, he delivered the speech from the portico of the Old Peoria Courthouse. Thousands of people assembled for this speech, and it followed upon a speech earlier in the day by Senator Stephen Douglas. Douglas had taken for his themes popular sovereignty, Kansas-Nebraska, and the repeal of the prohibition against slavery north of the 36th degree 30 minute parallel, as specified by the Louisiana Purchase. The prohibition had become law as part of the Missouri Compromise of 1820, but was effectively reversed by the Kansas-Nebraska Act that Douglas had shepherded through Congress earlier in the year. With his three-hour-and-ten-minute torchlit speech in the dark hours of October 16, 1854, Mr. Lincoln changed the course of his life, and changed the course of American history.

For six years following Peoria, Mr. Lincoln, as a private citizen, with two failed tries at the US Senate from Illinois, maintained his antislavery campaign. Much of the argument and the themes, most of the rhetoric, which come later in the Lincoln-Douglas debates of 1858 and other important speeches, can be traced from the Peoria speech. Lincoln himself, as editor, made sure it would be immortalized in print. Mr. Lincoln understood the importance of the Peoria speech and personally oversaw its publication in the *Illinois Daily Journal* between the 21st and 28th of October 1854.[23] At the heart of the Peoria speech was the core of Mr. Lincoln's public philosophy—his dedication to the principles of the Declaration of Independence.

The Old Peoria Courthouse: Turning point

The idea for writing a book about Lincoln's Peoria speech occurred to me around 1983, during my second reading of Basler. It took another two decades to begin serious work on the manuscript. I wanted not only to highlight the speech, but also to demonstrate the way in which the Peoria speech defined Lincoln's subsequent campaign against slavery, and his statecraft during the Civil War.

By 2005, I had read most of the Lincoln canon. I was possessed by the idea of writing *Lincoln at Peoria: The Turning Point.* "There are other books which consider the Peoria speech and Lincoln-Douglas in 1854," I told Bruce Cole of *Humanities* magazine. "To the best of my knowledge," I continued, "mine is the first book to be completely devoted to an analytical narrative of the history in which the Peoria speech takes place, and then traces the themes of the speech through 1865. I was trying to avoid only a rhetorical and philosophical analysis of the speech itself or of 1854 alone. I try to spell out an underlying narrative and the consequences of the speech until the assassination."[24] With the impending arrival of the Lincoln bicentennial, Cole had noticed a shift in the scholarship toward the rivalry between Lincoln and Douglas, and inquired why that was the case. I answered, "The seriousness of Douglas and Lincoln has a lot to do with it, and the slowly dawning realization that these politicians were not exclusively reflecting their own self-interests. Instead, conscious reflection and rationally motivated convictions helped lead to these debates."[25]

The words I gave the *New Republic* in 1983 still ring true: "I am struck by the Lincoln experience. He was unusual for an ideologue in that he was a good inside politician. And he was relentless. He made unavoidable the irrepressible conflict. Lincoln didn't know the context in which it would occur, the timing of the event, but he knew it would happen."[26]

In a later profile for the *Greenwich Time*, I would talk with journalist Anne Semmes about the enduring interest that scholars, including myself have for Lincoln.

> Hovering over the whole history of Mr. Lincoln's American pilgrimage, there still lingers the enigma of a very private man—the impenetrable shadow of Mr. Lincoln's profile.
>
> But in *him* we can surely say: the passions *were* regulated, not spent; the intellect focused, *not* dissipated. Though we scrutinize Lincoln's teaching, his matchless leadership, his formidable character, we still see both through a glass darkly. So we mine his papers, sap the memoirs left by those who knew him, plumb his personal relationships. But he escapes us. Surely we know about his humble parents, his lack of formal education, his discreet but towering ambition. But we wonder that—unlike the Adamses, the Roosevelts, the Kennedys, the Bushes—no descendants carried on his legacy of national leadership. Like a luminous comet, he had for a twinkling thrust himself before our eyes, the eyes of the world, there to dissolve into the vasty deep whence he came.[27]

In the end, President Lincoln did give up his life, but he never gave up the principle by which he believed the Union was worth living. And even this he had foreseen. On

February 22, 1861, as he made his first inaugural journey to Washington, DC, Lincoln was asked to raise the flag at Independence Hall in Philadelphia. It was George Washington's birthday. The chairman of the city's select council, famed attorney Theodore Cuyler, introduced him at the ceremony. In response to Cuyler's concerns about the looming conflict, Mr. Lincoln replied:

Gilder Lehrman Institute of American History GLC05136.10

The Vasty Deep...

> Mr. Cuyler—I am filled with deep emotion at finding myself standing here in the place where were collected together the wisdom, the patriotism, the devotion to principle, from which sprang the institutions under which we live. You have kindly suggested to me that in my hands is the task of restoring peace to our distracted country. I can say in return, sir, that all the political sentiments I entertain have been drawn, so far as I have been able to draw them, from the sentiments which originated, and were given to the world from this hall in which we stand. I have never had a feeling politically that did not spring from the sentiments embodied in the Declaration of Independence. (Great cheering.) I have often pondered over the dangers which were incurred by the men who assembled here and adopted that Declaration of Independence—I have pondered over the toils that were endured by the officers and soldiers of the army, who achieved that Independence. (Applause.) I have often inquired of myself, what great principle or idea it was that kept this Confederacy so long together. It was not the mere matter of the separation of the colonies from the mother land; but something in that Declaration giving liberty, not alone to the people of this country, but hope to the world for all future time. (Great applause.) It was that which gave promise that in due time the weights should be lifted from the shoulders of all men, and that all should have an equal chance. (Cheers.) This is the sentiment embodied in that Declaration of Independence.

Now, my friends, can this country be saved upon that basis? If it can, I will consider myself one of the happiest men in the world if I can help to save it. If it can't be saved upon that principle, it will be truly awful. But, if this country cannot be saved without giving up that principle—I was about to say I would rather be assassinated on this spot than to surrender it. (Applause.)

Now, in my view of the present aspect of affairs, there is no need of bloodshed and war. There is no necessity for it. I am not in favor of such a course, and I may say in advance, there will be no blood shed unless it be forced upon the Government. The Government will not use force unless force is used against it. (Prolonged applause and cries of "That's the proper sentiment.")

My friends, this is a wholly unprepared speech. I did not expect to be called upon to say a word when I came here—I supposed I was merely to do something towards raising a flag. I may, therefore, have said something indiscreet, (cries of "no, no"), but I have said nothing but what I am willing to live by, and, in the pleasure of Almighty God, die by.[28]

I came to admire not only Mr. Lincoln's political principles, but also his economic policies. He believed there is not, of necessity, any such thing as the free hired laborer being fixed to that condition for life. In a February 1995 article for the *Wall Street Journal*, I quoted Lincoln on the subject:

The prudent, penniless beginner in the world labors for wages awhile, saves a surplus with which to buy tools or land for himself; then labors on his own account for awhile, and at length hires another new beginner to help him. This is the just, and generous, and prosperous system, which opens the way to all—gives hope to all, and . . . energy, and progress, and improvement of conditions to all.

Lincoln's economic legacy has had a powerful effect on world history. Without our 16th president there would have been separate slave states and free states; and thus no integrated North American economy in which emerged the most powerful free-market, commercial civilization the world has ever known. Without pre-eminent American industrial power—which Lincoln self-consciously advocated—the means would not have been available to contain Imperial Germany in 1917 as it reached for European hegemony. Neither would there have been a national power strong enough to destroy its global successor, Hitler's Nazi Reich in 1945, nor to crush the aggressions of Imperial Japan. And in the end, there would have been no world power to oppose and overcome the Soviet Communist empire during the second half of our century. World conquest—based on the invidious distinctions of race and class, the goal of the malignant world powers of our era—was prevented by the force and leadership of a single country, the perpetual union of the American states.[29]

As much as I admired his simple articulation of American economic ideas, my primary interest in President Lincoln remained with his political principles and the remarkable effect his actions had upon subsequent events. In a series of articles for the *Wall Street Journal* I wrote about Lincoln's far-reaching impact in the light of contemporary history. I wanted to demonstrate how much history can hinge upon the earnest efforts of committed people, saying:

> For Mr. Lincoln, politics was not merely a struggle for personal power and prestige, but, instead, a campaign of first principles. He declared that neither blood ties, nor racial homogeneity, nor ancestral territory—the origin of all previous nations—had grounded the new nation on the shores of the Atlantic. Instead, the sheet anchors of the republic were the declared truths of human equality and the unalienable right to life and to liberty. unalienable rights made the American birthright unique among great nations, bestowing upon the American people, a nation of immigrants, a common patrimony.[30]

It is clear that if the Union armies had not won the Civil War, and Lincoln had not persisted and prevailed, and slavery had not been abolished when it was, then the American model would never have inspired emerging nations around the world. We became what Lincoln called the "last, best hope of earth." His leadership and subsequent Civil War victory set the moral framework for future historical triumphs—including victories over the Third Reich and communism, systems dependent upon societal separation based on race, class and other factors.

There is much to learn from Abraham Lincoln—just as Mr. Lincoln learned much from his own study of history, concentrating as it did on America's Founding. But there is also much to learn from Mr. Lincoln's focus on the future. With Bill Buckley in attendance, I had much earlier delivered a speech on Lincoln the prophet. Years later, the *Stamford Advocate* published my article on the same theme wherein I noted that Theodore Roosevelt had once said that "Lincoln saw into the future with the prophetic imagination usually vouchsafed only to the poet and the seer."

"And there is something holy in Lincoln's words," I continued, "which still have that special ring even across the centuries. In the early part of his administration, he sent the following message to Congress:

> The dogmas of the quiet past are inadequate to the stormy present. . . . The occasion is piled high with difficulty, and we must rise with the occasion. As our cause is new, so we must think anew, and act anew. We must disenthrall ourselves, and then we shall save our country . . .[31]

In his First Annual Message to Congress, Lincoln declared that "the struggle of today is not altogether for today—it is for a vast future also."[32] He would continue this theme in his Second Annual Message to Congress: "In times like the present, men should utter nothing for which they would not willingly be responsible through time and eternity."[33] Then in his widely reprinted letter to James Conkling in 1863,

Lincoln wrote: "Thanks to all. For the great Republic—for the principle it lives by and keeps alive—for man's vast future—thanks to all."[34]

WINSTON CHURCHILL—SAVIOR OF A NATION

After decades spent studying and writing about the premier American statesman of the nineteenth century, it seemed logical to study the leadership of the premier English-speaking statesman of the twentieth century. I had been interested in Churchill all my life. As I told the *Churchill Bulletin* in 2016, "My interest in Churchill began in early boyhood. I was born in central Pennsylvania in August of 1938. The radio was then widespread. I remember the latter part of the Second World War when I was five, six, and seven. My family would listen to reports, on the radio, of the battlefield struggles in Europe. Churchill was a hero in our family. He still is."[35]

Like Abraham Lincoln, Winston Churchill was an ambitious man whose political career stalled during a decade "in the wilderness." Like Lincoln, Churchill maintained his commitment to his principles even when they were unfashionable. They were both deeply committed to liberty, and strongly opposed to those who would deny freedom to others.

As a young man, I was impressed by his boldness as First Lord of the Admiralty in World War I, and by the way his leadership as prime minister in the spring and summer of 1940 sustained and inspired the spirit of British patriotism. Like Lincoln, he provided a model for what hard work and determination could accomplish. From Lincoln and Churchill, one also learned the importance of a reputation for honorable conduct.

Menpes, Mortimer. War Impressions. London: Adam & Charles Black, 1901

Winston Churchill: On the mountain and in the field

I was enchanted when I learned that Churchill was in fact half-American. In a speech he delivered to Congress, in December of 1941, the prime minister declared: "I shall always remember how each Fourth of July my mother would always wave an American flag before my eyes."[36] In 1918, while World War I was still being fought in deadly earnest, Churchill declared that "great harmony exists between the spirit and language of the Declaration of Independence and all we are fighting for now. A similar harmony exists between the principles of that Declaration and all that the British people have wished to stand for and have in fact achieved."[37] It was altogether natural, therefore, that my own history studies would extend to the author of *The History of English Speaking Peoples*. In its third and last volume, *Age of Revolution*, Churchill recognized the historical antecedents to the Declaration, and the implacable determination that the Founders had mustered to defend them. "The Declaration," as he then wrote, "was in the main a restatement of the principles which had animated the Whig struggle against the later Stuarts and the English Revolution of 1688, and it now became the symbol and rallying centre of the Patriot cause. Its immediate result was to increase the number of Loyalists, frightened by this splendid defiance. But the purpose of the colonies was proclaimed. The waverers were forced to a decision. There was no turning back."[38]

Like Lincoln, Churchill was a student of history. Like Lincoln, Churchill mustered his pen in defense of human liberty and the dignity of the individual. Like Lincoln, Churchill mobilized a nation to fight wars of unimaginable bloodshed and misery. Like Lincoln, Churchill's life demonstrated how the man in charge gets the blame for what goes wrong, and the credit for what goes right.

As with Mr. Lincoln, my study of Prime Minister Churchill deepened my appreciation of his wartime leadership—and of the alliance he forged domestically to lead Britain and the Allies to victory over Nazi Germany. My study of Churchill led to two books. The first, *Churchill, Roosevelt & Company*, was a study of the web of transatlantic relationships that sustained the Allied countries at both the top level between Winston Churchill and Franklin D. Roosevelt, and among their numerous civilian and military aides.

Like Lincoln, Churchill would not rest from the detailed prosecution of the war. The prime minister was all-in for the war he was fighting—all the time. Both leaders understood the need to mobilize both a nation and a team of leaders to wage war, unrelenting war. Their judgment in selecting subordinates and forging alliances was critical to success because there have always been concerns in America about the intentions of the United Kingdom.

"The Anglo-American alliance originated in the First World War, and is effective to this present day," I told Bob Marchant in a 2017 *Greenwich Time* interview. "There's a sense that there's a special relationship, based on a special trust, between English-speaking people. Whereas the truth was: It was a very, very tough alliance to put together. From the very beginning there was mutual mistrust. There was Anglophobia in the president's own cabinet, and there was condescension toward the former Colonials among the British elites. This mistrust had to be eliminated for the alliance to be effective."[39]

Named prime minister in May 1940, Churchill had resolved that he *must* have an Anglo-American alliance. While shaving, he said to his son Randolph, "I will drag the Americans in."[40] But in fact, it would be Japan and Germany on December 8 and 11, 1941, who would drag America into World War II by declarations of war against the United States.

Always, I was inspired and guided by the scholarship of historians who went before me. I met Martin Gilbert—Churchill's definitive biographer—through Larry Arnn, an American scholar then at the Claremont Institute who worked with Gilbert in preparing Churchill's collected works for publication. I learned from Gilbert to be a "slave to the facts." In a 2016 interview with the *Chartwell Bulletin*, I acknowledged that "This was his standard, a very difficult one to uphold. I do allow my opinions more leeway than the great Sir Martin, but he was certainly one of the best historians of the twentieth century."[41] I also met Gilbert's successor, Andrew Roberts, whose several books on Churchill were in all a *tour de force*.

My research on the Anglo-American alliance of World War II led naturally to a second book, *Lincoln & Churchill: Statesmen at War*, a comparative study of the wartime leadership of America's commander-in-chief during the Civil War, and Britain's leader in World War II.

Early on in the book, I summarize my findings, writing that "the primary similarity between Mr. Churchill and Mr. Lincoln, as war leaders, was their self-confidence to chart the strategy of the war, to suffer setbacks without giving up, to sustain the union in Lincoln's case and the British nation in Churchill's case, come what may. Each held himself responsible for the outcome of the war, no matter the odds. They never believed that the generals could fight it without their guidance. In my opinion, they were correct."[42]

Doris Kearns Goodwin: Teammate

Neither Lincoln nor Churchill was willing to stop short of complete victory—for their cause, and for freedom. They did so while respecting democracy and building coalitions, as I noted in an essay for the *Daily Beast* in 2018. "Lincoln and Churchill faced similar challenges," I wrote. "They needed to maintain unity and support within their own skeptical party even as they reached across the aisle to broaden that support. It was a delicate task that required political dexterity."[43]

Jason Emerson's book review for the *American Spectator* highlighted the essential point: the stalwart nature of both leaders. "But in the end," Emerson wrote, "one of the great takeaways from *Lincoln & Churchill* is both men's inspiring character, and their indomitable will to win that made victory possible. 'Neither the United States in 1860 nor Britain in 1939 had been well prepared for the cataclysms that would overtake them,' as Lehrman writes. 'Nothing could have made Lincoln or Churchill entirely ready for the challenges each would have to overcome.' Yet overcome them they did. As Lincoln said in 1862, 'I expect to maintain this contest until successful, or till I die, or am conquered, or my term expires, or Congress or the country forsakes me.'"[44] Churchill made a similar point in 1940 when, facing a major Cabinet division between appeasement of Hitler and fighting a war, Churchill had said, "Every man of you would rise up and tear me down from my place if I were for one moment to contemplate parley or surrender. If this long island history of ours is to end at last, let it end only when each one of us lies choking in his own blood upon the ground."[45]

My colleague, the historian Doris Kearns Goodwin, reviewed the book for me. "For years," she said, "I have longed to be in the same room with Abraham Lincoln and Winston Churchill. And now Lewis Lehrman has given all of us that chance with this sweeping, yet intimate study of the war leadership of both remarkable men.[46]

With Lincoln and Churchill, you are always in good company.

CHAPTER 16

Collaborating on History

The past, unlike the ephemeral present and unpredictable future, is the true reality.
—David Brion Davis, 2004[1]

American history is composed of the stories of our heroes and heroines—the unknown soldiers, and the nameless slaves and immigrants who created this country. Many of their names were not found in my history books one generation ago. I wanted to change that, and set about doing so.

One cannot be a fully informed American citizen without a strong foundation in American history. As everyone knows, the one thing about the past is that it is always present. I never lost the fascination with American history that I formed as a child. When I was on the road, whether for business or politics, I always carried my history books along with me.

My attraction to American history led to the founding of several institutions with my cofounder, philanthropist-businessman Richard Gilder. Dick came on board one day when he was walking down the hall past my office. Looking in the door, he found I wasn't studying investments. "What are you doing, Lew?" he asked. I told him I was reading a catalog of important documents in American history. He thought it was interesting, and told me he had been studying the restoration of American battlefields.

"Dick," I said, "you can't bring a battlefield into a classroom and teach it, but you can find a soldier's diary and study it to gain insight into how the battlefield soldiers thought." He was intrigued.

Together, in the years that followed, we founded the Lincoln and Soldiers Institute, the Gilder Lehrman Institute of American History, the Gilder Lehrman Center on Slavery, Resistance and Abolition at Yale, and the Gilder Lehrman Collection. In 1997, we were awarded honorary degrees from Gettysburg College. We helped to create four prizes: the Lincoln Prize, the Frederick Douglass Prize, the George Washington Book Prize, and the American Military History Prize. We would do so with the help of a multitude of other American history teachers, many at the more than thirty-four thousand Gilder Lehrman affiliate schools across the United States. Today, more than 25 percent of all US schools are Gilder Lehrman affiliates, and they can be found in all fifty states and seventy foreign countries. Each one shares our passion for this great nation's heritage.

The two Yale history majors

FINDING THE RIGHT PARTNER

I had first met Dick Gilder after I took Rite Aid public in 1968. He had come down to see me at our headquarters in Shiremanstown, Pennsylvania, looking to invest. Dick was an outstanding salesman, extremely energetic, very shrewd, and always asking questions that were very difficult to answer.

Our friendship developed when I later moved to New York. Dick and I recognized our philosophical agreements on certain political issues, and the importance of growth for the American economy, and people from all walks of life. When Bill Hammett became president of the Manhattan Institute in 1980, I recommended Dick to be chairman of the board, a position he held for several years. Dick was also very supportive of my gubernatorial campaign in 1982.

Our friendship left an impression on those with whom we worked. Daniel Jordan of Monticello saw our relationship in this light: "Lew had the gift of friendship with Dick. I never heard a cross word. I never heard either say anything negative about the other. . . . It was an amazing relationship.[2]

Dick and I, both history majors at Yale, had recognized that history had lost its academic cachet in the last part of the twentieth century. "You could graduate from almost every college in America today, without a course in American history,"[3] Dick noted. We not only shared a vision regarding the importance of historical knowledge, we also shared a trust and a common political philosophy that allowed a strong partnership to develop.

The honorary degree from Gettysburg College

George W. Bush Presidential Library and Museum

The faith of the founders is true:
Richard Gilder and I receive The National Endowment for the Humanities Award from President and Mrs. George W. Bush

About thirty-six years after we first met, Dick and I went to the White House to accept the National Humanities Medal. In November 2005, we were among about twenty medal recipients honored in an Oval Office ceremony. On that morning, I felt again that almost every success I could ever have arises from the fact that I can say that I am an American citizen.

The two days that Louise and I enjoyed in Washington were a testament to the patience and warmth of President George W. Bush and his wife Laura—and the amount of time they devoted to American history. Those two days were also a testament to an extraordinary partnership that began with that providential visit Dick Gilder made to my office in 1968.

COLLECTING AMERICAN HISTORY

I had started collecting American documents at Yale in 1961. One of the first I purchased contained Lincoln's signature. He had signed as A. Lincoln, voluntary captain, for some equipment borrowed from the American government. In the 1960s, you could buy interesting documents for just a few dollars. For me, it was always all about Lincoln and the American Founders. I bought my first significant document through the Abraham Lincoln bookstore in Chicago, a bookstore run by an expert on Mr. Lincoln.

When I became a partner at Morgan Stanley in 1987, I was able to expand the scope of my collecting. I concentrated especially on the colonial period, Revolutionary period, antebellum period, and Civil War period—the years that laid the foundations and re-foundations of our country. The Collection's expansion was documented by author David Howard. "In 1988," Howard wrote, "Myron Kaller read a newspaper interview with Barton Biggs, the global investment strategist for Morgan Stanley, in which Biggs advised that investors put a percentage of their money into collectibles. Myron wrote Biggs a letter: Perhaps Morgan Stanley should practice what it preached and start a collection of historic documents—a collecting field on the verge of taking off. Biggs brought the letter to Lewis Lehrman, a managing director."[4] Thus began a long and productive partnership with Myron and his son Seth, who works with us to this very day.

For a 1995 book based on his research in our collection, David Brion Davis, Sterling Professor of History at Yale, aptly described the nature of American document collecting, writing: "For the professional historian acclimated to public and university archives, it is astounding to learn that vast quantities of invaluable American source material have been and still are scattered about in private hands, in Europe as well as America, available for purchase."[5] I too was amazed at the availability of what might be thought of as priceless documents. The problem had been how to find sufficient funds for such investments.

That was when Dick Gilder joined my efforts.

Together, we were able to employ a network of agents—in Europe as well as America—and to acquire an almost immediate reputation among dealers in rare books and manuscripts for prompt payment. I also earned a reputation for being able to differentiate authentic documents from fakes. At the beginning, we kept a low profile. I decided that we should always work through dealers. In June of 2000, my friend the historian Harold Holzer interviewed Dick and me for *American Heritage* magazine. In the interview, Dick recalled: "Lew adopted a kind of classic financial posture: He stormed the market. It was his strategy, which I endorsed, to push prices up suddenly so as to cause shock in the market and have a lot of documents become available, like leaves falling from trees. That's precisely what occurred. He also set up a triple vetting system, to check carefully for forgeries."[6]

Unfortunately for Dick, this strategy would reveal that his copy of the Stonewall Jackson Bible was not the genuine article. As I told Harold, "The Bible was right here in this very office. Dick took it out to show it to me. I didn't say it then and there, but there's an old saw among historical manuscript people that there are seven original Stonewall Jackson Bibles. It was always plausible that Dick's was one of the seven—or one of seven hundred."[7] Dick was good natured about the discovery. "So of course it came back a complete forgery," he confided. "I was worried. Should I at least tell the people who were married with it that it was a fake? But I haven't. I hope by now the statute of limitations applies."[8]

Dick and I formed a partnership to expand the Collection and make the materials available for scholars, teachers, and public exhibitions. The Gilder Lehrman Collection developed very rapidly. I knew the canon of American history, and I knew the dealers. Soon, we were able to assemble an organization to reach dealers across the country, and to vacuum historical documents out of the attics and basements. Our goal was to move historical manuscripts into an institution where they would be accessible for scholars and students. In that same 2000 interview, Dick would tell Harold Holzer how I had said to him "'You know, collecting battlefields is nice, but collecting documents is really important. With a little support the battlefields will stay there whether you collect them or not. But this could be the last chance to put together something really big and important.' And, frankly, [Lew] talked to me about the speculative aspect, which I admit is always nine-tenths of what I'm interested in. I don't have the knowledge Lew has, but I sensed this was a huge opportunity. Lew organized the team."[9]

As I previously noted, it was through Barton Biggs that I had met the Kallers. Myron and his son Seth were then dealers in coins. At the time, Seth was planning to go to law school. Instead, he formed Kaller Historical Documents soon after he graduated from the University of Pennsylvania. I then hired him to represent us to the dealers and auction houses. He then prepared an inventory of available documents for purchase. Seth did a wonderful job keeping our fingerprints off his purchases, but we were building the collection at Mach speed. Soon, the news got out that we were buyers, high bidders, and known for prompt payment. As the price for historic documents grew, more documents became available.

The power of my partnership with Dick had to do with our complete agreement on goals. Dick and I had decided to establish the canon of American history. We had to start with the colonial period and carry on through Reconstruction. We did not

Seth Kaller: Like father like son

concentrate on the twentieth century until about five years later, in 1995.

By 1990, Dick and I had created the Lincoln Prize, and began full-bore collecting together. The critical juncture was when our capital combined behind this modest exercise I had begun. It has since become *the* major effort to collect American historical documents, and to make them available to history teachers.

It is a transformative experience of American history when you teach students by focusing on the great documents. They are revealing in a way that can't be summarized in a textbook. Dick and I believed that rather than presenting a liberal or conservative interpretation of American history, we should mobilize these documents for students to make up their own minds. In a 2007 article on the collection, Emily Sherwood noted, "The Gilder-Lehrman partnership traces its roots some twenty years back in time, when mutual investment opportunities brought the two men together and they discovered that they shared a deep passion for history. (Both had been history majors at Yale, but six years apart.) Like J.P. Morgan, who had purposefully set out to be one of the largest collectors of American antiquities, they devised a plan to systematically accumulate manuscript letters, diaries, maps, photographs, and other documents that would reflect, in a very human way, the social and political history of the United States."[10]

Our first purchase was a pamphlet from the Revolutionary War. We collected a lot of pamphlets at the beginning. We then upgraded the Collection to very important American documents. When we did that, we gave the pamphlets away to museums. There have always been a lot of pamphlets concentrated on the Revolutionary period.

Putting the Collection together was a team effort that became a larger team effort over the years. Paul Romaine, the founding curator, was very well qualified. He did a professional job organizing the collection.

Sandra Skordrud Trenholm, an alumna of Gettysburg College, joined the staff in 1995 and took over as curator-in-chief in 2001.

Sandy notes, "It surprises people to learn that there is relatively little in the Collection about economic history. Many people assume that would be one of Lew's primary historical interests. But Lew's vision for the Collection is based on the ideals of the Declaration of Independence. He has stated several times that the Collection is the story of freedom in the United States. It shapes everything I do at Gilder Lehrman. There have been moments where we do not live up to the ideals of the Declaration, but we can always find examples of individuals pushing the cause of freedom forward."[11]

We did not just buy everything. I remained focused on value. When one of the twenty-five copies of the Dunlap Declaration of Independence was auctioned, we bid it up by phone to $7 million before pulling out. It was a game of chicken, and I won. One year later, I got a call offering me the very same Declaration. I was not a buyer. We already had William Stone's Declaration of Independence, the one commissioned by John Quincy Adams. I had bet the other bidder would come to me if he got bored with a $7 million piece of paper. We were not bored, but nor did we need another copy of the Declaration, especially not at that price. Although the Dunlap Broadside is historic—printed on the night of July 4th, 1776—the Stone Declaration is the one best known to history. For three years Stone worked to complete it, finally unveiling it in 1823. An exact facsimile of the calligraphic original, the Stone Declaration may be a "press copy," produced by "moistening an ink original and pressing the original against paper to transfer an ink offset." In 1881, the National Academy of Sciences declared that the poor condition of the original Declaration was the "result of a wet copy technique, but there is no way to confirm the claim."[12]

Dick and I continually maintained our commitment to collecting the canon of American history. We wanted depth and breadth but did not want to devote valuable resources to copies of the same document. We built what David Brion called the "Manhattan magnet" to pull in documents from across America and around the world. The formula was simple. Dick and I ponied up the capital, and I set out using my knowledge of the canon of American history to acquire the most important documents. Professor Davis was pleasantly surprised by his first visit to the Collection in 1995. At the time, it was still housed at the

David Brion Davis: Founder of global slavery studies

Pierpont Morgan Library in New York, where Dick and I were both trustees. In an appendix to his book, *The Boisterous Sea of Liberty: A Documentary History of America from Discovery Through the Civil War* (2000), Professor Davis described his first memorable encounter with the Collection, saying:

> I soon discovered that a genuine exploration of the tens of thousands of documents (now exceeding an estimated sixty thousand[13] separate items—documents, letters, manuscripts, prints, photographs) would require many months of concentrated effort. Indeed, it almost seemed as if a team of the most renowned American historians, having access to the Library of Congress and all the archives of the major university libraries and historical societies, had selected representative documents to illustrate important themes, events, conflicts, [and] tragedies . . .
>
> No less remarkable the materials ranged from letters of Washington, Franklin, Jefferson, the two Adamses, Marshall, Jackson, and Lincoln—some of which have never been printed—to the letters and archives of former slaves, unknown soldiers, and eloquent women such as Mercy Otis Warren and Lucy Knox, the wife of Washington's secretary of war. Immense special collections such as the Livingston-Redmond Family Papers, including documents in English, French, Dutch and Algonkian, shed light on the manorial system and political intrigues of upstate New York from the early colonial period to the mid-nineteenth century. And the rich meanings conveyed by pen were complemented by a wealth of pictorial imagery that ranges from cartoons, broadsides, and prints to dazzling Civil War photographs. In the forty-odd years I had devoted to historical research, in Britain, France, Brazil, the West Indies, and many American states, I had never encountered such a breathtaking single collection. And I was particularly struck by the vivid way the manuscripts documented the origins and history of the struggle against slavery that finally led to the Civil War. How on earth, I kept wondering, had Richard Gilder and Lewis E. Lehrman acquired and made public such a priceless window to the American past?[14]

The Collection's strength is in seventeenth-, eighteenth-, and nineteenth-century American history, the antebellum era, Civil War, and Reconstruction. We are still weak in the twentieth century, but have worked with Jim Basker and Sandy Trenholm to rectify that. Sandy notes that "Most of our recent acquisitions have been 20th century. Both researchers and teachers are looking for the 'untold' stories. What I have come to realize is that they are looking for the role of the individual in history, and that is the core of the Collection. The how and the why of history."[15] Documents in the Collection include a letter describing Columbus's discoveries and President Gerald Ford's pardon of the recently resigned President Richard Nixon. I got the most pleasure from buying the Thirteenth Amendment, signed by Mr. Lincoln. We eventually bought three signed copies for the Collection. Sometimes, one just isn't enough.

The Letters of Henry and Lucy Knox was a major acquisition—given that it constituted over ten thousand items, and provided valuable insights into many of America's Founders. We committed to keeping the documents at the Morgan Library for ten years. Sandra Trenholm described the significance of the Knox collection: "It is certainly a wealth of information for the founding era. The correspondence between Lucy and Henry Knox is a favorite among students and teachers. Through those letters, we are able to bring the issues and events of the Revolutionary War down to the personal level. It showcases how much people had at stake and what they were willing to risk."[16]

After building the Collection over fifteen years, Dick and I donated it in stages to the Gilder Lehrman Institute of American History, so the documents could be fully integrated into the Institute's work. A committee now presides over new purchases for the Collection. This committee does collectively what I once did alone, and Jim Basker has now taken the leadership role. The work of the Gilder Lehrman Institute of American History has made an impression on not just the public, but on the Institute's staff as well.

Susan Saidenberg was one of the key staff members involved in making the Collection widely available. In particular, she developed some of our signature teaching tools, saying that "Opportunities to work with the Collection over the years nurtured my love of American history and fueled my passion to share it with students, teachers and the general public. It was a privilege to develop the History in a Box publications and traveling exhibitions based on documents in the collection. I am grateful to Lew and Dick for building an archive, and donating it to the Institute."[17]

Susan and I had met at the opening reception for "Free at Last," a traveling panel exhibition on the abolition of slavery at Federal Hall in 1996. The Institute hired her the next year. From that first encounter, she and I returned again and again to the theme of "traveling panel exhibitions, and the opportunity to share scholarship and documents with teachers and students in schools where they did not have access to primary documents." Susan flourished at the Gilder Lehrman Institute, writing that "Lew was very supportive of developing traveling exhibitions. Over the years we received notes from parents, students and teachers that the chance to see the image of a document written by Lincoln in an exhibition was inspiring."[18]

Traveling exhibitions remain an important offering of Gilder Lehrman today. We have seven different ones on different topics and two more in preparation. In the most recent year, they visited more than 50 different sites across the country. We also have exhibitions on our web site, where three million people visit each year.

THE LINCOLN PRIZE

One of the Gilder Lehrman Institute's original purposes was the selection of the winner of the Lincoln Prize, awarded annually for the finest scholarly work in English on Abraham Lincoln, the American Civil War soldier, or a related subject. The Prize generally goes to a book author, but other contributions to scholarship are also eligible. The Prize is supervised and awarded by the five trustees of the Gilder Lehrman

Phil Hamilton: Master of research

Institute chosen to focus on the Lincoln Prize. These trustees then appoint a jury each year of three historians or qualified specialists to make recommendations. Although the first prize was awarded in 1991, I had been laying the foundations for almost ten years.

In the mid-1980s, I had opened communications with Gettysburg College professor Gabor Boritt. Phil Hamilton, a graduate of Gettysburg studying for his master's in history at George Washington University, had worked with me at Citizens for America. Phil made the original introduction, and recently wrote down the details saying that "Lew queried me [in early 1985] about my experiences at Gettysburg College where I was a history major. And he immediately followed up asking if I knew the Civil War professor there. I replied 'yes', his name was Gabor Boritt, who had started his career at the college during my junior year, and that I had taken his Civil War class . . . I do remember that Lew knew about Gabor's book *Lincoln and the Economics of the American Dream* (1978). I don't believe Lew had read it yet, and so my first direct assignment from him was to get him a copy of that book!"[19]

A native of Hungary, Gabor had fled the country after participating in the Hungarian Revolution of 1956. Emigrating to the United States, he read the story of Abraham Lincoln and became entranced with the man and his writings. After earning his PhD at Boston University, Gabor settled at Gettysburg, where he founded its Civil War Institute. Dick Gilder once categorized Gabor as "an entrepreneurial historian with the audacity and courage to think of something new."[20]

A few years later, Gabor and Gettysburg College seemed natural partners for the project that Dick and I were contemplating. In 1989, I asked Dick if he wanted to go with me to Gettysburg. We flew down on a puddle jumper to meet with Gabor and Gordon Haaland, then president of the college.[21] Dick and I proposed an annual prize for scholarship on Abraham Lincoln and the Civil War. Gabor suggested the award should be $5,000. Dick and I said, "No way. It should be $50,000, to demonstrate how important American history is." Dick had originally wanted the prize to be called the Lincoln and Soldiers Prize as he was interested in the common soldier. I felt the

Janet Riggs: An outstanding president of Gettysburg College

Lincoln Prize was a much better name, and after a short debate, Dick remembers that I "suggested, 'Let's create the Lincoln and Soldiers Institute, and it will present the Lincoln Prize.'" And that was, in Dick's estimation, "a very fair compromise."[22]

Janet Riggs is also a former president of Gettysburg College. As such, she was an ex-officio member of the Lincoln and Soldiers Institute Board of Trustees. When she wrote down her recollection of the origins of the Lincoln Prize, she noted that "I met Lew in the early '90s when I was a faculty member working for President Gordon Haaland as his executive assistant. I helped to coordinate meetings for Gettysburg College's Board of Trustees and attended those meetings while Lew was serving on the Board. [Haaland] was convinced Gettysburg College was 'missing the boat' by not embracing its history and connection to the American Civil War, and he was very interested in Gabor's idea of establishing the Lincoln Prize. Gabor founded the Civil War Institute and worked with Lew and Dick to found the Lincoln Prize with much encouragement from Gordon. Since that time, Gettysburg has built a Civil War Era Studies program that is quite distinctive and attracts a wide variety of students."[23]

The inaugural announcement of the Lincoln Prize was made in April 1990 at the National Portrait Gallery in Washington. It was held in the Great Hall of what had once been the federal Patent Office Building, where the reception for President Lincoln's second inauguration was held in 1865. For that reason we thought it was a suitable location.

At the 1990 announcement, I observed, "Scholars often work a lifetime to produce a great work which never receives sufficient compensation. In a commercial society, the rewards for great scholarship should be financial as well as psychic."[24]

In opening the 1991 dinner at Gettysburg College at which the first Lincoln Prize was awarded, I said: "Richard Gilder, Gabor Boritt, and I, in creating the Lincoln and Soldiers Institute, hope to honor specific publicists of American history who shall draw out the significance of those simple soldiers, North and South who, here, gave their lives. We can also hope that aspiring peoples the world over shall learn from

Ken Burns: In the visual vanguard of Civil War studies

the sacrifices made for them by those warriors of the nearby battlefield who gave their last full measure for those truths which alone can set men free."[25]

The expected winner of the Lincoln Prize was the author of a book, but the Prize rules provided for other categories. The first Lincoln Laureate was actually Ken Burns, the creator of the *Civil War* film series on PBS. Burns quickened the imagination of some forty million Americans, getting them to focus on the centrality and momentousness of Lincoln and the Civil War. The three-member Lincoln Prize jury that year set the standard for excellence in future juries, including Robert V. Bruce of Boston University, James M. McPherson of Princeton, and *New York Times* columnist Tom Wicker. In accepting the prize, Burns recognized that his was not a solo achievement, saying "Film's a collaborative act. I know who brung me to the dance."[26]

In her recollections, Janet Riggs also described the way in which the prize selection worked, saying that she "always very much liked the fact that the jury was not supposed to select the finalist(s). Rather they are asked to provide commentary on each book, answer questions, and leave the selection of the winner to the trustees. Each year in which I was involved, the trustees engaged in serious, thoughtful, respectful deliberation. I always found our meetings to be uplifting."[27]

Winners of the Lincoln Prize over the years have included America's premier historians: Kenneth Stampp, 1992 (*The Peculiar Institution*); David Herbert Donald, 1996 (*Lincoln*); James McPherson, 1998 (*For Cause and Comrades: Why Men Fought in the Civil War*); Douglas L. Wilson, 1999 *(Honor's Voice: The Transformation of Abraham Lincoln*); John Hope Franklin and Loren Schweninger, 2000 (*Runaway Slaves: Rebels in the Plantation)*; Doris Kearns Goodwin, 2006 (*Team of Rivals: The Political Genius of Abraham Lincoln)*; Michael Burlingame, 2010 (*Abraham Lincoln: A Life*); Eric Foner, 2011 (*The Fiery Trial: Abraham Lincoln and American Slavery)*; James Oakes, 2013 (*Freedom National: The Destruction of Slavery in the United States, 1861–1865)*; and Allen C. Guelzo, 2014 (*Gettysburg: The Last Invasion*). In 2014, Steven Spielberg received a Special Achievement Prize for his movie, *Lincoln*.[28]

The Prize allowed me to discover new scholarship and develop working relationships with many outstanding American history scholars. Among them was Monticello's Doug Wilson, whom I met at an award ceremony. Doug and I hit it off right away, and later he wrote down his memories of the event. "I first met Lew," he began, "at the Lincoln Prize dinner in 1999, when I was first honored as a laureate . . . I already knew and very much admired Dick Gilder, but what struck me so forcibly about his partner at this first meeting was how remarkably gracious and complimentary he was to me personally, leaving no doubt that he admired my book, *Honor's Voice,* and appreciated the work that went into it and what I was trying to accomplish in writing it. Like any author, I have always been grateful to hear the testimony of approving readers, but I can truly say that I have never encountered a reader, before or since, who made me feel as he did at our first meeting, that he was the one who was grateful, and that I had done him a great service in writing *Honor's Voice*. And I should add that I say this not as a tribute to my book, but to Lew Lehrman."[29]

The relationships developed from the Lincoln Prize benefitted both Dick and me—and the general public—but also provided resources, and a spotlight for the authors and scholars, highlighting their achievements. With a few exceptions, the Lincoln Prize was awarded annually at a Union League Club dinner in New York—in the grand ballroom presided over by a splendid portrait of Abraham Lincoln. At first, I was master of ceremonies, but when Jim Basker proved himself worthy of the honor, I appointed him to the office, which he has held down to this very day.

Douglas Wilson:
Friend and scholar

James McPherson:
Pioneer of Civil War Studies

Steven Spielberg: *Lincoln*'s intimate director

Gabor became part of the administration of the Lincoln Prize. Gordon Haaland and Janet Riggs provided outstanding support. Diane Brennan and the late Tina Grim handled the complex logistics of both the Prize and the dinner.

Janet Riggs made a few other notable remarks about the significance of the Lincoln Prize, saying that "the Prize has inspired more scholarship about Lincoln and the Civil War Era than there might otherwise be. I also believe that the public has learned more about Lincoln (and the Civil War) than they would have otherwise, as a result of the scholarship that's been produced and the publicity associated with the Prize. The dinner has brought the Gilder Lehrman Institute of American History's essay contest winners, young people from across the country, into the Lincoln 'orbit' so to speak, teaching them about leadership and inspiring an interest in American history."[30]

Diane Brennan also appreciated the mutual support the Lincoln Prize generates for the subject and its teachers, saying "Historians over the years have benefited from the Prize, the Gilder Lehrman Institute, and from Lew and Dick. When the trustees of the Prize decided to make sure finalists and honorable mentions were named in the press releases and acknowledged at the dinner, they were actually helping advance the career of some young historians."[31] Diane used the example of Barbara Gannon to make her case, specifically with respect to Barbara's 2012 dissertation *The Won Cause: Black and White Comradeship in the Grand Army of the Republic.* "Barb was not the typical historian," Diane noted, "she had completed her undergraduate degree and then went to work for the government for several years before deciding to attend graduate school. Gannon benefited professionally from this honor and it helped her scholarship reach the non-academic."[32]

THE GILDER LEHRMAN INSTITUTE OF AMERICAN HISTORY

Dick and I found American history to be inspiring. We wanted to share that inspiration with the teachers of American history, and with their students. So, in 1994, we refounded the Gilder Lehrman Institute of American History, with a broader mission than just the Lincoln Prize. We now aim to successfully advance the study of American history in our own unique way.

As I explained to C-SPAN's Brian Lamb, "The Gilder Lehrman Institute of American History . . . was sort of an organic outgrowth of the work that Dick and I did together on building the collection. And in order to deploy the collection, in order to make it a mechanism for teaching American history, we felt we needed an enterprise—active enterprise. And thus, the name Gilder Lehrman Institute of American History."[33] We organized seminars for teachers; supported and produced publications and traveling exhibitions; sponsored lectures by historians; developed electronic media projects for scholars and the public; created history-centered high schools and Saturday academies for New York City students; established research centers at universities and libraries; and granted and oversaw fellowships for scholars to work in the Gilder Lehrman Collection and in other archives of American history. "And that," I told Lamb, "gave rise to our relationship with David Brion Davis, a—probably *the* founder—I think, in fact, *the founder* of modern global slavery studies and, in particular, the Atlantic slave trade."[34]

Davis was among the first—and the most distinguished—historians recruited to teach our teacher seminars. Here he describes the experience:

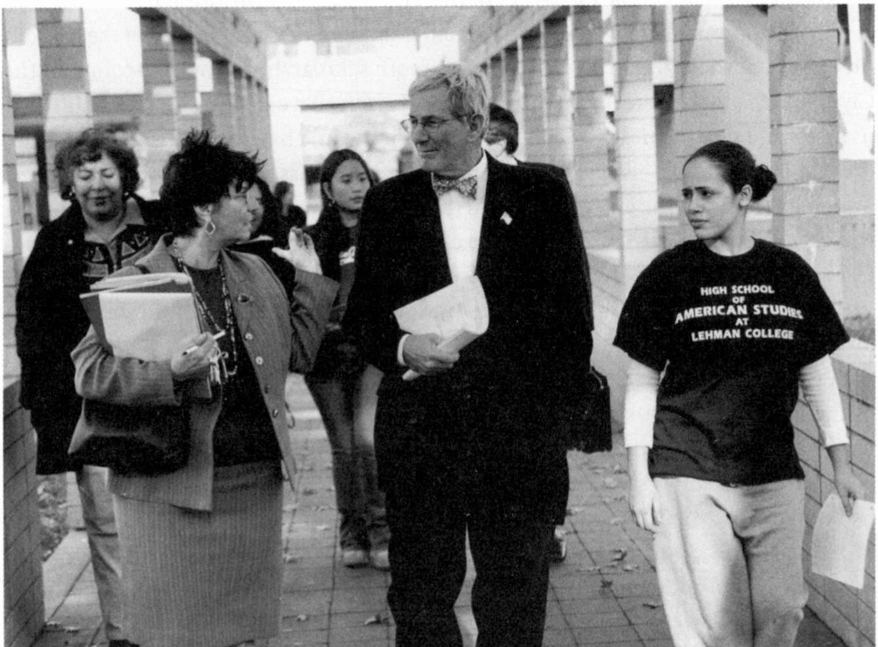

Gilder Lehrman Institute of American History

My partner Richard Gilder with teachers and students

> The teachers turned out to be extraordinarily excited, appreciative, and highly motivated. Some members of each year's class let me know how they had incorporated slavery and abolition into their high-school curricula. I therefore eagerly expanded my teaching notes into a large new lecture course on New World slavery for Yale undergraduates. Then as I approached retirement, various friends urged me to . . .'translate' the lecture course into a book designed for general readers. This assignment turned out to be far more difficult and to take far longer than I anticipated, but *Inhuman Bondage* is the gratifying result.
>
> Meanwhile, the Gilder Lehrman Institute moved on to invite dozens of the nation's greatest historians, in universities extending from Stanford to Harvard, to teach similar courses on a variety of subjects in American history. Dick Gilder and Lew Lehrman, aided by such wise and capable directors as James Basker and Lesley Herrmann, have made an unprecedented contribution to the nation-wide teaching of American history.[35]

The Collection worked in tandem with the Gilder Lehrman Institute, developing programs that made its documents available to students in different formats. The Collection has now been fully digitized, including even a soldier's bible—providing access at very affordable rates to subscribing libraries all over the world. Staff at the Institute and Collection have worked together to provide innovative ways to engage students. Sandra Trenholm observed that, "The Spotlight on Primary Sources that we develop for the website is one of the most popular resources that Gilder Lehrman offers. Teachers who come to the Collection through workshops, our First Friday program or field trips love using our materials and exposing their students to the 'real stuff' of history."[36]

Seeing the value of the Institute's work, Monticello's Daniel Jordan called it "a big candle in the dark. Every survey tells you that school kids don't know American history and don't care. School kids are more likely to be able to tell you the names of the three stooges than the three branches of government."[37] We consider that problem our challenge, and the team at the Gilder Lehrman Institute meets that challenge every day.

With a clear idea of the goals for the Institute, Sandy Trenholm attains them through constant engagement directly with children. She wrote a couple of notes recently to describe her approach to field trips and student engagement, saying:

> Lew has also stated the importance of close reading of the documents. I developed our field trip program with this in mind. We do not tell students what to think or what to look for. We ask them what they think, what questions they have, and we guide them with questions designed to develop their critical thinking and analytical skills. Teachers have reported that we are students' favorite field trip and that they talk about the materials we show them for months.
>
> There have been so many moments where students have made connections, or had an epiphany while working with our materials. . . . The documents are

a tangible link to our history. You can often view the content online, but it is quite a different experience when viewing the materials in person. No matter what age, people's reactions to the documents are often very visceral. They often ask, "Is this the real? The really real one?" People experience amazement, disbelief, and sometimes even a bit of giddiness, as if they had just met their favorite celebrities. They [the original documents that is] humanize history.

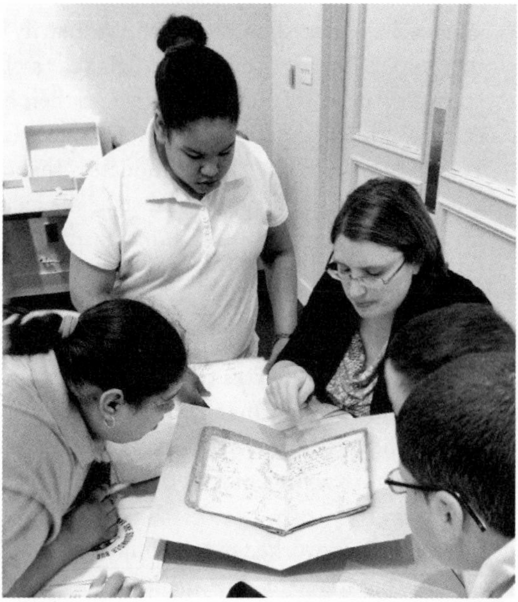

Sandra Trenholm: Outstanding Lincoln student and "Curator-in-Chief"

When discussing the Declaration of Independence, we show a copy printed in August of 1776 by Peter Timothy who committed an act of treason against the British crown when he put his name in the colophon. We ask guests if they would have done that. This prompts a conversation about what people risked by openly supporting the Declaration. As one middle schooler succinctly stated, "I think there would be repercussions for that." Students ask about Timothy's family and often state they would support the Declaration if they didn't have families to worry about. This document and Timothy's story help students understand the personal risks and sacrifices that people have taken in the past.

When examining images from the Civil Rights Movement, a group of 8th grade students remarked on how young some of the protesters looked. We asked them, "how do you think their families felt?" They discussed how the families were probably proud, scared, and worried all at the same time. One student remarked that it was the first time he thought of civil rights leaders having families.

Several years ago, we gave a presentation for the winners of the National History Teacher of the Year award. The program was attended by the winners (both the current and past winners), their families, school administrators, and the students who nominated them. During the presentation we featured numerous documents, including the Thomas Burpee Collection of Civil War soldiers' letters. We explained that letters from family members rarely survive because soldiers had to carry all their belongings with them and that they had to carefully choose what they saved. In addition to discussing Burpee's service and his death at Cold Harbor, we also showed them letters from his two young

> sons, Lucien (age 7) and Charley (age 4). Charley's letters were only scribbles, but his mother had translated one "Charley loves his father very much."
>
> The educators became very excited about the historic example of prewriting and how it hadn't changed much over time. One student became very quiet and looked thoughtful. I asked him what he was thinking and he responded "I thought you said letters from home didn't usually survive." He paused for a second before continuing, "They must have meant the world to him." One of the teachers gasped and the room, which had been filled with excited chatter, fell silent.[38]

Such moments of inspiration confirmed our sense of the importance of our work at the Gilder Lehrman Institute. They were a regular occurrence.

The day after one of our Lincoln Prize dinners, Diane Brennan and I joined a Gilder Lehrman Institute trip to the Academy of American Studies in New York City. Diane's observations were keen, and her eye for significance was aroused. This is how she recalls the events:

> As we entered the building we were greeted by the principal Michael Serber. [Sitting] in Michael's office he told us about the connection with the Gilder Lehrman Institute of American History, Lewis Lehrman, and Dick Gilder . . . how much they helped the school and the students. Shortly after, Principal Serber escorted us to the school's auditorium for a program involving the student body. Gabor Boritt spoke to the students about his journey to America. [John Hope] Franklin, [Loren] Schweninger and [Allen] Guelzo discussed with the

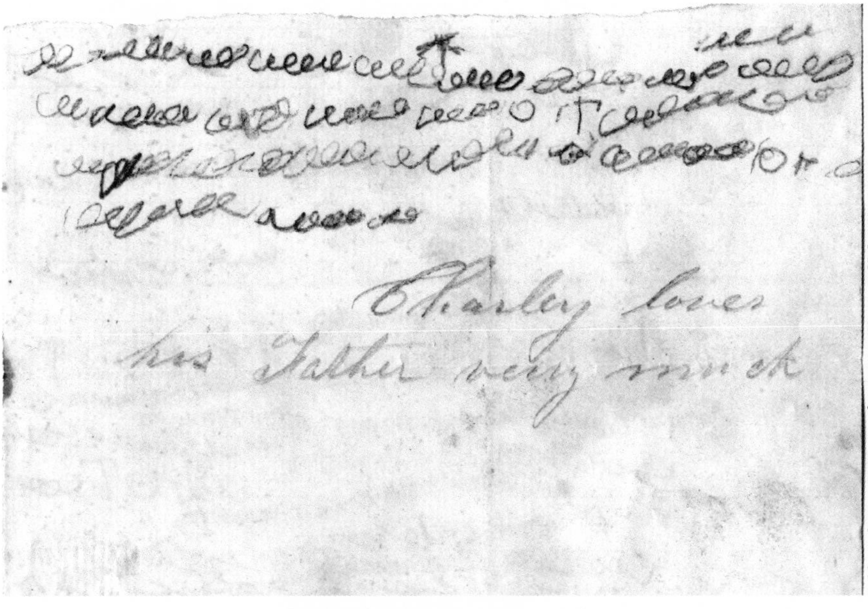

Gilder Lehrman Institute of American History, GLC02744.296

"Charley loves his father. . . ."

students their prize-winning books and scholarship. It was truly amazing to see how well-educated these students were about American history. Many of the students were first generation Americans, and English was not their first language. This was a moment I understood the mission of Lew, Dick, and the Gilder Lehrman Institute of American History."[39]

Diane Brennan: Coordinator of the Lincoln Prize

I was especially inspired that day, seeing all the chairs full for an 8:30 a.m. lecture. By way of introducing the other speakers, I delivered a presentation based on Professor Davis's work comparing Alexander Hamilton and Thomas Jefferson. In the question and answer period I asked the students who would be their preference for president, Jefferson or Hamilton? Ninety percent of the students present answered Hamilton. Maybe it was because they were first-generation Americans themselves. It also appeared to me that those who were especially poor answered for Hamilton. These children were already clear that Hamilton was a self-made man of the people, and they resonated with his struggle. This sentiment prevailed among American schoolchildren way before the *Hamilton* musical came out.

Teaching from the actual documents

David McCullough: Presidential Medal of Freedom winner

The positive impact of the Institute's work on students has enabled it to attract resources far beyond that which Dick and I could provide alone. In addition to building a network of scholars, teachers, and affiliate schools, one of President Jim Basker's challenges has been to build a broad network of support, beginning with a Board committed to the Institute's work.

Daniel Jordan, the former president of the Thomas Jefferson Foundation and one of the earliest members of our board, gave a good description of our development. "The initial board was small and strictly inside. When it decided to expand, I believe I was the first outside trustee. Jim [Basker] and I then recruited David McCullough, [who] was [also] on the board of Monticello. David has crusaded to help young Americans to have a greater appreciation of their heritage. For a long time, the board was very small, with full participation, and thus I had a front row seat. I was invited to share ideas with [Executive Director] Leslie Hermann about the creation of what became the Gilder Lehrman Institute. [We then] made the transition from Founders board to Resource board. The initial premise we had was to get a small group that had real gravitas. We aimed high. We didn't have any luck. Jim began to recommend people who loved history. He sought very different people such as John Nau . . . North America's largest beer distributor, Houston-based, UVA graduate, very philanthropic, and close to the Bush family."[40]

Jordan was skeptical of the strategy at first; however, he came around quickly, saying "I always had a bias against businesspeople in history. I learned that there were people like Dick and Lew who actually read more history than I did. We had these board meetings and these businesspeople wanted to talk about the latest book about history."[41]

Another man we have been fortunate to recruit to the board is my former colleague from Morgan Stanley, Bob Niehaus. Of his work on the board, Bob said it was "both a privilege and an honor to . . . play a small role in the explosive growth in interest, viewing and use of one of the great American History archives. The Institute's decision . . . to digitize and make readily available the entire archive of original documents for both students and teachers is one of the great success stories in American education over the past several decades. Lew and Dick's passion for American History, their shrewd assembling of the historical archives and their selection of the very capable Professor James Basker to lead and build an organization to make the materials accessible and of interest to tens of millions of Americans is an astonishing and incredible feat."[42]

PARTNERING WITH MONTICELLO

One of the Institute's key partnerships developed serendipitously with the Thomas Jefferson Foundation at Monticello. In 1987, an Arkansas businessman purchased a bust of Thomas Jefferson created by Jean-Antoine Houdon at a Christie's auction. Jefferson had posed for the bust in 1789 while serving as America's foreign minister in Paris. At the time of the auction, the Thomas Jefferson Foundation was the losing bidder. A few years after the purchase, the new owner hit hard times, and put the bust back on the market. I learned that it was for sale and consulted with Dick—who raised serious doubts about whether it was appropriate for a collection of documents.

Dick told the story to C-SPAN's Brian Lamb in 2005: "One day, I got a call from [Lew] because he—on any important purchase, you know, he's . . . well-mannered, wants to call me and let me have some of the blame, so he said, 'There's this Houdon bust of Mr. Jefferson's come on the market.' I was a no. I was not a trustee of Monticello. I've been since, but I wasn't at the time. And Lew said, 'It's going to cost, you know, seven figures—low seven—it's going to be in the millions.' And I said, 'Lew, don't we have enough on our plate to collect documents and maps and broadsides and all that? I mean, once you get into works of art, isn't that a whole 'nother league? But I'll leave it to—I'm against it, but I'll leave it to you.' So, of course he bought it. And it was a fabulous acquisition."[43]

Dick was fond of telling the story about his objections—and how I ignored them to pay $3 million for the bust. In the same interview with C-SPAN he said "I love to tell this story because it makes Lew look good, it makes me look like willing to go along, you see? I mean, in other words, if you don't have the brainpower, find someone who does. I've had fabulous partners—and especially Lew—in my life." In truth, he was proud of the way the purchase opened a special new partnership for Dick and the Collection. We had asked the Monticello curator, Susan Stein, to vet the "portrait," and thus began a long and fruitful collaboration. As Dick told C-SPAN, "It got us involved with Monticello."[44]

© Thomas Jefferson Foundation at Monticello

Thomas Jefferson by Jean-Antoine Houdon

Knowing about our purchase of the bust, Daniel P. Jordan, then president of the Thomas Jefferson Foundation, invited

Daniel Jordan: Jefferson's man at GLI

us down to see what they were doing at Monticello. Soon, Dick joined the Monticello board as a trustee, calling it "one of the top boards I've ever been on. They accomplished so much in these last 10 years, and had begun, well before I got on the board, with the momentum."[45]

"When Dick realized that we had a serious-minded board, he signed on," recalled Dan. "They loaned the [Houdon] bust for the big [Jefferson] exhibit in 1993. Dick thought the only reason to be on a history board was to do something big. The capacity of the board determines the capacity of the program. With a resource board, you can do anything. We had capacity on the Monticello board when Dick served. David McCullough had been on the Monticello board. I remember sitting on a bench with Jim [Basker] and David talking about the importance of [David] becoming involved [with the Gilder Lehrman Institute]."[46]

Thus, through Monticello, we got to know the incomparable David McCullough, who eventually became a valuable board member for the Gilder Lehrman Institute. We also got to know Professor Douglas Wilson, who would eventually move from work on Thomas Jefferson at Monticello to work on Abraham Lincoln at Knox College. "I first heard about Lew Lehrman in 1996 while working at Jefferson's Monticello," Wilson recalled. "At that time, I had the oversight of Monticello's scholarly and educational programs, and we had been approached by the Gilder Lehrman Institute about offering an ambitious, high-quality summer seminar for teachers. I knew Dick Gilder, because he was an active and generous member of Monticello's board of directors, though I knew nothing about the other member of the partnership, Lewis Lehrman. But happily, Monticello's director, Dan Jordan, knew all about him, and proceeded to fill me in."[47]

Our work at Monticello had the ancillary benefit of creating another partnership—that with Buford Scott, husband of my childhood friend, Susie Bailey Scott. Susie recently shared her perspective on those events with me, stating that "Buford started the Jefferson Scholars Program at the University of Virginia. Buford and Lew share a love of history. Lew became interested in some historic programs here in Richmond. He donated a [Rembrandt Peale] portrait of George Washington to the State Capitol. Buford and he served on the boards for the American Civil War Museum and the Capitol Foundation."[48]

We watched the work that Monticello was doing on educational programs and its International Center for Jefferson Studies. We admired the way that they professionalized their operations and moved from a "friends and family" board to a resources board. In short, the Houdon purchase turned into a learning experience that enriched and enlivened both organizations, and everyone involved.

Susie and Buford Scott: Tried and true friends

FINDING THE RIGHT LEADER

By the mid-1990s Dick and I had a lot of initiatives going on. I suggested a review of everything. We asked Professor James Basker of Barnard College to conduct that review. We knew he was an active educational entrepreneur, having established the hugely successful and well-respected Oxbridge Summer School program for international students interested in exploring the great British universities. We felt sure he would be a strong leader for a new business. We were also impressed that Jim was very active in Title I Academics, and that his wife is equally dedicated to the same Title I children. I have always been particularly interested in reaching those most at risk, for they have the most to gain from knowing the history of America's promise to its people.

From our first meeting, Jim and I hit it off. Jim's memory of that day is delightful. "I first met Lew in 1995 at a concert at the Morgan Library," he began.

> Lew invited me to lunch at the Racquet Club, probably in the spring of 1996. It was one of the most embarrassing days of my life.
>
> It was pouring rain. The traffic was backed up Park Avenue. I got out of the cab and without an umbrella ran for the club. I arrived looking like a drowned rat, 20 minutes late for lunch. Lew couldn't have been more gracious. It was the first touch of his grace. From that first conversation it was about ideas. We went straight to what he was doing with the Gilder Lehrman Institute and a discussion about document-based learning.
>
> I had built an education business in Europe, starting in 1984. Later in 1996, Dick and Lew stunned me by asking me to provide an outside perspective on

James Basker: All-time greatest entrepreneur of education

> the Gilder Lehrman enterprises. They blew me away—offering $25,000 for a month's work. I visited all their enterprises, institutional partners, and leaders. I ended up working another month and producing a 10-page report. Lew and Dick took me to another level. It was hugely empowering.[49]

After Jim had completed his work, I suggested we should hire him. I remember the moment clearly. Dick asked Jim to lunch. At lunch, Dick said to him: "Lew and I like your ideas."[50] During the rest of lunch, we worked out the details. Jim later memorialized the rest of the conversation, saying, "[Dick] wanted me to quit Barnard and 'come do this.' I explained: 'I've worked all my life to be a professor.' He told me to go talk to my wife. Lew understood what it was like to be a professor. He said Dick should have asked me to go half-time. I ended up going half-time at Barnard and two-thirds at Gilder Lehrman."[51] In 1997, we made Jim president and CEO of the Gilder Lehrman Institute of American History, and began to centralize our work through him. It was an inspired choice. Jim Basker is probably the finest academic entrepreneur in the country. He would have been successful in any field, but especially diplomacy.

Jim became a full partner as soon as he joined the Institute. He was modest, hard-working; he had all the virtues and talents the job required. He was honorable as well as honest. Apparently, he appreciated my style as well, saying: "Lew's advice and his example have been the most valuable to me in the last two decades. I learned discipline and diplomacy by watching him. [Lew] taught me to listen."[52]

Jim had an open mind for the best of the American traditions. He had an enormous respect for Lincoln. He was very much interested in helping the impoverished. He may be the very best head of a charitable organization in the United States. Under Jim's leadership, the number of Gilder Lehrman–affiliated high schools grew from just a handful to over thirty thousand, and he has tirelessly secured the necessary resources to successfully support the effort.

Among Jim's other accomplishments, in 2005 he set up the George Washington Book Prize with Washington College in Maryland and the Regents of Mount Vernon. The very first prize recipient was Ron Chernow for his monumental book *Hamilton* (2004). Other winners have included Stacy Schiff, 2006 (*A Great Improvisation: Franklin, France, and the Birth of America*); Annette Gordon-Reed, 2009 (*The Hemingses of Monticello: An American Family*); Pauline Maier, 2011 *(Ratification: The People Debate the Constitution: 1787–1788*); and Flora Fraser, 2016 (*The Washingtons: George and Martha, "Join'd by Friendship, Crown'd by Love*").

Leading up to the creation of the George Washington book prize, I had developed a partnership with Gay Gaines, the eighteenth regent of the Mount Vernon Ladies' Association, who had joined the Regents board in 2000 as Florida's vice regent. I also got to work with James C. Rees, the longtime president of Mount Vernon, who had significantly expanded Mount Vernon's educational offerings and resources. In 2012, I developed the Gay Gaines Distinguished Visiting Fellowship at Mount Vernon to fund an annual lecture series. The first Fellow was Richard R. Beeman, the

Gay Gaines: Whirlwind of success and former regent of Mt. Vernon

John Walsh Centennial Professor of History at the University of Pennsylvania.

Dick Gilder let Jim and me set the stage for the Institute's work, and generously assured that the resources were there to sustain it. "You know, I wouldn't have thought it would be where it was five years ago," Dick told Brian Lamb in 2000. "The thing is," he continued, "Jim Basker has had so many darn good ideas and Lew and I are in the wonderful position of saying, 'That a boy Jim, keep it up, Jim, that's terrific, you should do more.' . . . I know this sounds a little fatuous, but if we can keep attracting the people we can, they're going to make us look fabulous. Lew makes me look good now."[53] The three of us had tremendous respect for each other and studiously avoided any conflicts amongst ourselves while resolving external problems.

THE GILDER LEHRMAN CENTER AT YALE

For years, the subject of slavery was neglected by the American academy. In 1998, Dick and I established the Gilder-Lehrman Center for the Study of Slavery, Resistance and Abolition at Yale University. We were already well acquainted with the brilliant scholarship of Professor David Brion Davis. Although Professor Davis taught for forty-seven years, only late in his career was slavery deemed worthy of a semester-long course.

In March of 1994, Professor Davis had given a speech at the Morgan Library sponsored by the Gilder Lehrman Institute. In notes I received from him, he painted a picture of the event, remarking that his speech had been "on the origins and significance of New World slavery.

> Fortunately, the audience included Dick Gilder and Lewis Lehrman, two highly successful Yale alumni who are passionately interested in history and who had succeeded in collecting tens of thousands of original historical documents ranging from Columbus to modern times. After my lecture, Dick and Lew immediately asked my wife and me to join them and some friends for dinner. It was then that they finalized plans for founding the Gilder Lehrman Institute

of American History and asked me to teach a summer seminar on the subject of my lecture to a class of thirty or so schoolteachers. Greatly aided by a former doctoral student, close friend, and future co-author, Professor Steven Mintz, I taught the Gilder Lehrman slavery course seven times from 1994 to 2001."[54]

From that original lecture at the Morgan Library, the Yale Center was born. As Yale defined the new research institute, "The Gilder Lehrman Center at Yale promotes the study of slavery, slave resistance, and the abolition of slavery in academic scholarship, school curricula, and public education programs by such means as conferences, publications, fellowships, prizes and lectures. The Center, which is part of the Yale Center for International and Area Studies, seeks to promote a better understanding of all aspects of the Atlantic Slave System, including the Africans' resistance to enslavement, the black and white abolitionist movements, and of the ways in which slavery finally came to an end."[55]

With Davis at the helm, the Center had instant credibility. One of its first acts was to begin the annual Frederick Douglass Book Prize for the best new book on slavery, resistance, and abolition. At the first prize dinner in 1999, I observed from the podium that:

> No American statesman, but for Mr. Lincoln, understood so well as Mr. Douglass the world-scale historical mutation wrought by the American Civil War. Up from slavery, this gifted black man wrote, "no republic is safe that . . . denies to any of its citizen's equal rights, and the equal means to maintain them."
>
> What was theory before this War has been made fact by this war? Who among us will deny that Mr. Douglass was an authentic and intrepid warrior, bearing quill and rhetoric for weapons?
>
> And he was ever ready for the fight of his faith. In the event, he was not found wanting. "Men of color, to arms," he exhorted bondmen and freeman alike. And in the Thirteenth, Fourteenth, and Fifteenth Amendments to the Constitution of the United States, the great trial of arms had bought him his birthright—and an exhilarating personal victory.
>
> For there he stood, at the second inaugural of the sixteenth president of the United States. There, at the White House, he described himself as "a man among men." There, before the assembled white multitude, President Lincoln called out to him, modestly and totally unselfconsciously, "here comes my friend Frederick Douglass."[56]

I concluded my brief remarks by observing "what extraordinary tales remain to be told of the migration of the African people to America, of their way of life here—slave and free, and of their unique contributions to the making of the American nation and of American culture. Above all, Dick and I believe that the telling of this tale must be inspired by American historians—by their impeccable scholarship—by means of unflinching, deep, honest research."[57]

Frederick Douglass: Mr. Lincoln's friend

Professor Davis was the ideal person to lead this intellectual effort at Yale—because it was work he was already doing and had been doing for decades. He was, as mentioned, the pioneer of global slavery studies, and a great exemplar of classical English prose and original scholarship. At Yale, he created an enterprise for the ages in the Gilder Lehrman Center.

THE IMPORTANCE OF HISTORY

Professor Davis was unequivocal in his writing, and forthright in his views about the importance of history. Some of his remarks resemble feelings I also expressed in my Carnegie Teaching Fellowship essay, "Why Study History."[58] In a 2006 talk at the Morgan Library, he began:

> I would like to say a few words in opposition to the view, expressed nowadays by far too many educators, that history is a boring and antiquarian diversion, that we should "let bygones be bygones," "free" ourselves from a dismal and oppressive past, and concentrate on a fresh and better future. I have long and fervently believed that a consciousness of history is one of the key factors that distinguishes us from all other animals—I mean the ability to transcend an illusory sense of *now*, of an eternal present, and to strive for an understanding of the forces and events that made us what we are. Such an understanding is the prerequisite, I believe, for all human freedom. Obviously history can be used in ideological ways to justify the worst forms of aggression and oppression. But that fact underscores the supreme importance of freeing ourselves from such distortions and searching, as far as possible, for a true and balanced picture of the past.[59]

Davis's definitive works include *The Problem of Slavery in Western Culture* (1966, Pulitzer Prize), *In the Image of God: Religion, Moral Values, and Our Heritage of Slavery* (2001), and *Inhuman Bondage: The Rise and Fall of Slavery in the New World* (2006). His work earned him the National Humanities Medal in 2014.

Davis took up some of the same themes in an October 2003 letter to me in which he wrote, "there are simply no words that can be adequate in honoring what you and Dick have done and have been doing to enrich and to disseminate knowledge of our past. Aside from my long admiration for George Santayana, who famously said 'Progress, far from consisting in change, depends on retentiveness. . . . Those who cannot remember the past are condemned to fulfill it' (usually mistranslated as 'repeat it'), I've long believed that the thing that most significantly distinguishes us from our animal ancestors is our understanding of our past. And the past, unlike the ephemeral present and unpredictable future, is the true 'reality.'"[60]

In June 2004, Yale University president Richard C. Levin announced that David Blight would succeed Davis. Blight had joined the Yale faculty in 2002 after teaching at Amherst College for more than a decade. Blight won the Frederick Douglass Prize for his *Race and Reunion: The Civil War in American Memory* (2001). Among Blight's other books were two pathbreaking works on Douglass: *Frederick Douglass's Civil War* (1989) and *Frederick Douglass: Prophet of Freedom* (2018), which won both the Lincoln Prize and the Pulitzer Prize.

Under Professor Blight, the Center continues to thrive. As Professor Davis observed in 2009: "David Blight has expanded and greatly enriched the activities of the [Gilder Lehrman] Center. . . . From international conferences and countless lectures to Connecticut school classrooms, from interaction with teachers and ongoing bibliographies to the Douglass Prize, the Gilder Lehrman Center has helped to transform slavery from being a minor chapter in U.S. 'Southern history' into both a global subject and one of the unhappy foundations of our own past—something we must come to terms with."[61]

FINDING A HOME FOR THE COLLECTION

One of our central goals was to rescue important manuscripts from private obscurity and make them available for scholarly and educational purposes. So, in 1992 we decided to put the rapidly expanding Gilder Lehrman Collection on deposit at the Morgan Library for ten years. It was a pleasure and an honor to be able to work with my former partner at Morgan Stanley, Parker Gilbert, once again. Parker had been chairman of the board of Morgan Stanley during my career there. This time he joined our efforts in his capacity as CEO of the Morgan Library.

By the turn of the millennium, however, Dick Gilder, Jim Basker, and I were looking for a new home for the Gilder Lehrman Collection. The dignified and genteel Morgan Library was no longer an appropriate repository. We wanted a place where we could keep the collection, and use it for teaching—a venue where students would be welcome. We wanted to relocate the Collection to an institution such as the New-York Historical Society, which was more focused on student education programs, especially in American history

The New York Public Library's president Paul LeClerc had wanted the Collection moved to his library, one of America's premier research institutions. Although we were grateful for the offer, once Jim Basker was named president of the Gilder Lehrman Institute, we began negotiations with the New-York Historical Society. One of its founders had been Albert Gallatin, who served as treasury secretary under Presidents Thomas Jefferson and James Madison. Although he was an intellectual rival of America's first treasury secretary, Alexander Hamilton, Gallatin was also one of the founders of America's economic system.

Dick and I entered most projects as a team. So in 2003 we both joined the board of the New-York Historical Society, which was then experiencing difficulties with its vision and finances. We got deeply involved in the restoration of the Society's principal location on Central Park West, but our contributions to its financial and intellectual resources may have been even more significant. Location was a major decision, because we knew we would have to invest at least a million dollars in the creation of a vault to protect the Collection. We decided to commit and came up with several ideas to announce our decision.

In preparation for the bicentennial of Alexander Hamilton's death by duel in July of 1804, Dick and I hatched the idea of hosting an exhibit at our new location. Along with Gallatin, Hamilton had also been a founder of the New-York Historical Society, as well as the Anti-Slavery Society of New York. The exhibit would commemorate both the Society's founding and the anniversary of the duel. As I later told C-SPAN's Brian Lamb, Hamilton "was a man for all seasons even though he had his flaws."[62]

In fact, Hamilton was the quintessential New Yorker. From an obscure beginning, Hamilton rose to prominence as the founder of institutions like the *New York Post* and the Bank of New York. I had written about the consequences of his immigration to New York for a 1999 essay in the *New Criterion,* saying:

> Hamilton really was the proverbial self-made man. Born in 1757 (or perhaps 1755), the illegitimate son of a feckless Scot and another man's wife, he spent his early years in the slave and sugar culture of the West Indies. His father abandoned his errant mother when Hamilton was nine, and young Alexander was then apprenticed to an export-import merchant at Christiansted; two years later, his mother's death left him on his own. He immigrated to the colonies when he was fifteen and was educated at King's College (now Columbia University). Within two decades this enterprising young man rose from utter obscurity to become one of the most celebrated American statesmen in the history of the republic. Having learned early on to love Plutarch, Hamilton, it seems, was ever guided by Demosthenes; "Wise politicians march at the head of affairs," rarely awaiting "the event, to know what measures to take; but the measures which they have taken, ought to produce the event."[63]

Hamilton was one of the greatest of the Founders, but he had virtually disappeared from the American pantheon as early as the post–New Deal period because Roosevelt was a Jeffersonian.

Jim remembers the phone call in August 2003, wherein Dick and I sprang the idea to curate the exhibit upon our ever-creative colleague:

"Lew and Dick called me when I was on vacation in Oregon. 'We're in discussion about a big exhibition at the New-York Historical Society.' They asked me if it was possible to prepare in a year. I was on the spot. I said yes. Lew, Dick, and their friend Roger Hertog guaranteed the funds to put it on. We had big summit meetings each week with about 25 people."[64]

For the exhibit, I recruited Richard Brookhiser to do the script. Rick had written *Alexander Hamilton, American* in 1999, and thereby launched the revival of Alexander Hamilton as one of the most creative and productive Founders. He also "understood the need to deliver copy quickly,"[65] as Jim Basker remembered. During the 1982 gubernatorial campaign, I had gotten to know Brookhiser, who covered

Richard Brookhiser: The man responsible for the Hamilton renaissance

the campaign for *National Review.* A brilliant student and English major at Yale, Rick was one of the best historians chronicling America's Founders. He was also happy to have me join the field, writing an article saying that "New York's loss was the country's gain because Lew, free from the distractions of office, turned to his first love, history. Here is one instance of his ardor and eye for detail. We were talking about Lincoln's Peoria speech. I said 'it was long—three hours long.' Lew said, 'three hours and ten minutes.' Of course, he had read it himself, and timed it—the marriage of passion and precision."[66]

"Hamilton was the perfect topic," recalls Jim. "Lew had been steeped in the Hamiltonian idea—the quintessential outsider."[67] It was the right idea. Hamilton *is* the American idea. To further dramatize Hamilton's life, we even commissioned a bronze statue of the Hamilton-Burr duel. The exhibit was called "Alexander Hamilton: The Man Who Made Modern America." When it opened in

The New-York Historical Society, Kim Crowley sculptor

Bronze statues of the Hamilton-Burr duel

September 2004, I said: "Shall we all raise our glass to Alexander Hamilton? May I say for the evening 'We are all Hamiltonians.'"[68]

The Hamilton exhibit provided one "bookend" to the revival of the New-York Historical Society. As Jim said, "that exhibit drew people out and rehabilitated Hamilton and the New-York Historical Society."[69]

THE INSTITUTE BRINGS HAMILTON TO SCHOOLCHILDREN

Perhaps one of the most iconic contributions of the Gilder Lehrman Institute to the study of history has been our partnership with Lin-Manuel Miranda. With help from the Rockefeller Foundation, we were able to make the groundbreaking musical *Hamilton* accessible to tens of thousands of economically disadvantaged students. This effort dramatically broadened the appeal of American history to a true cross-section of the American young adult population.

In April 2004, Ron Chernow's *Alexander Hamilton* had been released—further stimulating interest in the man who set up America's financial system and wrote most of the *Federalist Papers*. Chernow's book on Hamilton is a path-breaking book. It covers his life in its entirety, from exalted achievement to some of the more disappointing aspects, like the adulterous affair which he himself exposed to the public in order to save his reputation as a punctilious secretary of the treasury.

It was Chernow's book that stimulated Lin-Manuel Miranda to write and stage the blockbuster musical *Hamilton*. Chernow also had the idea to bring Lin-Manuel, his father Luis, and Hamilton producer Jeffrey Seller to meet Jim Basker in our office. The relationship took off immediately. Impressed by the enormous educational potential

Lin-Manuel and Luis Miranda: The famous playwright and his father, cofounders of EduHam

of a partnership, Jim cultivated the relationship. Soon thereafter, Luis Miranda joined our board, and helped the Gilder Lehrman Institute form a partnership with the Rockefeller Foundation to bring thousands of students into the theater for new inspiration and insights into America's Founding. The *Hamilton* Education Program, informally dubbed "EduHam," drew notice from both academic and theater circles. A 2019 *Broadway World* article documented how the partnership was forged, saying:

> The groundbreaking 2015 musical, HAMILTON, made everybody stand up and take notice when its instant popularity made getting tickets to the show virtually impossible for the average American. This inequity tugged at Miranda's heartstrings so deeply, that he found a way to make this important story accessible to everyone—hence—the HAMILTON Education Project, affectionately known as EduHam, was born. [It is] a five-year program which has already blessed the lives of over 50,000 Title I students annually.
>
> Miranda and his father Luis took their brainchild to the Gilder Lehrman Institute of American History, whose mission it is to promote the knowledge and understanding of American history through educational programs and resources. Armed with a grant from the Rockefeller Foundation, the Mirandas, along with Alexander Hamilton Biographer, Ron Chernow, Producer, Jeffery Sellers (sic), and Gilder Lehrman President, James Basker devised the curriculum that would not only give kids a fun day out at the theater, but would turn them into active learners, grounding them in a more meaningful way to learn about their founding fathers.[70]

In *Hamilton,* Lin-Manuel magnified a typical immigrant success story. Black and Hispanic people can own the Alexander Hamilton story—mental agility, ambition, and desire to serve your country can lead to success. Anyone who has laudable ambition can succeed. Those who have seen the play, or even just heard about it, can appreciate its moral. Hamilton was an inspired man, a brave officer, a successful lawyer, and a true American Horatio Alger story. In 2015, the George Washington Prize's first-ever "special achievement award" was presented to Lin-Manuel Miranda for creating the smash musical.

The second "bookend" to the revival of the New-York Historical Society came more than a decade later with the appointment of historian Andrew Roberts as the Lehrman Institute Fellow at the New-York Historical Society. He lifted the Society's historical credentials to a new high. As a scholar of World War II, Andrew was a brilliant, respected conservative who wrote outstanding biographies of Napoleon and Winston Churchill, as well as *A History of the English-Speaking Peoples Since 1900* (2007). As of 2022, Andrew has now become Lord Roberts of Belgravia, taking his seat in the House of Lords on nomination by the Conservative Party in Parliament.

The appointment in 2004 of Louise Mirrer as New-York Historical Society president was also triumphal. We knew each other because she had once been City University of New York's executive vice chancellor for academic affairs. At that time,

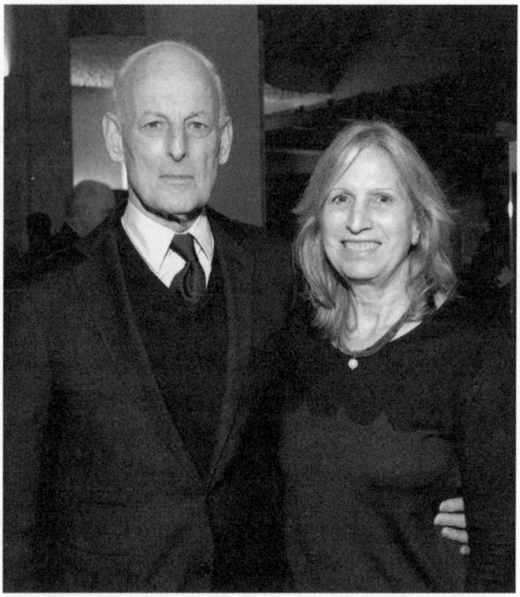

Louise Mirrer: superb director of the New-York Historical Society

I was considering an appointment to be chairman of the City University of New York board of trustees, to replace distinguished literary scholar, Anne A. Paolucci. Louise has done a magnificent job as chief executive. Strong, disciplined, and inspired, Louise has been to the New-York Historical Society what Jim Basker has been to the Gilder Lehrman Institute of American History.

Indeed, Louise and Pam Schafler—who became a member of the NYHS board in 2010—proved perhaps the most inspired team of any historical institution in America. Only Sandra Trenholm and I know the Gilder Lehrman Collection better than Pam.

Dick and I did draw some criticism for our involvement at the New-York Historical Society, in particular from City University of New York professor Mike Wallace. Wallace is a specialist in New York City history, and wrote an essay for the *New York Review of Books* in May 2003 that was critical of the Hamilton exhibit. That prompted an article in the *New York Times* in July 2004, wherein Wallace alleged that we were bent on imposing a conservative agenda on the New-York Historical Society.

Louise Mirrer, however, defended her organization's independence, saying that "as Professor Wallace well knows, the most recent appointees to the Society's board include David Blight, Yale professor and specialist in slavery, resistance, and abolition; Henry Louis Gates Jr., Harvard professor and head of the W.E.B. DuBois Institute; the filmmaker Ric Burns; and Bernard Schwartz, a major supporter of the Democratic Party. These appointments hardly give evidence to the claim Professor Wallace makes about the ideological influences at the society."[71]

David Brion Davis also came to the defense of the Gilder Lehrman Institute in his letter to the editor, saying:

> I would like to correct a serious misunderstanding that could be conveyed by the first long footnote in [Wallace's] review of the New-York Historical Society's exhibition on Alexander Hamilton [*NYRB*, February 10]. My concern has nothing to do with the Hamilton exhibition or the New-York Historical Society, but rather with the invaluable Gilder Lehrman Institute of American History,

which is emphatically not a right-wing or conservative organization, and which is surely not taking over the New-York Historical Society.

As a leftish Democrat (and a longtime contributor to the *New York Review*), I have worked quite closely with Dick Gilder, Lew Lehrman, and the GLI since 1994, teaching summer seminars on slavery and antislavery for high school teachers, co-editing a large "interpretive anthology" based on their extraordinary collection of documents (*The Boisterous Sea of Liberty*), and from 1998 to 2004 serving as director of Yale University's Gilder Lehrman Center for the Study of Slavery, Resistance, and Abolition. Despite our major political differences, I have never encountered even the most subtle attempt at ideological influence of any kind with respect to my teaching, writing, co-curating a national exhibition on slavery, or making proposals as a member of the Advisory Board of the Gilder Lehrman Institute of American History. The one time Mr. Gilder made a "political" suggestion, it was quite radical—he suggested that we add the word "Resistance" to the title of Yale's center, after he learned that African slaves rebelled on about 10 percent of the Atlantic slave ships.[72]

In the summer of 2004, Wallace successfully drew attention to his complaints with coverage in the *New York Times* and the *Wall Street Journal*. Eric Gibson wrote the article for the *Journal*, saying "The *New York Times* ran two articles intimating that the whole thing was a kind of hostile takeover of a small institution by ego-driven tycoons determined to bend it to their conservative point of view. Mr. Gilder responds that such speculation is nonsense. The museum needed to switch gears, he says, because it had an unpromising future. The visitor count was flat and expenses were on the rise. 'It was only a matter of time' before the society would go back into the red, he notes. 'And there was no vision being executed. There were just a lot of small, inconsequential—we thought—shows when you had this great opportunity.'"[73]

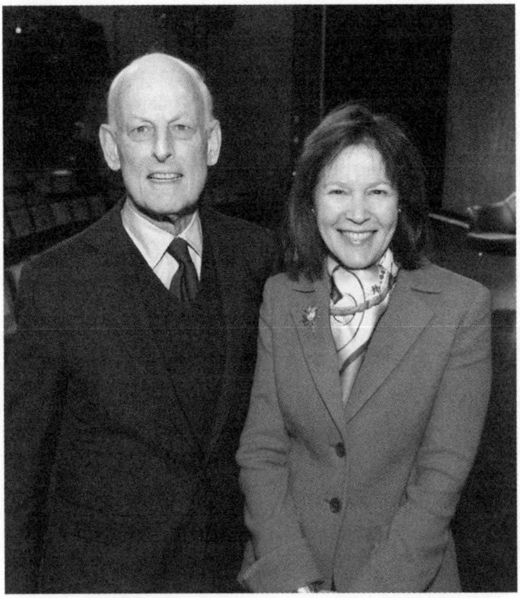

Pam Schafler: Expert on the Collection

Over time, critical suspicion about the Gilder Lehrman Institute and its founders dissipated. In 2017, liberal New York historian Kevin Baker said "we're far apart on ideology. But I've loved what [Lehrman] and his collaborators have done at the New York Historical Society, it's a great place for popular history. . . . What they've done is keep people engaged, and it doesn't seem like they're grinding any ideological axe."[74]

One of the historians with whom I worked closely over three decades was the prolific Harold Holzer, whose resume included campaign work for Mario Cuomo. Harold had worked for six years in Cuomo's administration before he joined the Metropolitan Museum of Art, rising to become senior vice president for public affairs. In 1990, when he was executive vice president of the New York State Urban Development Corporation, Holzer acted as a liaison between Mario Cuomo's administration and the Gilder Lehrman Collection. The Cuomo Administration wanted to borrow our copies of the Emancipation Proclamation and the Thirteenth Amendment for a special exhibit at the New York State Museum. That October, I spoke alongside Governor Mario Cuomo to a conference of scholars. The subject of the conference included the book *Lincoln on Democracy*, edited by Cuomo and Holzer.

These were some of my remarks.

> The living memory of our greatest statesman moves us to gather in this hall, amidst Mr. Lincoln's own writings to celebrate a new book dedicated to the intellectual legacy of a single man. And it is fitting that we should do this. For who among us could have been the same American if Mr. Lincoln had not given that "last full measure" of devotion to the American proposition—the idea that all human beings are created equal, and that legitimate government can thus be based only upon their consent. If, as he argued, the Declaration of Independence is the authentic American proposition, then surely Mr. Lincoln upheld this doctrine for all future time by his thoughts, his words, and his deeds.[75]

Harold later reminded me of what he referred to as "a humbling moment" at a separate event. "Lew is a born matchmaker," Harold said. "He brings the disparate elements of the field together and thaws longtime freezes. The year I was fortunate enough to earn the Lincoln Prize, Lew hosted my wife and me at his table and included a scholar with whom, I confess, I have not gotten along well over the years. 'Is this meant to bring us together?' I asked him. 'Yes,' he replied. 'Shake hands!' It wasn't quite the Arafat-Begin handclasp at Camp David," Harold joked, "but it was nice and a long time coming. And it was Lew's way of saying to us, I think, and not a bad lesson to learn: Now *both* you guys have earned the highest professional honor in the field. How about showing some personal honor as well?"[76]

INSPIRING HISTORIANS AND HISTORY TEACHERS

One of the greatest joys of my work at the Gilder Lehrman Institute has been the opportunity to interact with historians—both those with established reputations, and those whose reputations have yet to be established.

Through the work of the Gilder Lehrman Institute and the decisions regarding four major book awards, I have been able to meet, converse, and debate with the premier historians of Great Britain and the United States. It has been an unparalleled privilege and opportunity for me—having once taught as a Carnegie History Fellow at Yale and Woodrow Wilson Fellow at Harvard—to sit again with Yale's eminent scholars. I never forgot the way that professors at Yale and Harvard had mentored me, and adopted some of their best techniques.

One of the British scholars I was privileged to know was Correlli Barnett. From 1977 to 1995, Barnett was Keeper of the Churchill archives at Churchill College, Cambridge. In 1972, Barnett had published *The Collapse of British Power.* I thought it was one of the best historical volumes I had ever read. I wrote him right away. On my next trip to England, I met him. He invited me to lunch with some Cambridge dons, hosted by the Master of Churchill College. Barnett was not a PhD, so he was never fully accepted by the established historians of Cambridge and Oxford. He was by then an older man. Our relationship was similar to the one I had developed with Jacques Rueff. Barnett, who opposed American policy in the Middle East, was not a proponent of the Anglo-American Alliance. His basic argument was that the United States created vacuums when it helped topple the Middle East dictatorships. He was very smart, and very learned, always equipped with the facts.

Around the turn of the millennium, Rhodes Professor of American History at Oxford University, Richard Carwardine, had penned an impressive book called, simply *Lincoln*. He sent me the British issue of the book, and I worked with him to convince a premier US press to republish the book in America. The book went on to win the Lincoln Prize. We first met at the Awards Ceremony, where Richard brought down the house. As he recalled: "I struggled to keep my composure when accepting the Lincoln Prize. The emotion of a Welsh Nonconformist Liberal—as you described me—could not be suppressed. When Linda and I talked with you that evening we found and admired in you a gracious, clear-eyed, and vigorous champion of not only Lincoln studies, but also history's capacity to shape engaged and thoughtful citizenship." Professor Carwardine would later invite me to speak at Oxford University. "While I was in post there," he wrote on the occasion, "I loved introducing visitors to Corpus Christi College and the Rothermere American Institute, twin centres of my Oxford career. No guest was more gracious, or appreciative, or a more galvanising speaker than yourself."[77]

Richard Carwardine: The Welsh nonconformist liberal

A few years later, when I met Andrew Roberts at the New-York Historical Society, I immediately decided that he was the most interesting British historian since Barnett. He was brilliantly articulate, a master of twentieth-century history, and a master of Churchill's biography. He was very patriotic, *and* very pro-American. I thought he would be ideal as a distinguished Lehrman Fellow at the New-York Historical Society. Andrew delivered the first set of nine lectures on war leadership. The second and third nine were on Winston Churchill. His lectures have all been sell-outs, and he has become known as an "American historian."

Lord Andrew Roberts of Belgravia: The Lehrman Institute Distinguished Fellow at the New-York Historical Society

Phil Hamilton, my executive assistant at CFA, and the man who had introduced me to Gabor Boritt, would go on to become a respected historian and head of the history department at Christopher Newport University in Virginia. Of our early days, Phil remembered with particular fondness our working together in Washington, DC in the mid-1980s.

> Young and just starting out, I certainly admired Lew and greatly valued his advice and counsel. I especially remember the one time I was tasked to drive Lew from DC to his farm in Pennsylvania. . . . As we entered Pennsylvania, our discussions turned to American history and the importance of land and land-ownership to the Founding Fathers. And I recall that discussion as an important moment guiding me back toward the study of history. In short, our brief time together that evening helped start me along the career path I've traveled down ever since.[78]

Much as I have admired his growth in the profession, it was a particular pleasure to see Phil mine the archives of General Henry Knox at the Gilder Lehrman Collection. With the insights so gained, Phil wrote *The Revolutionary War Lives and Letters of Lucy and Henry Knox* (2017), a definitive portrait of the patriot who served not only as George Washington's chief artillery officer in the Revolutionary War, but also as the nation's first secretary of war.

Gilder Lehrman Institute of American History, GLC02437.10731_0

General Henry Knox, President Washington's secretary of war

Phil also became one of the first college professors to become involved in the seminars of the Lehrman American Studies Center (LASC) at the Intercollegiate Studies Institute (ISI). I founded the Center in 2006, and named my former Hill classmate General Josiah Bunting president.

Under another initiative of the ISI, twenty fellows assembled in the James Madison Program at Princeton University. Professor Robbie George, the McCormick Professor of Jurisprudence, was the director of the James Madison Program in American Ideals and Institutions. The Madison program welcomed conservative historians and political scientists who were not welcome elsewhere. Respected historians—such as Gordon S. Wood of Brown University, David Hackett Fischer of Brandeis, and Walter McDougall of the University of Pennsylvania were part of the faculty of the program.

I had come to know ISI president Ken Cribb when he worked in the Reagan Administration. In the ISI, I found the kind of intellectual partners with whom I could collaborate and leverage resources. By bringing together young historians, economists, and political philosophers, we provided them with their own opportunity to collaborate and build courses grounded in America's Founding Principles. As the Center's president, General Josiah Bunting observed, "Lehrman American Studies Center graduates are creating the kind of momentum necessary for a return to the traditional teaching of the American Founding that is so desperately needed today on America's college campuses."[79]

Robbie George: Outstanding philosopher and McCormick Professor of Jurisprudence at Princeton

With General Bunting, I was able to organize the fourth in the Gilder-Lehrman quartet of great history prizes. The Gilder Lehrman Military History

Allen Guelzo: Redeeming scholar, author of *Redeemer President*

Michael Burlingame: The historian's historian

Prize at the New-York Historical Society was founded to restore military history to a prominent place in American history. In the twentieth century, academics had colluded to eliminate military history from university curricula. The prize provided me with contact to an expanding set of historians. These included those whose works were considered for the prize, as well as those who served on the juries, such as British historians Andrew Roberts and Flora Fraser, founder of the Elizabeth Longford Prize for Historical Biography. Flora had also won the Washington Prize in 2016 for *The Washingtons: George and Martha: Partners in Friendship and Love*. In 2014, Professor Allen Guelzo won the inaugural Military History Prize for his monumental book *Gettysburg, The Last Invasion*.

Historians need to nurture future historians if we are to preserve America's historical legacy. In 2006, I told the ISI Fellows that "At Princeton, great teachers meet to bestow the American legacy upon their younger colleagues who will go on to teach America's first principles—these the indispensable grounds of American patriotism and preeminence."[80]

Professor Michael Burlingame describes my concerns on the subject in these words: "The Lincoln Prize has helped significantly to counteract one of the more baleful trends in the historical profession: the notion that it is unfashionable to write about dead white males, especially great men like Lincoln and Churchill. . . . Instead, [history] is supposedly influenced far more by vast, impersonal forces. [Mr. Lehrman's establishment of] the Hay-Nicolay Prize for the best dissertation on Lincoln has . . . served to counteract that trend."[81]

In 2007 I encouraged the Princeton fellows again, saying "What extraordinary tales remain to be told and taught by *you*—and by scholars, the world over—of the history and destiny of America—of our way of life here—of the contributions of unsung soldiers, plain working people, and inspired leaders. And so, to *you*, the teachers of our countrymen, gathered in this room, I wish to say that it is I who am grateful to be at work with *you*, telling one of the most moving stories ever told—the American story—above all, having the chance myself to invoke the principle, the truth, that gave it birth—that we are endowed by our Creator with the unalienable right to life—and the unalienable right to liberty."[82] I have no doubt about the ultimate victory of the American way of life—the faith of our fathers—living still.[83]

For my grandchildren

CHAPTER 17

Advice as Epilogue

Arnold Toynbee did *not* coin the phrase that has often been attributed to him, namely "history is just one damned thing after another." The distinguished British historian knew better. He had too much respect for history. In fact, he devoted twelve volumes to his book, *The Study of History.*

In *Civilization on Trial*, Toynbee wrote that "civilizations, I believe, come to birth and proceed to grow by successfully responding to successive challenges. They break down and go to pieces if and when a challenge confronts them which they fail to meet."[1]

As it is with civilizations, so it is with people. We must respond to challenges or we fail. I have always been competitive. I have sought to meet my challenges and to help others to meet theirs. Growing up in a commercial family, I learned to respect hard work, thrift, competition, and success. Growing up in the world, I was influenced by generations of mentors and teachers.

What I here attempt is to summarize the maxims which have guided my life, and to some extent will guide those of my children, grandchildren, and great-grandchildren. With any luck, they will also guide Americans in the future. A great life, after all, must add up to more than just one damn thing after another.

WORK, WORK, WORK

At Rite Aid, I was always citing the example of Mr. Lincoln. If our team would make a mistake or suffer a loss, I'd quote Mr. Lincoln from election night in November 1858: "It's a slip, not a fall."[2]

"Work, work, work, is the main thing," was Abraham Lincoln's advice to a young lawyer. Work can make up for natural disadvantages. To my children and the children of family friends, I would cite Mr. Lincoln's advice constantly. My wife Louise suffered gladly under that phrase . . . just as I had suffered gladly under my mother's "Be that as it may." After all, one translation of my mother's aphorism might be: "Quit complaining, and get back to work."

All through school, my children were interested in getting good grades. I would often tell them the story of Mr. Lincoln who gave advice to a young man starting out as a lawyer. In the middle of the 1860 presidential campaign, Mr. Lincoln wrote to J. M. Brockman: "Yours of the 24th. asking 'the best mode of obtaining a thorough knowledge of the law' is received. The mode is very simple, though laborious, and tedious. It is only to get the books, and read, and study them carefully. Begin with Blackstone's Commentaries, and after reading it carefully through, say twice, take up Chitty's Pleadings, Greenleaf's Evidence, & Story's Equity in succession. Work, work, work, is the main thing."[3] The truth bears repeating.

Whenever the kids wanted advice from me about their homework or grades, I told them I'm not so much interested in whether you get an A or a B, just as long as you get an A for effort . . . because Mr. Lincoln said, "work, work, work!" I continue to drum that maxim into any young person who will listen. It's one of those sharp truths which are boring to young people because they think there's got to be an easier way.

It may not be easy, but it is simple. In 1969, I offered a kind of paraphrase of Lincoln's original advice to my nephew, writing: "The system is a very simple one. Work your ass off. Master your subjects and go into every test well prepared. Such a procedure will result in an A average."[4]

Five decades later, I wrote another young relative: "Work hard, select the best teachers, and you will come out a most educated man."[5] I was consistent when I wrote another relative: "Given your focus and hard work, you will be successful. There will be many ups and downs but primarily onward and upward."[6]

I wrote one of my teenagers then away from home at school: "You will discover much about yourself in the next year or two, much about your goals, much about the world. . . . But in all your discovering, never forget the stones from which your foundation was built; never forget the unremitting labor with which you and your family toiled with these stones; never also forget the great houses you have yet to build to fulfill your promise, to develop your talents, to avail your own world of the great gifts you have received from the Lord."[7]

The theme was never exhausted. To another nephew I wrote "you have the knowledge, more importantly, the passion, even more decisive, the desire to work, work, work."[8] In my letters to my children, I urged them: "Do your best even though the full motivation is not there because of self-interest. . . . Motivation comes also from virtue—that is: do a good job for its own sake."[9]

SET GOALS AND A PATH TO REACH THEM

My grandfather had no assets and no English when he arrived by ship to New York in 1896 at sixteen years old. He boarded at first with a family relation, another "Louis Lehrman" in Brooklyn.

A decade later he had married and owned a store in Steelton, Pennsylvania. Another decade later, he had saved enough to start a wholesale business. His was the classic immigrant success story. He did well, but he also did good. Not only his family, but his community benefitted.

When his Brooklyn benefactor and namesake died in 1917, my grandfather helped to take care of his family. It was that kind of benevolence with which he would mark his life. Grandfather endured much—including the mental illness of his wife—but he persevered to raise three children, created a prosperous business, and left a legacy of generosity and grace. I learned from my mother and grandfather to be a gentleman.

In 1977, I set my own eyes on the governorship of New York. Over the next five years, I patiently laid the groundwork for what I knew would be an unlikely undertaking. I had no name recognition and no political office. What I had was a vision and a will. My rivals had their own assets and resources. Still, I think my example taught my children to "pursue your dreams," as all my children would acknowledge.

This "will" I had was often touched on in various campaign articles.

"In our discussion, we found out one of the things that has made him tick and be so successful," wrote *Suffolk Life*'s David Willmott. "Where others see problems, he sees opportunities. What others see as impossible, he says, 'can do.' . . . He is approaching his bid for the governorship with the same style and substance."[10]

My habits for success and drive were not always well understood. The *New York Post*'s Arthur Greenspan called it a "zeal that some observers feel borders on obsession."[11] I was the "type of business executive you read about in *Fortune* magazine and grimace," as Judy Watson of United Press International had observed during the campaign. "Lehrman rises at 4:30 a.m., jogs, and breakfasts lightly while scanning several newspapers. By 8 a.m., he's doing business over a second breakfast. Of course, it's early to bed."[12]

On the whole, however, I think people respected my effort. Maurice Carroll said my "impressive debut in big-time politics reflects one of his salient characteristics: single-mindedness. His decision to enter politics came, he says, after he had spent 13 years at Rite Aid and become a millionaire at least 50 times over." "'I was approaching 40," I told Maurice, "'I believed that with financial independence there were other things I could do.'"[13]

There will be roadblocks, potholes, and detours along the way. The key is to maintain focus on your goals. In 1855, Mr. Lincoln advised another aspiring attorney: "Always bear in mind that your own resolution to succeed is more important than any other one thing."[14] When young men sought his advice, he always put the power in *their* hands. For example, in 1858, he wrote yet another aspiring attorney: "If you wish to be a lawyer, attach no consequence to the place you are in, or the person you are with; but get books, sit down anywhere, and go to reading for yourself. That will make a lawyer of you quicker than any other way."[15]

"We grow or die," I have told my children. Aim high. Ambition to succeed is a virtue. Eliza remembers my message this way: "Stay committed to what you are good at, and become an expert."[16] Thomas highlighted one of my other favorite principles, saying "There are those who work out of necessity, and others who work out of a desire for excellence. Always seek excellence in your work. Do not measure the success of a man by how much money or material wealth he has made or created. True success lies in helping others through work and service."[17]

Lindsley, Harvey B, photographer. Portrait of Harriet Tubman. New York. Courtesy of the Library of Congress Prints & Photographs Division.

Harriet Tubman: "Never lost a passenger"

Gilder Lehrman Institute of American History, GLC06391.20_0

Sojourner Truth: Well-named Black woman first to sue a white man, and win in court

FIND MODELS FOR YOUR LIFE AND LEARN FROM THEM

My earliest models other than my family members were found in the classroom—teachers such as Elsie B. Diven and Garrett Greene. I later found my models in business, politics, and history. I admired entrepreneurs like John D. Rockefeller Sr. and railroad tycoon E. H. Harriman. Rockefeller built one of the great empires of business history. I read his two-volume biography by Allan Nevins, and applied some of the lessons of his career to Rite Aid.

Innovative businessmen built chain stores like Kresge and Woolworth, and today Sam Walton of Walmart. The first chain grocery store was built by Huntington Hartford. These men succeeded because they had good ideas and executed them well. They also provided models for me which I used at Rite Aid.

I found other models in English history like Benjamin Disraeli, who "climbed the greasy pole" of politics until he occupied No. 10 Downing Street. I admired the way that Winston Churchill also climbed that greasy pole over four decades, slipping on occasion, but never giving up. They were slips, not falls.

I was impressed by General Washington's courage and coolness under pressure. He had both resilience and derring-do. And he had the character to match.

I admired the courage and persistence of women like abolitionists Harriet Tubman, and Sojourner Truth. Similarly, I admired the strength and gumption of suffragettes like Susan B. Anthony, who persisted year after year until women's suffrage became the law of the land a dozen years after her death. As Anthony famously declared: "Failure is impossible."[18]

PERSEVERE WITH PATIENCE AND GRIT

You must play your part—recognizing that special something which is your "great thing" to pursue. Having set your goal, persevere no matter how great the obstacles. The process is intuitive rather than analytic.

You have to know how to lose as well as win. To the son of a friend, I wrote: "I have observed you and I am confident that you know how to win and to lose. And that you will get stronger and more confident as the years go by. . . . The game of life is played for the long run. Very often the people who looked good in one game, or with one girl, don't look very good when they get much older and that's what you should be interested in—playing the game of life for the long run."

From monetary history, I knew that a new gold standard would require a president ready to take executive action. That never happened, but I never gave up. I learned, however, that my reach was farther than my command.

Obstacles arise and obstacles must be overcome. "Remember, every CEO goes through crises of personal confidence, especially when there are big setbacks," I wrote to one young colleague. "You should have absolutely no doubts about your executive ability to build this enterprise. You have prevailed through the crisis. Banish the doubts."[19]

In June 1862, President Lincoln took the time to write West Point cadet Quintin Campbell, the son of Mary Lincoln's cousin: "Your good mother tells me you are feeling very badly in your new situation. Allow me to assure you it is a perfect certainty that you will, very soon, feel better—quite happy—if you only stick to the resolution you have taken to procure a military education. I am older than you, have felt badly myself, and know, what I tell you is true. Adhere to your purpose and you will soon feel as well as you ever did. On the contrary, if you falter, and give up, you will lose the power of keeping any resolution, and will regret it all your life. Take the advice of a friend, who, though he never saw you, deeply sympathizes with you, and stick to your purpose."[20]

Mr. Lincoln himself had persevered from an unpromising start in life in the backwoods of Indiana. "There I grew up," he said. "There were some schools, so called; but no qualification was ever required of a teacher, beyond 'readin, writin, and cipherin,' to the Rule of Three. If a straggler supposed to understand latin, happened to so-journ in the neighborhood, he was looked upon as a wizzard. There was absolutely nothing to excite ambition for education. Of course when I came of age I did not know much. Still somehow, I could read, write, and cipher to the Rule of Three; but that was all. I have not been to school since. The little advance I now have upon this store of education, I have picked up from time to time under the pressure of necessity."[21]

NURTURE SINCERITY AND TRUST . . . AND THEREBY INFLUENCE

I learned a lot by watching my mother and grandfather. Grandpa took everyone seriously. When he was asked to help, he was there. I learned the virtue of sincere charm. You want partners and colleagues to want you around because you are likable. Treat coworkers as true colleagues. Get to know them. Take a sincere interest in them and their families, and they will stay with you through life, especially the hard knocks.

You have to demonstrate sincerity. But the only way to come across as sincere is *to be sincere*, like Mr. Lincoln. Sincerity is fundamental, I advised one young friend. "You and I must always work hard to get rid of our impatience and harshness; but when we hurt people, then we must realize it and make *sincere* amends. . . .You have done that; and it makes me confident that you can be and will be a really big person."

On Washington's Birthday in 1842, Mr. Lincoln observed in one of his great speeches that "a drop of honey catches more flies than a gallon of gall. So with men. If you would win a man to your cause, first convince him that you are his sincere friend. Therein is a drop of honey which catches his heart, which, say what he will, is the high road to his reason, and which, when once gained, you will find but little trouble in convincing his judgment, or to command his action."

I learned to remember names. Jonathan Clark was a fellow Yalie, one year ahead of me. He became a managing partner at America's first-class law firm, Davis Polk. During the campaign, he asked me down to meet with the law partners. As I walked in, he introduced me to each partner, individually. When the meeting was over, I said goodbye to everybody by name, with a personal word. It made a big impression on Jonathan, who always reminds me about this story whenever we get together. People will never forget the fact that you do not forget their names.

"In 1982, twenty-two years after we graduated from Yale," recalled my former roommate Marty Gibson, "you were campaigning for New York State's Governorship . . . you made a stop in Corning, New York, where Ginger and I were living when I was with Corning Glass. Ginger went to a political luncheon. She did not realize you were the guest of honor and was shocked to see you give a stemwinder of a speech. Afterward, she approached you, your first words were: 'Ginger Taylor—what are you doing here?'"

Jonathan Clark: All-around athlete and distinguished lawyer

My sincere attempts to connect with everyone did not go unnoticed or, thankfully, unappreciated. Phil Hamilton was part of the annual ISI Summer Institutes at Princeton every year, where I would attend and participate. "Lew would also always mingle with the fellows," he remembered, "before and during the lunches and dinners. And the fellows always appreciated both his generosity as well as his graciousness. In these conversations, Lew would always ask them about their careers to date, their research interests, etc. As always, he listened closely to their answers and asked specific follow-up questions about their scholarly interests, their institutions, or their specific approaches to teaching."[22]

Keeping in touch with those you meet is another important demonstration of your sincere interest in their lives. Andrei Bogolubov was both amused and impressed by my methods, writing that his first job at CFA was to help produce letters and other communications in the wake of Lew's travels.

> Every CFA activist, donor, GOP official, and member of the media he met along the way received a personal letter of thanks. When I became Lew's executive assistant, I learned that he produced a steady stream of correspondence written by hand in bold strokes of a marker on postcard stationery so thick you could panel your house with it. We dispatched countless of these "Lew-grams," often attached to articles, to a remarkably eclectic array of correspondents. Robert Mundell the economist. Wall Street titans Julian Robertson and Barton Biggs, American politicians, foreign intellectuals, a Carmelite nun, police officers, and a host of New Yorkers who supported his gubernatorial campaign and simply stayed in touch.[23]

Ultimately, sincerity is rooted in the truth, and in being honest. Deja Hickcox still remembers a time early in her tenure when she answered the phone:

> It was someone with whom [Lew] spoke frequently and fondly. When I went in to tell him who it was, he didn't want to talk to the person. Not knowing what to say, I picked up the caller, and told them that he was out of town. After I hung up, [Lew] called me into his office, having heard the whole exchange because my desk was right outside of his office. He gently, but with all seriousness said, "Oh no, you've made a mistake. You didn't tell the truth. Never miss a chance to tell the truth." . . . In that moment, I felt so very guilty about not having been truthful, especially to one of Lew's friends, but it is a lesson that sticks with me to this day, some 15 years later, and I say it all the time to my child and their friends. I thought it was such a simple way to put such an important lesson: "Never miss a chance to tell the truth."[24]

DO THE RESEARCH

When I wanted to master economics, I read the masters—Aristotle, Augustine, Aquinas, Adam Smith, Alexander Hamilton, Jean-Baptiste Say, John Maynard Keynes, Charles Rist, Jacques Rueff, Robert Triffin, Henry Hazlitt, and Joseph Schumpeter among others. Few people have any idea that economics has such a long history. But without that history, the citizen is lost, often at the mercy of the unhinged abstractions of modern intellectuals.

When I wanted to master Lincoln, I read all nine volumes of Basler's *Collected Works of Abraham Lincoln three times* over a period of thirty years. I didn't just read. I studied, especially given those volumes amount to the autobiography of the man himself. I read Basler the way I read Rueff. If you work hard enough, you can master any subject.

As a young stock picker, I learned to do my research. I was always interested in the details. Your eye can catch a detail that is especially important to you, and not to others.

"Yours will be a great future," I wrote to a young friend. "Preparing for vocation is similar to arriving at a busy corner with traffic going many ways. Make sure you look both ways before you step off the curb."[25]

TEACH AND MENTOR

As a student, I was lucky to have great teachers. I once aspired to teach full-time and got a taste of teaching at Yale and Harvard. But I learned that one did not need to be called "professor" to be a teacher. At Rite Aid, I was, in essence, the head teacher in charge of learning, and then teaching, how to open and operate our stores and business. In fact, I wrote the operating manuals for almost every department in the company after around 1968.

Julian Robertson, whom I met through Barton Biggs, was a mentor to many. In one of Morgan Stanley's big conferences, Barton asked me to give the keynote speech. Julian was there. We became very good friends. In 1980, he launched Tiger Management, and turned a couple bucks into a $22 billion asset management firm. Julian was a brilliant evaluator of people who launched the careers of several lions of Wall Street—such as Steve Mandel, Andreas Halvorsen, and my son Thomas Lehrman.

Josie and the Tiger, Julian Robertson

Lizzy Trotta: Ambitious for the good

All my life, I've consciously tried to be helpful to young people. A lifelong friend from Wall Street and the campaign days, Langdon Cook once wrote to me about his son, who had worked for me one summer at CFA. "[Young] Lang had a very educational and exciting summer working for Citizens for America when he was a student at Middlebury College. And he and you have maintained your own friendship, with you as a great mentor, following his writing career and sending him a congratulatory note from time to time, or contacting Lyn and me and asking us to pass on a good word from you."[26]

Anna Halpine of the World Youth Alliance remembers a trip to our Mechanicsburg farm in her early twenties. "I spent a weekend at the farm," she wrote, "where I shot clay pigeons for the first time. The first shot (my first ever) was a total miss. Lew came beside me and showed me how to hold the gun and aim. The next four pigeons were hit straight down the center. That memory captures so much of our relationship; his confidence, friendship and support has helped me to hit our targets."[27]

Frank Trotta's daughter, Lizzy, came and worked for me after school during her high school years. Lizzy is a talented, tenacious young woman, and recently I wrote to congratulate her on a promotion. She replied thoughtfully:

> [Y]ou have seen yourself as a student, particularly a student of history and the economy. But I have always seen you as a teacher. You taught me about hard work by giving me my first job at Lehrman & Co. While at Lehrman & Co. you taught me about the importance of research and planning. These lessons I have taken with me to every classroom and job I have been in since. But the most valuable lesson is how to treat people. I will never forget how kind you have been to me. Even with all you do, you were never too busy to stop what you were doing to greet me with a hug—hello—to take me to lunch to strategize about my college applications or my next internship, to send me a congratulatory note with every small success I had. You are a great man, a leader in our country, yet you were always generous with your valuable time, even giving it to someone who could do nothing for you in return.[28]

I tried to mentor others, including the young men and women hired as part of the teams we put together. My colleague at Ten Squared Chris Potter appreciated my efforts, saying "Lew was always teaching, always building something in other people." When Chris and I took a trip to Singapore together with my son Thomas, there were many "meetings and business discussions," he recalled. "But the part that I remember most was how carefully Lew spent his free time coaching and teaching Thomas."[29]

Chris also remembers being my student himself:

> In early 2000, as the dot-com bubble was bursting, I naively trusted two unscrupulous Canadian brokers and invested in several of their failing companies. This was a big judgement error on my part, and it cost Ten Squared a lot of money. When this all became clear during a meeting with one of these companies, Lew asked to meet with me privately afterwards. I remember sitting across from him and being surprised to not see anger or disappointment in his eyes. He had every right to be upset with me but there was none of that in his expression or his words. Almost anyone else would have unloaded on me. Not Lew. He spoke calmly, made sure we were on the same page, and that was that. His restraint was an incredibly generous act that was meant to teach instead of punish. When I think about this and the other times when Lew could easily have gotten impatient or dismissive with me, yet chose not to, those are the times when I learned the most from him. I know Lew is many things to many people, but at his core he is a teacher.[30]

On the occasion of my eightieth birthday, my longtime partner Frank Trotta, made a thoughtful toast in which he said:

> The lessons in business I have learned from you are orders of magnitude greater than I learned (or could have learned) at Columbia Business School. You have taught me so much—and not "strictly business." It inspired me watching you and Louise raise five very special children. The examples you have set "in every significant respect" made me a better parent and a better man.[31]

It is heartening to know my example was a good one for such a man as Frank Trotta.

Frank and Chris were not the only young colleagues on whom I hope I made a decent impression. Deja Hickcox and I worked closely together on the production of all of my books, among other projects. "Working with Lew," she reflected:

> I feel I've learned to become a better writer, more thorough in my follow through, and I've learned what it takes to get a job done—not being afraid to use a little "elbow grease." I also feel that Lew has such high standards and such high expectations for all of us that it forces us to be better people to ensure we live up to those expectations. His expectations of me, and of the staff here at the office, based on the workplace culture he has created . . . has made me organize myself in a way where I am best suited to try and meet those expectations. . . .[32]

Trish Blake, reflecting on her departure from the Lehrman staff when her husband's work relocated him, recalled feeling like I was being asked to leave my family.

> However, I soon discovered that my training in Washington, DC, New York, and Greenwich had prepared me well for the journey ahead. The lessons I had learned and experience I had gained as a result of my tenure with the Lehrman organization allowed me to forge ahead with confidence and competence—and have always caused me to look back with the most profound sense of gratitude, happiness and appreciation.[33]

My godson, the young John Britton, is the son of my closest friend and advisor. In April 1998, young John wrote about how he had launched Lafayette Street Fund:

> I began with four investors, each subscribing $100,000. Lew was one of those. I will never forget that vote of confidence in me. I remain, to this very day, grateful for that. Lew was also a great supporter of Select Equity Funds in general. His observations about partnerships and the business of investing in stocks was invaluable.[34]

John was a talented investor in his own right, and went on to become an incredibly gifted artist. He also now plays a significant role as chairman of the Finance Committee on the board of the Gilder Lehrman Institute of American History.

John Britton II: Artist of success

Teaching is a way to discover talent. In 1995, I was privileged to be invited to teach a Lincoln seminar at Gettysburg College. The most outstanding student of my Lincoln Seminar was a young woman named Sandy Skordrud. Sandy's senior thesis was on Lincoln's education, and its reflection in his writing. "I looked into how the books Lincoln read as a child and young adult shaped his writing style. When I was meeting with Lew to go over my research," she recalled, "he asked me what I intended to do with the rest of my life. That was quite a daunting question for a second semester senior. I told him I didn't want to be a lawyer and didn't think I was cut out to be a teacher, but wanted to do research."[35]

I told her I knew of something she might be interested in. "Lew asked for my resume. At the time, the internet was in its infancy, and I had no idea who he was or about the Collection."[36] I hired her on the spot. She joined the Gilder Lehrman Collection, then also in its infancy, and a few years later became its curator-in-chief, a position she holds to this day. She also went on to pioneer our unique Book Break program.

Sammy MacFarlane and I have enjoyed a close relationship since his teenage years when he began visiting and working at my farm each summer. I consider him an adopted godson. After one visit, Sammy wrote me:

Sammy MacFarlane: One of Sam Reeves's talented grandsons

Engraved by Alexander Hay Ritchie after the painting by Francis Bicknell Carpenter. Modified by Kathleen McQuaid Holdridge, KathodeRay Media.

First reading of the Emancipation Proclamation

> My great gains are the treasured lessons you've inspired that I will carry with me for many years. I've learned in my talks with you how to give someone your full attention and ask thoughtful questions. And I've learned in observing you how to seek a range of interests and pursue whatever they may be with passion and intention. Above all, I think of a quote from a man you know as well as any, which I believe perfectly exemplifies your spirit and a spirit I hope to equal—"I do the very best I know how—the very best I can; and I mean to keep on doing so until the end."[37]

This quote, from a famous statement of Abraham Lincoln on the futility of responding to criticism, reminds me that I, too, expect this, my own book, to be controversial. As Lincoln, said, immediately following the above, "If the end brings me out all right, what is said against me won't amount to anything. If the end brings me out wrong, ten angels swearing I was right would make no difference." Both of these priceless Lincoln aphorisms are from a book by Francis Bicknell Carpenter called *Six Months at the White House*. Carpenter was an artist, famous for his painting, *First Reading of the Emancipation Proclamation*. Later turned into an engraving by Alexander Hay Ritchie, it is one of my favorite Lincoln era images. See if you can spot the modification in this photograph of the engraving.

PREPARE AND PERSIST

Louise turned down my first marriage proposal. I did not give up, although I gave her space for a time. I persisted, and the rest is history.

Mr. Lincoln lost his first race for the State Legislature, his first two races for Congress, and two elections for US senator. Still, he persisted. In August of 1864, he advised General Ulysses S. Grant,[38] then besieging Richmond and Petersburg, Virginia: "Hold on with a bulldog grip, and chew and choke as much as possible."[39]

Inevitably, one will encounter difficulties. The test of character is how one handles those difficulties. As I wrote to a young friend: "There's much anguish and ecstasy in the successes and failures of business and investment. You should learn a little about these emotions early. Do not overdo it, or you will lose your peace of mind. Always remember, invest to the sleeping point."[40]

As I wrote to another: "I believe you are headed in the right direction. You continue to challenge yourself on the ski slopes and on the football fields. There, you will find that no man can stand against you when you are determined to win—but prepared to lose, and able to lose as gracefully as you are able to win."[41]

In 2013, I wrote still another godchild: "Do not waste time on all the 'gut' courses at college which enable young men to waste their time. Most of those young men have trouble getting jobs and I hope you will be well-prepared, ambitious, and a self-starter."[42]

Chris Potter was with me at a speech I gave in Washington. It was July of 2013, and I was emphasizing the importance of moving our policy objectives forward. Later, Chris remembered:

"In the Q&A someone asked a pessimistic question, something like 'how will anything ever get done given how ineffective Congress has become?' Lew took no time to answer sternly and confidently (which I wrote down word for word because it was such a great response), 'Things happen . . . Statesmen rise . . . Congress gets its act together.' Lew never had time for defeatism. It was 'march forward,' never 'backwards' or in place."[43]

Frank Trotta remembered that I gave the same advice after I sold all of my shares in Rite Aid. Never look back. For example, I do not advocate a "return" to the gold standard. Instead, I promote "going forward to gold." Indeed, my book *The True Gold Standard, A Monetary Reform Plan without Reserve Currencies* includes numerous improvements on all previous gold standards, as well as a commentary on why they are necessary which is based on modern statistical analysis and historical research. As Mr. Lincoln observed in his Second Annual Message to Congress: "The dogmas of the quiet past are inadequate to the stormy present."[44]

Gilder Lehrman Institute of American History, GLC07808.037_0

Ulysses S. Grant: Second-in-Command after Lincoln

After one of our regular lunches, I spoke with Anna Halpine about her work. She remembers our conversation this way: "Lew showed me his early portrait of Churchill, a man we both love. Believing then the trust and confidence he had confirmed in me, I promised what I can reiterate today: 'that we will fight on the beaches, in the cities, in the schools for the world, until we gain victory or die choking in our blood.' Lew is a man of valor; he has encouraged me in my moments of darkness and has been a true friend."[45]

I wonder if many people realize that Winston Churchill's most famous words on the subject of persistence, namely "Never give in," were originally spoken to students. The demands of teaching well brings out the best in people. It is an order of magnitude more difficult to teach well than to simply criticize. On October 29, 1941, in the midst of World War II, Prime Minister Churchill addressed the students of Harrow saying:

> You cannot tell from appearances how things will go. Sometimes imagination makes things out far worse than they are; yet without imagination not much can be done. Those people who are imaginative see many more dangers than perhaps exist; certainly many more than will happen; but then they must also pray to be given that extra courage to carry this far-reaching imagination.
>
> But for everyone, surely, what we have gone through in this period—I am addressing myself to the School—surely from this period of ten months, this is the lesson:
>
> Never give in. Never give in. Never, never, never, never—in nothing, great or small, large or petty—never give in, except to convictions of honour and good sense. Never yield to force. Never yield to the apparently overwhelming might of the enemy. . . .
>
> Do not let us speak of darker days: let us speak rather of sterner days. These are not dark days; these are great days—the greatest days our country has ever lived; and we must all thank God that we have been allowed, each of us according to our stations, to play a part in making these days memorable in the history of our race.[46]

PROMOTE AND KEEP TALENT

People work for me for a long time. No one works for me for a couple of years. Mary Shroy worked from 1964 to 1975. Carla Saunders worked from 1976 to 1985. Susan Tang began working on February 29, 1980, and has been with me ever since, now over forty years. Deja Hickcox has worked with me for seventeen years and is still with me. Steve Szymanski worked for twenty-five years, and Frank Trotta for thirty-five years before they each retired.

Jerry Shoemaker worked for me at the farm for twenty-five years. Tom and Sue Zerbe have been there for twenty years. Victor Arce has been with me for twenty-five years, and his wife Stella for about twelve.

In the midst of the Civil War, President Lincoln had a staff of four aides, sometimes just two. Most were young men under thirty whom he had mentored. Two of his most devoted assistants, John G. Nicolay and John Hay, went on to write a ten-volume biography of their boss.

It is important to treat people as colleagues. If they have children, look out for them—taking a sincere interest in them, writing references, understanding when they have a birth or death in the family, paying them well, never trying to cut corners. Phil Hamilton remembered some of my best practices from his time at CFA:

> One night I was working late on some project and, as soon as I was finished, I was supposed to bring it over to him at La Brasserie, the French restaurant across the street from CFA's office. I did as requested, and when I was shown to the table (where he was dining, I believe with Frank Trotta and Terry Henry), Lew insisted that I join them for dinner. I was thinking, this restaurant is several grades above my pay level, but I gladly joined them. Even though I was still

Gilder Lehrman Institute of American History, GLC05111.02.0112_0 and GLC05111.02.0114_0

John Nicolay and John Hay: Mr. Lincoln's chief secretaries

> relatively new to CFA and the junior-most member of the staff, Lew made sure to include me in all of the conversations and discussions. I don't exactly remember what specific topics we discussed, but I recall Lew's great kindness toward me.[47]

Andrei Bogolubov was also grateful for such moments of camaraderie and counsel at work, writing that our occasional chartered flights home were "the best part of my CFA experience. It was very cool for a young man to fly on a private jet. But more importantly, Lew would always talk to me for a while. In the darkened cabin, sharing a plate of sandwiches and a six pack of beer, we spoke of everything from the sublime to the ridiculous. I learned a lot from Lew on those flights that I will never forget."[48]

Ever since that time, he continued, Andrei has "counseled young people starting in their careers to focus on *who* you work for, and don't worry about the job title. And I tell them about the time I worked for Lew and what it meant to me as a professional and as a man."[49]

I've tried to hire quality people and establish a good relationship with everyone who works with me, where possible. I believe in setting a good example for employees, children, and grandchildren—and always to be a gentleman.

RETAIN YOUR CHARACTER AND PRINCIPLES

"The men who achieve the most are the men who learned and practiced the difference between right and wrong, hard work and idleness, courage and cowardice, determination and defeat," as I wrote to my godson. "The truly meaningful things, which you will come to respect because of your sound mind and sound body, are the products of character and effort."[50]

General Washington was a great man. Mr. Lincoln was a great man. I believe that being honorable is a prerequisite to being a great man. In his final debate with Stephen A. Douglas on October 15, 1858, Lincoln declared his view of honor, and the purpose to which he dedicated his:

> It is the eternal struggle between these two principles—right and wrong—throughout the world. They are the two principles that have stood face to face from the beginning of time; and will ever continue to struggle. The one is the common right of humanity, and the other the divine right of kings.[51]

Mr. Lincoln never abandoned that struggle.

Nothing is worth doing except honorable things. Your reputation for honorable conduct is all-important. It gives you the credibility to influence events without being a bully. Eliza distills my philosophy this way: "Dad taught me early on, you don't need to be remembered as being right, be remembered as doing the right thing."[52]

In notes he took for a law lecture, Mr. Lincoln concerned himself with the popular belief that lawyers are too often dishonest. His advice to aspiring young law students in response is priceless: "Let no young man choosing the law for a calling for a moment yield to the popular belief—resolve to be honest at all events; and if in your own judgment you cannot be an honest lawyer, resolve to be honest without being a lawyer. Choose some other occupation, rather than one in the choosing of which you do, in advance, consent to be a knave."[53]

Andrei Bogolubov developed a clear understanding of certain insights I had shared with him during our work together. When he wrote them down I was delighted. These distillations of principle are especially useful for the study of economics, but also generally applicable. I usually reserve such lessons for oral transmission, but Andrei did such a good job writing them down that I include them here for all.

"Lew once told me that all false priesthoods are opaque," Andrei began. "The false and the evil does indeed come packaged in concepts and words that are hard to decipher and require interpretation by an adept—a false priest. True priesthood is as plainspoken and clear as the Bible, the Declaration of Independence, or the speeches of Abraham Lincoln."[54] I had learned to beware false priesthoods from my study of Jacques Rueff, and I am pleased to see that his advice is not lost on others.

"All debts are repaid in the short term," Andrei also remembered me saying. "You start paying for what you do even if you think you got away without a cost. So if you do bad things, you will pay for them in misery, misfortune, guilt and despair. These are the wages of sin in the world which we pay on this earth well before we face a final judgment."[55]

Andrei found my teachings to be "profound lessons in life for a young man. To sort through the opaque and seek out the simple truths at the heart of things. To look for the clarity of the good, the true and the beautiful. And to cleave to these things in life because what you do matters greatly. You shall reap what you sow."[56]

In this way, one can live with a good conscience, and, as I observed in a 2007 speech at Princeton University, "The well-formed conscience is also the simplest, least expensive, and most efficient economic regulator of a free social order. In the end, a lasting free market order depends on the formation of right conduct deep in the character of each citizen."[57]

The importance of enduring values is the invisible thread connecting all of my life's work. Daniel Horowitz seized upon this aspect of my character for his book, *On the Cusp.* I don't know that I can summarize my commitments better than he did when he wrote:

> As a writer and activist, [Lehrman's] views in many ways resembled those of most conservatives, advocating as he did dismantling communist governments in order to expand freedom, defending free market capitalism, and opposing abortion. His most distinctive contributions came with his advocacy of the gold standard and the grounding of his politics in the writings of Abraham Lincoln. *What united Lehrman's commitment to Catholicism, the gold standard, and Lincoln is a belief in absolute, enduring values.*[58]

DON'T HESITATE AND DON'T WAIT

Careful readers might remember that during one of our anniversaries in London, Louise and I looked at seventeenth- and eighteenth-century American silverware. We saw a pair of Queen Anne candlesticks. They were perfect. I told Mr. Shrubsole that I would give him $50 as a deposit. I came back the next day, but they were gone. Someone had made a higher bid. When you see something that you really want and can afford, don't hesitate. And when you make a decision, stick to it. Don't hesitate, and don't wait.

I applied the same lessons to the development of the Gilder Lehrman Collection—and it is one reason why the Collection is so comprehensive and unique. When I called Dick Gilder to discuss the possibility of purchasing Jean-Antoine Houdon's bust of Thomas Jefferson, Dick had expressed his doubts. He had reminded me that we were predominantly a collection of documents, not statuary. But afterwards, Dick always delighted in remembering that after I hung up with him, I ignored him, and immediately arranged the purchase of the bust for $3 million. It was valued several years later for $12 million. I was simply applying the lesson I had learned on my honeymoon.

Nothing aggravated President Lincoln quite so much as generals who did not seize their opportunities. He gnashed his teeth when General George McClellan did not follow up his victory at Antietam in September of 1862. When General George Meade failed to follow up quickly after the Battle of Gettysburg, Lincoln composed, but wisely did not send this letter to him:

> You fought and beat the enemy at Gettysburg; and, of course, to say the least, his loss was as great as yours—He retreated; and you did not; as it seemed to me, pressingly pursue him; but a flood in the river detained him, till, by slow degrees, you were again upon him. You had at least twenty thousand veteran troops directly with you, and as many more raw ones within supporting distance, all in addition to those who fought with you at Gettysburg; while it was not possible that he had received a single recruit; and yet you stood and let the flood run down, bridges be built, and the enemy move away at his leisure, without attacking him.[59]

The president was much aggrieved. "Again, my dear general, I do not believe you appreciate the magnitude of the misfortune involved in Lee's escape—He was within your easy grasp, and to have closed upon him would, in connection with our other late successes, have ended the war—As it is, the war will be prolonged indefinitely."[60]

Lincoln was right. A failed opportunity meant the Civil War would continue for another twenty-one months. Huge numbers of men and women were lost from this oversight. He was also right, however, to withhold the letter, seeking neither to crush Meade's honor, nor to diminish his effectiveness to fight another day.

But opportunities disappear. It is vital to take advantage of them while they exist.

ALIGN INTERESTS

There was an alignment of interests with my partners throughout my career. I looked carefully at what was important to that partner, and was ready to compromise. I understood that relationships are important. Alignment is necessary so that one can understand what reasonable people will arrive at objectively. It is the basis for sound agreements and good partnerships.

With Bob Bartley of the *Wall Street Journal* and Barton Biggs of Morgan Stanley, I was aligned in challenging monetary orthodoxy.

Congressman Jack Kemp and I agreed on much, but he had his own agenda. In Jack's case, the misalignment was more personal, and so it was very difficult to overcome with compromise. With his erstwhile aide John Mueller however, our productive alignment of vision included the ability to work well together and a sense of mutual honor.

FIND THE RIGHT PARTNERS

We all need partners, whether in our personal or religious lives. From The Hill School onward, I found friends for life. I was fortunate at twenty-five to find the perfect partner for life in Louise Lombard Stillman.

In our professional lives, sometimes partners don't work out. In my research on the gold standard, my first writing partner did not work out. Luckily, my next writing partner was John Mueller, with whom I developed a relationship that has lasted four decades.

Our collaboration was fruitful in large part because between us we succeeded in reuniting two critical elements of the Rueff Model. Most of Rueff's earliest writings were groundbreaking analyses of the two greatest economic policy problems—inflation and unemployment. But during and after the Second World War, Rueff's great works focused primarily on the rigorous development of monetary theory, and trying to influence both domestic French economic policy and international monetary reform.

Through the vehicle of an economic and financial-market forecasting firm, John and I were able to test and illustrate Rueff's theories with empirical forecasts, thus reuniting the two major strands in Rueff's writings. For example, the main difference between the first and second editions of *The True Gold Standard* consists of several very specific appendices with charts done by Mueller. These charts show the close correspondence over the whole of American history between the greatest long-term price stability and the least year-to-year price volatility under the constitutional metallic monetary standards, silver and gold.

Similarly, Dick Gilder proved the perfect partner for our work on American history. I still miss him. I remember so fondly one of our exchanges during a 2000 interview, wherein we went back and forth. He started the conversation by saying:

> Back in the late sixties I had just started my investment firm, and Lew was then running the Rite Aid drugstore company. Some friends and I went down to Pennsylvania to view the company and meet the principals. We were impressed with Lew, so we bought some stock. I think I sold it about a month later. That was a bad mistake; it went a lot higher. Later, when Lew decided to move to New York, he was re-introduced to me by mutual friends, this time as a potential client. I recommended a stock, and Lew placed quite a nice order. About a month later the stock dropped ten points. Flinching, I called Lew to tell him, but he just said, "Why don't we buy some more?" So I realized he was a very superior fellow, with enough confidence in me to screw up not once but twice. After that we started comparing notes on a lot of things [and eventually, domestic politics].
>
> *Lehrman:* We grew closer in the seventies. I had established The Lehrman Institute for economic and foreign policy studies, and we believed in the same things. When I decided to run for governor of New York, one of the first people I went to was Dick. I remember, of all the friends and acquaintances I could gather, only three or four thought running for governor was a sane idea.

Gilder: I was not among them. [Laughs.]

Lehrman: Dick and I shared common beliefs. It was the age of Jimmy Carter, pessimism, malaise, stagflation, and Henry Kissinger and the theory of American decline. We wanted America to grow again.[61]

Over the years, Dick and I were able to build a partnership based on mutual understanding and trust. In Professor James Basker we discovered a full partner who enabled us to execute our vision. In Jim we also found the most outstanding intellectual partner we could have wanted. Through our partnership with Daniel Jordan, former head of Monticello, we learned how to transform ourselves into an organization with a broad base of support.

My Yale classmate, John Britton, was an ever loyal, ever thoughtful, trustworthy, ever wise colleague until his death far too young. His wise counsel often challenged my own ideas, but his analytical judgment was invaluable—at no time more than in 1976 when he was a confidential sounding board as I contemplated a shift from Rite Aid to an independent career. In his unique but direct style, he laid out the "four principal components:

1. Household
2. Institute (and other eleemosynary)
3. Asset Management
4. Politics[62]

John then went on to strategize what kind of a structure was necessary to support all these activities.

He also had a wonderful sense of wry humor. Once I asked him to be vice-chair on an important Catholic charitable committee. He wrote me back in June of 1981:

> Thank you for your nice letter about the Cardinal's dinner. It sounds like a very interesting and worthwhile affair. I will be happy to be Chairman of the Vice Committee, although I didn't realize that the Cardinal went in for that kind of thing at his dinners. Nevertheless, I suppose that what you must do to entertain people these days has changed like everything else. I will count on you to let me know the specifics of what you would like to have arranged. As you know, when they made me a limited partner, they limited my resources as well as my faculties.[63]

John signed off, "Your prickly, but devoted friend."

Partners sometimes need to be prickly. But when the package includes unshakeable honesty and delightful irony, that person should be embraced, especially when he is capable of both intellectual and financial audits. The other lesson here is always to understand humor and employ it. It helps to relax everybody.

I have been unusually fortunate in enterprising partners. President Lincoln found his "team of rivals" with which to conduct the Civil War. Winston Churchill constructed a coalition government with members of the Labour and Liberal parties. He kept in harness a coalition with an American president and a Russian dictator.

Good partners may be hard to find, and hard to manage, but they are well worth pursuing.

KEEP FAMILY FIRST

The greatest satisfaction that Louise and I have had has been raising five children and our grandchildren. When things go well, it is the most fulfilling of human acts. Our children are now between forty-three and fifty-three years of age. Nothing compares with seeing your children grow up into manhood and womanhood. My advice to them: "Marry well, and master the problems that inevitably crop up."

We forget family at our peril, as I reminded one son: "At eighteen years of age, one of the worst afflictions develops in each of us . . . And it is this: self-centeredness; forgetfulness of family; lassitude about communications especially with one's mother; a sense of self-sufficiency which can become 'hubris'; and the inevitable 'nemesis' which follows."[64]

During the days at Citizens for America, Andrei Bogolubov was struck by the fact that I "was not extravagant when we traveled for CFA. We flew economy class on outbound flights from New York or Washington. But on return flights, if commercial flights could not get us home until very late or only the next morning, [Lew] chartered a plane to get home to his family as soon as possible. On one such flight, Lew told me that not once in his life did he ever stop for drinks or to socialize after work before going home to his family. It was one of Lew's first principles of family—make them your priority."[65]

Mary MacKenzie, a longtime member of my staff, recognized this commitment as well. "To say that I have learned so much from you is an understatement," she began. "It is not only through your example of the importance of professionalism and integrity in business, but it is also through the importance of keeping family first."[66]

As a parent, you hope the example you set for your children makes an impression. My son Peter picked up the following: "Consistency of hard work, consistency of having a positive mood each day, the value of work and the value of money, humility, great manners. Mom and Dad never swore in front of us, always practiced great manners, and I learned a lot just by watching the way they handled themselves with friends and guests."[67]

Eliza also felt Louise and I were committed to family first. She said we had "the greatest integrity of any two people I have ever known. Their unshakable commitment to truth, hard work and to a life filled with honorable pursuit, no matter the direction, has had an indelible stamp on the development of my character."[68] My son Lee remembered a few other fortunate maxims: "As a writer, read your work out loud. As a businessman, respect those who have already made their mistakes."[69]

MAKE A LEGACY

Each of us finds our own guidelines for life. In my files from the late 1970s, I kept some guidelines for my own conduct:[70]

1. Set an example of what you expect from others.
2. Emphasize the future rather than the past or present.
3. Look for, and deal with, causes rather than symptoms.
4. Admit, and learn from making a mistake.
5. Don't pass the buck.
6. Consider both the long-run and short-run results.
7. Everyone involved should benefit.
8. Legal and ethical means should be used to achieve legal and ethical ends.
9. The dignity of every individual should be respected.
10. Try to understand others, and make yourself understood by them.

Looking back, I see that my marriage was everything. Without Louise, nothing could have been achieved. Personal growth comes in stages. In my case, the stages were early family life, followed by grade school in Harrisburg, boarding school at Hill, study at Yale, the Carnegie Fellowship, the Woodrow Wilson Fellowship at Harvard, the responsibility of building a business, marriage after two years of courtship, and five children.

The most important aspect was my marriage and building a family.

I hope that future generations will remember that I was an honorable man—hard working, focused entirely on the family, and holding myself to the highest moral standards.

Leland Lehrman: Pilgrim

CHAPTER 18

The Children and Grandchildren

R. LELAND LEHRMAN (BORN 1969)

A father's evaluation: *A story about pilgrim's progress. When he gets inspired, he is a fireball.*

I remember like yesterday the birth of our firstborn, Leland. I was on the road working when I got a call from Louise that the water had broken. I headed straight for the hospital. It was the pre-modern period in which fathers were not in the delivery room.

I waited in the reception room. Lee was very healthy, but Louise had had a typically hard labor. Thrilled by his birth, Louise used to call him "Punkin." Soon thereafter, I discovered that another arrival would come just as the first one lost his fuzzy hair.

Lee was precocious—an astonishingly effective student as a young man. He finished the collected works of Sherlock Holmes when he was a mere child of nine years old. He distinguished himself at Exeter. From the earliest days, he was interested in the Federal Reserve. He was engaged with and eager to discuss the world. We had wonderful talks about history, faith, and the stock market.

Lee also had a gift for language—as exemplified by the essay he wrote for an application to Yale. He was a great student. I was proud when he went out for lacrosse in high school—and learned the sport from scratch.

In 1985, Lee and I took a trip around Cape Cod on our bicycles. I had not kept up my conditioning and could not carry on by the third day. It was a wonderful trip, staying at bed-and-breakfasts, but I ended up in the hospital. Fortunately, I recovered quickly.

Lee spent a year at Eton in England, at the end of which I wrote a note to him in June of 1988 regarding what I told others asking after him: "He has a heavier beard than his father . . . He is much taller . . . He has mastered Eton . . .He has a much stronger aesthetic sensibility than I—music, painting, English studies . . . He is preparing for A levels and will do well, all things considered. He has developed no new bad habits, so far as I can tell . . . He is good looking when his hair is cut and brushed, when he stands up straight, and when he smiles . . . He is thoughtful, generous, and polite . . . He has a religious soul . . . I cannot wait until he comes home . . . ."[1]

A few years earlier we had toured England looking at schools and different landmarks. Lee and I will never forget those days, about which he remembered having "a beer or two in a beautiful old village, and then driving down the wrong side of the road in England somewhere. When we discovered our error, we quickly pulled off the road, and laughed until we cried."[2]

Lee's skills and interests had a wide bandwidth—from philosophy to painting to composing to farming. "Continue to study life and thought," I urged him, "not only from men and nature, but from the prose and poetry, from the scholarship that your spirit and intellect need for nourishment. . . . Exercise your writing muscle, your reading muscle, yes even your math muscle. Buy the *New York Times*, the *Wall Street Journal* from time-to-time and observe the world around you which you cannot see, but which you can know from reading deeply and widely and thinking on these things."[3]

"Manhood," I wrote him, "means understanding our dual nature for good and evil; for great things and small; for virtue and license; for the divine and the diabolical. But manhood also means understanding that *most* of life is *never* so dramatic. . . . Most of life is lived 'in between'; and by that I mean working hard; doing one's daily tasks on time; obeying small rules and deferring sometimes to fools; getting a job; marrying; daily work at raising children . . . I write this because, like me, you have a philosophical tendency! Philosophers dwell abstractly between the *Great* and *Small*. But real people live happily (and sadly) 'in between.'"[4]

Lee fulfilled his promise as a boy by learning to understand human nature. Acting on his understanding of the world, he had no time for investment success. He was after bigger game.

JOHN STILLMAN LEHRMAN (BORN 1970)

A father's evaluation: *John is happy most of the time in a canoe, and in the outback. He is a powerful and youthful man.*

After St. Paul's School where he played lacrosse, John went to the University of Montana to get a degree in wildlife biology. In 1987, Johnny and I went down the Colorado River in Arizona on a raft. Here, John was the teacher as we hiked the side canyons of the Grand Canyon. We learned from disaster as John remembered it—"surviving a wipeout boat launch portage on the Henry's Fork River that knocked our guide's tooth out."[5]

John taught me some of the basic skills of a woodsman. His first peer-like comment was: "Deal with it, Dad." We finished the trip by visiting Las Vegas—which neither one of us liked.

John and Louise went to Alaska and had a wonderful time. John found his calling as an outdoorsman. He was fascinated by natural history and has been dedicated to passing on his passion and skills to others. For twenty seasons, John worked as an instructor and manager at the Keewaydin Camps in Northern Canada. He is the epitome of modesty and humility.

Johnny made me proud when he built a backcountry ski chalet named Downing Mountain Lodge from scratch. This Montana lodge overlooks the Bitterroot Valley through which Lewis and Clark traveled in 1805 on their expedition to the Pacific.

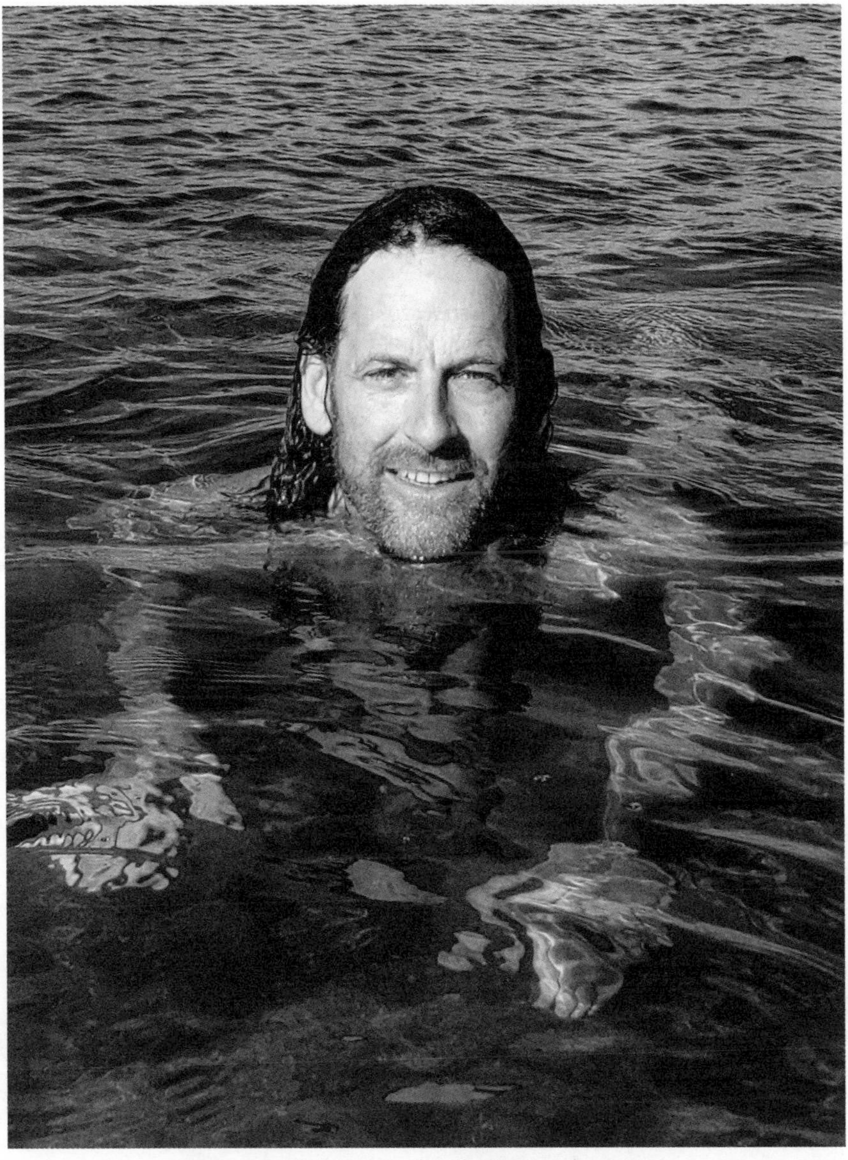

John Lehrman: Gentle as a lamb, all-around skier

Johnny has served as head guide at Bitterroot Backcountry Ski Guides and was also appointed as a National Park Service guide.

THOMAS DUDLEY LEHRMAN (BORN 1972)

A father's evaluation: *All-around athlete, and classic success story.*

Thomas was, like all of my children, a good-looking lad; and he was nursed as were all of our children by his mother. But it quickly became obvious that something was wrong with Thomas. He couldn't hold down his food and he began to lose weight. It was clear that he was starving, and we were mystified. The doctors could not diagnose what was wrong with him. We took him to specialists and they were mystified. He was shrinking before our very eyes.

One night, Louise poked me in the ribs and she said, "Hey, Lew, here it is. Thomas has pyloric stenosis." I said, "Pyloric what?" She said, "Thomas has pyloric stenosis. That is why he is starving, why he cannot hold down his food. There is this muscle between his small intestine and his stomach which has closed off so he cannot digest food. Nutrition does not find its way into his body."

I said, "How do you know that?" She said, "It says so right here in this book." And indeed, I read it and it seemed like Louise was right.

When we took Thomas to the hospital, he was twenty-three weeks old. There, his condition was diagnosed as . . . pyloric stenosis. He was operated on immediately, and today he thrives. In fact, he is a veritable hurricane of activity.

An expert didn't define his condition and save his life. Louise, in all of her wisdom, and with the intuition of natural motherhood, perceived it and remedied it.[6]

Thomas Lehrman and family: Swinging for the fences, prudently

Thomas was both a survivor—and a thriver. He learned his work habits by observing Louise and me at work. He distinguished himself at Groton where he was quarterback of the football team, center middie on the lacrosse team, and starting left wing on the hockey team. Like Lee, he also got good grades on the academic side of his life.

For our father and son trip, we decided to go to Scotland and Paris. We played a little golf and a lot of tennis. "We golfed Scotland's Gleneagles and had to turn back after running out of balls by the sixth hole," recalled Thomas. "While Dad was always a ball player, somehow golf never made it onto the list of preferred sports."[7]

In truth, we were both bored by golf. We took just one lesson. Thomas announced: "Dad, it's time to go to Paris," and off we went. In Paris we saw the entire Louvre in one day by trotting from one painting to another. We did not have a lot of time for art, either. In Paris, we met some of my friends including Paul Fabra and Passerose Rueff-Pigeat, the daughter of Jacques Rueff.

In 1998 Thomas founded the Gerson Lehrman Group after majoring in history at Duke University, and working for two years at Tiger Management. After graduation from Yale Law School in 2004, and service as director of the Office of WMD Terrorism in the State Department, Thomas returned to New York where he started mentoring and investing in early-stage entrepreneurs. This work eventually led to the formation with two partners of Teamworthy Ventures, a seed to growth-stage venture investment firm. During the fall of 2022, he was a visiting lecturer at Yale Law School where he taught the course Networks, Law, and Entrepreneurial Strategy. Along the way, he has devoted himself to advancing educational opportunity by cofounding the first public charter school in Brooklyn and serving on two other charter school network boards, as well as on the boards of various other Catholic and independent educational institutions.

He has also picked up his father's interest in natural philosophy and history, studying both the doctors of the Church and the most eclectic of the modern schoolmen.

ELIZA DISOSWAY LEHRMAN (BORN 1975)

A father's evaluation: *Eliza is best on a horse, and when inspired she can do anything.*

Eliza was a driven young woman who was tagged "Eliza Do-a-lot." When she was at Brearley School she had a project to research a public figure. She created a traditional scroll out of the entire life of President Ronald Reagan. I was so impressed with the scroll and her illustrations that I personally handed it to the president. President Reagan responded with a gracious, handwritten letter:

> Thank you very much for my pictorial biography and for choosing me as the subject of your school assignment. I am honored.
>
> Eliza, you might know this but when a President leaves office, there is a Presidential library & museum in his name. All his official papers and photos & mementos are displayed there. Your scroll will be in that museum.

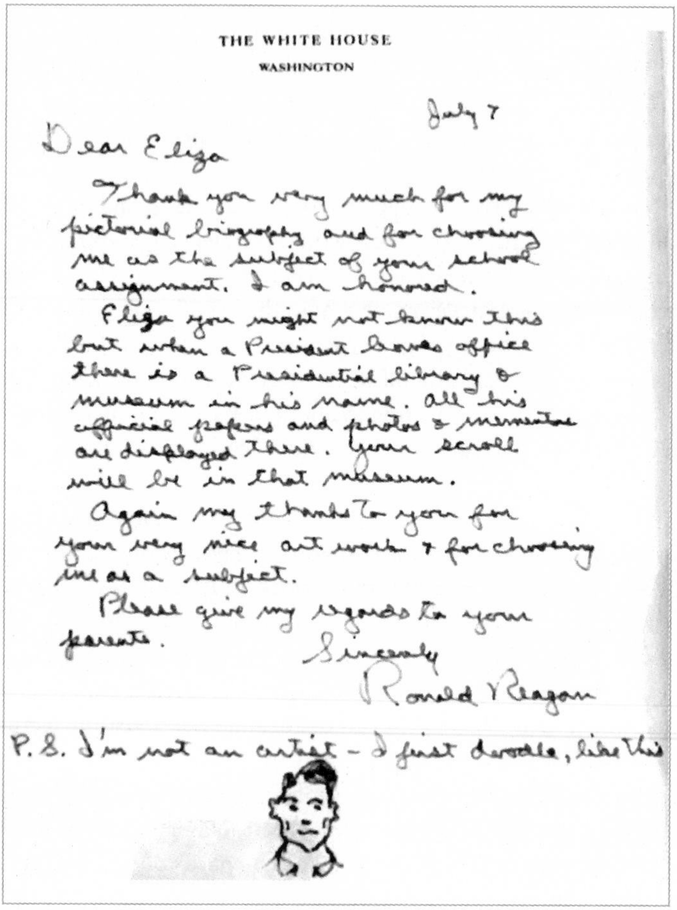

THE WHITE HOUSE
WASHINGTON

July 7

Dear Eliza

Thank you very much for my pictorial biography and for choosing me as the subject of your school assignment. I am honored.

Eliza you might not know this but when a President leaves office there is a Presidential library & museum in his name. All his official papers and photos & memento are displayed there. Your scroll will be in that museum.

Again my thanks to you for your very nice art work & for choosing me as a subject.

Please give my regards to your parents.

Sincerely
Ronald Reagan

P.S. I'm not an artist – I just doodle, like this

Letter from President Ronald Reagan to Eliza

Again, my thanks to you for your very nice artwork and for choosing me as a subject.

Please give my regards to your parents.

Sincerely,

Ronald Reagan

P.S. I'm not an artist—I just doodle, like this.[8]

Eliza and I signed up for a twelve-day horse ride in Ireland for our father-daughter trip. "The day trips were a solid six-plus hours on horseback," she recalled. "At this time, Dad was in his marathon shape, but he also would have some back soreness from too many hours in the saddle. So I would set out on horseback with the group from one [bed-and-breakfast] to the next, and Dad would run the distance and meet me there!"[9]

I remember not going on one ride because it was raining. I don't like being wet. But Eliza toughed it out the whole time. She is a very tough-minded girl, rain or shine.

Eliza out West

Of all the children, Eliza has the best work habits. She has been working to the limit of her capacity since she went to Brearley. Eliza was a fine athlete; her championship sport is show jumping. She professionalized her horsemanship at Garrison Forrest, where she received her secondary education before going on to Penn State, and then graduating from the University of Virginia.

Eliza began riding as a baby when she was just six months old. I carried her in the saddle in front of me. I would walk, trot, and canter, and she was never afraid. She has become an accomplished horsewoman, regularly competing at the Grand Prix level, maneuvering high up in the Olympic orbit. Although the boys were interested, active sportsmen, only Eliza is a professional competitive athlete.

Eliza Lehrman: Champion

As an adult, Eliza found both her profession and her husband, Filip de Wandel, on the show jumping circuit. Together, they founded Five Way Farm to train and sell show jumping horses.

Eliza's self-confidence is reflected in my memory of her decision to move to Europe. As I remember those fleeting years gone by, one unforgettable vision of Eliza emerges. I now draw down this vision from memory, wherein it has lingered long. A remembrance of things past—that special day was peopled by Louise and Eliza, but few others—it comes back to me clearly now, cast in the dialogue of the moment:

The curtain opens—

"Mom, Pop, I am moving to Belgium."

"Oh, yes, uh, of course; Belgium . . . Yes . . . but what will you do there? You have a flourishing horse business, here . . . in America."

"Pop, I'm taking my horses to Belgium . . ."

"Uh—yes, of course . . . horses to Belgium . . .—But how in the world will you do that, Eliza?"

"Mom, Pop—Come see me off. I depart June 15. I leave from Coker Farm . . ." *Exit Eliza*

I look then at Louise. "Oh goodness, all the way to Belgium? . . . How will she safely move all those horses? They are very valuable, easily injured . . . How will they be supervised, crossing an ocean, moving through many foreign borders, among hostile bureaucrats manning the crossings?"

June 15 arrives. We go to see Eliza at the stable. There she stands, booted and shirted for work—in the horse stalls—with a trucker at her side, a hearty man twice her size. They move toward an immense tractor trailer. Now they load each horse. I am told by the groomsman that the driver will go to the airport.

Whereupon I ask Eliza:

"Who will supervise these horses in the air and then transport them deep into the countryside of Belgium?"

Setting her boots, with that determined assurance, for which she is justly famous: "Pop, I do . . . I supervise them."

"But how do you do that?"

"I ride shotgun on the tractor-trailer. I load the horses into steerage on the cargo plane, each into his stall space. Then I mount the airplane with the horses. I fly with them; I sleep with them; I unload them upon arrival; I truck with them—the cheapest way—into Holland, then I cross the border into Belgium."

"There, I arrive safely—Filip de Wandel awaiting me—with Lena, with Antoine, and his sisters."

I look at Louise. I do suppress a lump in my throat. But there came no sympathy from my intrepid bride of fifty-seven years. Louise, of course, would do the very same thing—even today.[10]

Peter Lehrman: Iron Man

PETER RUEFF LEHRMAN (BORN 1979)

A father's evaluation: *Peter is hot on Thomas's trail, the daredevil of the family, whether it be waterskiing or mastering the mechanics of the motorcycle. Peter also has very promising children: early to bed, early to rise, doing homework promptly. Hard work in between.*

I clearly remember it. Louise and I were walking home to Park Avenue and 73rd Street. Out of the blue, she announces, "by the way, we're going to have another baby." I was surprised. She was already three months pregnant, but I hadn't noticed. Louise thought I wasn't quite with it.

Peter was still in a stroller when we visited Jackson, Wyoming, to ski. Not ready for the slopes, he surveyed his surroundings. Pointing to a Labrador retriever, much like the ones we had at home, I still remember Peter saying, "Big black doggy over there who is my friend." We always had Labradors at home, and they really are very friendly.

Peter was the last one out of the house. Every night after dinner, we would go to our favorite confectionery store. Every night, we would race all the way—until he finally beat me. I remember noticing that he really was an athlete. Just this past summer, in 2022, Peter completed the Ironman Triathlon in Lake Placid—4.8 miles swimming, 112 miles biking in the mountains, and a full marathon to finish. And he was smiling all the way.

Louise and I were fortunate to have him home in Greenwich where he finished his secondary education at The Brunswick School. Although fairly casual in grade school, he became an outstanding student at the University of Virginia. After five years as an executive at the Gerson Lehrman Group, Peter went to Stanford Business

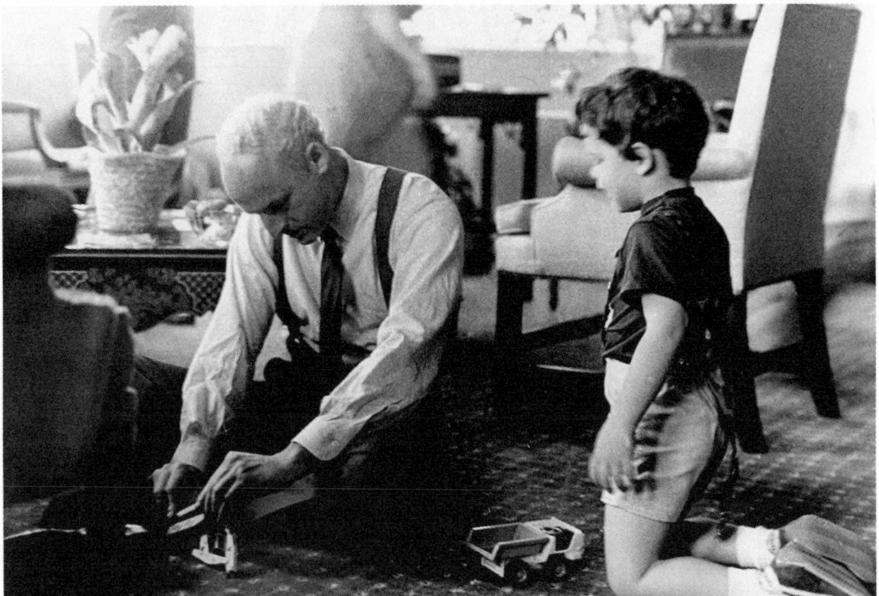

Peter Pumpkin playing

School in 2006. After graduation in 2008, Peter founded Axial Markets, a business-to-business platform connecting companies with sources of capital.

I must say I was touched when he sent me this note in 2019:

"The breadth of your life is far and away the most astonishing accomplishment. To have excelled so significantly in so many parts of your life—work, family, politics, public service, philanthropy, Lincoln, five children, Mom, academic distinction, writing books, gold, monetary policy, investing, personal fitness and marathoning—For me it's the breadth of achievement that is so inspiring."[11]

What can I add to such an outstanding preferment?

THE GRANDCHILDREN

Lincoln Eliot Lehrman

His initials are the same as mine: LEL. It was planned that way. His father, Peter, told me he will be known as LEL the Second. He's a healthy boy, now two years of age. With his father's encouragement, he's already riding a motorcycle as his father and Uncle Thomas did before him. The motorcycle is plastic, but it has fast wheels, and he can go down the hill at their house. I saw it with my own eyes—and at a rate of speed that would raise the hair on your head.

Sadie Louise Lehrman

Sadie Louise is a beautiful child, with wide blue eyes and a gentle manner. Dreamy and imaginative, playful and gently courageous, she is named in part for her

Fifteen grandchildren

grandmother Louise. She has also followed her grandmother's footsteps into the fifth generation of Brearley School students.

Caroline Louise Marjorie Lehrman

Caroline Louise is named for her grandmothers on both sides of the family. Caroline is a very bright child, and she finds great joy in writing. She reads at the level of a fifth grader, though she is actually but a charming, sweet eight-year-old. She is very playful, and she loves her grandfather, too.

Reed Wadsworth Lehrman

Reed is named for the Wadsworth family from whom Eve Auchincloss Wadsworth, Peter's wife, stems. It is fitting that our families should be so related, as William Watson Wadsworth was a hero to all of us. Reed is a sensitive child and uncommonly risk-taking. He's always been sympathetic with me because he knows I'm struggling with Parkinson's. He is at the Buckley School, where his father went before him through the eighth grade.

Lawrence Baudoin Lehrman

Lawrence's middle name comes from King Baudoin of Belgium with whom the Grace family of his mother Mara was very close. Mara spent a year living with them in Belgium as a young girl. They treated her as family, and she wanted to recognize them in a salient manner by naming Lawrence a Baudoin. He is thoughtful and a sweetheart, loves sports and music, and is kind to everyone.

Eleanor Auchincloss Lehrman

Eleanor is the first child of Peter Rueff, whose own name is taken from the friendship Louise and I had with Jacques Rueff. Eleanor has become very close to her brother Reed. They are happy together, and don't necessarily need any company. Mischievous and bright, she loves to joke around, and has fun with everything, especially gymnastics.

Forest Radovan Lehrman

Forest is the fourth of Leland's clan. He is unusually bright and sets a torrid pace for all of Lee's children. He is especially interested in science. If we have any grandchild involved in space travel, Forest will be that man. He is modest, unassuming, and a good-looking boy. He is already taller than his father who is six feet tall. He gets the top grades at the Waldorf School he attends in Massachusetts and has just finished building his own computer, his sights set on MIT.

James William Lehrman

James's middle name comes from William Grace, the name of his grandfather. He is a natural at sports and enjoys a good debate. He played competitive tennis at a young age and is now close to a scratch golfer. He's a scrappy fellow who also loves to fish and hunt.

Jasmine Lehrman

Jasmine is named for the sweet-smelling flower, and she certainly is sweet. She is the third child of Leland and Vera, and she loves to track and fish. She can even catch a trout with her bare hands. She's happy alone in the woods, pecking her way to a living, and thrives in the summer when she becomes a camp counselor at Woodland Ways in upstate New York.

Isabel Grace Lehrman

Isabel is the second of Mara and Thomas Lehrman's clan. She is a beautiful girl, loves the theater, and excelled in English and theology in high school. She was involved in the school play every year at Sacred Heart, where she played the roles of Cardinal Richelieu and Mr. Wormwood. She also captained the varsity tennis team and helped to start the Sacred Heart Hockey Program. Now at Duke, she's very mature, and has very similar study habits to her Aunt Eliza. She's disciplined and gets good grades.

Rose Lida Lehrman

Rose is the second child in Leland and Vera's clan. She graduated with honors and every department award from the Interlochen School for the Arts in Michigan. The school concentrates on a general curriculum and specializes in the arts, especially those associated with film, music, and theater. She has a lovely voice, but I've only heard it once. She's a little bit shy, but modesty becomes her.

Peter Lewis Lehrman

Peter is a giant among our family. He might continue to grow, and if he does, the only child who could soon exceed his height is Forest. Peter Lewis is named for his paternal grandfather and his maternal great-grandfather, Peter Grace, who was also a dear friend of mine. He was the first in the family to get a perfect score on his SATs. He loves to hunt and fish like James with whom he spends a lot of time, and he worked as a counselor at Teton Valley Ranch Camp. He is an exceptionally bright young man, and he works very hard. He's a very disciplined student, and he has a lovely hand on the piano like Leland. He is a super-athlete, and sailing in Maine was a keen interest in high school. He is currently studying at Duke University, pursuing both classical studies and computer science. He volunteers in various student groups, and recently returned from study abroad in Rome.

Berenika Lehrman

Berenika is the oldest among Lee and Vera's clan. She is very, very bright. The only question is how will she make the best of it since she has so many interests and already makes enough money to chart her own path. At my suggestion, she went to Oxford one summer with the Oxbridge program. There, she won the prize for outstanding dramatic work in a Shakespeare play.

Kestrel May Lehrman

Kestrel is the second of two in Johnny's clan. She just completed her degree at the University of Hawaii. She got an ample scholarship to go there. She got good grades by hard work and a practical intelligence. She and her sister Cree have grown together, and along with Johnny their father, they constitute a vital clan. Kestrel is an extremely warm person, and she is devoted to her father.

Cree Callahan Lehrman

Cree is the oldest of our grandchildren. She's a gifted people person, who started and succeeded at running her own business. She's very pretty and a voracious reader, constantly working to improve herself and her prospects. Lately she has been collaborating with her cousin, Dr. Leland Stillman, working on creating healthy travel and adventure experiences.

This is the true family of which Louise and I are very proud. We're so proud of our five children and fifteen grandchildren, all of whom exhibit all the virtues, some greater, some smaller.

Hallelujah.

WILLIAM WATSON WADSWORTH

No account of my life would be quite complete without mentioning the fictional characters I created for my children, and the stories I told about them. They were, of course, based on truth, and although William Watson Wadsworth is not the only such character, he did become the most famous. The older characters in my children's stories, Homo Erectus, Neanderthal, Pithecanthropus, and Australopithecus were rather more quaint. Here, I include the reminiscences of John and Sam Britton, who were old enough at the time I told these stories to remember the details:

> William Watson Wadsworth is the indelible protagonist of an oral story tradition that my Godfather, Lewis Lehrman, brought to life. WWW, as he was affectionately known in shorthand, was the epitome of everything we boys wanted in an action hero: Smart; athletic; well-equipped and deadly in the pursuit of justice when the urgent occasion called.
>
> WWW came to life in the bedtime rituals of family gatherings. The Lehrmans and the Brittons, lifelong friends dating back to the early sixties, would gather at each other's homes with six boys and a girl packed into bunkrooms in Winhall, Vermont, or in beds at a farm near Mechanicsburg, PA. In the evenings, as the children prepared for bed, a hallowed tradition would commence. A parent would turn down the lights; conversation would peter out; kids either tucked into bed or sitting on gathered couches would get comfortable and perk

up an ear. They knew that something great was coming. Parents stood in doorways to hear the impending tale.

Quietly, a story began, emanating from the darkness, improvised by the narrator, and yet as flowing and as compelling as any well-crafted novel. These were oral tradition action stories of the highest order. The fact that they were conjured by the darkened narrator without so much as a pause or a glance at notes was something not lost on us children. This made it all the more powerful, because this, evidently, was a simple recitation of facts, an apparently reluctantly revealed truth that children were perhaps too young to hear, but who could be trusted with the information. We were privileged to hear of such grave matters, and we were rapt.

There were no televisions or radios in these houses. There certainly were no video games or cellphones with social media. There were childhood activities and plenty of athletic endeavor that created a deep nod by the hour of 8:30 PM. It was at this time that we children, dressed in pajamas and well fed, were heading off to bed. Our send-off was a story from the pantheon of WWW.

The stories themselves followed a consistent narrative arc: WWW, in his office on the top floor of the Pan Am (now Met Life) building on 42nd Street in New York received an urgent call. The caller explained an emergency that required immediate intercession. This scenario might involve an abduction; a theft; a malevolent army under the leadership of a dark dictator. At all events, the situation was grave and called for our hero to jump into action. He did so by flying off the top of the Pan Am building in a (strap-on helicopter), armed with little besides his Bowie knife. He outwitted every army and every trap. He solved every problem set before him; he prevailed against long odds and delivered justice against malevolent actors the world over. Even at this moment, there can be no doubt that WWW has slipped through military lines . . . and is approaching the latest demonic despot . . . prepared to deliver justice and blood with his silent Bowie blade.

WWW was a towering hero of my childhood. I am forever grateful to my Godfather, my Uncle Lew, for creating him.[12]

The young Lehrman, poet and scholar

Appendix: Early Writings

WHY STUDY HISTORY?

On April 11, 1960, I completed the following essay for acceptance to the Carnegie Teaching Fellowship at Yale University.

Why Study History?

The question is not: why read history? For here the answer is obvious: for enjoyment. Nor is the question: why write history? For the response is self-evident: to communicate knowledge and understanding. The question, why study history, is not simply answered. It is provocative! The question evokes cries of "pedantry," "ivory tower," "useless," and finally "unimportant." The word *study* elicits a curious response from the critics of historians. A word so controversial demands a definition. To study is to inquire in a disciplined manner into the nature and extent of one's field of interest. Thus, *to study* is an irritating infinitive for the amateur, "useless" for Ortega's "Barbarian,"[1] pedantic for Isaiah Berlin's "hedgehog."[2]

Now, the study of history is a professional occupation. It could not be otherwise by its very definition. This simple categorization may suffice to dispel once for all the inane criticisms directed at the historian. That is, the professional usually best understands the nature and reason for his work. Perhaps an analogy will clarify this point. Only an architect designs a building, an engineer a bridge, a philosopher a systematic philosophy. The nature of each profession is on a specific level of organization having its own laws and functions; e.g., a philosopher assumes the "law of contradiction," and he cannot prove it without a circular argument. Lack of proof does not demand abandonment of this law, for without it there would be no truth; i.e., no contradictory ideas. Now, if an engineer were to demand that the philosopher prove the validity of the law of contradiction as conclusively as the engineer the efficacy of his principles by the construction of a usable bridge, the latter would merely demonstrate his ignorance of the philosophical problem involved in this law.

In the same manner the historian makes certain assumptions with regard to the study of history. To articulate these assumptions would no more convince the critic of *this* study than the philosopher would the critic of the "law of contradiction." The historian may enumerate his *raisons d'etre*, but these are assumptions rather than proofs of the worth of his profession. It is an unrealized

The question is not: why read history? For here the answer is obvious: for enjoyment. Nor is the question: why write history: For the response is self-evident: to communicate knowledge and understanding. The question, why study history, is not simply answered. It is provocative! The question evokes cries of "pedantry", "ivory-tower", "useless", and finally "unimportant." The word study elicits a curious response from the critics of historians. A word so controversial demands a definition. To study is to inquire in a disciplined manner into the nature and extent of one's field of interest. Thus, to study is an irritating infinitive for the amateur, "useless" for Ortega's "Barbarian", pedantic for Isaiah Berlin's "hedgehog."

Now, the study of history is a professional occupation. It could not be otherwise by its very definition. This simple catergorization may suffice to dispel once for all the inane criticisms directed at the historian. That is, the professional usually best understands the nature and reason for his work. Perhaps an analogy will clarify this point. Only an architect designs a building, an engineer a bridge, a scientist a betatron, a philosopher a systematic philosophy. The nature of each profession is on a specific level of organization having its own laws and functions; e.g., a philosopher assumes the "law of contradiction," and he cannot prove it without a circular argument. Lack of proof does not demand abandonment of this law, for without it there would be no truth; i.e., no contradictory fact that one rarely demands of science or technology its *raisons d'etre*. Why study science is to most a puerile question. This is simply because the world has come to identify a profession's *raisons d'etre* with its degree of practicality: truth varies directly with the production potential of the hypothesis. This statement is no more justifiable today than it was before Francis Bacon. It contains an assumption: that production and science are identical with progress or, at least, utility. What has been forgotten is that science, technology, and industrialization are only utilitarian or better, amoral. It is at this point that the historian and philosopher step in.

These two professionals retain, interpret, and construct the course of meaning of human enterprise. This function is no more questionable than the law of contradiction, no more suspect than the amorality of science. The study of history is a disciplined inquiry into the nature and process of the dynamic interrelations of men and institutions *on earth*. This task could never be categorized as amoral, nor suspect for circular justification. The historian assumes only one thing: that the human enterprise is a phenomenon worthy of disciplined consideration. Scientists have for two hundred and seventy-five years made extensive use of Newton's *Principia*. His principles are the groundwork of the engineer's working knowledge. Without Newton the modern world is almost inconceivable! Yet we do not merely examine Newton as mathematician and physicist. We pay little attention to him as philosopher. We do regard much of Western history that followed him as bearing the imprint of his influence. That is, Newton is important because he is an historical figure. His creation was in part a result of, but more importantly a powerful force in history. With this simple admission we have summoned the historian. "Enter the inner chamber," and discover in what way Newton was related to Copernicus, Brahe, Kepler; in what way he influenced Voltaire, Montesquieu, Kant; in what way Newton influenced the course of Western thought; how the social sciences drew upon his "summa" for inspiration; why industrialization and democracy are indebted to him.

In a word, Newton functioned in an historical context. The subsequent historical context functioned differently after he appeared. Hence, mention this scientist's name and one has *summoned* the historian. The historian's *raison d'etre* is nothing else than a qualified response to a universal subpoena.[3]

AN EARLY INTELLECTUAL AUTOBIOGRAPHY

Sometime in late 1960 or early 1961 I wrote the following essay for the Woodrow Wilson Fellowship at Harvard. I made some accurate predictions.

Continuity and change usually characterize one's intellectual interests. In my case the weight of change shifts the balance—enormously. My major intellectual interests are no older than two years, partly a result of factors quite beyond my comprehension. Perhaps the contemporaneity of my interests is the result of an age-old predicament. One "thinks" before one studies; one "knows' before one speculates.

This adolescent presumption of knowledge characterized my intellectual method until my twentieth year—and still haunts me at undisciplined moments during undisciplined arguments. I suggested that I was not fully aware of the reasons for the precipitous change in my intellectual orientation during the last two years. I implied that the dawning awareness of the adolescent nature of my quest for certainty may in part explain this change. More important, the decision to abandon football and basketball for the books should explain a great deal more.

These, however, are simply factors, or better, conditions which laid the groundwork for a significant change of attitude. The catalysts which activated these conditions are less difficult to isolate. Certain men, professors, exploited these conditions. These men are the primary factors which explain my intellectual reorientation. They guided and shaped my interests, if at times they did not change them.

A serious academic career would have been, for me, unthinkable as little as two years ago if certain men had not radically altered my intellectual postures, directions, interests. My grandfather and my father had "appointed" their descendant to medical school, where he might carry on a family tradition. This "appointment" was rejected by the appointee, along with much intellectual "excess baggage."

I withdrew from pre-medicine and entered more seriously into the study of history. Three men now make their appearance: Professor Robert Lopez, Professor Charles Garside, Professor Ralph Turner. They guided and shaped my direction of study: cultural and intellectual history. They disabused me of my rather "Ptolemaic" notions of history; they "removed" me from the United States and England—to Han China, Reformation Germany, Mediaeval Italy, Ancient Sumer. This "Copernican" revolution constituted the single greatest alteration in my vision of the world.

Without this radical intellectual reorientation, occasioned by the influence of these men, I would have been neither a serious history major nor a Carnegie Teaching Fellow in that department. The study of history is at this moment a continuous, self-sustaining interest, compelling me to consider seriously this subject, and the teaching of it, as a career. However, historians were simply the first to capture my imagination.

It was not until my senior year that the hegemony of historiography was questioned and contested. The new intellectual drift is again rather easy to explain. Two men appear: Professor Brand Blandshard and more important Professor John Smith. Philosophers both, they exerted upon me the magnetic attraction that their profession must have for all historians, who at one time or another are mired in the infinite "mud" of history. Though very superficially wallowing in this mud, I nevertheless felt the relief inherent in the discovery of a new method of search, that search for the elusive, always fleeting comprehension and definition of reality.

Mr. Blandshard and Mr. Smith seemed somehow to define their goal, beat a path in that direction, and arrive at home more swiftly than their colleagues in the History Department. The "vertical ascent" of the philosopher appeared less tenuous than the "horizontal" search of the historian. The influence of these two men was less significant, though no less permanent than that of Garside, Turner, and Lopez. The result has been a continuous interest in the philosophy of religion, which grew out of my relationship with Professor Smith. It was the necessary complement to my previous method of search, i.e., the study of history combined with the search for a standpoint from which to understand and evaluate this study.

I might now end an autobiography of this sort. To do so would result in a serious omission: This omission would render the motives for my future plans incomplete. This past summer witnessed in me the fulfillment of a deep and frustrated ambition. The nature of the ambition was political. As a boy I cherished the possibility of one day entering politics. My grandfather nourished this whim, unknowingly. He had been involved somewhat in Pennsylvania politics; and it was his interest that inspired mine. As a senior at Yale Professor Turner, again unwittingly, encouraged my ambitions. Politics for him was the source of all argument.

In July 1960, I began working for a Democratic candidate, Endicott Peabody, who was running in the Gubernatorial primary in the state of Massachusetts. He lost. Yet, in the process, we campaigned the entire state. I became, with a stroke of good fortune, his "factotum." Through him I learned a great deal about the profession to which I had for so long a time aspired. It was a revealing experience. The cobwebs of romance disappeared and I was swiftly initiated into the methods of the "marketplace."

History, philosophy, and the political marketplace characterize my overriding present interests. They lead logically into my plans for the future. I am now inquiring into the possibility of combining the two fields of study: law and history. I should like to achieve graduate degrees in both. With them I should then aspire to teach legal and intellectual history. Perhaps I might have the opportunity, in the far future, to fulfill the political demands placed, in one way or another, on every citizen in this country. This is, indeed, a peripheral ambition, though, nonetheless, a very alive and personal aspiration.

TWO POEMS

The following poems were discovered by Leland inside two of my Yale philosophy books. I wrote the first poem on the inside front cover of *The Fall*, by Albert Camus. The second I inscribed into the inside back cover of *The Thought and Art of Albert Camus*, by Thomas Hanna. They were written around 1960, were untitled, and are here published mostly unedited.

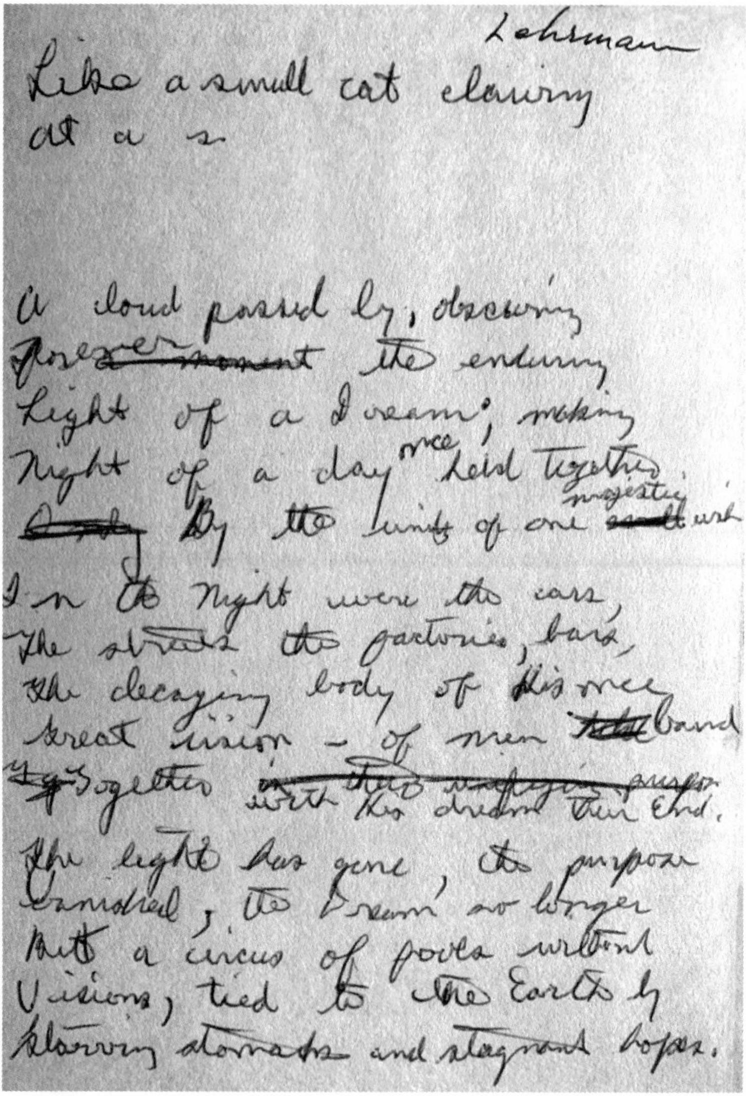
Lehrman

Like a small cat clawing
at a s

A cloud passed by, obscuring
~~forever moment~~ the enduring
Light of a Dream; making
Night of a day once held together
By the winds of one majestic wish

In the Night were the cars,
The streets the factories, bars,
The decaying body of this once
Great vision – of men band
together ~~in their majestic purpose~~ with this dream their End.
The light has gone, the purpose
Vanished, the Dream no longer
But a circus of fools without
Visions, tied to the Earth by
Starving stomachs and stagnant hopes.

This dream…

Poem written on the inside front cover of *The Fall*, by Albert Camus

A cloud passed by, drawing
Forever the enduring
Light of a Dream; making
Night of a day once held together
By the unity of one majestic wish.

In the night were the cars,
The streets the factories, bars,
The decaying body of this once
Great vision - of men bound
Together with this dream their end.

The light has gone, its purpose
Vanished, the dream no longer
But a circus of fools without
Visions, tied to the Earth by
Starving stomachs and stagnant hopes.[4]

Poem written on the inside back cover of *The Thought and Art of Albert Camus*

One stops his daily living
And looks about him,
To enjoy his moment of
Consciousness apart from all.

At this point we do wonder
Why, or what's the use; our life.
If there be any essence
There, or just mere nothingness.

That man of France says at that
Point when weary of our "habit"
We come awake and conscious,
Think on the worth of things.

Why is it then this thing be true?
Why is it that men ponder,
When all of life's about them
And they cannot feel its worth?

To the man Camus I say:
At this break with "habit",
Men become then "conscious'
And like he says distinguishable.

Not the absurdity of life I say yet
Is this reason for doubt
Not even that empty knowing
Of estrangement from the earth.

It is more this break with habit;
Brings on this kind of depth
Because he has equated "Habit"
With unconsciousness and indifference!

Thus when quitting habit or routine,
Nothingness descends upon us, not because
We question life, but life has now
Confronted us in all its full dimensions.

Size not absurdity is what frightens us,
Absurdity comes and goes just as
We lay down and pick up life's toils,
And what is more, life's toils are not enough,
It's conscious makes the difference.[5]

The author and the editor

NOTES

Acknowledgments

1. Abraham Lincoln, "Letter to J. M. Brockman dated September 25, 1860." In *The Collected Works of Abraham Lincoln*, eds. Roy P. Basler, Marion Delores Pratt, and Lloyd A. Dunlap (New Brunswick, NJ: Rutgers University Press, 1959), 4: 121.
2. Two famous statements by Churchill contributed to the title of this book. The first is "Study history, study history, in it lies all the secrets of statecraft," which appears in James Humes's book, *Churchill, Speaker of the Century* (New York: Stein and Day, 1980), vii. The second statement is "A joint committee leads to weak and faltering decisions—or rather indecisions. Why, you may take the most gallant sailor, the most intrepid airman, or the most audacious soldier, put them at a table together—what do you get? The sum of their fears." This latter statement was Churchill privately criticizing the Chiefs of Staff system, November 16, 1943, which is available to view in context at *Finest Hour*, the website of the Winston Churchill Society: https://winstonchurchill.org/publications/finest-hour/finest-hour-134/churchill-on-war/.

Chapter 1: Walking West on East 80th Street

1. D. Gilbert Lehrman, correspondence with author's team, February 26, 2019.
2. Lewis E. Lehrman, "Roots and Revolution," speech, 85th Pennsylvania Society Dinner, New York, NY, December 10, 1983.
3. Michael Moore, letter to author's team, July 2018.
4. "Louise Stillman Becomes Bride: 1958 Debutante and Lewis E. Lehrman Are Wed Here," *New York Times*, May 28, 1966.
5. Susan Bailey Scott, correspondence with author's team, April 22, 2019.
6. Alan Finder, "The Different Strides in Race for Governor: Lehrman's 'Controlled Passion,'" *Newsday*, October 24, 1982. See also George Arzt, "The Wife I Love, by Lew Lehrman," *New York Post*, October 21, 1982.
7. Dierdre LeFaye, "Jane Austen's Letters," *Persuasions* 14 (1992), 88.
8. Lewis E. Lehrman, "Toast on the Occasion of 50th Wedding Anniversary," speech, Colony Club, New York, NY, May 27, 2016.

Chapter 2: The Sum of It All

1. National Conference of Catholic Bishops, *Economic Justice for All: Pastoral Letter on Catholic Social Teaching and the U.S. Economy* (Washington, DC: US Catholic Conference, 1986), viii.
2. The source of this precept is Jacques Rueff as expressed throughout his entire body of work.
3. These (Chitty, et al.) were some of Abraham Lincoln's favorite primary sources.
4. Abraham Lincoln, "Speech at Chicago, Illinois, July 10, 1858." In *Collected Works of Abraham Lincoln*, 2: 499.
5. Thomas Jefferson, "Inscription on the Northwest Wall of the Jefferson Monument," Monticello website, https://www.monticello.org/research-education/thomas-jefferson-encyclopedia/quotations-jefferson-memorial/.
6. Henry Lee, *A Funeral Oration in Honor of the Memory of George Washington, Late General of the Armies of the United States. Prepared and Delivered at the Request of Congress at the German Lutheran Church, Philadelphia, on Tuesday the 26th December, by Major*

General Henry Lee, One of the Representative of the State of Virginia (New Haven, CT: Read & Morse, 1800), 19.
7. George Washington, *Washington's Farewell Address, Webster's First Bunker Hill Oration, Lincoln's Gettysburg Address*, ed. Charles Robert Gaston (Boston: The Athenaeum Press, Ginn and Company Proprietors, 1919), 12.
8. This chapter was originally written in the form of two speeches which I have edited and updated for this book. The originals of these and many of my other writings can be found online at my website lewiselehrman.com.

Chapter 3: Getting Started

1. Martha Hurwitz, letter to author, July 26, 1976.
2. D. Gilbert Lehrman, correspondence with author's team, February 26, 2019.
3. Lois Lehrman Grass, "Living Legacy Project," interview by Michael Greenwald, Rose Lehrman Arts Center, Harrisburg, PA, October 1, 2009.
4. Lewis E. Lehrman, letter to godson, December 3, 1975.
5. Maurice Carroll, "The New York Gubernatorial Campaign: A Referendum with National Overtones; The New Right," *New York Times Magazine*, October 31, 1982, 62.
6. Joe Palooka was a comic strip created by Pennsylvania native Ham Fisher.
7. "Maybe I just had my fist up, looking for a fight." Lewis E. Lehrman, conversation with Leland Lehrman, April 18, 2022.
8. Jean Chappel, *Harrisburg Patriot*, 1951.
9. Susan Bailey Scott, correspondence with author's team, April 22, 2019.
10. Susan Bailey Scott, letter to author, October 1, 1991.
11. Sir Walter Scott, *Lay of the Last Minstrel*, Canto VI, My Native Land (Edinburgh: Archibald Constable and Co., 1805).
12. Abraham Lincoln, "Address Delivered at the Dedication of the Gettysburg Cemetery, November 19, 1863." In *Collected Works of Abraham Lincoln*, 7: 23.
13. Wheeler T. Daniels, letter to author, July 2018.
14. Leslie Wayne, "Lehrman's Path to the Race for Governor," *New York Times*, October 21, 1982.
15. Laurie Bennett, "A Love of Competition—A Willingness to Spend to Win," *Rochester Times Union*, September 7, 1982.
16. *Quod erat demonstrandum:* Latin for "which was to be demonstrated." Often abbreviated as Q.E.D., the statement may appear at the conclusion of a text to signify that the author's overall argument has just been proven. "Quod Erat Demonstrandum," Wex—Legal Information Institute (Cornell Law School), accessed February 23, 2023, https://www.law.cornell.edu/wex/quod_erat_demonstrandum.
17. Wayne, "Lehrman's Path to the Race for Governor."
18. Daniels, letter to author, July 2018.
19. Martin Gibson, letter to author, July 2018.
20. Charles Moore, letter to author, July 2018.
21. Lewis E. Lehrman, "Commencement Address," The Hill School, Pottstown, PA, May 22, 1983.
22. John P. Britton (friend of author), letter to author, January 7, 1981.
23. A. Bartlett Giamatti, "Class of 1960 Notes," *Yale Alumni News*, December 1976.
24. Lewis E. Lehrman, letter to A. Bartlett Giamatti, December 27, 1976.
25. Robert P. Moncreiff, *Bart Giamatti: A Profile* (New Haven and London: Yale University Press, 2017), 70.
26. A. Bartlett Giamatti, letter to author, August 5, 1977.
27. Lewis Lehrman, "Noble and Brown-Bearded," *Yale Daily News*, October 14, 1978, 5.
28. Anson Beard, letter to author, July 2018.

29. Daniel Horowitz, *On the Cusp: The Yale College Class of 1960 and a World on the Verge of Change* (Amherst and Boston: University of Massachusetts Press, 2015), 8.
30. Ibid.
31. Karen Heller, "A Hurricane Named Lew," *Rochester Democrat and Chronicle*, June 6, 1982.
32. John C. MacMurray, letter to author, July 2018.
33. Matt Freeman, correspondence with author's team, March 26, 2019.
34. Ibid.
35. Ibid.
36. Ibid.
37. Lewis E. Lehrman, "A Teaching Fellow Tells His Story," *Yale Alumni Magazine*, May 1961, 12–13.
38. Roy L. Hill, ed., "Malcolm X Proclaims Muhammad as Man of the Hour," *Rhetoric of Racial Revolt* (Denver: Golden Bell Press, 1964), 304–17.
39. Howard Gillette, Jr., *Class Divide: Yale '64 and the Conflicted Legacy of the Sixties* (Ithaca and London: Cornell University Press, 2015), 19, 234 note 68.
40. Lewis E. Lehrman, letter to son, December 15, 1992.
41. Daniel P. Jordan, correspondence with author's team, April 12, 2019.
42. From his PhD dissertation later came a book, John P. Britton, *Models and Precision: The Quality of Ptolemy's Observations and Parameters* (New York and London: Garland Publishing, 1992).
43. Stan Luxenberg, "A Meeting of Minds and Millions," *Change*, September 1979, 17.
44. Ludwig Dehio, *The Precarious Balance: The Politics of Power in Europe 1494–1945* (London: Chatto & Windrus, 1963).
45. Ibid. For more on the importance of the Suez Canal to British policy, see Sir Anthony Eden, *Full Circle: The Memoirs of Anthony Eden* (London: Cassell & Company, Ltd, 1963).
46. Horowitz, *On the Cusp*, 229–30.
47. Heller, "A Hurricane Named Lew."
48. Bill Hutchinson, correspondence with author's team April 15, 2019; Lewis E. Lehrman, conversation with author, February 27, 2019.
49. Ibid.
50. Captain Heyward W. Riley, letter to author, January 17, 1964.
51. Major H. W. Gleason, letter to author, July 26, 1968.
52. Lewis E. Lehrman, "The 2153rd Becomes the 441st," *United States Army*, July 1969.
53. Jonathan Bush, letter to author, August 15, 1969.

Chapter 4: Down to Business

1. Robert Lehrman, letter to Barbara Weinberg, December 11, 1981.
2. Paul B. Beers, *Harrisburg Evening News*, March 2, 1981.
3. Michael Kramer, "Who Is This Guy Lew Lehrman?," *New York*, April 5, 1982, 26.
4. Desmond FitzGerald, letter to author, July 2018.
5. Rite Aid Corporation, *Prospectus*, filed April 26, 1968.
6. Wayne, "Lehrman's Path to Race for Governor."
7. "Grass, Rite Aid Founder, Dies at 82," *Chain Drug Review*, September 8, 2009.
8. Richard Gilder and Lewis E. Lehrman, interview by Brian Lamb, *Q&A*, C-SPAN, May 19, 2005.
9. "Jet Propulsion in Drug Discounting," *Discount Merchandiser*, August 1971, 43.
10. Ibid., 40–41.
11. Tim Noonan, correspondence with author's team, May 9, 2019.
12. John Szelest, correspondence with author's team, April 3, 2019.
13. Tim Noonan, correspondence with author's team, May 9, 2019.
14. John Szelest, correspondence with author's team, April 3, 2019.

15. Richard M. Nixon, 'The Challenge of Peace,'" national address, Washington, DC, August 15, 1971, https://www.presidency.ucsb.edu/documents/address-the-nation-outlining-new-economic-policy-the-challenge-peace.
16. Richard M. Nixon on price controls and the gold standard, quoted in Daniel Yergin and Joseph Stanislaw, *The Commanding Heights: The Battle Between the Government and the Marketplace that is Remaking the Modern World*, (New York: Simon & Schuster, 1998), 62.
17. Richard B. Cheney and Liz Cheney, *In My Time, A Personal and Political Memoir* (New York, Threshold Editions, 2011), 60.
18. "Tropical Storm Agnes: A 'Five-Day Dance of Havoc,'" *Patriot News* (Harrisburg, PA), June 21, 2021, https://www.pennlive.com/life/2017/06/tropical_storm_agnes_197_a_fiv.html.

Chapter 5: The Farm and the Family

1. Lehrman, "Roots and Revolution," speech.
2. John P. Britton (friend of author), letter to author, October 12, 1978.
3. Thomas D. Lehrman, correspondence with author, May 12, 2020.
4. Eliza D. Lehrman, correspondence with author, May 12, 2020.
5. Peter R. Lehrman, correspondence with author, May 15, 2020.
6. Eliza D. Lehrman, correspondence with author, May 12, 2020.
7. R. Leland Lehrman, correspondence with author, May 15, 2020.
8. Peter R. Lehrman, correspondence with author, May 12, 2020.
9. John S. Lehrman, correspondence with author, May 12, 2020.
10. Thomas D. Lehrman, correspondence with author, May 12, 2020.
11. Peter R. Lehrman, correspondence with author, May 15, 2020.
12. Eliza D. Lehrman, correspondence with author, May 12, 2020.
13. Thomas D. Lehrman, correspondence with author, May 12, 2020.
14. Eliza D. Lehrman, correspondence with author, May 12, 2020.
15. Peter R. Lehrman, correspondence with author, May 15, 2020.
16. R. Leland Lehrman, correspondence with author, May 15, 2020.
17. Peter R. Lehrman, correspondence with author, May 12, 2020.
18. Eliza D. Lehrman, correspondence with author, May 12, 2020.
19. Thomas D. Lehrman, correspondence with author, May 12, 2020.
20. John S. Lehrman, correspondence with author May 12, 2020.
21. As far as I know, my time still stands as a record unequaled by any member of my immediate family or close friends.
22. John D. Britton (godson of author), correspondence with author, March 27, 2019.
23. Ibid.
24. Lewis E. Lehrman, letter to son, September 19, 1990.
25. Ibid.

Chapter 6: The Lehrman Institute

1. Luxenberg, "A Meeting of Minds and Millions," 17.
2. Edmund Newton, "RX for Albany?," *Soho News*, January 19, 1982.
3. Heller, "A Hurricane Named Lew."
4. Bennett, "A Love of Competition."
5. Lise Bang-Jensen, "Lehrman Rivals Trained at His Think Tank," *Knickerbocker News* (Albany, NY), July 26, 1982.
6. Newton, "RX for Albany?"
7. Sidney Blumenthal, "The Wake of the Cold War," *Washington Post*, June 14, 1988.
8. Lewis E. Lehrman, letter to David P. Calleo, March 28, 1975.
9. Luxenberg, "A Meeting of Minds and Millions," 17.
10. Ibid.
11. Ibid.

12. Jacques Rueff, "The West Is Risking a Credit Collapse," *Fortune*, July 1961, 126.
13. Lewis E. Lehrman, interview by James C. Roberts, "The Case for a Return to the Gold Standard: An Exclusive Interview with Lewis Lehrman," *Human Events*, May 23, 1981, 1.
14. Lewis E. Lehrman, "The Creation of International Monetary Order," in *Money and the Coming World Order*, ed. David P. Calleo (New York: A Lehrman Institute Book published by New York University Press, 1976), 71–120.
15. Christopher S. Chivvis, *The Monetary Conservative: Jacques Rueff and Twentieth-Century Free Market Thought* (DeKalb: Northern Illinois University Press, 2010), 7.
16. Lewis E. Lehrman, "The Federal Reserve and the Dollar," *Cato Journal*, Spring/Summer 2014, 417.
17. I explain why pricing gold too low leads to unemployment in chapter 14, in the section called "The Hidden Problem of the Reserve Currency," see page 273.
18. Stanley W. Stillman, "IMF Curtain-Raiser, Interview with Jacques Rueff," draft of article for *Time*, September 25, 1972.
19. Ibid.
20. Lewis E. Lehrman, "Presentation of the First Jacques Rueff Memorial Prize to Paul Fabra," speech, The Lehrman Institute and the Association Jacques Rueff, Palais de Luxembourg, Paris, November 15, 1979.
21. It was this same reverence for "ordered liberty" that Calvin Coolidge spoke of when honoring George Washington at the dedication of Mount Rushmore some fifty years earlier.
22. Gilles Coville, "Les Fils Spirituels de Jacques Rueff," *Le Nouvel Economiste*, October 15, 1979, 78.
23. Lewis E. Lehrman, "Jacques Rueff, the Age of Inflation, and the True Gold Standard," speech, Assemble Nationale, Paris, November 7, 1996.
24. Ibid.
25. Michael Barone, "A Clash of Ideas in New York," *Washington Post*, October 19, 1982.
26. Lewis E. Lehrman, "Presentation of the Second Jacques Rueff Memorial Prize to Robert Mundell," speech, The Lehrman Institute and the Association Jacques Rueff, Palais de Luxembourg, Paris, October 20, 1983.
27. Newton, "Rx for Albany?"
28. Glenn Frankel, "As Their Support Thins, Candidates Run on Faith," *Washington Post*, March 12, 1996.
29. Lewis E. Lehrman, letter to Robert Bartley, October 29, 1974.
30. Lehrman, "Creation of International Monetary Order," in *Money and the Coming World Order*, 72–73.
31. Walter Bagehot, 1826–1877, British economist and writer, founder of the *National Review* and editor-in-chief of the *Economist*.
32. Lewis E. Lehrman, letter to Robert Bartley, November 16, 1978.
33. Lewis E. Lehrman, "Jack Kemp Oral History Project," interview by Morton Kondracke, *Jack Kemp Foundation*, December 14, 2011, 4–5.
34. Dan Morgan, "Getting Our Ideology in The Wall Street Journal," *Washington Post*, February 15, 1981.
35. Lewis E. Lehrman, letter to Maxwell M. Rabb, April 10, 1980.
36. Lewis E. Lehrman, personal conversation with Alan Greenspan, date unknown.
37. Lewis E. Lehrman, letter to Paul Volcker, April 21, 1980.
38. Lewis E. Lehrman, letter to Jack Kemp, March 29, 1976.
39. John D. Mueller, letter to author, July 2018.
40. Lewis E. Lehrman, "Jack Kemp Oral History Project," December 14, 2011, 8.
41. Lewis E. Lehrman, "The Decline and Fall of the Public Interest in New York," The Lehrman Institute's Seminar on Local Government presentation, The Lehrman Institute, New York, NY, January 25, 1975.
42. Thomas C. Hayes, "How Executives View Reagan," *New York Times*, July 18, 1980.

43. Luther F. Bliven, "Win by Reagan Held Boon to NY," *Syracuse Post Standard*, August 9, 1980.
44. Lewis E. Lehrman, "From Reagan, No Free Bike . . . But a Ride to Work," *Daily News* (New York, NY), September 18, 1980.
45. For details on the gold standard and Jim Grant's analysis, please see chapter 14.
46. This was a phrase Moynihan had borrowed from Winston Churchill's father, though he never cited the source.
47. Lewis E. Lehrman, "Conservative Reform and Coherent Economic Policy," *USA Today*, September 1981, 17–18.
48. Brian Domitrovic, *Econoclasts: The Rebels Who Sparked the Supply-Side Revolution and Restored American Prosperity* (Wilmington, DE: ISI Books, 2009), 211.
49. Rowland Evans and Robert Novak, *The Reagan Revolution: An Inside Look at the Transformation of the U.S. Government* (New York: E.P. Dutton, 1981), 118.
50. Lewis E. Lehrman, memo to file, December 15, 1980.
51. Michael Kramer, "When Lewis Lehrman Talks, Ronald Reagan Listens," *New York*, February 9, 1981, 20.
52. Lewis E. Lehrman, "The Struggle for Financial Order at the Onset of the Reagan Presidency," memo prepared at the request of E. Pendleton James for the Reagan Transition, November 6, 1980.
53. Domitrovic, *Econoclasts*, 214.
54. David A. Stockman, "Jack Kemp Oral History Project," interview by Morton Kondracke, *Jack Kemp Foundation*, December 8, 2011, 8.
55. Sidney Blumenthal, "David Stockman, the President's Cutting Edge," *New York Times Magazine*, March 15, 1981, 84.
56. James K. Glassman, "Back to the Gold Standard?" *Atlantic Monthly*, February 1981, 32.
57. Rowland Evans and Robert Novak, "Stockman's 90-Day Mission," *Advocate-Messenger* (Danville, KY), December 30, 1980.
58. David A. Stockman, *The Triumph of Politics: Why the Reagan Revolution Failed* (New York: Harper & Row, 1986), 97.
59. Ibid., 98.
60. Lewis E. Lehrman, "Jack Kemp Oral History Project," December 14, 2011, 14.
61. Leonard Silk, "Economic Scene; Gold Standard As Inflation Curb," *New York Times*, December 26, 1980.
62. Tom Redburn, "Return to Gold Standard: Old Idea Is Slowly Gaining a New Following," *Los Angeles Times*, April 5, 1981.
63. Silk, "Economic Scene; Gold Standard as Inflation Curb."
64. For more detail, see John D. Mueller, *Redeeming Economics: Rediscovering the Missing Element* (Wilmington, DE: ISI Books, 2010).
65. John M. Berry, "Supply-Side Syndrome: More Know of It Than About It," *Washington Post*, March 15, 1981.
66. Jude Wanniski, "Lehrman on Gold," *Polyconomics*, Supply-Side University, August 24, 2001, www.polyconomics.com/ssu/ssu-010824.htm.
67. Donald T. Regan, *For the Record: From Wall Street to Washington* (New York: Harcourt Brace Jovanovich, 1986), 146.
68. Ibid.
69. Steven R. Weisman, "White House; Behold, an Alliance on the Supply Side," *New York Times*, July 20, 1984.

Chapter 7: Into Politics

1. Brian Moss, "Closeup: Lew Lehrman," *Daily News,* August 4, 1985. I have paraphrased the quote here.

2. Lee Cannon, *Ronnie and Jesse: A Political Odyssey* (Garden City, NY: Doubleday, 1969), 99.
3. John B. Connally, letter to author, October 2, 1981.
4. Samuel G. Freedman, *The Inheritance: How Three Families and America Moved from Roosevelt to Reagan and Beyond* (New York: Simon & Schuster, 1996), 334–35.
5. Ibid., 335.
6. Tim Carey, correspondence with author's team, April 23, 2019.
7. Frederic U. Dicker, "He Passed the Bucks, and Bucked the Pros," *Albany Times Union*, June 18, 1982.
8. Freedman, *Inheritance*, 340.
9. Ibid., 335.
10. Tim Carey, correspondence with author's team, April 23, 2019.
11. Bennett, "A Love of Competition."
12. Michael Clements, "Lehrman Begins with a Flurry," *Rochester Democrat and Chronicle*, January 17, 1982.
13. Manley J. Anderson, "State GOP Party Out to Create a New Image," *Jamestown* (NY) *Post-Journal*, May 2, 1978.
14. Lois Uttley, "GOP Mans 'Listening Posts,'" *Knickerbocker News* (Albany, NY), June 6, 1978.
15. Steve Spero, "Platform Chief to Blend Views to Appeal to Voters," *Binghamton Press & Sun-Bulletin*, March 10, 1978.
16. Maile Hulihan, "Less Government Control Repeated Plea to Lehrman," *Utica Dispatch*, April 7, 1978.
17. Gus Bliven, "GOP Platform Chairman to Conduct 50 Hearings," *Syracuse Post Standard*, March 29, 1978.
18. Lewis E. Lehrman, "Republican State Platform," speech to Republican State Convention, Americana Hotel, New York, NY, June 13, 1978.
19. Carroll, "New York Gubernatorial Campaign," 25.
20. Ibid.
21. Ibid.
22. "Inflation Main Problem, Lehrman Tells Republicans," *Cobbleskill Times-Journal*, March 7, 1979.
23. Jim O'Hara, "GOP Spokesman Sees a Revolt Over Inflation," *Elmira Star-Gazette*, April 6, 1979.
24. John Maines, "GOP's Economic Aide Hits Government Rules," *Ithaca Journal*, April 6, 1979.
25. "GOP Advice: Start Locally," *Corning Leader*, April 5, 1979.
26. Ibid.
27. Lewis E. Lehrman, quoted in Mark Vosburgh, "GOP Needs a Winner, Not a New Platform, Advisor Says," *Daily Star*, June 11, 1979.
28. Stephen Goldstein, "Lehrman Rallies GOP at Colonie Dinner," *Schenectady Gazette*, February 15, 1979.
29. Ibid.
30. Jim O'Hara, "Rising Star Unnoticed," *Elmira Sunday Telegram*, April 15, 1979.
31. "Lehrman Says Working People Have the Answers," *Courier-Journal* (Palmyra, NY), August 3, 1979.
32. "Small Businesses Are Backbone of the Nation," *Owego Pennysaver Press* (Owego, NY), February 12, 1980.
33. Ibid.
34. Jim Wright, "Possible Candidate Hopeful on Economy," *Binghamton Press and Sun-Bulletin*, February 8, 1980.
35. Ibid.

36. Don Knorr, "Inflation the Key Issue, State GOP Official Says," *Utica Observer-Dispatch*, March 11, 1980.
37. Clark Walter, "Tioga Talk: Taxes Chase Industry," *Binghamton Press and Sun-Bulletin*, February 7, 1980.
38. William F. Buckley Jr., letter to author, December 2, 1980.
39. William F. Buckley Jr., "Mercy Killing as Cure for Bureaucracy," *Daily News* (New York, NY), December 4, 1980.
40. Lincoln would have accepted the Oregon governorship, but his wife Mary was against it.
41. Heller, "A Hurricane Named Lew."
42. Rowland Evans and Robert Novak, "The President's Daughter," *Indianapolis News*, August 24, 1981.
43. Mike Milmoe, "A Lehrman Preacher," *Chittenango-Bridgeport Times* (Chittenango, NY), July 6, 1982.
44. William O. Winans, direct mailer to Republicans, August 25, 1981.
45. John M. Caher, *King of the Mountain: The Rise, Fall, and Redemption of Chief Judge Sol Wachtler* (Amherst, NY: Prometheus Books, 1998), 62.
46. David M. Smick, "Jack Kemp Oral History Project," interview by Morton Kondracke, *Jack Kemp Foundation*, January 19, 2012, 28.
47. Rowland Evans and Robert Novak, "Brzezinski Seating a Reagan Message?," *Boston Globe*, October 11, 1981.
48. Dick Zander, "Washington's Loss Could Be a Gain for NY Republicans," *Newsday*, July 31, 1981.
49. William F. Buckley Jr., "Lehrman for Governor," *Daily News* (New York, NY), October 20, 1981.
50. Lewis E. Lehrman, letter to William F. Buckley Jr., October 20, 1981.
51. Karl Ottosen, confidential memo to Jonathan Bush, November 4, 1981.
52. R. L. McManus Jr., "Anderson Drops GOP Run," *Albany Times-Union*, December 4, 1981.
53. Augusta Schneider, letter to author, November 1982.
54. Susan Tang, correspondence with author, August 9, 2019.
55. Freedman, *Inheritance.*
56. Ibid., 357.
57. Lewis E. Lehrman, memo to campaign staff, March 1982.
58. Ibid.
59. Karl Ottosen, correspondence with author's team, April 23, 2019.
60. Tim Carey, correspondence with author's team, April 23, 2019.
61. Beth Fallon, "Now, the GOP Palace Is Up for Grabs," *Daily News* (New York, NY), June 18, 1982.
62. George Marlin, *Fighting the Good Fight: A History of the New York Conservative Party* (South Bend, IN: St. Augustine's Press, 2002), 260–61.
63. Karl Ottosen, correspondence with author's team, April 23, 2019.
64. Ibid.
65. George Borrelli, "Regan Calls Conservatives Key to Bid for Governor," *Buffalo Evening News*, December 4, 1981.
66. Ray Herman, "NYC Parley Illustrates Conservatives' Strength," *Buffalo Courier-Express*, December 20, 1981.
67. Ray Herman, "Conservatives Looking to Give Nod to Lehrman," *Buffalo Courier-Express*, December 13, 1981.
68. Ray Herman, "Lehrman Stoking Up for Long Haul," *Buffalo Courier-Express*, December 20, 1981.
69. Ibid.

70. George Borrelli, "Regan Encounters Snag with Conservative Party," *Buffalo Evening News*, December 20, 1981.
71. Maurice Carroll, "Top Conservatives Pick Lehrman for Governor," *New York Times*, December 30, 1981.
72. Ibid.
73. Ibid.
74. John J. O'Leary, *Playing It Well: The Life and Times of Jack O'Leary*, Part 2 (Trafford, 2012), 207.
75. Dick Zander, "Open Conservative Vote Urged," *Newsday*, March 29, 1982.
76. Frank Lynn, "Conservatives and a Political Gamble in New York; News Analysis," *New York Times*, January 26, 1982.
77. Ibid.
78. Dick Zander, "Candidate Lehrman Raises Some Doubts for GOP Leaders," *Newsday*, March 26, 1982.
79. Ibid.
80. Marlin, *Fighting the Good Fight*, 262.
81. Clements, "Lehrman Begins with a Flurry."
82. Marlin, *Fighting the Good Fight*, 261.
83. Associated Press, "Comptroller to Seek GOP Gubernatorial Nod," *Poughkeepsie Journal*, December 31, 1981.
84. Ibid.
85. Maurice Carroll, "Regan Announces He Will Seek GOP Nomination for Governor," *New York Times*, December 31, 1981.
86. Ibid.
87. Associated Press, "$600,000 Campaign for GOP Nod," *Elmira Star-Gazette*, January 2, 1982.
88. Lewis Lehrman for Governor, campaign commercial, January 4, 1982.
89. Frank Lynn, "Three-Front Gubernatorial Free-For-All," *New York Times*, January 10, 1982.
90. Luther F. Bliven, "GOP Leaders Reject Clark Overture," *Syracuse Post-Standard*, January 7, 1982.
91. Michael Kramer, "Koch-22: The Great Scramble to Succeed Carey," *New York*, February 15, 1982, 36.
92. Ray Herman, "How Lehrman Learned the Ways of a Politician," *Buffalo Courier Express*, January 24, 1982.
93. Harrison Rainie, "Prez Won't Take Bite of Primary Dogfights," *Daily News* (New York, NY), January 6, 1982.
94. Kramer, "Koch-22," 36.

Chapter 8: Through the Primary

1. Frank Lynn, "Lehrman Starts His Run in GOP Governor Race," *New York Times*, January 12, 1982.
2. Lewis E. Lehrman, "Announcement of Candidacy," speech, Grand Central Terminal, New York, NY, January 11, 1982.
3. Beth Fallon, "Lew Who?," *Daily News* (New York, NY), January 13, 1982.
4. Richard Meislin, "Lehrman Seeking Governorship Armed with a Marketing Plan," *New York Times*, January 11, 1982.
5. Ibid.
6. John Omicinski, "'It was Time to Smell the Roses,' says Aide," *Rochester Democrat and Chronicle*, January 16, 1982.
7. Frank Lynn, "Rosenbaum, a 'Rockefeller Republican,' Seeking Governorship," *New York Times*, February 2, 1982.

8. Michael Clements, "Republican Race for Governor Underway," *Rochester Democrat & Chronicle*, December 27, 1981.
9. Richard Wirthlin, poll commentary, internal campaign memo, Decision Making Information, February 6, 1982.
10. Ibid.
11. Michael Clements, "Regan Assails Lehrman Inexperience," *Rochester Democrat and Chronicle*, February 9, 1982.
12. Associated Press, "Kemp Endorses Regan in Governor's Race," *Elmira Star-Gazette*, February 11, 1982.
13. Rowland Evans and Robert Novak, "Voice Memo Creates Anger," *Asheville* (NC) *Citizen-Times*, February 16, 1982.
14. Richard Benedetto, "Regan Out of Contest He Started Timidly," *Binghamton Press and Sun-Bulletin*, March 12, 1982.
15. Ibid.
16. George Borrelli, "Regan Foes, Allies Say His Campaign Being Run Poorly," *Buffalo Evening News*, February 19, 1982.
17. Benedetto, "Regan Out of Contest He Started Timidly."
18. Ibid.
19. Richard Benedetto, "Regan to Seek Re-Election as Comptroller," *Journal News* (West Nyack, NY), March 13, 1982.
20. John Toscano and Sam Roberts, "Regan, On Way Out, Claws the Fat Cats for Not Stroking Him," *Daily News* (New York, NY), March 13, 1982.
21. Ray Herman, "Regan's People Blinked First," *Buffalo Courier-Express*, March 14, 1982.
22. Dick Zander, "Regan Dropping Governor Bid," *Newsday*, March 12, 1982.
23. Mark Gruenberg, "Lehrman 'In Governor's Race to Stay,'" *Middletown* (NY)*Times-Herald Record*, March 11, 1982.
24. Rowland Evans and Robert Novak, "'Certain Trumpet' Sought," *The Tribune* (Scranton, PA), March 31, 1982.
25. Frank Lynn, "State Republican Leaders Weigh Party's Chances in November; News Analysis," *New York Times*, March 27, 1982.
26. Phil Roura and Tom Poster, "Curran: Have Bucks, Will Run for Governor," *Daily News* (New York, NY), January 25, 1982.
27. Sam Roberts, "The Outsider with the Inside Track," *Sunday News Magazine*, *Daily News* (New York, NY), September 19, 1982, 19.
28. Marc Humbert, "What's with Talk About Loyalty Oaths," Associated Press, *Lockport Union Sun*, June 10, 1982.
29. Michael Kramer, "All-Star Family Feud," *New York*, June 7, 1982, 21.
30. Steve Geimann, "Lehrman Confident He'll Win in Swing Through Binghamton," *Binghamton Press and Sun-Bulletin*, June 10, 1982.
31. R. Emmett Tyrrell, "He Stands Out in the Crowd," *Finger Lakes Times* (Geneva, NY), June 9, 1982.
32. Andy Logan, "Around City Hall; Tuning Up," *New Yorker*, July 12, 1982, 75.
33. Maurice Carroll, "GOP Gathers for 'Wide Open' State Convention," *New York Times*, June 15, 1982.
34. Tim Carey, correspondence with author's team, April 23, 2019.
35. Michael Clements, "Emery Won't Consider Running in 2nd Spot," *Rochester Democrat and Chronicle*, June 16, 1982.
36. Ben De Forest, "'Christmas in July' for Lehrman," Associated Press July 2, 1982.
37. George Borrelli, "Kemp, Rukowski and Farley Join in Endorsing Lehrman Bid," *Buffalo Evening News*, July 2, 1982.
38. "Emery Endorses Lehrman For Governor," press release, Friends of Jim Emery, July 8, 1982.

39. Michael Clements, "Emery's Role Varied in Gubernatorial Race," *Rochester Democrat and Chronicle*, October 30, 1982.
40. Marc Humbert, "GOP Candidate Lehrman: 'I Welcome a Primary,'" Associated Press, July 9, 1982.
41. Ibid.
42. Roberts, "Outsider with the Inside Track."
43. Ray Herman, "A Test of Lehrman's Strategy," *Buffalo Courier Express*, August 8, 1982.
44. George Arzt, "GOP Gov Hopefuls Go for the Throat," *New York Post*, August 20, 1982.
45. Ray Herman, "Good Political Theater," *Buffalo Courier-Express*, August 22, 1982.
46. Ed Stransenback, "Politically Untested Lehrman Visits North Country," *Plattsburgh Press-Republican*, August 23, 1982.
47. Kerwin C. Swint, *Dark Genius: The Influential Career of Legendary Political Operative and Fox News Founder Roger Ailes* (New York: Union Square Press, 2008), 85.
48. Ibid., 86.
49. George Borrelli, "It Cost Him a Lot, But Lehrman Won Recognition," *Buffalo Evening News*, September 10, 1982.
50. Ibid.
51. Martin Schram, "Even Before the Preliminaries, Koch and Lehrman Are Sparring," *Washington Post*, September 21, 1982.
52. Carroll, "New York Gubernatorial Campaign," 23.
53. Kevin McCoy, "Lew's Army, Media Blitz, Sealed the Bid," *Journal News* (West Nyack, NY), September 24, 1982.
54. Ibid.

Chapter 9: Running the Race

1. "Republicans with a Harder Face," *Economist*, July 24, 1982, 30.
2. "Lehrman Pledges to Veto New Taxes If Elected," *New York Times*, October 17, 1982
3. Richard Wolf, "Lehrman Running uphill," *Journal News* (West Nyack, NY), October 31, 1982
4. John Buckley, correspondence with author's team, April 12, 2019.
5. Sam Roberts, "Mario Cuffs Lew in Round 1," *Daily News* (New York, NY), October 8, 1982.
6. Ibid.
7. Marc Humbert, "Governor Rivals Come in Clawing," *Binghamton Press and Sun-Bulletin*, October 8, 1982.
8. Murray Kempton, "Lehrman Could Win Through Principle, Cuomo's Best Tool," *Newsday*, October 8, 1982.
9. George Borrelli, "Something Odd Happened in Final Days of Campaign," *Buffalo Evening News*, November 14, 1982
10. Andy Logan, "Around City Hall: Starting Over," *New Yorker*, December 27, 1982.
11. John Buckley, letter to author, July 2018.
12. John Omicinski, "Lehrman Bid Fails at Wire," *Binghamton Press and Sun-Bulletin*, November 3, 1982.
13. Lewis E. Lehrman, "Concession Speech," press conference, New York, NY, November 3, 1982.
14. Richard Wolf and Adam J, Nagourney, "Lew Hints: You'll Hear from Me," *Journal News*, November 4, 1982.
15. Beth Fallon, "We'll Be Hearing More About Lehrman," *Daily News* (New York, NY), November 5, 1982.
16. The story of Rockefeller's Canadian votes was an old saw among New York's political elite. In this case, I'm using it to point out that my race also influenced Canadian politics.
17. Dick Zander, "Runaway Becomes Horse Race," *Newsday*, November 4, 1982.

18. Fallon, "We'll Be Hearing More About Lehrman."
19. Carroll, "The New York Gubernatorial Campaign."
20. "Biggest Winner Who Lost," *Washingtonian*, December 1982.
21. Robert Novak, "A New Idea from the GOP Right," *Washington Post*, November 5, 1982.
22. Lisa McCormack, "The Right Wing's Mr. Nice Guy," *Washington Times*, October 9, 1984.
23. Richard Vigilante, "The Right Strategy: Unite and Conquer," *Newsday*, February 22, 1993.
24. Eliza D. Lehrman, correspondence with author, May 12, 2020.
25. "Mario Cuomo for New York," *New York Times*, October 28, 1982.
26. E.J. Dionne, "A New Race in New York," *Washington Post*, May 23, 2000.
27. Richard Wolf, "Lehrman Running Uphill," *Journal News* (West Nyack, NY), October 31, 1982.
28. Paul A. Fisher, "The Wanderer ask Lew Lehrman about . . .," *St. Paul Wanderer*, May 30, 1985.
29. Harold Holzer, letter to author, July 2018.
30. Associated Press, "Lehrman Banks on Voters Not Fearing His Wealth," *Binghamton Press and Sun-Bulletin*, January 11, 1982.
31. Roberts, "Outsider with the Inside Track," 6.
32. Lewis E. Lehrman, "Commencement Address," speech, Eisenhower College of Rochester Institute of Technology, Rochester, NY, May 24, 1982.
33. Steve Geimann, "Party Started Before Polls Closed," *Poughkeepsie Journal*, September 24, 1982.
34. Jeff Simon, "Roger Ailes Was the Master Alchemist," *Buffalo News*, May 18, 2017.
35. Paul Winston, Winston Tailors, June 14, 2016, https://www.styleforum.net/threads/suspenders-or-belts-for-suits-when-everyone-takes-off-their-jacket.524719/

Chapter 10: Citizens for America

1. Lehrman, "Conservative Reform and Coherent Economic Policy."
2. R. Emmett Tyrrell, correspondence with author's team, April 9, 2019.
3. Alan Eyesen, "Lew Lehrman: Selling the Conservative Gospel," *Empire State Report*, October 1984.
4. Lewis E. Lehrman, Keynote Address, *10th Annual Conservative Political Action Conference*, Washington, DC, February 18, 1983.
5. Lewis E. Lehrman, "Commencement Address," speech, Babson College, Boston, MA, May 18,1981.
6. Lewis E. Lehrman, "Capitalism: Only One Cheer," *Crisis*, April 2000, 31-2.
7. Clements, "Lehrman Begins With a Flurry."
8. Lewis E. Lehrman, speech to the Philadelphia Society, April 1983.
9. Ronald Brownstein, "What Makes Lehrman Run?," *National Journal*, December 29, 1984, 2437.
10. Sidney Blumenthal, "Let Lehrman Be Reagan," *New Republic*, December 5, 1983, 16.
11. McCormack, "The Right Wing's Mr. Nice Guy."
12. Marc Humbert, "Lehrman and the Think-Tank Connection," *Ithaca Journal*, September 20, 1982.
13. Jeff Bell, "Jack Kemp Oral History Project," interview by Morton Kondracke, *Jack Kemp Foundation*, July 15, 2011.
14. Marc Humbert, "Lehrman Says Budget Stand Cost Him Federal Post," *Journal News* (West Nyack, NY), October 18, 1982.
15. Kramer, "When Lewis Lehrman Talks, Ronald Reagan Listens," 22.
16. Lewis E. Lehrman, letter to Ronald Reagan, January 23, 1982.
17. Ronald Reagan, *Reagan: A Life in Letters*, eds. Kiron K. Skinner, Annelise Anderson, Martin Anderson (New York: Free Press, 2003), 310.

18. Dick Zander, "Lehrman Declares Candidacy," *Newsday*, January 12, 1982.
19. E. J. Dionne, "The New York Gubernatorial Campaign: A Referendum with National Overtones; The Old Liberalism," *New York Times Magazine*, October 31, 1982, 24
20. Ibid.
21. Alan Emory, "'Elitist Economists' Rile Lehrman," *Watertown Daily Times*, March 13, 1982.
22. John Shanahan, "Reagan Won't Campaign for Lehrman," *Poughkeepsie Journal*, September 29, 1982.
23. Jane Perlez, "Aide Says Reagan Visit for Lehrman Is Unlikely," *New York Times*, September 28, 1982.
24. Adam J. Nagourney, "Cuomo, Lehrman Debate a Free-For-All," *Journal News* (West Nyack, NY), October 8, 1982.
25. Sam Roberts, Lew Lehrman States His Case," *Daily News*, October 24, 1982.
26. Arthur Greenspan, "Lew Blames Carter for Economic Woes," *New York Post*, October 9, 1982.
27. Ibid.
28. Michael Clements, "For Lehrman, Reagan Is a Political Hot Potato," *Rochester Democrat and Chronicle*, October 10, 1982.
29. Lewis E. Lehrman, *This Week with David Brinkley*, ABC News, October 24, 1982.
30. Associated Press, "Candidates Debate Reaganomics," *Poughkeepsie Journal*, October 31, 1982.
31. Richard Wolf, "Lehrman Raps Reagan," *Journal News* (West Nyack, NY), October 29, 1982.
32. Roberts, "Lew Lehrman States His Case."
33. Carroll, "New York Gubernatorial Campaign," 25.
34. Marcia Kramer and Sam Roberts, "Lew Rips GOP Economic Plan," *Daily News* (New York, NY), November 21, 1982.
35. John Lofton, "Lehrman Ready to Catch the Flag," *Human Events*, March 5, 1983.
36. Bill Peterson, "Direct Mail Writes New Chapter in How to Run a Political Campaign," *Washington Post*, November 17, 1982.
37. "Charles Z. Wick: Diplomacy Hollywood-Style," Association for Diplomatic Studies and Training, https://adst.org/oral-history/fascinating-figures/charles-z-wick-diplomacy-hollywood-style.
38. Brownstein, "What Makes Lehrman Run?" 2439.
39. Saul Friedman, "Reagan Finds Citizen's Lobby Help," Knight-News Service, December 9, 1983.
40. Blumenthal, "Let Lehrman Be Reagan," 16.
41. James M. Perry, "Cuomo-Lehrman Race in New York Is Vigorous, Seems Close," *Wall Street Journal*, October 21, 1982.
42. "Conservative Crusade," *Arizona Republic*, November 30, 1983.
43. Jeffrey Hart, "Would you Believe Lewis Lehrman in '88?" *Daily American* (Somerset County, PA), August 6, 1983.
44. Blumenthal, "Let Lehrman Be Reagan," 18.
45. Ibid., 19.
46. Brownstein, "What Makes Lehrman Run?" 2441.
47. Blumenthal, "Let Lehrman Be Reagan," 15.
48. Fred Barnes, "Lehrman to Head New Group Promoting Reagan Policies," *Baltimore Sun*, June 18, 1983.
49. "After the Crowds, the Monument Endures," *Baltimore Sun*, August 28, 1983.
50. John McLaughlin, "Lew Lehrman Neither Bends Nor Accommodates," *Binghamton Press and Sun*-Bulletin, October 22, 1982.
51. Ibid.
52. Ronald Reagan, "May 19, 1983," *The Reagan Diaries* (New York: HarperPerennial, 2009), 154.

53. Blumenthal, "Let Lehrman Be Reagan," 15.
54. Andrei Bogolubov, correspondence with author's team, September 29, 2019.
55. Ronald Reagan, "December 7, 1983," *White House Diaries*, website, Ronald Reagan Presidential Foundation and Institute, https://www.reaganfoundation.org/ronald-reagan/white-house-diaries/diary-entry-12071983/.
56. Stanley Engelberg, "Lehrman Takes to Road for Conservative Cause," *New York Times*, May 5, 1985.
57. "The Story Behind 'Citizens for America," *Human Events,* December 1, 1984.
58. R. Emmett Tyrrell, "Lehrman Taking 'Paul Revere' Role to Rally the Nation's Conservatives," *Times Leader* (Wilkes-Barre, PA), November 30, 1983.
59. James Flagg, "Lehrman Spreads the Gospel of the Right, *Express* (Easton, PA), October 12, 1983.
60. John Distaso, "New Conservative Lobby Created," Union Leader (Manchester, NH), October 14, 1983.
61. Ronald Reagan, "July 11, 1984," *The Reagan Diaries* (New York: Harper Perennial, 2009), 254.
62. "The Story Behind 'Citizens for America,'" *Human Events*, December 1, 1984.
63. Lisa McCormack, "The Two Hollywoods, East and West, Meet," *Washington Times*, January 22, 1985.
64. "Tax Reform Now on Nation's 'Front Burner,'" *Washington Times*, January 4, 1985.
65. Ronald Reagan, letter to author, May 30, 1985.
66. "Resistance Groups Issue Declaration," *Washington Times*, June 6, 1985.
67. Lewis E. Lehrman, "A Moral Case for Star Wars," *New York Times*, February 19, 1985.
68. Lewis E. Lehrman and Gregory A. Fossedal, "How to Decide About Strategic Defense," *National Review*, January 31, 1986, 37.
69. Andrew Ferguson, "A Lobbyist's Progress," *Weekly Standard*, December 20, 2004, 21.
70. Sidney Blumenthal, "Staff Shakeup Hits Conservative Group," *Washington Post*, July 27, 1985.
71. Andrei Bogolubov, correspondence with author's team, September 27, 2019.
72. Ronald Reagan, remarks at Reception for Citizens for America, November 13, 1986.
73. Lewis E. Lehrman, "For the Reagan Doctrine," *New York Times*, January 21, 1987.
74. John Buckley, correspondence with author's team, October 30, 2019.
75. Ibid.
76. Ibid.
77. "In Case You Wondered…20 Questions Normally Not Asked in Political Debates," *Newsday*, October 24, 1982.
78. Schram, "Even Before the Preliminaries, Koch and Lehrman Are Sparring."
79. George Borrelli, "It Cost Him a Lot, But Lehrman Won Recognition," *Buffalo Evening News*, September 18, 1982
80. Andrei Bogolubov, correspondence with author's team, September 27, 2019.
81. Paul J. Browne, "Lehrman Consumed by Desire to Be Governor," *Watertown Daily Times*, March 13, 1982.

Chapter 11: Spreading Wings

1. "When a man knows he is to be hanged in a fortnight, it concentrates his mind wonderfully."—Samuel Johnson, September 19, 1777, quoted in James Boswell, *The Life of Samuel Johnson, L.L.D.* (London: Henry Baldwin for Charles Dilly, in the Poultry, 1791).
2. R. Leland Lehrman, correspondence with author, May 12, 2020.
3. Lewis E. Lehrman, interviewed by Rick Johns, *American Economic Council Report*, July 1981, 7.

Chapter 12: Faith in Action

1. Lehrman, "Capitalism: Only One Cheer," 32.
2. Ibid.
3. George Washington, *Washington's Farewell Address, Webster's First Bunker Hill Oration, Lincoln's Gettysburg Address*, 12.
4. Susan Bailey Scott, correspondence with author's team, April 22, 2019.
5. "Twins Mark Bar Mitzvah; Lehrman Boys to Be Honored Tonight," *Harrisburg Patriot*, October 26, 1951.
6. Meislin, "Lehrman Seeking Governorship Armed with a Marketing Plan."
7. Sam Roberts, "Seating Chart for a Most Awkward Dinner Party," *New York Times*, October 27, 2016.
8. Georgia Dullea, "Mrs. Lehrman and Mrs. Cuomo: New Lives," *New York Times*, October 25, 1982.
9. "Inner-City Schools: Cardinals' Concern Praised as Fund Tops $1.8 Million," *Catholic New York*, December 15, 1983.
10. Susan Heller and David W. Dunlap, "New York Day by Day, A Conversion," *New York Times*, April 16, 1985.
11. Moss, "Closeup: Lew Lehrman."
12. Daniel Lazare, "Once in Politics, Lehrman Shuns the Limelight," *New York Observer*, July 31, 1989.
13. Rowland Evans and Robert Novak, "Regan Says Reagan's European Trip Was in Trouble from Very Beginning," *Hattiesburg* (MS) *American*, April 21, 1985.
14. William F. Buckley Jr., "The Perils of Baptism," *New York Post*, April 23, 1985.
15. John D. Mueller, letter to author, July 2018.
16. Trish Blake, correspondence with author's team, March 31, 2019.
17. Chris Potter, correspondence with author's team, July 15, 2019.
18. Andrei Bogolubov, correspondence with author's team, September 27, 2019.
19. Lewis E. Lehrman, "Faith and the Future of Capitalism," *Wall Street Journal*, April 16, 1993.
20. "Neither let us be slandered from our duty by false accusations against us, nor frightened from it by menaces of destruction to the Government nor of dungeons to ourselves." Abraham Lincoln, "Address at Cooper Institute, New York City, February 27, 1860." In *Collected Works of Abraham Lincoln*, 3: 550.
21. Michael Kramer, "Battle of the Brains," *New York*, November 1, 1982, 35.
22. Lewis E. Lehrman, speech, Pepperdine University, Malibu, CA, November 26, 1984.
23. Lewis E. Lehrman, *News Chronicle* (Shippensburg, PA), November 13, 1986.
24. Lewis E. Lehrman, "Commencement Address," Thomas Aquinas College, Santa Paula, CA, June 7, 1986.
25. Lewis E. Lehrman, "The Right to Life, and the Restoration of the American Republic," *National Review*, August 26, 1986, 25–26.
26. Lewis E. Lehrman, "The Declaration of Independence and the Right to Life," *American Spectator*, April 1987, 21.
27. Lewis E. Lehrman, "The Declaration of Independence and the Right to Life," *Human Life Review*, Summer 1987, 78.
28. Lewis E. Lehrman, "Rule of Lawlessness," *Crisis*, June 1989, 33.
29. Lewis E. Lehrman, "On Original Intent," *American Spectator*, September 22, 1986
30. Clarence Thomas, "Why Black Conservatives Should Look to Conservative Policies," speech, The Heritage Foundation, Washington, DC, June 18, 1987.
31. Lewis E. Lehrman, "Slavery and Abortion," speech, Catholic Campaign for America, Philadelphia, PA, September 21, 1996.
32. Lewis E. Lehrman, "Slavery and Abortion," *Crisis*, September 1996, 24.

33. Bill Slocum, "Lehrman Still Pursues 'Right-Minded' Goals," *Greenwich* (CT) *News*, October 24, 1991.
34. Ibid.
35. Lehrman, "Slavery and Abortion," speech.
36. Ibid.
37. Lewis E. Lehrman, "Abraham Lincoln, Slavery, and Abortion," speech, Connecticut Catholic Forum, April 28, 1991.
38. Lewis E. Lehrman, speech, Legatus, October 22, 1992.
39. Lehrman, "Slavery and Abortion," speech.
40. Anna Halpine, letter to author, July 2018.

Chapter 13: Business and I

1. Lewis E. Lehrman, letter to Jonathan Bush, March 21, 1979.
2. George W. Bush, letter to Lewis E. Lehrman, August 1, 1979.
3. Daniel F. Cuff, "Lehrman to Join Morgan Stanley," *New York Times*, March 19, 1987.
4. Lewis E. Lehrman, "On the Occasion of the Memorial Service of Barton M. Biggs," speech, Christ Church, Greenwich, CT, September 7, 2012.
5. Bob Niehaus, letter to author, July 2018.
6. Susan Tang, correspondence with author, August 9, 2019.
7. Trish Blake, correspondence with author's team, March 31, 2019.
8. Beard, letter to author, July 2018.
9. Susan Tang, correspondence with author, August 9, 2019.
10. Trish Blake, correspondence with author's team, March 31, 2019.
11. Deja Hickcox, correspondence with author, July 10, 2019.
12. Chris Potter, correspondence with author's team, July 15, 2019.
13. Ibid.
14. Chis Potter, letter to author, July 2018.
15. Chris Potter, correspondence with author's team, July 15, 2019.
16. Steve Szymanski, correspondence with author's team, May 14, 2020.
17. Frank Trotta, correspondence with author, 2002.
18. Steve Bodow, "Investing; It's Not What They Know, but Whom," *New York Times*, December 23, 2001.

Chapter 14: Forward to Gold

1. Daniel Webster, "A Speech Delivered in the Senate on the 25th of May, 1832, on the Bill for Renewing the Charter of the Bank of the United States," *The Works of Daniel Webster*, Volume III, 18th ed. (Boston: Little, Brown and Company, 1881), 394.
2. The essays are also available at my website: lewiselehrman.com.
3. Lewis E. Lehrman, "A Glittering Economy," *Washington Post*, July 22, 1981.
4. Lehrman, "A Glittering Economy."
5. Lewis E. Lehrman, "The Case for the Gold Standard," *Wall Street Journal*, July 30, 1981.
6. Lewis E. Lehrman, letter to Daniel Moynihan, May 1977.
7. Simon London, "Lunch with the FT—Milton Friedman: The Long View," *Financial Times (Financial Times Magazine* supplement, Issue No. 7), June 7, 2003, 12–13.
8. Lewis E. Lehrman, "Monetary Policy, the Federal Reserve System, and Gold," *Morgan Stanley Investment Research*, January 25, 1980, 5-6. This paper, and my other Morgan Stanley papers have been archived online at www.lewiselehrman.com/morganstanley.
9. John Mueller, "Jack Kemp Oral History Project," interview by Morton Kondracke, *Jack Kemp Foundation*, January 18, 2012.
10. World War I caused the suspension of the gold standard because some of the major countries were not solvent.

11. Jim would later write Bagehot's biography: James Grant, *Bagehot: The Life and Times of the Greatest Victorian* (New York: W.W. Norton and Company, 2019).
12. James Grant, *Money of the Mind: Borrowing and Lending in America from the Civil War to Michael Milken* (New York: Farrar Straus Giroux, 1992), 317–18.
13. Domitrovic, *Econoclasts*, 244.
14. Lewis E. Lehrman, "How to End Inflation," *Washington Post*, January 18, 1981.
15. James K. Glassman, "Back to the Gold Standard?" *Atlantic Monthly*, February 1981, 32.
16. Lewis E. Lehrman, "The Means to Establishing Financial Order," *Wall Street Journal*, February 18, 1981.
17. Lewis E. Lehrman, "Case for a Return to the Gold Standard," interview.
18. Lewis E. Lehrman, remarks to the American Economic Council, July 1981.
19. Ibid.
20. US Congress. *Congressional Record.* 1981. 97th Cong., 1st sess. Vol. 127, pt. 122.
21. Lewis E. Lehrman, "Should the U.S. Return to the Gold Standard?" *Christian Science Monitor*, September 21, 1981.
22. Lewis E. Lehrman, "Pro and Con: Time to Return to the Gold Standard?" *U.S. News & World Report*, September 7, 1981, 71.
23. Lewis E. Lehrman, "Turning Silver into Gold," *Leaders*, October-November-December 1981.
24. Jeff Bell, "An Inside Look at the Reagan Revolution, Part I," interview by Brian Maher, *Daily Reckoning*, June 6, 2016, https://dailyreckoning.com/85145-2/.
25. Ibid.
26. Leonard Silk, "Economic Scene: Clash Over Gold Standard," *New York Times*, April 29, 1981.
27. Lewis E. Lehrman, "The Return of Gold," memo to Edwin Meese, July 9, 1981.
28. Tom Redburn, "Return to Gold Standard: Old Idea Is Slowly Gaining a New Following," *Los Angeles Times*, April 5, 1981.
29. Lewis E. Lehrman, "Jack Kemp Oral History Project," December 14, 2011
30. Ibid.
31. Robert Novak, *The Prince of Darkness: 50 Years Reporting in Washington* (New York: Crown Form, 2007), 421.
32. Thomas O'Donnell, "Return of the Golden Rule?," *Forbes*, June 8, 1981, 33.
33. Lehrman, "Return of Gold," memo.
34. William Safire, "It's Gold Standard Time," *Chicago Tribune*, September 13, 1981.
35. Robert D. Hershey, Jr., "Notion of Reviving Gold Standard Debated Seriously in Washington," *New York Times*, September 18, 1981.
36. *Report to the Congress of the Commission on the Role of Gold in the Domestic and International Monetary Systems*, 2 vols. (Washington, DC: US Government Printing Office, March 1982).
37. Caroline Atkinson, "Gold Bugs Buzz, Don't Bite," *Washington Post*, September 19, 1981.
38. David Howden and Joseph T. Salerno, eds., *The Fed at One Hundred: A Critical View of the Federal Reserve System* (New York: Springer, 2014), 75.
39. Seth Lipsky, letter to author, July 2018.
40. Anna J. Schwartz, *Money in Historical Perspective* (Chicago: University of Chicago Press, 1987), 328–29.
41. "Supply Siders vs. Monetarists," *Business Week*, August 24, 1981, 80.
42. Lewis E. Lehrman, "Should We (and Could We) Return to the Gold Standard?" *New York Times*, September 6, 1981. The best source regarding the rationality of the operations of markets is George Gilder's book *Wealth and Poverty* (1981). In the book, Gilder shows that markets are superior to central planning and are more ethical too. Adam Smith's classic text *The Wealth of Nations* also makes important points in this regard. In citing Smith, however, I want to be careful not to endorse wholesale his controversial "invisible

hand" argument. See my article in the April 2000 issue of *Crisis*, "Capitalism: Only One Cheer," for a more complete treatment of the subject: https://www.crisismagazine.com/vault/capitalism-only-one-cheer.

43. Lewis E. Lehrman, "The Guru of Gold," interview by A. F. Ehrbar, *Fortune*, November 30, 1981, 98.
44. Jerome Idaszak, "Gold Standard Stirs A Revived Debate," *Newsday*, September 27, 1981.
45. In this regard, the gold standard can improve relations with natural resources, because it does not produce the rush to extract and spend associated with inflation.
46. Lewis E. Lehrman, interview by Jim Cook, *IRI Insights*, Fall 1981.
47. The Gold Commission was authorized by a provision of an October 7, 1980 (P.L. 96-389) and was amended to extend the date to submit the report on September 30, 1981 (P.L. 97-47).
48. *Report to the Congress of the Commission on the Role of Gold in the Domestic and International Monetary Systems*, 2 vols. (Washington, DC: US Government Printing Office, March 1982), 19.
49. Donald T. Regan, "Cover Letter, March 31, 1982," *Report to the Congress of the Commission on the Role of Gold in the Domestic and International Monetary Systems,* 2 vols. (Washington, DC: US Government Printing Office, March 1982), iii.
50. Schwartz, *Money in Historical Perspective* , 329.
51. Ibid., 324.
52. Domitrovic, *Econoclasts*, 211.
53. "Golden Opportunity: Lew Lehrman on Stocks, Bonds, and Economics," interview by Kathryn M. Welling, *Barron's*, April 18, 1983, 8.
54. Ibid.
55. Lewis E. Lehrman, "A Flat Tax Would Stimulate Growth," *New York Times*, February 24, 1985.
56. Lewis E. Lehrman, "Tax Lessons at the State Level," *Wall Street Journal*, August 2, 1985.
57. George Schultz, letter to author, August 2, 1985.
58. Charles Rist was Jacques Rueff's teacher and friend. For more information on the issue of prewar parity, please see the article by Jacques Rueff, "The West Is Risking a Credit Collapse," *Forbes*, July 1961.
59. Lewis E. Lehrman, "Protectionism, Inflation, or Monetary Reform: The Case for Fixed Exchange Rates and a Modernized Gold Standard," *Morgan Stanley Investment Research*, November 1985.
60. Lewis E. Lehrman, "Back to Gold: Giving Up the 'Order of the Jungle'" *Challenge*, January/February 1986, 22.
61. Lewis E. Lehrman, "To Move Forward, Go Back to Gold," *New York Times*, February 9, 1986.
62. Lewis E. Lehrman, "An Exorbitant Privilege," *National Review*, November 21, 1986, 42.
63. Lewis E. Lehrman, remarks at US Congressional Summit on Debt and Trade, Washington, DC, December 4, 1986.
64. Lewis E. Lehrman, "Trade War or Monetary Reform?" *Wall Street Journal*, January 28, 1987.
65. As I contemplated this section prior to publication, I realized that given how long ago these events happened, I am not sure I have been able to recall every detail correctly. The meeting with both men, however, and the general subject matter are a matter of fact.
66. Robert A. Jaeger qtd in. Lewis E. Lehrman, "Gold in a Global Multi-Asset Portfolio," *Morgan Stanley Asset Management*, March 4, 1988, 1.
67. Paul Fabra, "Les Fils Spirituels Americains de Jacques Rueff," *Le Monde*, July 10, 1990.
68. Lewis E. Lehrman, "The Curse of Being a Reserve Currency," *Wall Street Journal*, January 4, 1993.
69. Lewis E. Lehrman and John D. Mueller, "How the 'Reserve' Dollar Harms America," *Wall Street Journal*, November 21, 2014.

70. Ibid.
71. Lewis E. Lehrman, "The Federal Reserve, Dollar Disorders, and Market Forecasting," speech at Grant's Spring Credit Conference, New York, NY, May 14, 1991.
72. Lewis E. Lehrman and John Mueller, "Redeem Us with a Cross of Gold," *Wall Street Journal*, July 8, 1994.
73. Lewis E. Lehrman, "A New (and Improved) Bretton Woods," remarks at Empower America Conference, Georgetown University, Washington, D.C., September 8, 1994.
74. Lewis E. Lehrman and John Mueller, "Go Forward to Gold," *National Review*, December 15, 2008, 40.
75. Lewis E. Lehrman and John Mueller, "Why Real Monetary Reform Can—and Must—Be Done Now," *Washington Examiner*, March 11, 2011.
76. Lewis E. Lehrman, "Fiat Money, Fiat Inflation," *Weekly Standard*, March 21, 2011, 16.
77. Lewis E. Lehrman, "To End the Age of Financial Disorder, Forward to a Modernized Gold Standard," remarks to Grant's Spring Conference, Plaza Hotel, New York, NY, March 29, 2011.
78. Lewis E. Lehrman, "Monetary Reform: The Key to Spending Restraint," *Wall Street Journal*, April 26, 2011.
79. Allan H. Meltzer, *A History of the Federal Reserve* (Chicago: University of Chicago Press, 2003, 2010).
80. Lewis E. Lehrman, "The Nixon Shock Heard 'Round the World," *Wall Street Journal*, August 15, 2011.
81. Lewis E. Lehrman, *Churchill, Roosevelt & Company: Studies in Character and Statecraft* (Guilford, CT: Stackpole Books, 2017).
82. Lewis E. Lehrman, testimony before Hearing of the Subcommittee on Domestic Monetary Policy & Technology, Washington, DC, September 20, 2012.
83. Lewis E. Lehrman, "The Case for a Modernized Gold Standard," *American Spectator*, October 2012, 21–22.
84. Lewis E. Lehrman, "Summary of the Monetary Reform Plan," in *The True Gold Standard* (New York: TLI Books, 2013), i.
85. James D. Grant, email to author, January 24, 2012.
86. Newt Gingrich, Republican Presidential Primary debate, Tampa, FL, January 23, 2012.
87. Lewis E. Lehrman, "Join the Alliance for a Sound Dollar," *New York Sun*, January 29, 2012.
88. Lewis E. Lehrman, "The Demise of Money and Credit," *American Spectator*, May 2013, 35.
89. Lewis E. Lehrman and John D. Mueller, "Fiscal Fitness," *Weekly Standard*, February 25, 2013, 17.
90. Paul Brodsky, "The Lehrman Standard," *American Spectator*, June 2013, 54.
91. Lehrman, "Summary of the Monetary Reform Plan," in *The True Gold Standard*, iii.

Chapter 15: Getting Right with the Founders

1. Lewis E. Lehrman, "Introduction of Richard Gilder," remarks at the Arthur Schlesinger Lecture, Gilder Lehrman Institute of American History, New York, NY, February 22, 1995.
2. Barone, "Clash of Ideas in New York."
3. Lewis E. Lehrman, "On Jaffa, Lincoln, Marshall, and Original Intent," *University of Puget Sound Law Review*, Spring 1987, 343.
4. See chapter 12 titled "Faith in Action."
5. Daniel P. Jordan, correspondence with author's team, April 12, 2019.
6. Lewis E. Lehrman, "Blessed, to the Latest Generation," speech, Bissell Fellow Program, The Hill School, Pottstown, PA, February 21, 1991.
7. Lewis E. Lehrman, "Jefferson May Have Drafted the Declaration of Independence But He Wasn't Happy Being Edited," *Fox News*, May 7, 2015, https://www.foxnews.com/

opinion/jefferson-may-have-drafted-the-declaration-of-independence-but-he-wasnt-happy-being-edited.

8. Lehrman, "Roots and Revolution," speech.
9. Lehrman, "Commencement Address," speech, Thomas Aquinas College, Santa Paula, CA, June 7, 1986.
10. Moss, "Closeup: Lew Lehrman."
11. Winston S. Churchill, "Sinews of Peace," speech, Westminster College, Fulton, MO, March 5, 1946, https://www.nationalchurchillmuseum.org/sinews-of-peace-iron-curtain-speech.html.
12. Lehrman, "Roots and Revolution," speech.
13. Ibid.
14. Lewis E. Lehrman, speech, Pepperdine University, Malibu, CA, November 26, 1984.
15. Lewis E. Lehrman, "Whither American History and American Capitalism," speech, ISI Lehrman American Studies Center Summer Institute, Princeton, NJ, June 19, 2007.
16. Lewis E, Lehrman, "Alexander Hamilton: Precocious and Preeminent," *New Criterion*, May 1999, 33.
17. Lewis E. Lehrman, "Justice James Wilson of Cumberland County," *Cumberland County History* (Carlisle, PA), Summer 1994, 19.
18. Ibid., 23.
19. Lewis E. Lehrman, *The American Founders* (The Lehrman Institute, 2013), iii.
20. Gordon S. Wood, *Revolutionary Characters: What Made the Founders Different* (New York: Penguin Press, 2006), 246.
21. Abraham Lincoln, "First Inaugural Address—Final Text, dated March 4, 1861." In *Collected Works of Abraham Lincoln*, 4: 271.
22. Abraham Lincoln, "Letter to Jesse W. Fell, Enclosing Autobiography, December 20, 1859." In *Collected Works of Abraham Lincoln*, 3: 512.
23. Abraham Lincoln, "Speech at Peoria, Illinois, October 16, 1854." In *Collected Works of Abraham Lincoln*, 2: 248–83.
24. Bruce Cole, "History Unfiltered," *Humanities*, July/August 2008, 53.
25. Ibid.
26. Blumenthal, "Let Lehrman Be Reagan," 19.
27. Anne W. Semmes, "Lew Lehrman: On Life, Liberty, and Lincoln," *Greenwich* (CT) *Time*, July 3, 2014.
28. Abraham Lincoln, "Speech in Independence Hall, Philadelphia, PA, February 22, 1861." In *Collected Works of Abraham Lincoln*, 4: 241.
29. Lewis E. Lehrman, "Work Is the Main Thing," *Wall Street Journal*, February 10, 1995.
30. Lewis E. Lehrman, "Listen to Mr. Lincoln," *Wall Street Journal*, February 12, 1996.
31. Lewis E. Lehrman, "Lincoln Looked into Future," *Stamford Advocate*, February 16, 2020.
32. Abraham Lincoln, "First Annual Message to Congress, December 1, 1861." In *Collected Works of Abraham Lincoln*, 5: 53.
33. Abraham Lincoln, "Second Annuial Message to Congress, December 1, 1862." In *Collected Works of Abraham Lincoln*, 5: 535.
34. Abraham Lincoln, "Letter to James C. Conkling, August 26, 1863." In *Collected Works of Abraham Lincoln*, 6: 410.
35. "Lewis Lehrman Analyzes Two Great Leaders," *Churchill Bulletin*, February 26, 2016, https://winstonchurchill.org/publications/churchill-bulletin/bulletin-093-mar-2016/mr-churchill-mr-lincoln/.
36. Winston S. Churchill, quoted in Frank Costogliola, *Roosevelt's Lost Alliances: How Personal Politics Helped Start the Cold War* (Princeton, NJ and Oxford: Princeton University Press, 2012), 154.

37. Winston S. Churchill, "Liberty Day Meetings, July 4, 1918," The Churchill Project at Hillsdale College, https://winstonchurchill.hillsdale.edu/churchill-on-july-4th/.
38. Winston S. Churchill, *A History of the English Speaking Peoples, Vol. 3, The Age of Revolution* (London: Cassell and Company , 1957), 154, 156.
39. Robert Marchant, "Greenwich Executive Continues to Tell America's Story," *Greenwich* (CT) *Time*, March 18, 2017.
40. Martin Gilbert, *The Churchill War Papers* (London: Heinemann, 1994), 2: 70–71.
41. "Lewis Lehrman Analyzes Two Great Leaders."
42. Lewis E. Lehrman, *Lincoln & Churchill: Statesmen at War* (Guilford, CT: Stackpole Books, 2018).
43. Lewis E. Lehrman, "How Lincoln and Churchill Put National Unity First," *Daily Beast*, May 11, 2019, https://www.thedailybeast.com/how-lincoln-and-churchill-put-national-unity-first.
44. Jason Emerson, "Two Historical Giants at War," *American Spectator*, March 1, 2018, https://spectator.org/two-historical-giants-at-war/.
45. Winston S. Churchill, speaking to his non-Cabinet ministers, May 28, 1940, available from Richard M. Langworth, "Martin on Churchill: No One Ever Left without Feeling a Braver Man," March 30, 2022, https://richardlangworth.com/john-martin.
46. Doris Kearns Goodwin, review of *Lincoln & Churchill Statesmen at War* (Guilford, CT: Stackpole Books, 2018).

Chapter 16: Collaborating on History

1. David Brion Davis, letter to author, October 7, 2003.
2. Daniel P. Jordan, correspondence with author's team, September 12, 2019.
3. Robert Marchant, "Man of History Continues to Tell America's Story," *Greenwich* (CT) *Time*, May 17, 2017.
4. David Howard, *Lost Rights: The Misadventures of a Stolen American Relic* (Boston and New York: Houghton Mifflin, 2010), 168.
5. David Brion Davis, *Boisterous Sea of Liberty: A Documentary History of America from Discovery through the Civil War* (Oxford and New York: Oxford University Press, 1998), 562.
6. Harold Holzer, "Prizing History: An Interview with Richard Gilder and Lewis," *American Heritage*, May/June 2000, 96–97.
7. Ibid., 97.
8. Ibid., 97.
9. Ibid., 96.
10. Emily Sherwood, "Richard Gilder and Lewis Lehrman Make History Come Alive," *Education Update*, June 2007, 3.
11. Sandra Trenholm, correspondence with author, September 30, 2019.
12. Catherine Nicholson, "The Stone Engraving: Icon of the Declaration," *Prologue Magazine*, Fall 2003, Vol. 35, No. 3.
13. The current total number of artifacts in the Gilder Lehrman Collection is 86,466.
14. Davis, *Boisterous Sea of Liberty*, 561.
15. Sandra Trenholm, correspondence with author's team, September 30, 2019.
16. Ibid.
17. Susan Saidenberg, correspondence with author's team, August 7, 2019.
18. Ibid.
19. Phil Hamilton, correspondence with author's team, March 25, 2019.
20. Holzer, "Prizing History," 97.
21. "Puddle jumper" is an affectionate nickname for light aircraft.
22. Holzer, "Prizing History," 97.
23. Janet Riggs, correspondence with author's team, August 8, 2019.
24. David Streitfeld, "A Few Choice Words," *Washington Post*, February 17, 1991.

25. Lewis E. Lehrman, "Remarks at the Inaugural Lincoln Prize Dinner," Gettysburg College, Gettysburg, PA, February 9, 1991.
26. United Press International, "PBS Series 'Civil War' Wins First Lincoln Prize," February 9, 1991.
27. Janet Riggs, correspondence with author's team, August 8, 2019.
28. A full list of all the winners of the Lincoln Prize can be found on the Gilder Lehrman Institute of American History's Lincoln Prize page: https://www.gilderlehrman.org/programs-and-events/national-book-prizes/gilder-lehrman-lincoln-prize.
29. Douglas Wilson, correspondence with author's team, April 1, 2019.
30. Janet Riggs, correspondence with author's team, August 7, 2019.
31. Diane Brennan, correspondence with author's team, March 21, 2019.
32. Ibid.
33. Richard Gilder and Lewis E. Lehrman, interview by Brian Lamb .
34. Ibid.
35. David Brion Davis, "Remarks Concerning *Inhuman Bondage*: *The Rise and Fall of Slavery in The New Wold*," speech, Morgan Library, New York, NY, June 7, 2006.
36. Sandra Trenholm, correspondence with author's team, September 30, 2019.
37. Daniel P. Jordan, correspondence with author's team, September 12, 2019.
38. Sandra Trenholm, correspondence with author's team, September 30, 2019.
39. Diane Brennan, correspondence with author's team, March 21, 2019.
40. Daniel P. Jordan, correspondence with author's team, September 12, 2019.
41. Ibid.
42. Bob Niehaus, letter to author, July 2018.
43. Richard Gilder and Lewis E. Lehrman, interview by Brian Lamb.
44. Ibid.
45. Ibid.
46. Daniel P. Jordan, correspondence with author's team, September 12, 2019.
47. Douglas Wilson, correspondence with author's team, April 1, 2019.
48. Susan Bailey Scott, correspondence with author's team, April 22, 2019.
49. James G. Basker, correspondence with author's team, June 12, 2019.
50. Ibid.
51. Ibid.
52. Ibid.
53. Richard Gilder and Lewis E. Lehrman, interview by Brian Lamb.
54. Davis, "Remarks Concerning *Inhuman* Bondage."
55. "Gilder Lehrman Center History," Yale Macmillan Center: Gilder Lehrman Center for the Study of Slavery, Resistance, and Abolition, https://glc.yale.edu/about-us/gilder-lehrman-center-history.
56. Lewis E. Lehrman, "Frederick Douglass Prize," speech First Annual Frederick Douglass Prize Ceremony, Yale Club, New York, NY, September 26, 1999.
57. Ibid.
58. See Appendix of this book.
59. Davis, "Remarks Concerning *Inhuman Bondage*".
60. David Brion Davis, letter to author, October 7, 2003.
61. David Brion Davis, letter to Lewis E. Lehrman and Richard Gilder, December 20, 2009.
62. Richard Gilder and Lewis E. Lehrman, interview by Brian Lamb.
63. Lewis E. Lehrman, "Alexander Hamilton: Precocious & Preeminent," *New Criterion*, May 1999, 31.
64. James G. Basker, correspondence with author's team, June 12, 2019.
65. Ibid.
66. Richard Brookhiser, letter to author, July 2018.

67. James G. Basker, correspondence with author's team, June 12, 2019.
68. Gary Shapiro, "Honoring Hamilton," *New York Sun*, September 9, 2004.
69. James G. Basker, correspondence with author's team, June 12, 2019.
70. Angelle Albright, "EDUHAM: Offering Every Kid a Shot! at Saenger Theatre," *Broadway World*, April 3, 2019, https://www.broadwayworld.com/new-orleans/article/BWW-Feature-EDUHAM-OFFERING-EVERY-KID-A-SHOT-at-Saenger-Theatre-20190403.
71. Louise Mirrer, in David Brion Davis and Louise Mirrer, "'That Hamilton Man:' An Exchange," *New York Review of Books*, May 26, 2005.
72. David Brion Davis, in Davis and Mirrer, "That Hamilton Man."
73. Eric Gibson, "They Do Know Much About History," *Wall Street Journal*, July 30, 2004.
74. Kevin Baker, quoted in Robert Marchant, "Greenwich Executive Continues to Tell America's Story," *Greenwich* (CT) *Time*, May 18, 2017.
75. Lewis E. Lehrman, "Remarks to Conference," speech, *Lincoln on Democracy* conference, New-York Historical Society, New York, NY, October 1990.
76. Harold Holzer, correspondence with author's team, July 22, 2019.
77. Richard Carwardine, letter to author, July 2018.
78. Phil Hamilton, letter to author, July 2018.
79. Josiah Bunting III, quoted in "Lewis E. Lehrman: Reinvigorating the Teaching of America's Founding Principles," *Canon*, Fall 2008, 56.
80. Lewis E. Lehrman, "The Restoration of American History," speech, ISI Lehrman American Studies Center Summer Institute, Princeton University, June 20, 2006.
81. Michael Burlingame, correspondence with author's team, March 30, 2019.
82. Lewis E. Lehrman, "Whither American History and American Capitalism," speech, ISI Lehrman American Studies Center Summer Institute, Princeton, NJ, June 19, 2007.

Chapter 17: Advice as Epilogue

1. Lehrman, "Roots and Revolution," speech.
2. Arnold J. Toynbee, *Civilization on Trial* (New York: Oxford University Press, 1948), 56.
3. Abraham Lincoln, quoted in *Inside Lincoln's White House: The Complete Civil War Diary of John Hay*, Michael Burlingame and John R Turner Ettlinger, eds. (Carbondale and Edwardsville: Southern Illinois University Press, 1999), 244.
4. Abraham Lincoln, "Letter to J. M. Brockman dated September 25, 1860." In *Collected Works of Abraham Lincoln*, 4: 121.
5. Lewis E. Lehrman, letter to nephew, October 15, 1969.
6. Lewis E. Lehrman, email to grand-nephew, April 7, 2020.
7. Lewis E. Lehrman, letter to nephew, December 4, 2013.
8. Lewis E. Lehrman, letter to son, September 1988.
9. Lewis E. Lehrman, email to nephew, March 31, 2014.
10. Lewis E. Lehrman, letter to son, January 27, 1988.
11. David J. Willmott, "Listen to Lehrman and Save," *Suffolk Life*, January 27, 1982.
12. Arthur Greenspan, "For Lew, 'Lose' Doesn't Exist," *New York Post*, July 12, 1982.
13. Judy Watson, "'Unknown' Drugstore Tycoon to Run for Governor," *United Press International*, November 9, 2981.
14. Carroll, "New York Gubernatorial Campaign," 25.
15. Abraham Lincoln, "Letter to Isham Reavis dated November 5, 1855." In *Collected Works of Abraham Lincoln*, 2:327.
16. Abraham Lincoln, "Letter to William H. Grigsby dated August 3, 1858." In *The Collected Works of Abraham Lincoln*, ed. Roy P. Basler (New Brunswick: Rutgers University Press, 1959), 2: 535.
17. Eliza D. Lehrman, correspondence with author, May 12, 2020.
18. Thomas D. Lehrman, correspondence with author, May 12, 2020.

19. Lynn Sherr, *Failure Is Impossible: Susan B. Anthony in Her Own Words* (New York: Times Books, 1995).
20. Lewis E. Lehrman, email to Anna Halpine, September 18, 2017.
21. Abraham Lincoln, "Letter to Quintin Campbell, June 28, 1862." In *Collected Works of Abraham Lincoln*, 5: 288.
22. Abraham Lincoln, "To Jesse W. Fell, Enclosing Autobiography" In *Collected Works of Abraham Lincoln*, 3: 512. Mr. Lincoln might have added that he was, however, an inveterate reader of newspapers.
23. Phil Hamilton, correspondence with author's team, March 26, 2019.
24. Andrei Bogolubov, correspondence with author's team, September 27, 2019.
25. Deja Hickcox, correspondence with author, July 10, 2019.
26. Lewis E. Lehrman, letter to godson, June 17, 2011.
27. Langdon Cook, letter to author, July 2018.
28. Anna Halpine, letter to author, July 2018.
29. Elizabeth Trotta, letter to author, July 2018.
30. Chris Potter, correspondence with author's team, July 15, 2019.
31. Ibid.
32. Frank Trotta, toast to Lewis E. Lehrman, July 2018.
33. Deja Hickcox, correspondence with author, July 10, 2019.
34. Trish Blake, letter to author, July 2018.
35. John D. Britton, correspondence with author's team, March 27, 2019.
36. Sandra Trenholm, correspondence with author's team, September 30, 2019.
37. Ibid.
38. Sammy MacFarlane, letter to author, December 6, 2018.
39. Along with Mrs. Diven, Jim Grant also thought I would have made a good general. He wrote me in July 2018, saying: "If Lew had not become an entrepreneur, corn farmer, public intellectual, historian, biographer, candidate for high office, adviser to the Reagan administration, patron of history, collector and curator of rare American historical documents, Catholic layman, father, grandfather, husband and helpmeet of the former Louise Stillman, monetary speculator (Wikipedia chooses the circumlocution, "banker")—if he had not become each and every one of those things, what might he have become? Why he would have become a general. His soldierly bearing, patriotism, depth of strategic knowledge and love of country would have raised him to the top of the military chain of command. But one unfortunate incident barred his way. Under questioning by his Army recruiter, Lew answered that he had earned a B.A. at Yale university, and an M.A. at Harvard. It was a fact, but the recruiter wasn't born yesterday. He stared at the intense young man across the desk. If he was telling the truth, he would certainly be good for nothing in the Army. If not, he would go no further than a private."
40. Abraham Lincoln, "Letter to Ulysses S. Grant, August 15, 1864." In *Collected Works of Abraham Lincoln*, 7: 499.
41. Lewis E. Lehrman, letter to godson, May 27, 2011. If this statement is not clear, it means invest in such a way that your decisions do not keep you up at night.
42. Lewis E. Lehrman, letter to godson, November 7, 1979.
43. Lewis E. Lehrman, letter to godson, December 19, 2013.
44. Chris Potter, correspondence with author, July 15, 2019.
45. Abraham Lincoln, "Annual Message to Congress, December 1, 1862." In *Collected Works of Abraham Lincoln*, 5: 537.
46. Anna Halpine, letter to author, July 2018.
47. Winston S. Churchill, "Never Give In, Never, Never, Never," speech, Harrow School, October 29, 1941, accessed at: https://www.nationalchurchillmuseum.org/never-give-in-never-never-never.html.

48. Phil Hamilton, correspondence with author's team, March 25, 2019.
49. Andrei Bogolubov, correspondence with author's team, September 27, 2019.
50. Ibid.
51. Lewis E. Lehrman, letter to godson, November 7, 1978.
52. Abraham Lincoln, "Final Debate with Stephen Douglas, October 15, 1858." In *Collected Works of Abraham Lincoln*, 3: 315.
53. Eliza D. Lehrman, correspondence with author, May 12, 2020.
54. Abraham Lincoln, "Fragment: Notes for a Law Lecture, July 1, 1850." In *Collected Works of Abraham Lincoln*, 2: 82.
55. Bogolubov, correspondence with author's team, September 30, 2019.
56. Ibid.
57. Ibid.
58. Lewis E. Lehrman, "Whither American History and American Capitalism," speech, ISI Summer Institute, Princeton, NJ, June 19, 2007.
59. Horowitz, *On the Cusp*, 230.
60. Abraham Lincoln, "Letter to George G. Meade, July 14, 1863." In *Collected Works of Abraham Lincoln*, 6: 327–28.
61. Ibid.
62. Holzer, "Prizing History," 96.
63. John P. Britton, letter to author, July 12, 1976.
64. John P. Britton, letter to author, June 8, 1981.
65. Lewis E. Lehrman, letter to son, April 18, 1988.
66. Bogolubov, correspondence with author's team, September 30, 2019.
67. Mary MacKenzie, letter to author, July 2018.
68. Peter R. Lehrman, correspondence with author, May 15, 2020.
69. Eliza D. Lehrman, correspondence with author, May 12, 2020.
70. R. Leland Lehrman, correspondence with author, May 15, 2020.
71. Lewis E. Lehrman, memo to file, 1970s.

Chapter 18: The Children and Grandchildren

1. Lewis E. Lehrman, letter to R. Leland Lehrman, June 7, 1988.
2. R. Leland Lehrman, correspondence with author, May 15, 2020.
3. Lewis E. Lehrman, letter to R. Leland Lehrman, September 19, 1988.
4. Lewis E. Lehrman, letter to R. Leland Lehrman, April 1987.
5. John S. Lehrman, correspondence with author, May 12, 2020.
6. Lewis E. Lehrman, memo to file, 1980.
7. Thomas D. Lehrman, correspondence with author, May 12, 2020.
8. Ronald Reagan, letter to Eliza D. Lehrman, July 7, 1983.
9. Eliza D. Lehrman, correspondence with author, May 12, 2020.
10. Lewis E. Lehrman, toast to Eliza, speech, Greenwich, CT, November 5. 2011.
11. Peter R. Lehrman, correspondence with author, May 15, 2020.
12. John D. Britton, letter to author, July 2018. John D. Britton; correspondence with author's team, March 27, 2019; Sam Britton, correspondence with author's team.

Appendix: Early Writings

1. Jose Ortega y Gasset, *The Revolution of the Masses* (London: Allen and Unwin, 1969). Ortega's barbarian is a reference to the philosopher's own critique of both the "mass-man" and the overspecialized scientist in his book, *The Revolt of the Masses*. http://xahlee.

org/wordy/p/Barbarism_of_Specialization.html and https://en.wikipedia.org/wiki/The_Revolt_of_the_Masses.

2. Isaiah Berlin, *The Hedgehog and The Fox* (London: Weidenfeld & Nicolson, 1953). Isaiah Berlin's book *The Hedgehog and the Fox* is based on the ancient Greek saying, "a fox knows many things, but a hedgehog knows one big thing." According to the Princeton University Press, "Although there have been many interpretations of the adage, Berlin uses it to mark a fundamental distinction between human beings who are fascinated by the infinite variety of things and those who relate everything to a central, all-embracing system." https://press.princeton.edu/books/paperback/9780691156002/the-hedgehog-and-the-fox.
3. Some of the inspiration for this essay, especially the section on Isaac Newton, comes from Franklin Baumer, ed., *Main Currents of Western Thought: Readings in Western European Intellectual History from the Middle Ages to the Present* (New York: Alfred A. Knopf, 1952).
4. A rare critique of contemporary American culture, this poem and Lehrman's thought is best understood in the light of the second poem, see next endnote. —R. L. Lehrman
5. In this poem, Lehrman challenges existentialist philosophy from a poetic standpoint. First, note his reverence for the "Great vision—of men bound/Together with this dream their end" as described in the first poem—a dream that is clearly American in spirit. With that in mind, one can see that in this second poem, Lehrman is stating that the dream of America is more appealing as a philosophy and as a poetic than the idea that life and civilization are absurd. Although his critique of existentialist philosophy may be reductionist, Lehrman makes an understandable case that both the work of life, as well as the dream of America can be made good by the same consciousness that under existentialism despairs of life's meaninglessness. "It's conscious[ness that] makes the difference," he concludes. In the same vein, Lehrman starts with a great question: "Why is it that men ponder, when all of life's about them and they cannot feel its worth." Indeed. —R. L. Lehrman.

BIBLIOGRAPHY

Aquinas, St. Thomas. 1981. *The Summa Theologica*. English Dominican Provincial Translation. 5 vols. Westminster, MD: Christian Classics.

Augustine, 1950. *City of God*. New York: Modern Library.

Barnett, Correlli. 1972. *The Collapse of British Power*. New York: William Morrow & Company, Inc.

Baumer, Franklin. 1952. *Main Currents of Western Thought: Readings in Western European Intellectual History from the Middle Ages to the Present*. New York: Alfred A. Knopf.

Berlin, Isaiah. 1953. *The Hedgehog and the Fox*. London: Weidenfeld & Nicolson.

Blackstone, William. 1765. *Commentaries on the Laws of England*. 8 vol. Oxford: Clarendon Press.

Boswell, James. 1791. *The Life of Samuel Johnson, L.L.D.* London: Henry Baldwin for Charles Dilly, in the Poultry.

Britton, John P. 1992. *Models and Precision: The Quality of Ptolemy's Observations and Parameters*. New York and London: Garland Publishing.

Burns, Elizabeth (Gertrude Behanna). 1968. *The Late Liz: The Autobiography of an Ex-Pagan*. Revised. New York: Meredith Press.

Caher, John M. 1998. *King of the Mountain: The Rise, Fall, and Redemption of Chief Judge Sol Wachtler*. Amherst, NY: Prometheus Books.

Cannon, Lee. 1969. *Ronnie and Jesse: A Political Odyssey*. Garden City, NY: Doubleday.

Cheney, Richard B., and Liz Cheney. 2011. *In My Time: A Personal and Political Memoir*. New York: Threshold Editions.

Chitty, Joseph. 1828. *A Treatise on the Parties to Actions and On Pleading with Second and Third Volumes Containing Precedents of Pleading*. 3 vol. Philadelphia: Carey, Lea and Carey.

Chivvis, Christopher S. 2010. *The Monetary Conservative: Jacques Rueff and Twentieth-Century Free Market Thought*. DeKalb: Northern Illinois University Press.

Churchill, Randolph, and Martin Gilbert. 1966-1988. *Winston S. Churchill*. 8 vols. London: Heinemann.

Churchill, Winston S. 1957. *A History of the English Speaking Peoples: The Age of Revolution*. Vol. 3. 4 vols. London: Cassell and Company.

Cleveland, Harold V., Charles P. Kindleberger, and Lewis E. Lehrman. 1976. *Money and the Coming World Order*. Edited by David P. Calleo. New York: New York University Press.

Costogliola, Frank. 2012. *Roosevelt's Lost Alliances: How Personal Politics Helped Start the Cold War*. Princeton, NJ and Oxford: Princeton University Press.

Davis, David Brion. 1998. *Boisterous Sea of Liberty: A Documentary History of America from Discovery Through the Civil War*. Oxford and New York: Oxford University Press.

Dehio, Ludwig. 1963. *The Precarious Balance: The Politics of Power in Europe 1494–1945*. London: Chatto & Windrus.

Domitrovic, Brian. 2009. *Econoclasts: The Rebels Who Sparked the Supply-Side Revolution and Restored American Prosperity*. Wilmington, DE: ISI Books.

Eden, Sir Anthony. 1963. *Full Circle: The Memoirs of Anthony Eden*. London: Cassell & Company, Ltd.

Evans, Rowland, and Robert Novak. 1981. *The Reagan Revolution: An Inside Look at the Transformation of the U.S. Government*. New York: E.P. Dutton.

Freedman, Samuel G. 1996. *The Inheritance: How Three Families and America Moved from Roosevelt to Reagan and Beyond*. New York: Simon & Schuster.

Friedman, Milton, and Anna J. Schwartz. 1963. *A Monetary History of the United States: 1867–1960.* Princeton, NJ: Princeton University Press.

Gilbert, Sir Martin. 1994. *The Churchill War Papers.* Vol. 2. London: Heinemann.

Gilder, George. 1981. *Wealth and Poverty.* New York: Basic Books.

Gillette, Jr., Howard. 2015. *Class Divide: Yale '64 and the Conflicted Legacy of the Sixties.* Ithaca, NY and London: Cornell University Press.

Goodwin, Doris Kearns. 1976. *Lyndon Johnson and the American Dream.* New York: Harper & Row.

———. 2005. *Team of Rivals: The Political Genius of Abraham Lincoln.* New York: Simon & Schuster.

Grant, James D. 2019. *Bagehot: The Life and Times of the Greatest Victorian.* New York and London: W.W. Norton and Company.

———. 1992. *Money of the Mind: Borrowing and Lending in America from the Civil War to Michael Milken.* New York: Farrar Straus Giroux.

Hay, John. 1999. *Inside Lincoln's White House: The Complete Civil War Diary of John Hay.* Edited by Michael Burlingame and John R. Turner Ettlinger. Carbondale and Edwardsville: Southern Illinois University Press.

Horowitz, Daniel. 2015. *On the Cusp: The Yale College Class of 1960 and a World on the Verge of Change.* Amherst and Boston: University of Massachusetts Press.

Howard, David. 2011. *Lost Rights: The Misadventures of a Stolen American Relic.* Boston and New York: HarperCollins.

Howden, David, and Joseph T. Salerno. 2014. *The Fed at One Hundred: A Critical View of the Federal Reserve System.* New York: Springer.

Humes, James. 1980. *Churchill: Speaker of the Century.* New York: Stein and Day.

Jaffa, Harry V. 1959. *Crisis of the House Divided: An Interpretation of the Issues of the Lincoln-Douglas Debates.* New York: Doubleday & Co.

Kent, James. 1828. *Commentaries on American Law.* 4 vol. New York: O. Halstead.

Keynes, John Maynard. 1920. *The Economic Consequences of the Peace.* New York: Harcourt, Brace and Howe.

Langston, Thomas S. 1992. *Ideologues and Presidents: From the New Deal to the Reagan Revolution.* Baltimore: Johns Hopkins University Press.

Lee, Henry. 1800. *A Funeral Oration in Honor of the Memory of George Washington, Late General of the Armies of the United States.* New Haven, CT: Read & Morse.

Lehrman, Lewis E. 2017. *Churchill, Roosevelt & Company: Studies in Character and Statecraft.* Guilford, CT: Stackpole Books.

———. 2013. *Lincoln "By Littles".* The Lehrman Institute.

———. 2018. *Lincoln & Churchill: Statesmen at War.* Guilford, CT: Stackpole Books.

———. 2008. *Lincoln at Peoria: The Turning Point.* Mechanicsburg, PA: Stackpole Books.

———. 2013. *Money, Gold, and History.* The Lehrman Institute.

———. 2013. *The American Founders.* The Lehrman Institute.

———. 2012. *The True Gold Standard: A Monetary Reform Plan without Official Reserve Currencies.* Second Edition. The Lehrman Institute.

Lehrman, Lewis E., Harold V. Cleveland, and Charles P. Kindleberger. 1976. *Money and the Coming World Order.* Edited by David P. Calleo. New York: New York University Press.

Lewis, Sinclair. 1922. *Babbitt.* New York: Harcourt, Brace and Company.

Lincoln, Abraham. 1953. *The Collected Works of Abraham Lincoln.* Edited by Roy P. Basler, Marion Delores Pratt, and Lloyd A. Dunlap. 9 vols. New Brunswick, NJ: Rutgers University Press.

Malcolm X, 1964. "Malcolm X Proclaims Muhammad as Man of the Hour." In *Rhetoric of Racial Revolt,* edited by Roy L. Hill, 304–17. Denver: Golden Bell Press.

Marlin, George. 2002. *Fighting the Good Fight: A History of the New York Conservative Party.* South Bend, IN: St. Augustine's Press.
Meltzer, Allan H. 2003, 2010. *A History of the Federal Reserve.* 2 vols. Chicago: University of Chicago Press.
Moncreiff, Robert P. 2017. *Bart Giamatti: A Profile.* New Haven, CT: Yale University Press.
Mueller, John D. 2010. *Redeeming Economics: Rediscovering the Missing Element.* Wilmington, DE: ISI Books.
Novak, Robert. 2007. *The Prince of Darkness: 50 Years Reporting in Washington.* New York: Crown Form.
O'Leary, John J. 2012. *Playing It Well: The Life and Times of Jack O'Leary, Part 2.* Trafford.
Ortega y Gasset, Jose. 1969. *The Revolution of the Masses.* London: Allen and Unwin.
Paul, Ron, and Lewis E. Lehrman. 1982. *The Case for Gold: A Minority Report of the U.S. Gold Commission.* Cato Institute.
Reagan, Ronald. 2003. *Reagan: A Life in Letters.* Edited by Kiron K. Skinner, Annelise Anderson, and Martin Anderson. New York: Free Press.
———. 2009. *The Reagan Diaries.* Edited by Douglas Brinkley. New York: HarperPerennial.
Regan, Donald T. 1986. *For the Record: From Wall Street to Washington.* New York: Harcourt Brace Jovanovich.
Rueff, Jacques. 1967. *Balance of Payments: Proposal for the Resolution of the Most Pressing World Economic Problem of Our Time,* translated by Jean Clément. New York: Macmillan.
———. 1929. *From the Physical to the Social Sciences,* translated by Herman Green. Baltimore: Johns Hopkins University Press.
———. 1977. *Œuvres Complètes de Jacques Rueff.* Vol. 1, *De L'Aube Au Crépuscule.* Paris: Plon.
———. 1979. *Œuvres Complètes de Jacques Rueff.* Vol. 2, bk. 1. *Théorie Monétaire.* Paris: Plon.
———. 1979. *Œuvres Complètes de Jacques Rueff.* Vol. 2, bk. 2. *Théorie Monétaire.* Paris: Plon.
———. 1979. *Œuvres Complètes de Jacques Rueff.* Vol. 3, bk. 1. *Politique Economique.* Paris: Plon.
———. 1980. *Œuvres Complètes de Jacques Rueff.* Vol. 3, bk. 2. *Politique Economique.* Paris: Plon.
———. 1981. *Œuvres Complètes de Jacques Rueff.* Vol. 4. *L'Ordre Social.* Paris: Plon.
———. 1964. *The Age of Inflation,* translated by A. H. Meeus and F. G. Clarke. Chicago: H. Regnery Co.
———. 1973. *The Gods and the Kings: A Glance at Creative Power,* translated by George Robinson and Roger Glémet. New York: Macmillan.
———. 1972. *The Monetary Sin of the West,* translated by Roger Glémet. New York: Macmillan.
Rueff, Jacques and Fred Hirsch. 1965. "The Role and the Rule of Gold: An Argument," *Essays in International Finance* 47, Princeton, NJ: Princeton University.
Schwartz, Anna J. 1987. *Money in Historical Perspective.* Chicago: University of Chicago Press.
Scott, Sir Walter. 1805. "Canto VI, My Native Land." In *Lay of the Last Minstrel.* Edinburgh, Scotland: Archibald Constable and Co.
Sherr, Lynn. 1995. *Failure Is Impossible: Susan B. Anthony in Her Own Words.* New York: Times Books.
Skidelsky, Robert. 2003. *John Maynard Keynes 1883–1946: Economist, Philosopher, Statesman.* Unabridged. London: Macmillan.
Smith, Adam. 1776. *An Inquiry Into the Nature and Causes of the Wealth of Nations.* 2 vol. London: W. Strahan.
Stockman, David A. 1986. *The Triumph of Politics: Why the Reagan Revolution Failed.* New York: Harper & Row.
Story, Joseph. 1833. *Commentaries on the Constitution of the United States.* 3 vol. Boston: Hilliard, Gray and Co.
Swint, Kerwin C. 2008. *Dark Genius: The Influential Career of Legendary Political Operative and Fox News Founder Roger Ailes.* New York: Union Square Press.
Toynbee, Arnold J. 1948. *Civilization on Trial.* New York: Oxford University Press.

Washington, George. 1919. "Farewell Address to the People of the United States." In *Washington's Farewell Address, Webster's First Bunker Hill Oration, Lincoln's Gettysburg Address*, edited by Charles Robert Gaston. Boston: The Athenaeum Press, Ginn and Company Proprietors.

Webster, Daniel. 1881. "A Speech Delivered in the Senate on the 25th of May 1832 on the Bill for Renewing the Charter of the Bank of the United States." In *The Works of Daniel Webster, Volume III*, by Daniel Webster. Boston: Little, Brown and Company.

Wood, Gordon S. 2006. *Revolutionary Characters: What Made the Founders Different.* New York: The Penguin Press.

Yergin, Daniel, and Joseph Stanislaw. 1998. *The Commanding Heights: The Battle Between the Government and the Marketplace That Is Remaking the Modern World.* New York: Simon & Schuster.

INDEX